VOLUME ONE
PREPARING & PROTECTING THE SAINTS
IN THE LAST DAYS

WORDS FROM THE PROPHETS
TO INSPIRE & WARN

Compiled by Arlene Kay Butler

ISBN # 0-9660284-1-4

Published & Distributed by Nelson Book
HC-61 Box 1056
Malta, ID   83342
1-800-388-4512

Italics have been added by the author. Quotes have been verified from the original source or through the Infobase Collector's Library. For future revisions if there are any suggestions, or additions you would like to suggest please contact the publisher.

Additional copies may be ordered from the above address.

TABLE OF CONTENTS

Publisher's Foreword iv

Preface v

Introduction vi

1. The Dispensation of the Fulness of Times 1

   — Joseph Smith, Dispensation Head 15

2. Protection & Preparation 27

3. Government & the Constitution 147

4. The Gospel Preached in All the World 223

   — Missionary Work 223

   — Time of the Gentiles 234

   — The 144,000 248

5. The Gathering of Israel 259

Index 297

PUBLISHER'S FOREWORD

The three volumes in this series are a partial fulfillment of the publisher's thirty-year quest to better understand the glorious times surrounding the Second Coming of the Lord Jesus Christ.

Additional quotes by the apostles and prophets concerning the future events of our times may be submitted with primary source documentation to the publisher for possible inclusion in an expanded version of this work at the following address: Nelson Book, HC 61, Box 1056, Malta, ID 83342.

I would like to express sincere thanks to Arlene Kay Butler for her tireless efforts over the past seven years in compiling these quotes.

Zeldon Nelson
Publisher & President of Nelson Book

PREFACE

The words of the Lord and the prophets are beautiful! In these books I do not interpret them nor comment on them. They speak for themselves! The book only contains quotes from apostles, prophets, and the scriptures. The quotes are organized under subject in different chapters. Due to the overlap of subject matter, the quotes could not be organized within the chapter into more defined subjects. The quotes in each chapter are organized chronologically according to the date the individual was sustained as an apostle, i.e. beginning with Joseph Smith and ending with the newest sustained apostle. This also helps provide a time perspective. The "Apostle and Prophet List" gives the date an apostle was ordained. Due to copyright restrictions, some quotes are condensed and say "See" before the reference indicating a need to refer to the original source for full information.

In the 1986 Priesthood Manual it states: "The Lord has revealed a great deal concerning his Second Coming, and he expects his Saints to search out and understand the signs of the times (p. 210-211)."

When I started I had no thought of compiling a book, but desired to understand the last days. As I read every book available on the subject instead of the events and doctrines becoming plainer, I found that the fog became even thicker. I determined that it might be more understandable if I could read just what the prophets, apostles, and scriptures had said on the subject. So I started collecting quotes and organizing them on my computer according to subject. When I obtained the gospel CD-Rom, I was able to thoroughly research by methodically scanning every key word imaginable checking tens of thousands of quotes.

President Lorenzo Snow tells us: "Knowledge helps us withstand difficulties. God bless this people is my prayer continually, especially in the obtaining of knowledge and intelligence from heaven, so that we may be able to withstand the difficulties, trials, and afflictions which may arise in our path." (Teachings of Lorenzo Snow, p.30, October 5, 1889.)

In 2 Nephi 25:7-8 it says "in the days that the prophecies of Isaiah shall be fulfilled men will know of a surety, at the times when they shall come to pass", and " I know that they shall be of great worth unto them in the last days; for in that day shall they understand them".

I hope this book will help you understand the events surrounding the "Great and dreadful day of the Lord", and as you read you will be filled with a sense of joy and hope for truly it is a "Great Day" for the saints. I am grateful to my Heavenly Father, for his love, guidance, and protection, and allowing "a small and weak thing" to contribute to His work (Joel 2:28-29).

Arlene Kay Butler

INTRODUCTION

I felt the most fitting introduction to this book was, of course, the words of the prophets! Why should we make the effort to study and understand the prophecies of the last days? The Lord himself tells us:

"What I the Lord have spoken, I have spoken, and I excuse not myself; and though the heavens and the earth pass away, my word shall not pass away, but shall all be fulfilled, whether by mine own voice or by the voice of my servants, it is the same." (D&C 1:38.)

"And the voice of warning shall be unto all people, by the mouths of my disciples, whom I have chosen in these last days." (D&C 1:4.)

Some saints avoid studying the last days because some of the prophecies are frightening. The benefit of studying the revelations is indicated in the scripture 'If ye are prepared ye shall not fear.' (D&C: 38:30). President Romney said: "It is my opinion that the Latter-day Saints, because of the knowledge they have received in the revelations, are better prepared to meet the perplexities of our times than any other people. We know more about the difficulties which are coming, and we have the key to their solution." (Marion G. Romney, Conference Report, October 1961, p. 58.)

Will the many prophecies of the last days be fulfilled? "The manner in which our Father and our God has spoken concerning the great work of the last days with which we are identified, is very remarkable. When we examine the prediction of the holy prophets, it is wonderful how plainly everything connected with this work, so far, has been fulfilled; and as we have been told this morning—and we are told whenever the Spirit of God rests down upon the Elders of this Church to speak concerning the future—we have the strongest assurance that can be given by God to any people that as that which has been predicted in the past has been completely fulfilled up to the present time, so all the predictions which have been made connected with this work, or concerning it, will also be fulfilled to the very letter; not one word will fail, not one iota of the word of God concerning Zion will fall to the ground unfulfilled." (George Q. Cannon, JD, Vol.25, p. 318-319, October 5, 1884)

As you read and study these books you will find a beautiful continuity as the foretold events fit together. But what about some of the obvious discrepancies? "We must admit that there are many mysteries of the kingdom. I am sure that the Lord will reveal them as fast as we are ready for them. We have enough to save and exalt us now. A small percentage of the people are living up to those teachings. The Brethren are united on all policies and programs, but when they go beyond the revealed word and they enter the field of conjecture, there will come differences of opinion." (The Teachings of Spencer W. Kimball, p. 532, May, 31,1948.)

Why is this dispensation so special that God's prophets have given it so much attention? "But there is this difference between the dispensation in which we are engaged and other dispensations which have preceded it: we have the promise of God that His work introduced in this the dispensation of the fulness of times shall never be overthrown, so that this dispensation differs in this respect from every dispensation which has preceded it. There is no stopping this work. Men may fight it, they may kill those who advocate it, and use every means in their power against it; but the fight of Jehovah has gone forth concerning it, and it will spread and increase and will gather within its pale every honest soul throughout the earth sooner or later, not making war, not attacking, not assaulting, but by the power of divine truth and by the spirit that accompanies it, bearing testimony to every honest soul. And as these troubles increase of which Brother Woodruff has spoken—for they will increase, in our own land, too; they have increased, and they will increase—men will become unsettled in their minds as to what they will do and where they will seek for protection; for the day will come when stable government in these United States will be very hard to find. The elements are already operating that will produce this instability. Men will be glad to seek refuge, glad to seek protection, glad to live in any place where men and women are honest and true, and where the principles which Brother Woodruff has announced, the principles of true liberty are maintained, and God grant that they may be ever maintained." (George Q. Cannon, JD, Vol.22, p. 180, June 12, 1881)

To the youth of the church President Benson gave this special instruction and warning. It is interesting to note that the youth of 1979 are today's mothers, fathers, teachers, and leaders.

"For nearly six thousand years, God has held you in reserve to make your appearance in the final days before the Second Coming of the Lord. Every previous gospel dispensation has drifted into apostasy, but ours will not. True, there will be some individuals who will fall away; but the kingdom of God will remain intact to welcome the return of its head—even Jesus Christ. While our generation will be comparable in wickedness to the days of Noah, when the Lord cleansed the earth by flood, there is a major difference this time. It is that God has saved for the final inning some of his strongest children, who will help bear off the Kingdom triumphantly. And that is where you come in, for you are the generation that must be prepared to meet your God.

All through the ages the prophets have looked down through the corridors of time to our day. Billions of the deceased and those yet to be born have their eyes on us. Make no mistake about it— you are a marked generation. There has never been more expected of the faithful in such a short period of time as there is of us. Never before on the face of this earth have the forces of evil and the forces of good been as well organized. Now is the great day of the devil's power, with the greatest mass murderers of all time living among us. But now is also the great day of the Lord's power, with the greatest number ever of priesthood holders on the earth. And the showdown is fast approaching.

Each day the forces of evil and the forces of good pick up new recruits. Each day we personally make many decisions that show where our support will go. The final outcome is certain —the forces of righteousness will finally win. What remains to be seen is where each of us personally, now and in the future, will stand in this fight—and how tall we will stand. Will we be true to our last days, foreordained mission?" (Ezra Taft Benson, "In His Steps", BYU, March 4, 1979.)

As I've compiled this book, I have seen more clearly how certain apostles and prophets had certain "missions or gifts". You are probably aware that one of Ezra Taft Benson's was government and the constitution. Did you know that Orson Pratt's was the last days? In the D&C 34:5-6 the Lord says to Orson "you are called of me to preach my gospel—preparing the way of the Lord for his second coming." Hyrum M. Smith said in the Doctrine and Covenants Commentary on section 34 (p. 178-179), this was Orson Pratt's mission. In his sermons and writings, the dominant note is always the coming of the Lord.

Orson Pratt's teachings were so prolific and beautifully detailed, I knew he had to have seen the last days. Then I found his testimony of that fact. "The Lord our God has therefore fulfilled that which he spoke; and as I said this work, instead of being nearly accomplished, nearly fulfilled, and all things brought about according to the purposes of the Almighty, only the foundation, as it were, is now laid, and instead of being gathered in a little company of 150,000, by and bye we shall be gathered in hundred of thousands and even millions. Now do you believe it? I not only believe it but know it will come to pass just as much as a great many other things which have already been fulfilled since the promises were uttered and published in this book. I knew they would come to pass, for God has revealed these things to me, and given me a knowledge of them, and I also know concerning the future of this people, as also do a great many of our brethren that have received testimonies concerning these matters." (Orson Pratt, JD, Vol. 21, p. 135-136, September 7, 1879.)

This prophecy of Heber C. Kimball's is my favorite quote not only because it covers many aspects of the last days in a detailed way (I could include it in almost every chapter), but because it is already being fulfilled.

"An army of Elders will be sent to the four quarters of the earth to search out the righteous and warn the wicked of what is coming. All kinds of religions will be started and miracles performed that will deceive the very elect if such were possible. Our sons and daughters must live pure lives so as to be prepared for what is coming.
After a while the gentiles will gather to this place by the thousands, and Salt Lake City will be classed among the wicked cities of the world. A spirit of speculation and extravagance will take possession of the Saints, and the result will be financial bondage.
Persecution comes next and all true Latter-Day Saints will be tested to the limit. Many will apostatize and others will stand still, not knowing what to do. Darkness will cover the earth and gross darkness the minds of the people. The judgments of God will be poured out upon the wicked to the extent that our Elders from far and near will be called home, or in other words the gospel will be taken from the Gentiles and later on be carried to the Jews.
The western boundary of the State of Missouri will be swept so clean of its inhabitants that as President Young tells us, 'When you return to that place, there will not be left so much as a yellow dog to wag his tail.'
Before that day comes, however, the Saints will be put to tests that will try the integrity of the best of them. The pressure will become so great that the more righteous among them will cry unto the Lord day and night until deliverance comes.
Then the Prophet Joseph and others will make their appearance and those who have remained faithful will be selected to return to Jackson County, Missouri and take part in the building of that beautiful city, the New Jerusalem." (Heber C. Kimball, Deseret News, May 23, 1931.)

Through it all, remember this poem by Edward Everett Hale:

"I am only one, but I am one.
I can't do everything, but I can do something.
What I can do, that I ought to do,
And what I ought to do,
By the grace of God, I shall do!"

CHAPTER ONE

THE DISPENSATION OF THE FULLNESS OF TIMES

"When I contemplate our position as Latter-day Saints, and the responsibilities that we are under, I feel that our hearts and our souls should be drawn out in thanksgiving to God. We should labor for the building up of the Kingdom of God and for the establishment of His work; for we have been called of God and appointed to take this kingdom in the latter days and bear it off. We have promises given unto us that no other dispensation or generation of men ever had. It has been promised us that we shall possess the kingdom and the greatness of the kingdom, and it will never be overthrown, but will remain until Jesus Christ, the great lawgiver to Israel, comes to reign over His people. Therefore, we need not think that we have nothing to do. We have a great work before us, and it will require all our exertions and all our talents and ability to perform it. We must seek for the Spirit of God to assist us; for without this Spirit we can accomplish but very little."
(Wilford Woodruff, Collected Discourses, Vol. 1, May 19, 1889.)

Joseph Smith, History of the Church, Vol. 1, Introduction, p. xxiii.

"Theologically a dispensation is defined as one of the several systems or bodies of law in which at different periods God has revealed his mind and will to man, such as the Patriarchal Dispensation, the Mosaic Dispensation, or the Christian Dispensation. The word is also sometimes applied to the periods of time during which the said laws obtain. That is, the period from to Noah is usually called the Patriarchal Dispensation. From Noah to the calling of Abraham, the Noachian Dispensation; and from Abraham to the calling of Moses, the Abrahamic Dispensation. But the word dispensation as connected with the Gospel of Jesus Christ means the opening of the heavens to men; the giving out or dispensing to them the word of God; the revealing to men in whole or the part the principles and ordinances of the Gospel; the conferring of divine authority upon certain chosen ones, by which they are empowered to act in the name, that is, in the authority of God, and for Him. That is a dispensation as relating to the Gospel; and the Dispensation of the Fullness of Times is the dispensation which includes all others and gathers to itself all things which bear any relation whatsoever to the work of God. Also it is the last dispensation, the one in which will be gathered together in one all things in Christ, both which are in heaven, and which are on earth; even in Him. It is the dispensation which will see fulfilled all the decrees of God respecting the salvation of men and the redemption of the earth itself; and bears such relation to all other dispensations of the Gospel as the ocean does to all earth's streams. It receives and unites them all in itself."

Joseph Smith, History of the Church, Vol. 4, Introduction, p. 39.

"Respecting the place of Adam in the Priesthood and his relationship to the dispensations of that Priesthood to our earth, the Prophet said: 'Commencing with Adam, who was the first man, who

1

is spoken of in Daniel as being the 'Ancient of Days', or in other words, the first and oldest of all, the great, grand progenitor of whom it is said in another place he is Michael, because he was the first and father of all, not only by progeny, but the first to hold the spiritual blessings, to whom was made known the plan of ordinances for the salvation of his posterity unto the end, and to whom Christ was first revealed, and through whom Christ has been revealed from heaven, and will continue to be revealed from henceforth. Adam holds the keys of the dispensation of the fullness of times; i.e., the dispensation of all the times have been and will be revealed through him from the beginning to Christ, and from Christ to the end of all the dispensations that are to be revealed. `Having made known unto us the mystery of His will, according to His good pleasure which He hath purposed in Himself' that in the dispensation of the fullness of times He might gather together in one all things in Christ, both which are in heaven, and which are on earth; even in him (Ephesians, 1st chap., 9th and 10th verses). Now the purpose in Himself in the winding up scene of the last dispensation is that all things pertaining to that dispensation should be conducted precisely in accordance with the preceding dispensations. And again. God purposed in Himself that there should not be an eternal fullness until every dispensation should be fulfilled and gathered together in one, and that all things whatsoever, that should be gathered together in one in those dispensations unto the same fullness and eternal glory, should be in Christ Jesus; therefore He set the ordinances to be the same forever and ever, and set Adam to watch over them, to reveal them from heaven to man, or to send angels to reveal them. * * * * These angels are under the direction of Michael or Adam, who acts under the direction of the Lord. * * * * There are many things which belong to the powers of the Priesthood and the keys thereof, that have been kept hid from before the foundation of the world; they are hid from the wise and prudent to be revealed in the last times."

Joseph Smith, History of the Church, Vol. 4, p. 426.

"The dispensation of the fullness of times will bring to light the things that have been revealed in all former dispensations; also other things that have not been before revealed. He shall send Elijah, the Prophet, etc., and restore all things in Christ."

Joseph Smith, History of the Church, Vol.5, p. 151.

"It is sufficient to know, in this case, that the earth will be smitten with a curse, unless there is a welding link of some kind or other between the fathers and the children, upon some subject or other: and behold, what is that subject? It is the baptism for the dead. For we without them cannot be made perfect; neither can they without us be made perfect. Neither can they nor we be made perfect without those who have died in the gospel also; for it is necessary, in the ushering in of the dispensation of the fullness of times, which dispensation is now beginning to usher in, that a whole and complete, and perfect union, and welding together of dispensations, and keys, and powers, and glories should take place, and be revealed, from the days of Adam even to the present time; and not only this, but those things which never have been revealed from the foundation of the world, but have been kept hid from the wise and prudent, shall be revealed unto babes and sucklings in this the dispensation of the fullness of times."

Joseph Smith, History of Joseph Smith, Deseret News, Vol. 4, #30, p. 172.

2

"Elijah was the last prophet that held the keys of the priesthood, and who will, before the last dispensation, restore the authority and deliver the keys of the priesthood, in order that all the ordinances may be attended to in righteousness. It is true the Savior had authority and power to bestow this blessing; but the sons of Levi were too prejudiced."

Teachings of the Prophet Joseph Smith, p. 158.

"Adam stands at the head of all dispensations, he being the presiding high priest (under Christ) over all the earth."

Teachings of the Prophet Joseph Smith, p. 169.

"This, then, is the nature of the priesthood; every man holding the presidency of his dispensation, and one man holding the presidency of them all, even Adam; and Adam receiving his presidency and authority from the Lord."

Teachings of the Prophet Joseph Smith, Section Four, 1839–42, p. 231.

"The building up of Zion is a cause that has interested the people of God in every age; it is a theme upon which prophets, priests and kings have dwelt with peculiar delight; they have looked forward with joyful anticipation to the day in which we live; and fired with heavenly and joyful anticipations they have sung and written and prophesied of this our day; but they died without the sight; we are the favored people that God has made choice of to bring about the Latter-day glory; it is left for us to see, participate in and help to roll forward the Latter-day glory, 'the dispensation of the fulness of times, when God will gather together all things that are in heaven, and all things that are upon the earth,' 'even in one,' when the Saints of God will be gathered in one from every nation, and kindred, and people, and tongue, when the Jews will be gathered together into one, the wicked will also be gathered together to be destroyed, as spoken of by the prophets; the Spirit of God will also dwell with His people, and be withdrawn from the rest of the nations, and all things whether in heaven or on earth will be in one, even in Christ. The heavenly Priesthood will unite with the earthly, to bring about those great purposes; and whilst we are thus united in one common cause, to roll forth the kingdom of God, the heavenly Priesthood are not idle spectators, the Spirit of God will be showered down from above, and it will dwell in our midst. The blessings of the Most High will rest upon our tabernacles, and our name will be handed down to future ages; our children will rise up and call us blessed; and generations yet unborn will dwell with peculiar delight upon the scenes that we have passed through, the privations that we have endured; the untiring zeal that we have manifested; the all but insurmountable difficulties that we have overcome in laying the foundation of a work that brought about the glory and blessing which they will realize; a work that God and angels have contemplated with delight for generations past; that fired the souls of the ancient patriarchs and prophets; a work that is destined to bring about the destruction of the powers of darkness, the renovation of the earth, the glory of God, and the salvation of the human family. (May 2, 1842.) DHC 4:608-610."

Joseph Smith, Journal of Discourses, Vol. 2, p. 64-65, October 8, 1854.

"Angels will have a part in the work of the last days. What are they to do? Says the

Saviour—'The kingdom of heaven is likened unto a man which sowed good seed in his field: but while men slept, his enemy came and sowed tares among the wheat, and went his way.' He let them grow together until the time of harvest; then He 'will say to the reapers, Gather ye together first the tares, and bind them in bundles and burn them: but gather the wheat into my barn.' The field is the world. Who are the reapers? The angels are the reapers; and still, angels, you say, are coming to earth no more. This won't do, for the reapers are the angels, the good seed are the children of the kingdom, and the tares are the children of the wicked one, and the enemy that sowed them is the devil. In another place it is said. 'And he shall send his angels with a great sound of a trumpet, and they shall gather together his elect from the four winds, from one end of heaven to the other.'"

Joseph Smith, Journal of Discourses, Vol. 7, p. 81-82, August 28, 1859.
   "In the last dispensation of the fullness of times all other dispensations will be consolidated. It will be the winding-up dispensation of this earth, introduced before the great and terrible day of the Lord comes. It will be a dispensation that will take hold of the fathers back to the earliest ages of the world. It will be a dispensation in which the keys that were committed to the Apostles in the ancient days will be delivered to chosen ones—a dispensation in which all the keys and powers held by all the ancient Prophets will be delivered—a dispensation that will reach back unto the days of Moses, and that will take hold of patriarchal keys, and the righteous institutions of those that lived in the days of the flood, and back to the days of our father Adam; and there will be keys and powers restored once revealed to him. All these dispensations could not be perfected without the grand dispensation of the fullness of times that will encompass all the inhabitants of the earth, of all ages and generations, in one vast general assembly. All things in heaven, recollect, and all things on the earth that are in Christ are to be gathered in one."

Brigham Young, Journal of Discourses, Vol. 8, p. 134-135, July 29, 1860.
   "Do you understand that what the Lord will perform in the latter days will be done quicker than in the former days? He suffered Noah to occupy one hundred and twenty years in building the ark. Were he to command us to build an ark, he would not allow so long a time for completing it."

Discourses of Brigham Young, p. 442.
   "This Kingdom they (the wicked) cannot destroy, because it is the last dispensation—because it is the fulness of times. It is the dispensation of all dispensations, and will excel in magnificence and glory every dispensation that has ever been committed to the children of men upon the earth. The Lord will bring again Zion, redeem his Israel, plant his standard upon the earth, and establish the laws of his Kingdom, and those laws will prevail."

Orson Pratt, Journal of Discourses, Vol. 17, p. 265-266, November 15, 1874.
   "It is literally a dispensation of gathering, not merely a gathering together of those who are here on the earth in the flesh; but before it is completed all things in Christ which are in heaven will also be gathered and united with those who are in Christ on the earth. We have but barely commenced in this glorious dispensation. The Church has been organized, by divine revelation, angels have appeared, the apostolic authority has been restored by the ministration of angels, and the

kingdom of God has been set up in fulfillment of the promise made to the ancient Prophet Daniel—a kingdom which shall never be destroyed, never again be rooted out of the earth and never be committed to another people, but it shall continue forever, while all human governments, of whatever name they shall be, will be rooted out of the earth by the divine judgments that will take place as the kingdom of God rolls forth among the nations. This is clearly foretold by nearly all the Prophets whose words are recorded in the divine Scriptures. They have spoken of the day when the Gospel should be restored; they have spoken of the period in which the kingdom of God should be set up and what it should accomplish; they have spoken of the signs that should be made manifest in those days both in the heavens and upon the earth; they have told us concerning the gathering, not only of the literal descendants of Israel, from the four quarters of the earth, but also of the gathering of all the Saints."

Orson Pratt, Journal of Discourses, Vol. 18, p. 61, July 25, 1875.

"The dispensation of the fullness of times is to bring about one of the grandest events that our earth has ever experienced—the union of all things in Christ, both in heaven and upon earth. Are the Saints in Christ? As many of you as have been baptized into Christ and have put on Christ, consequently if you are in Christ, if you live in the dispensation of the fullness of times, you will be required to take part in this great and grand gathering together of those who are on the earth. But how about all things in Christ in heaven, are they to come too? That is what I have been explaining. When Christ comes the inhabitants of heaven will come with him. The spirits of the righteous of all dispensations, who have not already received a resurrection, will then come forth, and when the trump of the archangel shall sound, the dead in Christ shall rise first. Then those spirits which appear in the heavens will take possession of their renewed immortal bodies which will spring forth from the tomb, and they will be with those who are gathered here on the earth. Then the dispensation will be complete—all things in Christ, whether in heaven or on earth, will be gathered in one."

John Taylor, Journal of Discourses, Vol. 21, p. 241-242, March 21, 1880.

"We are living in the dispensation which is emphatically called the dispensation of the fulness of times, which we are informed from the scriptures has been 'spoken of by all the holy prophets since the world was;' and this being the case, the dispensation in which we live embraces necessarily all that was contained in any and all of the other dispensations that have existed in all the ages preceding ours; and that consequently whatever organizations, manifestations, revelations or communications that have ever come from God to the human family in their times and dispensations, we may consistently expect to be embodied in this one. And, therefore, in some respects, as I stated before, the dispensation or time in which we live differs in many particulars from those in which God has communicated to man."

John Taylor, Journal of Discourses, Vol. 22, p. 299, August 28, 1881.

"We have had in the different ages various dispensations; for instance what may be called the Adamic dispensation, the dispensation of Noah, the dispensation of Abraham, the dispensation of Moses and of the Prophets who were associated with that dispensation; the dispensation of Jesus Christ; when he came to take away the sins of the world by the sacrifice of himself, and in and through those various dispensations, certain principles, powers, privileges and Priesthoods have been developed. But in the dispensation of the fullness of times a combination or a fullness, a completeness of all those dispensations was to be introduced among the human family. If there was anything pertaining to the Adamic, (or what we may term more particularly the patriarchal) dispensation, it would be made manifest in the last days. If there was anything associated with Enoch and his city, and the gathering together of his people, or of the translation of his city, it would be manifested in the last days. If there was anything associated with the Melchizedek Priesthood in all its forms, powers, privileges and blessings at any time or in any part of the earth, it would be restored in the last days. If there was anything connected with the Aaronic Priesthood, that also would be developed in the last times. If there was anything associated with the Apostleship and Presidency that existed in the days of Jesus, or that existed on this continent, it would be developed in the last times; for this is the dispensation of the fullness of times, embracing all other times, all principles, all powers, all manifestations, all Priesthoods and the powers thereof that have existed in any age, in any part of the world, for 'Those things which never have been revealed from the foundation of the world, but have been kept hid from the wise and prudent, shall be revealed unto babes and sucklings in this the dispensation of the fullness of times.'"

John Taylor, Journal of Discourses, Vol. 23, p. 28, March 5, 1882.
    "We are living in peculiar times; we are operating in an eventful era; we are associated with a peculiar dispensation, and we have a labor to perform which in many respects differs from that of all other ages or times. The dispensation that we are connected with is called in Scripture the dispensation of the fullness of times in which, it is recorded, God will gather together all things in one, whether they be things on the earth or things in the heavens. There are ideas associated with this dispensation that are in many respects distinct, and dissimilar from those that have been enunciated and proclaimed in former ages and dispensations; and inasmuch as the present dispensation is to embrace everything that has been connected with all past dispensations—all the prominent features as well as the minor ones that characterized the Church and kingdom of God in former days, that were essentially necessary to its growth and development—must re-appear in connection with the work of God in this our day. If the manifestations and developments of other dispensations have been made known to us, we have had revealed to us doctrines, theories, organizations and systems that have existed among the whole of them; because it is emphatically the dispensation of the fullness of times. If they had anything that was peculiarly characteristic in the days of the ancient Patriarchs, we have the same revealed to us. If they had anything prominent and important in the dispensation of Noah, we have it, and if Noah was called upon to preach the Gospel to the world in his day, before its destruction, so are we."

Wilford Woodruff, Journal of Discourses, Vol. 13, p. 161-162, December 12, 1869.
    "They are not perfect without us, we are not perfect without them. There is no period in the whole history of the world, no dispensation of God to man, that is fraught with such interest as the dispensation in which we live; there never has been. No prophets, no apostles or inspired men in any age of the world ever had the privilege of laying the foundation of the Zion of God to remain on the earth to be thrown down no more for ever. In every other dispensation of the world the people have

risen up against God and His Christ, against the kingdom and against the Priesthood, and have overthrown the messengers of heaven, and put to death every man who has borne the kingdom of God, and the kingdom has been taken from the earth. This is true of every age, except that of Enoch. He built up a kingdom and gathered together the people after laboring and preaching three hundred and sixty-five years. He perfected a city, which was called the city of the Zion of God. But behold and lo, the nations of the earth awoke and found that Zion had fled! The Lord took it to Himself; took it away from the earth. The people were righteous; they had become sanctified and the Lord took them away out of the power of the wicked. Zion could not remain on the earth; there was not power sufficient to withstand the assaults of the wicked; or if there was, the time had not come when the Lord would make use of the children of men; or there were not enough of the children of men willing to take hold and manifest those principles in their lives so that they could remain on the earth. But in the latter days he will do so. He has sworn it by Himself, because there is none greater to swear by. He has declared it through the mouth of every prophet that has ever lived on the earth, whose writing we possess, both in the Bible and Book of Mormon, as well as in those glorious revelations in the Book of Doctrine and Covenants given through the mouth of Joseph Smith the prophet. These saying are true. We as a people should exercise faith in them, no matter what may be transpiring in the outside world. We have had the powers of wicked men and devils to contend with. We may say that the devil is mad; he is stirred up against Zion; he knows that his reign will last but a little season longer."

Wilford Woodruff, Journal of Discourses, Vol. 17, p. 245-246, October 9, 1874.

"This is the only dispensation that God has ever established that was foreordained, before the world was made, not to be overcome by wicked men and devils. All other dispensations have been made war upon by the inhabitants of the earth, and the servants and Saints of God have been martyred. This was the case with Jesus and the Apostles in their day. The Lord have that good old Prophet Enoch, President of the Zion of God, who stood in the midst of his people three hundred and sixty five years, a view of the earth in its various dispensations, showing him that the time would come when it would groan under the wickedness, blasphemy, murders, whoredoms and abominations of its inhabitants. The Prophet asked the Lord whether there would ever be a time when the earth should rest; and the Lord answered that in the dispensation of the fulness of times the earth would fill the measure of its days, and then it would rest from wickedness and abominations, for in that day he would establish his kingdom upon it, to be thrown down no more for ever. Then a reign of righteousness would commence and the honest and meek of the earth would be gathered together to serve the Lord, and upon them would rest power to build up the great Zion of God in the latter days. These things were also shown to Abraham, and many others of the ancient servants of God had glimpses of them by vision, revelation and the inspiration of the Spirit of God, and what they saw, or an account of what they saw, has been left on record."

Wilford Woodruff, Journal of Discourses, Vol. 18, p. 36-37, June 27, 1875.

"I say to the Latter-day Saints, we should be faithful to our God. We are blessed above all the people that breathe the breath of life upon the earth, and we are blessed above all other dispensations and generations of men, for the Lord has put into our hands the power to build up his

Zion upon the earth, never more to be thrown down, and this is what no other generation has ever been called to do. But although this is the mission of the Latter-day Saints, we have a continual warfare to wage—a warfare with the powers of darkness, and a warfare with ourselves. The ancients had a similar experience to pass through—they had their day of trials, troubles and tribulations. Enoch labored three hundred and sixty-five years in building up Zion, and he had the opposition of the whole world. But the Lord blessed him so that he maintained his ground for that length of time, and gathered together a few out of the nations of the earth, and they were sanctified before the Lord, and he had to take them away, and the saying went forth—'Zion is fled.' So you may trace down all the Prophets. Read the history of Ezekiel, Jeremiah, Isaiah and others, and you will find that it was a warfare with them all the way through. And so with Jesus and the Apostles. But all those dispensations have passed and gone into the spirits world, and they have their eyes upon us, and in fact God our heavenly Father and all under him—the whole heavenly host, have their eyes turned towards the Latter-day Saints, because this is the great dispensation of which Adam, Enoch and all the ancient patriarchs and Prophets have spoken, in which shall take place the final redemption of the House of Israel, the restoration of their kingdom, the rebuilding of their city and Temple, the restoration of their oracles and Priesthood, of the Urim and Thummim, and the preparation for the final winding up scene in the last days; all these things will take place in the dispensation in which we are permitted to live."

Wilford Woodruff, Journal of Discourses, Vol. 22, p. 333, October 8, 1881.

"Now, I will refer to a thing that took place with me in Tennessee. I was in Tennessee in the year 1835, and while at the house of Abraham O. Smoot, I received a letter from Brothers Joseph Smith and Oliver Cowdery, requesting me to stay there, and stating that I would lose no blessing by doing so. Of course, I was satisfied. I went into a little room and sat down upon a small sofa. I was all my myself and the room was dark; and while I rejoiced in this letter and the promise made to me, I became wrapped in vision. I was like Paul; I did not know whether I was in the body or out of the body. A personage appeared to me and showed me the great scenes that should take place in the last days. One scene after another passed before me. I saw the sun darkened; I saw the moon become as blood; I saw the stars fall from heaven; I saw seven golden lamps set in the heavens, representing the various dispensations of God to man—a sign that would appear before the coming of Christ. I saw the resurrection of the dead. In the first resurrection those that came forth from their graves seemed to be all dressed alike, but in the second resurrection they were as diverse in their dress as this congregation is before me today, and if I had been an artist I could have painted the whole scene as it was impressed upon my mind, more indelibly fixed than anything I had ever seen with the natural eye. What does this mean? It was a testimony of the resurrection of the dead. I had a testimony. I believe in the resurrection of the dead, and I know it is a true principle. Thus we may have dreams about things of great importance, and dreams of no importance at all."

Wilford Woodruff, Collected Discourses, Vol. 2, October 6, 1890.

"We are in the last dispensation. . . It is a great day, and the eyes of all the heavens are over us, and the eyes of God Himself and all the patriarchs and prophets. They are watching over you with feelings of deep interest, for your welfare; and our prophets who were slain and sealed their testimony with their blood, are mingling with the Gods, pleading for their brethren. Therefore, let us be faithful, and leave events in the hands of God, and He will take care of us if we do our duty."

Wilford Woodruff, Collected Discourses, Vol. 5, October 19, 1896.

"Joseph Smith continued visiting myself and others up to a certain time, and then it stopped. The last time I saw him was in heaven. In the night vision I saw him at the door of the temple in heaven. He came and spoke to me. He said he could not stop to talk with me because he was in a hurry. The next man I met was Father Smith; he could not talk with me because he was in a hurry. I met half a dozen brethren who had held high positions on earth, and none of them could stop to talk with me because they were in a hurry. I was much astonished. By and by I saw the Prophet again, and I got the privilege to ask him a question. 'Now,' said I, 'I want to know why you are in a hurry. I have been in a hurry all through my life; but I expected my hurry would be over when I got into the kingdom of heaven, if I ever did.' Joseph said: 'I will tell you, Brother Woodruff. Every dispensation that has had the Priesthood on the earth and has gone into the celestial kingdom, has had a certain amount of work to do to prepare to go to the earth with the Savior when He goes to reign on the earth. Each dispensation has had ample time to do this work. We have not. We are the last dispensation, and so much work has to be done, and we need to be in a hurry in order to accomplish it.' Of course, that was satisfactory to me, but it was new doctrine to me."

Erastus Snow, Journal of Discourses, Vol. 20, p. 181, April 6, 1879.

"The rendering of this 24th chapter of Matthew is somewhat imperfect in King James' translation; the events connected with the destruction of Jerusalem and the dispersion of the Jews seem to be intermingled with the events that were to precede and accompany the second advent of the Savior. In the new translation of this chapter by the Prophet Joseph Smith, which may be found in the Pearl of Great Price, the difference is made very plain, and the figure of the fig tree and the second coming of the Son of Man and the generation referred to therein is made applicable, not to the period of the destruction of Jerusalem, but to the time of the second coming of the Son of Man. And the new translation reads, in speaking of the putting forth of the fig-tree and the signs that should precede the coming of the Son of Man, 'Verily, I say unto you, this generation, in which these things shall be shewn forth, shall not pass away, till all I have told shall be fulfilled.' From the reading of the new and correct rendering it will be seen that, instead of the things spoken of being fulfilled in the generation in which the prophecy was made—which is the inference—the application is transferred at once from the generation in which the Savior was speaking to the generation who should witness the signs of the times therein set forth."

George Q. Cannon, Journal of Discourses, Vol. 22, p. 180, June 12, 1881.

"But there is this difference between the dispensation in which we are engaged and other dispensations which have preceded it: we have the promise of God that His work introduced in this the dispensation of the fulness of times shall never be overthrown, so that this dispensation differs in this respect from every dispensation which has preceded it. There is no stopping this work. Men may fight it, they may kill those who advocate it, and use every means in their power against it; but the fight of Jehovah has gone forth concerning it, and it will spread and increase and will gather within its pale every honest soul throughout the earth sooner or later, not making war, not attacking, not assaulting, but by the power of divine truth and by the spirit that accompanies it, bearing testimony to every honest soul."

Charles W. Penrose, Conference Report, October 1911, p. 48.

"We are living in the dispensation of the fulness of times, and in this dispensation—the grandest and greatest of all, will be gathered in one all things that are in Christ, not only His people gathered from the various nations to Zion to build it up, to prepare the place for His feet, but the hosts that have passed away, whom He will bring with Him. Not only are the people to be gathered together, but the glorious truths which have been made manifest in the ages that are past will all be brought forth in the dispensation in which we are living, and things kept old from the foundation of the world will be made manifest; for the Lord has promised it, and His promises never fail of fulfillment."

Joseph Fielding Smith Jr., The Way to Perfection, p. 278.

"Many things have taken place during the past one hundred years to impress faithful members of the Church with the fact that the coming of the Lord is near. The Gospel has been restored. The Church has been fully organized. The Priesthood has been conferred upon man. The various dispensations from the beginning have been revealed and their keys and authorities given to the Church. Israel has been, and is being gathered to the land of Zion. The Jews are returning to Jerusalem. The Gospel is being preached in all the world as a witness to every nation. Temples are being built and ordinance work for the dead as well as for the living is performed in them. The hearts of the children have turned to their fathers, and they are seeking after their dead. The covenants which the Lord promised to make with Israel in the latter days have been revealed and thousands of gathered Israel have entered into them. Thus the work of the Lord is advancing, and all these things are signs of the near approach of our Lord."

Joseph Fielding Smith, The Way to Perfection, p. 283-284.

"If the great and dreadful day of the Lord was near at hand when Elijah came, we are just one century nearer it today. 'But no! Elijah, you are wrong! Surely one hundred years have passed, and are we not better of today than ever before? Look at our discoveries, our inventions, our knowledge and our wisdom! Surely you made a mistake!' So many seem to think, and say, and judging by their actions they are sure that the world is bound to go on in its present condition for millions of years before the end will come. Talk to them; hear what they have to say—these learned men of the world. 'We have had worse times,' they say. 'You are wrong in thinking there are more calamities now than in earlier times. There are not more earthquakes, the earth has always been quaking but now we have facilities for gathering the news which our fathers did not have.' 'These are not signs of the times: things are not different from former times.' And so the people refuse to heed the warnings the Lord so kindly gives to them, and thus they fulfil the scriptures."

Joseph Fielding Smith Jr., Doctrines of Salvation, Vol. 1, p. 161.

"The first dispensation of the gospel was given to Adam . . .Enoch had a dispensation granted to him, and through his faithfulness be and his people were translated. Noah received a dispensation of warning when the whole world had fallen into apostasy . . .To Abraham was given a dispensation, and with him the Lord made a special covenant that through him and his posterity all nations of the earth should be blessed. . . . Moses was given a dispensation of gathering and led Israel from Egypt to their promised land. John the Baptist was given the dispensation of preparation before the coming of our Redeemer, and Jesus Christ granted a dispensation of the gospel to his disciples in the restoration of its fullness and the commission that they should go into all the world and preach the gospel."

Joseph Fielding Smith Jr., Doctrines of Salvation, Vol. 1, p. 163.
    "The dispensation of the meridian of time is the name given to the dispensation of the ministry of Christ and his apostles. It is so called because our Lord came into the world in the meridian of its mortal history. By revelation we know that it was about 4,000 years from the time of the fall of Adam to the birth of Christ and that it will be about 3,000 years, plus 'a little season' from his birth until the end of the mortal earth. We are now living near the close of the sixth thousandth year, or the period known as the 'last days,' or the time immediately preceding the second advent of Jesus Christ."

Joseph Fielding Smith Jr., Doctrines of Salvation, Vol. 2, p. 112-113.
    "This day of preparation by turning the hearts of the fathers to the children and of the children to the fathers, it is very evident from the context, is reserved until the last days, or the day of restitution of all things. It is an event to take place, according to the plain prediction, shortly preceding the great and dreadful day of the Lord. . . . However, before it comes there is to be some mighty work performed by the restoration of Elijah's authority, which is so potent that it will save the earth from destruction, or from being smitten with a curse."

Joseph Fielding Smith Jr., Doctrines of Salvation, Vol. 2, p. 117.
    "But what was the nature of his (Elijah's) mission to the earth in these latter days? It was to restore power and authority which once was given to men on the earth and which is essential to the complete salvation and exaltation of man in the kingdom of God. . . .This priesthood holds the keys of binding and sealing on earth and in heaven of all the ordinances and principles pertaining to the salvation of man, that they may thus become valid in the celestial kingdom of God."

Joseph Fielding Smith Jr., Doctrines of Salvation, Vol. 2, p. 154.
    "What was the promise made to the fathers that was to be fulfilled in the latter-days by the turning of the hearts of the children to their fathers? It was the promise . . . that the time should come when the dead should be redeemed. And the turning of the hearts of the children is fulfilled in the performing of the vicarious temple work and in the preparation of their genealogies."

Joseph Fielding Smith Jr., Doctrines of Salvation, Vol. 2, p. 244.
    "The responsibility resting upon the members of the Church in this dispensation is far greater than that given to any other dispensation. This being the last dispensation, it is our responsibility to labor, not only for ourselves, but also for all the righteous dead of all other dispensations for whom

the work has to be done. Moreover, the Lord has revealed to us things which no other dispensation had relating to the kingdom of God."

Joseph Fielding Smith Jr., Doctrines of Salvation, Vol. 3, p. 94.
"The sacrifice of animals will be done . . . when the temple spoken of is built; at the beginning of the millennium . . . blood sacrifices will be performed long enough to complete the fullness of the restoration in this dispensation. Afterwards sacrifice will be of some other character."

Joseph Fielding Smith Jr., Doctrines of Salvation, Vol. 3, p. 135.
"The President of the Church holds the keys over all the Church. In him is concentrated the power of the priesthood. He holds all the keys of every nature, pertaining to the dispensation of the fullness of times. All the keys of former dispensations which have been revealed are vested in him."

James E. Talmage, The Articles of Faith, p. 21.
"It is further evident from the scriptures that the dispensation of the Gospel in the latter days is to be one of restoration and restitution, truly a 'dispensation of the fullness of times.' Paul declares it to be the good pleasure of the Lord, 'That in the dispensation of the fullness of times he might gather together in one all things in Christ, both which are in heaven, and which are on earth; even in him.' This prediction finds a parallel in an utterance of the prophet Nephi: 'Wherefore, all things which have been revealed unto the children of men shall at that day be revealed.' And in accord with this is the teaching of Peter: 'Repent ye therefore, and be converted, that your sins may be blotted out, when the times of refreshing shall come from the presence of the Lord; And he shall send Jesus Christ, which before was preached unto you: Whom the heaven must receive until the times of restitution of all things, which God hath spoken by the mouth of all his holy prophets since the world began.'"

John A. Widtsoe, Evidences and Reconciliations, p. 93-94.
"For example, modern revelation declares that these are the last days. This period of the earth's history may be recognized by several signs: The fullness of the gospel will be restored and preached to all the world (D&C 39:11; 1:23); work will be done for the spirits of the dead (D&C 76:73; 124:29-36; also Sections 127 and 128); mighty, natural events will take place, from the darkened sun to tremendous earthquakes, and the whole earth will be in commotion and many will be destroyed because of wars, pestilence, and fear. (D&C, Sections 29, 45, 49, 84, 87, 88) These are also signs of the coming of the Lord Jesus Christ. (D&C 45:39) All who fear the Lord will anxiously look for these signs as they appear. (D&C 45:39) Yet, despite these signs, none shall know the exact time of His coming."

Teachings of Ezra Taft Benson, p. 19.
"This is the last and great dispensation in which the great consummation of God's purposes will be made, the only dispensation in which the Lord has promised that sin will not prevail. The Church will not be taken from the earth again. It is here to stay. The Lord has promised it and you are a part of that Church and kingdom—the nucleus around which will be builded the great kingdom

of God on the earth. The kingdom of heaven and the kingdom of God on the earth will be combined together at Christ's coming—and that time is not far distant. How I wish we could get the vision of this work, the genius of it, and realize the nearness of that great event. I am sure it would have a sobering effect upon us if we realized what is before us. ('I'll Go Where You Want Me to Go,' Church News [November 23, 1946]: 8.)"

Teachings of Ezra Taft Benson, p. 172.
"This is the dispensation of the fullness of times. Every other gospel dispensation from the days of Adam through the ancient Apostles has drifted into apostasy. But our dispensation is different. We have been assured by the Lord that the kingdom of God, The Church of Jesus Christ of Latter-day Saints, will remain on earth to prepare the way and meet the kingdom of heaven when the Lord comes again. ('Our Obligation and Challenge,' Regional Representatives Seminar, Salt Lake City, Utah, September 30, 1977.)"

Teachings of Ezra Taft Benson, p. 555.
"Our young people are not just ordinary people. They are not just run-of-the-mill. They are choice spirits. President Wilford Woodruff said this: 'The Lord has chosen a small number of choice spirits of sons and daughters out of all the creations of God, who are to inherit this earth; and this company of choice spirits have been kept in the spirit world for six thousand years to come forth in the last days to stand in the flesh in this last dispensation of the fullness of times, to organize the kingdom of God upon the earth, to build it up and to defend it and to receive the eternal and everlasting priesthood [of God].' (Title of Liberty, p. 197.)"

LeGrand Richards, A Marvelous Work and a Wonder, p. 35.
"It is the pronouncement of The Church of Jesus Christ of Latter-day Saints that this is the dispensation of the fullness of times, and that through the restitution of all things, the Lord has made provision to 'gather together in one all things in Christ, both which are in heaven, and which are on earth.' This restitution of all things will, however, not be complete until the end of the thousand years of the personal reign of Christ upon the earth when death will be destroyed. (See 1 Corinthians 15:24-26.) There is no other such plan in the world today."

Bruce R. McConkie, Mormon Doctrine, "Dispensation of the Fullness of Times", p. 200.
"Every key, power, and authority necessary ... has already been restored in this dispensation."

Bruce R. McConkie, Mormon Doctrine, "Dispensations" p. 200.
"Gospel dispensations are those periods of time during which the Lord reveals ... the gospel."

Bruce R. McConkie, The Mortal Messiah, Vol. 3, p. 441.
"Ours is the dispensation of desolation and war . . . climaxed by a worldwide Armageddon."

See Bruce R. McConkie, The Millennial Messiah, p. 88-89.
"What is it that shall be restored in the times of restitution of all things? It is the keys of

creation . . . presidency . . . to gather Israel . . . sealing power . . . apostolic commission . . .It is every key, power, and authority ever possessed by any prophet . . .It is also governments and kingdoms. It is lands and properties and peoples. The church and kingdom of God on earth is to be set up again. . . .The Book of Mormon shall come forth, including the sealed portion. The lost portions of the Bible shall again be read . . . once again men shall speak a pure language."

See Bruce R. McConkie, The Millennial Messiah, p. 109-110.
"The times of restitution . . . is the age of restoration, the age in which God has promised to restore all things, all truths, all powers ... restore the earth itself to its primeval and paradisiacal state."

Bruce R. McConkie, The Millennial Messiah, p. 111-112.
"The dispensation of the fullness of times was opened in the spring of 1820 when the Father and the Son appeared to Joseph Smith, and it will not be closed until 'the Lord shall come'".

Bruce R. McConkie, The Millennial Messiah, p. 117.
"The dispensation of the fullness of times is the greatest of all the dispensations. In it the gospel shall be preached to more people than in all previous dispensations combined. . . .In it Israel shall be gathered and a people prepared for our Lord's return."

Bruce R. McConkie, A New Witness for the Articles of Faith, p. 626-627.
"The promise is not that all things will be restored before the Second Coming, but that the age of restoration will commence . . . Many things—indeed, most things will be restored after he comes."

Bruce R. McConkie, A New Witness for the Articles of Faith, p. 629.
"This promised Elias is, in effect, all of the angelic ministrants who have come . . . Someone came from each of these ancient dispensations to bring to us what was had among mortals in his day."

Neal A. Maxwell, All These Things Shall Give Thee Experience, p. 121.
"Staying close to the prophets will be vital since, in some ways, the last days in this last dispensation may come to resemble the first days in this dispensation. The middle period through which the Church has recently passed has been essentially a pleasant period—full of growth, understanding, and even some acclaim from the world. But the last days, although they will be characterized by much growth, will also be characterized by much tribulation and difficulty. There will be both wonderful and awful things."

JOSEPH SMITH, DISPENSATION HEAD

Joseph Smith, History of the Church, Vol. 3, p. 50.

"Now, then, we can see that this deliverer is a kind of harbinger or forerunner, that is, one that is sent to prepare the way for another, and this deliverer is such a one, for he comes to turn away ungodliness from Jacob, consequently he must receive a dispensation and an authority suitable to his calling, or he could not turn away ungodliness from Jacob, nor fulfill the Scriptures. But the words of the prophets must be fulfilled, and in order to do this, to this messenger must be given the dispensation of the fullness of times, according to the prophets. For Paul says again, in speaking of the dispensation of the fullness of times, 'Having made known unto us the mystery of His will, according to His good pleasure, which He hath purposed in Himself: that in the dispensation of the fullness of times, He might gather together in one all things in Christ, both which are in heaven, and which are on earth; even in Him.'(Ephesians, 1: 9-10). And Isaiah says, 'And it shall come to pass in that day, that the Lord shall set His hand again the second time to recover the remnant of His people.' (Isaiah 11:11). Now is the time that the deliverer shall come out of Zion and turn away ungodliness from the house of Israel. Now the Lord has said that He would set His hand the second time, and we ask, for what, but to recover the house of Jacob? For what have they fallen? Most assuredly they have broken the covenant that God had made with their fathers, and through their fathers with them. For Paul says, 'Thou wilt say then, The branches were broken off, that I might be grafted in. Well; because of unbelief they were broken off, and thou standest by faith. Be not highminded, but fear.' (Romans 11:18, 20.)"

Brigham Young, Journal of Discourses, Vol. 7, p. 289, October 9, 1859.

"From the day that the Priesthood was taken from the earth to the winding-up scene of all things, every man and woman must have the certificate of Joseph Smith, junior, as a passport to their entrance into the mansion where God and Christ are— I with you and you with me. I cannot go there without his consent. He holds the keys of that kingdom for the last dispensation—the keys to rule in the spirit-world; and he rules there triumphantly, for he gained full power and a glorious victory over the power of Satan while he was yet in the flesh, and was a martyr to his religion and to the name of Christ, which gives him a most perfect victory in the spirit-world. He reigns there as supreme a being in his sphere, capacity, and calling, as God does in heaven."

Brigham Young, Journal of Discourses, Vol. 15, p. 138-139, August 24, 1872.

"If we ask who will stand at the head of the resurrection in this last dispensation, the answer is—Joseph Smith, Junior, the Prophet of God. He is the man who will be resurrected and receive the keys of the resurrection, and he will seal this authority upon others, and they will hunt up their friends and resurrect them when they shall have been officiated for, and bring them up."

Discourses of Brigham Young, p. 108.

"It was decreed in the counsels of eternity, long before the foundations of the earth were laid, that he, Joseph Smith, should be the man, in the last dispensation of this world, to bring forth the word of God to the people, and receive the fullness of the keys and power of the Priesthood of the

Son of God. The Lord had his eyes upon him, and upon his father, and upon his father's father, and upon their progenitors clear back to Abraham, and from Abraham to the flood, from the flood to Enoch, and from Enoch to Adam. He has watched that family and that blood as it has circulated from its fountain to the birth of that man. He was foreordained in eternity to preside over this last dispensation."

Discourses of Brigham Young, p. 321-322.

"This people are mostly gathered from what are termed the laboring and middle classes. We have not gathered into this Church men that are by the world esteemed profound in their principles, ideas, and judgment. We have none in this Church that are called by them expert statesmen. How frequently it is cast at the Elders, when they are abroad preaching, that Joseph Smith, the founder of their Church and religion, was only a poor illiterate boy. That used to be advanced as one of the strongest arguments that could be produced against the doctrine of salvation, by the wise and learned of this world, though it is no argument at all. The Lord should have revealed himself to some of the learned priests or talented men of the age, say they, who could have done some good and borne off the Gospel by their influence and learning, and not to a poor, ignorant, unlettered youth. Not many wise, not many mighty, not many noble, speaking after the manner of men, are called; but God hath chosen the foolish things of the world to confound the wise, the weak things of the world to confound the things that are mighty; and base things of the world—things which are despised by the world, hath God in his wisdom chosen; yea, and things which are not, to bring to naught things that are, that no flesh should glory in his presence."

Discourses of Brigham Young, p. 458.

"Joseph Smith has laid the foundation of the Kingdom of God in the last days; others will rear the superstructure."

John Taylor, Journal of Discourses, Vol. 18, p. 326, December 31, 1876.

"Then comes another personage, whose name is John the Baptist. He ordained the Prophet Joseph to that portion of the Priesthood of which he held the keys, namely, the Aaronic, or lesser Priesthood. Afterwards came Peter, James and John, who held the keys of the Melchizedek Priesthood, and of the dispensation of the fullness of times, they being the last in their day to whom it was committed, and therefor they came to him and revealed to him the principles pertaining to the Gospel, and the events to be fulfilled. Then we read again of Elias or Elijah, who was to act as a restorer, and who committed to him the powers and authority associated with his position. Then Abraham, who had the Gospel, and Priesthood and Patriarchal powers, in his day; and Moses, who stood at the head of the gathering dispensation in his day, and had these powers conferred upon him. We are informed that Noah, who was a Patriarch, and all in the line if the Priesthood, in every generation back to Adam, who was the first man, possessed the same. Why was it that all these people should be associated with all these dispensations, and all could communicate with Joseph Smith? Because he stood at the head of the dispensation of the fullness of times, which comprehends all the various dispensations that have existed upon the earth, and that as the Gods in the eternal worlds and the Priesthood that officiated in time and eternity had declared that it was time for the issuing forth of all these things, they all combined together to impart to him the keys of their several missions, that he might be fully competent, through the intelligence and aid afforded him through these several parties, to introduce the Gospel in all its fullness, namely, the dispensation of the fullness of times, when, says the Apostle Paul, 'He might gather all things in Christ, both which are in heaven and which are in earth even in him.' Consequently he stood in that position, and hence his familiarity with all these various dispensations and the men who administered in them. If you were to ask Joseph what sort of a looking man Adam was, he would tell you at once; he would tell you his size and appearance and all about him. You might have asked him what sort of men Peter, James, and John were, and he could have told you. Why? Because he had seen them."

Wilford Woodruff, Journal of Discourses, Vol. 16, p. 267, October 8, 1873.

"Keys Received by Joseph Smith. He received powers and keys from under the hands of Moses for gathering the house of Israel in the last days; he received under the hands of Elias the keys of sealing the hearts of the fathers to the children, and the hearts of the children to the fathers; he received under the hands of Peter, James, and John the apostleship, and everything belonging thereto; he received under the hands of Moroni all the keys and powers required of the stick of Joseph in the hands of Ephraim; he received under the hand of John the Baptist the Aaronic Priesthood, with all its keys and powers, and every other key and power belonging to this dispensation, and I am not ashamed to say that he was a prophet of God, and he laid the foundation of the greatest work and dispensation that has ever been established on the earth."

George Q. Cannon, Journal of Discourses, Vol. 23, p. 362, October 29, 1882.

"I present this matter before you that you may see that when Joseph died he had embodied in him all the keys and all the authority, all the powers and all the qualifications necessary for the head of a dispensation, to stand at the head of this great last dispensation. They had been bestowed upon him through the providences of God, and through the command of God to his faithful servants who lived in ancient days. There was no end scarcely, in many respects, to the knowledge that he received. He was visited constantly by angels; and the Son of God Himself condescended to come and minister unto him, the Father having also shown Himself unto him; and these various angels, the heads of dispensations, having also ministered unto him. Moroni, in the beginning, as you know, to prepare him for his mission, came and ministered and talked to him from time to time, and he had vision after vision in order that his mind might be fully saturated with a knowledge of the things of God, and that he might comprehend the great and holy calling that God has bestowed upon him. In this respect he stands unique. There is no man in this dispensation can occupy the station that he, Joseph did, God having reserved him and ordained him for that position, and bestowed upon him the necessary power. Think of what he passed through! Think of his afflictions, and think of his dauntless character! Did any one ever see him falter? Did any one ever see him flinch? Did any one ever see any lack in him of the power necessary to enable him to stand with dignity in the midst of his enemies, or lacking in dignity in the performance of his duties as a servant of the living God? God gave him peculiar power in this respect. He was filled with integrity to God; with such integrity as was not known among men. He was like an angel of God among them. Notwithstanding all that he had to endure, and the peculiar circumstances in which he was so often placed, and the great

17

responsibility that weighed constantly upon him, he never faltered; the feeling of fear or trembling never crossed him—at least he never exhibited it in his feelings or actions. God sustained him to the very last, and was with him, and bore him off triumphant even in his death."

Joseph Fielding Smith, Answers to Gospel Questions, Vol. 4, p.194.

"This name (Elias) is a title which is applied to several prophets, and has reference to their office as messengers sent to prepare the way for a greater work. John the Baptist is spoken of as Elias, because he prepared the way before the ministry of the Lord. Joseph Smith is an Elias because he was sent to prepare the way for the second coming of our Lord."

Joseph Fielding Smith Jr., Doctrines of Salvation, Vol. 1, p. 198-199.

"When Moroni appeared to Joseph Smith, he said that the time was at hand for the fulfillment of many of the prophecies relating to the last times. This angel quoted to the young man, Joseph Smith, part of the third and all of the fourth chapters of Malachi, with some variations from the reading as we find it in the King James translation of the Bible.

He also quoted the 11th chapter of Isaiah, saying that it was about to be fulfilled; also the 22nd and 23rd verses of the third chapter of Acts, and the second chapter of Joel, verses 28 to the end, which he said were shortly to be fulfilled. He also said that the time for the fullness of the gentiles would soon come in, and many other scriptures were quoted which pertain to the dispensation of the fullness of times."

Joseph Fielding Smith Jr., Doctrines of Salvation, Vol. 1, p. 221.

"We read in the scriptures that the testimony is not of force without the death of the testator—that is, in his particular case, and in the case of Christ. It was just as necessary that Hyrum Smith lay down his life a martyr for this cause as a witness for God as it was for Joseph Smith, so the Lord permitted them both to be taken in that way and both sealed their testimony with their blood. Both of them held the keys of the dispensation of the fullness of times jointly, and they will through all the ages of eternity."

Bruce R. McConkie, The Millennial Messiah, p. 339-341.

" 'What is the root of Jesse spoken of in the 10th verse of the 11th chapter? Behold, thus saith the Lord, it is a descendant of Jesse, as well as of Joseph, unto whom rightly belongs the priesthood, and the keys of the kingdom, for an ensign, and for the gathering of my people in the last days.'(Isa.).

. . . the prophet here mentioned is Joseph Smith, to whom the priesthood came, who received the keys of the kingdom, and who raised the ensign for the gathering of the Lord's people in our dispensation? And is he not also the 'servant in the hands of Christ, who is partly a descendant of Jesse as well as of Ephraim, or of the house of Joseph, on whom there is laid much power'? (D&C 113:4-6.)"

Neal A. Maxwell, Plain and Precious Things, p. 83.

"But surely Joseph, sophisticated in Egyptian politics, knew that a pharaoh would soon come who knew not Joseph nor his posterity. What, therefore, was the future of his seed? How understandable that Joseph would care so deeply about his posterity! No wonder he exclaimed over God's promise that a seer like Moses would be raised up from his seed in the last days to serve his seed. (See 2 Nephi 3:6-7.) And upon being told, as an indication of divine loyalty, that this seer would even bear his name, Joseph rejoiced. (See JST, Genesis 50:24-38.)"

SCRIPTURAL REFERENCES

JST Genesis 7:67
67 And the Lord said unto Enoch, As I live, even so will I come in the last days, in the days of wickedness and vengeance, to fulfil the oath which I made unto you concerning the children of Noah.

JST Genesis 14:34-35
34 And his people wrought righteousness, and obtained heaven, and sought for the city of Enoch which God had before taken, separating it from the earth, having reserved it unto the latter days, or the end of the world;
35 And hath said, and sworn with an oath, that the heavens and the earth should come together; and the sons of God should be tried so as by fire.

Isaiah 2:2-4
2 And it shall come to pass in the last days, that the mountain of the LORD's house shall be established in the top of the mountains, and shall be exalted above the hills; and all nations shall flow unto it.
3 And many people shall go and say, Come ye, and let us go up to the mountain of the LORD, to the house of the God of Jacob; and he will teach us of his ways, and we will walk in his paths: for out of Zion shall go forth the law, and the word of the LORD from Jerusalem.
4 And he shall judge among the nations, and shall rebuke many people: and they shall beat their swords into plowshares, and their spears into pruninghooks: nation shall not lift up sword against nation, neither shall they learn war any more.

Isaiah 11:10
10 And in that day there shall be a root of Jesse, which shall stand for an ensign of the people; to it shall the Gentiles seek: and his rest shall be glorious.

Micah 4:1-4
1 But in the last days it shall come to pass, [that] the mountain of the house of the LORD shall be established in the top of the mountains, and it shall be exalted above the hills; and people shall flow unto it.
2 And many nations shall come, and say, Come, and let us go up to the mountain of the LORD, and to the house of the God of Jacob; and he will teach us of his ways, and we will walk in his paths: for the law shall go forth of Zion, and the word of the LORD from Jerusalem.
3 And he shall judge among many people, and rebuke strong nations afar off; and they shall beat their swords into plowshares, and their spears into pruninghooks: nation shall not lift up a sword against nation, neither shall they learn war any more.
4 But they shall sit every man under his vine and under his fig tree; and none shall make [them] afraid: for the mouth of the LORD of hosts hath spoken [it].

The Dispensation of the Fulness of Times

Malachi 4:5-6

5 Behold, I will send you Elijah the prophet before the coming of the great and dreadful day of the LORD:

6 And he shall turn the heart of the fathers to the children, and the heart of the children to their fathers, lest I come and smite the earth with a curse.

Acts 2:17-21

17 And it shall come to pass in the last days, saith God, I will pour out of my Spirit upon all flesh: and your sons and your daughters shall prophesy, and your young men shall see visions, and your old men shall dream dreams:

18 And on my servants and on my handmaidens I will pour out in those days of my Spirit; and they shall prophesy:

19 And I will shew wonders in heaven above, and signs in the earth beneath; blood, and fire, and vapour of smoke:

20 The sun shall be turned into darkness, and the moon into blood, before that great and notable day of the Lord come:

21 And it shall come to pass, that whosoever shall call on the name of the Lord shall be saved.

Romans 15:12

12 And again, Esaias saith, There shall be a root of Jesse, and he that shall rise to reign over the Gentiles; in him shall the Gentiles trust.

Ephesians 1:9-10

9 Having made known unto us the mystery of his will, according to his good pleasure which he hath purposed in himself:

10 That in the dispensation of the fulness of times he might gather together in one all things in Christ, both which are in heaven, and which are on earth; even in him:

2 Timothy 3:1-7

1 This know also, that in the last days perilous times shall come.

2 For men shall be lovers of their own selves, covetous, boasters, proud, blasphemers, disobedient to parents, unthankful, unholy,

3 Without natural affection, trucebreakers, false accusers, incontinent, fierce, despisers of those that are good,

4 Traitors, heady, highminded, lovers of pleasures more than lovers of God;

5 Having a form of godliness, but denying the power thereof: from such turn away.

6 For of this sort are they which creep into houses, and lead captive silly women laden with sins, led away with divers lusts,

7 Ever learning, and never able to come to the knowledge of the truth.

2 Peter 3:3-4

3 Knowing this first, that there shall come in the last days scoffers, walking after their own lusts,

4 And saying, Where is the promise of his coming? For since the fathers fell asleep, all things continue as they were from the beginning of the creation.

2 Nephi 3:7-15
7 Yea, Joseph truly said: Thus saith the Lord unto me: A choice seer will I raise up out of the fruit of thy loins; and he shall be esteemed highly among the fruit of thy loins. And unto him will I give commandment that he shall do a work for the fruit of thy loins, his brethren, which shall be of great worth unto them, even to the bringing of them to the knowledge of the covenants which I have made with thy fathers.
8 And I will give unto him a commandment that he shall do none other work, save the work which I shall command him. And I will make him great in mine eyes; for he shall do my work.
9 And he shall be great like unto Moses, whom I have said I would raise up unto you, to deliver my people, O house of Israel.
10 And Moses will I raise up, to deliver thy people out of the land of Egypt.
11 But a seer will I raise up out of the fruit of thy loins; and unto him will I give power to bring forth my word unto the seed of thy loins—and not to the bringing forth my word only, saith the Lord, but to the convincing them of my word, which shall have already gone forth among them.
12 Wherefore, the fruit of thy loins shall write; and the fruit of the loins of Judah shall write; and that which shall be written by the fruit of thy loins, and also that which shall be written by the fruit of the loins of Judah, shall grow together, unto the confounding of false doctrines and laying down of contentions, and establishing peace among the fruit of thy loins, and bringing them to the knowledge of their fathers in the latter days, and also to the knowledge of my covenants, saith the Lord.
13 And out of weakness he shall be made strong, in that day when my work shall commence among all my people, unto the restoring thee, O house of Israel, saith the Lord.
14 And thus prophesied Joseph, saying: Behold, that seer will the Lord bless; and they that seek to destroy him shall be confounded; for this promise, which I have obtained of the Lord, of the fruit of my loins, shall be fulfilled. Behold, I am sure of the fulfilling of this promise;
15 And his name shall be called after me; and it shall be after the name of his father. And he shall be like unto me; for the thing, which the Lord shall bring forth by his hand, by the power of the Lord shall bring my people unto salvation.

2 Nephi 25:7-8
7 But behold, I proceed with mine own prophecy, according to my plainness; in the which I know that no man can err; nevertheless, in the days that the prophecies of Isaiah shall be fulfilled men shall know of a surety, at the times when they shall come to pass.
8 Wherefore, they are of worth unto the children of men, and he that supposeth that they are not, unto them will I speak particularly, and confine the words unto mine own people; for I know that they shall be of great worth unto them in the last days; for in that day shall they understand them; wherefore, for their good have I written them.

2 Nephi 26:14-24
14 But behold, I prophesy unto you concerning the last days; concerning the days when the Lord God

shall bring these things forth unto the children of men.

15 After my seed and the seed of my brethren shall have dwindled in unbelief, and shall have been smitten by the Gentiles; yea, after the Lord God shall have camped against them round about, and shall have laid siege against them with a mount, and raised forts against them; and after they shall have been brought down low in the dust, even that they are not, yet the words of the righteous shall be written, and the prayers of the faithful shall be heard, and all those who have dwindled in unbelief shall not be forgotten.

16 For those who shall be destroyed shall speak unto them out of the ground, and their speech shall be low out of the dust, and their voice shall be as one that hath a familiar spirit; for the Lord God will give unto him power, that he may whisper concerning them, even as it were out of the ground; and their speech shall whisper out of the dust.

17 For thus saith the Lord God: They shall write the things which shall be done among them, and they shall be written and sealed up in a book, and those who have dwindled in unbelief shall not have them, for they seek to destroy the things of God.

18 Wherefore, as those who have been destroyed have been destroyed speedily; and the multitude of their terrible ones shall be as chaff that passeth away—yea, thus saith the Lord God: It shall be at an instant, suddenly—

19 And it shall come to pass, that those who have dwindled in unbelief shall be smitten by the hand of the Gentiles.

20 And the Gentiles are lifted up in the pride of their eyes, and have stumbled, because of the greatness of their stumbling block, that they have built up many churches; nevertheless, they put down the power and miracles of God, and preach up unto themselves their own wisdom and their own learning, that they may get gain and grind upon the face of the poor.

21 And there are many churches built up which cause envyings, and strifes, and malice.

22 And there are also secret combinations, even as in times of old, according to the combinations of the devil, for he is the founder of all these things; yea, the founder of murder, and works of darkness; yea, and he leadeth them by the neck with a flaxen cord, until he bindeth them with his strong cords forever.

23 For behold, my beloved brethren, I say unto you that the Lord God worketh not in darkness.

24 He doeth not anything save it be for the benefit of the world; for he loveth the world, even that he layeth down his own life that he may draw all men unto him. Wherefore, he commandeth none that they shall not partake of his salvation.

2 Nephi 27:1-8

1 But, behold, in the last days, or in the days of the Gentiles—yea, behold all the nations of the Gentiles and also the Jews, both those who shall come upon this land and those who shall be upon other lands, yea, even upon all the lands of the earth, behold, they will be drunken with iniquity and all manner of abominations—

2 And when that day shall come they shall be visited of the Lord of Hosts, with thunder and with earthquake, and with a great noise, and with storm, and with tempest, and with the flame of devouring fire.

3 And all the nations that fight against Zion, and that distress her, shall be as a dream of a night

vision; yea, it shall be unto them, even as unto a hungry man which dreameth, and behold he eateth but he awaketh and his soul is empty; or like unto a thirsty man which dreameth, and behold he drinketh but he awaketh and behold he is faint, and his soul hath appetite; yea, even so shall the multitude of all the nations be that fight against Mount Zion.

4 For behold, all ye that doeth iniquity, stay yourselves and wonder, for ye shall cry out, and cry; yea, ye shall be drunken but not with wine, ye shall stagger but not with strong drink.

5 For behold, the Lord hath poured out upon you the spirit of deep sleep. For behold, ye have closed your eyes, and ye have rejected the prophets; and your rulers, and the seers hath he covered because of your iniquity.

6 And it shall come to pass that the Lord God shall bring forth unto you the words of a book, and they shall be the words of them which have slumbered.

7 And behold the book shall be sealed; and in the book shall be a revelation from God, from the beginning of the world to the ending thereof.

8 Wherefore, because of the things which are sealed up, the things which are sealed shall not be delivered in the day of the wickedness and abominations of the people. Wherefore the book shall be kept from them.

2 Nephi 28:7-14

7 Yea, and there shall be many which shall say: Eat, drink, and be merry, for tomorrow we die; and it shall be well with us.

8 And there shall also be many which shall say: Eat, drink, and be merry; nevertheless, fear God—he will justify in committing a little sin; yea, lie a little, take the advantage of one because of his words, dig a pit for thy neighbor; there is no harm in this; and do all these things, for tomorrow we die; and if it so be that we are guilty, God will beat us with a few stripes, and at last we shall be saved in the kingdom of God.

9 Yea, and there shall be many which shall teach after this manner, false and vain and foolish doctrines, and shall be puffed up in their hearts, and shall seek deep to hide their counsels from the Lord; and their works shall be in the dark.

10 And the blood of the saints shall cry from the ground against them.

11 Yea, they have all gone out of the way; they have become corrupted.

12 Because of pride, and because of false teachers, and false doctrine, their churches have become corrupted, and their churches are lifted up; because of pride they are puffed up.

13 They rob the poor because of their fine sanctuaries; they rob the poor because of their fine clothing; and they persecute the meek and the poor in heart, because in their pride they are puffed up.

14 They wear stiff necks and high heads; yea, and because of pride, and wickedness, and abominations, and whoredoms, they have all gone astray save it be a few, who are the humble followers of Christ; nevertheless, they are led, that in many instances they do err because they are taught by the precepts of men.

D&C 20:1

1 The rise of the Church of Christ in these last days, being one thousand eight hundred and thirty years since the coming of our Lord and Savior Jesus Christ in the flesh, it being regularly organized

and established agreeable to the laws of our country, by the will and commandments of God, in the fourth month, and on the sixth day of the month which is called April--

D&C 27:13

13 Unto whom I have committed the keys of my kingdom, and a dispensation of the gospel for the last times; and for the fulness of times, in the which I will gather together in one all things, both which are in heaven, and which are on earth;

D&C 112:30-32

30 For unto you, the Twelve, and those, the First Presidency, who are appointed with you to be your counselors and your leaders, is the power of this priesthood given, for the last days and for the last time, in the which is the dispensation of the fulness of times.

31 Which power you hold, in connection with all those who have received a dispensation at any time from the beginning of the creation;

32 For verily I say unto you, the keys of the dispensation, which ye have received, have come down from the fathers, and last of all, being sent down from heaven unto you.

D&C 113:3-6

3 What is the rod spoken of in the first verse of the 11th chapter of Isaiah, that should come of the Stem of Jesse?

4 Behold, thus saith the Lord: It is a servant in the hands of Christ, who is partly a descendant of Jesse as well as of Ephraim, or of the house of Joseph, on whom there is laid much power.

5 What is the root of Jesse spoken of in the 10th verse of the 11th chapter?

6 Behold, thus saith the Lord, it is a descendant of Jesse, as well as of Joseph, unto whom rightly belongs the priesthood, and the keys of the kingdom, for an ensign, and for the gathering of my people in the last days.

D&C 124:41

41 For I deign to reveal unto my church things which have been kept hid from before the foundation of the world, things that pertain to the dispensation of the fulness of times.

D&C 128:17-18

17 And again, in connection with this quotation I will give you a quotation from one of the prophets, who had his eye fixed on the restoration of the priesthood, the glories to be revealed in the last days, and in an especial manner this most glorious of all subjects belonging to the everlasting gospel, namely, the baptism for the dead; for Malachi says, last chapter, verses 5th and 6th: Behold, I will send you Elijah the prophet before the coming of the great and dreadful day of the Lord: And he shall turn the heart of the fathers to the children, and the heart of the children to their fathers, lest I come and smite the earth with a curse.

18 I might have rendered a plainer translation to this, but it is sufficiently plain to suit my purpose as it stands. It is sufficient to know, in this case, that the earth will be smitten with a curse unless there is a welding link of some kind or other between the fathers and the children, upon some subject

or other—and behold what is that subject? It is the baptism for the dead. For we without them cannot be made perfect; neither can they without us be made perfect. Neither can they nor we be made perfect without those who have died in the gospel also; for it is necessary in the ushering in of the dispensation of the fulness of times, which dispensation is now beginning to usher in, that a whole and complete and perfect union, and welding together of dispensations, and keys, and powers, and glories should take place, and be revealed from the days of Adam even to the present time. And not only this, but those things which never have been revealed from the foundation of the world, but have been kept hid from the wise and prudent, shall be revealed unto babes and sucklings in this, the dispensation of the fulness of times.

D&C: 128:20
20 And again, what do we hear? Glad tidings from Cumorah! Moroni, an angel from heaven, declaring the fulfilment of the prophets—the book to be revealed. A voice of the Lord in the wilderness of Fayette, Seneca county, declaring the three witnesses to bear record of the book! The voice of Michael on the banks of the Susquehanna, detecting the devil when he appeared as an angel of light! The voice of Peter, James, and John in the wilderness between Harmony, Susquehanna county, and Colesville, Broome county, on the Susquehanna river, declaring themselves as possessing the keys of the kingdom, and of the dispensation of the fulness of times!

D&C 135:3
3 Joseph Smith, the Prophet and Seer of the Lord, has done more, save Jesus only, for the salvation of men in this world, than any other man that ever lived in it. In the short space of twenty years, he has brought forth the Book of Mormon, which he translated by the gift and power of God, and has been the means of publishing it on two continents; has sent the fulness of the everlasting gospel, which it contained, to the four quarters of the earth; has brought forth the revelations and commandments which compose this book of Doctrine and Covenants, and many other wise documents and instructions for the benefit of the children of men; gathered many thousands of the Latter-day Saints, founded a great city, and left a fame and name that cannot be slain. He lived great, and he died great in the eyes of God and his people; and like most of the Lord's anointed in ancient time, has sealed his mission and his works with his own blood; and so has his brother Hyrum. In life they were not divided, and in death they were not separated!

Moses 7:65-66
65 And it came to pass that Enoch saw the day of the coming of the Son of Man, in the last days, to dwell on the earth in righteousness for the space of a thousand years;
66 But before that day he saw great tribulations among the wicked; and he also saw the sea, that it was troubled, and men's hearts failing them, looking forth with fear for the judgments of the Almighty God, which should come upon the wicked.

CHAPTER TWO
PROTECTION & PREPARATION

"I testify that as the forces of evil increase under Lucifer's leadership and as the forces of good increase under the leadership of Jesus Christ, there will be growing battles between the two until the final confrontation. As the issues become clearer and more obvious, all mankind will eventually be required to align themselves either for the kingdom of God or for the kingdom of the devil. As these conflicts rage either secretly or openly, the righteous will be tested. God's wrath will soon shake the nations of the earth and will be poured out on the wicked without measure. But God will provide strength for the righteous and the means of escape; and eventually and finally truth will triumph. I testify that it is time for every man to set in order his own house both temporally and spiritually." (Ezra Taft Benson, Ensign, November 1988, p. 87.)

Joseph Smith, History of the Church, Vol. 1, p. 279.

"Although the Lord has said, that it is His business to provide for His Saints in these last days, yet remember He is not bound so to do, unless we observe His sayings and keep them."

Joseph Smith, History of the Church, Vol. 2, p. 516.

" The salvation of the Saints one and all depends on the building up of Zion, for without this there is no salvation, for deliverance in the last days is found in Zion and in Jerusalem, and in the remnant whom the Lord our God shall call, or in other words, in the stakes which He shall appoint (Joel 2:32)."

Joseph Smith, Lectures on Faith, Lecture 6, p. 58.

"For a man to lay down his all, his character and reputation, his honor, and applause, his good name among men, his houses, his lands, his brothers and sisters, his wife and children, and even his own life also—counting all things but filth and dross for the excellency of the knowledge of Jesus Christ—requires more than mere belief or supposition that he is doing the will of God; but actual knowledge, realizing that, when those sufferings are ended, he will enter into eternal rest, and be a partaker of the glory of God."

Teachings of the Prophet Joseph Smith, Section Four, 1839-42, p. 161.

"Look to the Presidency and receive instruction. Every man who is afraid, covetous, will be taken in a snare. The time is soon coming, when no man will have any peace but in Zion and her stakes."

Teachings of the Prophet Joseph Smith, Section Four, 1839–42, p. 162.

"I explained concerning the coming of the Son of Man; also that it is a false idea that the Saints will escape all the judgments, whilst the wicked suffer; for all flesh is subject to suffer, and 'the righteous shall hardly escape;' still many of the Saints will escape, for the just shall live by faith; yet many of the righteous shall fall a prey to disease, to pestilence, etc., by reason of the weakness of the flesh, and yet be saved in the Kingdom of God. So that it is an unhallowed principle to say that such and such have transgressed because they have been prayed upon by disease or death, for all flesh is subject to death; and the Savior has said, 'Judge not, lest ye be judged.' (September 29, 1839.) DHC 4:11."

Teachings of the Prophet Joseph Smith, Section Six, 1843–44, p. 298.

"Now for the secret and grand key. Though they might hear the voice of God and know that Jesus was the Son of God, this would be no evidence that their election and calling was made sure, that they had part with Christ, and were joint heir with him. They then would want that more sure word of prophecy, that they were sealed in the heavens and had the promise of eternal life in the kingdom of God. Then, having this promise sealed unto them, it was an anchor to the soul, sure and steadfast. Though the thunders might roll and lightnings flash, and earthquakes bellow, and war gather thick around, yet this hope and knowledge would support the soul in every hour of trial, trouble and tribulation. Then knowledge through our Lord and Savior Jesus Christ is the grand key that unlocks the glories and mysteries of the kingdom of heaven."

Teachings of the Prophet Joseph Smith, Section Six, 1843–44, p. 331.

"I have tried for a number of years to get the minds of the Saints prepared to receive the things of God; but we frequently see some of them, after suffering all they have for the work of God, will fly to pieces like glass as soon as anything comes that is contrary to their traditions: they cannot stand the fire at all. How many will be able to abide a celestial law, and go through and receive their exaltation, I am unable to say, as many are called, but few are chosen. (DHC 6:183-185, Jan. 20, 1844.)"

Teachings of the Prophet Joseph Smith, Section Six, 1843-44, p. 365.

"In relation to the kingdom of God, the devil always sets up his kingdom at the very same time in opposition to God. Every man who has a calling to minister to the inhabitants of the world was ordained to that very purpose in the Grand Council. It is the testimony that I want that I am God's servant, and this people His people."

Teachings of the Prophet Joseph Smith, Section Six, 1843–44, p. 391.

"There is one principle which is eternal; it is the duty of all men to protect their lives and the lives of the household, whenever necessity requires, and no power has a right to forbid it, should the last extreme arrive, but I anticipate no such extreme, but caution is the parent of safety."

Proclamation of the Twelve, Messages of the First Presidency, Vol. 1, April 6, 1845, p. 253-254.

"This Spirit shall bear witness to you, of the truth of our testimony; and shall enlighten your minds, and be in you as the spirit of prophecy and revelation. It shall bring things past to your understanding and remembrance; and shall show you things to come.

It shall also impart unto you many great and glorious gifts; such as the gift of healing the sick, and of being healed, by the laying on of hands in the name of Jesus; and of expelling Demons; and even of seeing visions, and conversing with Angels and spirits from the unseen world.

By the light of this Spirit, received through the ministration of the ordinances—by the power and authority of the Holy Apostleship and Priesthood, you will be enabled to understand, and to be the children of light; and thus be prepared to escape all the things that are coming on the earth, and so stand before the Son of Man."

Brigham Young, Messages of the First Presidency, Vol. 2, p. 64.

"Of the day and the hour of the coming of Christ no man knoweth. It is not yet, neither is it far off; there are prophecies yet to be fulfilled before that event takes place; therefore, let no man deceive the Saints with vain philosophy and false prophecy; for false prophets will arise, and deceive the wicked, and, if possible, the good; but while the wicked fear and tremble at surrounding judgments, the Saints will watch and pray; and, waiting the final event in patience, will look calmly on the passing scenery of a corrupted world, and view transpiring events as confirmation of their faith in the holy gospel which they profess, and rejoice more and more, as multiplied signs shall confirm the approach of the millennial day."

Brigham Young, Journal of Discourses, Vol. 1, p. 107, May 8, 1853.

"I wish you to have faith to lay hold on the promises, and claim them as your own. If you have faith like the ancients, you might escape the edge of the sword, stop the mouths of the lions, quench the violence of fire, open the prison doors, and burst asunder iron fetters—all this could be accomplished by faith. But, lest you should not have faith, we have caused to be done that which has been done, in having this people prepared for any emergency that should arise. My advice is be on the watch all the time. Do not lie down, and go to sleep, and say all is well, lest, in an hour when you think not, sudden destruction overtake you."

Brigham Young, Journal of Discourses, Vol. 1, p. 171-172, July 31, 1853.

"As for this people fostering to themselves that the day has come for them to sell their guns and ammunition to their enemies, and sit down to sleep in peace, they will find themselves deceived, and before they know, they will sleep until they are slain. They have got to carry weapons with them, to be ready to send their enemies to hell cross lots, whether they be Lamanites, or mobs who may come to take their lives, or destroy their property. We must be so prepared that they dare not come to us in a hostile manner without being assured they will meet a vigorous resistance, and ten to one they will meet their grave."

Brigham Young, Journal of Discourses, Vol. 2, p. 311, July 8, 1855.

"If any man here is a coward, there are fine mountain retreats for those who feel their hearts beating, at every little hue and cry of the wicked, as though they would break their ribs.

After this year we shall very likely again have fruitful seasons. Now, you cowards, if there are any, hunt in these mountains until you find some cavern where no person can find you, and go there and store up grain enough to last you and your families seven years; then when the mob comes, take your wives and your children, and creep into your den, and there remain until the war is over.

Do not apostatize to save your lives, for if you do, you are sure to lose them. You may do some good by laying up a little more grain than you want, and by handing out a biscuit to a brave hearted soldier passing by, hungry and fatigued. I could hide myself in these mountains, and defy five hundred thousand men to find me. That is not all, I could hide this whole people, and fifty times more, in the midst of these mountains, and our enemies might hunt until they died with old age, and they could not find us. You who are cowards, lay up your crops another year and hide them away.

You know that almost every time that Gentiles address us in public, they are very mindful to caution the Latter-day Saints 'not to fight, now don't fight.' Have we ever wanted to fight them? No, but we have wanted to preach to them the Gospel of peace.

Again, they say, 'We are afraid that you, Latter-day Saints, are becoming aliens to the United States; we are afraid your hearts are weaned from the brotherhood down yonder.' Don't talk about weaning now, for we were weaned long ago, that is, we are or should be weaned from all wickedness and wicked men. I am so perfectly weaned that when I embraced 'Mormonism,' I could have left father, mother, wife, children, and every relation I had, and am weaned from everybody that will turn a deaf ear to the voice of revelation. We are already weaned, but remember, we are not weaned from the constitution of the United States, but only from wickedness, or at least we should be. Let every man and woman rise up in the strength of their God, and in their hearts ask no favors of the wicked; that is the way to live, and then let the wicked persecute, if they choose.

Are we going to fight? No, unless they come upon us and compel us either to fight or be slain."

Brigham Young, Journal of Discourses, Vol. 4, p. 203, February 1, 1857.
"Previous to the death of Joseph, he said that the time would come when the Saints would be glad to take a bundle, if they could get one, under their arms and start to the mountains, and that they would flee there, and that if they could pick up a change of linen they would be glad to start with that, and to go into the wilderness with anything, in order to escape from the destruction that is coming on the inhabitants of the earth. This we believed, or at least I did; though it seemed to be pretty hard that people should be obliged to leave their houses, farms, friends, and comforts that they had gathered around them, and run from them all."

Brigham Young, Journal of Discourses, Vol. 4, p. 343, June 7, 1857.
"Let us go to, then, and lay up in our store-houses, and prepare for the day of famine, of sorrow, and of trouble; for all those things written in the prophecies, in ancient days and in this our day, will surely come upon the inhabitants of the earth."

Brigham Young, Journal of Discourses, Vol. 4, p. 358, June 14, 1857.
"It is the liberal heart, the liberal feelings of men and women—of those who are full of faith in God that they will not suffer, because He will provide for His people in the last days. He has done so; but He will not provide for you and me, except we live our religion. If we will live our religion,

walk in the light of the Lord's countenance, day by day, so as to have fellowship with our Father and His Son Jesus Christ, by the power of the Holy Ghost, and with every good being in heaven and on earth, let me tell you that hell may spew and bellow, and the devils may howl, and they cannot scathe you and me any more than can a few crickets. But, to enjoy the protection of the Almighty, we have got to live our religion—to live so that we have the mind of Christ within us."

Brigham Young, Journal of Discourses, Vol. 4, p. 369-370, June 28, 1857.

"The world are determined to destroy the kingdom of God upon the earth: they wish to obliterate it. The kingdoms of darkness are determined to destroy this kingdom. In their feelings they are fighting you and me, and do not know that they are contending against Jehovah. They have not the least idea of that, but think they are contending against the 'Mormons.' They are not contending against you and me—they are contending against the God of heaven. Do you think he can manage his own affairs? 'Yes, if he only will,' you say. Do you think He can lead this people to victory and glory? 'O yes,' every heart responds, 'if He has a mind to.' Do you think we are safe in trusting in God? 'Yes, if the Lord will actually preserve us.'

How are you going to be assured of all this, and a great many more things? There is but one way—live so that you have the abiding witness within you that, if all the rest go to the devil, I am a servant of God, and will go into His presence. Let every man and woman take that course, and then the Lord will take care of the whole of them."

Brigham Young, Journal of Discourses, Vol. 8, p. 150-151, August 26, 1860.

"Can you discern and understand the dealings of the Lord with this people from the beginning? If we can understand this, it is indeed a matter of great rejoicing to us. All intelligent beings who are crowned with crowns of glory, immortality, and eternal lives must pass through every ordeal appointed for intelligent beings to pass through, to gain their glory and exaltation. Every calamity that can come upon mortal beings will be suffered to come upon the few, to prepare them to enjoy the presence of the Lord. If we obtain the glory that Abraham obtained, we must do so by the same means that he did. If we are ever prepared to enjoy the society of Enoch, Noah, Melchizedek, Abraham, Isaac, and Jacob, or of their faithful children, and of the faithful Prophets and Apostles, we must pass through the same experience, and gain the knowledge, intelligence, and endowments that will prepare us to enter into the celestial kingdom of our Father and God. How many of the Latter-day Saints will endure all these things, and be prepared to enjoy the presence of the Father and the Son? You can answer that question at your leisure. Every trial and experience you have passed through is necessary for your salvation."

Brigham Young, Journal of Discourses, Vol. 8, p. 279, June 3, 1860.

"God does not violate the agency he has given to man; wherefore let this be in the mouth of every Saint, 'The Lord shall have perfect dominion in my heart and affections;' then he will begin to reign in the midst of the people; but he cannot do so now. When we have faith to understand that he must dictate, and that we must be perfectly submissive to him, then we shall begin to rapidly collect the intelligence that is bestowed upon the nations, for all this intelligence belongs to Zion. All the knowledge, wisdom, power, and glory that have been bestowed upon the nations of the earth, from the days of Adam till now, must be gathered home to Zion."

Brigham Young, Journal of Discourses, Vol. 8, p. 283, June 7, 1860.

"It is written that in the latter days the age of man shall be as the age of a tree, when the Lord shall bring again Zion. The Prophet understood that what had been would be again; also that mankind would become blinder in the understandings, and make their days shorter and shorter, until they would become almost extinct; and that then the Lord would begin to revive his Spirit and power and Priesthood among his children; and when he could get a people that would hearken to his voice, he would begin to add to their days, to their intellect, to their stature, and to every power and virtue of life, as at first bestowed upon the human family."

Brigham Young, Journal of Discourses, Vol. 8, p. 339-340, January 20, 1861.

"We might refer to the prophecies and their fulfillment in these our own times; but this does not bear with so much weight upon my mind to tell the people what the Lord is doing and what he is going to do, as it does to urge the Latter-day Saints to faithfulness, to strict obedience, to every requirement of the Gospel of the Son of God, that we may be prepared for every event as it transpires, no matter whether the prophecies are fulfilled under our eyes or on the other side of the earth. No matter whether we live to see them fulfilled or fall to sleep before they are fulfilled, we must live prepared for the events that will take place preparatory to the coming of the Son of man."

Brigham Young, Journal of Discourses, Vol. 9, p. 2-3, April 6, 1861.

"I am thankful that we live to see this day, and have the privilege of assembling ourselves in these valleys. We are not now mingling in the turmoils of strife, warring, and contention, that we would have been obliged to have mingled in, had not the Lord suffered us to have been driven to these mountains—one of the greatest blessings that could have been visited upon us. It has been designed for many generations to hide up the Saints in the last days until the indignation of the Almighty be over. His wrath will be poured out upon the nations of the earth. We see the nations steadily driving along to the precipice. The Lord has spoken from the heavens, and he is about to fulfil the prophecies of his ancient and modern Prophets. He will bring the nations into judgment, and deal with them and make a full end of them. Do you wish to see it done today? Are you prepared for the crisis that will eventually come? No.

I have frequently thought upon the preparation that is necessary. Suppose the word should come, 'Return and build up the center Stake of Zion,' are we ready for it? No. I have often alluded to our mechanics. We have not a mechanic that would know how to lay the first stone for the foundation of the wall around the New Jerusalem, to say nothing about the temples of our God. Are you prepared for the day of vengeance to come, when the Lord will consume the wicked by the brightness of his coming? No. Then do not be too anxious for the Lord to hasten his work. Let our anxiety be centered upon this one thing, the sanctification of our own hearts, the purifying of our own affections, the preparing of ourselves for the approach of the events that are hastening upon us. This should be our concern, this should be our study, this should be our daily prayer, and not to be in a hurry to see the overthrow of the wicked. Be careful; for if they were all to be overthrown at once, how many would there be left that are called Saints? Not as many as I would have remain. We are prepared for the day that is approaching: let us then prepare ourselves for the presence of our Master—for the coming of the Son of Man. The wicked and the ungodly are preparing for their own utter overthrow, and the nation in which we live is doing so as fast as the wheels of time can roll, and ere long sudden destruction will come upon them. Seek not to hasten it, but be satisfied to let the Lord have his own time and way, and be patient. Seek to have the Spirit of Christ, that we may wait patiently the time of the Lord, and prepare ourselves for the times that are coming. This is our duty.

We are blessed in these mountains. This is the best place on the earth for the Latter-day Saints. Search the history of all the nations, and every geographical position on the face of the earth, and you cannot find another situation so well adapted for the Saints as are these mountains. Here is the place in which the Lord designed to hide his people. Be thankful for it; be true to your covenants; be faithful, each and every one."

Brigham Young, Journal of Discourses, Vol. 9, p. 138, July 28, 1861.
"When will Zion be redeemed? When will the Saviour make his appearance in the midst of his people? When will the veil be taken away, that we may behold the glory of God? Can any of you answer these questions? Yes, readily, when I tell you. The redemption of Zion is the first step preparatory to the two last-named events. Just as soon as the Latter-day Saints are ready and prepared to return to Independence, Jackson County, in the State of Missouri, North America, just so soon will the voice of the Lord be heard, 'Arise now, Israel, and make your way to the centre Stake of Zion.' Do you think there is any danger of our being ready before the Lord prepares the other end of the route? Do you believe that we, as Latter-day Saints, are preparing our own hearts, our own lives, to return to take possession of the center Stake of Zion, as fast as the Lord is preparing to cleanse the land from those ungodly persons who dwell there? You can read, reflect, and make your own calculations. If we are not very careful, the earth will be cleansed from wickedness before we are prepared to take possession of it. We must be pure to be prepared to build up Zion. To all appearance, the Lord is preparing that end of the route faster than we are preparing ourselves to go there."

Brigham Young, Journal of Discourses, Vol. 9, p. 191, February 2, 1862.
"It is necessary for us to sustain ourselves, or we will be left in poverty, nakedness, and distress, as a consequence of war and the breaking up of the general government."

Brigham Young, Journal of Discourses, Vol. 9, p. 272, April 6, 1862.
"When the Lord cuts off every resource from this people, only that which is immediately around them, they can then live as well if not better than they do now, and attain to a state of self sustenance much sooner than if he should continue to plead with them to rise up in their strength and do as they ought toward becoming independent before all foreign temporal facilities are entirely cut off. Enoch was three hundred and sixty-five years in getting a people ready to receive the blessings the Lord had to bestow upon them, but in the latter days his work will be cut short in righteousness. Were the Lord to be as indulgent with us as many want him to be, and continue to bear with the sins of the wicked, I presume it would take him fully as long to prepare the people in his day, but he will not wait so long. The Lord can oblige this people to come to the standard he wishes them to reach,

but I have very little faith that many will attain to it in the flesh."

Brigham Young, Journal of Discourses, Vol. 10, p. 250, October 6, 1863.

"Do you know that it is the eleventh hour of the reign of Satan on the earth? Jesus is coming to reign, and all you who fear and tremble because of your enemies, cease to fear them, and learn to fear to offend God, fear to transgress his laws, fear to do any evil to your brother, or to any being upon the earth, and do not fear Satan and his power, nor those who have only power to slay the body, for God will preserve his people."

Brigham Young, Journal of Discourses, Vol. 10, p. 294, May 15, 1864.

"The time is coming when your friends are going to write to you about coming here, for this is the only place where there will be peace. There will be war, famine, pestilence, and misery through the nations of the earth, and there will be no safety in any place but Zion, as has been foretold by the Prophets of the Lord, both anciently and in our day.

This is the place of peace and safety. We would see how it would be if the wicked had power here, but they have not the power. And they never will have, if we live as the Lord requires us to.

Buy flour, you who can; and you, sisters, and children too, when harvest comes, glean the wheat fields. I would as soon see my wives and children gleaning wheat, as anybody's. And then, when the people come here by thousands, you will be able to feed them. What will be your feelings, when the women and children begin to cry in your ears, with not a man to protect them? You can believe it or not, but the time is coming when a good man will be more precious than fine gold."

Brigham Young, Journal of Discourses, Vol. 10, p. 307, June 10-13, 1864.

"You have the finest climate there is anywhere in these mountains, therefore be encouraged, and take the advice so often given, to prepare for the day of want. If we will be faithful to our covenants, we may be sure that the Lord will give us seed time and harvest; and we will not suffer famine, unless we forsake the Priesthood of the Lord our God."

Brigham Young, Journal of Discourses, Vol. 10, p. 335-336, June 22-29, 1864.

"There is one principle I would like to have the Latter-day Saints perfectly understand—that is, of blessings and cursings. For instance, we read that war, pestilence, plagues, famine, etc., will be visited upon the inhabitants of the earth; but if distress through the judgments of God comes upon this people, it will be because the majority have turned away from the Lord. Let the majority of the people turn away from the Holy Commandments which the Lord has delivered to us, and cease to hold the balance of power in the Church, and we may expect the judgments of God to come upon us; but while six-tenths or three-fourths of this people will keep the commandments of God, the curse and judgments of the Almighty will never come upon them, though we will have trials of various kinds, and the elements contend with—natural and spiritual elements. While this people will strive to serve God according to the best of their abilities, they will fare better, have more to eat and to wear, have better houses to live in, better associations, and enjoy themselves better than the wicked ever do or ever will do."

Brigham Young, Journal of Discourses, Vol. 10, p. 336, June 22-29, 1864.

"I say to you, and would like to hear the brethren speak upon this subject, that the righteous have never suffered in temporal things like the ungodly. Search history and you will find it is so, whether with nations, neighborhoods, or individuals, from the day that Adam eat the forbidden fruit down to the present time. If you do not wish to go any farther back, look at the history of the Saints who have settled these valleys, and see it exemplified. History does not show that a colony was ever settled, either in North or South America, that had so little difficulty with the Indians as we have had. This is encouraging; and so it has been in our entire history. The wicked do not know how to enjoy life, but the closer we live to God the better we know and understand how to enjoy it. Live so that you can enjoy the spirit of the Lord continually."

Brigham Young, Journal of Discourses, Vol. 11, p. 130-131, August 1-10, 1865.

"And when we pray, let us not ask our Heavenly Father to do that for us which we would not help Him to do were it in our power. When our brethren, who have the cause of God at heart pray, we invariably hear them ask Him to cleanse the earth from sin, and sanctify it and prepare it for the Lord to dwell upon. While we thus pray, we should be employed in sanctifying ourselves first, and then in redeeming and sanctifying the earth, for this the work we are called to perform, aided by the Almighty. We pray the Lord to preserve the righteous and to let the wickedness of the wicked come to an end, and 'O Lord defend Thy people and fight their battles.' We should be prepared and be as ready and willing to defend ourselves as we are that the Lord should be ready and willing to defend us. We should be as ready and willing to fight our own battles as to have the Lord fight them for us. We should be just as willing to exercise the ability God has given to us to clothe ourselves, to build comfortable habitations for ourselves and our families, as He has been willing to bestow that ability upon us. We should be just as willing to learn to govern and control ourselves, and to abide in the truth, as we are to have the Lord assist us in doing so. When we fully perform our part, the Lord will not be backward in performing all that He has promised, if He should have to waste away and utterly destroy nations and kingdoms to do it.

We all believe that the Lord will fight our battles; but how? Will He do it while we are unconcerned and make no effort whatever for our own safety when an enemy is upon us? If we make no efforts to guard our towns, our houses, our cities, our wives and children, will the Lord guard them for us? He will not; but if we pursue the opposite course and strive to help Him to accomplish His designs, then will He fight our battles. We are baptized for the remission of sins; but it would be quite as reasonable to expect remission of sins without baptism, as to expect the Lord to fight our battles without our taking every precaution to be prepared to defend ourselves. The Lord requires us to be quite as willing to fight our own battles as to have Him fight them for us. If we are not ready for an enemy when he comes upon us, we have not lived up to the requirements of Him who guides the ship of Zion, or who dictates the affairs of his kingdom."

Brigham Young, Journal of Discourses, Vol. 11, p. 274, December 23, 1866.

"I never believed that the righteous have ever suffered as much as the wicked. Jesus Christ said to his disciples, 'These things I have spoken unto you, that in me ye might have peace. In the world ye shall have tribulation, but be of good cheer: I have overcome the world.' I admit that the

Saints anciently 'were . . . afflicted, tormented . . .' Yet in all this suffering and persecution, they were blessed and comforted and rejoiced though in tribulation."

Brigham Young, Journal of Discourses, Vol. 12, p. 121-122, August 17, 1867.

"So this people if they will take the counsels which the Lord gives to them through His servants with regard to their grain, and prepare for all contingencies to which they are subject in this mountainous country, we shall never see a famine; but if we neglect his counsel, refusing to hearken to good advice, we shall, by taking this course, bring distress upon ourselves and upon all who depend upon us for a subsistence. Let us pursue a course to preserve ourselves and avert every calamity. This we can do. It is not necessary for calamity to come upon us, if we will only take a course to prevent it."

Brigham Young, Journal of Discourses, Vol. 12, p. 161, February 16, 1868.

"We are here for the purpose of establishing the kingdom of God on the earth. To be prepared for this work it has been necessary to gather us out from the nations and countries of the world, for if we had remained in those lands we could not have received the ordinances of the Holy Priesthood of the Son of God, which are necessary for the perfection of the Saints preparatory to His coming."

Brigham Young, Journal of Discourses, Vol. 12, p. 231-232, May 17, 1868.

"Do not trifle with evil, or you will be overcome by it before you know. Our business is to build up the Zion of God on the earth. Do you think you will do it and go hand in hand with the wicked? No, never. I know you may say, and say truly, according to the parable spoken by Jesus to his disciples, when the bridegroom was coming, the cry was, 'Go ye out to meet him,' but while he tarried, they all slumbered and slept. And when they awoke with the cry, 'the bridegroom is here,' there were foolish virgins among them who had no oil in their lamps. He did not say that they would be among the ungodly. It is among those who are the bride, the Lamb's wife, that the foolish are to be found. But he never has instructed us to call on the ungodly, and those who would mob us, to make foolish virgins. Some may quote the parable of the wheat and the tares and say they must grow together. Let me tell you, the tares will be in the field, and many will think they are wheat, until harvest comes; but at no time has the Lord said, bring the wicked and ungodly among my people to scourge them; for they are capable of bringing upon themselves all the evil necessary to perfect the good."

Brigham Young, Journal of Discourses, Vol. 12, p. 241-242, July 25, 1868.

"I have never promised a famine to the Latter-day Saints, if we will do half right. You have never heard it drop from my lips that a famine would come upon this people. There never will, if we will only do half right, and we expect to do better than that. There is not another people on the earth whose faith and works are directed for the accomplishment of good like the Latter-day Saints. But we do not obey counsel as we should. Yet when we look at them and at others on the face of the earth, we have reason to say we are proud of the Latter-day Saints. But are we all we should be? No. We must learn to listen to the whispering of the Holy Spirit, and the counsels of the servants of God, until we come to the unity of the faith."

Brigham Young, Journal of Discourses, Vol. 12, p. 243-244, July 25, 1868.

"It is said, by some, that the Lord is not going to tell His servants to gather His people here to starve. That is true; but the Lord has said, 'Gather the poor from the nations;' and to the people here, 'Gather and save the produce I put within your reach, and prepare against a day of want.' Suppose a hundred thousand or a million of starving people were coming here, and we had only grain to last for a couple of years, with famine around; they would offer their gold and their silver and their plate and their precious things for bread to eat, and you would hand it out until all was gone. Then you could sit down and look at the riches you had got, until all would perish together with hunger. This would be so, unless the people act more wisely than they do now."

Brigham Young, Journal of Discourses, Vol. 12, p. 283-284, October 8, 1868.

"This people have got to be self-sustaining, if they believe in the revelations given to them. You will find by and by that this same Babylon, which the Saints of God are required to leave, will fall. Will there be anybody left on the face of the earth? Yes, probably millions. Who will they be? Why the servants and handmaidens of the Almighty, those who love and serve Him. Now, I will ask the question, suppose this is true concerning the gathering out of the Saints, and that Babylon, or a confused and wicked world, will cease its operations as they are now going on, and the time spoken of shall have come, when the merchants will mourn and weep because there is no one to buy their merchandise, will the inhabitants of Zion go Down to buy their silks and satins and keep up his trade? No. By and by there will be a gulf between the righteous and the wicked so that they can not trade with each other, and national intercourse will cease. It is not so now, they can pass from one to the other with ease. But if this is the Kingdom of God and if we are the Saints of God—I leave you all to judge for yourselves about this—are we not required to sustain ourselves and to manufacture that which we consume, to cease our bartering, trading, mingling, drinking, smoking, chewing and joining with all the filth of Babylon? You may judge for yourselves in relation to this. But I can say that we have been striving for twenty-one years in these valleys, and before we came here, to bring this people to this point. When we look at ladies and gentlemen we can see that their wants are many, but their real necessities are very few. Now, let the Latter-day Saints see that their necessities are supplied, and omit their wants for the present, and until we can manufacture what we want. We want you henceforth to be a self-sustaining people. Hear it, O Israel! hear it neighbors, friends and enemies, this is what the Lord requires of this people."

Brigham Young, Journal of Discourses, Vol. 12, p. 310, November 29, 1868.

"We look forward to the day when this people will be pure, holy and sanctified, and when we will be prepared to build up Zion. Are we prepared now? No, we are not. We are only professedly Latter-day Saints; practically, we are only so in part. To be a Saint is to be as Jesus was; to be assimilated to the spirit and character which He exhibited while here on earth. Now, I exhort the Latter-day Saints to live so that each and everyone may enjoy the spirit of the Lord Jesus day by day, that we may be one in all things, in temporal matters as well as spiritual."

Brigham Young, Journal of Discourses, Vol. 15, p. 1-4, April 28, 1872.

"Will he ever grant power to his Saints on the earth? Yes, they will take the kingdom, and possess it for ever and ever; but in the capacity they are now, in the condition that they now present themselves before God, before the world and before each other? Never, never! until we are sanctified, until we are filled with the wisdom of God, with the knowledge of God, will he bequeath the power that he has in reserve for his Saints; never will the Saints possess it until they are prepared to wield it with all that judgment, discretion, wisdom and forbearance that the Lord Almighty wields in his own capacity, and uses at his pleasure?"

Brigham Young, Journal of Discourses, Vol. 16, p. 45, May 18, 1873.

"Do you know that Babylon is going to fall? Her merchants will cry out, 'there is no one to buy our merchandise.' And if you and I do not learn how to take care of ourselves, and raise and manufacture what we consume, we shall have to go without. If you do not know how, go to work and learn how to knot, sew, weave, make ribbons, raise silk and make up and manufacture your own wearing apparel and all you need."

Brigham Young, Journal of Discourses, Vol. 19, p. 5-7, April 29, 1877.

"If we will faithfully mind our own concerns, live our religion, do good to all men, preach the Gospel to the nations of the earth, gather up the honest in heart, build up and establish Zion in the earth, send the Gospel to the House of Israel, and live and serve God in all things, all will be well with us, we have no cause for fear in the least. When the Lord deems it necessary that his servants should seal their testimony with their blood, in order that his word may be strengthened and of greater force in the earth, so let it be; they are received into the arms of Jehovah, they rejoice in the society of those who are waiting patiently until the trump shall sound, when the sleeping nations shall awake and their bodies come forth to be reunited with their spirits, and the faithful enter into a fullness of his glory. With them all is well, all is right."

Discourses of Brigham Young, p. 345.

"Should our lives be extended to a thousand years, still we may live and learn. Every vicissitude we pass through is necessary for experience and example, and for preparation to enjoy that reward which is for the faithful."

Discourses of Brigham Young, p. 298.

"The time will come that gold will hold no comparison in value to a bushel of wheat."

Discourses of Brigham Young, p. 350.

"When we look at the Latter-day Saints, we ask, is there any necessity of their being persecuted? Yes, if they are disobedient. Is there any necessity of chastening a son or a daughter? Yes, if they are disobedient. But suppose they are perfectly obedient to every requirement of their parents, is there any necessity of chastening them then? If there is, I do not understand the principle of it. I have not yet been able to see the necessity of chastening an obedient child, neither have I been able to see the necessity of chastisement from the Lord upon a people who are perfectly obedient.

Have this people been chastened? Yes, they have."

Life of Heber C. Kimball, p. 450, 1867.

"This Church has before it many close places through which it will have to pass before the work of God is crowned with victory. To meet the difficulties that are coming, it will be necessary for you to have a knowledge of the truth of this work for yourselves. The difficulties will be of such a character that the man or woman who does not possess this personal knowledge or witness will fall. If you have not got the testimony, live right and call upon the Lord and cease not till you obtain it. If you do not you will not stand.

Remember these sayings, for many of you will live to see them fulfilled. The time will come when no man nor woman will be able to endure on borrowed light. Each will have to be guided by the light within himself. If you do not have it, how can you stand?"

Heber C. Kimball, Deseret News, May 23, 1931.

"An army of Elders will be sent to the four quarters of the earth to search out the righteous and warn the wicked of what is coming. All kinds of religions will be started and miracles performed that will deceive the very elect if such were possible. Our sons and daughters must live pure lives so as to be prepared for what is coming.

After a while the gentiles will gather to this place by the thousands, and Salt Lake City will be classed among the wicked cities of the world. A spirit of speculation and extravagance will take possession of the Saints, and the result will be financial bondage.

Persecution comes next and all true Latter-Day Saints will be tested to the limit. Many will apostatize and others will stand still, not knowing what to do. Darkness will cover the earth and gross darkness the minds of the people. The judgments of God will be poured out upon the wicked to the extent that our Elders from far and near will be called home, or in other words the gospel will be taken from the Gentiles and later on be carried to the Jews.

The western boundary of the State of Missouri will be swept so clean of its inhabitants that as President Young tells us, 'When you return to that place, there will not be left so much as a yellow dog to wag his tail.'

Before that day comes, however, the Saints will be put to tests that will try the integrity of the best of them. The pressure will become so great that the more righteous among them will cry unto the Lord day and night until deliverance comes.

Then the Prophet Joseph and others will make their appearance and those who have remained faithful will be selected to return to Jackson County, Missouri and take part in the building of that beautiful city, the New Jerusalem."

Heber C. Kimball quoted by J. Golden Kimball, Conference Report, October 1930, p. 60.

"'Yes,' said Brother Heber (Kimball), 'the time is coming when we will be mixed up in these now peaceful valleys to that extent that it will be difficult to tell the face of a Saint from the face of an enemy against the people of God. Then is the time to look out for the great sieve, for there will be a great sifting time, and many will fall. For I say unto you there is a test, a Test, a TEST coming.'

He further said: 'This Church has before it many close places through which it will have to pass before the work of God is crowned with glory. The difficulties will be of such a character that the man or woman who does not possess a personal knowledge or witness will fall. If you have not got this testimony, you must live right and call upon the Lord, and cease not until you obtain it.'

'Remember these sayings: The time will come when no man or woman will be able to endure on borrowed light. Each will have to be guided by the light within themselves. If you do not have the knowledge that Jesus is the Christ, how can you stand?'"

Heber C. Kimball, Journal of Discourses, Vol. 2, p. 107-108, August 13, 1853.

"What do I care for what the world says? I care no more about it than I do for the squawking of a goose. It is none of their business if I have a mind to be a Saint, and keep the commandments of God; and as you have heard it said, so say I—the time will come in which you will dwell in peace and safety; and when the time comes that you will go back to Jackson County, you will be independent, and live without any opposition at all. Can the Lord do it? Yes. All the people are in His hands, and He can turn the nations as I can an obedient horse. They are governed and controlled by the Almighty at much as we are. What can they do against us? Why nothing whatever, but if we do not do right they will be a scourge in the hands of God to scourge us, just as the Indians are at this time. There never would have been a disturbance if this people had done as they were told."

Heber C. Kimball, Journal of Discourses, Vol. 2, p. 156, November 26, 1854.

"I would like to see the people take a course to make their own clothing, make their own machinery, their own knives and their own forks, and everything else we need, for the day will come when we will be under the necessity of doing it, for trouble and perplexity, war and famine, bloodshed and fire, and thunder and lightning will roll upon the nations of the earth, insomuch that we cannot get to them, nor they to us. If you do not believe me I want you to believe the Prophets; read the revelations that came through brother Joseph Smith, and through Daniel and Moses, and through Jesus, and through all the ancient Prophets. They spoke of these things, and declare they shall come to pass in the latter days. Well, what period is it now? Unto us it is the 'last days,' in which, the Lord says by His Prophets, when you hear of war, and rumors of war, it will not be long before you have it in your own land. Now are we as a people preparing and qualifying ourselves for that day, lest it overtake us as a thief in the night? It certainly will if we do not wake up from our slumber."

Heber C. Kimball, Journal of Discourses, Vol. 3, p. 227-228, March 2, 1856.

"Take this people as a people, throughout the valleys of the mountains, and I presume that they are the best people upon the face of the earth, and even here there is hardly a person but what takes a course to live from hand to mouth, that is, they will never lay up anything. This course will not answer for us, we must lay up grain against the famines that will prevail upon the earth. What shall we lay up that grain for? Shall we lay it up to feed the wicked? No, we shall lay it up to feed the Saints who gather here from all the nations of the earth, and for the millions of lovers of good and wholesome laws who will come from the old countries and from the United States, fleeing to this place for their bread, and I know it."

Heber C. Kimball, Journal of Discourses, Vol. 4, p. 6, June 29, 1856.

"Rejoice in all things brought forth in these last days, for the time will come when you will say that we indeed live in the last dispensation.

The trials in the last days will be numerous, but to the faithful they will be of but small moment, for they will live above these things, they will increase in power. The work of God is bound to increase, and just in that proportion will the devil's kingdom rise in power and strength, and walk up to battle against us. The adversary is bent on having a war with this people, we shall have him right by the side of us, and you will find that he will keep you very busy, if you strive to come off victorious."

Heber C. Kimball, Journal of Discourses, Vol. 4, p. 106, September 28, 1856.

"There will be millions on millions that will come much in the same way (handcarts), only they will not have hand carts, for they will take their bundles under their arms, and their children on their backs, and under their arms, and flee; and Zion's people will have to send out relief to them, for they will come when the judgments come on the nations. And you will find that judgments will be more sore upon this people, if they do not repent and lay aside their pride and their animosities, their quarrelling and contentions, their disputations among themselves."

Heber C. Kimball, Journal of Discourses, Vol. 4, p. 330, May 31, 1857.

"I speak of these things by way of encouragement to you, brethren and sisters. You are a good people: I respect you; I have pride in you, when you live your religion; but let us wake up. We have done first rate; but we can wake up more, and keep waking up, and attend to the things you have been told to attend to; and one of them is, to lay up stores of corn, wheat, oats, peas, beans, buck wheat, and every thing else that can be preserved; for you will see a day when you will want it; and it will be when we shall feel the effects of famine, and when the United States have not any food. And inasmuch as we are wise and prudent in this matter, we shall have power over them, and they cannot help themselves. And the day will come when the wicked shall not come here to impose upon our good feelings, and for us to nourish them, while they are infusing the poison of their corruption in our midst. I have borne and borne that wickedness until I will not bear it any longer."

Heber C. Kimball, Journal of Discourses, Vol. 5, p. 10, July 5, 1857.

"Lay up your stores, and take your silks and fine things, and exchange them for grain and such things as you need, and the time will come when we will be obliged to depend upon our own resources; for the time is not far distant when the curtain will be dropped between us and the United States. When that time comes, brethren and sisters, you will wish you had commenced sooner to make your own clothing. I tell you, God requires us to go into home manufacture; and, prolong it as much as you like, you have got to do it.

You will also see the day that you will wish you had laid up your grain, if you do not do it now; for you will see the day, if you do not take care of the blessings God has given to you, that you will become servants, the same as the world will.

We have told you this before. You have been exhorted, year after year, to prepare for hard times: you have been told of this often enough. We have told you that when hard times come again you won't have the privilege that you had last time of having food dealt out to you gratuitously, but you will have to pay for all you get. This will come to pass. I suppose there are many who don't believe it . . .

I will prove to you that I will put my faith with my works and lay up stores for my family and for my friends that are in the United States, and I will be to them as Joseph was to the people in the land of Egypt. Every man and woman will be a saviour if they will do as I say. You may write this down and send it to the States; for it will be published . . .

The day will come when the people of the United States will come lugging their bundles under their arms, coming to us for bread to eat. Every Prophet has spoken of this from the early ages of the world. Already we begin to see sickness, trouble, death, famine, and pestilence; and more yet awaits the nations of the wicked. Jesus said, When you hear of these things in foreign nations—destruction and desolation, you may then look forth for my coming, and know that it is nigh at hand. In relation to the world, our enemies, their soldiery, and their governors, I do not fear them, and I never did.

If you will do right—keep the commandments of God, I can say with all the propriety that any man, prophet, or apostle ever did, you shall never want for food, or raiment, or houses, or lands; and no power on the earth can injure you. There is no power that shall prevent our prosperity; for we shall increase, while every other power upon the earth that is opposed to this work and our God will go down. I just know it. Amen."

Heber C. Kimball, Journal of Discourses, Vol. 5, p. 19-20, April 6, 1857.
"If we sin, and do not repent, God will chastise us until we do repent of and forsake all sin; but He never will scourge us so long as we do right. I have said a hundred times that we never shall want for bread, meat, and the comforts of life, worlds without end, if we will only do right."

Heber C. Kimball, Journal of Discourses, Vol. 5, p. 21, April 6, 1857.
"As I have said, I know that we will see those things of which I have spoken—such famines as this world never beheld. Yes, we have got to see those scenes; but if we will keep our vows and covenants, the Lord will hold them off until we can prepare ourselves; and if you will wake up and do as you are told, you will escape."

Heber C. Kimball, Journal of Discourses, Vol. 5, p. 23, April 6, 1857.
"Then go to work and build up this kingdom, establish righteousness, and prepare yourselves for the famines that are coming upon the earth; for I tell you that they are coming.

Do you suppose that God would give revelations and tell us to warn the inhabitants of the earth of things which were coming speedily upon them, if He did not intend that those things should come? He said that they should feel them, and I know that they are bound to feel them; for they will not repent. Let us go to work and prepare for the thousands upon thousands who will come unto us."

Heber C. Kimball, Journal of Discourses, Vol. 5, p. 205, October 12, 1856.
"Let us take a course that will be pleasing to our Father, and lay aside our follies and our sins, and obtain favour with our God, that his angels may come and associate with us. They would do so

now, if you would believe and practice that which is laid before you day by day. And if you will strictly follow the leaders of this people, you never would want for clothing, nor for any of the comforts of life; for if it must needs be that we be protected and delivered from our enemies, God would cause a famine to scourge them, and would rain manna down from heaven to sustain us, as he did to the children of Israel. But he never will do that, until it is necessary to our salvation and deliverance."

Heber C. Kimball, Journal of Discourses, Vol. 6, p. 64, November 22, 1857.

"The righteous have got to provide for the righteous in the latter days, as Joseph in Egypt provided for his father's house and those that believed on him, like a good father providing for a good family, for good wives, and good children."

Heber C. Kimball, Journal of Discourses, Vol. 7, p. 234, August 28, 1859.

"With regard to grain, I will say, If you do not lay it up and keep it, you will be sorry in a day to come; for you will see hard times, trying times, plagues, and famines, and bloodshed. Be advised and provide in time, and while you have the opportunity."

Heber C. Kimball, Journal of Discourses, Vol. 7, p. 331, October 7, 1859.

"The Holy Ghost in the people of God will control not only our domestic animals, our families, our servants, and our handmaids, but it will control the armies of men that are in the world, the mountains, seas, streams of water, tempests, famines, and pestilence, and every destructive power, that they come not nigh unto us, just as much as we can keep sickness from us by the power of faith and prayer and good works. If we live our religion, we shall never suffer as the world suffers. We shall not be perplexed with famine and pestilence, with the caterpillar, and other destructive insects, which the Lord will send in the last days to afflict the wicked."

Heber C. Kimball, Journal of Discourses, Vol. 8, p. 89, June 7, 1860.

"Let it not be said that any portion of the people of this Territory have not wheat enough to last them until harvest. Let them be sure to do one thing, if God permit it—secure well the coming harvest, and be sure to lay up enough to last one, two, or three years. When we have done this, we have time then to beautify our gardens, cities, palaces, and playgrounds, and more thoroughly school our children. It is hard to improve when there is no bread. When a man has no bread, and his neighbours have none, he must have horrible feelings. The day will come when millions of people will flock to us for bread, and thousands of them will be honest; they will be the elect of God: they will come to us for salvation, either to this place or to Jackson County."

Heber C. Kimball, Journal of Discourses, Vol. 8, p. 257, December 16, 1860.

"If this people will take this course, and live their religion in all things, I can prophesy in the name of Israel's god that you will never have to fire a gun, for the Lord will send his angels to do the work of destruction among the wicked. The Almighty will lead the wicked as a man leads a horse, at pleasure. Brethren, why don't you live your religion, magnify your callings, and honour God in all things you do and say? Be humble and prayerful; be faithful to your duties at all times."

Heber C. Kimball, Journal of Discourses, Vol. 9, p. 54-55, April 14, 1861.

"The Almighty through his Prophets foretold that the nation would make war upon this people, and that he would come out of his hiding place, and pour out his judgments upon those that rebel against him, and who persecuted his people, and set themselves against his house. Then it shall go forth like a mighty whirlwind upon the face of the whole earth. In this country the North and the South will exert themselves against each other, and ere long the whole face of the United States will be in commotion, fighting one against another, and they will destroy their nationality. They have never done anything for this people, and I don't believe they ever will. I have never prayed for the destruction of this Government, but I know that dissolution, sorrow, weeping, and distress are in store for the inhabitants of the United States, because of their conduct towards the people of God. Then the judgments will go forth to the nations of the earth. I have an understanding of these things, and I sincerely hope that you comprehend as clearly as I do. If you do, you will strive to prepare for those things that are coming upon the earth in these last days."

Orson Hyde, Journal of Discourses, Vol. 5, p. 15-16, June 14, 1857.

"Let the Almighty shut down the gate of prosperity, as He will do, and a general dearth ensue, and they know that in Zion it is fruitful, and that the good things of the earth are produced there—let them know that there is bread, and you will see them coming here to pour out their treasures for a bit of bread; but if you shall not have it stored up for them, you will not do your duty. The Lord can do this. He can bring these things about; and, brethren, the test is right before us. It is not an imaginary thing, but it is actually coming to test us, to see whether we will, under these circumstances, abide the counsel that has been given to us."

Orson Hyde, Journal of Discourses, Vol. 20, p. 100-101, November 3, 1878.

"There is another important feature, my friends, connected with this subject that I cannot allow myself to omit. In the great rush of people to the Saints in the last days, all sorts, sizes, and of both sexes, will rush in upon us to escape the wrath of the elements, which will render a time of purification and cleansing, actually necessary. The chaff must be blown away, and they who laid us waste must go forth from us. The wicked and the ungodly must be far away. Now, what agencies must be employed to accomplish this important part of the programme. It is out of my power to inform you as to what means may be called in to requisition to effect this object. We know, however, that wind has something to do with the scattering of chaff. The departure of the ungodly from amongst the Saints may be voluntary in many cases."

Parley P. Pratt, Journal of Discourses, Vol. 3, p. 311, April 7, 1856.

"To sinners He has never made any promise, but that they shall be rewarded according to their works; but to the Saints that keep the commandments and abide in the Gospel of Jesus Christ, and to them that do believe and know His will, He has made these; but those who have known Him and in the day of tribulation forsaken His laws will be beaten with many stripes. To all those who stand firm and steadfast when the love of many shall wax cold because of the famine and pestilence, and great trials with which the Saints of God are to be tried before the judgments pass from the house of

God to the wicked, to all such He has made precious promises, and they will be fulfilled; and the promises concerning things to the house of Israel as well as to the Saints of the Most High will surely be fulfilled, for those promises hold good to the other side of the vail."

Orson Pratt, Deseret Evening News, Vol. 8, #265, Oct. 2, 1875, discourse delivered Sept. 26, 1875.

"The time will come, when we shall find ourselves restricted, and when it will be very important indeed for us to patronize home productions, and cease sending our millions abroad for importations, for the gate will be shut down, and circumstances will be such that we cannot bring things from abroad; and hence the necessity of the exhortation that we have received from time to time, to engage with all our hearts in the various branches of industry necessary to make us self-sustaining, and to carry them out with all the tact and wisdom which God has given to us, that we may become free and independent in all these matters, free before the heavens, and free from all the nations of the earth and their productions, so far as being dependent upon them is concerned. Then we will be a happy people, for we shall have an abundance of the good things of the earth, all that are necessary to eat and wear, all that are necessary to beautify and adorn our habitations, our cities, and our public buildings, or whatever may be necessary for the benefit and happiness of a great community, but not until that time shall come, for we are now taking a course that is calculated, in its very nature, to impoverish any people, for we are continually importing millions of dollars worth of foreign productions, while our exportations amount to but very little."

Orson Pratt, The Seer, p. 246-247.

"Let the Saints remember, that the Lord hath said, that the people of Zion are to be the only people upon the face of the whole earth, but what shall be at war one with another. They alone will escape if they observe diligently all the commandments of the Lord in the Book of Mormon, and in the other revelations which God has given or shall hereafter give; but if not, they will in no wise escape; for the Lord will chasten the Saints until they will learn to live by every word that proceedeth forth from His mouth. Those who call themselves Latter-Day Saints are no more precious in the sight of God than other people, unless they do better than others. Indeed, the greater the light against which the Saints sin, the greater and more severe must be their judgment, unless they repent. Therefore, let us fear before the Lord, and tremble exceedingly. If we have any of us sinned, let us go before Him, and confess our faults, and seek mercies and forgiveness at His hands. Let us put away every evil, and strive most earnestly to give heed to the word of truth; for how can we stand before Him unless we do this! The great and terrible day of the Lord is at hand, and all nations shall fear and tremble exceedingly; but if the Saints are prepared, it shall be a day of rejoicing and of great glory to them; it shall be the day of their redemption, and the commencement of a glorious reign, of which there shall be no end."

Orson Pratt, Journal of Discourses, Vol. 2, p. 264, April 7, 1855.

"Is there anything too great for us to suffer or endure, or any sacrifice too great for us to make to be prepared to receive blessings of this description? No. Then let us wake up, and be assured that just as soon as we prepare ourselves for these blessings, so soon they will be upon our heads. Do you suppose that these three Nephites have any knowledge of what is going on in this land? They know all about it; they are filled with the spirit of prophecy. Why do they not come into our midst? Because the time has not come. Why do they not lift up their voices in the midst of our congregations? Because there is a work for us to do preparatory to their reception, and when that is accomplished, they will accomplish their work, unto whomsoever they desire to minister. If they shall pray to the Father, says the Book of Mormon, in the name of Jesus, they can show themselves unto whatsoever person or people they choose. The very reason they do not come amongst us is, because we have a work to do preparatory to their coming; and just as soon as that is accomplished they are on hand, and also many other good old worthy ancients that would rejoice our hearts could we behold their countenances, and hear them recite over the scenes they have passed through, and the history of past events, as well as prophecy of the events to come."

Orson Pratt, Journal of Discourses, Vol. 3, p. 14-15, May 20, 1855.

"Here, then, we perceive that each will have his share of trials, either in the beginning or in the advanced state of the Church. We do not know what they will be, only so far as God has revealed in His word. He has told us that we should be visited with famine and sword, with pestilence and distress; all these are predicted, and laid before this people in the Book of Doctrine and Covenants. The Lord says, unless His servants should hearken to the words and counsels that He gives unto them, famine, trouble, and distress would overtake them."

Orson Pratt, Journal of Discourses, Vol. 3, p. 16, May 20, 1855.

"In order to do this, it is necessary for us, in our prosperity, to remember the Lord our God, for if men and women will not remember the Lord, when the heavens smile upon them, and when health is in their habitations—if they will not acknowledge the hand of God then, and be thankful for the blessings that they receive, you may be sure that they will not be so well prepared to endure trials, and to pass through adversities, as those who have, in the days of their prosperity, humbled themselves before the Lord, and acknowledged His hand in all things."

Orson Pratt, Journal of Discourses, Vol. 3, p. 17, May 20, 1855.

"A flowing stream is one that runs continually; and the Gentiles will, in that day, come to us as a flowing stream, and we shall have to set our gates open continually, they will come as clouds and as doves in large flocks. Do you suppose that the Gentiles are going to be ignorant of what is taking place? 'Now this will not be the case, they will perfectly understand what is taking place. The people will see that the hand of God is over this people; they will see that He is in our midst, and that He is our watchtower, that He is our shield and our defence, and therefore, they will say, 'Let us go up and put our riches in Zion, for there is no safety in our own nations.'

Those nations are trembling and tottering and will eventually crumble to ruin, and those men of wealth will come here, not to be baptized, but many of them will come that have never heard the servants of God; but they will hear that peace and health dwell among us, and that our officers are all peace officers, and our tax-gatherers men of righteousness."

Orson Pratt, Journal of Discourses, Vol. 3, p. 296, February 10, 1856.

"I am as convinced that the Lord will whip us into this diligent course, as I am that I am standing before you. Why? Because this is the kingdom, this is the people and the Church of the living God, and just as surely as He is our God, will He purify this people by famine, by war, by sickness, by death, by various judgments, and by the flame of devouring fire."

Orson Pratt, Journal of Discourses, Vol. 3, p. 303, April 6, 1856.

"If we had to depend upon our own faith alone, to bring about this latter-day work, it would be rather discouraging. The powers of darkness are so strong that our weak human natures might be overcome were it not for other powers that have great influence to aid and assist us. There are evil influences that are ever ready to throw iniquity in our path, and unless we were assisted by beings more powerful than we are, we should most certainly fail to accomplish the work assigned to us."

Orson Pratt, Journal of Discourses, Vol. 6, p. 204, January 24, 1859.

"In those days the Lord enabled Israel to overcome the Hittites, the Hivites, the Jebusites, etc. How easy it would have been for the Lord to have destroyed them by earthquake, or by fire, or by something of this kind! But he did not do it,—and why? Because he wanted to do several things at the same time: he wanted to destroy the wicked, and to see if his servants would flinch in the hour of danger. The Lord is going to defend this people, but not without their agency. He is not going to let us sit upon our easy chairs and not expose ourselves. If we were to do this, we should not be worthy of the kingdom of God. He offers the kingdom and says it is ours, upon certain conditions."

Orson Pratt, Journal of Discourses, Vol. 7, p. 189-190, July 10, 1859.

"But the Latter-day Saints are not in darkness; they are the children of light, although many of us will actually be asleep. We shall have to wake up and trim up our lamps, or we shall not be prepared to enter in; for we shall all slumber and sleep in that day, and some will have gone to sleep from which they will not awake until they awake up in darkness without any oil in their lamps. But, as a general thing, the Saints will understand the signs of the times, if they do lie down and get to sleep. Others have their eyes closed upon the prophecies of the ancient Prophets; and not only that, but they are void of the spirit of prophecy themselves. When a man has this, though he may appeal to ancient Prophets to get understanding on some subjects he does not clearly understand, yet, as he has the spirit of prophecy in himself, he will not be in darkness; he will have a knowledge of the signs of the times; he will have a knowledge of the house of Israel, and of Zion, of the ten tribes and of many things and purposes and events that are to take place on the earth; and he will see coming events, and can say such an event will take place, and after that another, and then another; and after that the trumpet shall sound, and after that certain things will take place, and then another trump shall sound, etc.; and he will have his eye fixed on the signs of the times, and that day will not overtake him unawares; but upon the nations it will come as a thief upon the mighty men and upon the chief captains, who will gather up their hosts upon the mountains, hills, and valleys of Palestine, to fight against the jews; and they will be as blind as the dumb ass; and right in the midst of their blindness the Lord will rend the heavens and stand his feet upon the Mount of Olives, and all the Saints will come with him, and the wicked will be destroyed from off the face of the earth."

Orson Pratt, Journal of Discourses, Vol. 7, p. 313, September 18, 1859.

"I recollect reading of Enoch's having gathered his people, and that their enemies came up against them to battle. What kind of weapons did Enoch use to destroy his enemies? It says, 'And he (Enoch) spake the word of the Lord, and the earth trembled, and the mountains fled, according to his command; and the rivers of water were turned out of their course, and the roar of the lions was heard out of the wilderness, and all nations feared greatly, so powerful was the word of Enoch, and so great was the power of language which God had given him.'

That was the power given to that Priesthood and authority which was conferred upon Enoch in the early ages of the world. It is also your privilege, ye servants of the living God, to obtain by faith the same blessings and the same power, that when you shall be appointed upon foreign missions, you can open your mouths by the power of the same Spirit that rested upon Enoch—that you can not only teach them what they shall do, but prophesy to the people and tell them what shall be in the future—tell them of the judgments and calamities that shall overtake the wicked. It is your privilege to prophesy to the great and to the low, to the king on his throne, to great men in high places, to the inhabitants of the earth, and to foretell that which shall befall their cities, villages, nations, countries, and kingdoms,—to foretell all these things, not by your wisdom, nor by the spirit of false prophecy, but by the power of that Spirit which rested on Enoch in ancient days. With such a qualification, you could go forth and perform the mission appointed to you acceptably in the sight of God.

What is the privilege of the servants of God that are remaining here in the midst of the settlements of Zion? It is our privilege to sanctify ourselves and have even greater power than those who go to the nations. Why? Because here is the great central place of gathering, and here should centre all the powers of the everlasting Priesthood. Here, in our midst, should be poured out the blessings of that Priesthood to their fullest extent. Here the servants of God should be clothed upon from on high with the glory of God, and be able to foretell all things which would be for the welfare and benefit of the children of Zion. All these blessings belong to the Priesthood here.

You have the keys of the Priesthood; you have the key-words of the Priesthood here; you have the signs of the Priesthood here; you have all the ordinances of the Priesthood here which have been revealed; you have learned the rules and laws of the Priesthood; and why not, ye Elders of Israel—ye servants of the Most High God, rise up in the power of the Priesthood and magnify your callings throughout the settlements in this Territory? Why give way to darkness, to debauchery, to low and degraded things, and mix with those who are calculated to fill you with the spirit of evil continually?

Why suffer a cloud of darkness to hover over your minds, even a cloud of thick darkness that is almost impenetrable? Why suffer your faith to die away, that you cannot prevail with the heavens and obtain the blessings of the Priesthood revealed in the last days?"

Orson Pratt, Journal of Discourses, Vol. 8, p. 48, April 8, 1860.

"One thing is certain—that every nation under the heaven will array itself against the kingdom of God. Inasmuch as some individuals among the nations receive it, they will muster their forces and try to destroy the Saints of the living God. To prepare for this, we must increase in the Spirit of God as our enemies increase in the spirit of darkness against us, and by the power of God proclaim in their ears a testimony that will overcome the wicked. There is no possibility of the wicked triumphing over this Latter-day Kingdom. There may be many who will have to fall—many who will have to suffer materially; but when we get to the home of the Saints of the living God, the wicked will cease from troubling us."

Orson Pratt, Journal of Discourses, Vol. 12, p. 342-346, December 27, 1868.

"I mention these things in order to impress one particular item upon the minds of the Latter-day Saints concerning the inheritance or possession of this land. The Lord not only made decrees in the early ages with the first colonists that came here, but He renewed these decrees every time He brought a colony here, that the people should serve Him, or they should be cut off from His presence, and you will find that God, in every instance, has remembered these decrees. And there is one thing remarkable in relation to the history of these nations, and that is the rapidity with which they departed from the faith and righteousness and the love of the true God. Sometimes they would, after some great judgement or scourge had fallen upon them, causing the death of many of them, repent and become a righteous people; and God would bless them again, and they would begin to rise up and prosper in the land. But perhaps in the course of three or four years a people that were almost wholly righteous would turn from their righteousness to folly, sin and wickedness, and bring down another heavy judgment on their heads. And thus generation after generation passed away among the former inhabitants of this land, and they had their ups and downs. Every time the majority of the people transgressed, a tremendous judgment would come upon them; and every time they repented before the Lord with all their hearts, He would turn away His wrath and begin to prosper them.

Now, these same decrees, which God made in relation to the former nations that inhabited this country, extend to us. 'Whatever nation,' the Lord said, 'shall possess this land, from this time henceforth and forever, shall serve the only true and living God, or they shall be swept off when the fullness of His wrath shall come upon them.' Since this ancient decree there are many nations who have come here. And lastly Europeans have come from what is termed the old world across the Atlantic. And lately the Chinese are beginning to come across the Pacific, and this continent is becoming extensively peopled. Many millions are already upon it. They have constructed many great and populous cities and have become very powerful on the face of the land; but they are nothing compared with the numerous hosts of the Jaredites that once spread over all the face of North America. But yet they are numerous, and are considered one of the most powerful nations on the face of the whole earth; and their resources are very great, and the prosperity which attended our forefathers in establishing settlements on the face of this land, in establishing a free government, with freedom of the press and religious worship, was very great.

They imagine to themselves that this prosperity is to continue for ever, that there is to be no end to their greatness. Now I can tell them, as I have told them ever since I was a boy, their greatness will not protect them; their present prosperity will not protect them. There is only one thing that will protect the nations that inhabit North and South America, and that is to turn to the Lord their God with all their hearts, minds and strength, and serve Him with full purpose of heart, and cease from all their wickedness. That will protect them. If they will do this they will spread forth and become ten times stronger and more powerful than they have ever been, and the Lord their God will bless them more abundantly than hitherto. But on the other hand if they will not do these things the decree that was made in ancient times is just as certain to be fulfilled as the sun shines in yonder heavens."

Orson Pratt, Journal of Discourses, Vol. 12, p. 344, December 27, 1868.

"But what shall become of this people? Shall we be swept off in the general ruin? Shall desolation come upon us? Shall we feel the chastening hand of the Almighty like those who will not repent? That will depend altogether upon our conduct. We have it within our power; God has granted it to us, to save ourselves from the desolation and calamities that will come upon the nation. How? By doing that which is right; by living honest before God and all men; by seeking after that righteousness that comes through the Gospel of the Son of God; by following after the law of Heaven; by doing unto others as we would have others do unto us; by putting away all the evils and abominations that are practiced by the wicked. If we do this prosperity will be upon the inhabitants of Utah; prosperity will be upon the towns and cities erected by this people, the hand of the Lord will be over us to sustain us, and we will spread forth. He will multiply us in the land; He will make us a great people, and strengthen our borders, and send forth the missionaries of this people to the four quarters of the earth to publish peace and glad tidings of great joy, and proclaim that there is still a place left in the heart of the American continent where there are peace and safety and refuge from the storms, desolations and tribulations coming upon the wicked. But on the other hand, Latter-day Saints, how great are the responsibilities resting upon us and upon our rising generations. If we will not keep the commandments of God, and if our rising generations will not give heed to the law of God and to the great light which has shone from Heaven in these latter days, but turn their hearts from the Lord their God and from the counsels of His priesthood, then we shall be visited like the wicked, then we shall have the hand of the Lord upon us in judgment; then that saying that the Lord has delivered in the Book of Doctrines and Covenants will be fulfilled upon us, 'that I will visit Zion, if she does not do right, with sore afflictions, with pestilence, with sword, with famine and with the flame of devouring fire.'

Now here we have the choice. It is within our reach; we can put forth our hand after prosperity, peace and the extension of our borders, and have all these things multiplied upon us, and the power of God within us; His arm to encircle round about to protect us from every harm and evil. And on the other hand we can reach forth the hand and partake of wickedness and bring desolation and destruction upon our borders. Which shall we do? We are agents; we are left to our own choice. God has said that He would plead with His people. I expect that He will. 'I will plead,' saith the Lord, 'with the strong ones of Zion until she overcomes and is clear before me.' There is some consolation in reading this declaration of the Lord. Though we have to receive great chastisement, though He has to plead with us by judgment, tribulation, famine, by the sword and by the vengeance of devouring fire, yet after all, when He has afflicted this people sufficiently, there will be some few that will be spared and will become clean before the Lord.

It is quite a consolation to read that the armies of Israel will eventually become sanctified, and as clear as the sun, as fair as the moon, and that their banners will become terrible to the nations of the wicked. Yet we may have to pass through, by our own wickedness, many calamities that may overtake us. I hope not; but I do not know. I may say that my hopes are strengthened in regard to this matter, for what do I behold here in this Territory? I behold a people that have been willing to sacrifice all that they have for the sake of the Gospel; that have been willing to forsake their native kingdoms and countries and to journey by sea and by land to come here to serve God. I see a people, the majority of whom are willing to give heed to the counsels of the servants of God that are in their midst. Hence I look for peace and prosperity, hence I look for the arm of the Lord to be extended in behalf of this people so long as there is a majority of them who desire to do right, so long as there is a majority who feel to unite their hearts to carry out the great principles of eternal truth and righteousness that have been revealed. So long will the Heavens be propitious, and we shall find favor in the sight of the Most High. But remember the inhabitants who once dwelt on the land; remember their afflictions and their calamities; remember that judgments were poured out upon them because they would not be obedient. Let them be an everlasting lesson to us who live in these latter times. Let us serve God and we shall be blest, we shall prosper if we keep His commandments."

Orson Pratt, Journal of Discourses, Vol. 15, p. 55-56, December 18, 1870.

"Notice, now, how completely it will sweep the proud and those who do wickedly from the face of this creation. The fire that proceeds forth from the presence of God at his second coming shall burn as an oven, and shall not only affect the mountains and the elements so as to melt them, but it will also consume the proud and them that do wickedly from the face of the globe. What effect will this intense heat have upon the righteous? No more than the heated furnace of Nebuchadnezzar had upon the Hebrews who were cast therein; and though it was heated seven times hotter than it was wont to be heated and slew those who cast their fellows into it, yet they who were thrown into it received no harm, not even the smell of fire on their garments. They were protected by a miracle, and the fire that slew their enemies was their preservation. So likewise when the Son of God shall burn up the wicked and consume their bodies to ashes, both root and branch, leaving no remnants of them among all people, nations and tongues, the righteous will be prepared to enter into the midst of this flaming fire without receiving any harm; indeed they will be caught up into the very presence of God, and they will be surrounded with a pillar of fire as Moses was when he came down from Mount Sinai, only to a far greater extent; but it will have no power over them, in fact it will be their protection and salvation, their glory, happiness and joy."

Orson Pratt, Journal of Discourses, Vol. 15, p. 335-336, January 26, 1873.

"The scourge of the Lord, we are told in this revelation, shall go forth by day and by night, and the report thereof shall vex all people. Among all those revelations concerning the scourges that were to go forth, the one which I have read was given long before the cholera broke out. The first year that we have any knowledge of that terrible plague, if I mistake not, was 1833, some four years after this revelation was given that the Lord would send forth scourges. He did send forth a scourge that seemed to sweep over all the nations of the earth. Did it come among the Latter-day Saints? It did. Why? Because they did not keep his commandments, and as the Destroyer was abroad laying waste the nations, the Latter-day Saints had to receive their share, I mean those among us who did not keep the commandments of the Lord. When we were journeying between Ohio and the state of Missouri, Joseph told us if we did not keep the commandments of God and hearken to his counsel we should die off like rotten sheep in that camp. There was no sickness among us at that time, and probably some in the camp did not believe that the words of the Prophet would be fulfilled; but after we had traveled a few weeks, and did not do that which we were told, we learned to our sorrow that the hand of the Lord was upon us, and found the words of the Prophet verified to the very letter, and numbers were laid low by cholera.

The Lord has told us in this book that he would scourge this people, and would not suffer them to go on in wickedness as he does the world. He will make a difference in this respect between those who profess his name and the world. The world may prosper. They have not the religion of Heaven among them; they have no revelators and prophets among them; they have not the baptism of the Holy Ghost, nor the gifts and blessings of God among them, and consequently though they transgress the revealed word of God, he suffers them to go on, apparently without checking them, until they are fully ripened in iniquity, then he sends forth judgment and cuts them off, instead of chastening them from time to time. Not so with the Saints. God has decreed, from the early rise of the Church, that we should be afflicted by our enemies, and by various afflictions, and he would contend with this people and chasten them from time to time until Zion should be clean before him."

Orson Pratt, Journal of Discourses, Vol. 15, p. 340-341, January 26, 1873.

"We are living in this Territory, comparatively at peace, but unless the Latter-day Saints live according to the light which God has revealed to them, they cannot escape. If God sends judgments upon the nations, he will send them upon us. If he cuts off the horses of the nations, as he has said in the Book of Mormon that he will, upon the face of this land, unless we keep his commandments he will cut off ours. If he visits the inhabitants of the earth with pestilence and blood, he will visit us in a similar manner unless we keep his commandments. If the inhabitants of the earth who know not God are to perish because of their wickedness, how much more will he visit those who have greater light and knowledge if they will not keep his commandments? The Lord sent forth the destroyer in ancient times to lay wast the firstborn of the Egyptians, pointing out the means by which his people might escape, and those who failed to do as they were commanded had no promise of being preserved; so in these days when judgments come, they will begin among his Saints, and those who have not attended to the word of wisdom and the laws of life that he has pointed out and have no claim to mercy and favor, God is no respecter of persons. They who have great light and yet sin will endure tribulation and indignation from his hand unless they repent. Amen."

Orson Pratt, Journal of Discourses, Vol. 15, p. 362-363, March 9, 1873.

"In order to bring about this, who knows how many chastisement God may yet have to pour out upon the people calling themselves Latter-day Saints? I do not know. Sometimes I fear, when I read certain revelations contained in this book. In one of them the Lord says, 'If this people will be obedient to all of my commandments, they shall begin to prevail against their enemies from this very hour, and shall not cease to prevail until the kingdoms of this world shall become the kingdoms of our God and his Christ.' That promise was given almost forty years ago. In the same paragraph it says—'Inasmuch as this people will not be obedient to my commandments and live by every word that I have spoken, I will visit them with sore afflictions, with pestilence, with plague, with sword and with the flame of devouring fire.' Is it not enough to make a person fear when God has spoken this concerning the Latter-day Saints? I do not know all things which await us. One thing I do know—that the righteous need not fear. The Book of Mormon is very express upon this subject. In the last chapter of the first book of Nephi, the Lord, through the Prophet, speaks concerning the building up of Zion in the latter days on the earth. He says his people should be, as it were, in great straits, at certain times, but said the Prophet, 'The righteous need not fear, for I will preserve them, if it must needs be that I send down fire from heaven unto the destruction of their enemies.' This will be fulfilled if necessary. Let the righteous among this people abide in their righteousness, and let them cleave unto the Lord their God; and if there are those among them who will not keep his commandments, they will be cleansed out by the judgments of which I have spoken. But if the majority of this people will be faithful, the Lord will preserve them from their enemies, from sword, pestilence and plague, and from every weapon that is lifted against them. God will shield us by his power, if we are to be led forth out of bondage as our fathers were led, at the first. This indicates that there may be bondage ahead, and that the Latter-day Saints may see severe times, and that unless we keep the commandments of God, we may be brought into circumstances that will cause our hearts to tremble within us, that is, those who are not upright before God. But if this people should be brought into bondage, as the Israelites were in ancient days, Zion must be led forth out of bondage, as Israel was at the first. In order to do this God has prophesied that he will raise up a man like unto Moses, who shall lead his people therefrom."

Orson Pratt, Journal of Discourses, Vol. 15, p. 367, March 9, 1873.

"Then the servants of God will need to be armed with the power of God, they will need to have that sealing blessing pronounced upon their foreheads that they can stand forth in the midst of these desolations and plagues and not be overcome by them. When John the Revelator describes this scene he says he saw four angels sent forth, ready to hold the four winds that should blow from the four quarters of heaven. Another angel ascended from the east and cried to the four angels, and said, 'Smite not the earth now, but wait a little while.' 'How long?' 'Until the servants of our God are sealed in their foreheads.' What for? To prepare them to stand forth in the midst of these desolations and plagues, and not be overcome. When they are prepared, when they have received a renewal of their bodies in the Lord's Temple, and have been filled with the Holy Ghost and purified as gold and silver in a furnace of fire, then they will be prepared to stand before the nations of the earth and preach glad tidings of salvation in the midst of judgments that are to come like a whirlwind upon the wicked."

Orson Pratt, Journal of Discourses, Vol. 16, p. 82, June 15, 1873.

"In order to prove this, I will refer you now to the 4th chapter of Isaiah. There we read—'And the Lord will create upon every dwelling-place in Mount Zion, and upon her assemblies, a cloud and smoke by day, and the shining of a flaming fire by night, and upon all the glory shall be for a defence. And there shall be a tabernacle in the day time for a shade from the heat and for a place of refuge, and for a covert from storm and from rain.' . . .

But in the latter days there will be a people so pure in Mount Zion, with a house established upon the tops of the mountains, that God will manifest himself, not only in their Temple and upon all their assemblies, with a visible cloud during the day, but when the night shall come, if they shall be assembled for worship, God will meet with them by his pillar of fire; and when they retire to their habitations, behold each habitation will be lighted up by the glory of God,—a pillar of flaming fire by night."

Orson Pratt, Journal of Discourses, Vol. 16, p. 83, June 15, 1873.

"Some people have supposed that the manifestation of the glory of God in the latter-days would not take place until Jesus comes in the clouds of heaven; but that is a mistake, it will take place before that time. Before the second advent of the Redeemer, the people of Zion will be acknowledged by God, as the great latter-day Church, that will be prepared for his coming, and they will hold the keys of power to teach mankind in the ways of the Lord. What will the rest of the people be doing? Says Isaiah, 'Behold the darkness shall cover the earth, and gross darkness the people.' That will be the distinction between Zion and the rest of the nations."

Orson Pratt, Journal of Discourses, Vol. 16, p. 151, August 16, 1873.

"Moreover, God has determined that in our day he will manifest his power again. When I say our day, I ought to say in the days of this last dispensation of the fullness of times. Before it closes up, it will turn out to be one of the most magnificent eras ever manifested to the world, so far as power is concerned. The Lord has taken this method for forty years past, to prepare us for what is coming. And if we will treasure up what the Lord has given, and suffer his will to be written in our hearts, and printed on our thoughts, and give heed to the teachings and counsel of the living oracles in our own midst, we will be prepared, that when the day of power does come, we shall not be overthrown."

Orson Pratt, Journal of Discourses, Vol. 16, p. 325, November 22, 1873.

"Six thousand years have nearly gone by, the world is getting aged, and Satan has accomplished almost all that the Lord intends that he shall accomplish, before the day of rest. With a work of such magnitude before them, the Latter-day Saints should be wide awake, and should not have their minds engaged in those fooleries in which many indulge at the present time. We should put these things away, and our inquiry should be;—'Lord, how can we prepare the way before thy coming? How can we prepare ourselves to perform the great work which must be performed in this greatest of dispensations, the dispensation of the fullness of times? How can we be prepared to behold the Saints who lived on the earth in former dispensations, and take them by the hand and fall upon their necks and they fall upon ours, and we embrace each other? How can we be prepared for this?' How can all things that are in Christ Jesus, both which are in heaven and on the earth, be assembled in one grand assembly, without we are wide awake?"

Orson Pratt, Journal of Discourses, Vol. 18, p. 170-171, March 26, 1876.

"If the Lord would prepare the way for the first coming, when he came apparently as a man, like other men; if he considered it important on that occasion to send one of the greatest Prophets that ever lived among men, why not also send Prophets or inspired men before the face of his second coming, to warn the inhabitants of the earth and prepare them for so great an event? I know what the traditions of the religious world are in regard to this matter—they consider that the day of Prophets has gone by, and that no more Prophets, Apostles, Revelators, or inspired men are to appear among the children of men. But it is very evident from a vast amount of Scripture that might be quoted, that there will be many Prophets in the latter days; indeed the time will come when the spirit will be poured out upon all living—all that have not been destroyed from the earth, all flesh; and the effects of that spirit, when it is poured out, will be to make Prophets of the people. Your sons and your daughters shall prophesy, and your old men shall dream dreams by the power of that spirit, and your young men shall see vision, all by the operations of the spirit that will be poured out upon all flesh. This is a prediction that must be fulfilled."

Orson Pratt, Journal of Discourses, Vol. 18, p. 228-229, August 26, 1876.
    "Says one, I will wait to see if God will do these things. But peradventure, while waiting, you may be cut asunder and your portion appointed among the unbelievers, where there are weeping, and wailing and gnashing of teeth. Woe unto them who wait to see if God will really fulfill the prophecies of his servants, and who repent not of their sins! But blessed are they who repent as soon as they hear the sound of the message, and who turn unto the Lord their God with all their hearts, for they shall be filled with the Holy Ghost, which bears record of the Father and the Son, and they shall be prepared for the dispensation of his providences, and hail his coming with great joy. The people of the antediluvian world waited one day too long; they waited until the flood came, when it was too late, and they were swept away, eight persons only escaping. The Savior, speaking of his second coming, said—'As it was in the days of Noah, so shall it be also in the days of the Son of Man. They did eat, they drank, they married wives, they were given in marriage, until the day that Noah entered into the ark, and the flood came and destroyed them all. Likewise also as it was in the days of Lot; they did eat, they drank, they bought, they sold, they planted, they builded. But the same day that Lot went out of Sodom, it rained fire and brimstone from heaven, and destroyed them all. Even thus shall it be in the day when the son of man in revealed.' Did the Lord raise up a Prophet and warn the antediluvians by new revelations? He did: and he did the same in the case of the people in the days of Lot. Will he do the same prior to his second coming? He will. He is doing it by means of his Gospel; revealed for the purpose of saving all who receive it, who gather to a place of safety, as Noah and those who believed his message did."

Orson Pratt, Journal of Discourses, Vol. 18, p. 365-366, May 13, 1877.
    "Now, his will must be done on the earth as it is in heaven, in order that that prayer which has been offered up by his people ever since it was revealed, may be fulfilled to the very letter. Hence the great necessity of the Latter-day Saints preparing themselves by being united, even as the hosts of heaven are. For remember that the Apostle Paul says, 'that in the dispensation of the fullness of times he might gather together in one all things in Christ, both which are in heaven and which are on the earth; even in him.' If then the General Assembly and Church of the Firstborn are to come down out of heaven to dwell on the earth, how important it is that the Latter-day Saints should be prepared to join this grand company, being united as they are, having no feeling of dissension, no division in their midst, no evil or corruption of any nature; no covetousness, no feeling of individuality in regard to wealth, but having all upon the alter ready to subserve the purposes of the Most high in building up his kingdom upon the earth."

Orson Pratt, Journal of Discourses, Vol. 21, p. 177-178, September 21, 1879.
    "I believe that the Latter-day Saints are the very best people on the face of our globe. Why?

Because they have been will to endure hardships, persecutions all the day long. They have been willing to leave their houses, their lands, their possessions, have been willing to see all fall into the hands of their enemies and flee to a desert country for the sake of their religion. Has God forgotten all these things? O, ye children of Zion! do you suppose that the Lord has forgotten, because many years have passed away, your tribulation, your sacrifices—if they can be called such—your mobbings and persecutions in times that are past? No. They are written as it were on the palms of his hands, they are printed indelibly upon the thoughts of his heart. He has all these things in remembrance, and a day of controversy is coming, and it is not far in the future—a controversy for Zion; a controversy with all the nations of the earth that fight against Mount Zion—the Lord has all these things in his mind, and he will fulfil them in his own due time and season."

Orson Pratt, Journal of Discourses, Vol. 21, p. 205-206, November 12, 1879.

"This being then the present condition of our earth, the present condition of the Latter-day Saints, and the work that is before them, to prepare them for the coming of the Lord, and for the redemption of the earth, what manner of persons ought you and I to be, to prepare for so great a change which is to come over the face of this creation? How ought we to act and conduct ourselves? How careful we ought to be in our doings, in all our conversations, in all our ways, to sanctify the Lord God in our hearts, to have an eye single to his glory, to keep his commandments in all things, to obey him with full purpose of heart, that we may be visited with more and more of that heavenly divine spirit, the Comforter, the Holy Ghost which we had confirmed upon us, by authority, through the laying on of hands. That Comforter should be nourished and cherished in our hearts. We should not grieve it. We should listen to its whisperings, and we should seek after more light, and knowledge, and truth. We must not expect the Holy Spirit to impart the future knowledge that will be necessary for the advancement of Latter-day Saints without any exertion of the mind on our part. In all things the Lord requires man as an agent to exert his faculties in order to obtain any blessing, of whatever nature it may be, whether it be the spirit of vision or the spirit of translating, or any other gift. We cannot let our minds remain dormant, taking no thought, expecting to be filled with the spirit of translation, or the spirit of inspiration, or revelation, or vision; but there must be an exertion of the mind, there must be an exercise of the agency of man and woman, in order that we may reach out after these great and glorious gifts, promised to us. And by and by, we will, after a school of experience has been given to us, find ourselves advanced to that degree, that the Lord will condescend to visit us by his angels—visit us by heavenly communications—visit us by visions—visit us more fully by the spirit of revelation, that the words of Isaiah may be fulfilled to the very letter. When speaking of the latter-day Zion, he says, 'Thy children shall all be taught of the Lord'—not being under the necessity of being taught by man, but all shall know the Lord from the least of them unto the greatest of them. This is the promise. All the children will be taught from on high, like the Nephite children in ancient days. We know how it was with them. The power of the Holy Ghost descended upon them, filling them, and encircling them round about, by a pillar of fire, and their tongues were loosed, even the tongues of babes and sucklings uttered forth great and marvelous things—far greater than that which Jesus had taught to them. The Lord operated upon them, to utter forth his knowledge, so that their fathers marvelled exceedingly."

John Taylor, Messages of the First Presidency, Vol. 3, p. 110-111, April 8, 1887.

"When the Lord, for any reason, turns His face away from His people, and is slow to hear their cries, thorough repentance on their part and a complete abandonment of their evil ways are sure to bring back His favor, and to cause His countenance to shine upon them. This has been the case in every age when God has had a people upon the earth. In our own day we have seen frequent illustrations of this. We have never feared for the people, nor for the prosperity of the work, when the Latter-day Saints have been fully alive to the duties and requirements of their religion. But when they have been careless and neglectful, or disobedient and hard in their hearts, then we have trembled; for when the Saints are in such a condition the displeasure of the Lord is sure to be awakened against them, and His scourges are likely to fall upon them. The Lord does not permit His enemies, nor the enemies of His people, to prevail over them for any length of time when they are living near unto Him and complying strictly with His will. All His promises, of the brightest and most glorious character, encouraging and hopeful, are given to those who keep His commandments and who seek earnestly to carry out in their lives the principles of salvation which He has revealed. When a people are in this condition their enemies cannot have much power over them."

John Taylor, Messages of the First Presidency, Vol. 3, p. 127.

"The afflictions which our Father permits to come upon us will be made light unto us and they will be made to appear as very trifling in comparison with the calamities that He has said shall come upon the ungodly inhabitants of the earth."

John Taylor, Journal of Discourses, Vol. 9, p. 238, April 28, 1861.

"We are in possession of the principles of eternal life, we are engaged in the work of the Lord here upon the earth, and whether it places us in difficulty, in danger, or in prosperity, it matters but very little if we understand correct principles, for we have commenced to live for ever. We have, or ought to have, drunk of the well, of which Jesus spoke when conversing with the woman of Samaria, which affords water that springs up into everlasting life. These are about my feelings in reference to our trials, privations, and also our prosperity. What is your life? What does it matter whether we die today, this week, or next year, so long as we are engaged in the work of God? The principles we have laid hold of are principles of eternal life, and whether we die today, or next week, or whether it is forty years hence, what does it matter so long as we are faithful to the callings whereunto the Lord has called us."

John Taylor, Journal of Discourses, Vol. 10, p. 118-119, February 22, 1863.

"If we do not understand everything in relation to every event of the past and the future, it is necessary we should know something about the things that now exist, something about the position of the world we live in, and something about our relationship to that God who still lives and will continue to live, and something about our interests in that redemption wrought out for us through the sacrifice of Jesus Christ, whose death and sufferings we are now commemorating. We should know enough about this to save ourselves and to know how to save the generation with which we are associated; enough to know how to save our families and to teach them the laws of life and the way that leads to God and exaltation; enough to know how to live and enjoy life and how to avoid the calamities that are coming upon the earth and how to prepare ourselves for celestial glory in the eternal worlds."

John Taylor, Journal of Discourses, Vol. 11, p. 158, October 7, 1865.

"As I before stated, we stand in a different position to the Almighty and to the world from that of any other people. To us God has revealed his will; He has opened the heavens to us; among us He has organized the Holy Priesthood, and revealed those principles which exist in the eternal world; of us He has made messengers of life and salvation, to us He has communicated his law, and from us He expects obedience and a ready co-operation with Him in bringing to pass those great events that must transpire in the building up and establishment of the kingdom of God in the last days. The Lord is anxious to do us good, to enlighten our minds, to inform our judgment, to unfold unto us His will, and to strengthen us and prepare us for the great events that must transpire in these last days. He is desirous to show us how to save ourselves, how to bless ourselves, temporally and spiritually, intellectually, morally, physically, politically and in every possible way that He is capable of bestowing his blessings upon fallen humanity. He is desirous to perform a great work upon the earth, to bring about a great revolution among men; to establish correct principles of every kind, and to make the earth and the inhabitants thereof fulfil the measure of their creation, and prepare all that are capable or worthy to receive everlasting life and exaltation in the celestial kingdom where he dwells. He is desirous of making use of us as his instruments in the development of this great work in which He has engaged."

John Taylor, Journal of Discourses, Vol. 11, p. 218-219, April. 7, 1866.

"The empires of the earth may be dissolved, and all the nations may crumble to pieces, and wars, and pestilence, and famine may stalk through the earth; this is not our affair; they are not our nations; they are not God's nations. Religionists may squabble, and contend, and quarrel, and live in difficulty, doubt, and uncertainty in relation to their affairs; but that is none of our business, it is entirely their own affair. There may be written upon the whole world, religious and political, 'Mene, mene, tekel, upharsin.' (Thou art weighed in the balances, and art found wanting) What is that to us? It is none of our affair. We are not associated with them; our interest is not bound up with them; they have nothing which we can sustain. In relation to all these matters we feel perfectly easy. If war goes forth and desolates the nations; if confusion exist among religious denominations; and if they should continue to act as they are doing, like perfect fools, it is their own business. The Pope may tremble on his throne, and be afraid that France or some other power will not sustain him; it is not our affair; we feel perfectly easy and tranquil; all is right with us, for we are in the hands of God, and it is his business to take care of his Saints; therefore, we feel perfectly easy, quiet, and peaceable in relation to all these matters."

John Taylor, Journal of Discourses, Vol. 17, p. 5, February 1, 1874.

"This nation and other nations will be overthrown, not because of their virtue, but because of their corruption and iniquity. The time will come, for the prophecies will be fulfilled, when kingdoms will be destroyed, thrones cast down and the powers of the earth shaken, and God's wrath will be kindled against the nations of the earth, and it is for us to maintain correct principles, political, religious and social, and to feel towards all men as God feels. He makes the sun to shine on the just as well as on the unjust; and if he has enlightened our minds and put us in possession of more correct principles than others have, let us be thankful and adore the God of Israel. Let us thank our heavenly Father for his goodness towards us in making us acquainted with the principles of the everlasting Gospel, and let us go on from strength to strength, from purity to purity, from virtue to virtue, from intelligence to intelligence; and when the nations shall fall and crumble, Zion shall arise and shine, and the power of God shall be manifest among his people. No man can overturn or permanently hurt those who do right. They may kill some of our bodies, but that is all they can do."

John Taylor, Journal of Discourses, Vol. 18, p. 282, November 5, 1876.

"In relation to events that will yet take place, the kind of trials, troubles, and sufferings which we shall have to cope with, it is to me a matter of very little moment; these things are in the hands of God, he dictates the affairs of the human family, and directs and controls our affairs; and the great thing that we, as a people, have to do is to seek after and cleave unto our God, to be in close affinity with him, and to seek for his guidance, and his blessing and Holy Spirit to lead and guide us in the right path. Then it matters not what it is nor who it is that we have to contend with, God will give us strength according to our day. There is no question in the hearts of all good Latter-day Saints about the future destiny of the Church and kingdom of God upon the earth; that with them is a settled fact. Neither does it concern them what this man or the other man may do, it makes no particular difference. God has a certain object to accomplish, and he will do it in his own way and in his own time. He holds the nations as dust in the balances; he will manipulate them and their affairs as he pleases, and they cannot help themselves; he will also manipulate the affairs of the Latter-day Saints, having his watchcare over them, as he ever has had over all his people. If we are found to be willing and obedient, and on the Lord's side for right, for truth, and integrity, for virtue and purity and holiness, adhering to the principles of truth and the laws of life, then God will be with us, and he will sustain all those who adhere to these principles; for be it remembered that these are the principles we profess to believe in, and those who are not governed by them he will move out of the way; they will drop down on the right hand and on the left as many have done before, and the pure and virtuous, the honorable and upright, will go forth from conquering to conquer until they shall accomplish all that God designs them to do on this earth; and when they get through he will supply their places with others, who will also take hold and roll forth the kingdom in all its majesty, until the things spoken of by all the holy Prophets be fulfilled; and hence in relation to these matters we cannot change the fiat of Jehovah, which has gone forth, nor alter his decrees."

John Taylor, Journal of Discourses, Vol. 19, p. 306-307, April 8, 1878.

"Will they have trouble? Yes. Will there be tribulations? Yes. Will nation be arrayed against nation? Yes. Will thrones be cast down and empires destroyed? Yes. Will there be war, and carnage, and bloodshed? Yes. But these things are with the people and with God. It is not for us; we have a mission to perform, and that is to preach the Gospel and introduce correct principles, to unfold the laws of God as men are prepared to receive them, to build up his Zion upon the earth, and to prepare a people for the time when the bursting heavens will reveal the Son of God, and when every creature on the earth and under the earth will be heard to say, blessing and glory, and honor, and power, and might, and majesty, and dominion be ascribed to him that sits upon the throne, and unto the Lamb forever."

John Taylor, Journal of Discourses, Vol. 20, p. 140, February 2, 1879.
"And although wars, commotions, troubles, difficulties, bloodshed, plagues, pestilence and famine will stalk over the earth, the nations totter and fall, thrones be cast down and the powers of the earth be shaken, yet God will protect Israel, he will maintain his people, if they will cleave to him and obey his laws and keep his commandments."

John Taylor, Journal of Discourses, Vol. 20, p. 266-267, March 2, 1879.
"And what is Zion? The pure in heart. We want to organize in such a way, and advocate and maintain such correct principles, that they will become the admiration of all honest men, who will flee that they can be protected and find safety and an asylum in Zion. What of that? Are we going to follow them then? No, no, no, we are not. Are we going to be governed by their notions? No, we are not. Are we going to mix up with their Babylonish ideas? No, we are not; we are going in for Israel and for the Church and kingdom of God, but we will protect every man in his rights so far as God gives us power to do so, but we will not mix up with their iniquities, their frauds and corruptions, that they are seeking in many instances to crowd in upon us; we want to be free from these evils, and put our trust in the living God and cleave to the right and the truth. If a man is a good man, won't I treat him right? Yes; but at the same time, our moral and social ideas are very different, and while I accord to them all the civil liberties that any reasonable men should want, I do not wish to be governed by his standard of morality, nor do I wish him to teach my children. Why? Simply because I do not wish them perverted. No Gentile or reasonable man would find fault with me for that. He does not want me to teach his children my faith. All right, he can keep them away, and I want to keep mine from his influences. Why? Because we are associated with things that are eternal in their consequences. We are aiming at the celestial glory. We believe they will get as big a glory as they are looking for, but it will not be that which we anticipate; therefore we don't want them to train our children and lead them down to death. We want to manage these things ourselves, but injure nobody. Is anybody injured by it? No. 'I cannot see as you see,' say some. All right, we cannot help that."

John Taylor, Journal of Discourses, Vol. 20, p. 307, July 6, 1879.
"That is the kind of feeling he had; that is the kind of feeling we want to possess, and feel that God is ours and we are his, and that we are associated with his Church and his kingdom, and are doing his will and carrying out his purposes upon the earth. And it is all the same with us then, whether in peace or war; nobody need have any trembling in the knees, for no power can harm the Saints of God if they continue to be followers of that which is good. The Psalmist says, 'Surely the wrath of men shall praise thee; the remainder of wrath shalt thou restrain.' He will turn and overturn, until ultimately the kingdoms of this world shall become the kingdoms of our God and His Christ; and he will rule for ever and ever. Whilst those that set themselves and run against the bosses of Jehovah's buckler, shall find that they have God to cope with, and that they are but potsherds of the earth, and that they will wilt and wither and die and be damned. There is no power on earth that can

hurt Israel as long as they shall be found doing what is right, obeying the commandments of God, keeping their covenants and preserving themselves in purity and honor before Him."

John Taylor, Journal of Discourses, Vol. 20, p. 309, August 24, 1879.

"We know what we are doing, whether other people do or not. This kingdom that has been spoken of will roll on. The word of the Lord has spoken it thousands of years ago. It will continue to roll on, and woe unto that man or that people who set their hands to fight against Zion for God will be after them. That people or nation will be wasted away. He will maintain the rights of this people, if they will fear Him and keep His commandments."

John Taylor, Journal of Discourses, Vol. 20, p. 318-319, October 6, 1879.

"When, therefore, we see these things progressing need we be astonished? I do not think we need be. Some of our people you know, who are a little shaky and get how? Why a little astride of the fence, and say 'good Lord and good devil,' not knowing into whose hands they will fall; when they see some of these things transpiring they are filled with amazement; but men who understand themselves, and who are in possession of the gift of the Holy Ghost and the Spirit of the living God, are looking for such things and they are not at all surprised."

John Taylor, Journal of Discourses, Vol. 21, p. 32-33, April 9, 1879.

"Are we capable, as Latter-day Saints, of fulfilling our destiny on the earth, and procuring a full temporal salvation and sustaining ourselves, on temporal principles without the interposition of the Almighty? I tell you no, we are not, no more than we are in regard to any other things. We read in the Scriptures of a time that is coming when there will be a howling among the merchants in Babylon, for men will not be found to buy their merchandise. This is in accordance with the prediction of John the Revelator. And the gold and the silver and the fine linen, etc., in Babylon will be of no avail. But before that time comes, we as a people must prepare for those events, that we may be able to live and sustain ourselves when in the midst of convulsions that by and by will overtake the nations of the earth, and among others, this nation. The time that is spoken of is not very far distant. 'He that will not take up his sword against his neighbor, must needs flee to Zion for safety.' And Zion herself must flee to the God of Israel and hide herself in the shadow of his wing, seeking for his guidance and direction to lead her in the right path, both as regards spiritual and temporal affairs; things social and things political, and everything pertaining to human existence. We are not prepared as a people today for the accomplishment of this object; we need the interposition and guidance of the Almighty. It is just as necessary that we be under his guidance in relation to these matters, as it is in regard to any other matters. Who made the earth? The same being that made the heavens. Who made our bodies? The same being that made our souls; and it takes the 'body and the spirit to make the soul of man.' We need not arrogate to ourselves any particular intelligence, whether of mercantile, manufacturing, chemical or scientific nature, for if there is anything good or intelligent, it is the Lord who has imparted it, whether man acknowledge it or not. We want to acknowledge the Lord in all things, temporal as well as spiritual."

John Taylor, Journal of Discourses, Vol. 21, p. 68-69, January 4, 1880.

"We ought to pray for these people, for those that are in authority, that they may be lead in the right way, that they may be preserved from evil, that they may administer the government in righteousness, and that they may pursue a course that will receive the approbation of heaven. Well, what else? Then we ought to pray for ourselves that when any plans or contrivances or opposition to the law of God, to the Church and kingdom of God, or to his people, are introduced, and whenever we are sought to be made the victims of tyranny and oppression, that the hand of God may be over us and over them to paralyze their acts and protect us, for as it is written, the wrath of man shall praise him, the remainder of wrath shall he restrain."

John Taylor, Journal of Discourses, Vol. 21, p. 100, April 13, 1879.

"And while nations shall crumble and thrones be cast down, and the God of heaven arise and shake terribly the earth, while the elements melt with fervent heat in fulfillment of ancient as well as modern prophecy; while these things are going on he will whisper, peace to Zion. But the judgments will begin at the house of God. We have to pass through some of these things, but it will only be a very little compared with the terrible destruction, the misery and suffering that will overtake the world who are doomed to suffer the wrath of God. It behooves us, as the Saints of God, to stand firm and faithful in the observance of his laws, that we may be worthy of his preserving care and blessing."

Orson Pratt, Journal of Discourses, Vol. 21, p. 278-279, June 20, 1880.

"The kingdom of heaven should be likened unto ten virgins; not the former kingdom that was to be built up, when he came on the earth in the flesh; that was not likened unto ten virgins; but at the time he should commence the great work of gathering, that wheresoever the main body of the kingdom is gathered together, from the four quarters of the earth, preparatory to his second coming, then, at that time, should the kingdom of heaven be likened unto ten virgins, which took their lamps and went forth—(signifying that they did not remain in their native lands) to meet the Bridegroom. It was a literal gathering out; and after they had gathered out, taking their lamps with them, they began to be sleepy, and it is written, 'they all slumbered and slept.' It was a time to sleep, a time of drowsiness; it is called midnight; but when all was silent, and when probably the world outside was not looking for anything very great, was careless and indifferent, a voice was heard in the depth of this silence, saying, 'Behold, the Bridegroom cometh; go ye out to meet him.' Then all those virgins awoke, both the wise and the foolish. The wise ones trimmed their lamps, and had some oil left; but the lamps of the foolish had gone out, because there was no oil in them. It seems that they had been so careless, that all the Spirit of God—which may be compared to the oil that gives brightness to the lamps—had gone out of them, and their lamps would not burn. 'Well,' said they, 'What shall we do?' We have been expecting the Bridegroom as well as you that are wise; we believed the Gospel, but really we have been too careless; the spirit has been withdrawn from us; there is no oil in our lamps; cannot you give us some? won't you sell us a little?' 'Oh, no,' say the wise ones, 'we almost fear we have not got enough for ourselves; if you want any, you had better go and buy of those who want to sell.' Hence, five that had gathered were foolish, and five were wise. The wise entered in with the Bridegroom, and the door was shut before the foolish ones could get in. But they afterwards arrived and begged to be admitted; and the question was asked. 'Who are ye?' 'We have been here among your people for a long time. Have we not cast out devils at a certain time? Have we not been on missions? Have we not healed the sick and done many wonderful works in your name?' What is the reply? 'I know you not.' Why? Because they have apostatized; they have lost the oil out of their lamps; they failed to be prepared for the coming of the Savior. Therefore they were bound, as it were, hand and foot, and delivered over to the wicked world, to suffer the same punishment as those that would not receive the truth, and perhaps even greater."

John Taylor, Journal of Discourses, Vol. 23, p. 337,October 29, 1882.
   "And if the families of Israel do this throughout all the land of Zion, all fearing God and working righteousness, cherishing the spirit of humility and meekness, and putting our trust in him, there is no power in existence that can injure us; for God will stand by and sustain his people, and he will deliver them out of the hands of their enemies. And as for the world I will say again, and as I have said on other occasions, I care not what they may say or what they may do; the wicked, whether men or nations can do no more than our Father in heaven permits them to do, and so long as we are doing that which is right before him, why should we fear—are we not in his hands, and is not the whole world in his hands, and can he not do with us and with them as seemeth him good."

John Taylor, Journal of Discourses, Vol. 24, p. 197-198, June 18, 1883.
   "Nevertheless, as I have said, it is necessary that we pass through certain ordeals, and that we be tried. But why is it that we should be tried? There is just the same necessity for it now that there was in former times. I heard the Prophet Joseph say, in speaking to the Twelve on one occasion: 'You will have all kinds of trials to pass through. And it is quite as necessary for you to be tried as it was for Abraham and other men of God, and (said he) God will feel after you, and He will take hold of you and wrench your very heart strings, and if you cannot stand it you will not be fit for an inheritance in the Celestial Kingdom of God.'"

John Taylor, Journal of Discourses, Vol. 24, p. 235.
   "This is the position that we as Priests of the Most High God ought to occupy. We should feel that we are not living for ourselves, but that we are living for God—living to accomplish His purposes. We are here to build up His Church and to purify it from all evil, that it may be presented before the Father as the bride, the Lamb's wife without spot or wrinkle. We are here to build up a Zion unto the Lord of Hosts—a Zion, which signifies the pure in heart—a people who will be prepared for the great events that are about to transpire upon this earth, and who will be able to stand the convulsions that will overthrow the world—and He has given us the Priesthood for that very purpose."

John Taylor, The Government of God, Chapter 11.
   "But the people would very reasonably be heard to enquire, what can we do? What hope have we? If war comes, we cannot either prevent or avoid it. If plague stalks through the earth, what guarantee have we of deliverance. You say you have come as messengers of mercy to us, and as the messengers of the nations. What shall we do? Let Isaiah answer: he has told the tale of war, and

defined the remedy. This shall be the answer of the messenger of the nations, that 'the Lord hath founded Zion, and the poor of his people shall trust in it.' (Isaish 14:32.) Yes, says Joel, when this great and terrible day of the Lord comes, there shall be deliverance in Mount Zion, and in Jerusalem, as the Lord hath said, and in the remnant whom the Lord shall call."

John Taylor, The Government of God, Chapter 11.

"As the world are ignorant of God and his laws, not having had any communication with him for eighteen hundred years; and as all those great and important events must transpire, and as the Lord says he will 'do nothing but what he reveals to his servants the Prophets,' it follows that there must be revelations made from God; and if so, as a necessary consequence, there must be prophets to reveal them to. How did God ever reveal his will and purposes to Enoch, Noah, Abraham, Moses, the Prophets, Jesus, and his Disciples, and they to the people. God's messengers made known his will, and the people obeyed, or rejected it. If they were punished by floods, fire, plagues, pestilence, dispersions, death, etc., it was in consequence of their disobedience. As God has dealt in former times, so will he in the latter, with this difference, that he will accomplish his purposes in the last days; he will set up his kingdom; he will protect the righteous, destroy Satan, and his works, purge the earth from wickedness, and bring in the restitution of all things. The above, while it is the only rational way, is evidently the only just, and Scriptural way. Some people talk about the world being burned up, about plagues, pestilence, famine, storm, and ruin, and all these things being instantaneous. Now it would not be just for the Lord to punish the inhabitants of the earth without warning. For if the world are ignorant of God, they cannot altogether be blamed for it; if they are made the dupes of false systems, and false principles, they cannot help it; many of them are doing as well as they can, while, as we have before stated, it would be unjust for the world to continue as it is. It would at the same time be as unjust to punish the inhabitants of the world for things that they are ignorant of, or for things over which they have no control. Before the Lord destroyed the inhabitants of the old world, he sent Enoch and Noah to warn them. Before the Lord destroyed Sodom and Gomorrah, he sent Lot into their midst. Before the Children of Israel were carried captive to Babylon, they were warned of it by the Prophets; and before Jerusalem was destroyed, the inhabitants had the testimony of our Lord, and his Disciples. And so will it be in the last days; and as it is the world that is concerned, the world will have to be warned. We will therefore proceed to examine the Scriptural testimony on this subject. John says in the Revelations, 'And I saw another angel fly in the midst of Heaven, having the everlasting Gospel to preach unto them that dwell on the earth; and to very nation and kindred, tongue and people, saying with a loud voice, fear God, and give glory to him, for the hour of his judgment is come, and worship him that made heaven and earth, the sea, and the fountains of waters. And there followed another angel, saying, Babylon the great is fallen.' (Revelations 14:6-8.) Here, then, a light bursts forth from the heavens; a celestial messenger is deputed to convey to me tidings of salvation; the everlasting Gospel is again to be proclaimed to the children of men; The proclamation is to be made to 'every nation, kindred, people, and tongue.' Associated with this, was to be another declaration, 'Fear God, and give glory to him, for the hour of his judgment is come. Thus, all were to have a fair warning, and afterwards Babylon falls—not before. From the above it is evident, that the everlasting Gospel will be restored, accompanied with a warning to the world."

Wilford Woodruff, Temples of the Most High, Dedicatory Prayer of the Salt Lake Temple, p. 132.

"Heavenly Father, when Thy people shall not have the opportunity of entering this holy house to offer their supplications unto Thee, and they are oppressed and in trouble, surrounded by difficulties or assailed by temptation and shall turn their faces towards this Thy holy house and ask Thee for deliverance, for help; for Thy power to be extended in their behalf, we beseech Thee to look down from Thy holy habitation in mercy and tender compassion upon them, and listen to their cries. Or when the children of Thy people, in years to come, shall be separated, through any cause, from this place, and their hearts shall turn in remembrance of Thy promises to this holy Temple, and they shall cry unto Thee from the depths of their affliction and sorrow to extend relief and deliverance to them, we humbly entreat Thee to turn Thine ear in mercy to them; hearken to their cries, and grant unto them the blessings for which they ask."

Wilford Woodruff, Messages of the First Presidency, Vol. 3, p. 164-165, April 6, 1888.

"It is a law (tithing) which, if properly observed, will prepare the Church of Christ against the day of vengeance and burning which will come upon the ungodly."

Wilford Woodruff, Messages of the First Presidency, Vol. 3, p. 175-176.

"Watch the signs of the times, and they will show the fulfillment of the words of the Lord. Let my servants call upon the Lord in mighty prayer, retain the Holy Ghost as your constant companion, and act as you are moved upon by that spirit, and all will be well with you. The wicked are fast ripening in iniquity, and they will be cut off by the judgments of God. Great events await you and this generation, and are nigh at your doors. Awake, O Israel, and have faith in God, and His promises, and He will not forsake you. I, the Lord will deliver my Saints from the dominion of the wicked, in mine own due time and way. I cannot deny my word, neither in blessings nor judgments. Therefore let mine anointed gird up their loins, watch and be sober, and keep my commandments. Pray always and faint not; exercise faith in the Lord and in the promises of God; be valiant in the testimony of Jesus Christ. The eyes of the Lord and the Heavenly Hosts are watching over you and your acts. Therefore be faithful until I come. I come quickly, to reward every man according with deeds done in the body."

Wilford Woodruff, Millennial Star, Vol. 51, p. 547, 1889.

"Zion is not going to be moved out of her place. The Lord will plead with her strong ones, and if she sins He will chastise her until she is purified before the Lord.

I do not pretend to tell how much sorrow you or I are going to meet with before the coming of the Son of Man. That will depend upon our conduct."

Wilford Woodruff, Journal of Discourses, Vol. 2, p. 197-198, February 25, 1855.

"I say I rejoice before the Lord this day that we have leaders in Israel that are qualified for their place and station to preside over this people, and who will seek their welfare, and are not afraid or ashamed to rebuke wickedness in high places, whether manifested by their brethren or neighbors, if they do wrong. Their minds are quick as the vivid lightning of heaven; they are filled with the visions of eternity; they are not asleep, but they comprehend the elements around them; they read and digest them, and they know exactly what course to pursue; the leaders of this people know what they are doing, what is approaching this people, and what is approaching the world: and we may all know the same things by reading the Scriptures, and by prayer, and through the ministering of the Holy Ghost conferred upon us. What man is there who reads the Scriptures, and believes that God means what He says, and says what He means, but what can see a flood of dreadful events ready to be poured out upon this generation with the rapidity of lightning. No man can escape the influence of these events that are about to burst upon the heads of this generation. The Gospel has gone forth, and when the nations are warned, another angel will cry, 'Babylon is fallen.' War, and famine, and the plague will overwhelm the nations of the earth, and none can escape."

Wilford Woodruff, Journal of Discourses, Vol. 6, p. 141, December 27, 1857.
"If we will do our duty and listen to those that are set to lead us, we shall find that the hand of God will be over us for our good, and it will be against those that are planning for our destruction; and God will strengthen and uphold this people until the day comes for the kingdom of God to spread itself abroad, and until the law of God is issued forth from Zion. We shall find that this will be the case; and inasmuch as we have these privileges and this faith, as Saints of the Most High, we should prize them and lay hold of them with one united heart, and not consider that the battle is to the strong or the race to the swift; for the Lord holds the destinies of all, and we are in his hands."

Wilford Woodruff, Journal of Discourses, Vol. 10, p. 15, July 27, 1862.
"When the spirit of the Gospel leaves any people it leaves them in a worse condition than it found them, the spirit of ferocity, darkness and war will take hold of that people, and the time will come when every man that does not take his sword against his neighbor will have to go to Zion for safety."

Wilford Woodruff, Journal of Discourses, Vol. 12, p. 13, May 19, 1867.
"The hand of God is in all the operations we are trying to carry out. We have to build up Zion independent of the wicked; we have got to become self-sustaining, and the Lord is inspiring His prophets to preach to us to lay the foundation for the accomplishment of this work. The day is not far distant when we shall have to take care of ourselves. Great Babylon is going to fall, judgment is coming on the wicked, the Lord is about to pour upon the nations of the earth the great calamities which He has spoken of by the mouths of His prophets; and no power can stay these things. It is wisdom that we should lay the foundation to provide for ourselves."

Wilford Woodruff, Journal of Discourses, Vol. 12, p. 279, July 19, 1868.
"Isaiah and Jeremiah and nearly all the prophets since the world began have foretold the gathering of the people in the last days to establish Zion, from which the law of the Lord should go forth to rule the nations of the earth, while the word of the Lord should go forth from Jerusalem. We are here to do these things, and to receive teachings and instructions that we may be prepared for the coming of the Son of Man. We are here to be shut up a little while in these chambers of the mountains, while the indignation of the Almighty passes over the nations. For this the Lord through his ancient servant said, 'Come out of her, my people, that ye be not partakers of her sins, and that

ye receive not of her plagues.'"

Wilford Woodruff, Journal of Discourses, Vol. 15, p. 277-279, January 12, 1873.

"These are only a beginning, their fullness has not yet opened upon the sons of men, but it is at their doors; it is at the doors of this generation and of this nation. And when the world rise up against the kingdom of God in these latter days, should the Saints have any fears? Should we fear because men, in their secret chambers, concoct plans to overthrow the kingdom of God? We should not. There is one thing we should do, and that is, pray to God. Every righteous man has done this, even Jesus the Savior, the Only Begotten of the Father in the flesh, had to pray, from the manger to the cross, all the way through; every day he had to call upon his Father to give him grace to sustain him in his hour of affliction and to enable him to drink the bitter cup."

Wilford Woodruff, Journal of Discourses, Vol. 15, p. 282, January 12, 1873.

"It is a day of warning, but not of many words, to the nations. The Lord is going to make a short work, or no flesh could be saved. If it were not for the manifestation of the power of God what would be the fate of his Zion and people? The same as in the days of Christ and his Apostles. The Lord has had Zion before his face from before the foundation of the world, and he is going to build it up. 'Who am I,' saith the Lord, 'That I promise and do not fulfill?' The Lord never made a promise to the sons of men which he has not fulfilled, therefore Latter-day Saints, you have all the encouragement in the world to sustain you in the faith that the Zion of God will remain on the earth. The work is in our hands to perform, the God of heaven requires it of us and if we fail to build it up we shall be under condemnation, and the Lord would remove us out of the way and he would raise up another people who would do it. Why? Because the Almighty has decreed that this work shall be performed on the earth, and no power on earth or in hell can hinder it."

Wilford Woodruff, Journal of Discourses, Vol. 15, p. 283-284, January 12, 1873.

"By and by great Babylon will fall and there will be wailing, mourning and sore affliction in her midst. The sons of Zion have got to stand in holy places to be preserved in the midst of the judgments that will shortly overtake the world."

Wilford Woodruff, Journal of Discourses, Vol. 16, p. 33, April 7, 1873.

"We have got either to make ourselves self-sustaining, or we shall have to go without a good many things that we now regard as almost indispensable for our welfare and comfort, for there is not a man who believes in the revelations of God but what believes the day is at hand when there will be trouble among the nations of the earth, when great Babylon will come in remembrance before God, and his judgments will visit the nations. When that day comes, if Zion has food and raiment and the comforts of life she must produce them, and there must be a beginning to these things."

Wilford Woodruff, Journal of Discourses, Vol. 17, p. 71-72, May 8, 1874.

"There are certain events awaiting the nations of the earth as well as Zion; and when these events overtake us we will be preserved if we take the counsel that is given us and unite our time, labor and means, and produce what we need for our own use; but without this we shall not be prepared to sustain ourselves and we shall suffer loss and inconvenience thereby."

Wilford Woodruff, Journal of Discourses, Vol. 18, p. 36-37, June 27, 1875.
"We are blessed above all the people that breathe the breath of life upon the earth, and we are blessed above all other dispensations and generations of men, for the Lord has put into our hands the power to build up his Zion upon the earth, never more to be thrown down, and this is what no other generation has ever been called to do. But although this is the mission of the Latter-day Saints, we have a continual warfare to wage—a warfare with the powers of darkness, and a warfare with ourselves."

Wilford Woodruff, Journal of Discourses, Vol. 18, p. 110, September 12, 1875..
"The parable of the ten virgins is intended to represent the second coming of the Son of Man, the coming of the bridegroom to meet the bride, the church, the Lamb's wife, in the last days; and I expect that the Savior was about right when he said, in reference to the members of the Church, that five of them were wise and five were foolish; for when the Lord of heaven comes in power and great glory to reward every man according to the deeds done in the body, if he finds one half of those professing to be members of his Church prepared for salvation, it will be as many as can be expected, judging by the course that many are pursuing."

Wilford Woodruff, Journal of Discourses, Vol. 18, p. 111, September 12, 1875.
"Where is the man, priest, or people, in the whole sectarian world, today, who believes in the literal fulfillment of the revelations of God contained in the Bible? If there is one I should like to see and converse with him. The whole Christian world profess to believe the Bible, and perhaps they do when it is shut. But open the Bible and read the declarations contained therein, concerning the last dispensation of the fullness of times, and where is the man who believes them? You can not find one, and it requires faith even among the Latter-day Saints to believe, the revelations of God, and to prepare themselves for those things which await the world."

Wilford Woodruff, Journal of Discourses, Vol. 18, p. 127, October 8, 1875.
"Know ye, Latter-day Saints, that the Lord will not disappoint you or this generation with regard to the fulfillment of his promises. No matter whether they have been uttered by his own voice out of the heavens, by the ministrations of angels, or by the voice of his servants in the flesh, it is the same; and though the earth pass away not one jot or tittle of his word will fall unfulfilled. There is no prophecy of Scripture of any private interpretation, but holy men of old spoke as they were moved upon by the Holy Ghost, and their words will be fulfilled to the very letter, and it certainly is time that we prepare ourselves for that which is to come. Great things await this generation—both Zion and Babylon. All these revelations concerning the fall of Babylon will have their fulfillment. Forty-five years ago, in speaking to the Church, the Lord said—'You are clean, but not all, and I am not well pleased with any who are not clean, because all flesh is corrupted before my face and darkness prevails among all the nations of the earth.' This causes silence to reign, and all eternity is pained. The angels of God are waiting to fulfill the great commandment given forty-five years ago, to go forth and reap down the earth because of the wickedness of men. How do you think eternity feels today?

Why there is more wickedness, a thousand times over, in the United States now, than when that revelation was given."

Wilford Woodruff, Journal of Discourses, Vol. 19, p. 363, June 30, 1878.

"Judgments await the world, but they heed not, and apparently do not care. With fire and sword the Lord will plead with all flesh, and as the prophet has said respecting this event, 'the slain of the Lord will be many;' and these things will overtake the world in an hour when they expect them not, when they will be crying peace, but alas, peace will have departed from them, and they left to devour and destroy each other. All these things are foretold and many of them are written in these revelations given in our day, and they are already being fulfilled before our eyes; and they will continue to be fulfilled, until all that is spoken of shall have come to pass. Therefore, I want to say to the Latter-day Saints: exercise faith in God, and exercise faith in his revelations, and read them and ponder over them, and pray earnestly that you may have a correct understanding of all that God has revealed, that you may grow in the light and knowledge of God, and see the importance of living your religion and of living uprightly before him."

Wilford Woodruff, Journal of Discourses, Vol. 21, p. 121-124, June 6, 1880.

"The Lord told Joseph Smith that he would prove us in all things, whether we would abide in his covenant even unto death, that we might be found worthy. The prophet sealed his testimony with his blood. That testimony is in force upon all the world and has been from the day of his death. Not one word of the Lord shall pass away unfulfilled. The unbelief in this generation will make no difference with regard to the building up of the kingdom of God. As it was in the days of Noah so shall also the coming of the Son of man be."

Wilford Woodruff, Journal of Discourses, Vol. 21, p. 126-127, June 6, 1880.

"Therefore I say to the elders of Israel, be faithful. We have had the priesthood given to us, and if we fail to use it right, we shall be brought under condemnation. Therefore, let us round up our shoulders and bear off the kingdom. Let us labor to obtain the Holy Spirit—and power of the Gospel of Jesus Christ—which has been put into our hands, and inasmuch as we do this, the blessing of God will attend our efforts."

Wilford Woodruff, Journal of Discourses, Vol. 21, p. 192-193, July 3, 1880.

"The Lord has called men to labor in his kingdom, and I wish the elders would look upon this subject as it is and realize our position before the Lord. Here we are a handful of people chosen out of some twelve or fourteen hundred millions of people; and my faith in regard to this matter is that before we were born, before Joseph Smith was born, before Brigham was born—my faith is that we were chosen to come forth in this day and generation and do the work which God has designed should be done. That is my view in regard to the Latter-day Saints and that is the reason why the apostles and elders in the early days of this Church had power to go forth without purse or scrip and preach the Gospel of Christ and bear record of his kingdom. Had it not been for that power we could not have performed the work. We have had to be sustained by the hand of God until to-day, and we shall be sustained until we get through, if we keep the commandments of God, and, if we do not, we shall fall, and the Lord will raise up other men to take our place. Therefore, I look upon it that we had a work assigned to us before we were born. With regard to the faithful leaders of this Church and kingdom, beginning with Joseph Smith, how many times have I heard men say in my travels—Why did God choose Joseph Smith, why did he choose that boy to open up this dispensation and lay the foundation of this Church? Why didn't he choose some great man, such as Henry Ward Beecher? I have had but one answer in my life to give to such a question, namely, that the Lord Almighty could not do anything with them, he could not humble them. They were not the class of men that were chosen for a work of this kind in any age of the world. The Lord Almighty chose the weak things of this world. He could handle them. He therefore chose Joseph Smith because he was weak, and he had sense enough to know it."

Wilford Woodruff, Journal of Discourses, Vol. 22, p. 334, October 8, 1881.
  "So I say with regard to Joseph Smith, he received his appointment from before the foundation of the world, and he came forth in the due time of the Lord to establish this work on the earth. And so it is the case with tens of thousands of the elders of Israel. The Lord Almighty has conferred upon you the Holy Priesthood and made you the instrument in His hands to build up this kingdom. Do we contemplate these things as fully as we ought? Do we realize that the eyes of all the heavenly hosts are over us? Then let us do our duty. Let us keep the commandments of God, let us be faithful to the end, so that when we go into the spirit world and look back upon our history we may be satisfied."

Wilford Woodruff, Journal of Discourses, Vol. 25, p. 11, January 6, 1884.
  "And there is a calmness prevailing among the Mormons—so called—that is a marvel and a wonder to the world. The world wonder why we are not excited over the opposition that is brought to bear upon us by the millions of people who inhabit this continent, as well as by the people of the nations of the earth. The reason of our calmness is—God is our friend, our lawgiver, our deliverer. If the Lord cannot sustain His work, we certainly cannot. But He can. He has always done it, and will do it to the end. Therefore I say to the Saints, fear not. Trust in God. Let not your hearts be faint. Let your prayers ascend to the ears of the Lord of Sabbath, day and night. Ask what you want. When you do that, the Lord will answer your prayers, if you ask what is right. There is where our strength lies. It is in God. I have no hope in anything else. But I do look upon the Latter-day Saints as occupying a most glorious position in this day and age of the world. This is the first time since God created the world that he has ever established a dispensation to remain on the earth until the coming of the Son of Man—to remain in power and strength and glory, until the Millennium, until He reigns whose right it is to reign. Behold what lies before you! Behold the power of God! Behold the prosperity of Zion! Behold the blessings which have rested upon your houses, your lands, your flocks and herds, your children—the blessings of the earth as well as of the heavens—in this mighty barren desert! Then should we have any doubts or fears with regard to the Kingdom of God? No! As a people we should rise up in faith and power before God, and make our wants known, and leave our destiny in His hands. It is there anyhow. It will remain there."

Wilford Woodruff, Collected Discourses, Vol. 1, October 6, 1889.

"Whatever sacrifices the Lord may require . . . of this people, will be met by the people. But ours is not a day of sacrifice. Our special calling is to build up Zion, and prepare the people to stand in holy places while the judgments of the Lord are being poured out upon the wicked."

Wilford Woodruff, Collected Discourses, Vol. 2, April 6, 1890.

"I would say to . . . all the inhabitants of this land . . . do not worry about these Latter-day Saints. . . . if these people are not the people of God, if this work has not been established by God Almighty, they will fall of themselves, they will be swept from the face of the earth by the judgments of God, when Great Babylon falls. But if they are of God, what can you do about it? . . . Have the nations forgotten that there is a God in Israel? Have they forgotten that there is a God . . . and that He governs and controls all these things? If He has set His hand to perform this work, there is no power on the face of the earth, or in hell, that can destroy it. . . . He holds our destiny and the destiny of all the world in His hands. But the great difficulty with this nation and with all nations is . . . they do not acknowledge the hand of God in any of these things. You see it in the history of the whole world and in the dealings of God with men and cities and nations, from the creation of the world.

Wilford Woodruff, Collected Discourses, Vol. 2, April 6, 1890.

"I tell you that thunders, that lightnings, that earthquakes, that storms, that cyclones, that pestilence and that famine are gathered together in the heaven of heavens, and the angels of God are ready to go forth when the testimony of the Elders of Israel is closed. Messengers will visit the earth that they cannot mob, that they cannot destroy, because they are the angels of God. These are eternal truths . . . and they will have their fulfillment. Prepare yourselves for the things that await us."

The Discourses of Wilford Woodruff, p. 166-167.

"So far as our temporal matters are concerned, we have got to go to work and provide for ourselves. The day will come when, as we have been told, we shall all see the necessity of making our own shoes and clothing and raising our own food, and uniting together to carry out the purposes of the Lord. We will be preserved in the mountains of Israel in the day of God's judgment. I therefore say to you, my brethren and sisters, prepare for that which is to come. You have a great future before you. There is a change coming over the world with regard to Zion. The day is coming when the world will say, 'Let us not go up to battle against Zion, for the inhabitants of Zion are terrible; wherefore we cannot stand.' They will find that the power of God is with this people. We want to prepare ourselves for this, and sanctify ourselves before the Lord that we may be prepared to carry out our mission. (October 8, 1894.)"

The Discourses of Wilford Woodruff, p. 212.

"We are in the last dispensation and fulness of time. It is a great day, and the eyes of all the heavens are over us, and the eyes of God himself and all the patriarchs and prophets. They are watching over you with feelings of deep interest, for your welfare; and our prophets who were slain, and sealed their testimony with their blood, are mingling with the Gods, pleading for their brethren. Therefore, let us be faithful, and leave events in the hands of God, and he will take care of us if we do our duty."

The Discourses of Wilford Woodruff, p. 229-230.

"Can you tell me where the people are who will be shielded and protected from these great calamities and judgments which are even now at our door? I'll tell you. The priesthood of God who honor their priesthood, and who are worthy of their blessings are the only ones who shall have this safety and protection. They are the only mortal beings. No other people have a right to be shielded from these judgments. They are at our very doors; not even this people will escape them entirely. They will come down like the judgments of Sodom and Gomorrah. And none but the priesthood will be safe from their fury. God has held the angels of destruction for many years, lest they should reap down the wheat with the tares. But I want to tell you now, that those angels have left the portals of heaven, and they stand over this people and this nation now, and are hovering over the earth waiting to pour out the judgments. And from this very day they shall be poured out. Calamities and troubles are increasing in the earth, and there is a meaning to these things. Remember this, and reflect upon these matters. If you do your duty, and I do my duty, we'll have protection, and shall pass through the afflictions in peace and in safety. Read the scriptures and the revelations. They will tell you about all these things. . . It's by the power of the gospel that we shall escape. (Young Womans Journal 5:512-513 - From the notable discourse delivered to the temple workers' excursion, Brigham City, June 24, 1894)."

The Discourses of Wilford Woodruff, p. 289.

"Joseph said: 'I will tell you, Brother Woodruff. Every dispensation that has had the priesthood on the earth and has gone into the celestial kingdom has had a certain amount of work to do to prepare to go to the earth with the Savior when he goes to reign on the earth. Each dispensation has had ample time to do this work. We have not. We are the last dispensation, and so much work has to be done, and we need to be in a hurry in order to accomplish it.'"

Lorenzo Snow, Journal of Discourses, Vol. 14, p. 308, January 14, 1872.

"Well, I do not feel materially concerned about anything that respects the advancement and prosperity of the kingdom of God. It is a matter that I have not contrived, nor my brethren; it is the Lord's affair. He has done this work. We never came to these valleys through our own designs and wishes; the Lord God Almighty brought us here, and when he wants us to leave these valleys, we are just as well prepared to leave as we were to come. We simply do what the Lord our God commands us. God loves his offspring, the human family."

Lorenzo Snow, Journal of Discourses, Vol. 14, p. 309, January 14, 1872.

"By and by the nations will be broken up on account of their wickedness, the Latter-day Saints are not going to move upon them with their little army, they will destroy themselves with their wickedness and immorality. They will contend and quarrel one with another, state after state and nation after nation, until they are broken up, and thousands, tens of thousands and hundreds of thousands will undoubtedly come and seek protection at the hands of the servants of God, as much so as in the days of Joseph when he was called upon to lay a plan for the salvation of the house of

Israel.

We have received revelation and, accordingly, we are here in these mountain valleys, and we are going to stay here. We shall cultivate our farms, and lay foundation for a time when the nations shall be broken up. Multitudes will then flee to these valleys of the mountains for safety, and we shall extend protection to them. You may say, shall you require them to be baptized and to become Latter-day Saints? Not by any means. . . . I am not anxious to make a 'Mormon' of him, not by any means; we extend the hand of charity just as far as people are willing to allow us; but when, as I said at the beginning, people are crowding upon us, persons who are determined to destroy us and have not the principles of humanity in their bosoms, we cannot exercise that charity in their behalf that we desire."

Lorenzo Snow, Journal of Discourses, Vol. 20, p. 332,October 6, 1879.

"And now all the Latter-day Saints have to do, all that is required of us to make us perfectly safe under all circumstances of trouble or persecution, is to do the will of God, to be honest, faithful and to keep ourselves devoted to the principles that we have received; do right one by another; trespass upon no man's rights; live by ever word that proceedeth from the mouth of God and his Holy Spirit will aid and assist us under all circumstances, and we will come out of the midst of it all abundantly blessed in our houses, in our families, in our flocks, in our fields—and in every way God will bless us. He will give us knowledge upon knowledge, intelligence upon intelligence, wisdom upon wisdom."

Lorenzo Snow, Journal of Discourses, Vol. 23, p. 290, October 5, 1882.

"In many instances of a similar nature where the destruction of the people of God seemed imminent, and there appeared no way of escape, suddenly there arose something or another that had been prepared for their salvation to avert the impending destruction. We find this in the case of the Israelites when led by Moses. When they came to the Red Sea and the Egyptian army in their rear threatened their destruction, there seemed no way of escape, but at the very moment when deliverance was required, behold, it appeared and they were delivered. So it has been and so it ever will be with us. Notwithstanding our difficulties may appear very great, yet there will be means provided for our escape if we ourselves perform the duties incumbent upon us as the children of God. But it may become necessary in the future—and this is the point I wish to make—for some of the Saints to act the part of Esther, the queen, and be willing to sacrifice anything and everything that is required at their hands for the purpose of working out the deliverance of the Latter-day Saints."

Lorenzo Snow, Journal of Discourses, Vol. 26, p. 367-368, January 10, 1886.

"I am not sorry, nor do I regret on account of the near approach of these fiery ordeals; the Church, no doubt, needs purifying—we have hypocrites among us—milk-and-water Saints—those professing to be Saints, but doing nothing to render themselves worthy of membership; and too many of us have been pursuing worldly gains, rather than spiritual improvements—have not sought the things of God with that earnestness which becomes our profession. Trials and afflictions will cause our hearts to turn towards our Father who has so marvelously wrought out our redemption and deliverance from Babylon."

Teachings of Lorenzo Snow, p. 30.

"Knowledge helps us withstand difficulties. God bless this people is my prayer continually, especially in the obtaining of knowledge and intelligence from heaven, so that we may be able to withstand the difficulties, trials, and afflictions which may arise in our path. (October 5, 1889)"

Teachings of Lorenzo Snow, p. 149.

"If you are on a moving train of cars, as long as you sit still and occupy your seat that train will take you to the point you wish to go; but if you step off the cars it will be dangerous, and it may be a long time before another train will come along. It is the same with us—if we are living right, doing our work, we are going along, and if we are keeping our covenants, we are doing the work of God and accomplishing His purposes, and we will be prepared for the time when Jesus the Son of God will come in honor and glory, and will confer upon all those who prove faithful all the blessings that they anticipate, and a thousand times more. (April 18, 1887)"

Teachings of Lorenzo Snow, p. 167-168.

"The united order is like Noah's ark. We should understand that the Lord has provided, when the days of trouble come upon the nations, a place for you and me, and we will be preserved as Noah was preserved, not in an ark, but we will be preserved by going into these principles of union by which we can accomplish the work of the Lord and surround ourselves with those things that will preserve us from the difficulties that are now coming upon the world, the judgments of the Lord. (5 October 1900, CR, p. 4-5.)"

Teachings of Lorenzo Snow, p. 179.

"Build up Zion, not Babylon. What did we come here for? We came to build up Zion, not to build up Babylon. The voice of the Almighty called us out from the midst of confusion, which is Babylon, to form a union and a lovely brotherhood, in which we should love one another as we love ourselves. When we depart from this purpose, the Spirit of God withdraws from us to the extent of that departure. But if we continue in the extent of those covenants which we made when we received the gospel, there is a corresponding increase of light and intelligence, and there is a powerful preparation for that which is to come. And because of our faithfulness and our adherence to the covenants we have made, the foundation upon which we stand becomes like the pillars of heaven— immovable. (May 6, 1889)"

Teachings of Lorenzo Snow, p. 184.

"The Saints must be prepared to return to Jackson County. A grand preparation is coming. Do you suppose that the Lord would ever send you and me back to Jackson County until He could feel perfectly assured that we would do those things which the people of Jackson County failed to do for lack of experience and faith? (CR, October 7, 1900, p. 62.)"

Erastus Snow, Journal of Discourses, Vol. 16, p. 206, September 14, 1873.

"Thus we learn, my friends, that the warning voice of God will go forth among the nations, and he will warn them by his servants; and by thunder, by lightning, by earthquake, by great hailstorms and by devouring fire; by the voice of judgment and by the voice of mercy; by the voice of angels and by the voice of his servants the Prophets; he will warn them by gathering out the righteous from among the wicked, and those who will not heed these warnings will be visited with sore judgments until the earth is swept as with the besom of destruction; and those who remain, in all the nations, tongues and kingdoms of the world, will heed the voice of warning and will accept the salvation sent unto them by the Lord through his servants."

Erastus Snow, Journal of Discourses, Vol. 19, p. 182-183, June 3, 1877.

"The Lord has taught us that by and by he will waste away the wicked and ungodly, or they will devour and destroy each other, when the righteous shall be gathered out through the preaching of the Gospel. And He designs his people to prepare while there is time, and while he gives them bread to sustain themselves. But if that time should come suddenly upon us in our present condition, who would be prepared for it? If the news was to reach us that Babylon was really going down, that a general war had overtaken her, causing distress of nations, and the closing up of her manufactories, and the struggle between capital and labor were again renewed, causing domestic and national trouble, and as a consequence we found our foreign supplies cut off, how many would begin to pray that Babylon might be spared a little longer?"

Erastus Snow, Journal of Discourses, Vol. 20, p. 372-373, October 8, 1879.

"As the light shone in darkness and the darkness comprehended it not, so might the same be said today. We are called to be the children of light. Blessed are they who continue in the light, for the day of the Lord will not overtake them as a thief in the night; but woe unto them that depart from, or reject that light that shines in the midst of the darkness, for the day cometh, and that speedily, when they will be overtaken as by a whirlwind. The command of the Lord to the Saints is to watch, for we know not the day nor the hour when the Son of man shall come. The precise time of his coming has not been revealed; the prophets were ignorant of it; it could not be declared to the apostles of the Lamb, and, indeed, the Savior said that not the angels, nor even he himself, knew the day or the hour of this important event. . . .

He told them; it was not for them to know the times and the seasons which the Father had put in his power. These things have been spoken that the Saints should watch and not fall asleep. The same idea is also set forth in the parable of the ten virgins, who were represented as having gone forth so meet the bridegroom, five of whom were wise and five foolish. The wise virgins took oil in their vessels, and were prepared to meet the bridegroom and to go with him into the marriage feast; the foolish virgins took no oil, they were unprepared, and were consequently shut out. This parable is expressly applicable to the time of the second coming of the Savior, showing us that however reluctant we may feel to admit it, we are plainly given to understand that a great portion of those who are counted virgins, of the Lord's people, who believe in his coming and who go forth to meet him, will slumber and sleep, and be locked out when he shall come. And it behooves all Saints to ask themselves the question which the disciples asked the Savior when he hold them the startling truth that one of them should betray him—'Lord, is it I?' And all those who are very anxious upon this point will be likely to be on the watch-tower, and not slumbering in that fatal hour."

Charles C. Rich, Journal of Discourses, Vol. 19, p. 376, June 30, 1878.

"Nearly half a century ago, when the Lord first commenced to reveal the principles of salvation to us his children, he began to tell us what was coming upon the earth; he predicted the overthrow of the kingdoms of this world, and he commissioned and sent forth his servants to bear testimony of his second coming and reign on the earth. He told us of earthquakes, of famine and pestilence, and of other judgments that must eventually overtake the wicked in their unrighteousness, and that was said at a time when the world was crying peace. But people are as blind concerning the fulfillment of prophecy in these days as they were anciently, when the Savior said of them 'they seeing see not; and hearing they hear not, neither do they understand.' Such has been the condition of all generations, notwithstanding the revelations, given to them have been plain and positive, and many have been fulfilled and many are being fulfilled. As it was with the overthrow of the Jews, so will it be in these last days. The Lord will fulfil his word, and he will fulfil all that he has said concerning his coming, whether we are prepared or not. He will overturn the kingdoms of this world, and will establish his kingdom, and the world of mankind cannot prevent it. It is for us to prepare ourselves for the dispensation of his providences by doing right, not by thinking so, or guessing so, or may be so, but by knowing what is right. We have the opportunity to learn what right is, and what is required of us, and we have the power to do it; and if we do not do it, surely we shall be found wanting."

Jedediah M. Grant, Journal of Discourses, Vol. 2, p. 146, April 2, 1854.

"Notwithstanding this display of the power of God in fulfilling His word, we need not expect the eyes of the inhabitants of the earth to be opened to understand the meaning of the astounding events that are transpiring around them, for one of the marked signs of the last days is, the blindness of the people; we are told they should have eyes and see not, and ears but hear not, and hearts but understand not. If in the days of Jesus this was true of the Jews and surrounding nations, it is doubly so now in relation to the nations with which we are acquainted.

Though the fulfilment of the words of the Prophets is clear and visible to us as the noonday sun in its splendor, yet the people of the world are blinded thereto; they do not comprehend nor discern the hand of the Lord. The Saints who live in the Spirit, walk by the Spirit, and are governed by the counsels of the Almighty, can see the working of the Lord."

Jedediah M. Grant, Journal of Discourses, Vol. 2, p. 147, April 2, 1854.

"Why is it that the Latter-day Saints are perfectly calm and serene among all the convulsions of the earth—the turmoils, strife, war, pestilence, famine, and distress of nations? It is because the spirit of prophecy has made known to us that such things would actually transpire upon the earth. We understand it, and view it in its true light. We have learned it by the visions of the Almighty—by that spirit of intelligence that searches out all things, even the deep things of God."

Daniel H. Wells, Journal of Discourses, Vol. 5, p. 44, March 22, 1857.

"Are we now prepared for the coming of the Son of Man and for the resurrection? Do we ever think of this? Brethren and sisters, let us be faithful, keep our covenants, and press onward until that time shall come. Important events and duties transpire quite as fast as we are prepared for them; therefore let us round up our shoulders—gird up our loins; and if we can bear greater burdens, there is more coming, and we shall have all that we can do."

Daniel H. Wells, Journal of Discourses, Vol. 9, p. 59, September 10, 1861.

"And now what is our duty? Shall we be like the world from which we have been gathered out? If this is our intention, we might as well have stayed in our native country, where we could have ripened for destruction as well as here. But if we have essayed to be servants of the Most High, to be his children, to be his chosen and peculiar people, and for which purpose we are gathered out from among the Gentile nations, let us not do as they do, but let us do according to the high behest of Heaven, who has given us an appointment, and called us forth to build up his kingdom in these last days. Let us follow implicitly the instructions of those whom God has appointed to guide our minds and direct our steps; or, to use other words, let us believe our religion and faithfully live it. Do we believe fully that God our Father has appointed men whom he influences day by day to lead forth his people, and direct them in all their spiritual and temporal labors, and do we so order our course as to correspond with the instructions given us? Or do we suppose we can entirely take our own way in temporal matters, according to the traditions of our fathers and the dictations of the spirit of the world, and at the same time please high Heaven, and do our duty faithfully in the building up of the kingdom of God? We think in spiritual 'Mormonism' we need direction and constant instruction by the authorized servants of God; but we think we know as much about temporal affairs as anybody."

Daniel H. Wells, Journal of Discourses, Vol. 16, p. 130, August 9, 1873.

"The Apostle said—'Come out of her, O my people, that ye be not partakers of her sins, that ye receive not of her plagues.' If we, after being gathered to Zion, still practice the vices and follies of the world, we might as well have stayed there, for these sins bring with them their punishment. The judgments of the Almighty follow sin as naturally as cause and effect in anything else, and the wicked nations of the world will feel retribution for the sins they commit, just as certain as they have an existence on the earth. There is no escape, except by forsaking their sins and obeying the commands of the Lord. We can not escape the plagues threatened to the sinner, even here in Zion, unless we refrain from sin and walk in the paths that the Lord marks out for us to walk in."

Daniel H. Wells, Journal of Discourses, Vol. 16, p. 130-131, August 9, 1873.

"The earth is defiled by the sins of its inhabitants, and destruction will certainly overtake them unless they forsake their evil ways, for the Lord will not suffer this thing to continue forever. This is not in the economy of heaven—none would be saved if it were permitted to be so. Satan would gain the ascendancy, and would dethrone the Almighty, if it could be suffered to go on. There must be a turning point—that has arrived, and the way of escape is made plain to the children of men. The God of heaven has revealed it in our day. We are the recipients of his mercy and of the principles of truth, and by complying strictly with the principles of the everlasting Gospel, which is the power of God unto salvation, we shall be preserved in the day of God's power; but we must observe the law of high heaven. If a man will persistently walk in the path of danger or into the fire, he will be burned and he knows it. Then why not take a different path? When the Lord points out the path of safety, his Saints must walk therein, or they will suffer the consequences. Some of us are captives to our own passions. We think we know best, and we oftentimes imagine that the Lord is far away, and that we are left to govern ourselves, and we yield to this and to that for the sake of a little transient pleasure, and we think that all will be well in the hereafter. We do not care particularly about the future, if we can only take care of ourselves today. We perhaps give way to some alluring spirit, in some quiet nook or corner, thinking we will be shielded if we do give way to some evil once in a while. There is a way to be shielded, but it is not by persisting in evil doing. We must turn from every evil way, then we have the assurance that God will forgive us."

Daniel H. Wells, Journal of Discourses, Vol. 18, p. 98, October 7, 1875.

"Now, we are here in obedience to a great command, a command given by the Almighty to his Saints to gather out from Babylon, lest they be partakers of her sins and receive of her plagues. But if we are going to partake of her sins in Zion, and to nourish and cherish the wicked and ungodly, what better shall we be for gathering? Shall we escape her plagues by so doing? No, there is no promise to that effect, but if we practice the sins and iniquities of Babylon here in Zion, we may expect to receive of her plagues and to be destroyed. We have duties to perform here, which devolve upon us as Saints of the Most High."

Daniel H. Wells, Journal of Discourses, Vol. 19, p. 369, June 1, 1878.

"There is an opposition to the Lord having on the earth a people, called by his name and doing his will. It has been so from the beginning. The Lord never had a people who were received with open arms by the world, admired, cherished and respected; on the contrary they have been persecuted or totally destroyed from off the earth. The wicked have invariably prevailed over the good; it might almost be said that the first bad man killed the first good man. The Latter-day Saints have had the same experience to pass through, and when a time of comparative peace has come around, as it has sometimes, they are apt to ask, 'What is the matter? Have we lost our faith, that the Adversary should thus let us alone?' There will come a time, however, in the history of the Saints, when they will be tried with peace, prosperity, popularity and riches."

Daniel H. Wells, Journal of Discourses, Vol. 23, p. 306-309, October 6, 1882.

"This great and marvelous work of the latter-days will be prolonged or hastened according to the faith and good works of the people engaged in it. If we pray, therefore, the Lord to hasten His work; to hasten the time when Zion shall be built up and redeemed; when the great and glorious Temple shall be erected to the name of the Most High God, and when His glory shall rest upon it in the form of a cloud by day and a pillar of fire by night, let our righteousness conform with our holy desires; let us so live as to call down the blessings of heaven upon us. For if we are faithful in all things, and are united, blessings cannot be withheld from us; the Lord is bound, according to the covenant, to hear the prayers of His faithful children. We have an example in the Book of Mormon of a man exercising such exceeding faith that his vision could not be withheld from penetrating behind the vail, when he saw the person of the Lord, and was there redeemed from the fall. The Lord is perfectly willing to bestow blessings upon His people, and to establish His work upon the earth, just as willing as His people can be to have him, and whenever the time comes that he finds that he has a people upon whom he can bestow these blessings, they will come. We need have no fears with regard to that; and, in fact, they do come now as fast as we can receive them and hold them in righteousness, and I think sometimes, they come too fast for a great many."

George Q. Cannon, Gospel Truth, Vol. 1, p. 84.

"There are powers engaged in preparing the earth for the events that await it and fulfilling all the great predictions concerning it which we know nothing of, and we need not think that it depends upon us Latter-day Saints alone and that we are the only agents in the hands of God in bringing these things to pass. The powers of heaven are engaged with us in this work. (JD 16:120-121, June 29, 1873.)"

George Q. Cannon, Journal of Discourses, Vol. 14, p. 125-126, April 8, 1871.

"Whence, I ask, my brethren and sisters, has this power come? Whence has it been derived? I attribute it to the blessings and the power and the authority and the keys which God gave unto his Saints, and which he commenced to give in the Temple at Nauvoo. The Elders of Israel there received keys, endowments and authority which they have not failed to exercise in times of extremity and danger; and clouds have been scattered and storms blown over, and peace and guidance, and all the blessings which have been desired have been bestowed upon the people, according to the faith that has been exercised. Others may attribute these things to other causes; but I attribute them to this, and I feel to give God the glory; and I trace these deliverances to the power that the Elders received in that temple and previously. I fully believe also, as I have said, that when this and other temples are completed, there will be an increase of power bestowed upon the people of God, and that they will, thereby, be better fitted to go forth and cope with the powers of darkness and with the evils that exist in the world and to establish the Zion of God never more to be thrown down."

George Q. Cannon, Journal of Discourses, Vol. 15, p. 299-300, January 12, 1873.

"But there is something that I dread more than active persecution. We have endured persecutions which have driven us from our home. Mobs have burned our houses, destroyed our corn and wheat fields, and torn down our fences; our men have been slain, and in some instances our women ravished. We have been driven as wild beasts are driven from the habitations of men, and compelled to flee to the wilderness. We have endured this, and we know that we can endure it, and live in the midst of it, for we have been tested. But we have not yet endured prosperity, we have not yet been tested in this crucible, which is one of the severest to which a people can be subjected. We have not been tested with abundance of property and wealth lavished upon us; and here, my brethren and sisters, is the point against which we have to guard more than all others, for there is more danger today to the Zion of God in the wealth that is pouring into and increasing in the hands of the Latter-day Saints, than in all the armies that have ever been mustered against us, or all the mobs that have been formed for our overthrow, from the organization of the Church until today. There is danger not in mines alone, not in the increase of strangers in our midst, not in the seducing influences which attend the presence of some of them, but in the fact that we ourselves are growing wealthy, and that it is natural for us to become attached to wealth, and for the mind of man to be allured by it, and by the influence which it brings. There is danger in this, and I look for the same results to follow this condition of affairs that formerly followed mobocracy. The mobs came upon us, and they cleansed from among us the hypocrites and cowards, and those who could not endure. The Gospel of Jesus

Christ, which brought persecutions, and called upon men to forsake houses and lands and everything that was dear to them, and to push out into the wilderness, had no attraction for the classes I have named, in the early history of the Church; and I expect that there will be attraction for the classes I have named, in the early history of the Church; and I expect that there will be attractions stronger than the Gospel to hypocrites and those weak in the faith in the present phase of our history, and that influences now operating will produce the same results as we have witnessed, that is, to cleanse the people of God. We have, therefore, at the present time, that at our doors, which menaces us with greater danger than mobs. I do not dread the results, but doubtless many, unless they are very careful, will have their hearts hardened and their eyes blinded by, and they will fall a prey to and be overcome by, these evils, which the adversary is seeking to pour upon us."

George Q. Cannon, Journal of Discourses, Vol. 16, p. 120-121, June 29, 1873.

"We in Salt Lake and elsewhere have ours upon the work that immediately attracts our attention; and while we, or all amongst us who are faithful, shall no doubt be instrumental in the hands of God, in bringing to pass his purposes and accomplishing the work he has predicted in connection with the ten tribes, the Lamanites, the Jews, and the Gentile nations, we need not think that these things depend upon us alone. There are powers engaged in preparing the earth for the events that await it and fulfilling all the great predictions concerning it, which we know nothing of, and we need not think that it depends upon us Latter-day Saints alone, and that we are the only agents in the hands of God in bringing these things to pass. The powers of heaven are engaged with us in this work."

George Q. Cannon, Journal of Discourses, Vol. 21, p. 77, October 5, 1879.

"It is our duty though to contend for more faith, for greater power, for clearer revelations, for better understanding concerning his great truths as he communicates them to us. That is our duty; that is the object of our lives as Latter-day Saints—to live so near unto him that nothing can happen to us but that we will be prepared for it beforehand."

George Q. Cannon, Journal of Discourses, Vol. 21, p. 268-270, November 2, 1879.

"Yet I believe that the power of God will be increased among us, that we will have manifestations of his power such as we never have before witnessed. For the day of God's power in the redemption of Zion will come. But I do not expect that to come upon us all of a sudden. I expect that it will be the natural result of the natural growth of the people in the things of God. I expect that we will go on step by step from one degree of knowledge, and of power, and of faith to another, until we shall be prepared to receive all the Lord has in store for us and be prepared to enter into that glory promised to the faithful Saints. The Lord has given unto his people and to his church every gift and every qualification and every key which is necessary to lead this people into the celestial kingdom of our father and our God. There is nothing wanting."

George Q. Cannon, Journal of Discourses, Vol. 24, p. 147, May 6, 1883.

"The nearer we approach unto God the more perfect we live in accordance with the revelations He has given, the more faith undoubtedly we will possess, the more God will hear us, the nearer the heavens will draw to us, the more the heavens will be opened to us to hear our cries and to answer our petitions. And, as I have said, the day will come, if we obey the laws that God has given, that Zion will be redeemed and the adversary will not have power over us to tempt us, and try us, an to afflict us as he does at the present time."

George Q. Cannon, Journal of Discourses, Vol. 25, p. 26-27, January 6, 1884.

"While Brother Woodruff was talking, I thought what an immense labor it is to endeavor to accomplish that which the Prophets have told us will be brought to pass in the last days. I look at this people so comparatively few in numbers, and at the immense work that is to be accomplished, and it seems an herculean, an impossible labor to the natural vision. It seems as if no human beings could accomplish it. But God has spoken concerning this work. His word has gone forth and it cannot fail. This work will be accomplished, and it will be accomplished by the operation of truth. As Brother Woodruff has said, there is a power connected with truth, that when brought to bear upon human beings, has the effect that he has described, and has the effect that the Prophets have predicted concerning the last days. There will be a power exercised in our behalf, increasing as we are prepared to receive it; for this people with all their weaknesses, and they are many, are nevertheless drawing nearer and nearer to God every day, and faith is increasing in their midst. A generation of boys and girls are growing up who will have greater faith than their predecessors, their parents, have had, and the work will continue to grow and spread. And there is this to be taken into consideration, God having predicted the ushering in of the last dispensation, knowing the odds that would have to be contended with in establishing it: God knowing this has reserved in the heavens to come forth at this time the noblest of His spirits, the men and women most capable of carrying out this work, and achieving the grand results the Prophets have predicted should be accomplished in the day and generation, preparatory to the coming of the Son of Man. God knowing this, in His wisdom and foreknowledge has prepared the way beforehand, and there will be men and women brought forth who will carry off this work in the way He designs, step by step, the adversary of God, that is the adversary of all truth, will have to recede. The struggle is between Satan and God. The struggle is for the supremacy of this earth, and you may depend upon it, it will not be given up without a mighty wrestle. The adversary has wielded this power now for nearly 2,000 years—1,400 years and upwards on this continent. For this period he has held undisturbed sway, it may be said—that is, if not entirely true it is nearly true in saying it has been undisturbed. There have occasionally some persons arisen who have endeavored to stem the tide of wickedness that the devil has caused to flow over the earth; but there has been no Priesthood on the earth, no organized church, no organized power, through whom God could operate, and you may depend upon it, now that there is one, there will be a mighty struggle. It will cost the best efforts of which we are capable, to lay the foundation so successfully that it shall not be overturned, to prepare the way for the coming of the Lord Jesus Christ."

George Q. Cannon, Journal of Discourses, Vol. 25, p. 274, August 31, 1884.

"Our only hope is our God; our only strength is in Him and in His providence, and He will deliver us. Let me say to you, that he has never yet failed to deliver us; and His promises are as firm and immovable as His eternal throne. We can rely upon Him with the utmost assurance that we shall not be deceived; but that in the direst extremity, in the darkest hour, in the midst of the deepest trials and afflictions, His arm will be extended in our behalf, and His providence be exerted to save and to deliver us. We can rest assured of this. Therefore, however dark the prospects may be, however gloomy, let us remember that He who sits on high knows our condition, and that He can deliver us. He will interpose at the very moment when it is needed and rescue us from every evil, and He will defeat and bring to naught, every plan and device which is concocted against the peace and prosperity of those who put their trust in Him and in the great work which He has established in the earth. This I can bear testimony to. I know whereof I speak. I know just as well as I know that I stand here, and that I am speaking to you, that the Latter-day Saints, this Church, or what we call the Zion of our God, will be delivered, and it will roll forth in mighty power, and it will accomplish all that has been predicted concerning it."

George Q. Cannon, Journal of Discourses, Vol. 26, p. 319, August 26, 1883.

"That there is no evil to-day that menaces Zion that we feel it difficult to cope with, that in this land to which God has led us, that is not traceable to ourselves and that does not have its origin in the reluctance of the people to comprehend and to obey the counsel which God has given through His servants ever since we came to these valleys. I leave it to every one of you to decide for yourselves under the spirit of God if this statement which I make is not abundantly true and sustained by facts. It is a sorrowful statement to make, but it is nevertheless a true statement. We have no dangerous or threatening evils to contend with that have not had their origin in the disobedience of some of the Latter-day Saints to the counsel which God has given them."

George Q. Cannon, Collected Discourses, Vol. 1, March 3, 1889.

"He (Nephi) saw that the Saints of God were not many . . . and that 'the whore of all the earth' arrayed itself against the Church of the Lamb and sought its destruction. But he says the righteous need not fear. We need not expect, therefore, anything different to this. The Book of Mormon would not be fulfilled unless we had just such things as these to contend with. . . . Consequently, instead of thinking that the work is going to be overcome, we should feel to rejoice that these events are taking place; and that, notwithstanding the mighty power that will be brought to bear against us . . . we shall prevail, and God will deliver us. He has laid the foundations of Zion, and they cannot be moved; and we shall go forward from one degree of strength to another, emerging from one trial, and perhaps in a short time entering upon another . . . until the kingdom of God will triumph in the earth . . . and the great whore of all the earth be destroyed. This is inevitable, for God has spoken it. . . . We need not, therefore, be discouraged at what we see and what we are passing through. But if we are united . . . . this power cannot prevail against us. Our opponents may secure temporary victories in places, and it may seem as though we were about to be overcome; but if we are united, I tell you that God our eternal Father will overrule these events for our good, and He will bring us great deliverance. But if we are divided, then we forge our own chains . . . . brethren, let us take a course to have our garments clean . . . so that . . . we can stand before His judgment seat and prove to Him that we have done our part towards holding up His Kingdom in the earth; that we have never done anything to weaken the influence of righteousness; . . .Let us . . . help build up this Kingdom . . .And leave the result with God. . . . We need not worry. We need not lie awake at nights. . . . He will take care of this Kingdom. He will overthrow Babylon. He will bind Satan."

George Q. Cannon, Collected Discourses, Vol. 1, July 21, 1889.

"These troubles that we now have are comparatively light to those that we shall have to meet with. But when they come we shall have the strength necessary to rise above them; for as they increase, our strength will increase in proportion. The forces which now antagonize us are insignificant compared with forces that we shall yet have to cope with, and with which we shall cope successfully. Threatening and formidable as the powers arrayed against us now may be because of our weak condition, we will find as we grow in strength, as we gain influence and power, the opposing forces will also increase, until, as I have said, it will not only be a nation, but it will be the whole world that will fight against Zion and will seek her destruction. And under those circumstances what will save us? Nothing will save us but the righteousness of the Latter-day Saints, and the power of God which that righteousness will bring forth."

George Q. Cannon, Collected Discourses, Vol. 2, February 23, 1890.

"And whatever our afflictions may be, whatever our trials may be, whatever we may have to endure, we can view the future with complacency, as far as we are concerned, and without fear; but our hearts may well be filled with sorrow and pity for the future of the children of men who reject the word of the Lord."

George Q. Cannon, Collected Discourses, Vol. 2, April 27, 1890.

"God knows everything connected with this work, from the beginning to the end. The troubles that we are now going through are all known to the Lord. He knew them before they took place. He knew the position we would be in. He knew how we would act. He knew it by His foreknowledge, which is infinite. He knows how these persecutions will terminate. He knows that salvation will come. He knows that Zion has been founded, never to be overthrown. He has told us this will be the case. The gates of hell will never prevail against the Zion of God. No matter what we may go through, no matter what we may have to endure, this is the infallible promise of the Lord Eternal which is made to us. Though we may go through the deep waters, though we may pass through the fiery furnace, though we may endure severe trials, God knows them all, and He has prepared for them all by His wonderful providence. He will overrule them for His glory and for the salvation of His people. All that is necessary for us is to do our duty; put our trust in Him, under all circumstances; not let our faith fail, but rely implicitly and continually upon His promises, and He will bring us off triumphant in the end."

George Q. Cannon, Collected Discourses, Vol. 2, October 5, 1890.

"Therefore, Latter-day Saints, go ahead and perform your duties carefully, consistently, and with a determination to do that which God requires at your hands. Do not look for some great cataclysm to occur, which will show all the world that this is the Kingdom of God. Perhaps such a thing will occur; but I will tell you what I have observed during my life—that God works in natural ways. His purposes come around seemingly perfectly natural—so natural that the world cannot see the hand of God in them. It requires faith and the Spirit of God to show these things."

Joseph F. Smith, Messages of the First Presidency, Vol. 3, p. 228.

"I want the Latter-day Saints to stop murmuring and complaining at the providence of God. Trust in God. Do your duty. Remember your prayers. Get faith in the Lord, and take hold and build up Zion. All will be right. The Lord is going to visit His people, and He is going to cut His work short in righteousness, lest no flesh should be saved. I say to you, watch the signs of the times, and prepare yourselves for that which is to come."

Joseph F. Smith, Conference Report, April 1880, p. 96.

"I further testify, that unless the Latter-day Saints will live their religion, keep their covenants with God and their brethren, honor the priesthood which they bear, and try faithfully to bring themselves into subjection to the laws of God, they will be the first to fall beneath the judgments of the Almighty, for his judgments will begin at his own house."

Joseph F. Smith, Journal of Discourses, Vol. 13, p. 342, November 12, 1870.

"I tell you, in the name of Israel's God, that this world and its inhabitants are doomed; their doom is sealed, and the only way of escape is the Gospel of the Son of God, the door to which is baptism for the remission of sins, after repenting of and forsaking every practice that tends to degrade and degenerate the human race. Nothing but this will save the world from the doom that is hanging over it, which God has decreed shall be poured out upon it. When the testimony of His servants has gone forth in the midst of its inhabitants."

Joseph F. Smith, Journal of Discourses, Vol. 19, p. 26-27, April 2, 1877.

"He is more willing to bestow blessings upon us than we are to use them properly when we obtain them, thus by our unworthiness we may prevent ourselves often from receiving the very blessings we desire, and that he is not only abundantly able, but willing and ready to shower upon us if we were worthy, for he cannot consistently bestow 'pearls upon swine.' No blessing or good will be withheld from those who are prepared and worthy to receive and make a wise use of it. The kingdom of God is to be enjoyed by the Saints—those who are righteous, not those who are wicked. If we prove unworthy, Zion will have to be redeemed by our children, who may be more worthy, while we may be kept, like the ancient children of Israel, wandering in the wilderness, enduring hardships, persecution and trials, until we shall have suffered the penalty of neglected, not to say broken and unfulfilled covenants."

Joseph F. Smith, Journal of Discourses, Vol. 20, p. 347, April 8, 1879.

"We should be prepared, not only to manufacture our own wearing apparel, but also to make all our mechanical and agricultural implements, our house-hold furniture, our building materials, our wagons, carriages and equipment, with all that is necessary for the righteous and legitimate use of man, that when Babylon shall fall we may be prepared for it, and not be found among those who shall wail and lament because 'no man buyeth her merchandise any more.'"

Joseph F. Smith, Journal of Discourses, Vol. 24, p. 251-252, August 19, 1883.

"It is for us to work righteousness; for, as President Young remarked in the Temple at St. George, in 1877, the more righteous we are, the more united we are; the more diligent we are in keeping the commandments of God, the less will be the power of our enemies; their power will diminish in proportion to our faithfulness. Yet our enemies will rage and their anger will increase against the work of the Lord; and I presume it is a true saying, that 'whom the gods would destroy they first make mad.' The heathen—the so-called Christian nations—will become mad with rage against the Latter-day Saints; and thus the world will go on until they are ripened for destruction. We can afford to be calm and patient and await God's deliverance; for we know that He is our friend; that He is on the side of the righteous; and that he will bring them off triumphant if they continue faithful, which may the Lord grant in the name of Jesus. Amen."

Joseph F. Smith, Collected Discourses, Vol. 3, July 16, 1893.

"I believe that it is our business to prepare against the day of famine, of pestilence, of tempests and earthquakes, and the time when the sea shall heave itself beyond its bounds. How shall we do it? By studying and carrying out the principles of true economy in our lives, and by a system of fraternity and love by which each one will help his brother, and all stand united, so that none shall suffer from want when it is within the power of others to alleviate it. One of the great promises that the Lord has made concerning His people, as contained in the Book of Doctrine and Covenants, is that they shall become the richest of all people. Now, how can this be fulfilled if every day we spend all that we earn, and borrow a little besides of our neighbor? The first thing we know, our farms will be in the hands of the money lender; and instead of being the richest of all people, we will be the hewers of wood and drawers of water, the menials and dependents of those who know enough to take care of their means."

Joseph F. Smith, Gospel Doctrine, p. 77.

"Now, we are thankful to the Lord that we are counted worthy to be taken notice of by the devil. I would fear very much for our safety if we had fallen into a condition where the devil ceased to be concerned about us. So long as the Spirit of the Lord is enjoyed by you, so long as you are living your religion, and keeping the commandments of the Lord, walking uprightly before him, I assure you that the adversary of souls will not rest easy; he will be discontented with you, will find fault with you, and he will arraign you before his bar; but that will not hurt you very much if you will just keep on doing right. You do not need to worry in the least, the Lord will take care of you and bless you, he will also take care of his servants, and will bless them and help them to accomplish his purposes; and all the powers of darkness combined on earth and in hell cannot prevent it. They may take men's lives; they may slay and destroy, if they will; but they cannot destroy the purposes of God nor stop the progress of his work. He has stretched forth his hand to accomplish his purposes, and the arm of flesh cannot stay it. He will cut his work short in righteousness, and will hasten his purposes in his own time. It is only necessary to try with our might to keep pace with the onward progress of the work of the Lord, then God will preserve and protect us, and will prepare the way before us, that we shall live and multiply and replenish the earth, and always do his will; which may God grant. (CR, Oct. 1905, p. 5-6.)"

Joseph F. Smith, Gospel Doctrine, p. 155.

"Leaders of the Church, then, should be men not easily discouraged, not without hope, and not given to forebodings of all sorts of evils to come. Above all things the leaders of the people should never disseminate a spirit of gloom in the hearts of the people. If men standing in high places sometimes feel the weight and anxiety of momentous times, they should be all the firmer and all the more resolute in those convictions which come from a God-fearing conscience and pure lives Men in their private lives should feel the necessity of extending encouragement to the people by their own hopeful and cheerful intercourse with them, as they do by their utterances in public places. It is a matter of the greatest importance that the people be educated to appreciate and cultivate the bright side of life rather than to permit its darkness and shadows to hover over them."

Moses Thatcher, Journal of Discourses, Vol. 26, p. 333-335, October 8, 1885.

"I will say when this nation, having sown to the wind, reaps the whirlwind; when brother takes up sword against brother; when father contends against son, and son against father; when he who will not take up his sword against his neighbor must needs flee to Zion for safety—then I would say to my friends come to Utah; for the judgments of God, commencing at the house of the Lord, will have passed away, and Utah, undisturbed, will be the most delightful place in all the Union. When war and desolation and bloodshed, and the ripping up of society come upon the nation, I have said to such, 'Come to Utah and we will divide our morsel of food with you, we will divide our clothing with you, and we will offer you protection.' I will tell you, my brethren and sisters, the day will come, and it is not far distant, when he who will not take up his sword against his neighbor, will have to flee to Zion for safety; and it is presupposed in this prediction that Zion will have power to give them protection."

Francis M. Lyman, Journal of Discourses, Vol. 25, p. 64-65, February 24, 1884.

"For we have no battles to fight if we be the Saints of our God. He will fight our battles if battles are to be fought. The wicked will slay the wicked and the righteous will be left free."

Francis M. Lyman, Journal of Discourses, Vol. 25, p. 65- 66.

"The blessing of the Lord has been over the land, and peace has reigned in it, and it will continue to reign if we but do the will of the Lord. He will over-rule and control all those agencies that may be brought against us from the outside, if we will but listen to the voice of counsel here at home."

Heber J. Grant, Message of the First Presidency, Conference Report, October 1942, p. 13.

"Satan is making war against all the wisdom that has come to men through their ages of experience. He is seeking to overturn and destroy the very foundations upon which society, government, and religion rest. He aims to have men adopt theories and practices which he induced their forefathers, over the ages, to adopt and try, only to be discarded by them when found unsound, impractical, and ruinous. He plans to destroy liberty and freedom—economic, political, and religious, and to set up in place thereof the greatest, most widespread, and most complete tyranny that has ever oppressed men. He is working under such perfect disguise that many do not recognize either him or his methods There is no crime he would not commit, no debauchery he would not set up, no plague he would not send, no heart he would not break, no life he would not take, no soul he would not destroy. He comes as a thief in the night; he is a wolf in sheep's clothing. Without their knowing it, the people are being urged down paths that lead only to destruction. Satan never before had so firm a grip on this generation as he has now."

Heber J. Grant, Messages of the First Presidency, Vol. 6, p. 173-174.
"When, as the Lord Himself has declared, plague, pestilence, famine, and death shall be poured out upon the nations for their wickedness, and when these shall break over our heads and our loved ones are smitten nigh to death, when hearts are torn and the anguish of grief almost overwhelms us, who can fathom the joy or measure the blessing of that father and mother who can stand before the Lord and say: 'We have kept Thy commandments. We and ours have lived the law. Vouchsafe Thy promised blessings unto us. We remember Thy word, `I, the Lord, am bound when ye do what I say.' Let Thy healing power rest upon our afflicted ones `that the destroying angel shall pass by them, as the children of Israel, and not slay them.'"

George Teasdale, Collected Discourses, Vol. 5, June 26, 1898.
"How are we living? Are we in harmony with these everlasting principles? For we are living in the last days—in the days of wickedness and vengeance. We are living in the days when the Lord is going to pour out His judgments upon the people of the world, preparatory to the second coming of the Messiah. Every intelligent man and woman realizes that the time is short, and that we have no time to waste."

George Albert Smith, Journal of Discourses, Vol. 3, p. 29, September 23, 1855.
"The Lord has said, in a revelation given through Joseph Smith, that it is His purpose to take care of His Saints. He also promised His people, in the commencement of the foundation of this Church, to sift them as with a sieve. Some of the old Prophets, in referring to the work of the last days, speak of the sieve of vanity."

George Albert Smith, Journal of Discourses, Vol. 3, p. 38, September 23, 1855.
"This spirit will in the end lead a man to destruction; and all that will preserve the Saints in the last days from the general destruction in the vortex of ruin to which the world is rushing, will be their unity with each other, their clinging with all their might, mind, and strength to the building up of this kingdom, and making it their only interest, that they may hang together as one; knowing the text we started on, that it is the Lord's business to provide for His Saints."

George Albert Smith, Journal of Discourses, Vol. 3, p. 289, April 6, 1856.
"The time is not far distant when millions of people will fly to these valleys as the only peaceful, plentiful place of refuge. Then it becomes the Saints to store up food for themselves, and for the hosts who will come here for sustenance and protection, for as the Lord lives they will flow here by thousands and millions, and seek bread and protection at the hands of this people."

George Albert Smith, Journal of Discourses, Vol. 4, p. 333, May 31, 1857.

"The Almighty God is at the helm; He rules His people, He governs and controls all men, and He can restrain the wicked at His pleasure; but let me tell you, if the designs of the spirit of the devil that reigns in the hearts of the wicked against us, prompting them to our destruction, could be executed, we would be exterminated from the face of the earth: but God limits their power, and as long as they cannot gratify their whole desires, just so long they may rage and foam; but if you put any trust whatever in man, if you rely on the arm of man to protect you, you will be disappointed. What protection have we ever had from the day we commenced to preach the Gospel to the present day? We expect nothing but the arm of the Almighty to protect His people; let us, therefore, put our trust in Him, and just let the devil howl."

George Albert Smith, Journal of Discourses, Vol. 9, p. 70-71, March 10, 1861.

"He does not wish us to go and slay our enemies, but he wants us to be upon the watchtower. He wants us to build towers, temples, houses, and everything that will make us comfortable; also to plant vineyards and oliveyards, and to watch over them. But when it comes to the wicked slaying the wicked, he has thus far caused the wicked to slay the wicked. The Saints have been and doubtless always will be spared this trouble, but they will have to face dangers—in many instances to lay down their lives for the Gospel's sake; and to such the Lord will give crowns of glory and endless life, even to all those that live according to the principles of eternal life. But we need not expect crowns of glory in this life. The blessings of light and life that are in the midst of the Saints are only to be had by living for them—by living our religion. There are hundreds and thousands that are willing to fight for their religion. The things that are required are for us to live our religion, walk in accordance with the principles of honesty and justice, that the light of the Holy Spirit may continually shine upon us, and that our religion shall be the uppermost thing in our minds all the day long."

George Albert Smith, Journal of Discourses, Vol. 12, p. 141, October 9, 1867.

"We all exercise faith that God may give to our President wisdom and understanding to foresee the evils with which we may be threatened, and to take measures to avert them. Suppose that he comes forward and tells us how to prepare, and we neglect his counsel, then the watchman is clear, and we are liable to the dangers and difficulties resulting from disobedience."

George Albert Smith, Journal of Discourses, Vol. 12, p. 142, October 9, 1867.

"Terrible destruction awaits the wicked. They will come to us by thousands by-and-by, saying—'Can you not feed us? Can you not do something for us?' It is said by the prophets they shall come bending, and shall say you are the priests of the Lord. What priest could administer greater earthly blessings than food to the hungry, who have fled from a country where the sword, famine, and pestilence were sweeping away their thousands? I look upon the subject of storing grain and other kinds of food as a very religious matter. How could a man who was half starved enjoy his religion? How on the face of the earth could a man enjoy his religion when he had been told by the Lord how to prepare for a day of famine, when, instead of doing so, he had fooled away that which would have sustained him and his family. I wish our brethren to lay this matter to heart, and not to rest until they have obeyed this particular item of counsel."

George Albert Smith, Journal of Discourses, Vol. 14, p. 13, May 6, 1870.

"It appears that we have gathered many to Zion who do not fully appreciate the great work of these days—namely, to place the people of God in a condition that they can sustain themselves, against the time that Babylon the Great shall fall. Some will say that it is ridiculous to suppose that Babylon, the 'Mother of Harlots,' is going to fall. Ridiculous as it may seem, the time will come when no man will buy her merchandise, and when the Latter-day Saints will be under the necessity of providing for themselves, or going without. 'This may be a wild idea,' but it is no more wild or wonderful than what has already transpired, and that before our eyes. When we are counseled to 'provide for your wants within yourselves,' we are only told to prepare for that day. When we are told, 'Unite your interests and establish every variety of business that may be necessary to supply your wants,' we are only told to lay a plan to enjoy liberty, peace and plenty."

Charles W. Penrose, Journal of Discourses, Vol. 24, p. 218, May 18, 1883.

"We are here in these mountains that we may escape these troubles; that we may not partake of the sins of Babylon, that we may not share in her plagues. God has called us out from the world that we may be different from the world; that the object we live for may be different from the object which men have in view in the world; that we may not live for worldly gain, but live for God, for humanity, for the spirit of the Gospel; live to gather Israel, live to build temples, live that we may attend to the ordinances pertaining to our own salvation and exaltation, and those that pertain to the salvation of our dead. That the word of God may be fulfilled; that His kingdom may be established upon the earth no more to be thrown down forever."

Orson F. Whitney, Saturday Night Thoughts, p. 188.

"Safety With The Priesthood.—The Almighty does not hurl the shafts of affliction against the righteous, especially helpless innocence; but in pursuance of his benevolent designs, and to affect the greatest good to the greatest number, he permits the destroyer to exercise his agency in a world where good and bad, old and young, all classes and all qualities, dwell. Some of the woes thus launched fall partly upon the choicest of God's children, unless faith be there—as doubtless he intends—faith and the power of the Priesthood, to intervene for their preservation. 'The just shall live by faith,' it is written, and the Priesthood is a shield to those who bear it and to those who honor its possessors."

Joseph Fielding Smith, Conference Report, October 1952, p. 60.

"Are we all prepared so that we will not be subject to the cunning craftiness of men, to the false doctrines that are in the world, the teachings that are contrary to the plan of eternal salvation? If we are not then we need to repent."

Joseph Fielding Smith Jr., The Way to Perfection, p. 280.

"The words of the prophets are rapidly being fulfilled, but it is done on such natural principles that most of us fail to see it."

Joseph Fielding Smith, Church History and Modern Revelation, Vol. 2, p.147.

"This revelation (Word of Wisdom) was also given as a warning to the saints against the evils which do and will exist in the hearts of conspiring men in the last days, and the Lord warned and had forewarned the saints that they might protect themselves against these wicked designs."

Joseph Fielding Smith, The Way to Perfection, p. 253.

"The continuation of the marriage covenant, and the family as a unit, was the crowning blessing in the restoration of the keys by the prophet Elijah. If there were no family organization approved of then the whole earth would be under a curse at the day of the coming of the Lord. What would be the need of the hearts of the fathers turning to their children and the hearts of the children to the fathers, if they were not to be united by some eternal union? It is the family eternally organized according to the law of God, which will save the earth from utter destruction when that great and dreadful day of the Lord shall come."

Joseph Fielding Smith, The Way to Perfection, p. 283.

"Yet the old world goes on about its business paying very little heed to all the Lord has said, and to all the signs and indications that have been given. Men harden their hearts and say 'that Christ delayeth his coming until the end of the earth.' (D&C 45:26.) They are 'eating and drinking, marrying and giving in marriage' according to the customs of the world, not of God, without one thought that the end of wickedness is near. Pleasure and the love of the world have captured the hearts of the people. There is no time for such people to worship the Lord or give heed to his warnings; so it will continue until the day of destruction is upon them. At no time in the history of the world has it been more necessary for the children of men to repent. We boast of our advanced civilization; of the great knowledge and wisdom with which we are possessed, but in and through it all, the love of God is forgotten!"

Joseph Fielding Smith Jr., Doctrines of Salvation, Vol. 1, p. 173.

"The disciples knew that the restitution was not to come until the approach of the second coming of Jesus Christ, and it was to be in that day that Elijah was to bring back to the earth his priesthood and restore to men the power to seal on earth and in heaven, so that mankind might have means of escape from the destruction which awaited the wicked in that great and dreadful day of the Lord. This great and dreadful day can be no other time than the coming of Jesus Christ to establish his kingdom in power on the earth, and to cleanse it from all iniquity. It will not be a day of dread and fear to the righteous, but it will be a day of fear and terror to the ungodly."

Joseph Fielding Smith Jr., Doctrines of Salvation, Vol. 1, p. 286.

"'And whoso treasureth up my word, shall not be deceived.' Therefore let us go to with our might in the labor of this Church, and in the study and understanding of the principles of the gospel, these principles of light; and as we study them, the Lord will reveal to us further light, until we shall receive the fulness, in due time, of the perfect day; and we shall not be under the necessity of being subject to doubt and seeking for advice when confronted by matters of this kind, because the Spirit of the Lord itself will teach us."

Joseph Fielding Smith Jr., Doctrines of Salvation, Vol. 2, p. 252.

"If we go into the temple, we raise our hands and covenant that we will serve the Lord and observe his commandments and keep ourselves unspotted from the world. If we realize what we are doing, then the endowment will be a protection to us all our lives—a protection which a man who does not go to the temple does not have."

Joseph Fielding Smith Jr., Doctrines of Salvation, Vol. 3, p. 16.

"There will be a separation between the righteous and the unrighteous. Those who will not keep the law of the Lord will deny the faith, for he will withdraw his Spirit from them if they do not repent . . .They must take one side or the other, for this separation must surely come."

Joseph Fielding Smith Jr., Doctrines of Salvation, Vol. 3, p. 27-28.

"It is not the will of the Lord that there should come upon the people disaster . . . but because man himself will violate the commandments . . . the Lord permits all of these evils to come upon him."

Joseph Fielding Smith Jr., Doctrines of Salvation, Vol. 3, p. 34.

"Remember the Lord says if we fail to keep his word, if we walk in the ways of the world, they (calamities) will not pass us by . . .We may escape these things through faithfulness."

Joseph Fielding Smith Jr., Doctrines of Salvation, Vol. 3, p. 37.

"All through the ages some of the righteous have had to suffer because of the acts of the unrighteous."

Joseph Fielding Smith Jr., Doctrines of Salvation, Vol. 3, p. 43-44.

"I do not think they (saints) are going to escape. . .The Lord made the promise to the Latter-day Saints that if they would keep his commandments, they should escape when these destructions like a whirlwind come suddenly . . .We are not keeping his commandments. Some of the Latter-day Saints are to the best of their ability, but many of them are not. . . .We are not half as good as we think we are. . . .We need to have our attention called to these conditions that we might repent and turn to the Lord with full purpose of heart lest these destructions come upon us."

Joseph Fielding Smith Jr., Doctrines of Salvation, Vol. 3, p. 55-56.

"We have been warned and forewarned of the great and dreadful day of the Lord . . .Is it not a fatal mistake for us to feel that this day is yet a long time off, that it is not to come in our generation, and therefore, we may in safety . . . seek after the things the world delights in. . .The Lord expects better things of us. He expects us to keep his commandments, and watch and pray."

John A. Widtsoe, Conference Report, April 1942. p. 33-34.

"Fear, which 'shall come upon every man,' is the natural consequence of a sense of weakness, also of sin. Fear is a chief weapon of Satan in making mankind unhappy. He who fears loses strength for the combat of life, for the fight against evil. Therefore, the power of evil ever seeks to engender fear in human hearts. . . .

As leaders in Israel, we must seek to dispel fear from among our people. A timid, fearing people cannot do their work well. The Latter-day Saints have a divinely assigned world-mission so great that they cannot afford to dissipate their strength in fear. The Lord has repeatedly warned His people against fear. Many a blessing is withheld because of our fears. He has expressly declared that men cannot stop his work on earth, therefore, they who are engaged in the Lord's latter-day cause and who fear, really trust man more than God, and thereby are robbed of their power to serve. . . .

In this world upheaval, in this day of wanton destruction, we, as a people must look upward. There must be trust and faith in our hearts. Hope must walk by our side."

John A. Widtsoe, Evidences and Reconciliations, p. 285.

"In the last days there are also great upheavals. Destruction and death stalk the highways of earth. There is danger all about. But, the tithepayer has claim upon protection. 'Verily it is a day of sacrifice, and a day for the tithing of my people; for he that is tithed shall not be burned. For after today cometh the burning.' (D&C 64:23, 24) The Lord in his mercy opens the windows of heaven upon his faithful children and repays a thousandfold according to their needs."

J. Reuben Clark, Jr., Conference Report, April 1937, p. 26.

"Let us straitly and strictly live within our incomes, and save a little. Let every head of every household see to it that he has on hand enough food and clothing, and, where possible, fuel also, for at least a year ahead. You of small means put your money in foodstuffs and wearing apparel, not in stocks and bonds; you of large means will think you know how to care for yourselves, but I may venture to suggest that you do not speculate. Let every head of every household aim to own his own home, free from mortgage. Let every man who has a garden spot, garden it; every man who owns a farm, farm it."

Harold B. Lee, Conference Report, April 1941, p. 121.

"There is no individual in the Church that knows the real purpose for which the program (welfare) then launched had been intended, but hardly before the Church has made sufficient preparation, that reason will be made manifest, and when it comes it will challenge every resource of the Church to meet it. I trembled at the feeling that came over me. Since that day that feeling has driven me on, night and day, hardly resting, knowing that this is God's will, this is His plan. The only thing necessary today is that the Latter-day Saints everywhere recognize these men, who sit here on the stand, as the fountainheads of truth, through whom God will reveal His will, that His Saints might be preserved through an evil day."

Harold B. Lee, Conference Report, April 1942, p. 87.

"We talk of security in this day, and yet we fail to understand that here on this Temple Block we have standing the holy temple wherein we may find the symbols by which power might be generated that will save this nation from destruction. Therein may be found the fulness of the blessings of the Priesthood."

Harold B. Lee, Welfare Conference, October 1966.

"Perhaps if we think not in terms of a year's supply of what we ordinarily would use, and think more in terms of what it would take to keep us alive in case we didn't have anything else to eat, that last would be very easy to put in storage for a year . . . just enough to keep us alive if we didn't have anything else to eat. We wouldn't get fat on it, but we would live; and if you think in terms of that kind of annual storage rather than a whole year's supply of everything that you are accustomed to eat which, in most cases, is utterly impossible for the average family, I think we will come nearer to what President J. Reuben Clark, Jr., advised us way back in 1937."

Harold B. Lee, Conference Report October 1970, p. 152.

"Now the only safety we have as members of this church is to do exactly what the Lord said to the Church in that day when the Church was organized. We must learn to give heed to the words and commandments that the Lord shall give through his prophet, 'as he receiveth them, walking in all holiness before me; . . . as if from mine own mouth, in all patience and faith.' (D&C 21:4-5.) There will be some things that take patience and faith. You may not like what comes from the authority of the Church. It may contradict your political views. It may contradict your social views. It may interfere with some of your social life. But if you listen to these things, as if from the mouth of the Lord himself, with patience and faith, the promise is that 'the gates of hell shall not prevail against you; yea, and the Lord God will disperse the powers of darkness from before you, and cause the heavens to shake for your good, and his name's glory.' (D&C 21:6.)"

Harold B. Lee, Stand Ye In Holy Places, p. 282.

"I am persuaded that the day of trial and tribulation, the time for testing the fidelity of the Latter-day Saints, is here as has been foretold. I am also convinced that you and I will not be prepared for living the celestial law in preparation for the Second Coming if we are not able to live the law of tithing, pay our fast offerings, and subscribe wholeheartedly to the workings of the welfare plan at the present time. In my mind there is grave doubt that any man can abide the day of the Second Coming who is not willing and able to follow the leadership of these men whom the Lord has appointed to counsel and guide us in this day."

Spencer W. Kimball, Conference Report, April 1960, p. 85.

"The answer to all of our problems—personal, national, and international—has been given to us many times by many prophets, ancient to modern. Why must we grovel in the earth when we could be climbing toward heaven! The path is not obscure. Perhaps it is too simple for us to see. We look to foreign programs, summit conferences, land bases. We depend on fortifications, our gods of stone; upon ships and planes and projectiles, our gods of iron—gods which have no ears, no eyes, no hearts. We pray to them for deliverance and depend upon them for protection."

Spencer W. Kimball, *The False Gods We Worship*, Ensign, June 1976, p. 6.

The Lord gave us a choice world and expects righteousness and obedience to his commandments in return. But when I review the performance of this people in comparison with what is expected, I am appalled and frightened. Iniquity seems to abound. . . . The Brethren constantly cry out against that which is intolerable in the sight of the Lord. . . That such a cry should be necessary among a people so blessed is amazing to me. . . .

Carnal man has tended to transfer his trust in God to material things . . .It is my firm belief that when we read the scriptures, and try to 'liken them unto ourselves', we will see many parallels between the ancient worship of graven images and behavioral patterns in our very own experience . . .

In spite of our delight in defining ourselves as modern, and our tendency to think we possess a sophistication that no people in the past ever had—in spite of these things, we are, on the whole, an idolatrous people—a condition most repugnant to the Lord. . . .

When enemies rise up, we commit vast resources to the fabrication of gods of stone and steel—ships, planes, missiles, fortifications—and depend on them for protection and deliverance. When threatened we become anti-enemy instead of pro-kingdom of God . . . We forget that if we are righteous the Lord will either not suffer our enemies to come upon us—and this is the special promise to the inhabitants of the land of the Americas (see 2 Ne. 1:7)—or he will fight our battles for us (Exodus 14:14, D&C 98:37 to name only two references of many)."

The Teachings of Spencer W. Kimball, p. 72.
"Security is not born of inexhaustible wealth but of unquenchable faith. And generally that kind of faith is born and nurtured in the home and in childhood."

The Teachings of Spencer W. Kimball, p. 114.
"Follow promptings of the Holy Ghost. There is only one safe and sure way for man to act. . . .The Lord has never condemned nor permitted destruction to any people until he has warned them. . . .One cannot say he did not know better. . . .Every normal person may have a sure way of knowing what is right and what is wrong. He may learn the gospel and receive the Holy Spirit, which will always guide him as to right and wrong. In addition to this, he has the leaders of the Lord's church."

The Teachings of Spencer W. Kimball, p. 363-364.
"Selflessness can bring Zion. May I suggest three fundamental things we must do if we are to 'bring again Zion,' three things for which we who labor for Zion must commit ourselves.

First, we must eliminate the individual tendency to selfishness that snares the soul, shrinks the heart, and darkens the mind. . . .

Second, we must cooperate completely and work in harmony one with the other. . .'Behold, . . .if ye are not one ye are not mine.' (D&C 38:27.). . .

Third, we must lay on the altar and sacrifice whatever is required by the Lord. We begin by offering a 'broken heart and a contrite spirit.' We follow this by giving our best effort in our assigned fields of labor and callings. . . .Finally we consecrate our time, talents, and means as called upon by our file leaders and as prompted by the whisperings of the Spirit. In the Church . . . we can give expression to every ability, every righteous desire, every thoughtful impulse, and in the end, we learn it was no sacrifice at all."

The Teachings of Spencer W. Kimball, p. 374.

"Maintain a year's supply. The Lord has urged that his people save for the rainy days, prepare for the difficult times, and put away for emergencies, a year's supply or more of bare necessities so that when comes the flood, the earthquake, the famine, the hurricane, the storms of life, our families can be sustained through the dark days. How many of us have complied with this? We strive with the Lord, finding many excuses: We do not have room for storage. The food spoils. We do not have the funds to do it. We do not like these common foods. It is not needed—there will always be someone to help in trouble. The government will come to the rescue. And some intend to obey but procrastinate."

Spencer W. Kimball, Faith Precedes the Miracle, p. 253-256.

"I believe that the Ten Virgins represent the people of the Church of Jesus Christ and not the rank and file of the world. All of the virgins, wise and foolish, had accepted the invitation to the wedding supper; they had knowledge of the program and had been warned of the important day to come. They were not the gentiles or the heathens or the pagans, nor were they necessarily corrupt and reprobate, but they were knowing people who were foolishly unprepared for the vital happenings that were to affect their eternal lives. . . .

Rushing for their lamps to light their way through the blackness, half of them found them empty. They had cheated themselves. They were fools, these five unprepared virgins. Apparently, the bridegroom had tarried for reasons that were sufficient and good. Time had passed, and he had not come. They had heard of his coming for so long, so many times, that the statement seemingly became meaningless to them. Would he ever come? So long had it been since they began expecting him that they were rationalizing that he would never appear. Perhaps it was a myth.

Hundreds of thousands of us today are in this position. Confidence has been dulled and patience worn thin. It is so hard to wait and be prepared always. But we cannot allow ourselves to slumber. The Lord has given us this parable as a special warning. . . .

Even the foolish ones trimmed their lamps, but their oil was used up and they had none to refill the lamps. They hastened to make up for lost time. Now, too late, they were becoming conscious of the tragedy of unpreparedness. They had been taught. They had been warned all their lives.

At midnight! Precisely at the darkest hour, when least expected, the bridegroom came. When the world is full of tribulation and help is needed, but it seems the time must be past and hope is vain, then Christ will come. The midnights of life are the times when heaven comes to offer its joy for man's weariness. But when the cry sounds, there is no time for preparation. . . .In the daytime, wise and unwise seemed alike; midnight is the time of test and judgment—and of offered gladness. . . .

The foolish asked the others to share their oil, but spiritual preparedness cannot be shared in an instant. The wise had to go, else the bridegroom would have gone unwelcomed. They needed all their oil for themselves; they could not save the foolish. The responsibility was each for himself.

This was not selfishness or unkindness. The kind of oil that is needed to illuminate the way and light up the darkness is not shareable. How can one share obedience to the principle of tithing; a mind at peace from righteous living; an accumulation of knowledge? How can one share faith or testimony? How can one share attitudes or chastity, or the experience of a mission? How can one share temple privileges? Each must obtain that kind of oil for himself.

The foolish virgins were not averse to buying oil. They knew they should have oil. They merely procrastinated, not knowing when the bridegroom would come.

In the parable, oil can be purchased at the market. In our lives the oil of preparedness is accumulated drop by drop in righteous living. Attendance at sacrament meetings adds oil to our lamps, drop by drop over the years. Fasting, family prayer, home teaching, control of bodily appetites, preaching the gospel, studying the scriptures—each act of dedication and obedience is a drop added to our store. Deeds of kindness, payment of offerings and tithes, chaste thoughts and actions, marriage in the covenant for eternity—these, too, contribute importantly to the oil with which we can at midnight refuel our exhausted lamps. Midnight is so late for those who have procrastinated."

Spencer W. Kimball, The Miracle of Forgiveness, p. 48.

"President Brigham Young expressed his fears that the riches of the world would canker the souls of his people in our own dispensation, when he said:

'Take courage, brethren . . . plow your land and sow wheat, plant your potatoes. It is our duty to preach the Gospel, gather Israel, pay our tithing and build temples. The worst fear I have about this people is that they will get rich in this country, forget God and His people, wax fat, and kick themselves out of the Church and go to hell. This people will stand mobbing, robbing, poverty, and all manner of persecution and be true. But my greatest fear is that they cannot stand wealth.'"

Spencer W. Kimball, The Miracle of Forgiveness, p. 318.

"While corridors are threatened and concessions are made, we live riotously, and divorce and marry in cycles, like the seasons. While leaders quarrel and editors write and authorities analyze and prognosticate, we break all the laws in God's catalog. While enemies filter into our nation to subvert and intimidate and soften us, we continue on with our destructive thinking 'It can't happen here.'"

Ezra Taft Benson, Conference Report, October 1961, p. 75

"Yes, perilous times are ahead, but if we do our duty in all things, God will give us inner peace and overrule all things for our good."

Ezra Taft Benson, BYU Speeches, February 28, 1962, p. 11.

"What can we do to prepare for what may lie ahead? Answers to this question have been repeated to our people many times, over the years. Here are some of them:
1. Get out of debt and live within your income.
2. Save what you can from your income.
3. Store at least one year's supply of food, clothing, and other household necessities.
4. Pay your tithes and offerings.
5. Support the welfare plan."

Ezra Taft Benson, Conference Report, April 1965, p. 121.

"Usually the Lord gives us the overall objectives to be accomplished and some guidelines to follow, but he expects us to work out most of the details and methods. The methods and procedures are usually developed through study and prayer and by living so that we can obtain and follow the promptings of the Spirit. Less spiritually advanced people, such as those in the days of Moses, had to be commanded in many things. Today those spiritually alert look at the objectives, check the guidelines laid down by the Lord and his prophets, and then prayerfully act—without having to be commanded 'in all things.' This attitude prepares men for godhood. . . .

Sometimes the Lord hopefully waits on his children to act on their own, and when they do not, they lose the greater prize, and the Lord will either drop the entire matter and let them suffer the consequences or else he will have to spell it out in greater detail. Usually, I fear, the more he has to spell it out, the smaller is our reward."

Ezra Taft Benson, Conference Report, April 1967, p. 61.
"Be Prepared. We have a duty to survive, not only spiritually but also physically. Not survival at the cost of principles, for this is the surest way to defeat—but a survival that comes from intelligent preparation. We face days ahead that will test the moral and physical sinews of all of us.

The scriptural parable of the five wise and the five foolish virgins is a reminder that one can wait too long before he attempts to get his spiritual and temporal house in order. Are we prepared?

A man should not only be prepared to protect himself physically, but he should also have on hand sufficient supplies to sustain himself and his family in an emergency. For many years the leaders of the Mormon Church have recommended, with instructions, that every family have on hand at least a year's supply of basic food, clothing, fuel (where possible) and provision for shelter. This has been most helpful to families suffering temporary reverses. It can and will be useful in many circumstances in the days ahead. We also need to get out of financial bondage, to be debt free."

Ezra Taft Benson, Conference Report, October 1973, p. 89.
"Here then is the key—look to the prophets for the words of God, that will show us how to prepare for the calamities which are to come."

Ezra Taft Benson, Conference Report, October 1973, p. 90.
"For the righteous the gospel provides a warning before a calamity, a program for the crises, a refuge for each disaster . . .The Lord has warned us of famines, but the righteous will have listened to the prophets and stored at least one year's supply of survival food."

Ezra Taft Benson, *"In His Steps"*, BYU, March 4, 1979.
"For nearly six thousand years, God has held you in reserve to make your appearance in the final days before the Second Coming of the Lord. Every previous gospel dispensation has drifted into apostasy, but ours will not. True, there will be some individuals who will fall away; but the kingdom of God will remain intact to welcome the return of its head—even Jesus Christ. While our generation will be comparable in wickedness to the days of Noah, when the Lord cleansed the earth by flood, there is a major difference this time. It is that God has saved for the final inning some of his strongest children, who will help bear off the Kingdom triumphantly. And that is where you come in, for you are the generation that must be prepared to meet your God.

All through the ages the prophets have looked down through the corridors of time to our day.

Billions of the deceased and those yet to be born have their eyes on us. Make no mistake about it— you are a marked generation. There has never been more expected of the faithful in such a short period of time as there is of us. Never before on the face of this earth have the forces of evil and the forces of good been as well organized. Now is the great day of the devil's power, with the greatest mass murderers of all time living among us. But now is also the great day of the Lord's power, with the greatest number ever of priesthood holders on the earth. And the showdown is fast approaching.

Each day the forces of evil and the forces of good pick up new recruits. Each day we personally make many decisions that show where our support will go. The final outcome is certain —the forces of righteousness will finally win. What remains to be seen is where each of us personally, now and in the future, will stand in this fight—and how tall we will stand. Will we be true to our last days, foreordained mission?"

Ezra Taft Benson, Conference Report, Ensign, November 1980, p. 33-34.
"There are blessings in being close to the soil, in raising your own food, even if it is only a garden in your yard and a fruit tree or two. Those families will be fortunate who, in the last days, have an adequate supply of food because of their foresight and ability to produce their own . . .

You do not need to go into debt to obtain a year's supply. Plan to build up your food supply just as you would a savings account. Save a little for storage each paycheck. Can or bottle fruit and vegetables from your gardens and orchards. Learn how to preserve food through drying and possibly freezing. Make your storage a part of your budget. Store seeds and have sufficient tools on hand to do the job. If you are saving and planning for a second car or a television set or some item which merely adds to your comfort or pleasure, you may need to change your priorities. We urge you to do this prayerfully and do it now. I speak with a feeling of great urgency. I have seen what the days of tribulation can do to people."

Ezra Taft Benson, Conference Report, Priesthood Leadership Meeting, Ensign, May 1986, p. 79-82.
"Such grim predictions by prophets of old would be cause for great fear and discouragement if those same prophets had not, at the same time, offered the solution. In their inspired counsel we can find the answer to the spiritual crises of our age . . .

In the word of God and through it we can find the power to resist temptation, the power to thwart the work of Satan and his emissaries . . .

The word of God, as found in the scriptures, in the words of living prophets, and in personal revelation, has the power to fortify the Saints and arm them with the Spirit so they can resist evil, hold fast to the good, and find joy in this life . . .

However diligent we may be in other areas, certain blessings are to be found only in the scriptures, only in coming to the word of the Lord and holding fast to it as we make our way through the mists of darkness to the tree of life.

And if we ignore what the Lord has given us, we may lose the very power and blessings which we seek."

Ezra Taft Benson, Conference Report, Oct. 1986, Ensign, Nov. 1986, p. 79.
"Many years before the coming of the Savior to this earth, the prophet Enoch saw the latter

days. He observed the great wickedness that would prevail on the earth at this time and foretold the `great tribulations' that would result from such wickedness; but in the midst of what was otherwise a very gloomy prophecy, the Lord promised, `But my people will I preserve' (Moses 7:61). How would He do so? Note what the Lord Himself promised He would do to preserve His people. He said: `And righteousness will I send down out of heaven; and truth will I send forth out of the earth, to bear testimony of mine Only Begotten, . . . and righteousness and truth will I cause to sweep the earth as with a flood, to gather out mine elect from the four quarters of the earth unto a place which I shall prepare' (Moses 7:62)."

Ezra Taft Benson, *"Righteousness Exalteth a Nation"*, Provo Freedom Festival, June 29, 1986.

"There are going to be difficult times in the nation, and even this nation will have to rely upon deity to be able to survive. And if we are going to survive it will require that we be righteous enough to justify the heavens in our behalf . . .

How do we prepare ourselves so God will intervene in our behalf in the days ahead? I would like to suggest 4 important things we can do.

1. We must both as individuals and as a nation look to God as our Maker and as the source of our freedoms and blessings. . . .

2. We must make the creation of quality family life a high priority in our lives . . .

3. We must become informed and knowledgeable citizens . . .

We must study and learn for ourselves the principles laid down in the constitution which have preserved our freedom for the last two hundred years. If we do not understand the role of government and how our rights are protected by the Constitution, we may accept programs or organizations that help erode our freedoms. An informed citizenry is the first line of defense against anarchy and tyranny.

We must teach our children about the spiritual roots of this great nation . . .

4. We must become actively involved in supporting, good, wise, and honest people for public office, and assume an active part in improving our communities."

Ezra Taft Benson, Ensign, May 1987, p. 4.

"The record of the Nephite history just prior to the Savior's visit reveals many parallels to our own day as we anticipate the Savior's second coming. The Nephite civilization had reached great heights. They were prosperous and industrious. They had built many cities with great highways connecting them. They engaged in shipping and trade. They built temples and palaces.

But, as so often happens, the people rejected the Lord. Pride became commonplace. Dishonesty and immorality were widespread. Secret combinations flourished because, as Helaman tells us, the Gadianton robbers `had seduced the more part of the righteous until they had come down to believe in their works and partake of their spoils' (Hel. 6:38). `The people began to be distinguished by ranks, according to their riches and their chances for learning' (3 Ne. 6:12). And `Satan had great power, unto the stirring up of the people to do all manner of iniquity, and to the puffing them up with pride, tempting them to seek for power, and authority, and riches, and the vain things of the world,' even as today (v. 15).

Mormon noted that the Nephites `did not sin ignorantly, for they knew the will of God concerning them' (v.18)."

Ezra Taft Benson, Ensign, November 1988, p. 87.

"I testify that as the forces of evil increase under Lucifer's leadership and as the forces of good increase under the leadership of Jesus Christ, there will be growing battles between the two until the final confrontation. As the issues become clearer and more obvious, all mankind will eventually be required to align themselves either for the kingdom of God or for the kingdom of the devil. As these conflicts rage either secretly or openly, the righteous will be tested. God's wrath will soon shake the nations of the earth and will be poured out on the wicked without measure. But God will provide strength for the righteous and the means of escape; and eventually and finally truth will triumph. I testify that it is time for every man to set in order his own house both temporally and spiritually."

Ezra Taft Benson, Conference Report, Ensign, May 1989, p. 4-7.

"The central feature of pride is enmity—enmity toward God and enmity toward our fellowmen. Enmity means 'hatred toward, hostility to, or a state of opposition.' It is the power by which Satan wishes to reign over us.

Pride is essentially competitive in nature. We pit our will against God's. When we direct our pride toward God, it is in the spirit of 'my will and not thine be done.' . . . The proud wish God would agree with them. They aren't interested in changing their opinions to agree with God's. . . .

Pride is a sin that can readily be seen in others but is rarely admitted in ourselves. Most of us consider pride to be a sin of those on the top, such as the rich and the learned, looking down at the rest of us. (See 2 Ne. 9:42.) There is, however, a far more common ailment among us—and that is pride from the bottom looking up. It is manifest in so many ways, such as faultfinding, gossiping, backbiting, murmuring, living beyond our means, envying, coveting, withholding gratitude and praise that might lift another, and being unforgiving and jealous.

Pride is a damning sin in the true sense of that word. It limits or stops progression. (See Alma 12:10-11.) The proud are not easily taught. (See 1 Ne. 15:3, 7-11.) They won't change their minds to accept truths, because to do so implies they have been wrong. . . . God will have a humble people. Either we can choose to be humble or we can be compelled to be humble."

Teachings of Ezra Taft Benson, p. 51.

"In our day, the Lord has revealed the need to reemphasize the Book of Mormon to get the Church and all the children of Zion out from under condemnation—the scourge and judgment (see D&C 84:54-58). This message must be carried to the members of the Church throughout the world. (CR, April 1986, Ensign, May 1986, p. 78.)"

Teachings of Ezra Taft Benson, p. 56.

"The Book of Mormon exposes the enemies of Christ. It confounds false doctrines and lays down contention (see I Nephi 3:12). It fortifies the humble followers of Christ against the evil designs, strategies, and doctrines of the devil in our day. The type of apostates in the Book of Mormon are similar to the type we have today. God, with His infinite foreknowledge, so molded the

Book of Mormon that we might see the error and know how to combat false educational, political, religious, and philosophical concepts of our time. ("The Book of Mormon Is the Word of God," Regional Representatives Seminar, Salt Lake City, Utah, April 4, 1986.)"

Teachings of Ezra Taft Benson, p. 59.

"If they saw our day, and chose those things which would be of greatest worth to us, is not that how we should study the Book of Mormon? We should constantly ask ourselves, 'Why did the Lord inspire Mormon or Moroni or Alma to include that in their records? What lesson can I learn from that to help me live in this day and age?' And there is example after example of how that question will be answered. For example, in the Book of Mormon we find a pattern for preparing for the Second Coming. A major portion of the book centerson the few decades just prior to Christ's coming to America. By careful study of that time period we can determine why some were destroyed in the terrible judgments that preceded His coming and what brought others to stand at the temple in the land of Bountiful and thrust their hands into the wounds of His hands and feet.

From the Book of Mormon we learn how disciples of Christ live in times of war. From the Book of Mormon we see the evils of secret combinations portrayed in graphic and chilling reality. In the Book of Mormon we find lessons for dealing with persecution and apostasy. We learn much about how to do missionary work. And more than anywhere else, we see in the Book of Mormon the dangers of materialism and setting our hearts on the things of the world. Can anyone doubt that this book was meant for us and that in it we find great power, great comfort, and great protection? (CR, Oct. 1986.)"

Teachings of Ezra Taft Benson, p. 60-61.

"We have not been using the Book of Mormon as we should. Our homes are not as strong unless we are using it to bring our children to Christ. Our families may be corrupted by worldly trends and teachings unless we know how to use the book to expose and combat the falsehoods in socialism, organic evolution, rationalism, humanism, and so forth. Our missionaries are not as effective unless they are 'hissing forth' with it. Social, ethical, cultural, or educational converts will not survive under the heat of the day unless their taproots go down to the fullness of the gospel which the Book of Mormon contains. Our Church classes are not as spirit-filled unless we hold it up as a standard. And our nation will continue to degenerate unless we read and heed the words of the God of this land, Jesus Christ, and quit building up and upholding the secret combinations which the Book of Mormon tells us proved the downfall of both previous American civilizations. (A Witness and a Warning, p. 6.)

Not only should we know what history and faith-promoting stories it contains, but we should understand its teachings. If we really do our homework and approached the Book of Mormon doctrinally, we can expose the errors and find the truths to combat many of the current false theories and philosophies of men. I have noted within the Church a difference in discernment, insight, conviction, and spirit between those who know and love the Book of Mormon and those who do not. That book is a great sifter. ("Jesus Christ—Gifts and Expectations," Christmas Devotional, Salt Lake City, Utah, December 7, 1986.)"

Teachings of Ezra Taft Benson, p. 65.

"I bless you with increased discernment to judge between Christ and anti-Christ. I bless you with increased power to do good and to resist evil. I bless you with increased understanding of the Book of Mormon. I promise you that from this moment forward, if we will daily sup from its pages and abide by its precepts, God will pour out upon each child of Zion and the Church a blessing hitherto unknown—and we will plead to the Lord that He will begin to lift the condemnation—the scourge and judgment. Of this I bear solemn witness. (CR, April 1986, Ensign, May 1986, p. 78.)"

Teachings of Ezra Taft Benson, p. 73-74.

"The voice of warning is unto all people by the mouths of His servants (see D&C 1:4). If this voice is not heeded, the angels of destruction will increasingly go forth, and the chastening hand of Almighty God will be felt upon the nations, as decreed, until a full end thereof will be the result. Wars, devastation, and untold suffering will be your lot except you turn unto the Lord in humble repentance. Destruction even more terrible and far-reaching than attended the last great war will come with certainty unless rulers and people alike repent and cease their evil and godless ways. God will not be mocked (D&C 63:58). He will not permit the sins of sexual immorality, secret murderous combinations, the killing of the unborn, and disregard for all His holy commandments and the messages of His servants to go unheeded without grievous punishment for such wickedness. The nations of the world cannot endure in sin. The way of escape is clear. The immutable laws of God remain steadfastly in the heavens above. When men and nations refuse to abide by them, the penalty must follow. They will be wasted away. Sin demands punishment."

Teachings of Ezra Taft Benson, p. 88.

"The Apostle Paul saw our day. He described it as a time when such things as blasphemy, dishonesty, cruelty, unnatural affection, pride and pleasure seeking would abound (see 2 Timothy 3:1-7). He also warned that 'evil men and seducers would wax worse and worse, deceiving and being deceived' (2 Timothy 3:12). Such grim predictions by prophets of old would be cause for great fear and discouragement if those same prophets had not, at the same time, offered the solution. In their inspired counsel we can find the answer to the spiritual crises of our age. ("The Power of the Word," address prepared [but not delivered] 1986.)"

Teachings of Ezra Taft Benson, p. 106-108.

"We live in difficult days—very difficult days. They are not improving. However, I do feel that there is some increase in the awakening to the dangers that face us. I am not sure that the awakening is going to be fast enough to avoid the disaster which could very seriously result in bloodshed, hardship, and much sorrow in this beloved country. (Salt Lake City, Utah, 8 April 1972.)"

We will live in the midst of economic, political, and spiritual instability. When these signs are observed—unmistakable evidences that His coming is nigh—we need not be troubled, but 'stand in holy places, and be not moved, until the day of the Lord come' (D&C 87:8). Holy men and women stand in holy places, and these holy places consist of our temples, our chapels, our homes, and stakes of Zion, which are, as the Lord declares, 'for a defense, and for a refuge from the storm, and from wrath when it shall be poured out without mixture upon the whole earth' (D&C 115:6). We must heed the Lord's counsel to the Saints of this dispensation: 'Prepare yourselves for the great day of the Lord' (D&C 133:10).

This preparation must consist of more than just casual membership in the Church. We must be guided by personal revelation and the counsel of the living prophet so we will not be deceived. Our Lord has indicated who, among Church members, will stand when He appears: 'At that day, when I shall come in my glory, shall the parable be fulfilled which I spake concerning the ten virgins' (D&C 45:56). (Come unto Christ, p. 115-116.)

There is a real sifting going on in the Church, and it is going to become more pronounced with the passing of time. It will sift the wheat from the tares, because we face some difficult days, the like of which we have never experienced in our lives. And those days are going to require faith and testimony and family unity, the like of which we have never had. (Grantsville Utah Stake Conference, September 1, 1974.)

Now, we are assured that the Church will remain on the earth until the Lord comes again—but at what price? The Saints in the early days were assured that Zion would be established in Jackson County, but look at what their unfaithfulness cost them in bloodshed and delay."

Teachings of Ezra Taft Benson, p. 107-108.

"In the light of these prophecies, there should be no doubt in the mind of any priesthood holder that the human family is headed for trouble. There are rugged days ahead. It is time for every man who wishes to do his duty to get himself prepared—physically, spiritually, and psychologically—for the task which may come at any time, as suddenly as the whirlwind. (God, Family, Country, p. 345-46.)

In striving to prepare a people who are ready to meet the Lord for His impending second coming, we are faced with wickedness which has never been as well organized, extensive, and subtle. Our day is becoming comparable to the days of Noah, when the Lord had to cleanse the earth by flood—only in our day it will be cleansed by fire. ("Our Obligation and Challenge," Regional Representatives Seminar, Salt Lake City, Utah, September 30, 1977.)"

Teachings of Ezra Taft Benson, p. 114-115.

"To the rulers and peoples of all nations, we solemnly declare again that the God of Heaven has established His latter-day kingdom upon the earth in fulfillment of prophecies. Holy angels have again communed with men on the earth. God has again revealed Himself from the heavens and restored to the earth His holy priesthood with power to administer in all the sacred ordinances necessary for the exaltation of His children. His Church has been reestablished among men with all the spiritual gifts enjoyed anciently. All this is done in preparation for Christ's second coming. The great and dreadful day of the Lord is near at hand. In preparation for this great event and as a means of escaping the impending judgments, inspired messengers have gone, and are going forth to the nations of the earth carrying this testimony and warning."

Teachings of Ezra Taft Benson, p. 117.

"While it is more difficult to live the truth, such as standing for free agency, some of us may in the not-too-distant future be required to die for the truth. But the best preparation for eternal life is to be prepared at all times to die—fully prepared by a valiant fight for right. (CR, April 1964, Improvement Era, June 1964, p. 504.)"

Teachings of Ezra Taft Benson, p. 134.

"Let me give you a crucial key to help you avoid being deceived. It is this—learn to keep your eye on the prophet. He is the Lord's mouthpiece and the only man who can speak for the Lord today. Let his inspired counsel take precedence. Let his inspired words be a basis for evaluating the counsel of all lesser authorities. Then live close to the Spirit so you may know the truth of all things."

Teachings of Ezra Taft Benson, p. 150.

"Stakes are to be a defense (see D&C 115:6). They do this as they unify under their local priesthood officers and dedicate themselves to do their duty and keep their covenants. Those covenants, if kept, become a protection from error, evil, or calamity.

Stakes are a defense for the Saints from enemies both seen and unseen. The defense is provided through priesthood channels that strengthen testimony and promote family solidarity and individual righteousness."

Teachings of Ezra Taft Benson, p. 151.

"The Book of Mormon prophet Nephi foresaw the day when the Saints would be scattered in stakes all over the world. He saw the time when the Lord would extend His protection to them when menaced by a storm of destruction which threatened their existence. Nephi prophesied: 'And it came to pass that I, Nephi, beheld the power of the Lamb of God, that it descended upon the saints of the church of the Lamb, and upon the covenant people of the Lord, who were scattered upon all the face of the earth; and they were armed with righteousness and with the power of God in great glory.' (1 Nephi 14:14.) (Geneva Switzerland Stake Creation, June 20, 1982.)"

Teachings of Ezra Taft Benson, p.151-152.

"Latter-day Saint chapels are more than just houses of worship. The stakes and districts of Zion are symbolic of the holy places spoken of by the Lord where His Saints are to gather in the last days as a refuge from the storm. You and your children will gather here to worship, to do sacred ordinances, to socialize, to learn, to perform in music, dance, drama, athletics, and to generally improve yourselves and one another."

Teachings of Ezra Taft Benson, p. 175.

"The aim of this organizing and concentration of resources is that the Church will be able to stand independent above all nations (which suggests that the Church will be self-governing, autonomous, and not reliant on human opinion or institutions for its temporal survival and support)—amidst a time when the wrath and judgments of God will be poured out on all nations (see D&C 78:13-14). ("The Energy Crisis," Salt Lake City, Utah, August 18, 1977.)"

Teachings of Ezra Taft Benson, p. 176.

"The Church will continue its opposition to error, falsehood, and immorality. The mission of the Church is to herald the message of salvation and make unmistakably clear the pathway to exaltation. Our mission is to prepare a people for the coming of the Lord. The power of God and the righteousness of the Saints will be the means by which the Church will be spared (see 1 Nephi 14:14-15). (CR, April 1980, Ensign, May 1980, p. 33-34.)"

Teachings of Ezra Taft Benson, p. 245.

"The Prophet Joseph Smith declared that the heavenly messenger Moroni, 'informed me of great judgments which were coming upon the earth, with great desolations by famine, sword, and pestilence; and that these grievous judgments would come on the earth in this generation' (Joseph Smith—History 1:45).

We live in a time when those days are imminent. Temples have been provided by a benevolent Father to protect us from these tribulations. Hear the promise given by President George Q. Cannon of the First Presidency: 'When other temples are complete, there will be an increase of power bestowed on the people of God, and they will, thereby, be better fitted to go forth and cope with the powers of darkness and with the evils that exist in the world and to establish the Zion of God never more to be thrown down' (Journal of Discourses, 14:126).

The Saints in this temple district will be better able to meet any temporal tribulation because of this temple. Faith will increase as a result of the divine power associated with the ordinances of heaven and the assurance of eternal associations. (Jordan River Utah Temple Cornerstone Laying, August 15, 1981.)"

Teachings of Ezra Taft Benson, p. 256.

"Let us make the temple a sacred home away from our eternal home. This temple will be a standing witness that the power of God can stay the powers of evil in our midst. Many parents, in and out of the Church, are concerned about protection against a cascading avalanche of wickedness which threatens to engulf Christian principles. I find myself in complete accord with a statement made by President Harold B. Lee during World War II. Said he: 'We talk about security in this day, and yet we fail to understand that . . . we have standing the holy temple wherein we may find the symbols by which power might be generated that will save this nation from destruction' (CR April 1942, p. 87).

Yes, there is a power associated with the ordinances of heaven—even the power of godliness —which can and will thwart the forces of evil if we will be worthy of those sacred blessings. This community will be protected, our families will be protected, our children will be safeguarded as we live the gospel, visit the temple, and live close to the Lord. (Atlanta Georgia Temple Cornerstone Laying, June 1, 1983.)"

Teachings of Ezra Taft Benson, p. 260.

"The Lord is not unmindful of the temporal salvation of His Saints. Some of us saw the welfare program developed from its inception. The full purpose and intent of this inspired program has hardly been realized, and when we have passed through some of the tribulations that are in store for the world, we will see that this inspired plan was necessary to bring the Church to a condition of independence. The Church must become independent of the world—or, in other words, wholly self-sufficient. I quote from the revelation which established the united order in the early days of the

Church, a revelation still awaiting fulfillment:

For verily I say unto you, the time has come, and is now at hand; and behold, and lo, it must needs be that there be an organization of my people, in regulating and establishing the affairs of the storehouse of the poor of my people, both in this place and in the land of Zion—

That you may come up unto the crown prepared for you, and be made rulers over many kingdoms. (D&C 78:3, 14-15.)

Apparently, there will be certain tribulations that will disrupt the nations of the world to the extent that the Church will have to be self-reliant. (Salt Lake City, Utah, June 6, 1980.)"

Teachings of Ezra Taft Benson, p. 263-264.

"Not only should we have strong spiritual homes, but we should have strong temporal homes. We should avoid bondage by getting out of debt as soon as we can, pay as we go, and live within our incomes. There is wisdom in having on hand a year's supply of food, clothing, fuel (if possible), and in being prepared to defend our families and our possessions and to take care of ourselves. I believe a man should prepare for the worst while working for the best."

Teachings of Ezra Taft Benson, p. 264.

"We must do more to get our people prepared for the difficult days we face in the future. Our major concern should be their spiritual preparation so they will respond with faith and not fear. 'If ye are prepared, ye shall not fear' (D&C 38:21). Our next concern should be for their temporal preparation. When the economies of nations fail, when famine and other disasters prevent people from buying food in stores, the Saints must be prepared to handle these emergencies. (Salt Lake City, Utah, 6 June 1980.)"

Teachings of Ezra Taft Benson, p. 265.

"For years we have been counseled to have on hand a year's supply of food. Yet there are some today who will not start storing until the Church comes out with a detailed monthly home storage program. Now, suppose that never happens. We still cannot say we have not been warned.

Should the Lord decide at this time to cleanse the Church—and the need for that cleansing seems to be increasing—a famine in this land of one year's duration could wipe out a large percentage of slothful members, including some ward and stake officers. Yet we cannot say we have not been warned."

Teachings of Ezra Taft Benson, p. 267.

"The times require that every officer of the Church be uniformly trained in principles of welfare, and that each one in turn train the rank and file until every individual is prepared for the calamities which are to come. I think it not extreme for me to say at this point that when all is written about the events to come, we may have hardly enough time to prepare, even if all our resources, spiritual and temporal, are taxed to the limit. ("The Training Challenge," General Welfare Services Committee, Salt Lake City, Utah, February 2, 1977.)"

Teachings of Ezra Taft Benson, p. 268.

"The strength of the Church welfare program lies in every family following the inspired direction of the Church leaders to be self-sustaining through adequate preparation. God intends for His Saints to so prepare themselves 'that the church may stand independent above all other creatures beneath the celestial world' (D&C 78:14). (God, Family, Country, p. 270-271.)"

Teachings of Ezra Taft Benson, p. 268.

"'When we really get into hard times,' said President J. Reuben Clark, Jr., 'where food is scarce or there is none at all, and so with clothing and shelter, money may be no good for there may be nothing to buy, and you cannot eat money, you cannot get enough of it together to burn to keep warm, and you cannot wear it.' (Church News, November 21, 1953, p. 4.)"

Teachings of Ezra Taft Benson, p. 289.

"Inspired leaders have always urged us to get out of debt, to live within our means, and to pay as we go—and this is sound advice for governments as well as individuals. History teaches that when individuals have given up looking after their own economic needs and transferred a large share of that responsibility to the government, both they and the government have failed. (The Red Carpet, p. 168-169.)"

Teachings of Ezra Taft Benson, p. 296.

"Some fathers leave solely to the mother or to the school the responsibility of shaping a child's ideas and standards. Too often television and movie screens shape our children's values. We should not assume that public schools always reinforce teachings given in the home concerning ethical and moral conduct. We have seen introduced into many school systems false ideas about the theory of man's development from lower forms of life, teachings that there are no absolute values, attempts to repudiate beliefs regarded as supernatural, permissive attitudes toward sexual freedom that give sanction to immoral behavior and 'alternative lifestyles,' such as lesbianism, homosexuality, and other perverse practices.

Such teachings not only tend to undermine the faith and morals of our young people, they also deny the existence of God, who gave absolute laws, and the divinity of Jesus Christ. Surely we can see the moral contradiction of some who argue for the preservation of endangered species but who also sanction the abortion of unborn humans. The Lord expects great things from the fathers of Israel. Fathers must take time to find out what their children are being taught and then take steps to correct false information and teaching. (Come unto Christ, p. 59.)"

Teachings of Ezra Taft Benson, p. 297.

"From the very beginning of recorded political thought, man has realized the importance of education as a tremendous potential for both good and evil. In a free and open society such as ours, a well-rounded education is an essential for the preservation of freedom against the chicanery and demagoguery of aspiring tyrants who would have us ignorantly vote ourselves into bondage. As the educational system falls into the hands of the in-power political faction or into the hands of an obscure but tightly knit group of professional social reformers, it is used not to educate but to indoctrinate."

Teachings of Ezra Taft Benson, p. 301.

"'My people are destroyed for lack of knowledge,' said the prophet Hosea (see Hosea 4:6). Let us not let it happen to us. First, let us do our homework, because action without the proper education can lead to fanaticism. But after we have done our homework, let us take action, because education without action can only lead to frustration and failure. (God, Family, Country, p. 380.)"

Teachings of Ezra Taft Benson, p. 302.

"We must be wise as serpents (see D&C 111:11); for as the Apostle Paul said, 'We wrestle against the rulers of darkness against spiritual wickedness in high places' (Ephesians 6:12). We are going through what J. Reuben Clark, Jr., once termed the greatest propaganda campaign of all time. We cannot believe all we read, and what we can believe is not all of the same value. We must sift. We must learn by study and prayer."

Teachings of Ezra Taft Benson, p. 337-338.

"It is not going to be enough just to accept the teachings, standards, and ideals of the Church passively. It will require real activity, real dedication to the principles of righteousness if we are to face the future unafraid. But if we have the courage, sound judgment, and the faith so to do, then no matter what happens we will be able to face any situation with courage and with faith and with the assurance that God will sustain us. I know that now is the time probably more than any other time in our lives to live the gospel. We should not be lulled away into false security as Nephi said many would be in the last days. We should not be pacified and feel in our hearts that we can sin a little, that we can attend to our meetings part of the time, that we can pay a token tithing, that we can live the gospel when it is convenient, and all will be well. We must not be 'at ease in Zion' and say 'Zion prospers, all is well' (2 Nephi 28:21, 24). But we must live the gospel plan in its fulness every day of our lives. Therein is safety. Therein will come a satisfaction which comes from righteous living which will enter our hearts, give us the courage and the strength that we need. There is no security in unrighteousness. The sinful always live in despair (see Moroni 10:22). (So Shall Ye Reap, p. 59-60.)"

Teachings of Ezra Taft Benson, p. 341.

"We have a responsibility of bearing off His kingdom, building up His Church, being a light to the world, and getting organized in a way that we will be a refuge from the storm. I don't mean rain or thunder. I mean the storm of sin that will be destructive of human life and government: 'For a defense, and for a refuge from the storm, and from wrath when it shall be poured out without mixture upon the whole earth' (D&C 115:6). And some of that wrath is going to be poured out upon the heads of the Latter-day Saints who have the gospel, but who refuse to live it and to maintain the standards which the Lord has provided us. I hope the number will be few. (Grantsville Utah Stake Conference, September 1, 1974.)"

Teachings of Ezra Taft Benson, p. 399-400.

"We live in that time of which the Lord spoke when He said that 'peace shall be taken from the earth, and the devil shall have power over his own dominion' (D&C 1:35). We live in that day which John the Revelator foresaw when "the dragon was wroth with the woman, and went to make war with the remnant of her seed, which keep the commandments of God and have the testimony of Jesus Christ" (Revelation 12:17). The dragon is Satan; the woman represents the Church of Jesus Christ. Satan is waging war against the members of the Church who have testimonies and are trying to keep the commandments. And while many of our members are remaining faithful and strong, some are wavering. Some are falling. Some are fulfilling John's prophecy that in the war with Satan, some Saints would be "overcome" (Revelation 13:7)."

Teachings of Ezra Taft Benson, p. 400-401.

"Great battles can make great heroes, but great heroes will make great battles. You will never have a better opportunity to be a greater hero in a more crucial battle than in the battle you will face today and in the immediate future. Be warned that some of the greatest battles you will face will be fought within the silent chambers of your own soul. David's battles in the field against the foe were not as critical as David's battles in the palace against a lustful eye. We will each find our own battlefield. The tactics that the enemy will use against us will vary from time to time; he will feel after our weak spots. We must be alert to the devil's devious designs, to the subtle sins and clever compromises as well as the obvious offenses."

Teachings of Ezra Taft Benson, p. 401-402.

"We live in an age when, as the Lord foretold, men's hearts are failing them, not only physically but in spirit (see D&C 45:26). Many are giving up heart for the battle of life. Suicide ranks as a major cause of death among college students. As the showdown between good and evil approaches, with its accompanying trials and tribulations, Satan is increasingly striving to overcome the Saints with despair, discouragement, despondency, and depression.

Yet, of all people, we as Latter-day Saints should be the most optimistic and the least pessimistic. For while we know that 'peace shall be taken from the earth, and the devil shall have power over his own dominion,' we are also assured that 'the Lord shall have power over his saints, and shall reign in their midst' (D&C 1:35-36). (CR, October 1974, Ensign, November 1974, p. 65.)

Throughout this great Christian nation there seems to be a desperate effort on the part of the adversary—through the great conspiracy, yes—and through other means also, to try to downgrade and depreciate and cheapen everything that's good and holy and pure and uplifting. You see evidence of it in every phase of our economic, social, and even spiritual life. It is a challenge to all of our ideals and traditions of the past. And it is all planned.

The adversary knows. He is smart. He knows this Church, and he knows where to strike, and today he is striking in two places particularly—at the home and the family—because he knows that no Church will ever be stronger than its families, and he knows that this nation will never rise above its homes. He knows that in large measure the home is where children are reared and trained and become good or bad. And so he is striking at the home and the family, trying to weaken that great, basic institution of the home.

He is emphasizing abortion, playing down the seriousness of divorce, playing up permissiveness, telling you to do what you feel like doing, regardless of the principle involved. He is promoting a permissive generation of parents—trying to get them to feel that they have no particular responsibility towards guiding their children, and that they should let the children have their own way, with no counseling. He doesn't like the home evening. He doesn't like family prayer. So he is trying to get us to concentrate our attention on the material things of the world, the styles of the world, the habits of the world, the cheapness of the world—anything to weaken our families and our homes. (Bear Lake Idaho Stake Conference, May 22, 1971.)"

Teachings of Ezra Taft Benson, p. 403-404.

"The Lord has on the earth some potential spiritual giants whom He saved for some six thousand years to help bear off the kingdom triumphantly and the devil is trying to put them to sleep. The devil knows that he probably won't be too successful in getting them to commit many great and malignant sins of commission. So he puts them into a deep sleep, like Gulliver, while he strands them with little sins of omission. And what good is a sleepy, neutralized, lukewarm giant as a leader?

We have too many potential spiritual giants who should be more vigorously lifting their homes, the kingdom, and the country. We have many who feel they are good men, but they need to be good for something—stronger patriarchs, courageous missionaries, valiant genealogists and temple workers, dedicated patriots, devoted quorum members. In short, we must be shakened and awakened from a spiritual snooze. ("Our Obligation and Challenge," Regional Representatives Seminar, Salt Lake City, Utah, September 30, 1977.)"

Teachings of Ezra Taft Benson, p. 404.

"Amid the encircling gloom, the kindly light of the Lord can lead us on (Hymns, 1985, no. 97)—can help expose and stop evil in some places, slow it down in others, give the forces of freedom the chance to become better entrenched, provide righteous alternatives, and develop faith and hope to keep on keeping on in the divine assurance that in the brightness of the Lord's coming, the darkness of Satan's conspiracy will eventually be fully exposed and destroyed. (God, Family, Country, p. 404.)

There is a conspiracy of evil. The source of it all is Satan and his hosts. He has a great power over men to 'lead them captive at his will, even as many as would not hearken' to the voice of the Lord (Moses 4:4). His evil influence may be manifest through governments; through false educational, political, economic, religious, and social philosophies; through secret societies and organizations; and through myriads of other forms. His power and influence are so great that, if possible, he would deceive the very elect (see Matthew 24:24). As the second coming of the Lord approaches, Satan's work will intensify through numerous insidious deceptions. (CR, April 1978, Ensign, May 1978, p. 33.)"

Teachings of Ezra Taft Benson, p. 406-407.

"It is from within the Church that the greatest hindrance comes. And so, it seems, it has been. Now the question arises, will we stick with the kingdom and can we avoid being deceived? Certainly this is an important question, for the Lord has said that in the last days the 'devil will rage in the hearts of men' (2 Nephi 28:20), and if it were possible he 'shall deceive the very elect' (see Joseph

Smith—Matthew 1:22). (Title of Liberty, p. 218.)"

Teachings of Ezra Taft Benson, p. 407.

"As the world becomes more wicked, a possible way to attain worldly success may be to join the wicked. The time is fast approaching when it will require great courage for Latter-day Saints to stand up for their peculiar standards and doctrine—all of their doctrine, including the more weighty principles such as the principle of freedom. Opposition to this weighty principle of freedom caused many of our brothers and sisters in the premortal existence to lose their first estate in the War in Heaven."

Teachings of Ezra Taft Benson, p. 408.

"War, famine, pestilences, earthquakes— these are conditions for which we must prepare our people. They are judgments to be poured out on the nations of the world because of the rejection of the gospel. 'And thus, with sword and by bloodshed the inhabitants of the earth shall mourn; and with famine, and plague, and earthquake, and the thunder of heaven, and the fierce and vivid lightning also, shall the inhabitants of the earth be made to feel the wrath, indignation, and chastening hand of an Almighty God, until the consumption decreed hath made a full end of all nations' (D&C 87:6)."

Teachings of Ezra Taft Benson, p. 413.

"Certainly spirituality is the foundation upon which any battle against tyranny must be waged. And because this is basically the struggle of the forces of Christ versus anti-Christ, it is imperative that our people be in tune with the supreme leader of freedom—the Lord our God. And men only stay in tune when their lives are in harmony with God. For apart from God we cannot succeed, but as a partner with God we cannot fail."

Teachings of Ezra Taft Benson, p. 480.

"To meet and beat the enemy will take clear heads and strong bodies. Hearts and hands grow strong based on what they are fed. Let us take into our bodies or souls only those things that would make us more effective instruments. We need all the physical, mental, and moral power we can get. Righteous concern about conditions is commendable when it leads to constructive action. But undue worry is debilitating. When we have done what we can, then let us leave the rest to God—including the worrying."

Teachings of Ezra Taft Benson, p. 480-481.

"We have a duty to survive, not only spiritually but also physically. Not survival at the cost of principles, for this is the surest way to defeat, but a survival that comes from intelligent preparation. We face days ahead that will test the moral and physical sinews of all of us. (God, Family, Country, p. 331.)"

Teachings of Ezra Taft Benson, p.507

"The revelation to produce and store food may be as essential to our temporal welfare today as boarding the ark was to the people in the days of Noah."

Teachings of Ezra Taft Benson, p. 562-563.

"Never has the Church had a more choice group of young people than at present, and Satan is well aware of who they are. He is doing everything in his power to thwart them in their destiny. He knows that they have been sent to earth in this crucial period of the world's history to build the kingdom of God and establish Zion in preparation for the second coming of the Lord Jesus Christ. Yes, our youth have an awesome challenge. ("Challenges for Leaders of Aaronic Priesthood," Young Men's General Presidency and Board, Salt Lake City, Utah, September 19, 1979.)"

Teachings of Ezra Taft Benson, p. 580.

"There are some in this land, among whom I count myself, whose faith it is that this land is reserved only for a righteous people, and we remain here as tenants only as we remain in the favor of the Lord, for He is the landlord as far as this earth is concerned. If we are to remain under heaven's benign protection and care, we must return to those principles which have brought us our peace, liberty, and prosperity. Our problems today are essentially problems of the Spirit."

Teachings of Ezra Taft Benson, p. 653.

"It will be increasingly valuable to have vocational skills—to be able to use our hands. The most essential temporal skills and knowledge are to be able to provide food, clothing, and shelter. Increasingly, the Lord, through His servants, is trying to get us closer to the soil by raising our own produce."

Teachings of Ezra Taft Benson, p. 706.

"Too often we bask in our comfortable complacency and rationalize that the ravages of war, economic disaster, famine, and earthquake cannot happen here. Those who believe this are either not acquainted with the revelations of the Lord, or they do not believe them. Those who smugly think these calamities will not happen, that they somehow will be set aside because of the righteousness of the Saints, are deceived and will rue the day they harbored such a delusion. The Lord has warned and forewarned us against a day of great tribulation and given us counsel, through His servants, on how we can be prepared for these difficult times. Have we heeded His counsel?"

Ezra Taft Benson, An Enemy Hath Done This, p. 232.

"Schools should be reminded that their primary field of competence is academic, not social adjustment, or world citizenship, or sex education."

Mark E. Petersen, Conference Report, October 1967, p. 68.

"But if we and our posterity reject religious instruction and authority, violate the rules of eternal justice, trifle with the injunctions of morality, and recklessly destroy the political constitution which holds us together, no one can tell how sudden a catastrophe may overwhelm us, that shall bury all our glory in profound obscurity."

Marion G. Romney, Conference Report, April 1951, p. 21-22.

"But we Latter-day Saints must not let ourselves be so engulfed with forebodings that we fail to obtain and enjoy such hope and courage as is within our reach—the hope and courage born of faith in the power of righteousness to ultimately triumph. I have boundless confidence in that power. I am persuaded beyond all doubt that the destiny of men and nations is in the hands of the Almighty, who has respect for righteousness, and not in the hands of conniving politicians whose wisdom has perished, whose understanding has come to naught, and who have no respect for righteousness. If it were not so, I should be in utter despair. I believe that the record and the word of God justify us in so placing our hope. . . .

I am persuaded that a complete surrender to the principles of righteousness would lift God's people out of the turmoil of this present world. Such has been the record in the past, as witness the experiences of Enoch and his people and the record of the Nephites following their visit from the risen Redeemer. I believe a similar performance by us in our day would bring the same results. I not only believe, but I know it would, and that it will yet be done."

Marion G. Romney, Conference Report, October 1958, p. 97.

"To provide an escape from our threatened destruction was one of the reasons specified by the Lord for restoring the gospel. '. . . knowing the calamity which should come upon the inhabitants of the earth,' he said, 'I the Lord, called upon my servant Joseph Smith, Jun., and spake unto him from heaven, and gave him commandments.'(D&C 1:17.) Obedience to the commandments here referred to the principles and ordinances of the gospel constitute the sure and only means of escaping the impending calamity. That the peoples of the earth will avail themselves of this means of escape is by no means certain. But whether they do or whether they do not they who know the truth are not dismayed, for they know that the promised blessings do not depend upon the conduct of others and that that peace promised by the Savior flows into the heart of every soul who keeps his commandments regardless of what others do."

Marion G. Romney, Conference Report, October 1961, p. 58.

"It is my opinion that the Latter-day Saints, because of the knowledge they have received in the revelations, are better prepared to meet the perplexities of our times than any other people. We know more about the difficulties which are coming, and we have the key to their solution."

Marion G. Romney, Conference Report, October 1961, p. 59.

"I am convinced that if we have the peace in our hearts the brethren have been talking about, we must learn how to preserve it in our hearts in the midst of trouble and trial. I know that if we lived the gospel, we would not have war. We would have peace if enough people lived the gospel, but for my single self I do not expect them to do so. I do not expect enough people to repent to spare the world from serious trouble, and I think the scriptures sustain this conclusion."

Marion G. Romney, Conference Report, October 1966, p. 53.

"Now, the basis for the hope and courage that will keep us from being troubled does not lie in the expectation that enough people will accept and obey the restored gospel to turn aside the oncoming calamities. Nor does it depend upon any such contingency. As already indicated, it lies in the assurance that everyone who will accept and obey the restored gospel of Jesus Christ shall reap the promised rewards, and this regardless of what others do. And certain it is that those who receive the blessings will have to prevail against great opposition, for the world in general is not improving. It is ripening in iniquity."

Marion G. Romney, Conference Report, October 1966, p. 53-54.

"Naturally, believing Christians, even those who have a mature faith in the gospel, are concerned and disturbed by the lowering clouds on the horizon. But they need not be surprised or frantic about their portent, for, as has already been said, at the very beginning of this last dispensation the Lord made it abundantly clear that through the tribulations and calamity that he foresaw and foretold and that we now see coming upon us, there would be a people who, through acceptance and obedience to the gospel, would be able to recognize and resist the powers of evil, build up the promised Zion, and prepare to meet the Christ and be with him in the blessed millennium. And we know further that it is possible for every one of us, who will, to have a place among those people. It is this assurance and this expectation that gives us understanding of the Lord's admonition, 'be not troubled.'"

Adam S. Bennion, Conference Report, April 1954, p. 96-97.

"As you read the history of the pioneers, it becomes increasingly clear with every page that you read, that they endured adversity and hardship. They could stand persecution; they could bear up under abuse; they could recover from the infliction of all kinds of harmful hatreds. That record is clear. The question before our generation is: Can we and our children endure prosperity and ease?"

Adam S. Bennion, Conference Report, April 1954, p. 100.

"One thing in common all these peoples had in their search for freedom to worship God—a schooling in hardship, persecution, sacrifice, that burned out from their souls the dross, leaving in them only the gold of loftiest character and faith, aye tried, tested, refined. God has never worked out his purposes through the pampered victims of ease and luxury and riotous living. Always He has used to meet the great crises in His work, those in whom hardship, privation, and persecution had built characters and wills of iron. God shapes His servants in the forge of adversity; He does not fashion them in the hot house of ease and luxury. (The Pioneers, p. 41.)"

Hugh B. Brown, Conference Report, October 1967, p. 113.

"And some of you young men are going to engage in that battle. Some of you are going to engage in the final testing time, which is coming and which is closer to us than we know. . . .

I want to say to you, brethren, that in the midst of all the troubles, the uncertainties, the tumult and chaos through which the world is passing, almost unnoticed by the majority of the people of the world, there has been set up a kingdom, a kingdom over which God the Father presides, and Jesus the Christ is the King. That kingdom is rolling forward, as I say, partly unnoticed, but it is rolling forward with a power and a force that will stop the enemy in its tracks while some of you live."

Hugh B. Brown, The Abundant Life, p. 91.

"My brethren and sisters, be prepared. All of this will happen. But before it does and while it is happening we are going to have some world-shaking events. When you consider that hundreds of millions of young people today are being relentlessly indoctrinated with the damnable doctrine that there is no God and that religion is an opiate; when you consider how well organized the anti-Christ has become and when you consider the challenge that lies ahead; when you see the hordes on the march and in many instances led by well-nigh maniacs—and I am measuring my words, for the Great Battle is to be between Christ and anti-Christ—your job is to prepare the coming generation of men to meet that onslaught. Unless you can impress into their very souls a knowledge of God and of His laws, His purposes, His program, a recognition of the fact that they are related to Him as His children, they will not be equal to the test."

Howard W. Hunter, Conference Report, Ensign, November 1992, p. 19.
    "But if we turn away our eyes from him in whom we must believe, as it is so easy to do and the world is so much tempted to do, if we look to the power and fury of those terrible and destructive elements around us rather than to him who can help and save us, then we shall inevitably sink in a sea of conflict and sorrow and despair."

Gordon B. Hinckley, Conference Report, Ensign, May 1992, p. 53.
    "We shall never be without a prophet if we live worthy of a prophet. The Lord is watching over this work. This is His kingdom. We are not as sheep without a shepherd. We are not as an army without a leader."

Boyd K. Packer, Conference Report, Ensign, May 1989, p. 59.
    "Teenagers also sometimes think, 'What's the use? The world will soon be blown all apart and come to an end.' That feeling comes from fear, not from faith. No one knows the hour or the day (see D&C 49:7), but the end cannot come until all of the purposes of the Lord are fulfilled. Everything that I have learned from the revelations and from life convinces me that there is time and to spare for you to carefully prepare for a long life."

Boyd K. Packer, Conference Report, Ensign, May 1994, p. 19.
    "The ultimate purpose of the adversary, who has 'great wrath, because he knoweth that he hath but a short time,' is to disrupt, disturb, and destroy the home and the family. Like a ship without a rudder, without a compass, we drift from the family values which have anchored us in the past. Now we are caught in a current so strong that unless we correct our course, civilization as we know it will surely be wrecked to pieces."

Bruce R. McConkie, Conference Report, Ensign, May 1979, p. 92-93.
    "For the moment we live in a day of peace and prosperity but it shall not ever be thus. Great trials lie ahead. All of the sorrows and perils of the past are but a foretaste of what is yet to be. And we must prepare ourselves temporally and spiritually. . . .
    We must do all we can to proclaim peace, to avoid war, to heal disease, to prepare for natural disasters—but with it all, that which is to be shall be....We can rest assured that if we have done all in our power to prepare for whatever lies ahead, he will then help us with whatever else we need...

We do not say that all of the Saints will be spared and saved from the coming day of desolation. But we do say there is no promise of safety and no promise of security except for those who love the Lord and who are seeking to do all that he commands. It may be, for instance, that nothing except the power of faith and the authority of the priesthood can save individuals and congregations from the atomic holocausts that surely shall be."

Bruce R. McConkie, Conference Report, Ensign, May 1980, p. 71-73.
"We see evil forces everywhere uniting to destroy the family, to ridicule morality and decency, to glorify all that is lewd and base. We see wars and plagues and pestilence. Nations rise and fall. Blood and carnage and death are everywhere. Gadianton robbers fill the judgment seats in many nations. An evil power seeks to overthrow the freedom of all nations and countries. Satan reigns in the hearts of men; it is the great day of his power.

But amid it all, the work of the Lord rolls on . . . Truly the world is and will be in commotion but the Zion of God will be unmoved. The wicked and ungodly shall be swept from the Church, and the little stone will continue to grow until it fills the whole earth. . . . There will yet be martyrs; the doors in Carthage shall again enclose the innocent. We have not been promised that the trials and evils of the world will entirely pass us by.

If we, as a people, keep the commandments of God; if we take the side of the Church on all issues, both religious and political; if we take the Holy Spirit for our guide; if we give heed to the words of the apostles and prophets who minister among us—then, from an eternal standpoint, all things will work together for our good."

Bruce R. McConkie, Mormon Doctrine, "Sealed in Forehead", p. 683.
"In the latter-days the servants of God would plead with the Lord to stay the tide of desolation and destruction 'till we have sealed the servants of our God in their foreheads.' With the restoration of the gospel, the power has again been given to seal men up unto eternal life, to place a seal on them so that . . . no matter what desolation sweeps the earth, yet they shall be saved."

Bruce R. McConkie, Mormon Doctrine, "Second Coming of Christ", p. 694.
"Behold, I come quickly means that when the appointed hour arrives, he will come with a speed and a suddenness which will leave no further time for preparation for that great day."

Bruce R. McConkie, Mormon Doctrine, "Signs of the Times", p. 720.
"Enoch saw that the restored kingdom would remain on earth to prepare a people for the Second Coming of the Lord. (Moses 7:60-66.)"

Bruce R. McConkie, Mormon Doctrine, "Signs of the Times", p. 728.
"Because of iniquity and greed. . . there will be depressions, famines, and a frantic search for temporal security . . . without turning to the Lord . . . We may expect to see the insatiable desire to get something for nothing result in further class legislation and more socialistic experiments."

Bruce R. McConkie, Doctrinal New Testament Commentary, Vol. 1, p. 475.

"True it is, as a general principle, that God sends disasters, calamities, plagues, and suffering upon the rebellious, and that he preserves and protects those who love and serve him. Such indeed were the very promises given to Israel—obedience would net them the preserving and protecting care of the Lord, disobedience would bring death, destruction, desolation, disaster, war, and a host of evils upon them. (Deut. 28:30.)"

Bruce R. McConkie, Doctrinal New Testament Commentary, Vol. 2, p. 326-327.

"Destruction awaits those who defile their bodies unless they repent. Shortly before the coming of Christ, the Nephites 'began to disbelieve in the spirit of prophecy and in the spirit of revelation; and the judgments of God did stare them in the face. . . .The Spirit of the Lord did no more preserve them; yea, it had withdrawn from them because the Spirit of the Lord doth not dwell in unholy temples—Therefore the Lord did cease to preserve them by his miraculous and matchless power, for they had fallen into a state of unbelief and awful wickedness.' (Helaman 4:23-25.)"

Bruce R. McConkie, The Promised Messiah, p. 457.

"We do not know and shall not learn either the day or the hour of that dreadful yet blessed day. We are expected to read the signs of the times and know thereby the approximate time of our Lord's return and to be in constant readiness therefor."

Bruce R. McConkie, The Mortal Messiah, Vol. 3, p. 440.

"In the latter-day age of restoration, when once again the glorious wonders of the gospel are available to men . . . the powers of evil will be unleashed as never before in all history. Satan will then fight the truth and stir up the hearts of men to do evil and work wickedness to an extent and with an intensity never before known."

Bruce R. McConkie, The Mortal Messiah, Vol. 3, p. 455.

"The flood of Noah and the destruction of Sodom and Gomorrah are types of the Second Coming. In Noah's day the normal affairs of life continued until the flood came to destroy the world that then was; in Lot's day, all went on, as was common among men, until the Lord rained fire and brimstone from heaven upon those wicked cities and destroyed their world. So shall it be with the destruction of the wicked, which is the end of the world. Such shall come without warning, as a thief in the night, where the wicked and ungodly are concerned. But with the elect of God, it is quite another matter. Though even they do not know the day or the hour, yet the season and the generation are clearly revealed."

Bruce R. McConkie, The Mortal Messiah, Vol. 3, p. 457-458.

"If there are to be wars and calamities, desolations and signs, let the elect view these things in their eternal perspective lest they remain as other men and reap the curses that shall be poured out without measure. If at our Lord's return the wicked will be as stubble and every corruptible thing shall be consumed by the brightness of his coming, how important it is to know how to escape the flames!"

Bruce R. McConkie, The Mortal Messiah, Vol. 4, p. 430-431.

"To prepare the way before the Lord is to bring to pass those things which must be done before he comes. It is to gather Israel, to build Zion, to proclaim the gospel to every nation and people; it is to prepare a people for that dread and glorious day. To prepare ourselves for that great day is to join with the saints, to gather with Israel, to dwell in Zion, to so live that we shall abide the day of his coming. Those who prepare the way before the Lord, by that very process prepare themselves for that which lies ahead. And those who are prepared shall be saved; they shall abide the day; their seed shall inherit the earth . . .Those who are not prepared have no such promises."

Bruce R. McConkie, The Millennial Messiah, p. 142.

"When the saints have done all that in their power lies, both to preach the everlasting word and to build up the eternal kingdom ... when the wars and desolations and carnality of men are about to overwhelm them—then the Lord will take over. By his own power he will destroy the wicked."

Bruce R. McConkie, The Millennial Messiah, p. 313.

"Satan will slay some of the righteous that their blood . . .may cry from the ground as a witness against those who fight against God. Yet, as a people the true saints shall prevail."

Bruce R. McConkie, The Millennial Messiah, p. 361-362

"As for Lot's wife, she looked back; that is, she turned again to the things of the world, and she too was destroyed . . . should any of the saints look back ... they will be burned with the wicked."

Bruce R. McConkie, The Millennial Messiah, p. 374-375.

"The disasters . . . are used by Him to temper and train us. . . to bring to us the conscious realization that we are dependent upon a Supreme Being for all things. . . as a means of judgment to punish us for evil deeds . . . to humble us so that perchance we will repent . . .

'Except the Lord doth chasten his People with many afflictions, yea, except he doth visit them with death and with terror, and with famine and with all manner of pestilence, they will not remember him.' (Hel. 12:3.)."

See Bruce R. McConkie, The Millennial Messiah, p. 502.

"There is a certain smugness in the Church, a feeling that all these things are for others, not for us . . . 'And upon my house shall it begin, and from my house shall it go forth, saith the Lord; First among those among you, saith the Lord, who have professed to know my name and have not known me, and have blasphemed against me in the midst of my house, saith the Lord.' (D&C 112:24-26.) Vengeance is for the wicked, in and out of the Church, and only the faithful shall be spared, and many of them only in the eternal perspective of things."

See Bruce R. McConkie, The Millennial Messiah, p. 546-547.

"Sometimes even the saints of the Most High become discouraged . . . some wonder if all their service and selflessness and sacrifice are worth the price. . . . forgotten that I have ordained all these things for your ultimate glory and blessing. . . .'Ye have said, It is vain to serve God: and what profit is it that we have kept his ordinance, and that we have walked mournfully before the Lord of hosts?' . . . .'Now we call the proud happy; yea, they that work wickedness are set up; yea, they that tempt God are even delivered.' (Malachi 3:13-15). . . .But soon their world will end."

Bruce R. McConkie, A New Witness for the Articles of Faith, p. 580-581.

"The children of Zion fail in their great mission for two reasons: (1) Oftentimes they set their hearts upon temporal things . . .(2) Others fail to live by the high standards of belief and conduct."

Bruce R. McConkie, A New Witness for the Articles of Faith, p. 608.

"The destructions preceding and attending the Second Coming will be to save the saints from the evils of the world."

L. Tom Perry, Conference Report, Ensign, November 1995, p. 36.

"Acquire and store a reserve of food and supplies that will sustain life. Obtain clothing and build a savings account on a sensible, well-planned basis that can serve well in times of emergency. As long as I can remember, we have been taught to prepare for the future and to obtain a year's supply of necessities. I would guess that the years of plenty have almost universally caused us to set aside this counsel. I believe the time to disregard this counsel is over. With events in the world today, it must be considered with all seriousness."

James E. Faust, Ensign, October 1992, p. 69-71.

"There seems to be developing a new civil religion. The civil religion I refer to is a secular religion. It has no moral absolutes. It is nondenominational. It is non-theistic. It is politically focused. It is antagonistic to religion. It rejects the historic religious traditions of America. It feels strange. If this trend continues, nonbelief will be more honored than belief. While all beliefs must be protected, are atheism, agnosticism, cynicism, and moral relativism to be more safeguarded and valued than Christianity, Judaism, and the tenets of Islam, which hold that there is a Supreme Being and that mortals are accountable to him? If so, this would, in my opinion, place America in great moral jeopardy."

Neal A. Maxwell, Conference Report, Ensign, May 1992, p. 39.

"Now, my brethren, 'these are (your) days' (Hel. 7:9) in the history of the Church. Mark well what kind of days they will be, days when, with special visibility, the Lord will 'make bare his holy arm in the eyes of all the nations' (D&C 133:3). God will also 'hasten' His work (D&C 88:73). He will also 'shorten' the last days 'for the elect's sake'; hence, there will be a compression of events (Matt. 24:22; JS-Matt. 1:20). Furthermore, 'all things shall be in commotion' (D&C 88:91). Only those in the process of becoming the men and women of Christ will be able to keep their spiritual balance."

Neal A. Maxwell, Conference Report, Ensign, November 1993, p. 20.

"In the days ahead, 'all things shall be in commotion' (D&C 88:91). We may even have nostalgia for past days of obscurity (see D&C 1:30). Amid a drumroll of developments, complex and converging world conditions will bring both trials and opportunities. Faithful Church members, however, will sense the crescendo in it all, even while being carried forward on the crest of breathtaking circumstances.

He whose name this church bears has promised that He will be in our midst (see D&C 6:32), lead us along (see D&C 78:18), go before us (see D&C 44:27; 84:88), and even fight our battles (see D&C 98:37). He has further counseled, 'Be not afraid of your enemies, for I have decreed in my heart . . . that I will prove you in all things, whether you will abide in my covenant, even unto death, that you may be found worthy' (D&C 98:14). So let us have patience and faith as did Lehi who saw pointing fingers of scorn directed at those who grasped the iron rod, which rod, ironically, some of those same fingers once grasped (see 1 Ne. 8:27, 33). But, said Lehi, 'we heeded them not.' So it should be with us! Brothers and sisters, being pointed in the right direction, we do not need to worry about being pointed at!"

Neal A. Maxwell, A Wonderful Flood of Light, p. 6.
"Flowing through the human condition too are many paradoxes and adverse linkages. As an example, the scriptures observe that, even among believers, 'hearts are set so much upon the things of this world' that they have neither time nor disposition to learn vital lessons (D&C 121:35). Jesus foretold that in the latter days the love of many would wax cold (see Matthew 24:12; D&C 45:27). That condition of less love means that there is more fear (see 1 John 4:17; Moroni 8:16). And the more iniquity—another feature of our love-lessened age—the more human despair (see Moroni 10:22), which is a close associate of fear."

Neal A. Maxwell, All These Things Shall Give Thee Experience, p. 41.
"There will be some tests that will be collective in nature as well as individual. President Harold B. Lee referred to the contrast between the tests in the early days of the Church and the tests of the latter period of this dispensation, which he characterized as 'a period of what we might call sophistication,' a period of time constituting a 'rather severe test.' This test, said President Lee, would be a special test for the youth of the Church—exceeding any test of affluence that previous generations of youth have passed through. (Instructor, June 1965, p. 217.)"

Neal A. Maxwell, All These Things Shall Give Thee Experience, p. 121-122.
"We cannot fully respond to the divine invitation, 'Come follow me,' unless we are willing to follow the Brethren. And it will be most helpful to us all if we renew and reassure ourselves by noting how it has always been the case—that the Lord has raised up men as His prophets who have just the cluster of talents needed for a particular time. It is no different in the culminating days of the dispensation of the fullness of time. The Lord measured and ordained these men before they came here. Knowing perfectly the conditions that would obtain, He has sent, and will send, men to match the mountains of challenges that are just ahead of us."

Neal A. Maxwell, All These Things Shall Give Thee Experience, p. 123.
"After He had spoken of some of the specific signs of His second coming, the Savior gave to His disciples, and to us all, the parable of the fig tree. He said that just as when the fig tree puts

forth its leaves, we may know that 'summer is nigh,' so we may be warned by certain signs that His second coming is nigh. (Matthew 24:32.) The 'summer' Jesus cited is now upon us, and you and I must not complain of the heat. Nor, indeed, should we let that heat, as Alma counseled, wither our individual tree of testimony. If we neglect to nourish the tree, 'when the heat of the sun cometh and scorcheth it,' it can prove fatal. (Alma 32:38.)"

Neal A. Maxwell, But for a Small Moment, p. 129.

"We should not be surprised, therefore, as such challenges emerge in our time and in our lives. We will likely have opportunities, again and again, to ponder the comforting and consoling words of the Lord to the Prophet Joseph Smith in Liberty Jail, 'My son, peace be unto thy soul' (D&C 121:7). Not that the afflictions will thereby be lessened. Surely of all the generations who have ever lived, those who live in the dispensation of the fulness of times cannot expect to be exempt from chastisement and trial (see Mosiah 23:21)."

Neal A. Maxwell, Deposition of a Disciple, p. 55.

"There is a further criterion that ought not to be ignored, one given by the Lord himself in these latter days in which he says, 'Behold, there are many called, but few are chosen. And why are they not chosen? Because their hearts are set so much upon the things of this world, and aspire to the honors of men, that they do not learn this one lesson.' (D&C 121:34-35.) It makes sense to me that the Lord would choose out of the world those who are (or who could become) different from the world and, therefore, could lead the world to a different outcome. We must be different in order to make a difference."

Neal A. Maxwell, Even As I Am, p. 4-5.

"Regarding eternal purpose, the words in this book are designed to help us to 'be of good cheer,' lest we be numbered among those whose hearts fail them in the last days. Some of the current causes for despair and discouragement should be no mystery: skepticism about the historicity of Jesus; the mistaken view that a value-free society is free; schools that lack moral content; family Bibles that go unread; and fewer and fewer families that are intact and nourishing, and so forth."

Neal A. Maxwell, Even As I Am, p. 17-18.

"For instance, while the virtue of patience, which was fully developed in Him, is never out of season, patience in tribulation will surely be a premiere virtue in the last days. Healthy self-denial in which He is the exemplar has always been important, but it is obviously relevant in a time of suffocating selfishness as so many empty their lives of meaning in a wrong-headed search for self-fulfillment. Submissiveness, in which Jesus showed the way, has always involved tutorial suffering, but this attribute becomes even more important at a time when our individual tutoring will be overlain with the tutoring of a whole people—for purposes wise unto the Lord."

Neal A. Maxwell, Even As I Am, p. 120.

"Before that reckoning moment, however, both your ministry and mine will unfold in the grim but also glorious circumstances of the last days.

Yes, there will be wrenching polarization on this planet, but also the remarkable reunion with our colleagues in Christ from the city of Enoch. Yes, nation after nation will become a house divided, but more and more unifying Houses of the Lord will grace this planet. Yes, Armageddon lies ahead —but so does Adam-ondi-Ahman!

Meanwhile, did not Jesus tell us what to expect by way of heat in the final summer? Did He not also say that He would prove our faith and our patience by trial?

Did He not provide a needed sense of proportion when He spoke of the comparative few who will find the narrow way leading to the strait gate? Did He not also say that His Saints, scattered upon all the face of the earth, would, in the midst of wickedness, commotion, and persecution, 'be armed with righteousness and with the power of God,' for He is determined to have 'a pure people'?

His work proceeds forward almost as if in the comparative calmness of the eye of a storm. First, He reigns in the midst of His saints; soon, in all the world.

So as the shutters of human history begin to close as if before a gathering storm, and as events scurry across the human scene like so many leaves before a wild wind, those who stand before the warm glow of the gospel fire can be permitted a shiver of the soul. Yet in our circle of certitude we know, even in the midst of all these things, that there will be no final frustration of God's purposes. God has known 'all things from the beginning; wherefore, He prepareth a way to accomplish all His works among the children of men.'"

Neal A. Maxwell, For the Power is in Them, p. 20.

"The chiliast, one who believes in a second coming of Christ that will usher in a millennial reign, has special challenges in reading signs. First, he is urged to notice lest he be caught unawares. Second, he must be aware of how many false readings and alarms there have been in bygone days, even by the faithful. For instance, has any age had more 'wonders in the sky' than ours, with satellites and journeys to the moon? Has any generation seen such ominous 'vapors of smoke' as ours with its mushroom clouds over the pathetic pyres of Hiroshima and Nagasaki? Yet there is 'more to come.' Our task is to react and to notice without overreacting, to let life go forward without slipping into the heedlessness of those in the days of Noah. It has been asked, and well it might be, how many of us would have jeered, or at least been privately amused, by the sight of Noah building his ark. Presumably, the laughter and the heedlessness continued until it began to rain—and kept raining! How wet some people must have been before Noah's ark suddenly seemed the only sane act in an insane, bewildering situation! To ponder signs without becoming paranoid, to be aware without frantically matching current events with expectations, using energy that should be spent in other ways these are our tasks."

Neal A. Maxwell, Meek and Lowly, p. 43.

"We do not live in an unexplainable world either. We need neither be drenched in despair nor resignedly 'eat, drink, and be merry, for tomorrow we die.' (2 Nephi 28:7-8.) Instead, we are volunteer participants in God's plan of salvation (Moses 6:62), which plan required the rescue mission by the Great Volunteer, Jesus Christ. Through Him and His atonement, there is an assured resurrection awaiting—not extinction. A worldwide millennium is impending, preceded by much misery and destruction, not total world annihilation. Divine determination so insures, and 'there is nothing that the Lord shall take in his heart to do but what he will do it.' (Abraham 3:17.)"

Neal A. Maxwell, Meek and Lowly, p. 89.

"Divine mercy is always operative. It may even cause God to hasten things. Jesus declared, for instance, that except the tribulations of the last days 'should be shortened' for the sake of the very elect, no flesh shall be saved. (Matthew 24:22.) When the full heat of the sun comes, 'summer is nigh' (Matthew 24:32), and the enveloping events will be blistering."

Neal A. Maxwell, Men and Women of Christ, p. 5.

"Nevertheless the conditioning of the world is fierce and unremitting. Its conventional wisdom and prevailing patterns of life-style are saturatingly portrayed in music, film, literature, and so forth. To compound the problem, there really are vexing 'evils and designs which do and will exist in the hearts of conspiring men in the last days' (D&C 89:4). This conspiracy plays to the cupidity and sensuality of the natural man, making it easier for some people to succumb by having their hearts 'set . . . upon the things of this world' (D&C 121:35)."

Neal A. Maxwell, Men and Women of Christ, p. 106-107.

"It takes faith to withstand the secular society. We who seek to serve in this day and time are, for instance, asked to be more loving at a time when the love of many waxes cold. We are asked to be more merciful, even as the Saints are persecuted. We are asked to be more holy as the world ripens in iniquity. We are asked to be more filled with hope in a world marked by growing despair because of growing iniquity. When, as in the world, there is more impatience, we are asked to be patient and full of faith even as other men's hearts fail them. We are asked to be peacemakers even as peace has been taken from the earth. We are asked to have enough faith to have fidelity in our marriage and chastity in dating even as the world celebrates sex almost as a secular religion."

Neal A. Maxwell, Notwithstanding My Weakness, p. 17-18.

"Moreover, Latter-day Saints need to remember that we who live now are being called upon to work out our salvation in a special time of intense and immense challenges—the last portion of the dispensation of the fullness of times during which great tribulation and temptation will occur, the elect will almost be deceived, and unrighteous people will be living much as they were in the days of Noah. It will be a time of polarization, as the Twelve fore saw in their declaration of 1845. Hardness of heart in many will produce other manifestations of hardness and coarseness. Civility will be one casualty of these conditions, and a lowered capacity to achieve reconciliation, whether in a marriage or between interest groups, will be another."

Neal A. Maxwell, Notwithstanding My Weakness, p. 18.

"Therefore, though we have rightly applauded our ancestors for their spiritual achievements (and do not and must not discount them now), those of us who prevail today will have done no small thing. The special spirits who have been reserved to live in this time of challenges and who overcome will one day be praised for their stamina by those who pulled handcarts."

Neal A. Maxwell, Notwithstanding My Weakness, p. 36.

"But we must make no mistake about it. The deceptions of the world will be clever and the pull of the world real and insistent. Life in the last days will be filled with tribulation and temptation and deception and polarization so much so that if it were possible, the very elect would be deceived. (Matthew 24:24-26.) In such darkness, so much greater is the need for God's laws and for the light of the gospel, for 'the commandment is a lamp; and the law is light.' (Proverbs 6:23.) Those of us seeking to progress, notwithstanding our weaknesses, dare not try to go forward lampless!"

Neal A. Maxwell, Notwithstanding My Weakness, p. 45.

"However, our hope, unless it is strong, can be at the mercy of our moods and can be badgered and bullied by events and by the contempt of the world, which we will experience in rather large doses in the irreligious last part of the last dispensation. Part of the contempt of the world comes because the worldly do not understand the things of the Spirit and regard such as foolishness and stupidity. Therefore, attacks on the Church are not always rebuttable in worldly terms. There are those who are multilingual but cannot communicate in the mother tongue of faith. Sometimes the best response is a certain silence, such as that of the Master before Pilate."

Neal A. Maxwell, Notwithstanding My Weakness, p. 124.

"The true believer knows, however, that Christ's glorious return will be preceded by much misery. But then the darkness will be broken by a millennial dawn and endless day. He understands, therefore, that the sooner he renounces the world, the sooner he can help to save some in it. Such an individual is the true believer in Christ!"

Neal A. Maxwell, Sermons Not Spoken, p. 38.

"Jesus also prophesied that in the last days, because of iniquity, the love of many would wax cold (Matthew 24:12). Yet we must not regard iniquity or human hardening and coarsening with a sense of inevitability."

Neal A. Maxwell, Things As They Really Are, p. 59-60.

"The eventual growth of the Church prior to Christ's second coming was foreseen by the Lord: 'But first let my army become very great, and let it be sanctified before me, that it may become fair as the sun, and clear as the moon, and that her banners may be terrible unto all nations.' (D&C 105:31.) Presumably 'very great' is something more than a church of a few million—though, to be sure, validity, not numeracy, is the first test."

Neal A. Maxwell, We Will Prove Them Herewith, p. 19.

"As described by Zephaniah, Church members in the last days live, though blessed with the light of the gospel, in a day of gloominess. (Zephaniah 1:15.) In these times of widespread commotion, disorder, unrest, agitation, and insurrection, the hearts of many will fail. (D&C 45:26; 88:91.) Others will be sorely tried but will, in their extremities, seek succor from seers as did the anxious young man who approached the prophet Elijah as ancient Israel was surrounded: 'Alas, my master! how shall we do?' The answer of today's prophets will be the same: 'Fear not: for they that

124

be with us are more than they that be with them.' Only when we are settled spiritually can we understand that kind of arithmetic. Only then will our eyes, like the young man's be opened. (2 Kings 6:15-17.)"

Neal A. Maxwell, We Will Prove Them Herewith, p. 80.

"Conditions before Jesus' second coming, we are further told, will resemble those in the days of Noah when there was a misdirected sense of self-sufficiency among the citizenry, a resistance to the words of the Lord's prophet, and a dangerous norm of wickedness as usual. The attitudes among some latter-day scoffers will reflect the same scornful self-sufficiency. Even the unmistakable signs will be discounted, because, said Peter, such people will say 'all things continue as they were.' (2 Peter 3:3-4.) Joseph Smith, in the inspired translation of the Bible, added, significantly, that these same latter-day scoffers would also deny the divinity of the Lord Jesus Christ, a sad reality that is well advanced even now. G.K. Chesterton has pointed out that when people cease to believe in God, instead of believing in nothing, what is far more dangerous is that they believe in anything."

Neal A. Maxwell, We Will Prove Them Herewith, p. 95.

"If one ever wondered at the seeming rapidity with which social, economic, and political changes occurred during the millennium of Book of Mormon history, this observation by Alberta Siegel is worth remembering: 'Every civilization is only 20 years away from barbarism. For 20 years is all we have to accomplish the task of civilizing the infants . . . who know nothing of our language, our culture, our religion, our values, or our customs of interpersonal relations.'"

Neal A. Maxwell, We Will Prove Them Herewith, p. 119-120.

"God's grace will be sufficient for us whatever our stage of spiritual maturity in the midst of temptation, persecution, tribulation, and even seeming deprivation, for He is the true Tutor pacing His pupils: 'Behold, ye are little children and ye cannot bear all things now; ye must grow in grace and in the knowledge of the truth.' (D&C 50:40.)"

Neal A. Maxwell, Wherefore Ye Must Press Forward, p. 13.

"It is no accident that the scriptures have preserved for us certain precious insights about the times in which Noah lived. Those were times, we read, that were 'filled with violence' (Genesis 6:11), and corruption abounded. There was apparently a sense of self-sufficiency, a condition to which Jesus called attention. (Matthew 24:36-41.) Jesus said this condition would be repeated in the last days. The people of Noah's time were desensitized to real dangers. So we may become in our time. Noah and those with him had to let go of their world or perish with it!"

Neal A. Maxwell, Wherefore Ye Must Press Forward, p. 64.

"There is probably a relationship between the sense of despair some feel and the prophecy that says that in the last days 'men's hearts shall fail them.' (D&C 45:26.) Another clue is in an Old Testament episode that links the failing of the heart to a loss of courage: 'and they were afraid'— because of anticipation of what was coming! (Genesis 42:28.) Anticipated anguish can disarm us and cause us to break even before the battle begins."

Neal A. Maxwell, Wherefore Ye Must Press Forward, p. 127-128.

"With regard to the signs that are preceding the second coming of Jesus, most will miss them and a few will overreact. Have you ever had the experience of looking at your watch without really noting what time it was? The world in its intense preoccupation will see some of the signs preceding the second coming without really noticing them."

M. Russell Ballard, Conference Report, Ensign, November 1992, p. 31.

"Although the prophecies tell us that these things are to take place, more and more people are expressing great alarm at what appears to be an acceleration of worldwide calamity. . . . These are difficult times, when the forces of nature seem to be unleashing a flood of 'famines, and pestilences, and earthquakes, in divers places.'. . . But regardless of this dark picture, which will ultimately get worse, we must never allow ourselves to give up hope! . . .

My message to you today . . . is simply this: the Lord is in control. He knows the end from the beginning. He has given us adequate instruction that, if followed, will see us safely through any crisis. His purposes will be fulfilled, and someday we will understand the eternal reasons for all of these events. Therefore, today we must be careful to not overreact, nor should we be caught up in extreme preparations, but what we must do is keep the commandments of God and never lose hope!. . .

Armed with the shield of faith, we can overcome many of our daily challenges and overpower our greatest weaknesses and fears, knowing that if we do our best to keep the commandments of God, come what may, we will be all right. Of course, that does not necessarily mean that we will be spared personal suffering and heartache. Righteousness has never precluded adversity."

Henry B. Eyring, Conference Report, April 1997, Ensign, May 1997, p. 26.

"He (Lehi) knew that the Savior holds responsible those to whom He delegates priesthood keys. With those keys comes the power to give counsel that will show us the way to safety. Those with keys are responsible to warn even when their counsel might not be followed. Keys are delegated down a line which passes from the prophet through those responsible for ever smaller groups of members, closer and closer to families and to individuals. That is one of the ways by which the Lord makes a stake a place of safety . . .

When we honor the keys of that priesthood channel by listening and giving heed, we tie ourselves to a lifeline which will not fail us in any storm. . . .

We are blessed to live in a time when the priesthood keys are on the earth. We are blessed to know where to look and how to listen for the voice that will fulfill the promise of the Lord that He will gather us to safety. I pray for you and for me that we will have humble hearts, that we will listen, that we will pray, that we will wait for the deliverance of the Lord which is sure to come as we are faithful."

SCRIPTURAL REFERENCES

JST Genesis 7:69-70

69 And great tribulations shall be among the children of men, but my people will I preserve; and righteousness will I send down out of heaven, and truth will I send forth out of the earth, to bear testimony of my mine Only Begotten; his resurrection from the dead; yea, and also the resurrection of all men,

70 And righteousness and truth will I cause to sweep the earth as with a flood, to gather out mine own elect from the four quarters of the earth unto a place which I shall prepare; an holy city, that my people may gird up their loins, and be looking forth for the time of my coming; for there shall be my tabernacle, and it shall be called Zion; a New Jerusalem.

JST Genesis 14:35

35 And hath said, and sworn with an oath, that the heavens and the earth should come together; and the sons of God should be tried so as by fire.

Proverbs 3:5-6

5 Trust in the LORD with all thine heart; and lean not unto thine own understanding.

6 In all thy ways acknowledge him, and he shall direct thy paths.

Isaiah 4:5-6

5 And the LORD will create upon every dwelling place of mount Zion, and upon her assemblies, a cloud and smoke by day, and the shining of a flaming fire by night: for upon all the glory [shall be] a defence.

6 And there shall be a tabernacle for a shadow in the daytime from the heat, and for a place of refuge, and for a covert from storm and from rain.

Isaiah 41:10-13

10 Fear thou not; for I am with thee: be not dismayed; for I am thy God: I will strengthen thee; yea, I will help thee; yea, I will uphold thee with the right hand of my righteousness.

11 Behold, all they that were incensed against thee shall be ashamed and confounded: they shall be as nothing; and they that strive with thee shall perish.

12 Thou shalt seek them, and shalt not find them, even them that contended with thee: they that war against thee shall be as nothing, and as a thing of nought.

13 For I the LORD thy God will hold thy right hand, saying unto thee, Fear not; I will help thee.

Jeremiah 46:28

28 Fear thou not, O Jacob my servant, saith the LORD: for I am with thee; for I will make a full end of all the nations whither I have driven thee: but I will not make a full end of thee, but correct thee in measure; yet will I not leave thee wholly unpunished.

Jeremiah 51:6
6 Flee out of the midst of Babylon, and deliver every man his soul: be not cut off in her iniquity; for this is the time of the LORD's vengeance; he will render unto her a recompence.

Daniel 12:1-2
1 And at that time shall Michael stand up, the great prince which standeth for the children of thy people: and there shall be a time of trouble, such as never was since there was a nation even to that same time: and at that time thy people shall be delivered, every one that shall be found written in the book.
2 And many of them that sleep in the dust of the earth shall awake, some to everlasting life, and some to shame and everlasting contempt.

Joel 2:28-32
28 And it shall come to pass afterward, that I will pour out my spirit upon all flesh; and your sons and your daughters shall prophesy, your old men shall dream dreams, your young men shall see visions:
29 And also upon the servants and upon the handmaids in those days will I pour out my spirit.
30 And I will shew wonders in the heavens and in the earth, blood, and fire, and pillars of smoke.
31 The sun shall be turned into darkness, and the moon into blood, before the great and the terrible day of the LORD come.
32 And it shall come to pass, that whosoever shall call on the name of the LORD shall be delivered: for in mount Zion and in Jerusalem shall be deliverance, as the LORD hath said, and in the remnant whom the LORD shall call.

Hosea 4:6
6 My people are destroyed for lack of knowledge: because thou hast rejected knowledge, I will also reject thee, that thou shalt be no priest to me: seeing thou hast forgotten the law of thy God, I will also forget thy children.

Malachi 3:8-11
8 Will a man rob God? Yet ye have robbed me. But ye say, Wherein have we robbed thee? In tithes and offerings.
9 Ye [are] cursed with a curse: for ye have robbed me, [even] this whole nation.
10 Bring ye all the tithes into the storehouse, that there may be meat in mine house, and prove me now herewith, saith the LORD of hosts, if I will not open you the windows of heaven, and pour you out a blessing, that [there shall] not [be room] enough [to receive it].
11 And I will rebuke the devourer for your sakes, and he shall not destroy the fruits of your ground; neither shall your vine cast her fruit before the time in the field, saith the LORD of hosts.

Matthew 24:22
22 And except those days should be shortened, there should no flesh be saved: but for the elect's sake those days shall be shortened.

Matthew 25:1-13

1 Then shall the kingdom of heaven be likened unto ten virgins, which took their lamps, and went forth to meet the bridegroom.

2 And five of them were wise, and five were foolish.

3 They that were foolish took their lamps, and took no oil with them:

4 But the wise took oil in their vessels with their lamps.

5 While the bridegroom tarried, they all slumbered and slept.

6 And at midnight there was a cry made, Behold, the bridegroom cometh; go ye out to meet him.

7 Then all those virgins arose, and trimmed their lamps.

8 And the foolish said unto the wise, Give us of your oil; for our lamps are gone out.

9 But the wise answered, saying, Not so; lest there be not enough for us and you: but go ye rather to them that sell, and buy for yourselves.

10 And while they went to buy, the bridegroom came; and they that were ready went in with him to the marriage: and the door was shut.

11 Afterward came also the other virgins, saying, Lord, Lord, open to us.

12 But he answered and said, Verily I say unto you, I know you not.

13 Watch therefore, for ye know neither the day nor the hour wherein the Son of man cometh.

Mark 13:32-37

32 But of that day and that hour knoweth no man, no, not the angels which are in heaven, neither the Son, but the Father.

33 Take ye heed, watch and pray: for ye know not when the time is.

34 For the Son of man is as a man taking a far journey, who left his house, and gave authority to his servants, and to every man his work, and commanded the porter to watch.

35 Watch ye therefore: for ye know not when the master of the house cometh, at even, or at midnight, or at the cockcrowing, or in the morning:

36 Lest coming suddenly he find you sleeping.

37 And what I say unto you I say unto all, Watch.

Luke 21:34-36

34 And take heed to yourselves, lest at any time your hearts be overcharged with surfeiting, and drunkenness, and cares of this life, and so that day come upon you unawares.

35 For as a snare shall it come on all them that dwell on the face of the whole earth.

36 Watch ye therefore, and pray always, that ye may be accounted worthy to escape all these things that shall come to pass, and to stand before the Son of man.

John 14:27

27 Peace I leave with you, my peace I give unto you: not as the world giveth, give I unto you. Let not your heart be troubled, neither let it be afraid.

Acts 2:21

21 And it shall come to pass, that whosoever shall call on the name of the Lord shall be saved.

Romans 8:31-32

31 What shall we then say to these things? If God be for us, who can be against us?

32 He that spared not his own Son, but delivered him up for us all, how shall he not with him also freely give us all things?

Ephesians 6:11-18

11 Put on the whole armour of God, that ye may be able to stand against the wiles of the devil.

12 For we wrestle not against flesh and blood, but against principalities, against powers, against the rulers of the darkness of this world, against spiritual wickedness in high places.

13 Wherefore take unto you the whole armour of God, that ye may be able to withstand in the evil day, and having done all, to stand.

14 Stand therefore, having your loins girt about with truth, and having on the breastplate of righteousness;

15 And your feet shod with the preparation of the gospel of peace;

16 Above all, taking the shield of faith, wherewith ye shall be able to quench all the fiery darts of the wicked.

17 And take the helmet of salvation, and the sword of the Spirit, which is the word of God:

18 Praying always with all prayer and supplication in the Spirit, and watching thereunto with all perseverance and supplication for all saints;

1 Thessalonians 5:2-6

2 For yourselves know perfectly that the day of the Lord so cometh as a thief in the night.

3 For when they shall say, Peace and safety; then sudden destruction cometh upon them, as travail upon a woman with child; and they shall not escape.

4 But ye, brethren, are not in darkness, that that day should overtake you as a thief.

5 Ye are all the children of light, and the children of the day: we are not of the night, nor of darkness.

6 Therefore let us not sleep, as [do] others; but let us watch and be sober.

1 Peter 4:17-18

17 For the time is come that judgment must begin at the house of God: and if it first begin at us, what shall the end be of them that obey not the gospel of God?

18 And if the righteous scarcely be saved, where shall the ungodly and the sinner appear?

Revelation 7:3-4

3 Saying, Hurt not the earth, neither the sea, nor the trees, till we have sealed the servants of our God in their foreheads.

4 And I heard the number of them which were sealed: and there were sealed an hundred and forty and four thousand of all the tribes of the children of Israel.

Revelation 13:10

10 He that leadeth into captivity shall go into captivity: he that killeth with the sword must be killed with the sword. Here is the patience and the faith of the saints.

Revelation 14:12

12 Here is the patience of the saints: here are they that keep the commandments of God, and the faith of Jesus.

Revelation 18:4

4 And I heard another voice from heaven, saying, Come out of her, my people, that ye be not partakers of her sins, and that ye receive not of her plagues.

1 Nephi 3:7

7 And it came to pass that I, Nephi, said unto my father: I will go and do the things which the Lord hath commanded, for I know that the Lord giveth no commandments unto the children of men, save he shall prepare a way for them that they may accomplish the thing which he commandeth them.

1 Nephi 14:1-4

1 And it shall come to pass, that if the Gentiles shall hearken unto the Lamb of God in that day that he shall manifest himself unto them in word, and also in power, in very deed, unto the taking away of their stumbling blocks—

2 And harden not their hearts against the Lamb of God, they shall be numbered among the seed of thy father; yea, they shall be numbered among the house of Israel; and they shall be a blessed people upon the promised land forever; they shall be no more brought down into captivity; and the house of Israel shall no more be confounded.

3 And that great pit, which hath been digged for them by that great and abominable church, which was founded by the devil and his children, that he might lead away the souls of men down to hell—yea, that great pit which hath been digged for the destruction of men shall be filled by those who digged it, unto their utter destruction, saith the Lamb of God; not the destruction of the soul, save it be the casting of it into that hell which hath no end.

4 For behold, this is according to the captivity of the devil, and also according to the justice of God, upon all those who will work wickedness and abomination before him.

1 Nephi 14:13-14

13 And it came to pass that I beheld that the great mother of abominations did gather together multitudes upon the face of all the earth, among all the nations of the Gentiles, to fight against the Lamb of God.

14 And it came to pass that I, Nephi, beheld the power of the Lamb of God, that it descended upon the saints of the church of the Lamb, and upon the covenant people of the Lord, who were scattered upon all the face of the earth; and they were armed with righteousness and with the power of God in great glory.

1 Nephi 22:16-17

16 For the time soon cometh that the fulness of the wrath of God shall be poured out upon all the children of men; for he will not suffer that the wicked shall destroy the righteous.

17 Wherefore, he will preserve the righteous by his power, even if it so be that the fulness of his

wrath must come, and the righteous be preserved, even unto the destruction of their enemies by fire. Wherefore, the righteous need not fear; for thus saith the prophet, they shall be saved, even if it so be as by fire.

1 Nephi 22:19
19 For behold, the righteous shall not perish; for the time surely must come that all they who fight against Zion shall be cut off.

1 Nephi 22:22
22 And the righteous need not fear, for they are those who shall not be confounded. But it is the kingdom of the devil, which shall be built up among the children of men, which kingdom is established among them which are in the flesh—

2 Nephi 6:13-14
13 Wherefore, they that fight against Zion and the covenant people of the Lord shall lick up the dust of their feet; and the people of the Lord shall not be ashamed. For the people of the Lord are they who wait for him; for they still wait for the coming of the Messiah.
14 And behold, according to the words of the prophet, the Messiah will set himself again the second time to recover them; wherefore, he will manifest himself unto them in power and great glory, unto the destruction of their enemies, when that day cometh when they shall believe in him; and none will he destroy that believe in him.

2 Nephi 28:19-22
19 For the kingdom of the devil must shake, and they which belong to it must needs be stirred up unto repentance, or the devil will grasp them with his everlasting chains, and they be stirred up to anger, and perish;
20 For behold, at that day shall he rage in the hearts of the children of men, and stir them up to anger against that which is good.
21 And others will he pacify, and lull them away into carnal security, that they will say: All is well in Zion; yea, Zion prospereth, all is well—and thus the devil cheateth their souls, and leadeth them away carefully down to hell.
22 And behold, others he flattereth away, and telleth them there is no hell; and he saith unto them: I am no devil, for there is none—and thus he whispereth in their ears, until he grasps them with his awful chains, from whence there is no deliverance.

2 Nephi 32:3
3 Angels speak by the power of the Holy Ghost; wherefore, they speak the words of Christ. Wherefore, I said unto you, feast upon the words of Christ; for behold, the words of Christ will tell you all things what ye should do.

Alma 9:13
13 Behold, do ye not remember the words which he spake unto Lehi, saying that: Inasmuch as ye

shall keep my commandments, ye shall prosper in the land? And again it is said that: Inasmuch as ye will not keep my commandments ye shall be cut off from the presence of the Lord.

Alma 9:25

25 And now for this cause, that ye may not be destroyed, the Lord has sent his angel to visit many of his people, declaring unto them that they must go forth and cry mightily unto this people, saying: Repent ye, for the kingdom of heaven is nigh at hand;

Alma 10:22-23

22 Yea, and I say unto you that if it were not for the prayers of the righteous, who are now in the land, that ye would even now be visited with utter destruction; yet it would not be by flood, as were the people in the days of Noah, but it would be by famine, and by pestilence, and the sword.

23 But it is by the prayers of the righteous that ye are spared; now therefore, if ye will cast out the righteous from among you then will not the Lord stay his hand; but in his fierce anger he will come out against you; then ye shall be smitten by famine, and by pestilence, and by the sword; and the time is soon at hand except ye repent.

Alma 12:10-11

10 And therefore, he that will harden his heart, the same receiveth the lesser portion of the word; and he that will not harden his heart, to him is given the greater portion of the word, until it is given unto him to know the mysteries of God until he know them in full.

11 And they that will harden their hearts, to them is given the lesser portion of the word until they know nothing concerning his mysteries; and then they are taken captive by the devil, and led by his will down to destruction. Now this is what is meant by the chains of hell.

Alma 36:3

3 And now, O my son Helaman, behold, thou art in thy youth, and therefore, I beseech of thee that thou wilt hear my words and learn of me; for I do know that whosoever shall put their trust in God shall be supported in their trials, and their troubles, and their afflictions, and shall be lifted up at the last day.

Alma 37:35-37

35 O, remember, my son, and learn wisdom in thy youth; yea, learn in thy youth to keep the commandments of God.

36 Yea, and cry unto God for all thy support; yea, let all thy doings be unto the Lord, and whithersoever thou goest let it be in the Lord; yea, let all thy thoughts be directed unto the Lord; yea, let the affections of thy heart be placed upon the Lord forever.

37 Counsel with the Lord in all thy doings, and he will direct thee for good; yea, when thou liest down at night lie down unto the Lord, that he may watch over you in your sleep; and when thou risest in the morning let thy heart be full of thanks unto God; and if ye do these things, ye shall be lifted up at the last day.

Alma 44:4

4 Now ye see that this is the true faith of God; yea, ye see that God will support, and keep, and preserve us, so long as we are faithful unto him, and unto our faith, and our religion; and never will the Lord suffer that we shall be destroyed except we should fall into transgression and deny our faith.

Alma 46:18

18 And he said: Surely God shall not suffer that we, who are despised because we take upon us the name of Christ, shall be trodden down and destroyed, until we bring it upon us by our own transgressions.

Alma 60:23

3 Do ye suppose that God will look upon you as guiltless while ye sit still and behold these things? Behold I say unto you, Nay. Now I would that ye should remember that God has said that the inward vessel shall be cleansed first, and then shall the outer vessel be cleansed also.

Alma 61:12-14

12 We would subject ourselves to the yoke of bondage if it were requisite with the justice of God, or if he should command us so to do.

13 But behold he doth not command us that we shall subject ourselves to our enemies, but that we should put our trust in him, and he will deliver us.

14 Therefore, my beloved brother, Moroni, let us resist evil, and whatsoever evil we cannot resist with our words, yea, such as rebellions and dissensions, let us resist them with our swords, that we may retain our freedom, that we may rejoice in the great privilege of our church, and in the cause of our Redeemer and our God.

Helaman 5:12

12 And now, my sons, remember, remember that it is upon the rock of our Redeemer, who is Christ, the Son of God, that ye must build your foundation; that when the devil shall send forth his mighty winds, yea, his shafts in the whirlwind, yea, when all his hail and his mighty storm shall beat upon you, it shall have no power over you to drag you down to the gulf of misery and endless wo, because of the rock upon which ye are built, which is a sure foundation, a foundation whereon if men build they cannot fall.

Helaman 12:2-3

2 Yea, and we may see at the very time when he doth prosper his people, yea, in the increase of their fields, their flocks and their herds, and in gold, and in silver, and in all manner of precious things of every kind and art; sparing their lives, and delivering them out of the hands of their enemies; softening the hearts of their enemies that they should not declare wars against them; yea, and in fine, doing all things for the welfare and happiness of his people; yea, then is the time that they do harden their hearts, and do forget the Lord their God, and do trample under their feet the Holy One—yea, and this because of their ease, and their exceedingly great prosperity.

3 And thus we see that except the Lord doth chasten his people with many afflictions, yea, except

he doth visit them with death and with terror, and with famine and with all manner of pestilence, they will not remember him.

Helaman 13:6

6 Yea, heavy destruction awaiteth this people, and it surely cometh unto this people, and nothing can save this people save it be repentance and faith on the Lord Jesus Christ, who surely shall come into the world, and shall suffer many things and shall be slain for his people.

Helaman 16:15-23

15 Nevertheless, the people began to harden their hearts, all save it were the most believing part of them, both of the Nephites and also of the Lamanites, and began to depend upon their own strength and upon their own wisdom, saying:

16 Some things they may have guessed right, among so many; but behold, we know that all these great and marvelous works cannot come to pass, of which has been spoken.

17 And they began to reason and to contend among themselves, saying:

18 That it is not reasonable that such a being as a Christ shall come; if so, and he be the Son of God, the Father of heaven and of earth, as it has been spoken, why will he not show himself unto us as well as unto them who shall be at Jerusalem?

19 Yea, why will he not show himself in this land as well as in the land of Jerusalem?

20 But behold, we know that this is a wicked tradition, which has been handed down unto us by our fathers, to cause us that we should believe in some great and marvelous thing which should come to pass, but not among us, but in a land which is far distant, a land which we know not; therefore they can keep us in ignorance, for we cannot witness with our own eyes that they are true.

21 And they will, by the cunning and the mysterious arts of the evil one, work some great mystery which we cannot understand, which will keep us down to be servants to their words, and also servants unto them, for we depend upon them to teach us the word; and thus will they keep us in ignorance if we will yield ourselves unto them, all the days of our lives.

22 And many more things did the people imagine up in their hearts, which were foolish and vain; and they were much disturbed, for Satan did stir them up to do iniquity continually; yea, he did go about spreading rumors and contentions upon all the face of the land, that he might harden the hearts of the people against that which was good and against that which should come.

23 And notwithstanding the signs and the wonders which were wrought among the people of the Lord, and the many miracles which they did, Satan did get great hold upon the hearts of the people upon all the face of the land.

3 Nephi 2:11-12

11 And it came to pass in the thirteenth year there began to be wars and contentions throughout all the land; for the Gadianton robbers had become so numerous, and did slay so many of the people, and did lay waste so many cities, and did spread so much death and carnage throughout the land, that it became expedient that all the people, both the Nephites and the Lamanites, should take up arms against them.

12 Therefore, all the Lamanites who had become converted unto the Lord did unite with their

brethren, the Nephites, and were compelled, for the safety of their lives and their women and their children, to take up arms against those Gadianton robbers, yea, and also to maintain their rights, and the privileges of their church and of their worship, and their freedom and their liberty.

3 Nephi 4:30
30 And they did rejoice and cry again with one voice, saying: May the God of Abraham, and the God of Isaac, and the God of Jacob, protect this people in righteousness, so long as they shall call on the name of their God for protection.

3 Nephi 10:12
12 And it was the more righteous part of the people who were saved, and it was they who received the prophets and stoned them not; and it was they who had not shed the blood of the saints, who were spared—

Mormon 1:13-14
13 But wickedness did prevail upon the face of the whole land, insomuch that the Lord did take away his beloved disciples, and the work of miracles and of healing did cease because of the iniquity of the people.
14 And there were no gifts from the Lord, and the Holy Ghost did not come upon any, because of their wickedness and unbelief.

Mormon 1:16-17
16 And I did endeavor to preach unto this people, but my mouth was shut, and I was forbidden that I should preach unto them; for behold they had wilfully rebelled against their God; and the beloved disciples were taken away out of the land, because of their iniquity.
17 But I did remain among them, but I was forbidden to preach unto them, because of the hardness of their hearts; and because of the hardness of their hearts the land was cursed for their sake.

Ether 2:8
8 And he had sworn in his wrath unto the brother of Jared, that whoso should possess this land of promise, from that time henceforth and forever, should serve him, the true and only God, or they should be swept off when the fulness of his wrath should come upon them.

D&C 1:35-6
35 For I am no respecter of persons, and will that all men shall know that the day speedily cometh; the hour is not yet, but is nigh at hand, when peace shall be taken from the earth, and the devil shall have power over his own dominion.
36 And also the Lord shall have power over his saints, and shall reign in their midst, and shall come down in judgment upon Idumea, or the world.

D&C 6:33-37
33 Fear not to do good, my sons, for whatsoever ye sow, that shall ye also reap; therefore, if ye sow

good ye shall also reap good for your reward.

34 Therefore, fear not, little flock; do good; let earth and hell combine against you, for if ye are built upon my rock, they cannot prevail.

35 Behold, I do not condemn you; go your ways and sin no more; perform with soberness the work which I have commanded you.

36 Look unto me in every thought; doubt not, fear not.

37 Behold the wounds which pierced my side, and also the prints of the nails in my hands and feet; be faithful, keep my commandments, and ye shall inherit the kingdom of heaven. Amen.

D&C 10:5

5 Pray always, that you may come off conqueror; yea, that you may conquer Satan, and that you may escape the hands of the servants of Satan that do uphold his work.

D&C 29:2

2 Who will gather his people even as a hen gathereth her chickens under her wings, even as many as will hearken to my voice and humble themselves before me, and call upon me in mighty prayer.

D&C 29:7-9

7 And ye are called to bring to pass the gathering of mine elect; for mine elect hear my voice and harden not their hearts;

8 Wherefore the decree hath gone forth from the Father that they shall be gathered in unto one place upon the face of this land, to prepare their hearts and be prepared in all things against the day when tribulation and desolation are sent forth upon the wicked.

9 For the hour is nigh and the day soon at hand when the earth is ripe; and all the proud and they that do wickedly shall be as stubble; and I will burn them up, saith the Lord of Hosts, that wickedness shall not be upon the earth;

D&C 33:10

10 Yea, open your mouths and they shall be filled, saying: Repent, repent, and prepare ye the way of the Lord, and make his paths straight; for the kingdom of heaven is at hand;

D&C 35:10-14

10 And the time speedily cometh that great things are to be shown forth unto the children of men;

11 But without faith shall not anything be shown forth except desolations upon Babylon, the same which has made all nations drink of the wine of the wrath of her fornication.

12 And there are none that doeth good except those who are ready to receive the fulness of my gospel, which I have sent forth unto this generation.

13 Wherefore, I call upon the weak things of the world, those who are unlearned and despised, to thrash the nations by the power of my Spirit;

14 And their arm shall be my arm, and I will be their shield and their buckler; and I will gird up their loins, and they shall fight manfully for me; and their enemies shall be under their feet; and I will let fall the sword in their behalf, and by the fire of mine indignation will I preserve them.

D&C 38:8-9

8 But the day soon cometh that ye shall see me, and know that I am; for the veil of darkness shall soon be rent, and he that is not purified shall not abide the day.

9 Wherefore, gird up your loins and be prepared. Behold, the kingdom is yours, and the enemy shall not overcome.

D&C 38:13-15

13 And now I show unto you a mystery, a thing which is had in secret chambers, to bring to pass even your destruction in process of time, and ye knew it not;

14 But now I tell it unto you, and ye are blessed, not because of your iniquity, neither your hearts of unbelief; for verily some of you are guilty before me, but I will be merciful unto your weakness.

15 Therefore, be ye strong from henceforth; fear not, for the kingdom is yours.

D&C 38:28-31

28 And again, I say unto you that the enemy in the secret chambers seeketh your lives.

29 Ye hear of wars in far countries, and you say that there will soon be great wars in far countries, but ye know not the hearts of men in your own land.

30 I tell you these things because of your prayers; wherefore, treasure up wisdom in your bosoms, lest the wickedness of men reveal these things unto you by their wickedness, in a manner which shall speak in your ears with a voice louder than that which shall shake the earth; but if ye are prepared ye shall not fear.

31 And that ye might escape the power of the enemy, and be gathered unto me a righteous people, without spot and blameless—

D&C 45:35

35 And I said unto them: Be not troubled, for, when all these things shall come to pass, ye may know that the promises which have been made unto you shall be fulfilled.

D&C 45:39

39 And it shall come to pass that he that feareth me shall be looking forth for the great day of the Lord to come, even for the signs of the coming of the Son of Man.

D&C 45:57

57 For they that are wise and have received the truth, and have taken the Holy Spirit for their guide, and have not been deceived—verily I say unto you, they shall not be hewn down and cast into the fire, but shall abide the day.

D&C 45:65-75

65 And with one heart and with one mind, gather up your riches that ye may purchase an inheritance which shall hereafter be appointed unto you.

66 And it shall be called the New Jerusalem, a land of peace, a city of refuge, a place of safety for the saints of the Most High God;

67 And the glory of the Lord shall be there, and the terror of the Lord also shall be there, insomuch that the wicked will not come unto it, and it shall be called Zion.

68 And it shall come to pass among the wicked, that every man that will not take his sword against his neighbor must needs flee unto Zion for safety.

69 And there shall be gathered unto it out of every nation under heaven; and it shall be the only people that shall not be at war one with another.

70 And it shall be said among the wicked: Let us not go up to battle against Zion, for the inhabitants of Zion are terrible; wherefore we cannot stand.

71 And it shall come to pass that the righteous shall be gathered out from among all nations, and shall come to Zion, singing with songs of everlasting joy.

72 And now I say unto you, keep these things from going abroad unto the world until it is expedient in me, that ye may accomplish this work in the eyes of the people, and in the eyes of your enemies, that they may not know your works until ye have accomplished the thing which I have commanded you;

73 That when they shall know it, that they may consider these things.

74 For when the Lord shall appear he shall be terrible unto them, that fear may seize upon them, and they shall stand afar off and tremble.

75 And all nations shall be afraid because of the terror of the Lord, and the power of his might. Even so. Amen.

D&C 58:26-29

26 For behold, it is not meet that I should command in all things; for he that is compelled in all things, the same is a slothful and not a wise servant; wherefore he receiveth no reward.

27 Verily I say, men should be anxiously engaged in a good cause, and do many things of their own free will, and bring to pass much righteousness;

28 For the power is in them, wherein they are agents unto themselves. And inasmuch as men do good they shall in nowise lose their reward.

29 But he that doeth not anything until he is commanded, and receiveth a commandment with doubtful heart, and keepeth it with slothfulness, the same is damned.

D&C 63:33-37

33 I have sworn in my wrath, and decreed wars upon the face of the earth, and the wicked shall slay the wicked, and fear shall come upon every man;

34 And the saints also shall hardly escape; nevertheless, I, the Lord, am with them, and will come down in heaven from the presence of my Father and consume the wicked with unquenchable fire.

35 And behold, this is not yet, but by and by.

36 Wherefore, seeing that I, the Lord, have decreed all these things upon the face of the earth, I will that my saints should be assembled upon the land of Zion;

37 And that every man should take righteousness in his hands and faithfulness upon his loins, and lift a warning voice unto the inhabitants of the earth; and declare both by word and by flight that desolation shall come upon the wicked.

D&C 63:58-59

58 For this is a day of warning, and not a day of many words. For I, the Lord, am not to be mocked in the last days.

59 Behold, I am from above, and my power lieth beneath. I am over all, and in all, and through all, and search all things, and the day cometh that all things shall be subject unto me.

D&C 64:24

24 For after today cometh the burning—this is speaking after the manner of the Lord—for verily I say, tomorrow all the proud and they that do wickedly shall be as stubble; and I will burn them up, for I am the Lord of Hosts; and I will not spare any that remain in Babylon.

D&C 68:6

6 Wherefore, be of good cheer, and do not fear, for I the Lord am with you, and will stand by you; and ye shall bear record of me, even Jesus Christ, that I am the Son of the living God, that I was, that I am, and that I am to come.

D&C 68:11

11 And unto you it shall be given to know the signs of the times, and the signs of the coming of the Son of Man;

D&C 77:9

9 Q. What are we to understand by the angel ascending from the east, Revelation 7th chapter and 2nd verse?

A. We are to understand that the angel ascending from the east is he to whom is given the seal of the living God over the twelve tribes of Israel; wherefore, he crieth unto the four angels having the everlasting gospel, saying: Hurt not the earth, neither the sea, nor the trees, till we have sealed the servants of our God in their foreheads. And, if you will receive it, this is Elias which was to come to gather together the tribes of Israel and restore all things.

D&C 78:7

7 For if you will that I give unto you a place in the celestial world, you must prepare yourselves by doing the things which I have commanded you and required of you.

D&C 78:11-14

11 Wherefore, a commandment I give unto you, to prepare and organize yourselves by a bond or everlasting covenant that cannot be broken.

12 And he who breaketh it shall lose his office and standing in the church, and shall be delivered over to the buffetings of Satan until the day of redemption.

13 Behold, this is the preparation wherewith I prepare you, and the foundation, and the ensample which I give unto you, whereby you may accomplish the commandments which are given you;

14 That through my providence, notwithstanding the tribulation which shall descend upon you, that the church may stand independent above all other creatures beneath the celestial world;

D&C 78:17-22

17 Verily, verily, I say unto you, ye are little children, and ye have not as yet understood how great blessings the Father hath in his own hands and prepared for you;

18 And ye cannot bear all things now; nevertheless, be of good cheer, for I will lead you along. The kingdom is yours and the blessings thereof are yours, and the riches of eternity are yours.

19 And he who receiveth all things with thankfulness shall be made glorious; and the things of this earth shall be added unto him, even an hundred fold, yea, more.

20 Wherefore, do the things which I have commanded you, saith your Redeemer, even the Son Ahman, who prepareth all things before he taketh you;

21 For ye are the church of the Firstborn, and he will take you up in a cloud, and appoint every man his portion.

22 And he that is a faithful and wise steward shall inherit all things. Amen.

D&C 85:3

3 It is contrary to the will and commandment of God that those who receive not their inheritance by consecration, agreeable to his law, which he has given, that he may tithe his people, to prepare them against the day of vengeance and burning, should have their names enrolled with the people of God.

D&C 87:6-8

6 And thus, with the sword and by bloodshed the inhabitants of the earth shall mourn; and with famine, and plague, and earthquake, and the thunder of heaven, and the fierce and vivid lightning also, shall the inhabitants of the earth be made to feel the wrath, and indignation, and chastening hand of an Almighty God, until the consumption decreed hath made a full end of all nations;

7 That the cry of the saints, and of the blood of the saints, shall cease to come up into the ears of the Lord of Sabaoth, from the earth, to be avenged of their enemies.

8 Wherefore, stand ye in holy places, and be not moved, until the day of the Lord come; for behold, it cometh quickly, saith the Lord. Amen.

D&C 88:73-75

73 Behold, I will hasten my work in its time.

74 And I give unto you, who are the first laborers in this last kingdom, a commandment that you assemble yourselves together, and organize yourselves, and prepare yourselves, and sanctify yourselves; yea, purify your hearts, and cleanse your hands and your feet before me, that I may make you clean;

75 That I may testify unto your Father, and your God, and my God, that you are clean from the blood of this wicked generation; that I may fulfil this promise, this great and last promise, which I have made unto you, when I will.

D&C 88:77-86

77 And I give unto you a commandment that you shall teach one another the doctrine of the kingdom.

78 Teach ye diligently and my grace shall attend you, that you may be instructed more perfectly in

theory, in principle, in doctrine, in the law of the gospel, in all things that pertain unto the kingdom of God, that are expedient for you to understand;

79 Of things both in heaven and in the earth, and under the earth; things which have been, things which are, things which must shortly come to pass; things which are at home, things which are abroad; the wars and the perplexities of the nations, and the judgments which are on the land; and a knowledge also of countries and of kingdoms—

80 That ye may be prepared in all things when I shall send you again to magnify the calling whereunto I have called you, and the mission with which I have commissioned you.

81 Behold, I sent you out to testify and warn the people, and it becometh every man who hath been warned to warn his neighbor.

82 Therefore, they are left without excuse, and their sins are upon their own heads.

83 He that seeketh me early shall find me, and shall not be forsaken.

84 Therefore, tarry ye, and labor diligently, that you may be perfected in your ministry to go forth among the Gentiles for the last time, as many as the mouth of the Lord shall name, to bind up the law and seal up the testimony, and to prepare the saints for the hour of judgment which is to come;

85 That their souls may escape the wrath of God, the desolation of abomination which awaits the wicked, both in this world and in the world to come. Verily, I say unto you, let those who are not the first elders continue in the vineyard until the mouth of the Lord shall call them, for their time is not yet come; their garments are not clean from the blood of this generation.

86 Abide ye in the liberty wherewith ye are made free; entangle not yourselves in sin, but let your hands be clean, until the Lord comes.

D&C 88:126

126 Pray always, that ye may not faint, until I come. Behold, and lo, I will come quickly, and receive you unto myself. Amen.

D&C 89:4

4 Behold, verily, thus saith the Lord unto you: In consequence of evils and designs which do and will exist in the hearts of conspiring men in the last days, I have warned you, and forewarn you, by giving unto you this word of wisdom by revelation--

D&C 90:3-5

3 Verily I say unto you, the keys of this kingdom shall never be taken from you, while thou art in the world, neither in the world to come;

4 Nevertheless, through you shall the oracles be given to another, yea, even unto the church.

5 And all they who receive the oracles of God, let them beware how they hold them lest they are accounted as a light thing, and are brought under condemnation thereby, and stumble and fall when the storms descend, and the winds blow, and the rains descend, and beat upon their house.

D&C 97:25-26

25 Nevertheless, Zion shall escape if she observe to do all things whatsoever I have commanded her.

26 But if she observe not to do whatsoever I have commanded her, I will visit her according to all

her works, with sore affliction, with pestilence, with plague, with sword, with vengeance, with devouring fire.

D&C 100:15

15 Therefore, let your hearts be comforted; for all things shall work together for good to them that walk uprightly, and to the sanctification of the church.

D&C 101:38

38 And seek the face of the Lord always, that in patience ye may possess your souls, and ye shall have eternal life.

D&C 101:67-69

67 Therefore, a commandment I give unto all the churches, that they shall continue to gather together unto the places which I have appointed.

68 Nevertheless, as I have said unto you in a former commandment, let not your gathering be in haste, nor by flight; but let all things be prepared before you.

69 And in order that all things be prepared before you, observe the commandment which I have given concerning these things—

D&C 101:82-95

82 There was in a city a judge which feared not God, neither regarded man.

83 And there was a widow in that city, and she came unto him saying: Avenge me of mine adversary.

84 And he would not for a while, but afterward he said within himself: Though I fear not God, nor regard man, yet because this widow troubleth me I will avenge her, lest by her continual coming she weary me.

85 Thus will I liken the children of Zion.

86 Let them importune at the feet of the judge;

87 And if he heed them not, let them importune at the feet of the governor;

88 And if the governor heed them not, let them importune at the feet of the president;

89 And if the president heed them not, then will the Lord arise and come forth out of his hiding place, and in his fury vex the nation;

90 And in his hot displeasure, and in his fierce anger, in his time, will cut off those wicked, unfaithful, and unjust stewards, and appoint them their portion among hypocrites, and unbelievers;

91 Even in outer darkness, where there is weeping, and wailing, and gnashing of teeth.

92 Pray ye, therefore, that their ears may be opened unto your cries, that I may be merciful unto them, that these things may not come upon them.

93 What I have said unto you must needs be, that all men may be left without excuse;

94 That wise men and rulers may hear and know that which they have never considered;

95 That I may proceed to bring to pass my act, my strange act, and perform my work, my strange work, that men may discern between the righteous and the wicked, saith your God.

D&C 109:38

38 Put upon thy servants the testimony of the covenant, that when they go out and proclaim thy word they may seal up the law, and prepare the hearts of thy saints for all those judgments thou art about to send, in thy wrath, upon the inhabitants of the earth, because of their transgressions, that thy people may not faint in the day of trouble.

D&C 109:46

46 Therefore, O Lord, deliver thy people from the calamity of the wicked; enable thy servants to seal up the law, and bind up the testimony, that they may be prepared against the day of burning.

D&C 112:24-26

24 Behold, vengeance cometh speedily upon the inhabitants of the earth, a day of wrath, a day of burning, a day of desolation, of weeping, of mourning, and of lamentation; and as a whirlwind it shall come upon all the face of the earth, saith the Lord.

25 And upon my house shall it begin, and from my house shall it go forth, saith the Lord;

26 First among those among you, saith the Lord, who have professed to know my name and have not known me, and have blasphemed against me in the midst of my house, saith the Lord.

D&C 115:6

6 And that the gathering together upon the land of Zion, and upon her stakes, may be for a defense, and for a refuge from the storm, and from wrath when it shall be poured out without mixture upon the whole earth.

D&C 121:34-40

34 Behold, there are many called, but few are chosen. And why are they not chosen?

35 Because their hearts are set so much upon the things of this world, and aspire to the honors of men, that they do not learn this one lesson—

36 That the rights of the priesthood are inseparably connected with the powers of heaven, and that the powers of heaven cannot be controlled nor handled only upon the principles of righteousness.

37 That they may be conferred upon us, it is true; but when we undertake to cover our sins, or to gratify our pride, our vain ambition, or to exercise control or dominion or compulsion upon the souls of the children of men, in any degree of unrighteousness, behold, the heavens withdraw themselves; the Spirit of the Lord is grieved; and when it is withdrawn, Amen to the priesthood or the authority of that man.

38 Behold, ere he is aware, he is left unto himself, to kick against the pricks, to persecute the saints, and to fight against God.

39 We have learned by sad experience that it is the nature and disposition of almost all men, as soon as they get a little authority, as they suppose, they will immediately begin to exercise unrighteous dominion.

40 Hence many are called, but few are chosen.

D&C 123:1-17

1 And again, we would suggest for your consideration the propriety of all the saints gathering up a knowledge of all the facts, and sufferings and abuses put upon them by the people of this State;

2 And also of all the property and amount of damages which they have sustained, both of character and personal injuries, as well as real property;

3 And also the names of all persons that have had a hand in their oppressions, as far as they can get hold of them and find them out.

4 And perhaps a committee can be appointed to find out these things, and to take statements and affidavits; and also to gather up the libelous publications that are afloat;

5 And all that are in the magazines, and in the encyclopedias, and all the libelous histories that are published, and are writing, and by whom, and present the whole concatenation of diabolical rascality and nefarious and murderous impositions that have been practised upon this people—

6 That we may not only publish to all the world, but present them to the heads of government in all their dark and hellish hue, as the last effort which is enjoined on us by our Heavenly Father, before we can fully and completely claim that promise which shall call him forth from his hiding place; and also that the whole nation may be left without excuse before he can send forth the power of his mighty arm.

7 It is an imperative duty that we owe to God, to angels, with whom we shall be brought to stand, and also to ourselves, to our wives and children, who have been made to bow down with grief, sorrow, and care, under the most damning hand of murder, tyranny, and oppression, supported and urged on and upheld by the influence of that spirit which hath so strongly riveted the creeds of the fathers, who have inherited lies, upon the hearts of the children, and filled the world with confusion, and has been growing stronger and stronger, and is now the very mainspring of all corruption, and the whole earth groans under the weight of its iniquity.

8 It is an iron yoke, it is a strong band; they are the very handcuffs, and chains, and shackles, and fetters of hell.

9 Therefore it is an imperative duty that we owe, not only to our own wives and children, but to the widows and fatherless, whose husbands and fathers have been murdered under its iron hand;

10 Which dark and blackening deeds are enough to make hell itself shudder, and to stand aghast and pale, and the hands of the very devil to tremble and palsy.

11 And also it is an imperative duty that we owe to all the rising generation, and to all the pure in heart—

12 For there are many yet on the earth among all sects, parties, and denominations, who are blinded by the subtle craftiness of men, whereby they lie in wait to deceive, and who are only kept from the truth because they know not where to find it—

13 Therefore, that we should waste and wear out our lives in bringing to light all the hidden things of darkness, wherein we know them; and they are truly manifest from heaven—

14 These should then be attended to with great earnestness.

15 Let no man count them as small things; for there is much which lieth in futurity, pertaining to the saints, which depends upon these things.

16 You know, brethren, that a very large ship is benefited very much by a very small helm in the time of a storm, by being kept workways with the wind and the waves.

17 Therefore, dearly beloved brethren, let us cheerfully do all things that lie in our power; and then may we stand still, with the utmost assurance, to see the salvation of God, and for his arm to be revealed.

D&C 133:4-5

4 Wherefore, prepare ye, prepare ye, O my people; sanctify yourselves; gather ye together, O ye people of my church, upon the land of Zion, all you that have not been commanded to tarry.
5 Go ye out from Babylon. Be ye clean that bear the vessels of the Lord.

D&C 133:57-59

57 And for this cause, that men might be made partakers of the glories which were to be revealed, the Lord sent forth the fulness of his gospel, his everlasting covenant, reasoning in plainness and simplicity—
58 To prepare the weak for those things which are coming on the earth, and for the Lord's errand in the day when the weak shall confound the wise, and the little one become a strong nation, and two shall put their tens of thousands to flight.
59 And by the weak things of the earth the Lord shall thrash the nations by the power of his Spirit.

D&C 134:11

11 We believe that men should appeal to the civil law for redress of all wrongs and grievances, where personal abuse is inflicted or the right of property or character infringed, where such laws exist as will protect the same; but we believe that all men are justified in defending themselves, their friends, and property, and the government, from the unlawful assaults and encroachments of all persons in times of exigency, where immediate appeal cannot be made to the laws, and relief afforded.

D&C 136:31

31 My people must be tried in all things, that they may be prepared to receive the glory that I have for them, even the glory of Zion; and he that will not bear chastisement is not worthy of my kingdom.

Moses 7:61

61 And the day shall come that the earth shall rest, but before that day the heavens shall be darkened, and a veil of darkness shall cover the earth; and the heavens shall shake, and also the earth; and great tribulations shall be among the children of men, but my people will I preserve;

CHAPTER THREE

GOVERNMENT & THE CONSTITUTION

"I warn you, unless we wake up soon and do something about the conspiracy, the communist-inspired civil rights riots of the past will pale into insignificance compared to the bloodshed and destruction that lie ahead in the near future.

Do not think the members of the Church shall escape. The Lord has assured us that the Church will still be here when He comes again. But has the Lord assured us that we can avoid fighting for freedom and still escape unscathed both temporally and spiritually? We could not escape the eternal consequences of our pre-existent position on freedom. What makes us think we can escape it here? . . .

It is the devil's desire that the Lord's priesthood stay asleep while the strings of tyranny gradually and quietly entangle us until, like Gulliver, we awake too late and find that while we could have broken each string separately as it was put upon us, our sleepiness permitted enough strings to bind us to make a rope that enslaves us.

For years we have heard of the role the elders could play in saving the constitution from total destruction. But how can the elders be expected to save it if they have not studied it and are not sure if it is being destroyed or what is destroying it? . . .

Now Satan is anxious to neutralize the inspired counsel of the Prophet . . .For example, he will argue, 'There is no need to get involved in the fight for freedom—all you need to do is live the gospel.' Of course this is a contradiction, because we cannot fully live the gospel and not be involved in the fight for freedom. . .

We know, as do no other people, that the Constitution of the United States is inspired — established by men whom the Lord raised up for that very purpose. We cannot— we must not— shirk our sacred responsibility to rise up in defense of our God-given freedom."

(Ezra Taft Benson, "Our Immediate Responsibility", BYU, October 25, 1966.)

Joseph Smith, History of the Church, Vol.6, p. 7.

"That when the Government ceases to afford protection, the citizens of course fall back upon their original inherent right of self-defense."

The Words of Joseph Smith, p. 279.

"The time would come when the Constitution and Government would hang by a brittle thread and would be ready to fall into other hands, but this people the Latter-day Saints will step forth and save it."

Words of Joseph Smith, p. 416, July 19, 1840.

"Even this nation will be on the very verge of crumbling to pieces and tumbling to the ground, and when the constitution is upon the brink of ruin this people will be the staff upon which the nation shall lean and they shall bear away the constitution away from the very verge of destruction. Then shall the Lord say go tell all my servants who are the strength of mine house, my young men and middle aged, come to the Land of my vineyard and fight the battle of the Lord. Then the Kings & Queens shall come, then the rulers of the Earth shall come, then shall all saints come yea the Foreign saints shall come to fight for the Land of my vineyard for in this thing shall be their safety and they will have no power to choose but will come as a man fleeth from a sudden destruction. . . . I know these things by the visions of the Almighty."

Brigham Young, Journal of Discourses, Vol. 2, p. 311, July 8, 1855.
"I say again that the constitution, and laws of the United States, and the laws of the different States, as a general thing, are just as good as we want, provided they were honored. But we find Judges who do not honor the laws, yes, officers of the law dishonor the law. Legislators and law makers are frequently the first violators of the laws they make. 'When the wicked rule the people mourn,' and when the corruption of a people bears down the scale in favor of wickedness, that people is nigh unto destruction."

Brigham Young, Journal of Discourses, Vol. 7, p. 15, July 4, 1854.
"Will the Constitution be destroyed? No: it will be held inviolate by this people; and, as Joseph Smith said, 'The time will come when the destiny of the nation will hang upon a single thread. At that critical juncture, this people will step forth and save it from the threatened destruction.' It will be so."

Brigham Young, Journal of Discourses, Vol. 8, p. 324, February 10, 1861.
"If our present happy form of government is sustained, which I believe it will be, it will be done by the people I am now looking upon, in connection with their brethren and their offspring. The present Constitution, with a few alteration of a trifling nature, is just as good as we want; and if it is sustained on this land of Joseph, it will be done by us and our posterity."

Brigham Young, Journal of Discourses, Vol. 9, p. 5, April 6, 1861.
"The whole Government is gone; it is as weak as water. I heard Joseph Smith say, nearly thirty years ago, 'They shall have mobbing to their heart's content, if they do not redress the wrongs of the Latter-day Saints.' Mobs will not decrease, but will increase until the whole Government becomes a mob, and eventually it will be State against State, city against city, neighbourhood against neighbourhood, Methodists against Methodists, and so on."

Brigham Young, Journal of Discourses, Vol. 10, p. 177, May 24, 1863.
"I am for the kingdom of God. I like a good government, and then I like to have it wisely and justly administered. The government of heaven, if wickedly administered, would become one of the worst governments upon the face of the earth. No matter how good a government is, unless it is administered by righteous men, an evil government will be made of it. The Lord has his eye upon all the kingdoms and nations of men, with their kings, governors and rulers, and he will sink the wicked to misery and woe, and we cannot help it."

Brigham Young, Journal of Discourses, Vol. 10, p. 191, May 31, 1863.

"When misuse of power has reached a certain stage, the divinity that is within the people asserts its right and they free themselves from the power of despotism. The nation that lifts itself up against God and rules in unrighteousness he will call to an account in his own way."

Brigham Young, Journal of Discourses, Vol. 11, p. 262-263, August 12, 1866.

"I hope and trust and pray that the government of our country may remain, because it is so good; but if they cut off this, and cast out that, and institute another thing, they may destroy all the good it contains. This, I hope, they will not do; they cannot do it. I expect to see the day when the Elders of Israel will protect and sustain civil and religious liberty and every constitutional right bequeathed to us by our fathers, and spread those rights abroad in connection with the Gospel for the salvation of all nations. I shall see this whether I live or die."

Brigham Young, Journal of Discourses, Vol. 12, p. 204-205, April 8, 1868.

"And I tell you further, Elders of Israel, that you do not know the day of your visitation, neither do you understand the signs of the times, for if you did you would be awake to these things. Every organization of our government, the best government in the world, is crumbling to pieces. Those who have it in their hands are the ones who are destroying it. How long will it be before the words of the prophet Joseph will be fulfilled? He said if the Constitution of the United States were saved at all it must be done by this people. It will not be many years before these words come to pass."

Discourses of Brigham Young, p. 358.

"Are we a political people? Yes, very political indeed. But what party do you belong to or would you vote for? I will tell you whom we will vote for: we will vote for the man who will sustain the principles of civil and religious liberty, the man who knows the most and who has the best heart and brain for a statesman; and we do not care a farthing whether he is a whig, a democrat, a barnburner, a republican, a new light or anything else. These are our politics."

Discourses of Brigham Young, p. 363.

"The Government of the United States is republican in form, and should be in its administration, and requires a man for President who is capable of communicating to the understanding of the people, according to their capacity, information upon all points pertaining to the just administration of the Government. He should understand what administrative policy would be most beneficial to the nation. He should also have the knowledge and disposition to wisely exercise the appointing power, so far as it is constitutionally within his control and select only good and capable men for the office. He should not only carry out the legal and just wishes of his constituents, but should be able to enlighten their understanding and correct their judgment. And all good officers in a truly republican administration will constantly labor for the security of the rights of all, irrespective of sect or party."

Heber C. Kimball, Journal of Discourses, Vol. 5, p. 217, September 6, 1856.

"We will yet save the Constitution of the United States. We will do it, as the Lord liveth, and we will save this nation, every one of them that will be saved. Brother Brigham Young and brother Joseph Smith stand at our head, and will do that thing, as the Lord liveth. Yes, we, as their children, with our children to assist us, will do it. We have got that power, and so have they, and will bear the kingdom off victoriously to every nation that is upon God's footstool; and I know it."

Orson Hyde, Journal of Discourses, Vol. 6, p. 152, January 3, 1858.

"It is said that brother Joseph in his lifetime declared that the Elders of this Church should step forth at a particular time when the Constitution should be in danger, and rescue it, and save it. This may be so; but I do not recollect that he said exactly so. I believe he said something like this—that the time would come when the Constitution and the country would be in danger of an overthrow; and said he, If the Constitution be saved at all, it will be by the Elders of this Church. I believe this is about the language, as nearly as I can recollect it.

The question is whether it will be saved at all, or not. I do not know that it matters to us whether it is or not: the Lord will provide for and take care of his people, if we do every duty, and fear and honour him, and keep his commandments; and he will not leave us without a Constitution."

Orson Hyde, Journal of Discourses, Vol. 6, p. 153-154, January 3, 1858.

"What Constitution shall we be governed by, when unprincipled men have destroyed the Constitution of our Union? I will tell you what we shall have: while we walk in the favour of God, we shall have a Constitution. The Constitution written in the Bible? No. In the Book of Doctrine and Covenants, or Book of Mormon? No. What kind shall we have, then? The Constitution that God will give us."

Orson Hyde, Journal of Discourses, Vol. 6, p. 369, July 4, 1854.

"When Justice is satisfied, and the blood of martyrs atoned for, the guardian angel of America will return to his station, resume his charge, and restore the Constitution of our country to the respect and veneration of the people; for it was given by the inspiration of our God."

Orson Pratt, Deseret Evening News, Vol. 8, #265, Oct. 2, 1875, discourse delivered Sept. 26, 1875.

"Now I am going to prophesy a little. The time is coming, when we will not be fettered by unjust laws that are imposed upon us. Why? Because the Lord intends, by his judgment, by wars among the nations that will not serve him, by famines, and pestilence, and by various judgments that will be sent forth, to waste away the nations of the earth that will not repent. This is what the Lord has decreed; it is written in the Book of Mormon, and it is published in the Book of Doctrine and Covenants, and we know their doom, and we know that it is very near at hand. It is not something to happen in a far distant period of the future, but it is right at the doors. God has sent forth his warning message in the midst of this nation, but they have rejected it and treated his servants with contempt; the Lord has gathered out his people from their midst, and has planted them here in these mountains; and he will speedily fulfill the prophecy in relation to the overthrow of this nation, and their destruction. We shall be obliged to have a government to preserve ourselves in unity and peace;

for they, through being wasted away, will not have power to govern; for state will be divided against state, city against city, town against town, and the whole country will be in terror and confusion; mobocracy will prevail and there will be no security, through this great Republic, for the lives or property of the people. When that time shall arrive, we shall necessarily want to carry out the principles of our great constitution and, as the people of God, we shall want to see those principles magnified, according to the order of union and oneness will prevails among the people of God. We can magnify it, and all will be united without having democrats or republicans and all kinds of religions; we can magnify it according to the spirit and letter of the constitution, though we are united in politics, religion, and everything else.

Well, then, to return to the prophesying, when the time shall come that the Lord shall waste away this nation, He will give commandment to this people to return and possess their own inheritances which they purchased some forty four years ago in the state of Missouri."

Orson Pratt, Journal of Discourses, Vol. 3, p. 71, July 8, 1855.

"'Did the Lord have a hand in the organization of the United States government?' asks the enquirer. Yes, the Lord had a hand in framing its Constitution. Why did not the Lord, at that time, introduce a perfect government—a theocracy? It was simply because the people were not prepared for it—they were too corrupt; and although they had more integrity, more virtue, more honesty, and more sympathy and feeling for that which is just and upright and good, than any other portion of the inhabitants of the earth, and probably more than a great many now have, yet they were far from being prepared for the government of God, which is a government of union.

They were far from that, consequently the Lord inspired them to introduce a government that He knew would be just suited to their capacity, and hence it was that He inspired Jefferson, Washington, Franklin, and others to introduce those measures which they did, and to carry them out, and they were such as were just suited to the conditions and circumstances of the people; hence the government of the United States we, as a people, venerate and defend.

Why do we do this? We do it because God had His hand in the organization of it; He controlled it so far as He could do so without interfering with the agency of man.

This government, then, was organized to suit the people and the circumstances in which they were placed, until they were prepared to receive a more perfect one.

But will the government of the United States continue for ever? No, it is not sufficiently perfect; and, notwithstanding it has been sanctioned by the Lord at a time when it was suited to the circumstances of the people, yet the day will come, (I will say it on my own responsibility and not that of this people,) the day will come when the United States government, and all others, will be uprooted, and the kingdoms of this world will be united in one, and the kingdom of our God will govern the whole earth, and bear universal sway; and no power beneath the heavens can prevent this taking place, if the Bible be true, and we know it to be true."

Orson Pratt, Journal of Discourses, Vol. 6, p. 204, January 24, 1859.

"The American continent never was designed for such a corrupt Government as the United States to flourish or prosper long upon it. After they should become ripened in iniquity, it was not intended they should continue. The Lord has designed another thing, and for this reason we are here in these mountains: the little stone has been rolling up hill."

Orson Pratt, Journal of Discourses, Vol. 15, p. 72-73, February 4, 1872.

"This prophecy of Daniel will give a true understanding of the matter to our wise men and statesmen, and all who desire to know the future destiny of the American government, the European governments, and all the kingdoms of the earth. Their destiny is total destruction from our earth, no matter how great or powerful they may become. Though our nation may grasp on the right hand and on the left; though it may annex the British possessions, and extend its dominions to the south and grasp the whole of this great western hemisphere, and although our nation shall become as powerful in population as in extent of territory, its destiny is foretold in the saying of the Prophet Daniel, 'They shall become like the chaff of the summer threshing floor, the wind shall carry them away and no place shall be found for them.' So with the kingdoms of Europe, so with the kingdoms of Western Asia and Eastern Europe."

Orson Pratt, Journal of Discourses, Vol. 24, p. 27-33, October 26, 1879.

"We never want to be freed from the Constitution of our country. It is built upon heavenly principles. It is established as firm as the rock of ages, and when those that abuse it shall moulder in corruption under the surface of the earth, the American Constitution will stand and no people can destroy it, because God raised it by our ancient fathers, and inspired them to frame that sacred instrument. The Constitution is one thing; corrupt politicians are another thing. One may be bright as the sun at noonday, the other as corrupt as hell itself; that is the difference. Because we have a good Constitution that is no sign that the strong arm of the law, founded upon that Constitution, will protect the minority as well as the majority. The politician may suffer the majority to trample upon the rights guaranteed by that Constitution to the minority. They have done it before, and perchance they will continue to do it until they are wasted away. Then will be fulfilled another saying in this same chapter which I have read—'For thou shalt break forth on the right hand and on the left; and thy seed shall inherit the Gentiles, and make the desolate cities to be inhabited.' Now, there are a great many cities in the United States that will not be totally destroyed when the inhabitants are swept off the surface of the earth. Their houses, their desolate cities will still remain unoccupied until Zion in her glory and strength shall enlarge the place of her tents, and stretch forth the curtains of her habitations. That is the destiny of this nation, and the destiny of the Latter-day Saints."

John Taylor, Messages of the First Presidency, Vol. 2, p. 346.

"You owe it to yourselves; you owe it to your posterity; you owe it to those of your co-religionists who, by this law, are robbed worse than even many of yourselves, of their rights under the Constitution; you owe it to humanity everywhere; you owe it to that free and constitutional form of government, which has been bequeathed to you through the precious sacrifices of many of your forefathers—to do all in your power to maintain religious liberty and free, republican government in these mountains, and to preserve every constitutional right intact, and not to allow, either through supineness or indifference, or any feeling of resentment or indignation because of wrongs inflicted upon you, any right or privilege to be wrested from you. Very many of you can take this oath with conscientiousness and entire truthfulness, as you could even if it were in a form which many of your traducers could not take without perjury; and yet there would be no impropriety, while you do take it, in protesting against it as a gross wrong imposed upon you. Then having done this, and everything else in your power to preserve constitutional government and full religious freedom in the land, you can safely trust the Lord for the rest. He has promised to fight your battles. His word has never failed. You have proved Him in times of trial and fierce persecution in the past, and He is the same God to day that He was then. He has neither gone to sleep, nor is He upon a journey; and if you are faithful to Him, He will as surely deliver you in the future, and fulfill all His promises to Zion, as He has delivered you in the past."

John Taylor, Conference Report, April 1880, p. 102.

"We will sustain the government in its administration, and be true to it, and maintain this position right along. And when division, strife, trouble and contention arise, we will try to still the troubled waters, and act in all honesty as true friends to the government; and when war shall exist among them, and there is no one found to sustain the remnants of liberty that may be left, the Elders of Israel will rally round the standard of freedom and proclaim liberty to all the world."

John Taylor, Journal of Discourses, Vol. 11, p. 92, March 5, 1865.

"We will stand by that constitution and uphold the flag of our country when everybody else forsakes it. We cannot shut our eyes to things transpiring around us. We have our reason, and God has revealed unto us many things; but never has he revealed anything in opposition to those institutions and that Constitution, no, never; and, another thing, he never will."

John Taylor, Journal of Discourses, Vol. 17, p. 5, February 1, 1874.

"This nation and other nations will be overthrown, not because of their virtue, but because of their corruption and iniquity. The time will come, for the prophecies will be fulfilled, when kingdoms will be destroyed, thrones cast down and the powers of the earth shaken, and God's wrath will be kindled against the nations of the earth, and it is for us to maintain correct principles, political, religious and social, and to feel towards all men as God feels. He makes the sun to shine on the just as well as on the unjust; and if he has enlightened our minds and put us in possession of more correct principles than others have, let us be thankful and adore the God of Israel."

John Taylor, Journal of Discourses, Vol. 20, p. 318-319, October 6, 1879.

"Need we be surprised that they should trample under foot the Constitution of the United States? No; Joseph Smith told us that they would do it. Many around me here knew long ago that they would do this thing and further knew that the last people that should be found to rally around that sacred instrument and save it from the grasp of unrighteous men would be the Elders of Israel! When, therefore, we see these things progressing need we be astonished? I do not think we need be."

John Taylor, Journal of Discourses, Vol. 20, p. 356-357, November 30, 1879.

"But this nation is laying the axe at the root of the tree and they then will crumble to pieces by and by. If they can stand it we can. If they can afford to treat us in this way, they will soon treat others in the same way. And they will tear away one plank of liberty after another, until the whole, fabric will totter and fall; and many other nations will be cast down and empires destroyed; and this nation will have to suffer as other will. And it will be as Joseph Smith once said, 'When all others forsake the Constitution, the Elders of this Church will rally around the standard and save its tattered shreds.' We will come to its rescue and proclaim liberty to all men."

John Taylor, Journal of Discourses, Vol. 21, p. 8, August 31, 1879.

"And then the day is not far distant when this nation will be shaken from centre to circumference. And now, you may write it down, any of you, and I will prophesy it in the name of God. And then will be fulfilled that prediction to be found in one of the revelations given through the Prophet Joseph Smith. Those who will not take up their sword to fight against their neighbor must needs flee to Zion for safety. And they will come, saying, we do not know anything of the principles of your religion, but we perceive that you are an honest community; you administer justice and righteousness, and we want to live with you and receive the protection of your laws, but as for your religion we will talk about that some other time. Will we protect such people? Yes, all honorable men. When the people shall have torn to shreds the Constitution of the United States the Elders of Israel will be found holding it up to the nations of the earth and proclaiming liberty and equal rights to all men, and extending the hand of fellowship to the oppressed of all nations. This is part of the programme, and as long as we do what is right and fear God, he will help us and stand by us under all circumstances."

John Taylor, Journal of Discourses, Vol. 21, p. 71, January 4, 1880.

"But do we propose to govern, interfere with, or rebel against the Government of the United States? No, we do not. That is not in the programme. Has God given us a law? Yes. All right we will get along and do the best we can, but we won't forsake our God. All who are willing to abide by the laws of God signify it by raising the right hand (unanimous vote). Now try and keep them. But will we fight against the United States? No, we will not. Well, how will these things be brought about? Don't you expect that the kingdoms of this world will become the kingdoms of our God and his Christ? Yes, I do, as much as I believe I am speaking to you and you are hearing me, and I not only believe it but know it. Well, now, how will that be brought about if you do not pitch in? We need not do this. There is plenty that will pitch in; there will be plenty of trouble by and by without our interference, when men begin to tear away one plank after another out of the platform of constitutional liberty; there will not be much to tie to. And how will you get along with them? We will leave them to get along with themselves. And how will that be? We are told the wicked shall slay the wicked, but says the Lord: 'It is my business to take care of the Saints.' God will stand by Israel, and Zion shall triumph and this work will go on until the kingdom is established and all nations bow to its standard."

John Taylor, Journal of Discourses, Vol. 22, p. 143, July 3, 1881.

"These secret combinations were spoken of by Joseph Smith, years and years ago. I have heard him time and time again tell about them, and he stated that when these things began to take place the liberties of this nation would begin to be bartered away. We see many signs of weakness which we lament, and we would to God that our rulers would be men of righteousness, and that those who aspire to position would be guided by honorable feelings—to maintain inviolate the Constitution and operate in the interest, happiness, well-being, and protection of the whole community. But we see signs of weakness and vacillation. We see a policy being introduced to listen to the clamor of mobs and of unprincipled men who know not of what they speak, nor whereof they affirm, and when men begin to tear away with impunity one plank after another from our Constitution, by and by we shall find that we are struggling with the wreck and ruin of the system which the forefathers of this nation sought to establish in the interests of humanity."

John Taylor, Journal of Discourses, Vol. 22, p. 229-230, June 26, 1881.
"But should this nation persist in violating their Constitutional guarantees, tear away the bulwarks of liberty, and trample upon the principles of freedom and human rights, that are sacred to all men, and by which all men should be governed, by and by the whole fabric will fall, and who will sustain it? We will, in the name of Israel's God. Of this the Prophet Joseph Smith prophesied long, long ago. This is the position we stand in. And if the Government of the United States can afford to oppress us, we can afford to suffer and grow strong."

John Taylor, Journal of Discourses, Vol. 23, p. 16, November 9, 1881.
"There are elements at work to uproot the government and destroy the foundation of society, and to take away the rights of men and pull down the bulwarks of this government, and scatter to the four winds the principles by which it has been governed, and to let loose the wildest passions of men. These are some of the things that are taking place. These are the elements that are at work to-day. They are running around, and through, and among the people almost everywhere. And it will not be long before there is trouble again in the United States. These inflated times will by and by bring about a great reaction, and then there will be trouble and difficulty; and so these things will continue to increase."

John Taylor, Journal of Discourses, Vol. 23, p. 62-63, April 9, 1882.
"The volcanic fires of disordered and anarchical elements are beginning to manifest themselves and exhibit the internal forces that are at work among the turbulent and unthinking masses of the people. Congress will soon have something else to do than to proscribe and persecute an innocent, law-abiding and patriotic people. Of all bodies in the world, they can least afford to remove the bulwarks that bind society together in this nation, to recklessly trample upon human freedom and rights, and to rend and destroy that great Palladium of human rights—the Constitution of the United States. Ere long they will need all its protecting influence to save this nation from misrule, anarchy and mobocratic influence. They can ill afford to be the foremost in tampering with human rights and human freedom, or in tearing down the bulwarks of safety and protection which that sacred instrument has guaranteed. It is lamentable to see the various disordered and disorganized elements seeking to overthrow the greatest and best government in existence on the earth. Congress can ill afford to set a pattern of violation of that Constitution which it has sworn to support. The internal fires of revolution are already smouldering in this nation, and they need but a spark to set them in a flame. Already are agencies at work in the land calculated to subvert and overthrow every principle of rule and government; already is corruption of every kind prevailing in high places and permeating

all society; already are we, as a nation, departing from our God, and corrupting ourselves with malfeasance, dishonor, and a lack of public integrity and good faith; already are licentiousness and debauchery corrupting, undermining and destroying society; already are we interfering with the laws of nature and stopping the functions of life, and have become the slayers of our own offspring, and employ human butchers in the shape of physicians to assist in this diabolical and murderous work. The sins of this nation, the licentiousness, the debauchery, the murders are entering into the ears of the Lord of Sabbath, and I tell you now, from the tops of these mountains, as a humble servant of the living God, that unless these crimes and infamies are stopped, this nation will be overthrown, and its glory, power, dominion and wealth will fade away like the dews of a summer morning. I also say to other nations of the earth, that unless they repent of their crimes, their iniquities and abominations, their thrones will be overturned, their kingdoms and governments overthrown, and their lands made desolate. This is not only my saying, but it is the saying of those ancient prophets which they themselves profess to believe; for God will speedily have a controversy with the nations of the earth, and, as I stated before, the destroyer of the Gentiles is on his way to overthrow governments, to destroy dynasties, to lay waste thrones, kingdoms and empires, to spread abroad anarchy and desolation, and to cause war, famine and bloodshed to overspread the earth."

John Taylor, Journal of Discourses, Vol. 23, p. 63-64, April 9, 1882.

"Besides the preaching of the Gospel, we have another mission, namely, the perpetuation of the free agency of man and the maintenance of liberty, freedom, and the rights of man. There are certain principles that belong to humanity outside of the Constitution, outside of the laws, outside of all the enactments and plans of man, among which is the right to live; God gave us the right and not man; no government gave it to us, and no government has a right to take it away from us. We have a right to liberty—that was a right that God gave to all men; and if there has been oppression, fraud or tyranny in the earth, it has been the result of the wickedness and corruptions of men and has always been opposed to God and the principles of truth, righteousness, virtue, and all principles that are calculated to elevate mankind. The Declaration of Independence states that men are in possession of certain inalienable rights, among which are life, liberty and the pursuit of happiness."

John Taylor, Journal of Discourses, Vol. 23, p. 238-240, August 20, 1882.

"In reading some of the histories pertaining to the dealings of God with man and the dealings of the devil with him you will find that Satan sought to rob man of his free agency, as many of his agents are seeking to do today; and for this cause Satan was cast out of heaven. God will have a free people, and while we have a duty to perform to preach the Gospel, we have another to perform, that is, to stand up in the defence of human rights—in the defence of our own rights, the rights of our children, and in defence of the rights of this nation and of all men, no matter who they may be, and God being our helper to maintain those principles and to lift up a standard for the honorable of this and other nations to flock to, that they may be free from the tyranny and oppression that is sought to be crowded upon them. This is a duty we have to perform, and in the name of Israel's God we will do it. It is a duty that our families demand of us; it is a duty that the honest in this nation demand of us, and that God demands of us; and we will try and carry it out, God being our helper. And if other people can afford to trample under foot the sacred institutions of this country, we cannot. And if other people trample upon the Constitution and pull it to pieces, we will gather together the pieces and rally around the old flag, or what is left of it, and proclaim liberty to the world, as Joseph Smith said we would."

John Taylor, Journal of Discourses, Vol. 23, p. 270, October 8, 1882.
    "We will leave the wicked in the hands of God: He will deal with them in his own way. We are told that the wicked shall slay the wicked; and one thing that I am sorry over in this nation is this: that they are striking at the tree of liberty and trying to fetter humanity and bring men into bondage, they are laying the axe at the root of this government, and unless they speedily turn round and repent and follow the principles they have sworn to sustain—the principles contained in the Constitution of the United States—they will be overthrown, they will be split up and divided, be disintegrated and become weak as water; for the Lord will handle them in his own way. I say these things in sorrow; but as sure as God lives unless there is a change of policy these things will most assuredly take place."

John Taylor, Journal of Discourses, Vol. 25, p. 215-217, June 29, 1884.
    "When the Government begins to break down the safeguards of society, tear in pieces the Constitution of the United States, and trample under foot the liberties of man, they are only preparing the nation for an utter overthrow. There are plenty of elements of discord and disintegration all around. Congress should not be the first to exhibit examples of lawlessness and the violation of Constitutional rights."

John Taylor, Journal of Discourses, Vol. 26, p. 155-157, February 1, 1885.
    "And while other men are seeking to trample the Constitution under foot, we will try to maintain it. We have prophecies something like this somewhere; that the time would come when this nation would do as they are now doing—that is, they would trample under foot the Constitution and institutions of the nation, and the Elders of this Church would rally around the standard and maintain those principles which were introduced for the freedom and protection of men. We expect to do that, and to maintain all correct principle. I will tell you what you will see by and by. You will see trouble, trouble, trouble enough in these United States. And as I have said before I say today, I tell you in the name of God, Woe! to them that fight against Zion, for God will fight against them. But let us be on the side of human liberty and human rights, and the protection of all correct principles and laws and government, and maintain every principle that is upright and virtuous and honorable, and let the world take the balance if they want, we don't want it. We will cleave to the truth, God being our helper, and try to introduce principles whereby the will of God will be done on earth as it is in heaven. And we will obey every institution of man for the Lord's sake so far as we can without violating our consciences and doing things that are wrong and improper."

John Taylor, The Gospel Kingdom, p. 166.
    "There are forces at work in the world that will in time overturn the world, which are today sapping the foundation of all government's and eating as a canker the foundation of all rule and dominion; and by and by their thrones will be cast down and nations and empires will be overturned, for God will arise to purge the world from its iniquities, its evils, and corruptions. And we have more

or less of the principles of insubordination among us."

John Taylor, The Gospel Kingdom, p. 310-311.

"By and by, you will find they will tear the Constitution to shreds, as they have begun now. They have started long ago to rend the Constitution of our country in pieces; and in doing so they are letting loose and encouraging a principle which will react upon themselves with terrible consequences. For if lawmakers and administrators can afford to trample upon justice, equity, and the Constitution of this country, they will find thousands and tens of thousands who are willing to follow in their wake in the demolition of the rights of man, and the destruction of all principles of justice, and the safeguards of the nation. But we will stand by and maintain its principles and the rights of all men of every color, and every clime. We will cleave to the truth, live our religion, and keep the commandments of God, and God will bless us in time and throughout the eternities that are to come. (JD 26:38-39, December 14, 1884.)"

Wilford Woodruff, Journal of Discourses, Vol. 19, p. 229, September 16, 1877.

"*An Incident at St. George Temple.* I will here say that two weeks before I left St. George, the spirits of the dead gathered around me, wanting to know why we did not redeem them. Said they, 'You have had the use of the Endowment House for a number of years, and yet nothing has ever been done for us. We laid the foundation of the government you now enjoy, and we never apostatized from it, but we remained true to it and were faithful to God.'

These were the signers of the Declaration of Independence, and they waited on me for two days and two nights. I thought it very singular, that notwithstanding so much work had been done, and yet nothing had been done for them. The thought never entered my heart, from the fact, I suppose, that heretofore our minds were reaching after our more immediate friends and relatives.

I straightway went into the baptismal font and called upon Brother McAllister to baptize me for the signers of the Declaration of Independence, and fifty other eminent men, making one hundred in all, including John Wesley, Columbus, and others. I then baptized him for every President of the United States, except three; and when their cause is just, somebody will do the work for them."

Wilford Woodruff, Journal of Discourses, Vol. 22, p. 345, October 23, 1881.

"We live in a government raised up by the God of heaven. We have a constitution that was given by inspiration from God to man. I believe it is the best human form of government that was ever given to the human family. Now, I say if our rulers and governors become corrupt and attempt to trample those principles under their feet; though the nation itself might go to pieces, yet it is beyond the power of man to destroy the principles of the constitution. They may destroy one another, yet the principles contained in that instrument will live, and the God of heaven will maintain them until Jesus Christ comes in the clouds of heaven to set up His throne in Jerusalem, and to reign on the earth a thousand years. . . .

Why, in the exercise of their religion, men must act: and it is straining points, it is overstepping the bounds of the Constitution to pass laws taking away the rights and privileges of any people because of their religion—because they happen to differ from their neighbors. Where will such a course land our government? I will tell you what it will do. It will rend the government in twain like unto a potter's vessel. It will lay the nation in the dust. It will overthrow the government. When they get through with the Mormons there will be somebody else to deal with. The Constitution is good enough for anybody. It is good enough for the Latter-day Saints. We have no principles but what are in accord with the Constitution of the United States and the laws of God. We are perfectly willing to trust ourselves and our interests in the hands of God, and to leave our nation in His hands also; for God will judge our nation; He will judge us; He will judge all the children of men and He will judge righteous judgment. What men sow they will reap. What measure they mete, it shall be measured to them again."

Wilford Woodruff, Journal of Discourses, Vol. 25, p. 11, January 6, 1884.

"And with regard to our nation, I leave them in the hands of God; but I would to God their eyes were open to see and understand the responsibilities that rest upon them. I would to God that the rulers of our land—the President of the United States, the Congress of the United States, the Supreme Court of the United States—would learn the responsibility the God of heaven will hold them to in the administration of those glorious principles laid down in the Constitution of the government of this country. The God of heaven will hold this nation, as well as all other nations, responsible for the manner in which these principles are used. If they misuse them, they will be held responsible, and will have to pay the bill. When innocent blood is shed, it costs something; and I would to God that our nation could understand the blessings they enjoy. There is no nation on the face of the earth that has the same liberty that is guaranteed to us by the Constitution of our country.

Have we any warfare with our Government? Have we any reproach to offer them? Not at all? I feel sorry that this nation should sow seeds which when ripe will bring destruction; for I know as God lives that if this or any other government departs from the principles of truth, becomes ripened in iniquity, forsakes the Lord, forsakes the principles of life and liberty, the God of heaven will hold it responsible. Judgments will come upon the wicked. When men depart from the principles of truth and cleave unto darkness and wickedness, they reap the whirlwind; they lay the foundation for desolation."

The Discourses of Wilford Woodruff, p. 188-189.

"As far as constitutional liberty is concerned, I will say, the God of heaven has raised up our nation, as foretold by his prophets generations ago. He inspired Columbus, and moved upon him to cross the ocean in search of this continent. . . .It is also well known how our forefathers found a home and an asylum in this land from the hand of persecution, and how they planted here the tree of liberty and jealously guarded it from the attempt of the mother country to uproot and destroy it. The hand of God was in this; and it is through the intervention of his providence that we enjoy today the freest and most independent government the world ever saw. And what was the object of this? It was to prepare the way for the building up of the kingdom of God in this the last dispensation of the fulness of times; and as long as the principles of constitutional liberty shall be maintained upon this land, blessings will attend the nation. (1889)"

Erastus Snow, Millennial Star, Vol. 47, p. 254, 1885.

"The time will come when this nation will trample the Constiution under foot, and override and set aside every one of its principles and safeguards in their attempts to crush and destroy this people. You can write this down in your note-books and keep it in mind, for it will surely come to pass."

Erastus Snow, Journal of Discourses, Vol. 24, p. 68, April 6, 1883.

"I deem it of much importance that these principles should be well understood and thoroughly impressed upon the minds of the Latter-day Saints throughout the world, and especially those dwelling upon this American Continent and within the pale of this government, that they may implant in the hearts of our children a love of freedom and human rights, and a desire to preserve them, and to aid in maintaining a defending them in all lawful and proper ways; and to study the constitutional laws of the land, and make others acquainted with them; knowing the principles contained therein, and of learning how to apply them to ourselves, to our children, and to our fellowmen who are willing to be governed thereby; study them that we may also learn how to use them in suppressing tyranny, misrule and other evils that affect mankind; for God has ordained this form of government in this age of the world, and has chosen His own instruments to further His great purposes on the earth—the organization of his Church, the proclamation of the everlasting Gospel, the establishment of His Zion, and bringing to pass His wonderful works which He predicted by the mouths of the ancient Prophets. And this political system and order of government is a power in His hands established, preserved and defended thus far by Him, which He will continue to use as long as the people are worthy of it, as long as they will maintain their integrity, uprightness and virtue; and at no time will the Latter-day Saints, as a people, ever stand approved before God in violating those principles or slackening their efforts to maintain and defend them. They are closely allied to the teachings of the ancient Prophets and Apostles, to the doctrines, practices and teachings of the Savior and His disciples, and they are the best means and aids of extending and promoting those principles on the earth. Whatever some may have thought of the mal-administration in our government and of the efforts of individuals and sometimes of large faction, to abridge the rights of the people, and of their blind zeal and efforts to reach the Latter-day Saints, and to stamp out the religion we profess—whatever may have been thought of the efforts of such individuals, cliques, or factions, and of their warfare trample under foot constitutional provisions of our Government—undermine the foundations upon which it rests—we must never in our feelings charge any of these things to this system of government, or to the principles enunciated is the Constitution, which we are commanded to observe and keep. We must charge it always where it belongs—to the bigotry, the ignorance, the selfishness, ambition and blind zeal of ignorant and corrupt politicians, their aiders and abettors, and all this should only serve to make us try more earnestly, anxiously and faithfully to combat such efforts upon constitutional grounds, calling upon God to help us therein."

Erastus Snow, Journal of Discourses, Vol. 26, p. 226-227, May 31, 1885.

"Well, we were told by the Prophet Joseph Smith, that the United States Government and people would come to this: that they would undermine one principle of the Constitution after another, until its whole fabric would be torn away, and that it would become the duty of the Latter-day Saints and those in sympathy with them to rescue it from destruction, and to maintain and sustain the principles of human freedom for which our fathers fought and bled. We look for these things to come in quick succession."

George Q. Cannon, Journal of Discourses, Vol. 18, p. 10-11, April 8, 1875.

"I expect to see the day when the Latter-day Saints will be the people to maintain constitutional government on this land. Men everywhere should know that we believe in constitutional principles, and that we expect that it will be our destiny to maintain them. That the prediction will be fulfilled that was made forty-four years ago the seventh of last March, wherein God said to Joseph Smith—'Ye hear of wars in foreign lands; but behold I say unto you, they are nigh, even at your doors, and not many years hence ye shall hear of wars in your own lands;' but the revelation goes on to say that the day will come among the wicked, that every man that will not take his sword against his neighbor, must needs flee unto Zion for safety. The causes are in operation to bring it about. We are not alone in the thought that the republic is drifting steadily in that direction; that we are leaving the old constitutional landmarks, and that the time is not far distant when there will be trouble in consequence of it, when there will be civil broils and strife; and, to escape them, we believe, men will be compelled to flee to the 'Mormons,' despised as they are now."

George Q. Cannon, Journal of Discourses, Vol. 20, p. 5-6, April 7, 1878.

"And as I have said often—for I have never failed to declare it—that the Latter-day Saints or 'Mormons' as we are called, expect it to be their destiny to uphold constitutional liberty on this continent, and to preserve our government and the forms thereof from overthrow and destruction. I have been taught from my boyhood that this was to be the destiny of the Latter-day Saints, and this people have been trained in the same belief, and we train our children to look forward to it, and to cherish the love of civil and religious liberty in their hearts, toleration for all men of every creed, of every nation, of every language and of every color, that all the sons and daughters of Adam, without exceptions, who dwell upon this broad land, may enjoy the inestimable blessing of liberty, and that it will be our favored and honored destiny, in the course of human events, unlikely as it may appear to-day to be the case, to preserve constitutional liberty in this land, which God has said shall be a land of liberty to all those who are righteous who dwell thereon. I have said, and I firmly believe, that the day will most assuredly come when the people of these mountains will become a great factor in the settlement of differences, in the preservation of human rights in the future, in the great contests which seem ready to burst upon us at any moment."

George Q. Cannon, Journal of Discourses, Vol. 20, p. 202-204, April 6, 1879.

"That is the kind of kingdom we have to contend for; that is the kind of kingdom we have to establish, and it is already provided for in the Constitution give unto us by God, and through the glorious labors of the fathers who aid the foundation of this government, who were inspired and raised by our Almighty Father for this express purpose. There is no liberty that a human being can desire, neither is there a right that can be exercised properly, that we do not have under the Constitution of our land. It needs no amendment about it; it is broad enough, if interpreted in its true spirit, to cover the individual, the continent, and the entire globe and furnish freedom for all."

George Q. Cannon, Journal of Discourses, Vol. 20, p. 339, October 6, 1879.

"It is not going to be a great while—and many of you will see it too—before there will be a great revolution in the earth. Just as sure as the Lord lives the day will come when there will be consternation not only in foreign nations but in our own nation. The people of this Republic are actually treading upon a volcano and they do not know how soon the fires may burst forth, how soon the governmental fabric of this nation, the most glorious the sun has ever shone upon, the best that man without the priesthood has had upon the earth, shall tumble. And why? Through the corruption of the people. The best government becomes the worst government when the people become corrupt, when bribery in high places rules, when political parties condescend to purchase votes. The power of a government is weakened when Senators, Representatives, and Presidents get their places by the use of money. Woe to a nation when this becomes the case. It is doomed and sooner or later it must fall. What is the remark respecting the election of United States Senators in many of the States? It is that a man cannot get that position except he be wealthy. What does that mean? Every one can draw his own conclusion. But that is not the worst feature either. There is disunion and animosity and the fires of sectional hatred burn fiercely. They may smoulder at times. They may not always appear on the surface. But let the breeze blow and quicken them into life and how fierce the flame burns."

George Q. Cannon, Journal of Discourses, Vol. 22, p. 136, July 3, 1881.

"Every man and woman who professes the faith of the Latter-day Saints, must love it, because, under it the development of the Kingdom of God is possible; for believing as we do that God inspired the founders of this government to perform the work which they accomplished; that He raised up men for the express purpose of achieving liberty upon this land, building up this grand fabric of free government, we must of necessity admire and have a deep attachment to its principles. While the people are pure, while they are upright, while they are willing to observe law, the best results must follow the establishment and maintenance of a government like this; but, on the other hand, if the people become corrupt, if they give way to passion, if they disregard law, if they trample upon consitutional obligations, then a republican form of government like ours becomes the worse tyranny upon the face of the earth."

George Q. Cannon, Journal of Discourses, Vol. 22, p. 180, June 12, 1881.

"And as these troubles increase of which Brother Woodruff has spoken—for they will increase, in our own land, too; they have increased, and they will increase—men will become unsettled in their minds as to what they will do and where they will seek for protection; for the day will come when stable government in these United States will be very hard to find. The elements are already operating that will produce this instability. Men will be glad to seek refuge, glad to seek protection, glad to live in any place where men and women are honest and true, and where the principles which Brother Woodruff has announced, the principles of true liberty are maintained, and God grant that they may be ever maintained."

George Q. Cannon, Journal of Discourses, Vol. 23, p. 104, November 20, 1881.

"But we came here to stay, here we expect to stay, and here we shall stay as long as we do right. And we shall not only stay here, but we shall spread abroad, and the day will come—and this is another prediction of Joseph Smith's—I want to remind you of it, my brethren and sisters, when good government, constitutional government—liberty—will be found among the Latter-day Saints, and it will be sought for in vain elsewhere; when the Constitution of this land and republican government and institutions will be upheld by this people who are now so oppressed and whose destruction is now sought so diligently. The day will come when the Constitution, and free government under it, will be sustained and preserved by this people."

George Q. Cannon, Journal of Discourses, Vol. 25, p. 274-275, August 31, 1884.

"For the day will come, and it is not far distant, when in our own nation, there will be civil strife, there will be domestic broils, there will be a withdrawal of peace, and men will yet have to come to the Latter-day Saints for that peace and that freedom from civil strife that cannot be found elsewhere. God revealed this and predicted it, upwards of fifty years ago, and it will, just as sure as He predicted it, be fulfilled to the letter. All we have to do is to take the course that He has pointed out to us, to keep His commandments, leaving the results with Him, and He will control all things for the glory of His name. We have been taught to believe that the time will come when constitutional government will be overthrown upon this land, and that it will be the province of the Latter-day to uphold those principles which God inspired the founders of this government to embody in the Constitution; and it seems to be fast approaching."

George Q. Cannon, Collected Discourses, Vol. 4, March 11, 1894.

"As a people we are utterly opposed to all forms of organization that contemplate, even in secret places, anything that will effect unfavorably the government of the United States. We are opposed to all factions that look to disorganization or to the impairing in any manner of the form of government and the liberties that we enjoy under it as citizens of the Republic. Our constant effort is to keep our people from joining these organizations."

George Q. Cannon, Collected Discourses, Vol. 5, April 5, 1897.

"God wants us to be a united people. I do not mean by this that we must all vote one ticket. But we can vote without quarreling and getting into a bad spirit. We should love the Lord, and be willing to be guided by Him, and we should listen to the voice of the Lord. What a power then the people would be! The Lord would come in a very little while; for the earth would be prepared for His coming. This is what we want; not for Latter-day Saints alone, but for this whole nation, which God loves, and which He established and made a free nation—the best, the strongest, and the most liberty-loving nation upon the face of the earth. And we love it because God has founded it. He raised up men to found it, and He gave it those forms of liberty which permitted this Church to be organized. This Church could not have been organized in any other land, or under any other form of government. Therefore, we love this land, we love this government, and we love the Constitution and the institutions of the land. We believe in the Constitution more than any other people, because we know it has been inspired of the Lord. Let not our people, therefore, divide, or go hither and thither after every will-o'-the-wisp there is in the land. The Lord wants us to be united, and wants the influence of this Church to be increased by the union of the people. He wants the influence of the

Priesthood of the Son of God elevated and strengthened in these mountains and among the nations. I tell it in great plainness, for it is the truth of heaven. And the possibilities that will result from this you cannot conceive of. God has chosen us expressly for this purpose and to do this work, and we cannot get out of it. Personally I tried to get out of this responsibility. The Lord revealed to me in my youth that I was to be an Apostle. In after years I besought Him that He would not choose me to hold this office, for I had seen what I would have to go through, and I shrunk from it. But we are chosen, and we cannot get out of it honorably."

Moses Thatcher, Journal of Discourses, Vol. 26, p. 334-335, October 8, 1885.

"There is no power in this land to turn this people against the government of the United States. They will maintain the Constitution of this country inviolate, and although it may have been torn to shreds they will tie it together again, and maintain every principle of it, holding it up to the downtrodden of every nation, kindred, tongue and people, and they will do it, too, under the Stars and Stripes. They will stand with their feet firmly upon the backbone of the American continent and maintain the principles which cost their fathers so much, and those principles cannot be taken away by men who violate their oath of office, and betray their trust."

Heber J. Grant, Improvement Era, July 1936. *Warning to Church Members,* p. 488.

"But Communism is not a political party nor a political plan under the Constitution; it is a system of government that is the opposite of our Constitutional government, and it would be necessary to destroy our government before Communism could be set up in the United States.

Since Communism, established, would destroy our American Constitutional government, to support Communism is treasonable to our free institutions, and no patriotic American citizen may become either a Communist or supporter of Communism.

To our Church members we say: Communism is not the United Order, and bears only the most superficial resemblance thereto; Communism is based upon intolerance and force, the United Order upon love and freedom of conscience and action; Communism involves forceful despoliation and confiscation, the United Order voluntary consecration and sacrifice.

Communists cannot establish the United Order, nor will Communism bring it about. The United Order will be established by the Lord in His own due time and in accordance with the regular prescribed order of the Church.

Furthermore, it is charged by universal report, which is not successfully contradicted or disproved, that Communism undertakes to control, if not indeed to proscribe the religious life of the people living within its jurisdiction, and that it even reaches its hand into the sanctity of the family circle itself, disrupting the normal relationship of parent and child, all in a manner unknown and unsanctioned under the Constitutional guarantees under which we in America live. Such interference would be contrary to the fundamental precepts of the Gospel and to the teachings and order of the Church.

Communism being thus hostile to loyal American citizenship and incompatible with true Church membership, of necessity no loyal American citizen and no faithful Church member can be a Communist.

We call upon all Church members completely to eschew Communism. The safety of our divinely inspired Constitutional government and the welfare of our Church imperatively demand that Communism shall have no place in America."

Heber J. Grant, Messages of the First Presidency, Vol. 6, p. 151,Conference Report, April 6, 1942, p. 90.

"We again warn our people in America of the constantly increasing threat against our inspired Constitution and our free institutions set up under it. The same political tenets and philosophies that have brought war and terror in other parts of the world are at work amongst us in America. The proponents thereof are seeking to undermine our own form of government and to set up instead one of the forms of dictatorship now flourishing in other lands. These revolutionists are using a technique that is as old as the human race,—a fervid but false solicitude for the unfortunate over whom they thus gain mastery, and then enslave them.

They suit their approaches to the particular group they seek to deceive. Among the Latter-day Saints they speak of their philosophy and their plans under it, as an ushering in of the United Order. Communism and all other similar isms bear no relationship whatever to the United Order. They are merely the clumsy counterfeits which Satan always devises of the gospel plan. Communism debases the individual and makes him the enslaved tool of the state to whom he must look for sustenance and religion; the United Order exalts the individual, leaves him his property, according to his family, according to his circumstances and his wants and needs, (D&C 51:3) and provides a system by which he helps care for his less fortunate brethren; the United Order leaves every man free to choose his own religion as his conscience directs. Communism destroys man's God-given free agency; the United Order glorifies it. Latter-day Saints cannot be true to their faith and lend aid, encouragement, or sympathy to any of these false philosophies. They will prove snares to their feet."

George Albert Smith, Conference Report, April 1947, p. 163.

"The Lord in his wisdom saw the necessity of giving us a nation in which we could thrive. In no other nation under heaven could the Church have been organized and gone forward as we have in this nation. The rounding of the United States was not an accident. The giving to us of the Constitution of the United States was not an accident. Our Heavenly Father knew what would be needed, and so he paved the way to give us the Constitution. It came under the influence of prayer, and he guided those who framed that wonderful document.

I hope that the membership of this Church will not be deceived into thinking that other plans, other forms of government, other systems of direction whatsoever, are desirable. I want to say to you without any hesitation that no form of government in the world can be compared favorably with the government God gave to us. This is his plan."

George Albert Smith, Conference Report, April 1948, p. 183.

"I am saying to you that to me the Constitution of the United States of America is just as much from my Heavenly Father as the Ten Commandments. When that is my feeling, I am not going to go very far away from the constitution, and I am going to try to keep it where the Lord started it, and not let anti-Christs come into this country that began because people wanted to serve God."

George Albert Smith, Journal of Discourses, Vol. 6, p. 85, November 29, 1857.

"An old principle, laid down from the earliest ages of British jurisprudence, from which we received our national institutions, is that allegiance is that ligament or thread which binds the subject to the sovereign, and that, for this allegiance, the sovereign, by an implied contract, owes, in turn, protection to the subject; and the very moment that the Government withholds its protection, that very moment allegiance ceases.

This is as old as the British constitution, and it is recognized as natural and eternal both in America and Great Britain; and you may trace this principle back through history to the earliest ages of man. The very moment a government ceases to protect its subjects, that moment they are at liberty to protect themselves."

David O. McKay, Conference Report, October 1939, p. 105.

"Latter-day Saints should have nothing to do with secret combinations and groups antagonistic to the Constitutional law of the land, which the Lord 'suffered to be established,' and which 'should be maintained for the rights and protection of all flesh, according to just and holy principles.'"

David O. McKay, Conference Report, April 1950, p. 37.

"In conclusion, I repeat that no greater immediate responsibility rests upon members of the Church, upon all citizens of this Republic and of neighboring Republics than to protect the freedom vouchsafed by the Constitution of the United States."

David O. McKay, BYU Speeches, May 18, 1960, p. 2.

"*Two Contending Forces.* Those forces are known and have been designated by different terms throughout the ages. 'In the beginning' they were known as Satan on the one hand, and Christ on the other.

In Joshua's time they were called 'gods of the Amorites,' for one, and 'the Lord,' on the other. Paul spoke of 'the works of the flesh' on the one hand, 'fruits of the spirit' on the other. They are often spoken of as 'selfishness' for one, 'life of service,' the other. In these days, they are called 'domination by the state,' on one hand, 'personal liberty,' on the other; communism on one hand, free agency on the other."

David O. McKay, Conference Report, April 1962, p. 125.

"J. Edgar Hoover, and I quote, says: 'There is no place here in America for part-time patriots. This nation is face to face with the greatest danger ever to confront it, a sinister and deadly conspiracy which can be conquered only by an alert, informed citizenry. It is indeed appalling that some members of our society continue to deplore and criticize those who stress the communist danger. Public indifference to this threat is tantamount to national suicide. Lethargy leads only to disaster. Knowledge of the enemy, alertness to the danger, everyday patriotism are the brick and mortar with which we can build an impregnable fortress against communism.'"

David O. McKay, *Statement Concerning the Position of the Church on Communism,* Priesthood Session, General Conference, April 9, 1966.

"The Church does not yield any of its devotion to or convictions about safeguarding the American principles and the establishments of government under federal and state constitutions and the civil rights of men safeguarded by these.

The position of this Church on the subject of Communism has never changed. We consider it the greatest satanical threat to peace, prosperity, and the spread of God's work among men that exists on the face of the earth. . . .

The entire concept and philosophy of Communism is diametrically opposed to everything for which the Church stands—belief in Deity, belief in the dignity and eternal nature of man, and the application of the gospel to efforts for peace in the world. Communism is militantly atheistic and is committed to the destruction of faith wherever it may be found. . . .

Communism debases the individual and makes him the enslaved tool of the state, to which he must look for sustenance and religion. Communism destroys man's God-given free agency.

No member of this Church can be true to his faith, nor can any American be loyal to his trust, while lending aid, encouragement, or sympathy to any of these false philosophies; for if he does, they will prove snares to his feet."

David O. McKay, Conference Report, October 1966, p. 5.

"Efforts are being made to deprive man of his free agency, to steal from the individual his liberty; and we must never forget that next to life itself free agency is the greatest gift of God to man."

David O. McKay, Conference Report, October 1968, p. 5.

"I believe that only through a truly educated citizenry can the ideals that inspired the founding fathers of our nation be preserved and perpetuated."

David O. McKay, Conference Report, October 1968, p. 6.

"We cannot, we must not, be insensible to the evil forces around us, and especially the communistic conspiracy, the avowed object of which is to destroy faith in God, to sow discord and contention among men with the view of undermining, weakening, if not entirely destroying, our constitutional form of government, and to weaken and subvert the ideals of our younger generation. When acts and schemes are manifestly contrary to the revealed word of the Lord, I feel, as do my associates, justified in warning our people against them."

David O. McKay, Gospel Ideals, p. 4-5.

"Religion is the most potent power in life. Spiritual development and moral integrity are fundamental in the lives not only of the Latter-day Saints but also of all who would build a community that will contribute to the safety and advancement of our republic or of any other nation. President Calvin Coolidge truly said that 'the government of a country never gets ahead of the religion of a country. There is no way by which we can substitute the authority of law for the virtue of man. Of course, we can help to restrain the vicious and furnish a fair degree of security and protection by legislation and police control, but the real reforms which society in these days is seeking will come as a result of our religious convictions or they will not come at all. Peace, justice, humanity, charity —these cannot be legislated into being. They are the results of a divine grace.' (CR, April 1934, p. 22 & CR, Oct. 1968, p. 8.)"

David O. McKay, Gospel Ideals, p. 304.
"Force rules in the world today; consequently, our government must keep armies abroad, build navies and air squadrons, create atom bombs to protect itself from the threatened aggression of a nation which seems to listen to no other appeal than compulsion. (CR, April 1950, p. 35.)"

David O. McKay, Gospel Ideals, p. 304.
"Individual freedom is threatened by international rivalries, interracial animosities, and false political ideals. Unwise legislation, too often prompted by political expediency, is periodically being enacted that seductively undermines man's right of free agency, robs him of his rightful liberties, and makes him but a cog in the crushing wheel of a regimentation which, if persisted in, will end in dictatorship. (CR, April 1950, p. 35.)"

David O. McKay, Gospel Ideals, p. 306.
"Of course there are errors in government which some would correct; certainly there are manifest injustices and inequalities; and there will always be such in any government in the management of which enter the frailties of human nature. If you want changes, go to the polls on election day. Express yourself as an American citizen, and thank the Lord for the privilege that is yours to have a say as to who shall serve you in public office. (CR, October 1939, p. 103-105.)"

David O. McKay, Gospel Ideals, p. 308.
"There is a danger even more menacing than the threat of invasion by a foreign foe. It is the unpatriotic activities and underhanded scheming of disloyal groups and organizations within our own borders. This country is so situated geographically that there need be little fear of invasion by an outside enemy. Furthermore, the government, knowing who and where the enemy is, can make ample preparation to meet his attacks. But the secret, seditious scheming of an enemy within our own ranks, hypocritically professing loyalty to the government, and at the same time plotting against it, is more difficult to deal with."

David O. McKay, Gospel Ideals, p. 312.
"Man's free agency is an eternal principle of progress, and any form of government that curtails or inhibits its free exercise is wrong. Satan's plan in the beginning was one of coercion, and it was rejected because he sought to destroy the agency of man which God had given him."

David O. McKay, Gospel Ideals, p. 319.
"Next to being one in worshiping God, there is nothing in this world upon which this Church should be more united than in upholding and defending the Constitution of the United States. (CR, October 1939, p. 105.)"

David O. McKay, Gospel Ideals, p. 486.

"The safety, the perpetuity of our government, or of an republican form of government, depends upon the safety and permanency of the home. Herein we get a glimpse of one thing in which this people may be the saviors, in a way, of this great nation. The home is the place where the perpetuation of the principles of liberty as well as the instructions in the gospel of Jesus Christ should be given to the children. When the home breaks up, then the children begin to wander off into sin. Then the law must reach out to bring them back and try to teach them some principles of service, and principles of true government; but, oh, how helpless, how helpless the state, when the home has failed! (CR, October 1917, p. 57.)"

Joseph Fielding Smith, Conference Report, April 1950, p. 159.

"The statement has been made that the Prophet said the time would come when this Constitution would hang as by a thread, and this is true.

Now I tell you it is time the people of the United States were waking up with the understanding that if they don't save the Constitution from the dangers that threaten it, we will have a change of government."

Joseph Fielding Smith, Church History and Modern Revelation, Vol. 2, p. 191-192.

"When we abide in the law which the Lord has approved, then we are free. It was his mighty hand which directed the founders of the government of the United States and gave this nation the constitution in the beginning. 'Nevertheless when the wicked rule,' saith the Lord, 'the people mourn.' (v. 9.) Even if the wicked rule, the saints do not have the right to take matters in their own hands in violation of the constitution in order to redress their wrongs. The constitutional law was given by inspiration for the purpose of protecting the rights of the citizens of the country. The Lord delights in freedom. Salvation is based upon this principle. There can be no compulsion in the kingdom of God. In the very beginning the Lord gave to man his freedom to act for himself to be an agent unto himself with the privilege, but not the right, to choose evil if he so desired, or to accept the truth which would make him free. In our government, we are taught to 'choose good and wise men' to hold office, and when they are chosen we should uphold them in their callings. As a people we have not lived up to this counsel. We have not always sought diligently and in prayer to know and choose wise and good men, but have turned from this course blindly because of political affiliation. Yet, when we do not seek humbly for wise and good men, 'whatsoever is less than these cometh of evil.'"

Joseph Fielding Smith, The Restoration of All Things, p. 247.

"On this earth the family is the unit which forms the government. Destroy the family and the government will perish. It must follow that in the government in heaven, thus officered by commissioned officers and subject to eternal laws, there must also be the family as the unit which forms that government, likewise there must be communities, cities and states, for earth is typical of things in heaven where all things are orderly. How could there be law and order with the family destroyed? The thought of such a thing on this earth as a progressive government, without the family is beyond the realm of reason. The laws governing in the kingdom of God are natural laws, for all the laws of nature are the laws of God. A government composed of individuals, without family ties is not the plan of the Lord either here or in heaven. In the eyes of the Lord individuals are not merely pawns controlled by the state."

Joseph Fielding Smith Jr., Doctrines of Salvation, Vol. 3, p. 315.
"Satan has control now. . . even in our own land. He is guiding the governments as far as the Lord will permit him. That is why there is so much strife, turmoil, and confusion . . .One master mind is governing the nations. It is not . . . the king or government of . . . any land; it is Satan himself."

Joseph Fielding Smith Jr., Doctrines of Salvation, Vol. 3, p. 317.
"I can see anarchy ahead of us. If we are going to permit men, in organized form, to desecrate the sacredness of the laws of this country and the Constitution . . . to take possession of that which does not belong to them, without protest, we are going to reap the whirlwind."

Joseph Fielding Smith Jr., Doctrines of Salvation, Vol. 3, p. 318.
"While it is a fact that men have turned from the Lord and have established their own governments, yet the Lord has never . . . wholly withdrawn and relinquished his rule and given over to the government of men the ruling of his earth without an accounting. He controls and directs, and he lets men go just as far as in his wisdom he desires they shall, and then he checks them."

Joseph Fielding Smith Jr., Doctrines of Salvation, Vol. 3, p. 361.
"Any member of this Church who will not sustain the established laws of the land is not only disloyal as a citizen of the government, but he is disloyal to his Church and disloyal to God. . . .We should be law-abiding . . . and at the same time have loyal hearts to the nations which bear rule."

Melvin J. Ballard, Conference Report, October 1938, p. 106.
"Thank the Lord for that promise. I am not afraid of any foreign foe disturbing this nation. Our perils will all come from within. It is true the Prophet saw even the Constitution hanging as by a thread, but, thank the Lord, he never saw the thread break. He saw this people become the savior and blessing of all flesh, not only the peoples of the United States. And after the experiments with dictatorships and other methods, they will, at last, when they have learned their lesson and are prepared for it, be willing to receive the Lord's offering, after much suffering."

J. Reuben Clark, Jr., Conference Report, April 1935, p. 93.
"To me, my brethren and sisters, that statement of the Lord, 'I have established the Constitution of this land,' puts the Constitution of the United States in the position in which it would be if it were written in this book of D&C itself. This makes the Constitution the word of the Lord to us. That it was given, not by oral utterance, but by the operation of his mind and spirit upon the minds of men, inspiring them to the working out of this great document of human government, does not alter its authority."

J. Reuben Clark, Jr., Conference Report, October 1941, p. 16.

"I have been preaching against Communism for twenty years. I still warn you against it, and I tell you that we are drifting toward it more rapidly than some of us understand, and I tell you that when Communism comes, the ownership of the things which are necessary to feed your families is going to be taken away from us. I tell you freedom of speech will go, freedom of the press will go, and freedom of religion will go.

I have warned you against propaganda and hate. We are in the midst of the greatest exhibition of propaganda that the world has ever seen, and all directed toward one end. Just do not believe all you read."

J. Reuben Clark, Jr., Conference Report, October 1942, p. 59.

"So, brethren, I wish you to understand that when we begin to tamper with the Constitution we begin to tamper with the law of Zion which God Himself set up, and no one may trifle with the word of God with impunity. . . .

I want to know what the man stands for. I want to know if he believes in the Constitution; if he believes in its free institutions; if he believes in its liberties, its freedom. I want to know if he believes in the Bill of Rights. I want to know if he believes in the separation of sovereign power into the three great divisions: the Legislative, the Judicial, the Executive. I want to know if he believes in the mutual independence of these, the one from the other. When I find out these things, then I know who it is who should receive my support, and I care not what his party tag is, because, brethren, if we are to live as a Church, and progress, and have the right to worship as we are worshipping here today, we must have the great guarantees that are set up by our Constitution. There is no other way in which we can secure these guarantees. You may look at the systems all over the world where the principles of our Constitution are not controlling and in force, and you will find there dictatorship, tyranny, oppression, and, in the last analysts, slavery.

. . .If we shall stand together we shall save the Constitution, just as has been foreseen, and if we do not stand together, we cannot perform this great task."

J. Reuben Clark, address at American Life Convention, Chicago, Illinois, October 7, 1943.

"Thus, and speaking in general terms, the Federal Government has reached down and touched the individual lives of the citizens in a multitude of matters which for a century and a half were held to be untouchable by that Government under those constitutional provisions which declared that the Federal Government is a government of delegated powers, and that unless powers are expressly given they are reserved by the people—who grant the powers—either to themselves or to their State Governments. Any proverbial school boy knows that the exercise by the Federal Government of a power not delegated to it by the people, is plain usurpation; so also he knows that any exercise by one department of the Federal Government of any power not expressly granted to it is a usurpation, whether that power be not granted at all to the Federal government by the people, or whether the people have in their Constitution granted that power to another department of the Government. These are merest commonplaces in constitutional law, but they are basic principles which are suffering daily violations.

Unless these usurpations are stopped, social, economic, and governmental chaos will come.

There are those who believe that the destructive influences wish chaos because they believe that out of it they can most easily build their projected communistic state here in America.

Now, obviously, if these unconstitutional practices and proceedings are to be stopped, if we are to regain our constitutional rights and the blessings of our free institutions, if we are to get back to the States and to the people the powers and rights that have been torn away from them, then we the people must assert ourselves,—through the courts, by the ballot, and in every other way open to us."

J. Reuben Clark, Jr., Conference Report, April 1944, p.116.

"Brethren, let us think about that, because I say unto you with all the soberness I can, that we stand in danger of losing our liberties, and that once lost, only blood will bring them back; and once lost, we of this Church will, in order to keep the Church going forward, have more sacrifices to make and more persecutions to endure than we have yet known, heavy as our sacrifices and grievous as our persecutions of the past have been."

J. Reuben Clark, Jr., address at Utah Wool Growers, Salt Lake City, Utah, January 24, 1945, p. 21.

"I have wished to bring together and to call to your attention a number of matters, the close relationship of which it is easy to miss, and to indicate to you that, so assembled, they make a pattern which cannot be accounted for except on the theory that some group of minds is working out a diabolical plan for the destruction of our liberties and freedom, our divinely inspired Constitution and the Government our fathers set up thereunder, and the wiping out of our constitutional guarantees and the free lives, the security, the happiness, and the blessings we have enjoyed thereunder."

J. Reuben Clark, Church News, December 14, 1946.

"Our present capital-labor relationship will surely lead us to economic destruction, and when that comes all the rest of our achievement will also disappear. Lincoln said we could not exist half slave and half free. He spoke politically. So we cannot exist half near-slave and half free economically. . . .

There are amongst us agents of an alien communistic ideology, and probably these agents are also, in considerable proportion, the paid agents of a foreign government. The purpose of these is to foment dissatisfaction, then disputes, then strikes and violence, then bloodshed, to the end of creating a condition of chaotic disorder, and then taking over our government and making us a member of a sovietized world."

J. Reuben Clark, Church News, November 22, 1947.

"In our course under the new gospel of interference with everything we do not like, we have gone forward and are going forward, as if we possessed all the good of human government, of human economic concept, of human comfort, and of human welfare, all of which we are to impose on the balance of the world, —a concept born of the grossest national egotism. In human affairs no nation can say that all it practices and believes is right, and that all that others have done that differs from what it has is wrong. Men inflict an unholy tragedy when they proceed on that basis. No man, no society, no people, no nation is wholly right in human affairs; and none is wholly wrong. A

172

fundamental principle of the operation of human society is to live and let live.

Yet, to repeat, we have entered into new fields to impose our will and concepts on others. This means we must use force, and force means war, not peace."

J. Reuben Clark, Church News, Sept 25, 1949.

"The plain and simple issue now facing us in America is freedom or slavery. . . .

Our real enemies are communism and its running mate, socialism. . . .

And never forget for one moment that communism and socialism are state slavery. . . .

Unfortunately, one thing seems sure, we shall not get out of our present difficulties without trouble, serious trouble. Indeed, it may well be that our government and its free institutions will not be preserved except at the price of life and blood. . . .

. . . the paths we are following that, if we move forward thereon, will inevitably lead us to socialism or communism, and these two are as like as two peas in a pod in the ultimate effect upon our liberties. . . .

We may first observe that communism and socialism—which we shall hereafter group together and dub Statism—cannot live with Christianity, nor with any religion that postulates a Creator such as the Declaration of Independence recognizes. The slaves of Statism must know no power, no authority, no source of blessing, no God, but the State. The State must be supreme in everything. . . .

. . . this country faces ahead enough trouble to bring us to our knees in humble, honest prayer to God for the help which he alone can give, to save us. . . .

Is any one so naive as to think that things will right themselves without a fight? There has been no more fight in us than there is in a bunch of sheep, and we have been much like sheep. Freedom was never brought to a people on a silver platter, nor maintained with whisk brooms and lavender sprays. . . .

And do not think that these usurpations, intimidations, and impositions are being done to us through inadvertence or mistake.

The whole course is deliberately planned and carried out; its purpose is to destroy the Constitution and our Constitutional government; then to bring chaos, out of which the new Statism with its slavery, is to arise, with a cruel, relentless, selfish, ambitious crew in the saddle, riding hard with whip and spur, a red-shrouded band of night riders for despotism. . . .

. . . if we do not vigorously fight for our liberties, we shall go clear through to the end of the road and become another Russia, or worse.

We have largely lost the conflict so far waged. But there is time to win the final victory, if we sense our danger and fight."

J. Reuben Clark, Jr., Vital Speeches 5:174-5 , quoted in "*Prophets, Principles, and National Survival*", (Newquist), p. 318-319, 1938.

"Reduced to its lowest terms, the great struggle which now rocks the whole earth more and more takes on the character of a struggle of the individual versus the state. Does the individual exist for the benefit of the State, or does the State exist for the benefit of the individual?. . .

This gigantic world-wide struggle, more and more takes on the form of a war to the death.

We shall do well and wisely so to face and so to enter it. And we must all take part. Indeed, we all are taking part in that struggle, whether we will or not. Upon its final issue, liberty lives or dies
. . .

In the economic field, this earth-wide conflict has taken the form of seizing without compensation from the man who has and giving to the man who has not, of taking from the worker the fruits of his work, and giving to the idler who does no work. It has from its very nature become an economic, uncompensated leveling downward, not upward, of the whole mass. This is the result in every country in which it has been tried. That this result may in one country be reaching by confiscatory taxation, and in another by direct seizure, is a mere matter of method. The result is the same. In some countries outright seizure and confiscation are already openly and shamelessly practiced. All is done in the name of the State, as if it were Deity—as if the State, not god, gave all."

J. Reuben Clark, Jr., Conference Report, October 1950, p. 171.
"Have you ever thought, and if you have not I suggest you do think about it, that if the civil government of any of our communities were to be suddenly wiped out, that the Church organization could govern the community if it were given the necessary civil sanction. To illustrate, our teachers who are to keep the Church in order, could act as the police force. Our bishops are authorized to hold court, the high council and the president of the stake another court, both of appellate and of original jurisdiction, with an appeal to the Presidency of the Church from that decision. And in the First Presidency of the Church, the President of the Church resides the power and authority to make all necessary rules and regulations for the government of the people. We have already, therefore, set up in this Church of ours, an organization of the Priesthood which could govern any community if it were given the necessary civil sanction, and if chaos should come, and if we travel along our present line far enough it will come, some of you may live to see the necessity of such an action as that."

J. Reuben Clark, Conference Report, April 1952, p. 80.
"If it (communism) comes here it will probably come in its full vigor and there will be a lot of vacant places among those who guide and direct, not only this government, but also this Church of ours."

J. Reuben Clark, "Some Fundamental Principles of Our Constitution", May 29, 1957, p. 34-43.
"In recent years the yen for a world-state in which we shall play a dominant part, has seemingly innoculated even some of our highest officials.

In furtherance of the general plan in contemplation of a world-state, we have made treaties of alliance containing obligations that infringed upon our sovereignty. We have made multipartite treaties—the League of Nations (which, when it was understood, the people rejected), the United Nations Charter, to which the Senate gave its advice and consent just one month and two days after its signature, the people having no time to examine its merits before it became operative. All of these surrendered some of our sovereignty. . . .

One now holding high government office is quoted as declaring:

`. . . congressional laws are invalid if they do not conform to the Constitution, whereas treaty laws can override the Constitution. Treaties, for example, can take powers away from the Congress and give them to the President; they can take powers from the States and give them to the Federal Government or to some international body and they can cut across the rights given the people by the Constitutional Bill of Rights.' (Frank E. Holman, Story of the Bricker Amendment, p 14-15.)

. . . It was never contemplated by the Framers that this (treaty-making) power should be subverted in an effort to destroy our independence as a nation and make us a subservient part of a world-state.

How earnestly Washington, a fond and wise `Father of his Country,' in his poignant Farewell Address, with prophetic admonition and warning, urged us against foreign entanglements and alliances: `Why,' he said, `by interweaving our destiny with that of any part of Europe, entangle our peace and prosperity in the toils of European ambition, rivalship, interest, humor, or caprice?'

How much more serious an interweaving of our destinies with the whole family of nations!

It has already been said that to an out-sider this new theory of treaty-law is a device to secure our participation in a world-state. The visionary beauties of this state, its advantages, its blessings to humanity, are dressed for us as if this were some modern concept now for the first time blossoming in the earth,—a sort of flower of paradise.

The Constitution is a part of my religion. . . .

It is His plan for the government of free men.

There will be no permanent peace until He comes to reign whose right it is to reign."

J. Reuben Clark, quoted in *"Prophets, Principles, and National Survival"*, (Newquist), p. 458.

"There seems no reason to doubt that such real approval as the Charter (United Nations) has among the people is based upon the belief that if the Charter is put into effect, wars will end . . . The Charter will not certainly end war. Some will ask — why not? In the first place, there is no provision in the Charter itself that contemplates ending war. It is true the charter provides for force to bring peace, but such use of force is itself war . . . The Charter is built to prepare for war, not to promote peace . . . The Charter is a war document not a peace document. . . .

Not only does the Charter Organization not prevent future wars, but it makes it practically certain that we will have future wars, and as to such wars it takes from us the power to declare them, to choose the side on which we shall fight, to determine what forces and military equipment we shall use in the war, and to control and command our sons who do the fighting."

Harold B. Lee, Conference Report, April 1950, p. 96.

"If we were united as a people in electing honorable men to high places in our civil government, regardless of the political party with which we have affiliation, we would be able to safeguard our communities and to preserve law and order among us. Our failure to be united means that we permit tyranny and oppression and taxation to the extent of virtual confiscation of our own property."

Harold B. Lee, Conference Report, October 1952, p. 18.

"It was Joseph Smith who has been quoted as having said that the time would come when the Constitution would hang as by a thread, and at that time when it was thus in jeopardy, the elders of this Church would step forth and save it from destruction.

Why the elders of this Church? Would it be sacrilegious to paraphrase the words of the Apostle Peter, and say that the Constitution of the United States could be saved by the elders of this Church because this Church and this Church alone has the words of eternal life? We alone know by revelation as to how the Constitution came into being, and we, alone, know by revelation the destiny of this nation. The preservation of 'life, liberty and the pursuit of happiness' can be guaranteed upon no other basis than upon a sincere faith and testimony of the divinity of these teachings."

Harold B. Lee, Youth & the Church, 1970, p. 219-220.

"To those of you who are striving to serve the God of this land and thus realize the promised blessings of national security, and yet who observe the flood of wickedness among the millions of this country who blaspheme the name of Jesus Christ rather than serve him, the Lord gives this comfort:

'Therefore, verily, thus saith the Lord, let Zion rejoice, for this is Zion—THE PURE IN HEART; therefore, let Zion rejoice, while all the wicked shall mourn. . . .The Lord's scourge shall pass over by night and by day, and the report thereof shall vex all people; yea, it shall not be stayed until the Lord come; . . . Nevertheless, Zion shall escape if she observe to do all things whatsoever I have commanded her. But if she observe not to do whatsoever I have commanded her, I will visit her according to all her works, with sore affliction, with pestilence, with plague, with sword, with vengeance, with devouring fire. (D&C 97:21-26.)"

Harold B. Lee, Youth & the Church, 1970, p. 219-221.

"Contained within the principles of that great heaven-inspired document is the message of this Church to the world in this fateful hour. Except the spirit of the Gospel of Jesus Christ and principles contained within the Constitution of the United States are inherent in world plans now being formulated, they are but building on sand and the Lord is not in that building. . . .

Where is that ideal which the world must pursue in setting up a world community? That ideal was written more than nineteen centuries ago by the Prince of Peace in these words: 'Thou shalt love the Lord thy God with all thy heart, and with all thy soul, and with all thy mind. This is the first and great commandment. And the second is like unto it, Thou shalt love thy neighbour as thyself. On these two commandments hang all the law and the prophets.' (Matthew 22:37-40.). . . .

A society in which men recognize no check upon their freedom soon becomes a society where freedom is in possession of only a few who lust for power and domination.   It was Abraham Lincoln who with uncanny foresight warned this nation against the logical results that could come from growing lawlessness where Caesars and Napoleons could be born to dictatorships within a democracy. Then as though he foresaw the probability of such an emergency, he points out our responsibilities in these solemn words: 'And when such an one does (spring up among us), it will require the people to be united with each other, attached to the government and the laws, and generally intelligent, successfully to frustrate his design.' (Abraham Lincoln, Man of God, p. 74.)"

Harold B. Lee, Prophet and Seer, 1985, p. 532.

"If the basic principles laid down in the Constiution were to be threatened, as is now a possibility, that we might come to (such) a time as when Abraham bargained with the Lord to save Sodom and Gomorrah from destruction, if he could find some righteous souls. Similarly, if such a downfall of the Constitution were imminent, the righteousness of this people might again importune the Almighty to save it because of their pleadings."

Ezra Taft Benson, Conference Report, October 1954, p. 121.

"So, today, I would like to throw out a challenge to the elders of Israel, my brethren of the priesthood, that we put forth an effort to prepare ourselves for statesmanlike work. The Prophet Joseph, as you will recall, had something to say regarding the important part which the elders of Israel would play in the safeguarding, if not the saving, of the Constitution of this land."

Ezra Taft Benson, Conference Report, October 1958, p. 99-100.

"It has been truly said by our present Chief Executive that, 'The federal government did not create the states of this Republic. The states created the federal government . . . —if the states lose their meaning our entire system of government loses its meaning and the next step is the rise of the centralized national state in which the seeds of autocracy can take root and grow. These are strong but true words.

The history of all mankind shows very clearly that if we would be free—and if we would stay free—we must stand eternal watch against the accumulation of too much power in government."

Ezra Taft Benson, BYU Speeches, May 24, 1961, p.7.

"We have heard that the Prophet Joseph said something about the time when the Constitution would be in danger. We do not know just what turn that will take. He also said something about the Elders of Israel rising to the challenge and helping to save the Constitution of this land. It is entirely possible that that may come about in a rather natural way. Our young people—as they mature and develop and take their positions in industry, in the professions, and in agriculture clear across this land—might represent the balance of power in a time of crisis, when they will stand up and defend those eternal principles upon which this Constitution has been established."

Ezra Taft Benson, Church News, September 2, 1961, p. 14.

"Others will say there is no danger in socialism - in policies that would weaken and destroy our private enterprise system. Socialism, they say, has no relationship to Communism.

It is my conviction that the paramount issue today is liberty against creeping socialism. Collectivized socialism is part of the Communist strategy. Communist dupes and left-wingers use every stratagem to make socialism sound appealing and seem inevitable. Their aims for the U.S. include greatly expanded wasteful spending, higher and higher taxes, increasingly unbalanced budgets, wild inflation followed by government controls over our economy and lives, greater centralization of power in Washington and so on ad infinitum.

We will never win our fight against Communism by making concessions to socialism."

Ezra Taft Benson, Conference Report, October 1961, p. 70.

"Today the devil as a wolf in a supposedly new suit of sheep's clothing is enticing some men, both in and out of the Church, to parrot his line by advocating planned government guaranteed security programs at the expense of our liberties. Latter-day Saints should be reminded how and why they voted as they did in heaven. If some have decided to change their vote they should repent—throw their support on the side of freedom—and cease promoting this subversion. . . .

He (Moroni) foresaw the rise of a great world-wide secret combination. . .He warned each gentile nation of the last days to purge itself of this gigantic criminal conspiracy which would seek to rule the world. . . .The Prophet Moroni described how the secret combination would take over a country and then fight the work of God, persecute the righteous, and murder those who resisted. Moroni therefore proceeded to describe the workings of the ancient 'secret combinations' so that modern man could recognize this great political conspiracy in the last days. . . .

The Prophet Moroni seemed greatly exercised lest in our day we might not be able to recognize the startling fact that the same secret societies which destroyed the Jaredites and decimated numerous kingdoms of both Nephites and Lamanites would be precisely the same form of criminal conspiracy which would rise up among the gentile nations in this day."

Ezra Taft Benson, BYU Speeches, February 28, 1962, p. 4-5.

"Meantime our people have come to look to the federal government as the provider, at no cost to them, of whatever is needful. If this trend continues, the states may be left hollow shells, operating primarily as the field districts of federal departments and depending upon the federal treasury for their support. . . .

Thomas Jefferson, while President of the United States, expressed what I hope and pray is the conviction of all of us. Mark carefully his wise declaration. 'I have sworn upon the altar of God eternal hostility against any form of tyranny over the minds and lives of men. To preserve our independence, we must not let our rulers load us with perpetual debt. We must take our choice between economy and liberty, or profusion and servitude. If we run into such debts, we must be taxed in our meat and drink, in our necessities and in our comforts, in our labors and in our amusements. If we can prevent the government from wasting the labor of the people under the pretense of caring for them, they will be happy.'

That government is best which governs the least, so taught the courageous founders of this nation. This simple declaration Is diametrically opposed to the all too common philosophy that the government should protect and support one from the cradle to the grave. The policy of the Founding Fathers has made our people and our nation strong. The opposite philosophy leads inevitably to moral decay."

Ezra Taft Benson, Conference Report, April 1962, p. 105.

"We must return to a love and respect for the basic spiritual concepts upon which this nation has been established. We must study the Constitution and the writings of the founding fathers.

Yes, we must protect the Lord's base of operations by moving away from unsound economic policies which encourage creeping socialism and its companion, insidious, atheistic communism. If we are to protect this important base we must as a nation live within our means, balance our budgets, and pay our debts. We must establish sound monetary policies and take needed steps to compete in world markets.

If we are to protect this American base, we must realize that all things, including information disseminated by our schools, churches, and government, should be judged according to the words of the prophets, especially the living prophet. This procedure coupled with the understanding which will come through the Spirit of the Lord, if we are living in compliance with the scriptures, is the only sure foundation and basis of judgment. Any other course of action leaves us muddled, despondent, wandering in shades of gray, easy targets for Satan."

Ezra Taft Benson, Conference Report, October 1962, p. 14.

"It is difficult for Americans to understand the danger to our liberty. It is generally outside the range of our experience. But we live today in an age of peril. We are threatened with the loss not only of material wealth but of something far more precious—our liberty itself.

Never before in the history of our country has there been a greater need for all of our people to take time to discover what is happening in the world. Every day decisions are being made affecting the lives of millions of human beings.

We as a people have never known bondage. Liberty has always been our blessed lot. Few of us have ever seen people who have lost their freedom—their liberty. And when reminded of the danger of losing our liberty and independence our attitude has usually been: It cannot happen here."

Ezra Taft Benson, Conference Report, October 1962, p. 17.

"It is almost unthinkable that any people would knowingly and willfully take on themselves the yoke of communist oppression ... As a people who have known only liberty, we are inclined to feel, it cannot happen here. We have become lulled away into a false security . . . I say to you it can happen here. It is happening here. We have retreated from the Monroe Doctrine. Our liberty is in danger. But we go blithely and gullibly on our way. Some of us fall for the Kremlin line as planned by the mass murderer, Khruschev and call patriots `extremists' and accuse courageous liberty-loving citizens of `dividing our people'."

Ezra Taft Benson, Conference Report, October 1963, p. 16.

"His (Satan's) main attack is still on free agency. When he can get men to yield their agency, he has them well on the way to captivity.

We who hold the priesthood must beware concerning ourselves, that we do not fall into the traps he lays to rob us of our freedom. We must be careful that we are not led to accept or support in any way any organization, cause or measure which, in its remotest effect, would jeopardize free agency, whether it be in politics, government, religion, employment, education, or any other field. It is not enough for us to be sincere in what we support. We must be right!'. . .

It was the struggle over free agency that divided us before we came here; it may well be the struggle over the same principle which will deceive and divide us again."

Ezra Taft Benson, Conference Report, October 1963, p. 19.

"Let us not be deceived in the sifting days ahead. Let us rally together on principle behind the prophet as guided by the promptings of the Spirit.

We should continue to speak out for freedom and against socialism and communism as President McKay has consistently admonished us. We should continue to come to the aid of patriots, programs and organizations which are trying to save our Constitution through every legal and moral means possible."

Ezra Taft Benson, BYU Speeches, December 10, 1963, p. 13.

"Today, Walt Whitman Rostow, who is the chief planner for the State Department, has expressed a dangerous point of view somewhat like this: We must do everything in our power to avoid irritating and antagonizing the Communists. They are, after all, merely rough and crude Socialists and we must avoid doing anything that would escalate into a war. In fact, what we should do is to help them to develop so that they will mature and outgrow their violent impulses. In this way the Communists will move somewhat over in our direction. At the same time we must move our country over toward the left with more and more socialism until, ultimately, the two will merge. Each country will then give up its armaments and armed forces and place them in the hands of a One-World Government. (See the book, A Proposal: Key to an Effective Foreign Policy, by Wait W. Rostow and Max F. Millikan, Harper, New York, 1957. An outgrowth of the Dartmouth Conference in the fall of 1960 and the Crimea Conference of May, 1961, was the pamphlet, Freedom from War, the United States Program for General and Complete Disarmament in a Peaceful World, U.S. State Department Publication No. 7277, Disarmament Series 5, released September, 1961, U.S. Government Printing Office.)

And Arthur Schlessinger, Jr., former professor of history at Harvard and now high in the councils of government, has said: 'There seems no inherent obstacle to the gradual advance of socialism in the U.S. through a series of New Deals,' and, that socialism appears quite practical as a long time proposition.

In either case the whole tendency is toward more and more GOVERNMENTISM, more and more centralization and less and less individual responsibility and freedom."

Ezra Taft Benson, BYU Speeches, December 10, 1963, p. 17.

"The scriptures tell us about the war in heaven over free agency—similar to the war we are going through now, where the devil's program was guaranteed security as opposed to the Lord's program of letting each choose for himself even if he makes the wrong choice. Once you understand these scriptures you will understand why the Presidents of the Church have opposed Communism, Socialism, and the Welfare State and you will see why you must oppose them, too, if you are in harmony with the word of the Lord."

Ezra Taft Benson, Conference Report, April 1965, p. 121.

"The Prophet Joseph Smith declared it will be the elders of Israel who will step forward to help save the Constitution, not the Church. And have we elders been warned? Yes, we have. And have we elders been given the guide lines? Yes indeed, we have. And besides, if the Church should ever inaugurate a program, who do you think would be in the forefront to get it moving? It would not be those who were sitting on the sidelines prior to that time or those who were appeasing the enemy. It would be those choice spirits who, not waiting to be 'commanded in all things,' used their own free will, the counsel of the prophets and the Spirit of the Lord as guidelines and who entered the battle 'in a good cause' and brought to pass much righteousness in freedom's cause. . . .

Brethren, if we had done our homework and were faithful, we could step forward at this time and help save this country. The fact that most of us are unprepared to do it is an indictment we will have to bear. The longer we wait, the heavier the chains, the deeper the blood, the more the persecution and the less we can carry out our God-given mandate and world-wide mission. The war in heaven is raging on earth today. Are you being neutralized in the battle?"

Ezra Taft Benson, BYU Speeches, May 10, 1966, p. 3.

"However, virtue is not the only basis for being singled out and promoted. As the world becomes more wicked, a possible way to attain worldly success may be to join the wicked. The time is fast approaching when it will require great courage for Latter-day Saints to stand up for their peculiar standards and doctrine—all of their doctrine, including the more weighty principles such as the principle of freedom. Opposition to this weighty principle of freedom caused many of our brothers and sisters in the pre-existence to lose their first estate in the war in heaven.

We are far removed from the days of our forefathers who were persecuted for their peculiar beliefs. Some of us seem to want to share their reward but are ofttimes afraid to stand up for principles that are controversial in our generation. We need not solicit persecution, but neither should we remain silent in the presence of overwhelming evils, for this makes cowards of men. We should not go out of the path of duty to pick up a cross there is no need to bear, but neither should we sidestep a cross that clearly lies within the path of duty."

Ezra Taft Benson, "Our Immediate Responsibility", BYU, October 25, 1966.

"Our Republic and Constitution are being destroyed while the enemies of freedom are being aided. How? In at least ten ways:

1. By diplomatic recognition and aid, trade and negotiations with the Communists.
2. By disarmament of our military defenses.
3. By destruction of our security laws and the promotion of atheism by decisions of the Supreme Court.
4. By loss of sovereignty and solvency through international commitments and membership in world organizations.
5. By undermining of local law enforcement agencies and Congressional investigating committees.
6. By usurpations by the Executive and Judicial branches of our Federal Government.
7. By lawlessness in the name of civil rights.
8. By a staggering national debt with inflation and a corruption of the currency.
9. By a multiplicity of executive orders and federal programs which greatly weaken local and state governments.
10. By the sacrifice of American manhood by engaging in wars we apparently have no intention of winning. . . .

I warn you, unless we wake up soon and do something about the conspiracy, the communist-inspired civil rights riots of the past will pale into insignificance compared to the bloodshed and destruction that lie ahead in the near future. . . .

As members of the Church we have some close quarters to pass through if we are to save our souls. . .The Lord is letting the wheat and the tares mature before he fully purges the church. He is testing you to see if you will be misled. The devil is trying to deceive the very elect.

Have you counted the cost if our countrymen, and especially the body of the priesthood, continue to remain complacent, misled through some of our news media, deceived by some of our officials, and perverted by some of our educators?"

Ezra Taft Benson, Conference Report, April 1967, p. 61-62.

"A man must not only stand for the right principles, but he must also fight for them. Those who fight for principle can be proud of the friends they've gained and the enemies they've earned. . . .

We are going through the greatest, most insidious propaganda campaign of all time. Even the character-destroying 'credibility gap' seems to be gaining respectability. We cannot believe all we read, and what we can believe is not all of the same value. We must sift. We must learn by study and prayer.

Study the scriptures and study the mortals who have been most consistently accurate about the most important things. When your freedom and your eternal welfare are at stake, your information best be accurate. . . .

Righteous concern about conditions is commendable when it leads to constructive action. But undue worry is debilitating. When we have done what we can do, then let's leave the rest to God."

Ezra Taft Benson, Conference Report, October 1967, p. 36.

"Total government is the objective of Communism. Without calling it by name, build Communism piece by piece through mass pressures for presidential decrees, court orders, and legislation that appear to be aimed at improving civil rights and other social reforms. If there is social, economic, or educational discrimination, then advocate more government programs and control.

And what if riots come? Then more government housing . . . welfare, government job training, and, finally, federal control over police. Thus the essential economic and political structure of Communism can be built entirely 'legally' and in apparent response to the wishes of the people who have clamored for some kind of solution to the problems played-up, aggravated, or created outright . . . After the machinery of Communism is firmly established, then allow the hidden Communists one by one to make their identities known. Liquidate first the anti-Communists and then the non-Communist sympathizers who are no longer needed in government. The total state mechanism can now openly and 'peacefully' be transferred into the hands of Communists. Such is the so-called proletarian revolution. Such has happened in other, once free, countries. It has already started here."

Ezra Taft Benson, Conference Report, October 1967, p. 38-39.

"But, in questions of money, great care should be taken not to accept grants from the federal government. Along with federal money, inevitably there will come federal controls and guidelines that not only may get local police embroiled in national politics, but may even lead to the eventual creation of a national police force. Every despotism requires a national police force to hold the people in line. Communism is no exception. Our local police should remain free from federal control."

Ezra Taft Benson, Conference Report, April 1968, p. 49-50.

"I do not believe the greatest threat to our future is from bombs or guided missiles. I do not think our civilization will die that way. I think it will die when we no longer care, when the spiritual forces that make us wish to be right and noble die in the hearts of men, when we disregard the importance of law and order. . . .

If America is destroyed, it may be by Americans who salute the flag, sing the national anthem, march in patriotic parades, cheer Fourth of July speakers—normally good Americans, but Americans who fail to comprehend what is required to keep our country strong and free—Americans who have been lulled away into a false security.

Great nations are never conquered from outside unless they are rotten inside. Our greatest national problem today is erosion, not the erosion of the soil, but erosion of the national morality—erosion of traditional enforcement of law and order. . . . In this blessed land we have exalted security, comfort, and ease above freedom."

Ezra Taft Benson, Conference Report, October 1968, p. 20-21.

"Once government steps over this clear line between the protective or negative role into the aggressive role of redistributing the wealth through taxation and providing so-called 'benefits' for some of its citizens, it becomes a means for legalized plunder. It becomes a lever of unlimited power that is the sought-after prize of unscrupulous individuals and pressure groups, each seeking to control the machine to fatten his own pockets or to benefit his favorite charity, all with the other fellow's money, of course. Each class or special interest group competes with the others to throw the lever of governmental power in its favor, or at least to immunize itself against the effects of a previous thrust. . . .In the end, no one is much further ahead, and everyone suffers the burdens of a gigantic bureaucracy and a loss of personal freedom. With each group out to get its share of the spoils, such governments historically have mushroomed into total welfare states. Once the process begins, once the principle of the protective function of government gives way to the aggressive or redistributive function, then forces are set in motion that drive the nation toward totalitarianism.

No government in the history of mankind has ever created any wealth. People who work create wealth. . . .Any attempt through governmental intervention to redistribute the material rewards of labor can only result in the eventual destruction of the productive base of society, without which real abundance and security for more than the ruling elite is quite impossible."

Ezra Taft Benson, Conference Report, October 1969, p. 61.

"Today we face insidious, devastating evils that are widespread. Aimed especially at the destruction of America—the last great bastion of freedom—with emphasis on our youth, the evils are everywhere, sponsored, promoted, and directed by the Communist conspiracy, fellow travelers, and dupes. Never has evil been presented in such an array of appealing forms. We face a most dangerous revolution in America, and it is now in progress. According to the FBI, 'It is well-planned, well-financed, and well-armed.'. . .

These atrocious, destructive evils are now revealed in our music, in our art, in sex perversion and so-called sex education in the schools, in destructive sensitivity training—a powerful form of Pavlovian brainwashing . . . These evils are prominent in the promotion of drugs . . . in TV, movie, and radio programs, in pornographic literature, in morally destructive paperback books . . .

These devilish forces 'led generally by dirty minds in dirty bodies,' seem to be everywhere. They are spreading into every segment of our social, economic, and religious life—all aimed at the destruction of one whole generation of our choice youth in preparation for the Communist takeover.

The godless Communists have declared, 'We are going to destroy the moral character of a generation of young Americans, and when we have finished you will have nothing with which to really defend yourself against us.'"

Ezra Taft Benson, *"America's Challenge Address"*, Boston, July 4, 1970.

"International Communism is the self-avowed enemy of every loyal American. It has declared war against us and fully intends to win. The war in which we are engaged is total. Although its main battlefields are psychological, political, and economic, it also encompasses revolution, violence, terror, and limited military skirmishes.

And now I wish to reveal one of the greatest tragedies of all time—and a fact that an increasing number of us are gradually coming to realize—and that is this: The growth and increasing success of communism around the world has been primarily the result of the support, yes, increasing support, which it has received from right within the United States, and particularly from our own government. . . .

Now some people may feel that this has just been stupidity on our part and the mistakes of mortal men who really mean well but did not realize what they were doing. I agree that there has been some stupidity on the part of some people—but consistency has never been a hallmark of stupidity. I believe it was Forrestal who said that if it were just stupidity, then we would have made a few more mistakes on our side now and then, because stupidity is not consistent."

Ezra Taft Benson, Conference Report, Ensign, July 1972, p. 60.

"Joseph Smith said that the Book of Mormon was the `keystone of our religion' and the `most correct' book on earth. (DHC, vol. 6, p. 56) This most correct book on earth states that the downfall of two great American civilizations came as a result of secret conspiracies whose desire was to overthrow the freedom of the people. `And they have caused the destruction of this people of whom I am now speaking', says Moroni, `and also the destruction of the people of Nephi.' (Ether 8:21)

Now undoubtedly Moroni could have pointed out many factors that led to the destruction of the people, but notice how he singled out the secret combinations, just as the Church today could point out many threats to peace, prosperity, and the spread of God's work, but it has singled out as the greatest threat the Godless conspiracy. There is no conspiracy theory in the Book of Mormon —it is a conspiracy fact."

Ezra Taft Benson, Conference Report, May 1976, p. 91.

"On April 6, 1789 . . . the Constitution of the United States went into operation as the basic law of the United States when the electoral college unanimously elected George Washington as the first president of the nation. This date, I believe, was not accidental."

184

The Government & the Constitution

Ezra Taft Benson, Conference Report, Ensign, November 1979, p. 33.

"I say with all the energy of my soul that unless we as citizens of this nation forsake our sins, political and otherwise, and return to the fundamental principles of Christianity and of constitutional government, we will lose our political liberties, our free institutions, and will stand in jeopardy before God.

No nation which has kept the commandments of God has ever perished, but I say to you that once freedom is lost, only blood—human blood—will win it back.

There are some things we can and must do at once if we are to stave off a holocaust of destruction.

First: We must return to worship the God of this land, who is Jesus Christ. He has promised that the righteous will be preserved by His power (see 1 Ne. 22:17). But we must keep the commandments of God.

Second: We must awaken to a sense of our awful situation, because of this secret combination which is among us (Ether 8:24). . . .

Third: We must do as the Lord commanded us by revelation in 1833: `Wherefore, honest men and wise men should be sought for diligently, and good men and wise men ye should observe to uphold; otherwise whatsoever is less than these cometh of evil' (D&C 98:10). . . .

Last: We must study the inspired Constitution and become involved in the political process ourselves . . .

I fully believe that we can turn things around in America if we have the determination, the morality, the patriotism, and the spirituality to do so."

Ezra Taft Benson, First Presidency Message (to be read in Sacrament meeting), Jan. 15, 1987.

"We encourage Latter-day Saints throughout the nation to familiarize themselves with the Constitution. They should focus attention on it by reading it and studying it. They should ponder the blessings that come through it. They should recommit themselves to its principles and be prepared to defend it and the freedom it provides (D&C 109:54).

Citizens of this nation are free to participate in efforts designed to warn of the threat of any force or power, theory or principle, that would deprive them of their freedom or the individual liberties vouchsafed by the Constitution.

Because some Americans have not kept faith with our Founding Fathers, the Constitution faces severe challenges. Those who do not prize individual freedom are trying to erode its great principles. We believe the Constitution will stand, but it will take the efforts of patriotic and dedicated Americans to uphold it. . . .We, as Latter-day Saints must be vigilant in doing our part to preserve the Constitution and safeguard the way of life it makes possible."

Ezra Taft Benson, Conference Report, Ensign, November 1987, p. 6-7.

"Unfortunately, we as a nation have apostatized in various degrees from different Constitutional principles as proclaimed by the inspired founders. We are fast approaching that moment prophesied by Joseph Smith when he said, 'Even this nation will be on the very verge of crumbling to pieces and tumbling to the ground, and when the constitution is upon the brink of ruin, this people will be the staff upon which the nation shall lean, and they shall bear the Constitution away from the very verge of destruction.' (July 19, 1840). . . .

I reverence the Constitution as a sacred document. To me it's words are akin to the revelations of God, for God has placed His stamp of approval upon it.

I testify that the God of heaven sent some of His choicest spirits to lay the foundations of the government, and He has now sent other choice spirits to help preserve it."

Ezra Taft Benson, Conference Report, Ensign, November 1988, p. 87.

"I testify that wickedness is rapidly expanding in every segment of our society. It is more highly organized, more cleverly disguised, and more powerfully promoted than ever before. Secret combinations lusting for power, gain, and glory are flourishing. A secret combination that seeks to overthrow the freedom of all lands, nations, and countries is increasing its evil influence and control over America and the entire world."

Teachings of Ezra Taft Benson, p. 23-24.

"Because a fallen condition was an essential part of this plan, an infinite, eternal sacrifice was also required to redeem us from this state. We are all familiar with the facts: how Lucifer—a personage of prominence—sought to amend the plan, while Jehovah sustained the plan. The central issue in that council, then, was: Shall the children of God have untrammeled agency to choose the course they should follow, whether good or evil, or shall they be coerced and forced to be obedient? Christ and all who followed Him stood for the former proposition—freedom of choice; Satan stood for the latter—coercion and force. Because Satan and those who stood with him would not accept the vote of the council, but rose up in rebellion, they were cast down to the earth, where they have continued to foster the same plan. The war that began in heaven is not yet over. The conflict continues on the battlefield of mortality. And one of Lucifer's primary strategies has been to restrict our agency through the power of earthly governments. Proof of this is found in the long history of humanity (see Teachings of the Prophet Joseph Smith, p. 357). (The Constitution: A Heavenly Banner, p. 2-3.)"

Teachings of Ezra Taft Benson, p. 42.

"The Doctrine and Covenants is important because it contains the revelations which helped lay the foundation of this great latter-day work. It speaks of many things. Government should hold inviolate the right and control of property (see D&C 134:2). This makes important reading in a day when government controls are increasing and people are losing the right to control their own property. (God, Family, Country, p. 338-339.)"

Teachings of Ezra Taft Benson, p. 186.

"I think the Lord expects us, as elders in Israel, to do much more than we have ever done in the past in order to help preserve and safeguard and save His base of operations for the continuation of His program, for His gospel to go to all the nations of the earth. I am sure that gospel is going to every nation under heaven. The message of the restored gospel which is intended for all our Father's children, whom He loves as we love our own children, even with a deeper love, is going to every nation, kindred, tongue, and people from this base of operations. That is why I am so concerned for this base to be safeguarded and protected and strengthened so that we can carry this message of salvation unto all men. (Salt Lake City, Utah, April 8, 1972.)"

Teachings of Ezra Taft Benson, p. 289.

"Inspired leaders have always urged us to get out of debt, to live within our means, and to pay as we go—and this is sound advice for governments as well as individuals. History teaches that when individuals have given up looking after their own economic needs and transferred a large share of that responsibility to the government, both they and the government have failed. (The Red Carpet, p. 168-69.)"

Teachings of Ezra Taft Benson, p. 298.

"There is absolutely nothing in the Constitution which authorized the federal government to enter into the field of education. Furthermore, the Tenth Amendment says: 'The powers not delegated to the United States by the Constitution, nor prohibited by it to the States, are reserved to the States respectively, or to the people.' Nothing could be more clear. It is unconstitutional for the federal government to exercise any powers over education.

The phrase federal aid to education is deceptive and dishonest. What is really meant is 'federal taxes for education.' The federal government cannot 'aid' education. All it can do is tax the people, shuffle the money from one state to another and skim off its administrative costs from the top. Only the people can aid education. They can do it safer, faster, and cheaper within their local communities than by going through the middleman in Washington. Federal taxes for education means federal control over education. No matter how piously the national planners tell us that they will not dictate policies to local school systems, it is inevitable that they will in the long run. In fact, they already are doing it. Whenever the federal government spends tax money for any purpose, it has an obligation to determine how and under what conditions that money is used. Any other course would be irresponsible."

Teachings of Ezra Taft Benson, p. 299-300.

"We are rearing a generation which does not seem to understand the fundamentals of our American way of life, a generation which is no longer dedicated to its preservation. Our people, both before and after they arrive at the age of the ballot, should understand what it is that has made America great. We can only appreciate freedom if we understand the comparative fruits thereof. It is one thing to win freedom, but its preservation is equally important. If reference is made continually to weaknesses of the private enterprise system without any effort to point out its virtues and the comparative fruits of this and other systems, the tendency in this country will be, as it has been in other countries, to demand that the government take over more and more of the economic and social responsibilities and make more and more of the decisions for the people. This can result in but one thing, slavery of the individual to the state. This seems to be the trend of the world today. (The Red Carpet, p. 219.)"

Teachings of Ezra Taft Benson, p. 344.

"Men receive blessings by obedience to God's law. And without obedience there is no blessing. Before the final triumphal return of the Lord, the question as to whether we may save our constitutional republic is simply based on two factors—the number of patriots and the extent of their obedience."

Teachings of Ezra Taft Benson, p. 387.
    "One of our most serious problems is the inferiority complex which people feel when they are not informed and organized. They dare not make a decision on these vital issues. They let other people think for them. They stumble around in the middle of the road trying to avoid being 'controversial,' and get hit by traffic going both ways. In this mighty struggle each of you has a part. Every person on the earth today chose the right side during the War in Heaven. Be on the right side now. Stand up and be counted. (Title of Liberty, p. 41.)"

Teachings of Ezra Taft Benson, p. 394.
    "Today you cannot effectively fight for freedom and moral principles and not be attacked, and those who think they can are deceiving themselves. While I do not believe in stepping out of the path of duty to pick up a cross I don't need, a man is a coward who refuses to pick up a cross that clearly lies within his path. No cross, no crown. No gall, no glory. No thorns, no throne."

Teachings of Ezra Taft Benson, p. 397.
    "Today the Christian constitutionalist mourns for his country. He sees the spiritual and political faith of his fathers betrayed by wolves in sheep's clothing. He sees the forces of evil increasing in strength and momentum under the leadership of Satan, the arch-enemy of freedom. He sees the wicked honored and the valiant abused. He senses that his own generation faces Gethsemanes and Valley Forges that may yet rival or surpass the trials of the early Apostles and the men of '76. And this gives him cause to reflect on the most basic of fundamentals—the reason for our existence. Once we understand that fundamental, the purpose for mortality, we may more easily chart a correct course in the perilous seas that are engulfing our nation."

Teachings of Ezra Taft Benson, p. 399.
    "In the War in Heaven the devil advocated absolute eternal security at the sacrifice of our freedom. Although there is nothing more desirable than eternal security in God's presence, and although God knew, as did we, that some of us would not achieve this security if we were allowed our freedom—yet the very God of Heaven, who has more mercy than us all, still decreed no guaranteed security except by a man's own freedom of choice and individual initiative."

Teachings of Ezra Taft Benson, p. 482.
    "Remember, it is the individual who is of supreme worth. His morals and character must be safeguarded if America is to continue as a great nation. You cannot build character and courage by taking away man's initiative and independence. It is a basic principle that you cannot help a man permanently by doing for him what he could do and should do for himself. Dependence upon the state for sustenance means the eventual surrender of political freedom. Therefore, shrink not from your duty in these important matters as your responsibility as an American is made clear to you. Accept

responsibility. Be grateful for work. Hesitate not to do your full share of it. (So Shall Ye Reap, p. 153.)"

Teachings of Ezra Taft Benson, p. 522.

"The home is the rock foundation, the cornerstone of civilization. No nation will rise above its homes, and no nation will long endure when the family unit is weakened or destroyed."

Teachings of Ezra Taft Benson, p. 553.

"We can never survive unless our young people understand and appreciate our American system which has given more of the good things of life than any other system in the world—unless they have a dedication that exceeds the dedication of the enemy. Character must become important in this country again. The old essentials of honesty, self-respect, loyalty, and support for law and order must be taught the younger generation."

Teachings of Ezra Taft Benson, p. 571.

"Our nation, the United States of America, was built on the foundation of reality and spirituality. To the extent that its citizens violate God's commandments, especially His laws of morality—to that degree they weaken the country's foundation. A rejection and repudiation of God's laws could well lead our nation to its destruction just as it has to Greece and Rome. It can happen to our country unless we repent."

Teachings of Ezra Taft Benson, p. 574.

"This nation will be preserved so long as we retain the same quality of faith in God that our founders manifested. Personal righteousness is essential to our liberty. The burden of self-government depends on our supporting wise and good representatives, exercising self-restraint, and keeping the commandments of God. ("The Faith of Our Founding Fathers," 1983, p. 25-26.)"

Teachings of Ezra Taft Benson, p. 582.

"Our complacency as a nation is shocking—yes, almost unbelievable! We are a prosperous nation. Our people have high-paying jobs. Our incomes are high. Our standard of living is at an unprecedented level. We do not like to be disturbed as we enjoy our comfortable complacency. We live in the soft present and feel the future is secure. We do not worry about history. We seem oblivious to the causes of the rise and fall of nations. We are blind to the hard fact that nations usually sow the seeds of their own destruction while enjoying unprecedented prosperity.

I say to you with all the fervor of my soul: We are sowing the seeds of our own destruction in America and much of the free world today. It is my sober warning to you today that if the trends of the past continue, we will lose that which is as priceless as life itself—our freedom, our liberty, our right to act as free men. It can happen here. It is happening here."

Teachings of Ezra Taft Benson, p. 582.

"The sad and shocking story of what has happened in America in recent years must be told. Our people must have the facts. There is safety in an informed public. There is real danger in a complacent, uninformed citizenry. This is our real danger today. Yes, the truth must be told even at the risk of destroying, in large measure, the influence of men who are widely respected and loved by the American people. The stakes are high. Freedom and survival is the issue."

Teachings of Ezra Taft Benson, p. 583.
 "The days ahead are sobering and challenging, and will require the faith, prayers, and loyalty of every American citizen. Our challenge is to keep America strong and free—strong socially, strong economically, and above all, strong spiritually, if our way of life is to endure. Indeed, it is America's only hope for life, liberty, and the pursuit of happiness!"

Teachings of Ezra Taft Benson, p. 589.
 "In times as serious as these, we must not permit fear of criticism to keep us from doing our duty. In the crisis through which we are now passing, we have been fully warned. This has brought forth some criticism. There are some of us who do not want to hear the message. It embarrasses us. The things which are threatening our lives, our welfare, our freedoms are the very things some of us have been condoning. (God, Family, Country, p. 358-59.)"

Teachings of Ezra Taft Benson, p. 593.
 "It is time we recognize, as a people, that this country rests on divinely inspired and uniquely formulated principles. Until 1791, no nation had all basic rights guaranteed and recognized by written contract. That is what the Constitution is—a contract between a sovereign people and their elected officials. It is high time these principles are not just acknowledged, but carried out. Indeed this is the only real hope for our survival as a free nation. ("A Warning to America," Washington D.C. Stake, July 3, 1979.)"

Teachings of Ezra Taft Benson, p. 594.
 "We must study and learn for ourselves the principles laid down in the Constitution which have preserved our freedoms for the last two hundred years. If we do not understand the role of government and how our rights are protected by the Constitution, we may accept programs or organizations that help erode our freedoms. An informed citizenry is the first line of defense against anarchy and tyranny. ("Righteousness Exalteth a Nation," Provo Utah Freedom Festival, June 29, 1986.)
 How can people who are ignorant of the principles and guarantees of American government stand up in defense of it and our rights under the Constitution? The fundamentals and processes of free government should be known to every schoolboy and his parents. No free people can ever survive if they are ignorant of and fail to understand the principles of free government!"

Teachings of Ezra Taft Benson, p. 599-600.
 "We must be careful that we do not trade freedom for security. Whenever that is attempted, usually we lose both. There is always a tendency when nations become mature for the people to become more interested in preserving their luxuries and their comforts than in safeguarding the ideals and principles which made these comforts and luxuries possible. ("Responsibilities of Citizenship,"

BYU Homecoming, Provo, Utah, October 22, 1954.)"

Teachings of Ezra Taft Benson, p. 601.

"I believe with all my heart the words of the American patriot Patrick Henry, who, on the eve of the American Revolution, said, 'There is a just God who presides over the destinies of nations and who will raise up friends to fight our battles for us.' Further, it is part of my faith that no people can maintain freedom unless their political institutions are founded on faith in God and belief in the existence of moral law. God has endowed men with certain inalienable rights, and no government may morally limit or destroy these."

Teachings of Ezra Taft Benson, p. 609.

"I support the doctrine of separation of church and state as traditionally interpreted to prohibit the establishment of an official national religion. But this does not mean that we should divorce government from any formal recognition of God. To do so strikes a potentially fatal blow at the concept of the divine origin of our rights, and unlocks the door for an easy entry of future tyranny. If Americans should ever come to believe that their rights and freedoms are instituted among men by politicians and bureaucrats, they will no longer carry the proud inheritance of their forefathers, but will grovel before their masters seeking favors and dispensations—a throwback to the feudal system of the Dark Ages.

The history of all mankind shows very clearly that if we would be free—and if we would stay free—we must stand eternal watch against the accumulation of too much power in government.

There is hardly a single instance in all of history where the dictatorial centralization of power has been compatible with individual freedom—where it has not reduced the citizenry to the status of pawns and mere creatures of the state. God forbid that this should happen in America. Yet I am persuaded that the continuation of the trend of the past could make us pallbearers at the burial of the states as effective units of government. ("Freedom Is Our Heritage," LDS Business and Professional Men's Association, Glendale, California, November 10, 1970.)"

Teachings of Ezra Taft Benson, p. 610.

"It is a firm principle that the smallest or lowest level that can possibly undertake the task is the one that should do so. First, the community or the city. If the city cannot handle it, then the county. Next, the state; and only if no smaller unit can possibly do the job should the federal government be considered. This is merely the application to the field of politics of that wise and time-tested principle of never asking a larger group to do that which can be done by a smaller group. And so far as government is concerned, the smaller the unit and the closer it is to the people, the easier it is to guide it, to correct it, to keep it solvent, and to keep our freedom.

It is well to remember that the people of the states of this republic created the federal government. The federal government did not create the states."

Teachings of Ezra Taft Benson, p. 611.

"Sooner or later, the accumulation of power in central government leads to a loss of freedom. Everyone knows, also, it is hard to end undesirable government programs after they have been established. If power is diffused, such cannot happen. Every schoolboy knows that this is why the founders of our country carefully divided power between state and federal levels.

Our traditional federal-state relationship, we must never forget, starts with a general presumption in favor of state and individual rights. Under the constitutional concept, powers not granted to the federal government are reserved to the states or to the people. This is in the Bill of Rights. It is one of the first ten amendments to the Constitution, insisted upon by a number of the states as a condition of ratification of the Constitution.

The framers of our Constitution knew that many forces would be at work toward the concentration of power at the federal level. They knew that it somehow seems easier to impose 'progress' on localities than to wait for them to bring it about themselves. Raids on the federal treasury can be all too readily accomplished by an organized few over the feeble protests of an apathetic majority. With more and more activity centered in the federal government, the relationship between the costs and the benefits of government programs becomes obscure. What follows is the voting of public money without having to accept direct local responsibility for higher taxes.

I know of no device of government which will lead more quickly to an increase in the number of federal programs than this. If this trend continues, the states may be left hollow shells, operating primarily as the field districts of federal departments and dependent upon the federal treasury for their support. (The Red Carpet, p. 147-48.)"

Teachings of Ezra Taft Benson, p. 613-614.
"If those who so carefully drafted the checks and balances into our Constitution could have looked into the future and seen what the Supreme Court of the United States would do to their masterpiece, they would have been dismayed. Through the process of supposedly 'interpreting' the Constitution, the Court has twisted beyond recognition just about every conceivable clause to justify the transfer of all sovereignty from the states to the federal government, to broaden the powers of the federal government beyond any definable limit, and then to make it possible for all such powers to fall into the hands of the executive branch of government. We may still give lip service to the checks and balances of our constitutional republic, but the phrase is now quite hollow.

We, the people, have allowed the government to ignore one of the most fundamental stipulations of the Constitution—namely, the separation of powers. In recent years, we have allowed Congress to fund numerous federal agencies. While these agencies may provide some needed services and protection of rights, they also encroach significantly on our constitutional rights. The number of agencies seems to grow continually to regulate and control the lives of millions of citizens.

What many fail to realize is that most of these federal agencies are unconstitutional. Why are they unconstitutional? They are unconstitutional because they concentrate the functions of the legislative, executive, and judicial branches under one head. They have, in other words, power to make rulings, enforce rulings, and adjudicate penalties when rulings are violated. They are unconstitutional because they represent an assumption of power not delegated to the executive branch by the people. They are also unconstitutional because the people have no power to recall administrative agency personnel by their vote. (The Constitution: A Heavenly Banner, p. 25-26.)

There is one and only one legitimate goal of United States foreign policy. It is a narrow goal, a nationalistic goal: the preservation of our national independence. Nothing in the Constitution grants that the president shall have the privilege of offering himself as a world leader. He is our executive; he is on our payroll; he is supposed to put our best interests in front of those of other nations. Nothing in the Constitution nor in logic grants to the president of the United States or to Congress the power to influence the political life of other countries, to 'uplift' their cultures, to bolster their economies, to feed their people, or even to defend them against their enemies. ("America at the Crossroads," Jackson, Mississippi, August 30, 1969.)

To get some idea of how we are flaunting the Constitution, see how the Constitution defines treason (see Article III, section 3). Then observe what we are doing to build up the enemy, this totally anti-Christ conspiracy. If we continue on this tragic course of aid and trade to the enemy, the Lord has warned us in the Book of Mormon of the consequences that will follow (Ether 8). Thank God for the Constitution. And may God bless the elders of Israel that when, as President John Taylor said, 'the people shall have torn to shreds the Constitution of the United States, the Elders of Israel will be found holding it up to the nations of earth and proclaiming liberty' (Journal of Discourses, 21:8). ("Jesus Christ—Gifts and Expectations," New Era, May 1975, p. 19.)"
Teachings of Ezra Taft Benson, p. 615.

"God placed a mandate upon His people to befriend and defend the constitutional laws of the land and see that the rights and privileges of all mankind are protected. He verified the declaration of the Founding Fathers that God created all men free. He also warned against those who would enact laws encroaching upon the sacred rights and privileges of free men. He urged the election of honest and wise leaders and said that evil men and laws were of Satan. (See D&C 98:5-10.) (God, Family, Country, p. 344.)"

Teachings of Ezra Taft Benson, p. 616.

"What can we do to preserve our Constitution, and how can we avoid being misled into doing those things that would actually help to destroy it? During October 1963 conference I spoke on the subject 'Be Not Deceived.' I said there were three keys one could use to avoid deception: first, the scriptures; second, the words of the prophets, especially the President of the Church (particularly the living one); and, third, the Holy Ghost. (Title of Liberty, p. 80.)

Learn about the Constitution, the Declaration of Independence, and other basic documents of our great country so that you can sustain them and the free institutions set up under them. The greatest watchdog of our freedom is an informed electorate. ("The Ten Commandments," New Era 8 [July 1978]: 39.)"

Teachings of Ezra Taft Benson, p.616-618

"As an independent American for constitutional government I declare that:

I believe that no people can maintain freedom unless their political institutions are founded upon faith in God and belief in the existence of moral law.

I believe that God has endowed men with certain inalienable rights as set forth in the Declaration of Independence and that no legislature and no majority, however great, may morally limit or destroy these; that the sole function of government is to protect life, liberty, and property, and anything more than this is usurpation and oppression.

I believe that the Constitution of the United States was prepared and adopted by men acting under inspiration from Almighty God; that it is a solemn compact between the peoples of the states of this nation that all officers of government are under duty to obey; that the eternal moral laws expressed therein must be adhered to or individual liberty will perish.

I believe it a violation of the Constitution for government to deprive the individual of either life, liberty, or property except for these purposes: to punish crime and provide for the administration of justice; to protect the right and control of private property; to wage defensive war and provide for the nation's defense; to compel each one who enjoys the protection of government to bear his fair share of the burden of performing the above functions.

I hold that the Constitution denies government the power to take from the individual either his life, liberty, or property except in accordance with moral law; that the same moral law which governs the actions of men when acting alone is also applicable when they act in concert with others; that no citizen or group of citizens has any right to direct their agent, the government, to perform any act that would be evil or offensive to the conscience if that citizen were performing the act himself outside the framework of government.

I am hereby resolved that under no circumstances shall the freedoms guaranteed by the Bill of Rights be infringed. In particular I am opposed to any attempt on the part of the federal government to deny the people their right to bear arms, to worship, to pray when and where they choose, or to own and control private property.

I maintain that every person who enjoys the protection of his life, liberty, and property should bear his fair share of the cost of government in providing that protection; that the elementary principles of justice set forth in the Constitution demand that all taxes imposed be uniform; and that each person's property or income be taxed at the same rate.

I believe that each state is sovereign in performing those functions reserved to it by the Constitution, and it is destructive of our federal system and the right of self-government guaranteed under the Constitution for the federal government to regulate or control the states in performing their functions or to engage in performing such functions itself.

I consider it a violation of the Constitution for the federal government to levy taxes for the support of state or local government; that no state or local government can accept funds from the federal government and remain independent in performing its functions, nor can the citizens exercise their rights of self—government under such conditions.

I believe that no treaty or agreement with other countries should deprive our citizens of rights guaranteed them by the Constitution.

I consider it a direct violation of the obligation imposed upon it by the Constitution for the federal government to dismantle or weaken our military establishment below that point required for the protection of the states against invasion, or to surrender or commit our men, arms, or money to control of foreign or world organizations or governments.

These things I believe to be the proper role of government. We have strayed far afield. We must return to basic concepts and principles—to eternal verities. There is no other way. The storm signals are up. They are clear and ominous.

It may cost us blood before we are through. It is my conviction, however, that when the Lord comes, the Stars and Stripes will be floating on the breeze over this people. May it be so, and may God give us the faith and the courage exhibited by those patriots who pledged their lives and fortunes and sacred honor that we might be free. (The Constitution: A Heavenly Banner, p. 33.)

The Lord told the Prophet Joseph Smith there would be an attempt to overthrow the country by destroying the Constitution. Joseph Smith predicted that the time would come when the Constitution would hang, as it were, by a thread, and at that time 'this people will step forth and save it from the threatened destruction' (Journal of Discourses, 7:15). It is my conviction that the elders of Israel, widely spread over the nation, will at that crucial time successfully rally the righteous of our country and provide the necessary balance of strength to save the institutions of constitutional government.

If the Gentiles on this land reject the word of God and conspire to overthrow liberty and the Constitution, their doom is fixed, and they 'shall be cut off from among my people who are of the covenant' (1 Nephi 14:6; 3 Nephi 21:11, 14, 21; D&C 84:114-15, 117). (God, Family, Country,

As we spread abroad in this land, bearers of this priesthood, men and women with high ideals and standards, our influence will spread as we take positions of leadership in the community, in the state, in the nation, in the world. We will be able to sit in counsel with others and we will be able to influence others in paths of righteousness. We will help to save this nation, because this nation can only be preserved on the basic of righteous living."

Teachings of Ezra Taft Benson, p. 619-620.

"It is the devil's desire that the Lord's priesthood stay asleep while the strings of tyranny gradually and quietly entangle us until, like Gulliver, we awake too late and find that while we could have broken each string separately as it was put upon us, our sleepiness permitted enough strings to bind us to make a rope that enslaves us.

For years we have heard of the role the elders could play in saving the Constitution from total destruction. But how can the elders be expected to save it if they have not studied it and are not sure if it is being destroyed or what is destroying it?"

Teachings of Ezra Taft Benson, p. 620.

"The Lord's priesthood has a mission to perform for liberty—loving people everywhere. We cannot, any more than Jonah of old, run away from our calling. If the people shall accept the Lord's solution of the world's problems, even as those who listened to a repentant Jonah, then all shall be well with them. If they do not, however, they will suffer the consequences. Our responsibility, as in Jonah's case, is to see to it that the people have a chance to choose decisively after they have been shown clearly the Lord's way and what the Lord expects of them. (See Jonah 1- 4.) (CR, October 1954, Improvement Era, December 1954, p. 922.)"

Teachings of Ezra Taft Benson, p. 620-622.

"Only in this foreordained land, under its God-inspired Constitution and the resulting environment of freedom, was it possible to have established the restored Church. It is our responsibility to see that this freedom is perpetuated so that the Church may more easily flourish in the future.

The Lord said, 'Therefore, I, the Lord justify you, and your brethren of my church, in befriending that law which is the constitutional law of the land' (D&C 98:6).

How then can we best befriend the Constitution in this critical hour and secure the blessings of liberty and ensure the protection and guidance of our Father in Heaven?

First and foremost, we must be righteous. John Adams said, 'Our Constitution was made only for a moral and religious people. It is wholly inadequate to the government of any other.' If the Constitution is to have continuance, this American nation, and especially the Latter-day Saints, must be virtuous.

The Book of Mormon warns us relative to our living in this free land: 'Wherefore, this land is consecrated unto him whom he shall bring. And if it so be that they shall serve him according to the commandment which he hath given; it shall be a land of liberty unto them; wherefore, they shall never be brought down into captivity; if so, it shall be because of iniquity; for if iniquity shall abound cursed shall be the land for their sakes, but unto the righteous it shall be blessed forever.' (2 Nephi 1:7.)

'And now,' warned Moroni, 'we can behold the decrees of God concerning this land, that it is a land of promise; and whatsoever nation shall possess it shall serve God, or they shall be swept off when the fulness of his wrath shall come upon them. And the fulness of his wrath cometh upon them when they are ripened in iniquity.' (Ether 2:9.)

Two great American Christian civilizations—the Jaredites and the Nephites—were swept off because they did not 'serve the God of the land, who is Jesus Christ' (Ether 2:12). What will become of our civilization?

Second, we must learn the principles of the Constitution in the tradition of the Founding Fathers. Have we read the Federalist Papers? Are we reading the Constitution and pondering it? Are we aware of its principles? Are we abiding by these principles and teaching them to others? Could we defend the Constitution? Can we recognize when a law is constitutionally unsound? Do we know what the prophets have said about the Constitution and the threats to it?

As Jefferson said, 'If a nation expects to be ignorant and free . . . it expects what never was and never will be.'

Third, we must become involved in civic affairs to see that we are properly represented. The Lord said that He 'holds men accountable for their acts in relation' to governments 'both in making laws and administering them' (D&C 134:1). We must follow this counsel from the Lord: 'Honest men and wise men should be sought for diligently and good men and wise men ye should observe to uphold; otherwise whatsoever is less than these cometh of evil' (D&C 98:10). Note the qualities that the Lord demands of those who are to represent us. They must be good, wise, and honest.

Fourth, we must make our influence felt by our vote, our letters, our teaching, and our advice. We must become accurately informed and then let others know how we feel. The Prophet Joseph Smith said: 'It is our duty to concentrate all our influence to make popular that which is sound and good, and unpopular that which is unsound. 'Tis right, politically, for a man who has influence to use it.... From henceforth I will maintain all the influence I can get' (History of the Church, 5:286).

I have faith that the Constitution will be saved, as prophesied by Joseph Smith. It will be saved by the righteous citizens of this nation who love and cherish freedom. It will be saved by the enlightened members of this Church—among others—men and women who understand and abide the principles of the Constitution."

Teachings of Ezra Taft Benson, p. 623.

"Part of the reason we may not have sufficient priesthood bearers to save the Constitution, let alone to shake the powers of hell, is because unlike Moroni, I fear, our souls do not joy in keeping our country free, and we are not firm in the faith of Christ, nor have we sworn with an oath to defend our rights and the liberty of our country (see Alma 48:17).

The Prophet Joseph Smith saw the part the elders of Israel would play in this constitutional crisis. Will there be some of us who won't care about saving the Constitution, others who will be blinded by the craftiness of men, and some who will knowingly be working to destroy it? He who has ears to hear and eyes to see can discern by the Spirit and through the words of God's mouthpiece that our liberties are being taken. (God, Family, Country, p. 399.)

To all who have discerning eyes, it is apparent that the republican form of government established by our noble forefathers cannot long endure once fundamental principles are abandoned. Momentum is gathering for another conflict—a repetition of the crisis of two hundred years ago. This collision of ideas is worldwide. The issue is the same that precipitated the great premortal conflict—will men be free to determine their own course of action or must they be coerced."

Teachings of Ezra Taft Benson, p. 631.

"Students of economics know that a nation cannot spend itself into prosperity. Nor can we preserve our prosperity and our free-enterprise system by following a reckless policy of spending beyond our income in peacetime. Critics forget that our free-enterprise system is based on solvent government and sound money. This is the road of common sense, the road of a sound defense—a sound defense against the enemies and forces that endanger freedom both at home and abroad. (The Red Carpet, p. 167.)"

Teachings of Ezra Taft Benson, p. 631.

"Some say the free-enterprise system is heartless and insensitive to the needs of those less fortunate individuals who are found in any society, no matter how affluent. What about the lame, the sick, and the destitute? Most other countries in the world have attempted to use the power of government to meet this need. Yet, in every case forced charity through government bureaucracies has resulted in the long run in creating more misery, more poverty, and certainly less freedom than when government first stepped in."

Teachings of Ezra Taft Benson, p. 637-638.

" Few policies are more capable of destroying the moral, political, social, and economic basis of a free society than the debauching of its currency. And few tasks, if any, are more important for the preservation of freedom than the preservation of a sound monetary system.

We must return to policies of fiscal responsibility which will regain the world markets we are losing and protect our private competitive economy. We must reverse our present dangerous fiscal policies. If we fail so to do, we will set off an international monetary debacle that could easily make the experience of the 1930s sink into insignificance.

The welfare state, towards which America is steadily moving, is not something new. History has recorded it in the ancient civilizations of Babylon, Greece, and Rome; and modernly in

Mussolini's Italy and Hitler's Germany. It is the program of all of today's Communist countries. It not only fails to provide the economic security sought for, but the welfare state always ended in slavery—and it always will. (The Red Carpet, p. 308.)"

Teachings of Ezra Taft Benson, p. 640.

"When the going gets rough, we mustn't rush to Washington and ask big brother to take care of us through price controls, rent controls, guaranteed jobs and wages. Any government powerful enough to give the people all that they want is also powerful enough to take from the people all that they have. And it is even possible that some of the government manipulators who have brought us into this economic crisis are hoping that, in panic, we, the American people, literally will plead with them to take our liberties in exchange for the false promise of 'security.' As Alexander Hamilton warned about two hundred years ago: 'Nothing is more common than for a free people, in times of heat and violence, to gratify momentary passions by letting into the government principles and precedents which afterward prove fatal to themselves' (Alexander Hamilton and the Founding of the Nation, p. 21). Let us heed this warning. Let us prepare ourselves for the trying time ahead and resolve that, with the grace of God and through our own self-reliance, we shall rebuild a monetary system and a healthy economy which, once again, will become the model for all the world."

Teachings of Ezra Taft Benson, p. 655.

"What can you and I do to preserve our God-given free way of life? First, let us all prize the treasures we have in this country. This is a choice land—all of America—choice above all others (1 Nephi 2:20). Blessed by the Almighty, our forebears have made it so. It will continue to be a land of freedom and liberty as long as we are able and willing to advance in the light of sound and enduring principles of right. Second, let us all do our part to stay free; let us stand eternal watch against the accumulation of too much power in government. Here in our free land let us preserve a true climate in which man can grow.

Third, let us all reaffirm our patriotism, our love of country. It is how we respond to public issues. Let us rededicate ourselves as patriots in the truest sense. Fourth, let us all help to build peace: True peace springs from within. Its price is righteousness, and to achieve righteousness we must so conduct ourselves individually and collectively as to earn the loyalty and devotion of other men. Finally, let us all rededicate our lives and our nation to do the will of God. With each of you, I love this nation. (Title of Liberty, p. 120-121.)"

Teachings of Ezra Taft Benson, p. 656.

"The fight for freedom is God's fight. Freedom is a law of God, a permanent law. And, like any of God's laws, men cannot really break it with impunity. So when a man stands for freedom he stands with God. And as long as he stands for freedom he stands with God. And were he to stand alone he would still stand with God—the best company and the greatest power in or out of this world. Any man will be eternally vindicated and rewarded for his stand for freedom.

There is no excuse that can compensate for the loss of liberty. Satan is anxious to neutralize the inspired counsel of the prophet and hence keep the priesthood off balance, ineffective, and inert in the fight for freedom. He does this through diverse means, including the use of perverse reasoning.

For example, he will argue, 'There is no need to get involved in the fight for freedom—all you need to do is live the gospel.' Of course this is a contradiction, because we cannot fully live the gospel and not be involved in the fight for freedom.

We would not say to someone, 'There is no need to be baptized—all you need to do is live the gospel.' That would be ridiculous because baptism is a part of the gospel. How would you have reacted if during the War in Heaven someone had said to you, 'Look, just do what is right; there is no need to get involved in the fight for free agency.' It is obvious what the devil is trying to do, but it is sad to see many of us fall for his destructive line.

The cause of freedom is a most basic part of our religion. Our position on freedom helped get us to this earth and it can make the difference as to whether we get back home or not."

Teachings of Ezra Taft Benson, p. 658.

"As important as are all other principles of the gospel, it was the freedom issue that determined whether you received a body. To have been on the wrong side of the freedom issue during the War in Heaven meant eternal damnation. How then can Latter-day Saints expect to be on the wrong side in this life and escape the eternal consequences? The War in Heaven is raging on earth today. The issues are the same: Shall men be compelled to do what others claim is for their best welfare or will they heed the counsel of the prophets and preserve their freedom?"

Teachings of Ezra Taft Benson, p. 659-661.

"The devil knows that if the elders of Israel should ever wake up, they could step forth and help preserve freedom and extend the gospel. Therefore the devil has concentrated, and to a large extent successfully, on neutralizing much of the priesthood. He has reduced them to sleeping giants. His arguments are clever. Here are a few samples.

'We really haven't received much instruction about freedom,' the devil says. This is a lie, for we have been warned time and again. . . .

'You want to be loved by everyone,' says the devil, 'and this freedom battle is so controversial you might be accused of engaging in politics.' Of course, the government has penetrated so much of our lives that one can hardly speak for freedom without being accused of being political. Some might even call the War in Heaven a political struggle—certainly it was controversial. Yet the valiant entered it with Michael (Revelation 12:7). Those who support only the popular principles of the gospel have their reward. And those who want to lead the quiet, retiring life but still expect to do their full duty can't have it both ways.

'Wait until it becomes popular to do,' says the devil, 'or, at least, until everybody in the Church agrees on what should be done.' This fight for freedom might never become popular in our day. And if you wait until everybody agrees in this Church, you will be waiting through the second coming of the Lord. Would you have hesitated to follow the inspired counsel of the Prophet Joseph Smith simply because some weak men disagreed with him? God's living mouthpiece has spoken to us—are we for him or against him? Where do you stand?

'It might hurt your business or your family,' says the devil, 'and besides, why not let the Gentiles save the country? They aren't as busy as you are.' Well, there were many businessmen who went along with Hitler because it supposedly helped their business. They lost everything. Many of us are here today because our forefathers loved truth enough that they fought at Valley Forge or crossed the plains in spite of the price it cost them or their families. We had better take our small pain now than our greater loss later. There were souls who wished afterwards that they had stood and fought with Washington and the Founding Fathers, but they waited too long—they passed up eternal glory. There has never been a greater time than now to stand up against entrenched evil. And while the Gentiles established the Constitution, we have a divine mandate to preserve it. But, unfortunately, today in this freedom struggle many Gentiles are showing greater wisdom in their generation than the children of light (Luke 16:8).

'Don't worry,' says the devil; 'the Lord will protect you, and besides, the world is so corrupt and heading toward destruction at such a pace that you can't stop it, so why try?' Well, to begin with, the Lord will not protect us unless we do our part. This devilish tactic of persuading people not to get concerned because the Lord will protect them no matter what they do is exposed by the Book of Mormon. Referring to the devil, it says: 'And others will he pacify, and lull them away into carnal security, that they will say: All is well in Zion; yea, Zion prospereth, all is well—and thus the devil cheateth their souls, and leadeth them away carefully down to hell' (2 Nephi 28:21).

I like that word carefully. In other words, don't shake them—you might wake them. The Book of Mormon warns us that when we see these murderous conspiracies in our midst, we should awaken to our awful situation (see Ether 8:24). Now, why should we awaken if the Lord is going to take care of us anyway? Let us suppose that it is too late to save freedom. It is still accounted unto us for righteousness' sake to stand up and fight. Some Book of Mormon prophets knew of the final desolate end of their nations, but they still fought on, and they saved some souls, including their own, by so doing. For, after all, the purpose of life is to prove ourselves, and the final victory will be for freedom (Abraham 3:24-25).

The last neutralizer that the devil uses most effectively is simply this: 'Don't do anything in the fight for freedom until the Church sets up its own specific program to save the Constitution.' This brings us right back to the scripture about the slothful servants who will not do anything until they are 'compelled in all things' (D&C 58:26). Maybe the Lord will never set up a specific Church program for the purpose of saving the Constitution. Perhaps if He set one up at this time it might split the Church asunder, and perhaps He does not want that to happen yet, for not all the wheat and tares are fully ripe (D&C 86:5-7)."

Teachings of Ezra Taft Benson, p. 665.

"The history of nations shows that the cycle of the body politic slowly but surely undergoes change. It progresses from bondage to spiritual faith, from spiritual faith to courage, from courage to freedom, from freedom to abundance, from abundance to selfishness, from selfishness to complacency, from complacency to apathy, from apathy to fear, from fear to dependency, from dependency to bondage. Every nation yearns for liberty, but too frequently its own self-indulgence precludes the possibility of freedom."

Teachings of Ezra Taft Benson, p. 668-669.

"History reveals why the great Roman Empire fell. These are the major reasons. Note them carefully and try to determine in your mind if there is anything in evidence in our own country today which smacks of these causes, which the historian Will Durant asserts were largely responsible for the fall of the great Roman Empire.

The first group of causes he lists as biological. These he considers the most fundamental. Mr. Durant claims they began with the educated classes, and started with the breakdown of the home and the family—the limitation of children, the refusal to assume the obligations of honorable parenthood, the deferment and avoidance of marriage. Sexual excesses were indulged in outside the marriage covenant. The practices of contraception and abortion became prominent; reduced fertility resulted. Sex ran riot and moral decay resulted.

Second, he mentioned the waste, among other things, of natural resources—mining, deforestation, erosion, neglect of irrigation canals. Most important he considered the negligence of harassed and discouraged men, the failure to teach high moral principles to the youth of the land—those principles which make for the building of character—and the sad neglect of our greatest single asset, our boys and girls.

Third, he lists rising costs of government—armies, doles, public works, expanding bureaucracy, a parasitic court, depreciation of the currency, and absorption of investment capital by confiscatory taxation. Is there anything suggestive in this summary? (The Red Carpet, p. 238-239.)"

Teachings of Ezra Taft Benson, p. 672-673.

"A government is nothing more nor less than a relatively small group of citizens who have been hired, in a sense, by the rest of us to perform certain functions and discharge responsibilities which have been authorized. It stands to reason that the government itself has no innate power nor privilege to do anything. Its only source of authority and power is from the people who have created it. This is made clear in the Preamble of the Constitution of the United States.

The important thing to keep in mind is that the people who have created their government can give to that government only such powers as they, themselves, have in the first place. Obviously, they cannot give that which they do not possess, so the question boils down to this: What powers properly belong to each and every person in the absence of and prior to the establishment of any organized governmental form? A hypothetical question? Yes, indeed! But, it is a question which is vital to an understanding of the principles which underlie the proper function of government.

The proper function of government is limited to those spheres of activity within which the individual citizen has the right to act. By deriving its just powers from the governed, government becomes primarily a mechanism for defense against bodily harm, theft, and involuntary servitude. It cannot claim the power to redistribute money or property, or to force reluctant citizens to perform acts of charity against their will. Government is created by the people. No individual possesses the power to take another's wealth or to force others to do good, so no government has the right to do such things either. The creature cannot exceed the creator. (The Constitution: A Heavenly Banner, p. 9.)

In general terms, the proper role of government includes such defensive activities as maintaining national military and local police forces for protection against loss of life, loss of property, and loss of liberty at the hands of either foreign despots or domestic criminals. It also includes those powers necessarily incidental to the protective function, such as the maintenance of courts where those charged with crimes may be tried and where disputes between citizens may be impartially settled; the establishment of a monetary system and a standard of weights and measures so that courts may render money judgments, taxing authorities may levy taxes, and citizens may have a uniform standard to use in their business dealings.

A category of government activity which today not only requires the closest scrutiny but which also poses a grave danger to our continued freedom is the activity not within the proper sphere of government. No one has the authority to grant such power as welfare programs, schemes for redistributing the wealth, and activities which coerce people into acting in accordance with a prescribed code of social planning. There is one simple test. Do I as an individual have a right to use force upon my neighbor to accomplish my goal? If I do have such a right, I may delegate that power to my government to exercise on my behalf. If I do not have that right as an individual, I cannot delegate it to government, and I cannot ask my government to perform the act for me. "

Teachings of Ezra Taft Benson, p. 674.

"History teaches that when individuals have given up looking after their own economic needs and transferred a large share of that responsibility to the government, both they and the government have failed. At least twenty great civilizations have disappeared. The pattern of their downfall is shockingly similar. All, before their collapse, showed a decline in spiritual values, in moral stamina, and in the freedom and responsibility of their citizens. They showed such symptoms as excessive taxation, bloated bureaucracy, government paternalism, and generally a rather elaborate set of supports, controls, and regulations affecting prices, wages, production, and consumption. (The Red Carpet, p. 168-169.)"

Teachings of Ezra Taft Benson, p. 676-677.

"Edmund Burke once said, 'All that is necessary for the triumph of evil is for good men to do nothing.' It is not enough that we wring our hands and moan about conditions in America. We must become responsible citizens and carry out our civic duty. We should be 'anxiously engaged' in good causes and leave the world a better place for having lived in it (D&C 58:27). ("Righteousness Exalteth a Nation," Provo Utah Freedom Festival, June 29, 1986.)"

Teachings of Ezra Taft Benson, p. 678-679.

"We should measure all proposals having to do with our national or local welfare by four standards: First, is the proposal, the policy, or the idea being promoted, right as measured by the gospel of Jesus Christ? I assure you it is much easier for one to measure a proposed policy by the gospel of Jesus Christ if he has accepted the gospel and is living it.

Second, is it right as measured by the Lord's standard of constitutional government? (See D&C 98:5.) Whether we live under a divinely inspired Constitution, as in the United States, or under some other form of government, the Lord's standard is a safe guide.

Third, we might well ask, Is it right as measured by the counsel of the living oracles of God? It is my conviction that these living oracles are not only authorized, but are also obligated to give counsel to this people on any subject that is vital to the welfare of this people and to the upbuilding of the kingdom of God.

Fourth, what will be the effect upon the morale and the character of the people if this or that policy is adopted? After all, as a Church, we are interested in building men and women and in building character. (God, Family, Country, p. 278-279.)"

Teachings of Ezra Taft Benson, p. 681.

"We must expose to the light of public inquiry those forces which would destroy our country and our way of life. We should pay no attention to the recommendations of men who call the Constitution an eighteenth-century agrarian document—who apologize for capitalism and free enterprise. We should refuse to follow their siren song of increasingly concentrating the powers of government in the chief executive, of delegating American sovereign authority to non-American institutions of the United Nations and pretending that it will bring peace to the world by turning our armed forces over to a United Nations worldwide police force. (Title of Liberty, p. 16.)"

Teachings of Ezra Taft Benson, p. 682-683.

"Ever since World War I, when we sent American boys to Europe supposedly 'to make the world safe for democracy,' our leaders in Washington have been acting as though the American people elected them to office for the primary purpose of leading the entire planet toward international peace, prosperity, and one-world government. At times, these men appear to be more concerned with something called world opinion or with their image as world leaders than they are with securing the best possible advantage for us, with showing that they are not 'nationalistic' in their views, that they are willing to sacrifice narrow American interests for the greater good of the world community. Patriotism and America—first have become vulgar concepts within the chambers of our State Department. It is no wonder that the strength and prestige of the United States has slipped so low everywhere in the world."

Teachings of Ezra Taft Benson, p. 684.

"At this particular moment in history the United States Constitution is definitely threatened, and every citizen should know about it. The warning of this hour should resound through the corridors of every American institution—schools, churches, the halls of Congress, press, radio, and television, and so far as I am concerned it will resound—with God's help.

Wherever possible I have tried to speak out. It is for this very reason that certain people in Washington have bitterly criticized me. They don't want people to hear the message. It embarrasses them. The things which are destroying the Constitution are the things they have been voting for. They are afraid of their political careers if these facts are pointed out. They therefore try to silence any who carry the message—anyone who will stand up and be counted. (Title of Liberty, p. 30.)"

Teachings of Ezra Taft Benson, p. 691.

"The conservative has faith in the human person to make his own decisions. The liberal has faith in the ability of Washington to make more and more decisions for us. The liberal would impose on the people his version of progress whether the people want it or not. Conservatives believe that the best way to achieve progress in our country is through individual effort and not government force, which in the end will destroy all progress and all freedom. In the long run we do things better for ourselves than the government can do them for us. Government serves best when it protects the freedom of the individual. But the moment the government steps in and dictates the economic or agricultural life of the nation, the individual's rights begin to diminish and are in danger ultimately of vanishing. (The Red Carpet, p. 211.)"

Teachings of Ezra Taft Benson, p. 692-693.

"We cannot afford to minimize the threat of socialism in America. We must be on guard against unsound theories and programs which strike at the very root of all we hold dear. We have lived too long under a government of controls. Government by control has extended into almost all of our economy and even invaded many of our personal freedoms. We must be made aware of this and be awakened to its dangers.

This major effort is to keep left-wing, bureaucratic planners away from control of our national government. They are leading us today toward more and more socialization of our entire economy, a weakening of the free-enterprise system, and an increase in the regulation and domination of the people of America. (The Red Carpet, p. 311.)

Today's Socialists—who call themselves egalitarians—are using the federal government to redistribute wealth in our society—not as a matter of voluntary charity, but as a so-called matter of right. One Housing, Education, and Welfare official said, 'In this country, welfare is no longer charity; it is a right. More and more Americans feel that their government owes them something.' (U.S. News and World Report, 21 April 1975, p. 49.) President Grover Cleveland said—and we believe as a people—that though the people support the government, the government should not support the people. ("A Vision and a Hope for the Youth of Zion," in 1977 Devotional Speeches of the Year [Provo, Utah: BYU, 1978], p. 77.)

Yes, we have traveled a long way down the soul-destroying road of socialism. (You young men and women today little realize that the federal government has taken over what once was the exclusive domain of the local government or the individual citizen.) How did it happen? Men of expediency ascended to high political offices by promising what was not theirs to give, and citizens voted them into office in the hopes of receiving what they had not earned. You can, therefore, see how the violation of one commandment—Thou shalt not covet—has weakened our entire system of government and led to a partial loss of liberty. ("Be True to God, Country, and Self," Young Adult Fireside, Logan, Utah, February 11, 1979.)

There is an evidence in our beloved country of certain trends and tendencies which strike at the very foundation of all we hold dear. The outlook for free enterprise in the world has never seemed so uncertain as now. A world survey by the New York Times shows that nationalization is growing rapidly, especially outside the Western Hemisphere. Many nations have a mixed economy brought about by an increase in state control and a corresponding weakening of the private-enterprise system. The seriousness of the situation demands careful reflection by all interested in the preservation and perpetuation of our system of individual free enterprise, predicated as it is on a democratic capitalistic economy under a republican form of government. ("Cooperative Goals," American Institute of Cooperation, Madison, Wisconsin, August 22, 1949.)

I fear for the future when I realize that our once-free institutions—political, economic, educational, and social—have been drifting into the hands of those who favor the welfare state, and who would 'centralize all power in the hands of the political apparatus in Washington. This enhancement of political power at the expense of individual rights, so often disguised as 'democracy' or 'freedom' or 'civil rights,' is 'socialism,' no matter what name tag it bears.' (Admiral Ben Moreell.) (Title of Liberty, p. 62.)"

Teachings of Ezra Taft Benson, p. 695-696.
"Many well-intentioned people are now convinced that we are living in a period of history which makes it both possible and necessary to abandon our national sovereignty, to merge our nation militarily, economically, and politically with other nations, and to form, at last, a world government which supposedly would put an end to war. We are told that this is merely doing between nations what we did so successfully with our thirteen colonies. This plea for world federalism is based on the idea that the mere act of joining separate political units together into a larger federal entity will somehow prevent those units from waging war with each other. The success of our own federal system is most often cited as proof that this theory is valid. But such an evaluation is a shallow one.
Sovereignty for a nation is hard to come by and even more difficult to retain. It cannot be shared, for then sovereignty becomes something else, and, for want of a better word, when sovereignty is lessened the end-product is internationalism. Sovereignty is neither more nor less than self-government. American self-government is blueprinted in the Constitution."

Teachings of Ezra Taft Benson, p. 696.
"The world is smaller, you say? True, it is, but if one finds himself locked in a house with maniacs, thieves, and murderers—even a small house—he does not increase his chances of survival by entering into alliances with his potential attackers and becoming dependent upon them for protection to the point where he is unable to defend himself. Perhaps the analogy between nations and maniacs is a little strong for some to accept. But if we put aside our squeamishness over strong language, and look hard at the real world in which we live, the analogy is quite sound in all but the rarest exceptions.

Teachings of Ezra Taft Benson, p. 697.
"Channing Pollock observed that most democracies last for about two hundred years. They are conceived and developed by simple, vigorous, idealistic, hard-working people who, unfortunately, with success become rich and decadent, learn to live without labor, depend more on the largess of big government, and end by trading domestic tyrants for foreign tyrants."

Teachings of Ezra Taft Benson, p. 697.
"Even among free nations we see the encroachment of government upon the lives of the citizenry by excessive taxation and regulation, all done under the guise that the people would not wilfully or charitably distribute their wealth, so the government must take it from them. We further observe promises by the state of security, whereby men are taken care of from the womb to the tomb rather than earning this security by the 'sweat of their brow' (Moses 5:1); deception in high places, with the justification that 'the end justifies the means'; atheism; agnosticism; immorality; and dishonesty. The attendant results of such sin and usurpation of power lead to a general distrust of government officials, an insatiable, covetous spirit for more and more material wants, personal debt

to satisfy this craving, and the disintegration of the family unit. Yes, we live today amidst the times the Savior spoke of, times when 'the love of many shall wax cold, and iniquity shall abound' (Matthew 24:12)."

Teachings of Ezra Taft Benson, p. 698-699.

"On the surface, the United Nations Charter and the structure of its various departments bears a strong resemblance to those of our own federal government. But the similarity goes no further than outward form. Whereas the United States is founded on the concept of limited government, the United Nations concept is one of unlimited government power with virtually no meaningful restraints to protect individual liberty.

For instance, article 4, section 4 of our Constitution states: 'The United States shall guarantee to every State in this union a Republican form of government.' This means a government with limited powers. The framers knew that the Union would not last if the individual states were allowed to become despotic and unrestrained. To provide protection against the creation of a super-federal government, the ninth amendment further stipulates: 'The enumeration in the Constitution of certain rights shall not be construed to deny or disparage others retained by the people.' And more of the same in the tenth amendment: 'The powers not delegated to the United States by the Constitution, nor prohibited by it to the States, are reserved to the States respectively, or to the people.'

Compare this with the ideological foundation upon which the United Nations is built. Instead of insuring that all member states have limited forms of government, the United Nations assumes that most of them have unlimited power over their subjects. The United Nations is not the least bit concerned over the fact that a majority of its members are governments which rule with police-state methods. Instead of assuming that any power not specifically mentioned in the Constitution is reserved to the individual citizens or their smaller governmental units, the United Nations operates under the doctrine that its charter is sufficiently vague and broad so as to authorize doing absolutely anything."

Teachings of Ezra Taft Benson, p. 699.

"Even if we assume that all of the people at the United Nations representing the various nations were of the highest moral caliber and prompted only by the most pure and selfless motives, there still is every reason to believe that the concentration into their hands of the absolute power of a nuclear monopoly, plus a military land, air, and naval force superior to any nation, would be a mighty tempting influence. In time, the flesh could weaken, even the best of men would be caught up in the inevitable struggle for world power, and finally, the whole planet would be subject to an unchallengeable dictatorship of the few over the many. True, such a development conceivably might not materialize for years, but it would materialize. The only legitimate question open to speculation is how soon."

Teachings of Ezra Taft Benson, p. 704.

"Until all nations follow the concept of limited government, it is unlikely that universal peace will ever be realized on this planet. Unlimited, power-grasping governments will always resort to force if they think they can get away with it. But there can be peace for America. As long as our leaders faithfully discharge their duty to preserve and strengthen the military, economic, and political independence of our republic, the world's petty despots will leave us alone. "

Ezra Taft Benson, God, Family, Country: Our Three Great Loyalties, p. 87.

"Some day we may be called upon as a people to exert great influence in helping to preserve the liberties and freedoms and blessings vouchsafed to us as a people in the Constitution of this land. Some of our inspired leaders have had words to say on that subject. I hope and pray that we will be ready when the time comes - in fact, I am inclined to feel sometimes it is going to be a gradual process. Maybe it is underway now. We will not be able to discharge our obligations unless we adhere strictly to the standards and ideals of the church and kingdom of God."

Ezra Taft Benson, The Red Carpet, p. 197.

"There is yet another threat to American freedom we should consider . . .

It is the current anti anti-communism drive and the branding as 'super-patriots,' 'fanatics' and 'right-wing extremists,' those who defend the freedom, traditions, and principles on which this great nation was founded. The implication is to make of them something that is evil."

Ezra Taft Benson, The Red Carpet, p. 199.

"That we might face up properly to such a campaign of lies and name-calling, we should accept the advice of Thomas Jefferson who warns us as follows:

'If we suffer ourselves to be frightened from our posts by mere lying, surely the enemy will use that weapon . . . The patriot like the Christian, must learn that to bear revilings and persecutions is a part of his duty; and in proportion as the trial is severe, firmness under it becomes more requisite and praiseworthy.'"

Ezra Taft Benson, This Nation Shall Endure, p. 43.

"Yes, I repeat, righteousness is an indispensable ingredient to liberty. Virtuous people elect wise and good representatives. Good representatives make good laws and then wisely administer them. This tends to preserve righteousness. An unvirtuous citizenry tends to elect representatives who will pander to their covetous lustings."

Ezra Taft Benson, This Nation Shall Endure, p. 94.

"Today, as government becomes increasingly dominant in our affairs, we are becoming more and more like ancient Rome before it crumbled and collapsed. We are choosing bread and circuses instead of facing the challenges that always test a free people."

Ezra Taft Benson, This Nation Shall Endure, p. 97.

"The government is manipulating our monetary system, and unless we return to fiscal responsibility, we can look forward to a highly dangerous economic crisis. If we are to beat inflation effectively, four vital steps must be taken:

1. Abolish wage and price controls permanently.
2. Stop all spending in excess of tax receipts and make annual payments on the debt.

3. Abrogate all extravagant and unnecessary government programs.

4. Reestablish the gold and silver standard.

. . .If our representatives and senators persist in shirking their duties in this regard, then we'll continue on the same course to economic disaster, and we'll end up with a controlled economy under a totalitarian form of government."

Ezra Taft Benson, This Nation Shall Endure, p. 99-100.

"Never since the days of the Civil War has this choice nation faced such a crisis. Throughout history, great civilizations have disappeared. In every case the pattern bears a grim similarity. First comes a decline in spiritual values, then a repudiation of economic and moral principles of integrity and responsibility, followed by the inevitable loss of freedom.

If we are to survive as an independent, sovereign nation, we must, as free Americans, follow sound economic and political policies, uphold and protect our hallowed Constitution, and live to the letter the virtues of frugality, integrity, loyalty, patriotism, and morality. Today, more than ever before, we need God's influence and guidance in every area of our lives."

Ezra Taft Benson, This Nation Shall Endure, p. 108.

"When government presumes to demand more and more of the fruits of man's labors through taxation, and reduces more and more his actual income by printing money and furthering debt, the wage earner is left with less and less with which to buy food and to provide housing, medical care, education, and private welfare. Individuals are then left without a choice and must look to the state as the benevolent supporter of these services. When that happens, liberty is gone."

Ezra Taft Benson, This Nation Shall Endure, p. 114.

"When will we learn the lesson that fiscal irresponsibility leads to a loss of self-government? When will we learn that when you lose economic independence, you lose political freedom. We have accepted a frightening degree of socialism in our country. . . .The amount of freedom depends upon the amount of federal control and spending. A good measurement is to determine the amount, or percentage, of income of the people that is taken over and spent by the state."

Ezra Taft Benson, This Nation Shall Endure, p. 116.

"Our major danger is . . . transferring responsibility from the individual, local, and state governments to the federal government. We cannot long pursue this present trend without its bringing us to national insolvency."

Ezra Taft Benson, This Nation Shall Endure, p. 132.

"No nation has ever perished that has kept the commandments of God. Neither permanent government nor civilization will long endure that violates these laws . . .Our problems today are essentially problems of the spirit. The solution is not more wealth, more food, more technology, more government, or instruments of destruction. . . .Repentance is the sovereign remedy to our problems."

Ezra Taft Benson, An Enemy Hath Done This, p. 120.

"In 1787 Edward Gibbon completed his noble work, The Decline and Fall of the Roman Empire. Here is the way he accounted for the fall: 1. The undermining of the dignity and sanctity of the home, which is the basis of human society. 2. Higher and higher taxes and the spending of public monies for free bread and circuses for the populace. 3. The mad craze for pleasure, sports becoming every year more and more exciting and more brutal. 4. The building of gigantic armaments when the real enemy was within the decadence of the people. 5. The decay of religion—faith fading into mere form, losing touch with life and becoming impotent to warn and guide the people. Is there a parallel for us in America today? Could the same reasons that destroyed Rome destroy America?"

Ezra Taft Benson, An Enemy Hath Done This, p. 151-163.

"The only way America can survive in this basically hostile and topsy-turvy world is to remain militarily, economically and politically strong and independent . . .Yet, many Americans have been led to believe that our country is so strong that it can defend, feed and subsidize half the world, while at the same time believing that we are so weak and `inter-dependent' that we cannot survive without pooling our resources and sovereignty with those we subsidize ."

Ezra Taft Benson, An Enemy Hath Done This, p. 172.

"(Americans) have forgotten that, right now, as a matter of calculated policy, the communists are perpetrating horrible atrocities every bit as sickening as those carried out in the torture chambers and gas ovens of the Nazi regime. . . .Because so many Americans have forgotten this fact . . . they are willing to accept the possibility of living under communism rather than run the risk of death in an unlikely nuclear war. Apparently they do not comprehend the object lesson of tens of thousands of people risking their lives to escape from behind the iron and bamboo curtains."

Ezra Taft Benson, An Enemy Hath Done This, p. 174-178.

"As it is used today by those who are its foremost advocates, the word `disarmament' can be defined simply as `the transfer of our national military apparatus to the control of the U.N. . . .

This is merely part of the overall plan to resolve our conflict with communism, not by victory over it, but by merging with it into a world body, since it will have a superior military force at its disposal, will become by definition a one-world government . . .

Lord Acton often has been summoned to remind us that `Power tends to corrupt and absolute power corrupts absolutely' (Essays on Freedom and Power, p. 364). . . . It needs to be applied to our thinking regarding the creation of al all-powerful international police force."

Ezra Taft Benson, An Enemy Hath Done This, p. 219.

" Those . . . who would have us believe that, somehow, if we just do a little more manipulating of our money, possibly even set up a world monetary system through the U.N., then we can avoid having to pay the fiddler. . .But such proposals are merely more of the same con game against the American people, and would not only fail to solve our economic problems, but could lead us into surrendering our economic independence as a nation to the dictates of a majority block in the U.N. which, conceivably, would be less interested in our recovery than in exploiting our misery."

Ezra Taft Benson, An Enemy Hath Done This, p. 332.

"The Book of Mormon points out how these ancient conspirators were able to fill the judgment seats, usurp power, destroy justice, condemn the righteous and let the guilty and the wicked go unpunished. Do you see any parallel between this and the present-day decisions of our Supreme Court? President McKay has stated that the Supreme Court is leading this Christian nation down the road to atheism. I believe the Court is also leading us down the road to anarchy and atheistic communism."

Ezra Taft Benson, An Enemy Hath Done This, p. 333.

"And so the crucial question is, `Has our nation upheld communism so that it could get power and gain?' And the tragic answer is, `Yes.' And so, unless we as a people can soon stop and reverse the disastrous course we are taking, then our nation shall be destroyed. For the sad truth is that communism would be insignificant in our country and the world today were it not for the consistent and persistent help which it is continuing to receive from right within our own government."

Mark E. Petersen, Church News, *"Editorial"*, April 16, 1950.

"To save the Constitution, either when it hangs by a thread or at any other time, our people must be fully prepared. Part of the preparation is that they shall understand the Constitution and be willing to accept the provisions set forth therein. Nobody is going to risk very much to save an instrument which he does not understand, nor is he going to jeopardize his life or property to preserve principles he does not accept.

If some day the elders of this Church will step forth and save the Constitution, then the elders of this Church must be fully conversant with the Constitution and be wholeheartedly converted to the high principles of free government which it embodies. Are we thus converted? Are we thus prepared?"

Mark E. Petersen, The Way to Peace, p. 44.

"The safety of America lies in acceptance of Jesus Christ. Preaching and living the Gospel is the surest defense of this nation. Enemies may rage, both within and without, but if the majority of Americans will continue to accept Christ and serve him to the best of their knowledge, he will protect them and preserve our nation."

Henry D. Moyle, Conference Report, October 1950, p. 93.

"Washington realized that religion and morality are the pillars which uphold the Constitution of the United States, and without which the Constitution would fall. Washington also realized and exemplified in his life the necessity for religion and morality in the lives of those charged with the responsibility of maintaining our Constitution, and without which men will be led away from the truth. Men will be led to follow the course which will ultimately destroy the Constitution rather than uphold it, against their very oaths of office, if they once throw off the cloak of morality and of religion. No one can fail to uphold the Constitution and be a good citizen, much less a worthy public officer. One who disregards the Constitution is not worthy of our patronage, politically or otherwise."

Marion G. Romney, Conference Report, April 1966, p. 98-99.

"Man is in the earth to be tested. The issue as to whether he succeeds or fails will be determined by how he uses his agency. His whole future, through all eternity, is at stake. Abridge man's agency, and the whole purpose of his mortality is thwarted. Without it, the Lord says, there is no existence. (See D&C 93:30.)"

Bruce R. McConkie, Mormon Doctrine, "Devil", p. 194.

"Satan's influence is also manifest in the world through governmental powers, particularly those in which dictatorship and compulsion are the rule. Political philosophies, as those which spread communistic and socialistic ideologies, are his propaganda vehicles."

Bruce R. McConkie, Mormon Doctrine, "The Laws of the Land", p. 437.

"Inspiration and divine guidance have been manifest in the creation . . . of the United States. This inspiration has not made the government of the United States synonymous with the government of God, and, so today we find civil law administered by men and spiritual law by the Church. Under present conditions there is and should be a complete separation of Church and state, and as long as such a separation continues, the saints are and should be subject to the laws of the land."

Bruce R. McConkie, Mormon Doctrine, "Signs of the Times", p. 726.

"The Lord's decree for this age is: 'The whole earth shall be in commotion.' (D. & C. 45:26.) Signs of this commotion are seen . . . in the unholy plots against our freedoms and free institutions; in the anarchy, rebellion, and crime that flow from great political movements which seek to destroy the agency of man and overthrow the governments of the world by force and violence."

See Bruce R. McConkie, A New Witness for the Articles of Faith, p. 625.

"There are those who would control, govern, and enslave the whole world if they could. . . .They are part of the church of the devil and will be overthrown when the Lord comes."

Bruce R. McConkie, A New Witness for the Articles of Faith, p. 687.

"Subjection to secular power does not constitute a divine approval of the system of government involved."

Neal A. Maxwell, Wherefore Ye Must Press Forward, p. 13.

"In a similar observation Samuel P. Huntington has warned: 'The vulnerability of democratic government in the United States thus comes not primarily from external threats, though such threats are real . . . but rather from the internal dynamics of democracy itself in a highly educated, mobilized, and participant society'. 'Democracy never lasts long,' John Adams observed. 'It soon wastes, exhausts, and murders itself. There never was a democracy yet that did not commit suicide.' That suicide is more likely to be the product of overindulgence than of any other cause."

Dallin H. Oaks, Ensign, October 1992, p. 63-64.

"When religion has a special constitutional right to its free exercise, religious leaders and churches should have more freedom than other persons and organizations, not less . . . religious-based values are just as legitimate a basis for political action as any other values. . . . churches and church leaders should be able to participate in public policy debates on the same basis as other persons and organizations, favoring or opposing specific legislative proposals or candidates . . .

The relationship in the world between church and state and between church leaders and politicians should be respectful and distant, as befits two parties who need one another but share the realization that a relationship too close can deprive a pluralistic government of its legitimacy and a divine church of its spiritual mission. Despite that desirable distance, government need not be hostile to religion or pretend to ignore God."

M. Russell Ballard, Ensign, October 1992, p. 65-69.

"Some people now claim that the Founding Fathers' worst fear in connection with religion has been realized; that we have, in fact, a state-sponsored religion in America today. This new religion, adopted by many, does not have an identifiable name, but it operates just like a church. It exists in the form of doctrines and beliefs, where morality is whatever a person wants it to be, and where freedom is derived from the ideas of man and not the laws of God. . . .

The values that made America great are, in reality, the commandments of God. . . .And if American democracy seems shaky today, it's only because that foundation has been eroded and weakened under the guise of separation of church and state."

SCRIPTURAL REFERENCES

Proverbs 29:2
 2 When the righteous are in authority, the people rejoice: but when the wicked beareth rule, the people mourn.

Ephesians 6:11-12
 11 Put on the whole armour of God, that ye may be able to stand against the wiles of the devil.
 12 For we wrestle not against flesh and blood, but against principalities, against powers, against the rulers of the darkness of this world, against spiritual wickedness in high places.

2 Nephi 1:7-9
 7 Wherefore, this land is consecrated unto him whom he shall bring. And if it so be that they shall serve him according to the commandments which he hath given, it shall be a land of liberty unto them; wherefore, they shall never be brought down into captivity; if so, it shall be because of iniquity; for if iniquity shall abound cursed shall be the land for their sakes, but unto the righteous it shall be blessed forever.
 8 And behold, it is wisdom that this land should be kept as yet from the knowledge of other nations; for behold, many nations would overrun the land, that there would be no place for an inheritance.
 9 Wherefore, I, Lehi, have obtained a promise, that inasmuch as those whom the Lord God shall bring out of the land of Jerusalem shall keep his commandments, they shall prosper upon the face of this land; and they shall be kept from all other nations, that they may possess this land unto themselves. And if it so be that they shall keep his commandments they shall be blessed upon the face of this land, and there shall be none to molest them, nor to take away the land of their inheritance; and they shall dwell safely forever.

2 Nephi 10:10-16
 10 But behold, this land, said God, shall be a land of thine inheritance, and the Gentiles shall be blessed upon the land.
 11 And this land shall be a land of liberty unto the Gentiles, and there shall be no kings upon the land, who shall raise up unto the Gentiles.
 12 And I will fortify this land against all other nations.
 13 And he that fighteth against Zion shall perish, saith God.
 14 For he that raiseth up a king against me shall perish, for I, the Lord, the king of heaven, will be their king, and I will be a light unto them forever, that hear my words.
 15 Wherefore, for this cause, that my covenants may be fulfilled which I have made unto the children of men, that I will do unto them while they are in the flesh, I must needs destroy the secret works of darkness, and of murders, and of abominations.
 16 Wherefore, he that fighteth against Zion, both Jew and Gentile, both bond and free, both male and female, shall perish; for they are they who are the whore of all the earth; for they who are not for me are against me, saith our God.

Mosiah 29:21-27

21 And behold, now I say unto you, ye cannot dethrone an iniquitous king save it be through much contention, and the shedding of much blood.

22 For behold, he has his friends in iniquity, and he keepeth his guards about him; and he teareth up the laws of those who have reigned in righteousness before him; and he trampleth under his feet the commandments of God;

23 And he enacteth laws, and sendeth them forth among his people, yea, laws after the manner of his own wickedness; and whosoever doth not obey his laws he causeth to be destroyed; and whosoever doth rebel against him he will send his armies against them to war, and if he can he will destroy them; and thus an unrighteous king doth pervert the ways of all righteousness.

24 And now behold I say unto you, it is not expedient that such abominations should come upon you.

25 Therefore, choose you by the voice of this people, judges, that ye may be judged according to the laws which have been given you by our fathers, which are correct, and which were given them by the hand of the Lord.

26 Now it is not common that the voice of the people desireth anything contrary to that which is right; but it is common for the lesser part of the people to desire that which is not right; therefore this shall ye observe and make it your law—to do your business by the voice of the people.

27 And if the time comes that the voice of the people doth choose iniquity, then is the time that the judgments of God will come upon you; yea, then is the time he will visit you with great destruction even as he has hitherto visited this land.

Alma 61:10-14

10 And now, behold, we will resist wickedness even unto bloodshed. We would not shed the blood of the Lamanites if they would stay in their own land.

11 We would not shed the blood of our brethren if they would not rise up in rebellion and take the sword against us.

12 We would subject ourselves to the yoke of bondage if it were requisite with the justice of God, or if he should command us so to do.

13 But behold he doth not command us that we shall subject ourselves to our enemies, but that we should put our trust in him, and he will deliver us.

14 Therefore, my beloved brother, Moroni, let us resist evil, and whatsoever evil we cannot resist with our words, yea, such as rebellions and dissensions, let us resist them with our swords, that we may retain our freedom, that we may rejoice in the great privilege of our church, and in the cause of our Redeemer and our God.

Helaman 4:22

22 And that they had altered and trampled under their feet the laws of Mosiah, or that which the Lord commanded him to give unto the people; and they saw that their laws had become corrupted, and that they had become a wicked people, insomuch that they were wicked even like unto the Lamanites.

Helaman 5:2-3

2 For as their laws and their governments were established by the voice of the people, and they who chose evil were more numerous than they who chose good, therefore they were ripening for destruction, for the laws had become corrupted.

3 Yea, and this was not all; they were a stiffnecked people, insomuch that they could not be governed by the law nor justice, save it were to their destruction.

Helaman 6:21-30

21 But behold, Satan did stir up the hearts of the more part of the Nephites, insomuch that they did unite with those bands of robbers, and did enter into their covenants and their oaths, that they would protect and preserve one another in whatsoever difficult circumstances they should be placed, that they should not suffer for their murders, and their plunderings, and their stealings.

22 And it came to pass that they did have their signs, yea, their secret signs, and their secret words; and this that they might distinguish a brother who had entered into the covenant, that whatsoever wickedness his brother should do he should not be injured by his brother, nor by those who did belong to his band, who had taken this covenant.

23 And thus they might murder, and plunder, and steal, and commit whoredoms and all manner of wickedness, contrary to the laws of their country and also the laws of their God.

24 And whosoever of those who belonged to their band should reveal unto the world of their wickedness and their abominations, should be tried, not according to the laws of their country, but according to the laws of their wickedness, which had been given by Gadianton and Kishkumen.

25 Now behold, it is these secret oaths and covenants which Alma commanded his son should not go forth unto the world, lest they should be a means of bringing down the people unto destruction.

26 Now behold, those secret oaths and covenants did not come forth unto Gadianton from the records which were delivered unto Helaman; but behold, they were put into the heart of Gadianton by that same being who did entice our first parents to partake of the forbidden fruit—

27 Yea, that same being who did plot with Cain, that if he would murder his brother Abel it should not be known unto the world. And he did plot with Cain and his followers from that time forth.

28 And also it is that same being who put it into the hearts of the people to build a tower sufficiently high that they might get to heaven. And it was that same being who led on the people who came from that tower into this land; who spread the works of darkness and abominations over all the face of the land, until he dragged the people down to an entire destruction, and to an everlasting hell.

29 Yea, it is that same being who put it into the heart of Gadianton to still carry on the work of darkness, and of secret murder; and he has brought it forth from the beginning of man even down to this time.

30 And behold, it is he who is the author of all sin. And behold, he doth carry on his works of darkness and secret murder, and doth hand down their plots, and their oaths, and their covenants, and their plans of awful wickedness, from generation to generation according as he can get hold upon the hearts of the children of men.

Helaman 6:37-40

37 And it came to pass that the Lamanites did hunt the band of robbers of Gadianton; and they did

preach the word of God among the more wicked part of them, insomuch that this band of robbers was utterly destroyed from among the Lamanites.

38 And it came to pass on the other hand, that the Nephites did build them up and support them, beginning at the more wicked part of them, until they had overspread all the land of the Nephites, and had seduced the more part of the righteous until they had come down to believe in their works and partake of their spoils, and to join with them in their secret murders and combinations.

39 And thus they did obtain the sole management of the government, insomuch that they did trample under their feet and smite and rend and turn their backs upon the poor and the meek, and the humble followers of God.

40 And thus we see that they were in an awful state, and ripening for an everlasting destruction.

Helaman 7:4-5

4 And seeing the people in a state of such awful wickedness, and those Gadianton robbers filling the judgment-seats—having usurped the power and authority of the land; laying aside the commandments of God, and not in the least aright before him; doing no justice unto the children of men;

5 Condemning the righteous because of their righteousness; letting the guilty and the wicked go unpunished because of their money; and moreover to be held in office at the head of government, to rule and do according to their wills, that they might get gain and glory of the world, and, moreover, that they might the more easily commit adultery, and steal, and kill, and do according to their own wills—

3 Nephi 5:4-6

4 And now it came to pass that when they had taken all the robbers prisoners, insomuch that none did escape who were not slain, they did cast their prisoners into prison, and did cause the word of God to be preached unto them; and as many as would repent of their sins and enter into a covenant that they would murder no more were set at liberty.

5 But as many as there were who did not enter into a covenant, and who did still continue to have those secret murders in their hearts, yea, as many as were found breathing out threatenings against their brethren were condemned and punished according to the law.

6 And thus they did put an end to all those wicked, and secret, and abominable combinations, in the which there was so much wickedness, and so many murders committed.

3 Nephi 7:1-6

1 Now behold, I will show unto you that they did not establish a king over the land; but in this same year, yea, the thirtieth year, they did destroy upon the judgment seat, yea, did murder the chief judge of the land.

2 And the people were divided one against another; and they did separate one from another into tribes, every man according to his family and his kindred and friends; and thus they did destroy the government of the land.

3 And every tribe did appoint a chief or a leader over them; and thus they became tribes and leaders of tribes.

4 Now behold, there was no man among them save he had much family and many kindreds and

friends; therefore their tribes became exceedingly great.

5 Now all this was done, and there were no wars as yet among them; and all this iniquity had come upon the people because they did yield themselves unto the power of Satan.

6 And the regulations of the government were destroyed, because of the secret combination of the friends and kindreds of those who murdered the prophets.

3 Nephi 9:9

9 And behold, that great city Jacobugath, which was inhabited by the people of king Jacob, have I caused to be burned with fire because of their sins and their wickedness, which was above all the wickedness of the whole earth, because of their secret murders and combinations; for it was they that did destroy the peace of my people and the government of the land; therefore I did cause them to be burned, to destroy them from before my face, that the blood of the prophets and the saints should not come up unto me any more against them.

Ether 2:7-12

7 And the Lord would not suffer that they should stop beyond the sea in the wilderness, but he would that they should come forth even unto the land of promise, which was choice above all other lands, which the Lord God had preserved for a righteous people.

8 And he had sworn in his wrath unto the brother of Jared, that whoso should possess this land of promise, from that time henceforth and forever, should serve him, the true and only God, or they should be swept off when the fulness of his wrath should come upon them.

9 And now, we can behold the decrees of God concerning this land, that it is a land of promise; and whatsoever nation shall possess it shall serve God, or they shall be swept off when the fulness of his wrath shall come upon them. And the fulness of his wrath cometh upon them when they are ripened in iniquity.

10 For behold, this is a land which is choice above all other lands; wherefore he that doth possess it shall serve God or shall be swept off; for it is the everlasting decree of God. And it is not until the fulness of iniquity among the children of the land, that they are swept off.

11 And this cometh unto you, O ye Gentiles, that ye may know the decrees of God—that ye may repent, and not continue in your iniquities until the fulness come, that ye may not bring down the fulness of the wrath of God upon you as the inhabitants of the land have hitherto done.

12 Behold, this is a choice land, and whatsoever nation shall possess it shall be free from bondage, and from captivity, and from all other nations under heaven, if they will but serve the God of the land, who is Jesus Christ, who hath been manifested by the things which we have written.

Ether 8:Heading

There is strife and contention over the kingdom—Akish forms an oath-bound secret combination to slay the king—Secret combinations are of the devil and result in the destruction of nations—Modern Gentiles are warned against the secret combination which shall seek to overthrow the freedom of all lands, nations, and countries.

Ether 8:18-26

18 And it came to pass that they formed a secret combination, even as they of old; which combination is most abominable and wicked above all, in the sight of God;

19 For the Lord worketh not in secret combinations, neither doth he will that man should shed blood, but in all things hath forbidden it, from the beginning of man.

20 And now I, Moroni, do not write the manner of their oaths and combinations, for it hath been made known unto me that they are had among all people, and they are had among the Lamanites.

21 And they have caused the destruction of this people of whom I am now speaking, and also the destruction of the people of Nephi.

22 And whatsoever nation shall uphold such secret combinations, to get power and gain, until they shall spread over the nation, behold, they shall be destroyed; for the Lord will not suffer that the blood of his saints, which shall be shed by them, shall always cry unto him from the ground for vengeance upon them and yet he avenge them not.

23 Wherefore, O ye Gentiles, it is wisdom in God that these things should be shown unto you, that thereby ye may repent of your sins, and suffer not that these murderous combinations shall get above you, which are built up to get power and gain—and the work, yea, even the work of destruction come upon you, yea, even the sword of the justice of the Eternal God shall fall upon you, to your overthrow and destruction if ye shall suffer these things to be.

24 Wherefore, the Lord commandeth you, when ye shall see these things come among you that ye shall awake to a sense of your awful situation, because of this secret combination which shall be among you; or wo be unto it, because of the blood of them who have been slain; for they cry from the dust for vengeance upon it, and also upon those who built it up.

25 For it cometh to pass that whoso buildeth it up seeketh to overthrow the freedom of all lands, nations, and countries; and it bringeth to pass the destruction of all people, for it is built up by the devil, who is the father of all lies; even that same liar who beguiled our first parents, yea, even that same liar who hath caused man to commit murder from the beginning; who hath hardened the hearts of men that they have murdered the prophets, and stoned them, and cast them out from the beginning.

26 Wherefore, I, Moroni, am commanded to write these things that evil may be done away, and that the time may come that Satan may have no power upon the hearts of the children of men, but that they may be persuaded to do good continually, that they may come unto the fountain of all righteousness and be saved.

D&C 38:28-30

28 And again, I say unto you that the enemy in the secret chambers seeketh your lives.

29 Ye hear of wars in far countries, and you say that there will soon be great wars in far countries, but ye know not the hearts of men in your own land.

30 I tell you these things because of your prayers; wherefore, treasure up wisdom in your bosoms, lest the wickedness of men reveal these things unto you by their wickedness, in a manner which shall speak in your ears with a voice louder than that which shall shake the earth; but if ye are prepared ye shall not fear.

D&C 98:5-10

5 And that law of the land which is constitutional, supporting that principle of freedom in maintaining rights and privileges, belongs to all mankind, and is justifiable before me.

6 Therefore, I, the Lord, justify you, and your brethren of my church, in befriending that law which is the constitutional law of the land;

7 And as pertaining to law of man, whatsoever is more or less than this, cometh of evil.

8 I, the Lord God, make you free, therefore ye are free indeed; and the law also maketh you free.

9 Nevertheless, when the wicked rule the people mourn.

10 Wherefore, honest men and wise men should be sought for diligently, and good men and wise men ye should observe to uphold; otherwise whatsoever is less than these cometh of evil.

D&C 101:77-80

77 According to the laws and constitution of the people, which I have suffered to be established, and should be maintained for the rights and protection of all flesh, according to just and holy principles;

78 That every man may act in doctrine and principle pertaining to futurity, according to the moral agency which I have given unto him, that every man may be accountable for his own sins in the day of judgment.

79 Therefore, it is not right that any man should be in bondage one to another.

80 And for this purpose have I established the Constitution of this land, by the hands of wise men whom I raised up unto this very purpose, and redeemed the land by the shedding of blood.

D&C 109:54

54 Have mercy, O Lord, upon all the nations of the earth; have mercy upon the rulers of our land; may those principles, which were so honorably and nobly defended, namely, the Constitution of our land, by our fathers, be established forever.

D&C 121:36-39

36 That the rights of the priesthood are inseparably connected with the powers of heaven, and that the powers of heaven cannot be controlled nor handled only upon the principles of righteousness.

37 That they may be conferred upon us, it is true; but when we undertake to cover our sins, or to gratify our pride, our vain ambition, or to exercise control or dominion or compulsion upon the souls of the children of men, in any degree of unrighteousness, behold, the heavens withdraw themselves; the Spirit of the Lord is grieved; and when it is withdrawn, Amen to the priesthood or the authority of that man.

38 Behold, ere he is aware, he is left unto himself, to kick against the pricks, to persecute the saints, and to fight against God.

39 We have learned by sad experience that it is the nature and disposition of almost all men, as soon as they get a little authority, as they suppose, they will immediately begin to exercise unrighteous dominion.

D&C 134:1-9

1 We believe that governments were instituted of God for the benefit of man; and that he holds men

accountable for their acts in relation to them, both in making laws and administering them, for the good and safety of society.

2 We believe that no government can exist in peace, except such laws are framed and held inviolate as will secure to each individual the free exercise of conscience, the right and control of property, and the protection of life.

3 We believe that all governments necessarily require civil officers and magistrates to enforce the laws of the same; and that such as will administer the law in equity and justice should be sought for and upheld by the voice of the people if a republic, or the will of the sovereign.

4 We believe that religion is instituted of God; and that men are amenable to him, and to him only, for the exercise of it, unless their religious opinions prompt them to infringe upon the rights and liberties of others; but we do not believe that human law has a right to interfere in prescribing rules of worship to bind the consciences of men, nor dictate forms for public or private devotion; that the civil magistrate should restrain crime, but never control conscience; should punish guilt, but never suppress the freedom of the soul.

5 We believe that all men are bound to sustain and uphold the respective governments in which they reside, while protected in their inherent and inalienable rights by the laws of such governments; and that sedition and rebellion are unbecoming every citizen thus protected, and should be punished accordingly; and that all governments have a right to enact such laws as in their own judgments are best calculated to secure the public interest; at the same time, however, holding sacred the freedom of conscience.

6 We believe that every man should be honored in his station, rulers and magistrates as such, being placed for the protection of the innocent and the punishment of the guilty; and that to the laws all men owe respect and deference, as without them peace and harmony would be supplanted by anarchy and terror; human laws being instituted for the express purpose of regulating our interests as individuals and nations, between man and man; and divine laws given of heaven, prescribing rules on spiritual concerns, for faith and worship, both to be answered by man to his Maker.

7 We believe that rulers, states, and governments have a right, and are bound to enact laws for the protection of all citizens in the free exercise of their religious belief; but we do not believe that they have a right in justice to deprive citizens of this privilege, or proscribe them in their opinions, so long as a regard and reverence are shown to the laws and such religious opinions do not justify sedition nor conspiracy.

8 We believe that the commission of crime should be punished according to the nature of the offense; that murder, treason, robbery, theft, and the breach of the general peace, in all respects, should be punished according to their criminality and their tendency to evil among men, by the laws of that government in which the offense is committed; and for the public peace and tranquility all men should step forward and use their ability in bringing offenders against good laws to punishment.

9 We do not believe it just to mingle religious influence with civil government, whereby one religious society is fostered and another proscribed in its spiritual privileges, and the individual rights of its members, as citizens, denied.

Moses 6:15

15 And the children of men were numerous upon all the face of the land. And in those days Satan

had great dominion among men, and raged in their hearts; and from thenceforth came wars and bloodshed; and a man's hand was against his own bother, in adminstering death, because of secret works, seeking for power.

CHAPTER FOUR

THE GOSPEL PREACHED IN ALL THE WORLD

"'Do you think there is calamity abroad now among the people?' Not much. All we have yet heard and all we have experienced is scarcely a preface to the sermon that is going to be preached. When the testimony of the Elders ceases to be given, and the Lord says to them, 'Come home; I will now preach my own sermons to the nations of the earth,' all you now know can scarcely be called a preface to the sermon that will be preached with fire and sword, tempests, earthquakes, hail, rain, thunders and lightnings, and fearful destruction." (Brigham Young, Journal of Discourses, Vol. 8, p. 123, July 15, 1860.)

MISSIONARY WORK

Joseph Smith, History of the Church, Vol. 2, p. 197.

"It is a sorrowful tale, but the Gospel must be preached, and God's ministers rejected: but where can Israel be found and receive your testimony, and not rejoice? Nowhere! The prophecies are full of great things that are to take place in the last days. After the elect are gathered out, destructions shall come on the inhabitants of the earth; all nations shall feel the wrath of God, after they have been warned by the Saints of the Most High. If you will not warn them, others will, and you will lose your crowns."

Teachings of the Prophet Joseph Smith, Section One, 1830–34, p. 43.

"Let the Elders be exceedingly careful about unnecessarily disturbing and harrowing up the feelings of the people. Remember that your business is to preach the Gospel in all humility and meekness, and warn sinners to repent and come to Christ.

Avoid contentions and vain disputes with men of corrupt minds, who do not desire to know the truth. Remember that 'it is a day of warning, and not a day of many words.' If they receive not your testimony in one place, flee to another, remembering to cast no reflections, nor throw out any bitter sayings. If you do your duty, it will be just as well with you, as though all men embraced the Gospel."

Teachings of the Prophet Joseph Smith, Section Two, 1834–37, p. 87.

"The servants of God will not have gone over the nations of the Gentiles, with a warning voice, until the destroying angel will commence to waste the inhabitants of the earth, and as the prophet hath said, 'It shall be a vexation to hear the report.'"

Teachings of the Prophet Joseph Smith, Section Two, 1834-37, p. 91.

"You need an endowment, brethren, in order that you may be prepared and able to overcome all things; and those that reject your testimony will be damned. The sick will be healed, the lame made to walk, the deaf to hear, and the blind to see, through your instrumentality. But let me tell you, that you will not have power, after the endowment to heal those that have not faith, nor to benefit them, for you might as well expect to benefit a devil in hell as such as are possessed of his spirit, and are willing to keep it: for they are habitations for devils, and only fit for his society. But when you are endowed and prepared to preach the Gospel to all nations, kindreds, and tongues, in their own languages, you must faithfully warn all, and bind up the testimony, and seal up the law, and the destroying angel will follow close at your heels, and exercise his tremendous mission upon the children of disobedience; and destroy the workers of iniquity, while the Saints will be gathered out from among them, and stand in holy places ready to meet the Bridegroom when he comes."

Brigham Young, Journal of Discourses, Vol. 8, p. 123, July 15, 1860.

"'Do you think there is calamity abroad now among the people?' Not much. All we have yet heard and all we have experienced is scarcely a preface to the sermon that is going to be preached. When the testimony of the Elders ceases to be given, and the Lord says to them, 'Come home; I will now preach my own sermons to the nations of the earth,' all you now know can scarcely be called a preface to the sermon that will be preached with fire and sword, tempests, earthquakes, hail, rain, thunders and lightnings, and fearful destruction."

Discourses of Brigham Young, p. 320.

"The Elders have also preached through the different nations of Europe so far as they were allowed to do so. In some countries the law would not permit them; but the Lord will yet revolutionize those nations until the door will be opened and the Gospel will be preached to all."

Parley P. Pratt, Journal of Discourses, Vol. 3, p. 186, August 26, 1855.

"Prior to this great destruction, the everlasting Gospel will be taught to them by the servants of God, by the testimony of men and angels, and by the testimony of Jesus Christ, and by the testimony of ancient and modern Prophets; by the testimony of Joseph Smith, and of the Apostles ordained by him, and by the testimony of ancient and modern Saints; by the testimony of the Ten Tribes; by the testimony of heaven and the testimony of earth; then shall the wicked be sent to their own place, and truth shall be established in the earth; and the voice of joy and gladness shall be heard with the meek of the earth."

Orson Pratt, Journal of Discourses, Vol. 6, p. 205, January 24, 1859.

"Then, brethren, you can go and preach to them, and say the power of God is with you, and say to the people, Look yonder, and behold the children of Zion delivered by the power of God; and then you will be respected. Then you can go to the palaces of the great and preach to the king upon his throne, to the great men, to the nobles, and rich men of the earth,; and many will fear, and receive your testimony, and flow to Zion, bringing their riches with them. But now you could not go into their fine palaces, nor find access to their rich and splendid mansions. You could not get them to hear you for one moment."

Orson Pratt, Journal of Discourses, Vol. 7, p. 185, July 10, 1859.

"There must be the interposition of the Almighty to make a change among the nations of the earth before this church can be established among all the nations and kingdoms of the Gentiles. This change will probably be brought about by war overturning all the governments and kingdoms of the Gentiles."

Orson Pratt, Journal of Discourses, Vol. 7, p. 185-186, July 10, 1859.

"There will be a time of peace—a time that will be more favourable to the promulgation of the Gospel, that you and I and whosoever of the servants of God he pleases may be sent to these European nations to fulfil the prophecy which I have referred to in the Book of Mormon, and establish the kingdom of God among all the nations of modern Europe. Where tyranny and oppression and all the horrors of despotism now reign, will be heard the Gospel of peace. Saints must be established in all those countries. Even in Russia, that place where they would almost put you to death if you brought a printed work of a religious nature into the empire,—in that country, where they will not suffer you to propagate the Bible unmolested, whose religion is established by law, has the Gospel of Jesus Christ to be preached. Yes, the Church of the Saints is to be established there; and after it is established, there they are to gather together in multitudes, like other nations, to fight against it; and so they will in Austria, Spain, Portugal, and in all the modern nations of Europe, as well as those nations that inhabit Asia and Africa. This war that is now taking place will not result in that dreadful extinction that is foretold in the Book of Mormon, and which will rage among all the nations and kingdoms of the Gentiles, or, in other words, among the nations of Christendom. The one is a war preparatory to the proclamation of the Gospel; the other is a war of terrible destruction, which will not better the condition of those who escape. The wars that are now taking place will have a tendency, in some measure, to open the way for the Elders of the Church of Jesus Christ to go and establish the Church and kingdom of God among those nations."

Orson Pratt, Journal of Discourses, Vol. 7, p. 186, July 10, 1859.

"The day will come when the nations of Europe will have warred among themselves sufficiently long, and those despotic governments are torn down, and when the hand of oppression and tyranny has been eased up, and when the principles of religious liberty have become more fully and more widely spread, that the Elders of this church will traverse all these nations; and then we shall have use for these Seventies that have been organizing so long."

Orson Pratt, Journal of Discourses, Vol. 8, p. 47, April 8, 1860.

"In speaking of the signs of the coming of the Son of Man, and of the preaching of the Gospel to all the world, the new translation reads as follows:—'Again shall this Gospel of the kingdom be preached in all the world for a witness, and then shall the end come.' Now, the word 'again' makes the thing all plain. It is as much as to say, You shall go forth, you shall preach to the people and declare my testimony among the nations of the earth; and after this there shall arise many false Christs and false prophets. Then shall follow many judgments and tribulations upon the face of the earth.

And after the world has been in darkness for centuries, again shall this Gospel of the kingdom be preached in all the world for a witness unto all nations; and then shall the end come. What end? I answer, the end of the wicked world—the destruction of the wicked from the face of our globe."

Orson Pratt, Journal of Discourses, Vol. 14, p. 65-66, March 26, 1871.
    "It is not only a Gospel to be preached to all the nations of the earth, but in connection with it you will have to make proclamation connected with it, to all people, to fear God and give glory to him, for the hour of his judgment is come.

Orson Pratt, Journal of Discourses, Vol. 15, p. 47, April 7, 1872.
    "John, who saw this angel restore the everlasting Gospel to be preached to all the nations, declares that another proclamation was closely connected with the preaching of the Gospel. What was it? 'The hour of his judgment has come'—the eleventh hour, the last time that God will warn the nations of the earth. 'The hour of God's judgment has come,' and that is the reason why the Gospel is to be so extensively preached among all people, nations and tongues, because the Lord intends through this warning to prepare them, if they will, to escape the hour of his judgment, which must come upon all people who will refuse to receive the divine message of the everlasting Gospel."

Orson Pratt, Journal of Discourses, Vol. 15, p. 366-367, March 9, 1873.
    "When the Temple is built the sons of the two Priesthoods, that is, those who are ordained to the Priesthood of Melchizedek, that Priesthood which is after the order of the Son of God, with all its appendages; and those who have been ordained to the Priesthood of Aaron with all its appendages, the former called the sons of Moses, the latter the sons of Aaron, will enter into that Temple in this generation, or in the generation that was living in 1832, and all of them who are pure in heart will behold the face of the Lord and that too before he comes in his glory in the clouds of heaven, for he will suddenly come to his Temple, and he will purify the sons of Moses and of Aaron, until they shall be prepared to offer in that Temple and offering that shall be acceptable in the sight of the Lord. In doing this, he will purify not only the minds of the Priesthood in that Temple, but he will purify their bodies until they shall be quickened, renewed and strengthened, and they will be partially changed, not to immortality, but changed in part that they can be filled with the power of God, and they can stand in the presence of Jesus, and behold his face in the midst of that Temple.
    This will prepare them for further ministrations among the nations of the earth, it will prepare them to go forth in the days of tribulation and vengeance upon the nations of the wicked, when God will smite them with pestilence, plague and earthquake, such as former generations never knew. Then the servants of God will need to be armed with the power of God, they will need to have that sealing blessing pronounced upon their foreheads that they can stand forth in the midst of these desolations and plagues and not be overcome by them. When John the Revelator describes this scene he says he saw four angels sent forth, ready to hold the four winds that should blow from the four quarters of heaven. Another angel ascended from the east and cried to the four angels, and said, 'Smite not the earth now, but wait a little while.' 'How long?' 'Until the servants of our God are sealed in their foreheads.' What for? To prepare them to stand forth in the midst of these desolations and plagues, and not be overcome. When they are prepared, when they have received a renewal of

their bodies in the Lord's Temple, and have been filled with the Holy Ghost and purified as gold and silver in a furnace of fire, then they will be prepared to stand before the nations of the earth and preach glad tidings of salvation in the midst of judgments that are to come like a whirlwind upon the wicked."

Orson Pratt, Journal of Discourses, Vol. 18, p. 59, July 25, 1875.

"One of the means which God will use to prepare the way before his second coming, is to send angels from heaven with a proclamation, not to benefit a few individuals, not for one nations alone, but to all the inhabitants of our globe, and that too before he comes. Do you want to know where this prediction is recorded? Let me refer to you the fourteenth chapter of the revelations given to St. John on Patmos. Did St. John behold, in vision, the coming of the Son of God? He did. How does he describe it in that fourteenth chapter? He said, as you will find by reading the chapter through, that he saw one sitting on a white cloud, having a sharp sickle in his hand. He had reference to the time when Jesus should come in the clouds of heaven; however, before John saw the personage sitting on the cloud, he saw a preparatory work commence, as it is declared in the sixth verse, in which the Prophet says—'I saw another angel fly in the midst of heaven, having the everlasting Gospel to preach unto them that dwell on the earth, unto every nation and kindred and tongue and people,' declaring that the hour of God's judgment was come."

Orson Pratt, Journal of Discourses, Vol. 18, p. 63-64, July 25, 1875.

"At the present time there are some nations who will not permit any religion to be proclaimed within their borders except that which is established by law. When God shall cast down thrones, which he will soon do; when he shall overturn kingdoms and empires, which time is very near at hand, then other governments will be formed more favorable to religious liberty, and the missionaries of this Church will visit those nations. . . .

And so we might enumerate what God is doing among these despotic powers, overturning and changing long-established usages and institutions, that His servants may go by His own command, to deliver the great and last message of the Gospel to the inhabitants of the earth, preparatory to the coming of his Son."

Orson Pratt, Journal of Discourses, Vol. 20, p. 150, March 9, 1879.

"Now let me point out some other things which will occur, before the coming of the Son of Man. The Lord has a controversy among all the nations of the gentiles. He has sent to them a warning. He has sent his servants to prophesy to them. He has sent them to preach and bear record of the truth. He has sent them to call upon the nations to repent, both high and low, rich and poor, religionist and non-religionist, priest and people, for all of them to repent and receive the Gospel in its fullness, and not only to do this, but to gather out from these nations. Will they hear? They will not. We know they will not; but this does not justify us in being slack in delivering our message. We have a responsibility placed upon us, and that responsibility we must fulfill, whether the people hear, or whether they forbear, we must warn them, so that they shall not have any excuse, when the tribulations shall come which I have named."

Orson Pratt, Journal of Discourses, Vol. 20, p. 150-151, March 9, 1879.

"The Lord, therefore has a controversy among them, the same as he had with the Egyptian nation, with this difference, that the Egyptians did not have the same length of time to consider the message which you have. They only had a few days, and if they would not repent and receive the word which Moses and Aaron delivered to them, well and good; and only a short time, a very few days were allowed them to decide this matter. You have had a portion of a whole generation. Your times are not quite yet fulfilled, and hence you have had the privilege to consider it from your childhood up to middle age, and some of you from middle age to old age, to see whether you will receive the latter-day message which God has sent or not. Now, the consequences will be, if you receive it, you will save yourselves by fleeing out from the midst of this nation. You will save yourselves and your children temporally speaking as well as spiritually. On the other hand, if you do not receive it, the Lord, who is long suffering, will, after he has borne with the people all the day long, withdraw his servants from your midst. When that day shall come there shall be wars, not such wars has have come in centuries and years that are past and gone, but a desolating war."

Orson Pratt, Journal of Discourses, Vol.20, p. 153-154, March 9, 1879.

"It is because of this, of the light that the nations have in their midst, which they will not receive that the Lord will visit them first; and when he has visited and overthrown them, he will lay his hand heavily upon the heathen nations in Asia, and also those who are in Africa, and they will be visited with severe judgment, but they will not be utterly destroyed. A portion of the heathen nations will be redeemed. Why? They will see the power and glory of God that will be manifested among the tribes of Israel, who will be gathered out from their midst and return to their own land. They will see the glory of God manifested as in ancient times and they will say, 'surely Jaggernaut is no longer my God.' 'Surely I will not worship crocodiles, nor serpents; neither will I worship the sun, or the moon, for there is a God manifested among that people, Israel, who is worthy of the natures and attributes of a God. I will cast my Gods to the moles and bats, and I will worship the God of Israel.' Then will be fulfilled that which was spoken by the prophet Ezekiel, 'then shall the heathen know that I the Lord am God.' And it will come to pass, after that period, when Jesus shall have raised all the righteous from their graves, that he will descend with all the hosts of heaven accompanying him, and will stand upon the Mount of Olives, and he will go out of Jerusalem, and the Jews will go out to the mount to meet him and will acknowledge him as their Messiah and King; and then it shall come to pass, that the heathen nations will also more fully recognize him as the true and only God."

John Taylor, Journal of Discourses, Vol. 19, p. 244-245, October 21, 1877.

"We profess to be Apostles of the Lord bearing his Gospel message to the nations of the earth; then let us exhibit a little more of the apostolic power and zeal when we go out among our fellow-men, realizing that we have got the light and life and power of God with us; and that we are sent to teach and not to be taught of men, to control circumstances, in a great measure, by the power of the Priesthood, instead of allowing ourselves to be controlled so much. We have not got through with the work, we have only just commenced it. Here are our fallen brethren, the Lamanites. What an extensive work opens up among them, which must yet be done, but which will not fairly commence until we approximate to the consummation of our mission to the Gentile world. And when we shall have introduced more fully the Gospel, and developed the purposes of the Almighty to this Branch of Israel, the Jews will be ready to receive the servants of God and the Gospel, which will then be proclaimed to them. And when we get through with Israel, there will remain the ten tribes to be restored, the earth to be redeemed and the kingdom of God to be established thereon; all of which must be done in order that the Scriptures may be fulfilled, and the designs of God consummated. Our work is mapped out before us, it is all designed and planned by him who rules above, and it is time that every Elder in Israel fully understood this fact that the Latter-day Saints have got to take a part in all this work, and that we are not here to attend to our own personal affairs merely, but, we are called to look after the interests of God, to build up his Zion and establish his kingdom on this his earth."

John Taylor, Journal of Discourses, Vol. 20, p. 23, July 7, 1878.

"But it is time we were waking up to a sense of the position we occupy before God; for the day is not far distant when we will hear of wars and rumors of wars; not only rumors of wars, but wars themselves—nation arrayed against nation and seizing one another by the throat, and blood will flow, and general carnage will be spread through the lands, and if you do not magnify your callings, God will hold you responsible for those whom you might have saved had you done your duty. How many of you can say, My garments are clean from the blood of this generation? I speak in behalf of the nations and the people thereof, and the honest in heart who are ignorant of God and his laws. He has called upon us to enlighten them, and to spread forth the truth, and send forth the principles of the Gospel, and point out the way of life. And it is for us to attend to these things, that we may secure the smiles and approbation of God."

John Taylor, Journal of Discourses, Vol. 20, p. 139-140, February 2, 1879.

"The Latter-day Saints feel as though they occupy a peculiar position in the world—that God has selected them from among the nations of the earth and gathered them together that he might place his name among them; and that in the coming struggle, in the great revolutions that shall transpire upon the face of the earth, it will be for them to manage, to direct, to control and adjust, and under the influence and guidance of the Spirit of the living God, to promulgate the principles of eternal truth to all people, that all mankind may have the opportunity of listening to the great and glorious principles that God has revealed to them, that they may be inducted into the laws of life and comprehend the principles of truth as they exist in the bosom of God; and holding the priesthood in all its various forms, organizations and powers, they feel that they are associated with the priesthood on the other side of the vail, who are interested in their welfare, in the progress of the work in which they are engaged, and in the accomplishment of the purpose which God has designed from before the commencement of the world. This is the kind of feeling that the Latter-day Saints are inspired with who comprehend their true position. And hence there are organizations of High Priests, Seventies, Elders and others, whose duty it is to go to nations of the earth to proclaim to all peoples the glad tidings of salvation. And whilst men ignorantly, and without knowledge, seek to persecute, proscribe and interfere with the rights of Israel, the God of Israel stands forth as their defender and will protect them under all circumstances, and every arm that is raised against them will fall, and every power that is marshalled against them will crumble to pieces, for he will assuredly take care of his people, and protect them in every emergency."

John Taylor, The Government of God, p. 95.

"Some people talk about the world being burned up, about plagues, pestilence, famine, sworn, and ruin, and all these things being instantaneous. Now it would not be just for the Lord to punish the inhabitants of the earth without warning. For if the world are ignorant of God, they cannot altogether be blamed for it; if they are made the dupes of false systems, and false principles, they cannot help it; many of them are doing as well as they can, while, as we have before stated, it would be unjust for the world to continue as it is. It would at the same time be as unjust to punish the inhabitants of the world for things that they are ignorant of, or for things over which they have no control. Before the Lord destroyed the inhabitants of the old world, he sent Enoch and Noah to warn them. Before the Lord destroyed Sodom and Gomorrah, he sent Lot into their midst. Before the Children of Israel were carried captive to Babylon, they were warned of it by the Prophets; and before Jerusalem was destroyed, the inhabitants had the testimony of our Lord, and his Disciples. And so will it be in the last days; and as it is the world that is concerned, the world will have to be warned."

John Taylor, The Government of God, p.101.

"The testimony of God is first to be made known, the standard is to be raised, the Gospel of the kingdom is to be preached to all nations, the world is to be warned, and then come the troubles. The whole world is in confusion, morally, politically, and religiously; but a voice was to be heard, 'come out of her, my people, that you partake not of her sins, and that ye receive not of her plagues.'"

Franklin D. Richards, A Compendium of the Doctrines of the Gospel, p. 206.

"The testimony of the elders is the great preparatory work for the destruction of the wicked in this dispensation. Their labors are 'To bind up the law and seal up the testimony, and to prepare the saints for the hour of judgment which is to come;' (D&C 88:84.) And, after their testimony, 'cometh wrath and indignation upon the people;' (vs. 88.)"

Charles W. Penrose, Journal of Discourses, Vol. 22, p. 95-96, May 1, 1880.

"I know that the Gospel will be preached to every creature. I know that the honest and truth-loving, who dare meet the frowns of men, who dare face popular opinion, will come out from the sects and parties of the earth and from the different nations and countries, and be baptized into this Church and receive the Holy Ghost, and thus be drawn near to God, and prepared for the advent of the Lord. They will come from all parts of the earth. This work will roll on. No government, or kingdom, or power, or president, or ruler, or monarch, can stop its progress. It is not the work of man. It is the work of the great God."

David O. McKay, BYU Speeches, May 18, 1960, p. 6.

"Can you not see many nations yet to hear the truth, students, Jew as well as Gentile, India and China both awaking, Russia enveloped with communism—a new religious freedom must come. God will overrule it, for that people must hear the truth, and truth in simplicity. Truly there is much for the Church to do in the coming century!"

Joseph Fielding Smith Jr., Doctrines of Salvation, Vol. 3, p. 7.
"When the time comes that the nations will cast the elders out . . .woe be unto them. . . . after the testimony of the elders will come wrath and indignation upon the people."

James E. Talmage, Jesus the Christ, p. 739-740.
"Their ministry (three Nephites) was to be extended to Jews and Gentiles, amongst whom they labor unrecognized as of ancient birth; and they are sent unto the scattered tribes of Israel, and to all nations, kindreds, tongues and peoples, from whom they have brought and are bringing many souls unto Christ, 'that their desire may be fulfilled, and also because of the convincing power of God which is in them.'"

Ezra Taft Benson, Improvement Era, June 1970, p. 96.
"It is in very deed a mandate to his church. It will be carried out. No power on earth or in hell can stop this work or thwart the purposes of the Lord to have his soul-satisfying gospel message go to his children. It may take war, commotion, disasters in many forms to bring it about. But the purposes of God will be achieved. His children will hear the gospel of salvation in his own due time."

Teachings of Ezra Taft Benson, p. 177.
"In modern revelation, the Lord has said, 'Behold, verily I say unto you, the angels are crying unto the Lord day and night, who are ready and waiting to be sent forth to reap down the fields' (D&C 86:5). He also said in this same revelation that He would 'let the wheat and the tares grow together until the harvest is ripe; then ye shall first gather out the wheat from among the tares, and after the gathering of the wheat, behold and lo, the tares are bound in bundles, and the field remaineth to be burned' (verse 7). This is the time to 'gather the wheat,' the millions of righteous people. ("Safety in the Face of Wickedness," Tokyo Japan Area Conference, August 8-10, 1975.)"

Teachings of Ezra Taft Benson, p. 187.
"Prophets of God, ancient and modern, have predicted that judgments would be poured out upon the world unless the people repented. Prophets and leaders of the Church from the days of the Prophet Joseph have spoken out clearly and courageously regarding the calamities, destructions, and plagues which would visit the earth unless the people repented of their evil ways. But now, before the greatest calamities come, is the time for all of us to unite, to 'lengthen our stride,' as President Spencer W. Kimball has indicated, to 'raise our sights,' and to get a vision of the magnitude and urgency of this great missionary work. ("Safety in the Face of Wickedness," Tokyo Japan Area Conference, August 8-10, 1975.)"

Teachings of Ezra Taft Benson, p. 188.
"We are commanded by God to take this gospel to all the world. That is the cause that must unite us today. Only the gospel will save the world from the calamity of its own self-destruction. Only

the gospel will unite men of all races and nationalities in peace. Only the gospel will bring joy, happiness, and salvation to the human family."

Ezra Taft Benson, This Nation Shall Endure, p. 180.

"We must never forget that the gospel message we bear to the world is to go forth to the world from this nation, and that gospel message can prosper only in an atmosphere of freedom. We must maintain and strengthen our freedom in this blessed land."

Bruce R. McConkie, Conference Report, Ensign, May 1980, p. 72.

"We see the Lord break down the barriers so that the world of Islam and the world of Communism can hear the message of the restoration . . .We see congregations of the covenant people worshipping the Lord in Moscow and Peking and Saigon. We see Saints of the Most High raising their voices in Egypt and India and Africa. We see stakes of Zion in all parts of the earth; and Israel the chosen people, gathering into these cities of holiness . . . to await the coming of their King. . . .

All that is yet to be shall go forward in the midst of greater evils and perils and desolations than have been known on earth at any time. . . . But amid it all, the work of the Lord rolls on. The gospel is preached and the witness is born. The elect of God forsake the traditions of their fathers and the ways of the world. The kingdom grows and prospers, for the Lord is with his people."

Bruce R. McConkie, The Mortal Messiah, Vol. 4, p. 360-361.

"In this summary we are reminded: (1) that when the gospel goes to the Lamanites, it will be a sign that the great latter-day work has begun; (2) that in that day the gospel will go to all the dispersed of Israel, including the lost tribes; (3) that its purpose will be to bring Israel unto Christ so they can call upon the Father in his name; (4) that the work will go forward in all nations so that the chosen seed may be gathered to the lands of their inheritances; and (5) that they shall go out, not as escapees from oppression or for political reasons, but in glory and beauty and truth—the Lord himself going before and preparing the way and being also their rearward."

Bruce R. McConkie, The Millennial Messiah, p. 136.

"When the prophetic word says the gospel shall be preached in every nation, it means every nation. It includes Russia and China and India. . . . And the Lord will not come until it does."

Bruce R. McConkie, The Millennial Messiah, p. 137-138.

"The Lord will use the wars . .. to open nations and kingdoms to the preaching of the gospel."

Bruce R. McConkie, The Millennial Messiah, p. 138.

"When nations and peoples gather to oppose us, we must preach the saving truths to them as Ammon and his brethren did to the Lamanites. There is nothing but the gospel that will soften the hearts of men and cause them to turn away from war, and from evil, and from opposition to God."

Bruce R. McConkie, The Millennial Messiah, p. 142.

"All the forces of evil men . . . shall rise to fight the truth. . . .Knowing these things, we cannot permit opposition, however powerful and severe, to deter us . . . to proclaim the gospel."

Bruce R. McConkie, The Millennial Messiah, p. 142.
"The gospel shall be preached everywhere . . . converts by . . . the millions will be made in all nations. . .Comparatively speaking, however, a few only in all nations will believe the restored truth."

Bruce R. McConkie, The Millennial Messiah, p. 143.
"When the saints have done all that in their power lies, both to preach the everlasting word and to build up the eternal kingdom . . . when the wars and desolations and carnality of men are about to overwhelm them—then the Lord will take over. By his own power he will destroy the wicked."

TIME OF THE GENTILES

Heber C. Kimball, Deseret News, May 23, 1931.

"The judgments of God will be poured out upon the wicked to the extent that our elders from far and near will be called home. Or, in other words, the gospel will be taken from the Gentiles and later on will be carried to the Jews."

Parley P. Pratt, Journal of Discourses, Vol. 3, p. 135-136, October 7, 1855.

"Now, when the times of the Gentiles are fulfilled there will be an uprooting of their governments and institutions, and of their civil, political, and religious polity. There will be a shaking of nations, a downfall of empires, an upturning of thrones and dominions, as Daniel has foretold, and the kingdom and power, and rule on the earth will return to another people, and exist under another polity, as Daniel has further foretold. But let me read it here, let Jesus speak in his own words, or the writer for him. Now understand that we have got down to the present time, that is sure with this prophecy, no man can mistake it. Jerusalem has been overthrown, and not one stone of that magnificent temple has been left upon another. A great portion of that nation fell by the edge of the sword, and the residue went captive among all nations, and their city has been trodden under foot of the Gentiles, and will be until their times are fulfilled, that is, until they have had their reign out. Then what will happen? We will read; 'And there shall be signs in the sun.' Has anybody seen them?—not away back among those other things; there were signs in the air then; Josephus tells you about it, and this book tells you about it, as I have been reading to-day in this chapter, about the signs which happened as a forerunner of the destruction of Jerusalem, and the Jews as a nation. Now after the Jews have remained among the Gentiles until the times of the Gentiles are fulfilled, as a forerunner of this latter overturn 'there shall be signs in the sun and in the moon.' Have any of you seen them during the last 30 years? I have. 'And in the stars.' Have you seen any signs in the stars? Think back for the last 30 years. 'And upon the earth distress of nations, with perplexity; the sea and the waves roaring, men's hearts failing them for fear, and for looking after those things which are coming on the earth, for the powers of heaven shall be shaken. And THEN'—not some other time. Are there any Millerites here who have been setting a time for the Son of Man to come? 'Then shall they see the Son of Man coming in a cloud, with power and great glory.' Not you, my disciples, whom I told a little while ago should be delivered up to the synagogues, and to prisons, and be beheaded, and suffer many things; not you whom I have warned to take heed lest you are deceived by false Christs that shall come to you; and when you should hear of wars and commotions to be not terrified, etc.; but Jesus Christ now directs his attention to another age; this does not refer to you my followers, you will be dead, and in paradise when these things that I now refer to shall take place. But THEY. Who? The people who shall live when the times of the Gentiles are fulfilled—when their reign is about to come to an end, the generation that will be alive when Jerusalem and the Jews are about to be restored, and the full end of all Gentile polity is about to usher in. 'Then shall they see,' those that shall live in those days. And what shall they see? 'The Son of Man coming in a cloud with power and great glory.'"

Orson Pratt, Journal of Discourses, Vol. 2, p. 261-262, April 7, 1855.

"Here then, we perceive the two distinctions, when the light begins to break forth; that is, when the Book of Mormon is translated, when the Church is organized, these events bring in the time of the Gentiles, and in the generation that the light breaks forth the times of the Gentiles shall be fulfilled. We are also told in the same revelation that the Jews who were to be scattered from old Jerusalem, should remain scattered, until the times of the Gentiles should be fulfilled; consequently, this is the reason why the Jews have not gathered since the rise of this Church. If they were gathered together—if they had assembled at old Jerusalem, it would have contradicted the prophecies and revelations God has given on this subject. They are to remain scattered, said the Lord, until the times of the Gentiles are fulfilled, and their times are to be fulfilled in the generation that their time comes in, or when the light of the fullness of the Gospel begins to break forth."

Orson Pratt, Journal of Discourses, Vol. 7, p. 186-187, July 10, 1859.

"And you have got to do a great deal of preaching before the times of the Gentiles are fulfilled; you have got to go and build up the Church of the Lamb of God among those nations, and set ministers over them, and go and build up more; and the High Priests that preside over them have got to purify their own hearts, and the Branches over which they preside to be prepared for the power of God that shall rest upon them in great glory, that when the multitudes gather to fight against them they may be armed with the power that comes from heaven, that will cause their thrones and their kingdoms to shake to their very centre."

Orson Pratt, Journal of Discourses, Vol. 7, p. 187-188, July 10, 1859.

"By-and-by, after you have fulfilled your missions to the nations of the Gentiles, and there will not any more of them repent,—that is, when you have fully accomplished all that is required of you in relation to them, you will have another mission, and so will the Twelve, and that is to the house of Israel that may be among those nations; I mean the literal descendants of Jacob—the Jews, and the descendants of the other tribes that may be scattered among those nations. There are some from the ten tribes among them; but the body of the ten tribes are in the north country. You will find a few among all these Gentile nations: you will have to direct your attention to them after you have fulfilled your mission among the Gentiles, and their times are fulfilled. You will have something to do among the Jews, and then will be a time of great power, such as you and I have not dreamed of. Indeed, we could not, with our narrow comprehensions of mind, perceive the power that will then follow. The Lord has told it in a revelation in the Book of Doctrine and Covenants. He has told us, before the rise of this Church, that in bringing forth this Gospel, it is a light that could not be hid in darkness: therefore, he says I must bring the fullness of my Gospel from among the Gentiles to the house of Israel; or, this light of the fullness of my Gospel will, as it were, be covered up and hid in darkness in many respects, and will not shine with that brilliancy, power, and greatness: it will not appear in that magnitude that it will when I bring it from the midst of the Gentiles to my people, O house of Israel. Again, the Lord says, in another revelation in the Book of Doctrine and Covenants, that when we have preached the Gospel faithfully to the Gentile nations, then cometh the day of my power; and we already know what the Psalmist says in regard to that day—'My people shall be willing in the day of my power.' The house of Israel have been unwilling in many generations past to receive the Gospel; but in the day of his power, you Seventies, that will go forth among the nations of Gentiles to hunt out the literal descendants of Jacob, will be armed with that glory, power, and majesty and clothed upon from on high to that degree that no power on earth can stay you; and then, in that day, the seed of Jacob will be willing to receive the testimony of the Gospel."

Orson Pratt, Journal of Discourses, Vol. 7, p. 188, July 10, 1859.

     "By-and-by, when the Lord has made bare his arm in signs, in great wonders, and in mighty deeds, through the instrumentality of his servants the Seventies, and though the instrumentality of the churches that shall be built up, and the nations and kingdoms of the earth have been faithfully and fully warned, and the Lord has fulfilled and accomplished all things that have been written in the Book of Mormon, and in other revelations pertaining to the preaching of the Gospel to the nations of the Gentiles and to the nations of Israel, by-and-by the Spirit of God will entirely withdraw from those Gentile nations, and leave them to themselves. Then they will find something else to do besides warring against the Saints in their midst—besides raising their sword and fighting against the Lamb of God; for then war will commence in earnest, and such a war as probably never entered into the hearts of men in our age to conceive of. No nation of the Gentiles upon the face of the whole earth but what will be engaged in deadly war, except the Latter-day Kingdom. They will be fighting one against another."

Orson Pratt, Journal of Discourses, Vol. 14, p. 61-62, March 26, 1871.

     "It may not be amiss to declare, in a very few words, the belief of the Latter-day Saints, in regard to the fulfilling of the times of the Gentiles; that is, what we understand by the fulfilling of their times. We believe, as was said this morning, that before the times of the Gentiles can possibly be fulfilled, a proclamation must come from heaven and be sounded in their ears—namely, that an angel must come from heaven and bring the everlasting Gospel, not for the Jews, the descendants of Israel, alone, but for every nation, kindred, tongue and people. Gentiles and Jews, all must hear it, for the prediction is that when the angel comes forth with that message from heaven, it is to be preached to all nations, kindreds, tongues and people. This, of course, includes Gentiles as well as Jews. We cannot, therefore, suppose that the times of the Gentiles will be fulfilled until after that event takes place. When the angel comes, when the servants of God are sent forth by Divine authority with a proclamation, and have fulfilled that prediction by declaring the everlasting Gospel to all the nations and kingdoms of the Gentiles, then their times will be fulfilled, and not before."

Orson Pratt, Journal of Discourses, Vol. 14, p. 66, March 26, 1871.

     "Again, says the Prophet, 'And the Lord shall utterly destroy the tongue of the Egyptian sea.' How? 'With his mighty power shall he shake his hand over the river and shall smite it in the seven streams and make men go over dryshod. And there shall be an highway for the remnant of his people which shall be left from Assyria like as it was to Israel in the day that he came up out of the land of Egypt.' The same thing, not a spiritual, but a literal transaction, as the Lord smote the tongue of the Egyptian sea in ancient days, and caused his people to go through on a highway in the midst of those mighty waters which stood like walls on each side of the assembly of Israel. So in the latter days he will not only cut off the tongue of the Egyptian sea, but the river in its seven streams will also be divided and men will go through dryshod. This is the testimony of the prophets concerning the events that are to take place when the times of the Gentiles are fulfilled."

Orson Pratt, Journal of Discourses, Vol. 14, p. 146-147, March 19, 1871.

"Then comes in another prediction concerning the destruction of the nations of the wicked. 'For the terrible one is brought to nought, and the scorner is consumed, and all that watch for iniquity are cut off, and all nations that fight against Mount Zion, will perish and vanish away.' When this marvelous work and a wonder is commenced, and its truths preached and fully declared to the nations, and they reject them, the desolation and destruction that were brought upon the ancient Jews for the rejection of the Gospel will, according to this prophecy, be visited upon the wicked of this generation. . . .

Thus you see, in that day, when the wicked will be so sorely afflicted the God of heaven will signally favor Israel. These things will transpire when we get through with the Gentiles, because the direct commandment of the Lord is, first to the Gentiles, and then to the house of Israel. And when the times of the Gentiles are fulfilled, then the Lord will restore the blessings he promised to Israel; he will then fulfill literally that which was uttered by the Psalmist David, 'Turn us again, O God of our salvation; how long will thou be angry with us? how long shall we have to suffer in consequence of our wickedness and the wickedness of our fathers?' Until truth shall spring out of the earth; until then your captivity must remain; until then your sufferings and great afflictions must continue. But when the Lord brings truth out of the earth and sends righteousness down from heaven he will again remember Israel; then the Gentile nations will be punished, and Israel be saved."

Orson Pratt, Journal of Discourses, Vol. 14, p. 332-333, February 11, 1872.

"But before Israel can be gathered, these records, according to the predictions contained in them, must be sounded abroad, not only to the great and powerful nation, the Republic of the United States, and the Canadas, but to all the nations of the Gentiles, that all may be left without excuse. Already the time has far gone by for this warning to the Gentiles. Forty-two years out of the generation has already passed, and the same generation to whom these records were revealed shall not pass away until the times of the Gentiles shall be fulfilled. When that period shall arrive, as I said in my lecture during the week, there will come a day of the Lord's especial power, the day of power spoken of by the psalmist David where he addresses the Lord, saying: 'Thy people shall be willing in the day of thy power.' Israel have never been willing to receive Jesus from the day that they were cut off as bitter branches that brought forth no good fruit, until the present period. Generation after generation has passed away, and they still remain in unbelief, and they still remain in their scattered condition among all the nations and countries of the earth. But when the day of the Lord's power shall come, when he shall send forth his servants with the power of the priesthood and apostleship to the nations and to the scattered remnants of the house of Israel that dwell in the islands of the sea afar off, he will show forth his power in that day in such a conspicuous manner that all Israel, as it were, will be saved. As it is written by the Apostle Paul, 'Blindness in part hath happened to Israel until the fullness of the Gentiles be come in, and so all Israel shall be saved.' All Israel in that day will hear the voice of the Lord and the voice of his servants; all Israel, in that day, will see the arm of the Lord made bare in signs and mighty wonders in effecting the restoration of his chosen people to their own land."

Orson Pratt, Journal of Discourses, Vol. 14, p. 333, February 11, 1872.

"Yet we are told by the present generation there is to be no more revelation, no more miracles, no more manifestations of the power of the Almighty, no more the voice of God speaking from the heavens, no more of the manifestations of his glory, or the showing of himself personally to his people. How wonderfully this generation of Christendom will be mistaken in that day when Israel will go again to their own land, and when the Lord God shall stretch forth his hand to the nations of the Gentiles, saying, 'Your times are fulfilled, my servants have been sent forth in your midst, they have declared the word of the Lord to you all the day long, but you would not hear or receive their testimony, now the summer is ended and your times are fulfilled. Now will I gather my people Israel from the four quarters of the earth.'"

Orson Pratt, Journal of Discourses, Vol. 15, p. 191, September 22, 1872.

"The question is, How will he bring about the fulfillment of the times of the Gentiles? I answered, by sending forth to them the stick of Joseph, written upon for Joseph, in connection with the Bible, by his servants who go forth to the nations of the earth. They will proclaim to all people, nations and tongues, to the Gentiles first, the fullness of the Gospel of the Son of God, contained in these two records. The testimony of two nations running together and growing into one is stronger than the testimony of one nation; and when the Lord makes the ancient continent of America bear record to the same great truths; when he unites the Bible of the Western hemisphere, with the Bible of the East, and sends it forth to the nations of the earth, it will be a witness, and evidence and a testimony sufficient to bring about what is termed the fullness of the Gentiles, or to fulfill their times.

This is the reason why, during forty-two years, God has restricted us to the Gentile nations, and would not suffer us to go with the Book of Mormon to the house of Israel until the times of the Gentiles were fulfilled. How much longer the Lord will bear with the Gentile nations I know not; but I do know that when they count themselves unworthy of eternal life, when the servants of God have thoroughly warned them by preaching to them the fullness of the Gospel of his Son, then the commandment will go forth from the Almighty to his servants—'turn from the Gentile nations and go to the dispersed of Israel. Go, ye fishers and ye hunters, and fulfill that which I spake by the mouth of mine ancient Prophets, that Jacob may no longer be made ashamed, that his face may no longer wax pale. Go and say to the house of Israel in the four quarters of the earth that the God of Jacob has again spoken. Go and tell them that that which he spake by the mouths their ancient Prophets is being fulfilled.' And they will go, and their proclamation will be to Israel the same as to the Gentiles, with the exception of gathering the Jews to old Jerusalem, instead of to the land of Zion."

Orson Pratt, Journal of Discourses, Vol. 16, p. 151-152, August 16, 1873.

"Now, that there is a day of power coming, every Latter-day Saint, who is acquainted with the predictions of the Prophets, is certain. He is expecting that it will come in the time specified in those revelations. God has said to us, in the Book of Doctrine and Covenants, that when the times of the Gentiles are fulfilled, then cometh the day of my power. 'Thy people will be willing,' says one of the ancient Prophets, 'in the day of thy power.' The Elders of this Church have gone forth among many nations. They rejoice in the power that is made manifest, in some measure. God has said that they should go and preach the Gospel to all nations of the earth; and that signs should follow them that believe. In my name they shall do many wonderful works. In my name they shall cast out devils, speak in other tongues; and the eyes of the blind shall be opened. The Elders have found this to be true. As far as the people have had faith, they have seen this power, in some measure, displayed. But this can not be said, comparatively, to be the day of his power. When the day of the power of the Lord shall come, then will be a time when not only the sick, the lame and the blind, but also the very elements will be wrought upon by the power of God, as the Lord has spoken, and be subservient to the commands of his servants."

Orson Pratt, Journal of Discourses, Vol. 16, p. 324-325, November 22, 1873.

"If he gives us any knowledge regarding chronology, depend upon it; and he has given us a great deal of information with regard to the signs of the times. If he has not given us the age of the world, he has given us that whereby we may know that we live in the generation in which the times of the Gentiles will be fulfilled. And then we have other revelations, showing that when their times are fulfilled there is a speedy and short work to be accomplished in the gathering of the house of Israel from the four quarters of the earth."

Orson Pratt, Journal of Discourses, Vol. 16, p. 352-353, January 25, 1874.

"Inquires one—'Why do you not go to the House of Israel, what have you Latter-day Saints been doing for forty years past? Have you gathered Israel?' No, we have not; if we had the Scriptures would not have been fulfilled. Why? Because the times of the Gentiles must first be fulfilled, and Jerusalem must be trodden down by them, until their times are fulfilled. What do you mean by their times being fulfilled, and the fullness of the Gentiles coming in? I mean just what the Lord means, that this Gospel, which God sends by the ministration of 'another angel' from heaven, must be preached to all nations, kindreds, tongues and people, to the Gentiles first; and when they get through with them, it will go to Israel, for the times of the Gentiles will then be fulfilled; in other words, when God shall speak to his servants, and say unto them—'It is enough, you have been faithful in your ministry, you have warned the nations, kindreds and tongues of the Gentiles sufficiently, now I call you to a still greater work, and will give you a new mission, not to go and preach to the Gentiles, but go to the remnants of the House of Israel wherever they can be found, and let your testimony be to them. Hunt them up from the four quarters of the earth, gather them out with a mighty hand and with an outstretched arm, and bring them back to their own land.' When that time shall come Israel will be gathered and not till then.

Inquires one—'How long will the Gospel still be preached to the Gentiles?' I do not know; I can give you certain limits, but within those limits I cannot decide. God told us in the early days of this Church, by new revelation, that the times of the Gentiles would be fulfilled in the generation then living upon the earth. Forth-three years of that generation have already gone by. How many more years it will be before their times are fulfilled I cannot tell; but I know the day is not far distant when young men, now living in these mountains, will be commissioned to go, not to the Gentiles, for their times will be fulfilled, but the Lord will say to them—'Go forth and fish and hunt up Israel in the four quarters of the earth. Go to the remnants of Joseph that are in South America, and scattered over this vast continent from the frozen regions of the north to Cape Horn in South America; go and teach them the Gospel, for they are a remnant of the tribe of Joseph: and his arm will be made bare in that day in such a manner that they will not reject the truth, and they will be grafted in again into their own olive tree, and become a righteous branch of the house of Israel.'"

Orson Pratt, Journal of Discourses, Vol. 17, p. 278, November 15, 1874.

"Finally, examine every point of evidence you can think of; take up, step by step, the various events that must take place—the preaching of the Gospel to the Gentiles to bring in their fullness that their times may be fulfilled; the preaching of it to the Jews; the preaching of it to the scattered tribes of Israel, and all the other events predicted in connection with this Latter-day work; take them up one by one, and see if this people have left one thing out of their faith that should characterize the dispensation of the fullness of times. Do the Scriptures foretell the gathering of the Jews from the four quarters of the earth? The Book of Mormon does the same thing. Do the Scriptures say that the Jews should remain scattered until the times of the Gentiles are fulfilled? The Book of Mormon and the Revelations given to this Church declare the same thing. Did the ancient Prophets and Apostles declare that the Gospel of the Kingdom should be preached to all nations, that the fullness of the Gentiles should come in before all Israel should be saved? This also is according to the faith of the Latter-day Saints' Church and is contained in our writings."

Orson Pratt, Journal of Discourses, Vol. 17, p. 286, September 20, 1874.

"To show more fully the time when this book should be brought to light, let me say that it is a latter-day work, and to prove it, I will read the following verses. 'The poor among men shall rejoice in the Holy One of Israel, for the terrible one is brought to naught, and the scorner is consumed, and all that watch for iniquity are cut off; all that make a man an offender for a word, or that lay a snare for him that reproveth in the gate, or that turn aside the just for a thing of naught.' All these are to be cut off. When? When they have heard the words of this book, when the proclamation has been sounded in their ears. When they are become fully ripened in iniquity, they will be cut off according to the declaration of the Prophet Isaiah. But their times must first be fulfilled; their fulness must come in, before these terrible judgments and destructions shall lay waste the nations of the Gentiles."

Orson Pratt, Journal of Discourses, Vol. 18, p. 64-65, July 25, 1875.

"After the times of the Gentiles are fulfilled, which period is set in the mind of God, another scene will open up before the world, in the grand panorama of the last days. What is that? The downfall of the Gentile nations. Says one—'Whom do you call Gentiles?' Every nations excepting the literal descendants of Israel. We, the Latter-day Saints, are Gentiles; in other words, we have come from among the Gentile nations, though many of us may have the blood of Israel within our veins. When God has called out the righteous, when the warning voice has been sufficiently proclaimed among these Gentile nations, and the Lord says 'It is enough,' he will also say to his servants—'O, ye, my servants, come home, come out from the midst of these gentile nations, where you have labored and borne testimony for so long a period; come out from among them, for they are not worthy; they do not receive the message that I have sent forth, they do not repent of their sins; come out from their midst, their times are fulfilled. Seal up the testimony among them and bind up the law.' What then? Then the word of the Lord will be—'O, ye, my servants, I have a new commission for you. Instead of going forth to convert the Gentile nations, go unto the remnants of the house of Israel that are scattered in the four quarters of the earth. Go and proclaim to them that the times of their dispersion are accomplished; that the times of the Gentiles are fulfilled; that the time has arrived for my people Israel, who have been scattered for generations in a dark and cloudy day, to gather unto their own homes again, and to build up old Jerusalem on its former heap. And then will commence the gathering of the Jews to old Jerusalem; then the ten tribes in the northern regions, wherever they may be, after having been concealed from the nations for twenty-five hundred years, will come forth and will return, as Jeremiah has said, from the north country."

Orson Pratt, Journal of Discourses, Vol. 18, p. 166, July 18, 1875.

"Because this book come forth to bring the house of Jacob from all the nations and kingdoms of the earth; and this will commence just as soon as the times of the Gentiles are fulfilled; not until then. We must be warned first; we Gentiles must hear the word first; and when we count ourselves unworthy of eternal life, and fight against the book, and against the Zion and people of God, behold the Lord will then remember the house of Jacob."

Orson Pratt, Journal of Discourses, Vol. 18, p. 176, March 26, 1876.

"The Lord also told them that when the fullness of the Gentiles had come, when their times were fulfilled, then his servants should be sent to all the scattered remnants of the house of Israel, who should be grafted in again; but first, the fullness of the Gentiles must come in. You know that Scripture which says—'The first shall be last, and the last shall be first.' Now the Gospel, when it was preached in ancient times, was preached first to the Jews, the house of Israel, to those of Israelitish origin, and when they counted themselves unworthy of eternal life, and rejected that Gospel, 'Lo' says Paul, 'we turn unto the Gentiles.' The Gentiles, then, heard it last; they were last to embrace the Gospel of the kingdom, and the Jews first, that is, as many of them as would believe and repent. But in the last days, when the angel brings the Gospel, it is reversed, and it is preached first to the Gentiles, to bring in their fullness, and to fulfill their times, and then it will be sent to the house of Israel."

Orson Pratt, Journal of Discourses, Vol. 18, p. 176-177, March 26, 1876.

"The great object of the angel in restoring the Gospel was, in the first place, to fulfill the times of the Gentiles. Inquires one—'What do you mean by that?' I mean that God will send this Gospel, restored by an angel, to every nations, kindred, people, and tongue in the Gentile world before he will permit his servants to go to the scattered remnants of Israel; and they will labor with, preach to and declare the work of God to the Gentile nations, and seek to bring them to a knowledge of the ancient Gospel, and to organize a Church among them, so far as they will hearken to and receive their testimony. Then, when the Gentile nations shall reject this Gospel and count themselves unworthy of eternal life, as the Jews did before them, the Lord will say—'It is enough, come away from them, my servants, I will give you a new commission, you shall go to the scattered remnants of the house

241

of Israel. I will gather them in from the four quarters of the earth, and bring them again into their own lands. They shall build Jerusalem on its own heap; they shall rear a Temple on the appointed place in Palestine, and they shall be grafted in again.' Now that, in short, is the nature of the great latter-day preparatory work for the coming of the Son of Man."

Orson Pratt, Journal of Discourses, Vol. 18, p. 225-226, August 26, 1876.

"This Gospel should be preached first to the nations of the Gentiles, and then the Lord would call in his servants and give them a special mission to the scattered remnants of the house of Israel, that are among the Gentile nations. You have not heard of our trying to convert the Jews. Why? Because God has decreed and determined that he will fulfill the times of the Gentiles first, in accordance with ancient prophecy. When that time arrives, the Lord will have prepared some of the Jewish nation to receive the Gospel, and then they will gather to their own land, and rebuild their city upon its former site. You doubtless will remember those words of the Saviour referring to the Jewish nations, which can be found in the 21st chapter of St. Luke—'For there shall be great distress in the land, and wrath upon this people. And they shall fall by the edge of the sword, and shall be led away captive into all nations: and Jerusalem shall be trodden down of the Gentiles, until the times of the Gentiles be fulfilled.' How and in what way will the Lord fulfill the times of the Gentiles? There must first be a revealed message, a Gospel message, sent to them. The preaching of this message is referred to in the 14th chapter of Revelations, by the Apostle John, who in vision saw the angel in the act of bring it to the earth. And we are told it was to be preached to all nations which may be said to be composed of the two peoples known as the Gentiles and the Jews. But the Lord has said that 'the last shall be first, and the first shall be last.' Jesus came to the lost sheep of the house of Israel, but they rejected him, and the Apostles were moved upon to say, 'Lo, we turn to the Gentiles;' and they did so, the Jews having proved themselves unworthy of eternal life, 'and the kingdom of God shall be taken from you,' says the Savior, 'and given to a nation bringing forth the fruits thereof.' The Gentiles, to whom the Gospel was to be given, received it, and the gifts and graces of the Church, which were before enjoyed by Israel, were now manifested among the Gentiles. But behold they corrupted themselves, after having received the kingdom, and Paul perceived the decline of their faith, which was the beginning of the great 'falling away,' which he, in his second epistle to the Thessalonians, said must be before the day of the Lord came. Also in the 11th Chapter of Romans, Paul speaks of the Gentiles who had received the Gospel as the wild olive tree, having been grafted into the tame olive tree, and cautions them in this language—'Because of unbelief, they (Israel) were broken off, and thou standest by faith. Be not high minded but fear. For if God spared not the natural branches, take heed lest he also spare not thee.' This, with other prophetic warnings of a similar character, was disregarded."

Orson Pratt, Journal of Discourses, Vol. 18, p. 226-227, August 26, 1876.

"The Scriptures say, the first shall be last, and the last shall be first. The Gentiles were the last to receive the Gospel in ancient times, but on its restoration by the angel in the last days, they are to receive it first, and then the Jews. But before the Jews receive it, the following words of the Savior must be fulfilled—Jerusalem shall be trodden down of the Gentiles, until the times of the Gentiles be fulfilled, when the Gospel again will revert to that people. What do you think will bring about the fulfillment of the times of the Gentiles? It must be the promulgations of the Gospel, which the angel brings, which is to be sounded in the hearts of the Gentile nations; all those receiving it are to gather out from this spiritual wickedness called Babylon the Great, because God has decreed her downfall. The overthrow of Babylon is spoken of in connection with the bringing of the Gospel by the angel, who declares also, 'the hour of his judgment is come.' Judgment upon whom? First, upon the Gentile nations, when their times are fulfilled, in what way? By visiting upon them famines, and pestilences, and earthquakes; nation rising against nation in war, etc, until the Gentile nations are overthrown. Or, to speak in the language of John, who declared that after the angel shall bring the Gospel, another angel shall follow, crying with a loud voice, saying, Babylon is fallen, is fallen, because she made all nations drink of the wine of the wrath of her fornication; she is fallen like a great millstone, cast into the depths of the sea, and no more place found for her.

How long will it be before the times of the Gentiles are fulfilled? This is a question I cannot fully answer. It will be in the generation that the angel comes. Forty-six years have already transpired, since the Lord sent his Gospel message to the Gentile nations; and for upwards of forty years the Saints have been gathering out from the midst of Babylon, in fulfillment of another prophecy of John—'And I heard another voice from heaven, saying, Come out of her, my people, that ye be not partakers of her sins, and that ye receive not of her plagues. For her sins have reached unto heaven, and God hath remembered her iniquities.' Remember, strangers and all, that this gathering of the people was not to result from a cunningly devised fable, or the natural scheming of man; but it should be in consequence of new revelation—a voice from heaven, commanding the people to come out from those nations where the Mother of Harlots has her seat."

Orson Pratt, Journal of Discourses, Vol. 20, p. 146, March 9, 1879.

"Having established his kingdom, he offers it first to these Gentile nations, if they will receive it; and when they shall account themselves unworthy of the kingdom, unworthy of eternal life, unworthy of the message which God has sent to them, and shall persecute his servants and his people all the day long and shall close up their sanctuaries, their Churches, and their chapels, their meeting houses, and their places of worship against this message, and when it can no longer find place among them, so as to bring them to a knowledge and understanding of the truth, the Lord will, after a while, designate by revelation, and say unto his servants, 'It is enough. You have been faithful in laboring in my vineyard, for the last time;' for it was the decree of heaven, that this shall be the last time, that he will labor in his vineyard. It is the eleventh hour the last warning that will be given to the nations of the earth, first to the Gentiles, and then to the House of Israel.

When they shall render themselves unworthy of this great and joyful message, that has been presented to them, the servants of God will, as I have already stated, have it revealed to them, to confine no longer their mission to the Gentiles; but they will receive a commission from the Almighty to go to the scattered remnants of the House of Israel, wherever they may be located."

Wilford Woodruff, Journal of Discourses, Vol. 2, p. 200, February 25, 1855.

"When the Gentiles reject the Gospel it will be taken from them, and go to the house of Israel, to that long suffering people that are now scattered abroad through all the nations upon the earth, and they will be gathered home by thousands, and by hundreds of thousands, and they will re-build

243

Jerusalem their ancient city, and make it more glorious than at the beginning, and they will have a leader in Israel with them, a man that is full of the power of God and the gift of the Holy Ghost; but they are held now from this work, only because the fullness of the Gentiles has not yet come in. Tens of thousands among the Gentile nations will receive the Gospel, but the majority of them will reject it, and then the Jews will receive it; and it will go to them with all the gifts, blessings, and powers it possessed when it was taken from them."

Wilford Woodruff, Journal of Discourses, Vol. 10, p. 220, June 2, 1863.

"I rejoice that the Lord still holds the door open, that we still have the privilege of sending the Elders to the nations; while this door remains open we shall continue to preach the Gospel to the Gentile world. When they reject it it will be taken from them and then we go to the Jews, and the ten tribes will come from the north to Zion to be crowned under the hands of the children of Ephraim. And the remnant of the Lamanites who are cursed below all humanity that we are acquainted with—who have been filled with the spirit of bloodshed which they have inherited from their fathers—they will embrace the Gospel in the due time of the Lord. They are of the house of Israel, and this spirit of war will be taken from them and they will become the children of God, but not until the Gentiles have entirely rejected the Gospel. Anciently it was preached to the Jews first and then to the Gentiles; in the latter times it will be first preached to the Gentiles and then to the Jews—the first shall be last and the last first."

Wilford Woodruff, Journal of Discourses, Vol. 14, p. 5, January 1, 1871.

"When I see the world making warfare against the Zion and people of God because they have borne record and testimony of his work on the earth I can tell pretty well what the end will be; I can see it. We are living in a time when the work of God is going to increase in interest every day until it is wound up. No man knows the day or the hour when Christ will come, yet the generation has been pointed out by Jesus himself. He told his disciples when they passed by the temple as they walked out of Jerusalem that that generation should not pass away before not one stone of that magnificent temple should be left standing upon another and the Jews should be scattered among the nations; and history tells how remarkably that prediction was fulfilled. Moses and the prophets also prophesied of this as well as Jesus. The Savior, when speaking to his disciples of his second coming and the establishment of his kingdom on the earth, said the Jews should be scattered and trodden under foot until the times of the Gentiles were fulfilled. But, said he, when you see light breaking forth among the Gentiles, referring to the preaching of his Gospel amongst them; when you see salvation offered to the Gentiles, and the Jews—the seed of Israel—passed by, the last first and the first last; when you see this you may know that the time of my second coming is at hand as surely as you know that summer is nigh when the fig tree puts forth its leaves; and when these things commence that generation shall not pass away until all are fulfilled."

Wilford Woodruff, Journal of Discourses, Vol.18, p. 38.

"And by and by the testimony of the Gospel will be sealed among the Gentiles, and the Gospel will turn to the whole house of Israel, and the judgments of God will back up the testimony of the Elders of this Church, and the Lord will send messengers who will go forth and reap down the earth.

The unbeliever may say that what we term judgments have always prevailed more or less among the nations, and that God has nothing to do with them, they are all natural. Well, if they have always prevailed, they will prevail to a greater extent in these last days than ever before, until everything that God has spoken shall come to pass. Judgments await the world, and they await this nation, and the day is as hand when the Lord will sweep the earth as with a besom of destruction."

Wilford Woodruff, Journal of Discourses, Vol. 18, p. 112, September 12, 1875.
    "Sometimes our neighbors and friends think hard of us because we call them Gentiles; but, bless your souls, we are all Gentiles. The Latter-day Saints are all Gentiles in a national capacity. The Gospel came to us among the Gentiles. We are not Jews, and the Gentile nations have got to hear the Gospel first. The whole Christian world have got to hear the Gospel, and when they reject it, the law will be bound and the testimony sealed, and it will turn to the house of Israel. Up to the present day we have been called to preach the Gospel to the Gentiles, and we have had to do it. For the last time we have been warning the world, and we have been engaged in that work for forty-five years."

Wilford Woodruff, Journal of Discourses, Vol. 18, p. 220-221, August 13, 1876.
    "This we declare is the kingdom which the Prophet Daniel saw in vision, never more to be thrown down or give to another people. In these mountains Zion is to be built up, in fulfillment of prophecy, and every jot and tittle that has been spoken of her must come to pass. The last is first, and the first will be last. The Gospel was first sent directly to the Jews; the Savior himself was of that lineage, through the loins of David. He came to his own, but they received him not. He was reproached of them, from the day of his birth until they crucified him on the cross. Consequently, the risen Redeemer commanded his Apostles to turn the Gentiles. They received the work and enjoyed the gifts and blessings of the Gospel, even the Comforter, the Holy Ghost; and the Priesthood continued with them until a portion of them became unworthy of it, through their falling away, while the faithful were harassed and persecuted to their death. The Gospel is now restored to us Gentiles, for we are all Gentiles in a national capacity, and it will continue with us if we are faithful, until the law is bound, and the testimony sealed, and the times of the Gentiles are fulfilled, when it will again revert to the Jews, whom the Lord will have prepared to receive it. They will gather to their own land, taking with them their gold and silver, and will re-build their city and temple, according to the prediction of Moses and the Prophets. When this time arrives, which is nigh, even at our doors, let the Gentile nations who reject the Gospel which is now sent to them, prepare to meet the judgments of an offended God! For when their cup is full even to the brim, the Lord will then remember the chastisement of the Jews, his favored people, and at whose hands they will have received double for their iniquities. Offenses must come, said the Savior, but woe unto them by whom they come. Woe unto the Gentiles, who have administered afflictions to the Jews for these many years! Woe unto them if they now reject this only means of salvation, for the awful calamities spoken of in these books, the Bible and Book of Mormon, will certainly befall them."

Joseph Fielding Smith Jr., Doctrines of Salvation, Vol. 3, p. 258.
    "The Lord said they (Jews) should remain scattered among the nations until the times of the

Gentiles were fulfilled. Moroni said the times of the Gentiles were about to be fulfilled, Today we are living in the transition period; the day of the Gentiles has come in, and the day of Judah and the remnant of downtrodden Israel is now at hand."

Ezra Taft Benson, The New Era, May 1982, p. 47.

"The Lord has designated these days in which we live as the 'times of the Gentiles'. The Gentile nations are the so-called Christian nations—North and South America and the European nations from which we came. The 'times of the Gentiles' refers to that period of time extending from when the gospel was restored to the world (1830) to when the gospel will again be preached to the Jews—after the Gentiles have rejected it. . . .

We will know when the times of the Gentiles are approaching fulfillment by these signs:

'And in that day shall be heard of wars and rumors of wars, and the whole earth shall be in commotion, and men's hearts shall fail them, and they shall say that Christ delayeth his coming until the end of the earth. And the love of men shall wax cold, and iniquity shall abound.' (D&C 45:26-7)

'And again, this gospel of the kingdom shall be preached in all the world, for a witness unto all nations, and then shall the end come, or the destruction of the wicked.' (J.S.T. Matthew 24:32)"

LeGrand Richards, Conference Report, October 1956, p. 26.

"There is a question with some as to when the times of the gentiles shall be fulfilled. The gospel came first to the Jews in the Meridian of Time, and then to the gentiles, and the promise was that in the latter days it would come first to the gentiles and then unto the Jews. But you will recall that the Lord did not wait until all the Jews were converted before he sent the gospel to the gentiles, through that marvelous vision and experience Peter had. It seems to me that if we wait until all the gentiles are converted before we take the gospel to the Jews, we shall never convert the Jews; and yet the Lord promised them that the fulness of his gospel would be preached unto them."

Bruce R. McConkie, Mormon Doctrine, "The Signs of the Times", p. 721.

"The fulfilling of the times of the Gentiles will not come at a specified moment; it will involve a period of time. We are living in that transition period. . . . 'Jerusalem shall be trodden down of the Gentiles, until the times of the Gentiles be fulfilled.' In December, 1917, General Allenby of Great Britain captured Jerusalem almost without opposition and for the first time in nearly 1900 years that city came out from . . . Gentile domination and was made available for the return of the Jews."

Bruce R. McConkie, Doctrinal New Testament Commentary, Vol. 1, p. 656.

"The times of the Gentiles, shall come to an end before our Lord returns in power and glory. Then, with his return, the times of the Jews shall begin; that is the era will commence in which the Jews shall accept the gospel and be blessed spiritually in an abundant way."

Bruce R. McConkie, The Mortal Messiah, Vol. 3, p. 441-442.

"He is here classifying all men as Jews or Gentiles. There are no others. Jews are the Israelites, no matter what their tribal ancestry . . .All other people are Gentiles, including Israelites who were not Jewish nationals as herein defined. In this sense Joseph Smith, a pit re Ephraimite, was a Gentile, and the Book of Mormon came forth as promised by way of the Gentile. In this sense those of us of Ephraim and Manasseh and other tribes who are already gathered with latter-day Israel are Gentiles. The Gentiles are the non-Jews within the meaning of words as here used.

The times of the Gentiles is the period during which the gospel will be preached to the Gentiles in preference to the Jews, and the times of the Jews is the similar period when the Jewish nationals, so to speak, will again receive the message of salvation that is in Christ. We are living in the times of the Gentiles, but that era is drawing to its close, and the gospel will soon go to the Jews.

In the generation in which the times of the Gentiles shall be fulfilled there shall be signs in the sun, and in the moon, and in the stars; and upon the earth."

Bruce R. McConkie, The Mortal Messiah, Vol. 4, p. 340-341.

"Except for a limited few, the great day of Jewish conversion will be in the millennial day, after they have seen him whom they crucified."

Bruce R. McConkie, A New Witness for the Articles of Faith, p. 633.

"We live in that generation, or age, when 'the times of the Gentiles [shall] be fulfilled,' although this will not be complete until the Lord comes. (D&C 45:30.)"

THE 144,000

Joseph Smith, History of the Church, Vol. 6, p. 196.

"I attended prayer-meeting with the quorum in the assembly room, and made some remarks respecting the hundred and forty-four thousand mentioned by John the Revelator, showing that the selection of persons to form that number had already commenced."

Teachings of the Prophet Joseph Smith, Section Two, 1834–37, p.75.

"If the first Seventy are all employed, and there is a call for more laborers, it will be the duty of the seven presidents of the first Seventy to call and ordain other Seventy and send them forth to labor in the vineyard, until, if needs be, they set apart seven times seventy, and even until there are one hundred and forty-four thousand thus set apart for the ministry."

Teachings of the Prophet Joseph Smith, Section Six, 1843–44, p. 366.

"It is not only necessary that you should be baptized for your dead, but you will have to go through all the ordinances for them, the same as you have gone through to save yourselves. There will be 144,000 saviors on Mount Zion, and with them an innumerable host that no man can number."

Orson Pratt, Journal of Discourses, Vol. 14, p. 242-243, August 20, 1871.

"This puts me in mind of a certain vision that John the Revelator had on the Isle of Patmos. On that occasion he saw one hundred and forty-four thousand standing upon Mount Zion, singing a new and glorious song; the singers seemed to be among the most happy and glorious of those who were shown to John. They, the one hundred and forty-four thousand, had a peculiar inscription in their foreheads. What was it? It was the Father's name. What is the Father's name? It is God—the being we worship. If, then, the one hundred and forty-four thousand are to have the name of God inscribed on their foreheads, will it be simply a plaything, a something that has no meaning? or will it mean that which the inscriptions specify?—that they are indeed Gods—one with the Father and one with the Son; as the Father and Son are one, and both of them called Gods, so will all His children be one with the Father and the Son, and they will be one so far as carrying out the great purposes of Jehovah is concerned. No divisions will be there but a complete oneness; not a oneness in person but a perfect oneness in action in the creation, redemption, and glorification of worlds."

Orson Pratt, Journal of Discourses, Vol. 16, p. 325, November 22, 1873.

"Then again, after the six thousand years have ended, before the Lord shall come while these trumpets are sounding, or about that time, we find that there is to be a great work among the nations—which will probably take place in the morning of the seventh thousand years. The ten tribes will have to come forth and come to this land, to be crowned with glory in the midst of Zion by the hands of the servants of God, even the Children of Ephraim; and twelve thousand High Priests will be elected from each of these ten tribes, as well as from the scattered tribes, and sealed in their foreheads, and will be ordained and receive power to gather out of all nations, kindreds, tongues and people as many as will come unto the general assemblage of the Church of the first-born. Will not that be a great work? Imagine one hundred and forty-four thousand High Priests going forth among the nations, and gathering out as many as will come to the Church of the first-born. All that will be done, probably, in the morning of the seventh thousand years."

Orson Pratt, Journal of Discourses, Vol. 18, p. 25, April 11, 1875.

"How long will they who come from the north countries tarry in the heights of Zion? Sometime. They have got to raise wheat, cultivate the grape, wine and oil, raise flocks and herds, and their souls will have to become as a watered garden. They will dwell in Zion a good while, and during that time, there will be twelve thousand chosen out of each of these ten tribes, besides twelve thousand that will be chosen from Judah, Joseph, and the remaining tribes, one hundred and forty-four thousand in all. Chosen for what? To be sealed in their foreheads. For what purpose? So that the power of death and pestilence and plague that will go forth in those days sweeping over the nations of the earth will have no power over them. These parties who are sealed in their foreheads will go forth among all people, nations and tongues, and gather up and hunt out the house of Israel, wherever they are scattered, and bring as many as they possibly can into the Church of the first-born, preparatory to the great day of the coming of the Lord. One hundred and forty-four thousand missionaries! Quite a host."

Orson Pratt, Journal of Discourses, Vol. 19, p. 320-321, October 7, 1867.

"In the visions of eternity that were shown to John, he beheld things that were to take place in future generations. Among other things that were shown to him, were the one hundred and forty-four thousand, standing on Mount Zion, who had been redeemed from among men. Who were they? Let us look at the inscription that John says was written on their foreheads. That will tell us that the name of their Father was written there. What was his name? God, translated into the English language. Ahman in the pure language. The Father's name John saw inscribed on the foreheads of the hundred and forty-four thousand who were singing the new song before the Lord. What would you think if you were to have the future opened to you as John had, and could see these men with the word God, inscribed in bright and shining characters upon each of their foreheads? Would you think that God was making fun of them by putting such an inscription there? Would you suppose the inscription was a mere form without any meaning? No: every man permitted to see these things would at once say, 'They are gods having been redeemed, and made like their Father.' This is what we believe. Then, when we come to personality, we not only believe in our personal Father, in His Son Jesus Christ, and in the Holy Ghost, as personages, but we also believe that in the eternity of eternities, in the heaven of heavens there will be innumerable millions of persons who will occupy that exalted station—each one being a personal god, as much so as the God of this creation—the Father of our spirits is."

John Taylor, The Gospel Kingdom, p. 29.

"Their 'Father's name,' bless me! that is GOD! Well done for Mormonism; one hundred and forty four thousand GODS, among the tribes of Israel, and, two living Gods and the Holy Ghost, for this world! Such knowledge is too wonderful for men, unless they possess the spirit of Gods. It unravels the little mysteries, which, like a fog, hide the serene atmosphere of heaven, and looks from world to world, from system to system, from universe to universe, and from eternity to eternity, where, in each, and all, there is a presidency of Gods, and Gods many, and lords many; and from time to time, or from eternity to eternity, Jesus Christ shall bring in another world regulated and saved as this will be when he delivers it up to the Father; and God becomes all in all. As John the Revelator said: 'And there shall be no more curse: but the throne of God and of the Lamb shall be in it; and his servants shall serve him.'"

Spencer W. Kimball, The Miracle of Forgiveness, p. 65.
"The importance of continence in the unmarried is underlined by the divine approval given it in the vision to John the Revelator, in which he saw the Lamb of God standing on Mount Zion and with him 144,000 having the Father's name written in their foreheads. Of these the voice from heaven said: 'These are they which were not defiled with women; for they are virgins and in their mouth was found no guile: for they are without fault before the throne of God.' (Rev. 14:4-5.)"

Bruce R. McConkie, Mormon Doctrine, "144,000", p. 546.
"These 144,000 are Gods, as the name on their foreheads specifies; their callings and elections have been made sure; they are exalted personages; they are 'redeemed from among men . . .They have attained perfection."

Bruce R. McConkie, Mormon Doctrine, "Tribes of Israel", p. 809.
"When John recorded his vision of the special mission for 12,000 of each of the tribes . . . for some reason that is not apparent left out the tribe of Dan. Scholars speculate that 'the tribe of Dan is not mentioned, perhaps because of a Jewish tradition that Antichrist was to come from the tribe.'"

Bruce R. McConkie, The Mortal Messiah, Vol. 3, Footnotes, p. 221.
"Though `there is none other God but one' for men on this earth to worship, yet `there be gods many, and lords many' throughout the infinite expanse of eternity. (1 Cor. 8:47.) That is, there are many exalted, perfected, glorified personages who reign as gods over their own dominions. John saw 144,000 of them standing with Christ upon Mount Zion, all `having his Father's name written in their foreheads' (Rev 14:1), which is to say that they were gods and were so identified by wearing crowns so stating. Indeed, to each person who overcomes and gains exaltation, Christ has promised: `I will write upon him the name of my God,' and he shall `sit with me in my throne, even as I also overcame, and am set down with my Father in his throne.' (Rev. 3:12, 21.)"

SCRIPTURAL REFERENCES

Matthew 20:16
16 So the last shall be first, and the first last: for many be called, but few chosen.

JST Matthew 24:32
32 And again, this gospel of the kingdom shall be preached in all the world, for a witness unto all nations, and then shall the end come, or the destruction of the wicked.

Mark 13:9-10
9 But take heed to yourselves: for they shall deliver you up to councils; and in the synagogues ye shall be beaten: and ye shall be brought before rulers and kings for my sake, for a testimony against them.
10 And the gospel must first be published among all nations.

Luke 21:24
24 And they shall fall by the edge of the sword, and shall be led away captive into all nations: and Jerusalem shall be trodden down of the Gentiles, until the times of the Gentiles be fulfilled.

JST Luke 21:24-5
24 Now these things he spake unto them, concerning the destruction of Jerusalem. And then his disciples asked him, saying, Master, tell us concerning thy coming?
25 And he answered them, and said, In the generation in which the times of the Gentiles shall be fulfilled, there shall be signs in the sun, and in the moon, and in the stars; and upon the earth distress of nations with perplexity, like the sea and the waves roaring. The earth also shall be troubled, and the waters of the great deep.

Romans 11:25
25 For I would not, brethren, that ye should be ignorant of this mystery, lest ye should be wise in your own conceits; that blindness in part is happened to Israel, until the fulness of the Gentiles be come in.

Revelation 7:3-4
3 Saying, Hurt not the earth, neither the sea, nor the trees, till we have sealed the servants of our God in their foreheads.
4 And I heard the number of them which were sealed: and there were sealed an hundred and forty and four thousand of all the tribes of the children of Israel.

Revelation 7:9
9 After this I beheld, and, lo, a great multitude, which no man could number, of all nations, and kindreds, and people, and tongues, stood before the throne, and before the Lamb, clothed with white robes, and palms in their hands;

Revelation 14:1-6

1 And I looked, and, lo, a Lamb stood on the mount Sion, and with him an hundred forty and four thousand, having his Father's name written in their foreheads.

2 And I heard a voice from heaven, as the voice of many waters, and as the voice of a great thunder: and I heard the voice of harpers harping with their harps:

3 And they sung as it were a new song before the throne, and before the four beasts, and the elders: and no man could learn that song but the hundred and forty and four thousand, which were redeemed from the earth.

4 These are they which were not defiled with women; for they are virgins. These are they which follow the Lamb whithersoever he goeth. These were redeemed from among men, being the firstfruits unto God and to the Lamb.

5 And in their mouth was found no guile: for they are without fault before the throne of God.

6 And I saw another angel fly in the midst of heaven, having the everlasting gospel to preach unto them that dwell on the earth, and to every nation, and kindred, and tongue, and people,

1 Nephi 13:42

42 And the time cometh that he shall manifest himself unto all nations, both unto the Jews and also unto the Gentiles; and after he has manifested himself unto the Jews and also unto the Gentiles, then he shall manifest himself unto the Gentiles and also unto the Jews, and the last shall be first, and the first shall be last.

1 Nephi 14:12-14

12 And it came to pass that I beheld the church of the Lamb of God, and its numbers were few, because of the wickedness and abominations of the whore who sat upon many waters; nevertheless, I beheld that the church of the Lamb, who were the saints of God, were also upon all the face of the earth; and their dominions upon the face of the earth were small, because of the wickedness of the great whore whom I saw.

13 And it came to pass that I beheld that the great mother of abominations did gather together multitudes upon the face of all the earth, among all the nations of the Gentiles, to fight against the Lamb of God.

14 And it came to pass that I, Nephi, beheld the power of the Lamb of God, that it descended upon the saints of the church of the Lamb, and upon the covenant people of the Lord, who were scattered upon all the face of the earth; and they were armed with righteousness and with the power of God in great glory.

1 Nephi 22:11

11 Wherefore, the Lord God will proceed to make bare his arm in the eyes of all the nations, in bringing about his covenants and his gospel unto those who are of the house of Israel.

2 Nephi 30:4-6

4 And then shall the remnant of our seed know concerning us, how that we came out from Jerusalem,

and that they are descendants of the Jews.

5 And the gospel of Jesus Christ shall be declared among them; wherefore, they shall be restored unto the knowledge of their fathers, and also to the knowledge of Jesus Christ, which was had among their fathers.

6 And then shall they rejoice; for they shall know that it is a blessing unto them from the hand of God; and their scales of darkness shall begin to fall from their eyes; and many generations shall not pass away among them, save they shall be a pure and a delightsome people.

3 Nephi 16:10-13

10 And thus commandeth the Father that I should say unto you: At that day when the Gentiles shall sin against my gospel, and shall reject the fulness of my gospel, and shall be lifted up in the pride of their hearts above all nations, and above all the people of the whole earth, and shall be filled with all manner of lyings, and of deceits, and of mischiefs, and all manner of hypocrisy, and murders, and priestcrafts, and whoredoms, and of secret abominations; and if they shall do all those things, and shall reject the fulness of my gospel, behold, saith the Father, I will bring the fulness of my gospel from among them.

11 And then will I remember my covenant which I have made unto my people, O house of Israel, and I will bring my gospel unto them.

12 And I will show unto thee, O house of Israel, that the Gentiles shall not have power over you; but I will remember my covenant unto you, O house of Israel, and ye shall come unto the knowledge of the fulness of my gospel.

13 But if the Gentiles will repent and return unto me, saith the Father, behold they shall be numbered among my people, O house of Israel.

3 Nephi 21:26-29

26 And then shall the work of the Father commence at that day, even when this gospel shall be preached among the remnant of this people. Verily I say unto you, at that day shall the work of the Father commence among all the dispersed of my people, yea, even the tribes which have been lost, which the Father hath led away out of Jerusalem.

27 Yea, the work shall commence among all the dispersed of my people, with the Father to prepare the way whereby they may come unto me, that they may call on the Father in my name.

28 Yea, and then shall the work commence, with the Father among all nations in preparing the way whereby his people may be gathered home to the land of their inheritance.

29 And they shall go out from all nations; and they shall not go out in haste, nor go by flight, for I will go before them, saith the Father, and I will be their rearward.

D&C 14:10

10 Wherefore, I must bring forth the fulness of my gospel from the Gentiles unto the house of Israel.

D&C 18:28

28 And if they desire to take upon them my name with full purpose of heart, they are called to go into all the world to preach my gospel unto every creature.

D&C 35:12-15

12 And there are none that doeth good except those who are ready to receive the fulness of my gospel, which I have sent forth unto this generation.

13 Wherefore, I call upon the weak things of the world, those who are unlearned and despised, to thrash the nations by the power of my Spirit;

14 And their arm shall be my arm, and I will be their shield and their buckler; and I will gird up their loins, and they shall fight manfully for me; and their enemies shall be under their feet; and I will let fall the sword in their behalf, and by the fire of mine indignation will I preserve them.

15 And the poor and the meek shall have the gospel preached unto them, and they shall be looking forth for the time of my coming, for it is nigh at hand—

D&C 39:11

11 And if thou do this, I have prepared thee for a greater work. Thou shalt preach the fulness of my gospel, which I have sent forth in these last days, the covenant which I have sent forth to recover my people, which are of the house of Israel.

D&C 43:24-27

24 O, ye nations of the earth, how often would I have gathered you together as a hen gathereth her chickens under her wings, but ye would not!

25 How oft have I called upon you by the mouth of my servants, and by the ministering of angels, and by mine own voice, and by the voice of thunderings, and by the voice of lightnings, and by the voice of tempests, and by the voice of earthquakes, and great hailstorms, and by the voice of famines and pestilences of every kind, and by the great sound of a trump, and by the voice of judgment, and by the voice of mercy all the day long, and by the voice of glory and honor and the riches of eternal life, and would have saved you with an everlasting salvation, but ye would not!

26 Behold, the day has come, when the cup of the wrath of mine indignation is full.

27 Behold, verily I say unto you, that these are the words of the Lord your God.

D&C 45:24-33

24 And this I have told you concerning Jerusalem; and when that day shall come, shall a remnant be scattered among all nations;

25 But they shall be gathered again; but they shall remain until the times of the Gentiles be fulfilled.

26 And in that day shall be heard of wars and rumors of wars, and the whole earth shall be in commotion, and men's hearts shall fail them, and they shall say that Christ delayeth his coming until the end of the earth.

27 And the love of men shall wax cold, and iniquity shall abound.

28 And when the times of the Gentiles is come in, a light shall break forth among them that sit in darkness, and it shall be the fulness of my gospel;

29 But they receive it not; for they perceive not the light, and they turn their hearts from me because of the precepts of men.

30 And in that generation shall the times of the Gentiles be fulfilled.

31 And there shall be men standing in that generation, that shall not pass until they shall see an

overflowing scourge; for a desolating sickness shall cover the land.

32 But my disciples shall stand in holy places, and shall not be moved; but among the wicked, men shall lift up their voices and curse God and die.

33 And there shall be earthquakes also in divers places, and many desolations; yet men will harden their hearts against me, and they will take up the sword, one against another, and they will kill one another.

D&C 58:64-65

64 For, verily, the sound must go forth from this place into all the world, and unto the uttermost parts of the earth—the gospel must be preached unto every creature, with signs following them that believe.

65 And behold the Son of Man cometh. Amen.

D&C 77:9-11

9 Q. What are we to understand by the angel ascending from the east, Revelation 7th chapter and 2nd verse?

A. We are to understand that the angel ascending from the east is he to whom is given the seal of the living God over the twelve tribes of Israel; wherefore, he crieth unto the four angels having the everlasting gospel, saying: Hurt not the earth, neither the sea, nor the trees, till we have sealed the servants of our God in their foreheads. And, if you will receive it, this is Elias which was to come to gather together the tribes of Israel and restore all things.

10 Q. What time are the things spoken of in this chapter to be accomplished?

A. They are to be accomplished in the sixth thousand years, or the opening of the sixth seal.

11 Q. What are we to understand by sealing the one hundred and forty-four thousand, out of all the tribes of Israel—twelve thousand out of every tribe?

A. We are to understand that those who are sealed are high priests, ordained unto the holy order of God, to administer the everlasting gospel; for they are they who are ordained out of every nation, kindred, tongue, and people, by the angels to whom is given power over the nations of the earth, to bring as many as will come to the church of the Firstborn.

D&C 88:80-96

80 That ye may be prepared in all things when I shall send you again to magnify the calling whereunto I have called you, and the mission with which I have commissioned you.

81 Behold, I sent you out to testify and warn the people, and it becometh every man who hath been warned to warn his neighbor.

82 Therefore, they are left without excuse, and their sins are upon their own heads.

83 He that seeketh me early shall find me, and shall not be forsaken.

84 Therefore, tarry ye, and labor diligently, that you may be perfected in your ministry to go forth among the Gentiles for the last time, as many as the mouth of the Lord shall name, to bind up the law and seal up the testimony, and to prepare the saints for the hour of judgment which is to come;

85 That their souls may escape the wrath of God, the desolation of abomination which awaits the wicked, both in this world and in the world to come. Verily, I say unto you, let those who are not the

first elders continue in the vineyard until the mouth of the Lord shall call them, for their time is not yet come; their garments are not clean from the blood of this generation.

86 Abide ye in the liberty wherewith ye are made free; entangle not yourselves in sin, but let your hands be clean, until the Lord comes.

87 For not many days hence and the earth shall tremble and reel to and fro as a drunken man; and the sun shall hide his face, and shall refuse to give light; and the moon shall be bathed in blood; and the stars shall become exceedingly angry, and shall cast themselves down as a fig that falleth from off a fig-tree.

88 And after your testimony cometh wrath and indignation upon the people.

89 For after your testimony cometh the testimony of earthquakes, that shall cause groanings in the midst of her, and men shall fall upon the ground and shall not be able to stand.

90 And also cometh the testimony of the voice of thunderings, and the voice of lightnings, and the voice of tempests, and the voice of the waves of the sea heaving themselves beyond their bounds.

91 And all things shall be in commotion; and surely, men's hearts shall fail them; for fear shall come upon all people.

92 And angels shall fly through the midst of heaven, crying with a loud voice, sounding the trump of God, saying: Prepare ye, prepare ye, O inhabitants of the earth; for the judgment of our God is come. Behold, and lo, the Bridegroom cometh; go ye out to meet him.

93 And immediately there shall appear a great sign in heaven, and all people shall see it together.

94 And another angel shall sound his trump, saying: That great church, the mother of abominations, that made all nations drink of the wine of the wrath of her fornication, that persecuteth the saints of God, that shed their blood—she who sitteth upon many waters, and upon the islands of the sea—behold, she is the tares of the earth; she is bound in bundles; her bands are made strong, no man can loose them; therefore, she is ready to be burned. And he shall sound his trump both long and loud, and all nations shall hear it.

95 And there shall be silence in heaven for the space of half an hour; and immediately after shall the curtain of heaven be unfolded, as a scroll is unfolded after it is rolled up, and the face of the Lord shall be unveiled;

96 And the saints that are upon the earth, who are alive, shall be quickened and be caught up to meet him.

D&C 90:9-11

9 That through your administration they may receive the word, and through their administration the word may go forth unto the ends of the earth, unto the Gentiles first, and then, behold, and lo, they shall turn unto the Jews.

10 And then cometh the day when the arm of the Lord shall be revealed in power in convincing the nations, the heathen nations, the house of Joseph, of the gospel of their salvation.

11 For it shall come to pass in that day, that every man shall hear the fulness of the gospel in his own tongue, and in his own language, through those who are ordained unto this power, by the administration of the Comforter, shed forth upon them for the revelation of Jesus Christ.

D&C 112:28

28 But purify your hearts before me; and then go ye into all the world, and preach my gospel unto every creature who has not received it;

D&C 133:8-10

8 Send forth the elders of my church unto the nations which are afar off; unto the islands of the sea; send forth unto foreign lands; call upon all nations, first upon the Gentiles, and then upon the Jews.

9 And behold, and lo, this shall be their cry, and the voice of the Lord unto all people: Go ye forth unto the land of Zion, that the borders of my people may be enlarged, and that her stakes may be strengthened, and that Zion may go forth unto the regions round about.

10 Yea, let the cry go forth among all people: Awake and arise and go forth to meet the Bridegroom; behold and lo, the Bridegroom cometh; go ye out to meet him. Prepare yourselves for the great day of the Lord.

D&C 133:16-18

16 Hearken and hear, O ye inhabitants of the earth. Listen, ye elders of my church together, and hear the voice of the Lord; for he calleth upon all men, and he commandeth all men everywhere to repent.

17 For behold, the Lord God hath sent forth the angel crying through the midst of heaven, saying: Prepare ye the way of the Lord, and make his paths straight, for the hour of his coming is nigh—

18 When the Lamb shall stand upon Mount Zion, and with him a hundred and forty-four thousand, having his Father's name written on their foreheads.

D&C 133:36-40

36 And now, verily saith the Lord, that these things might be known among you. O inhabitants of the earth, I have sent forth mine angel flying through the midst of heaven, having the everlasting gospel, who hath appeared unto some and hath committed it unto man, who shall appear unto many that dwell on the earth.

37 And this gospel shall be preached unto every nation, and kindred, and tongue, and people.

38 And the servants of God shall go forth, saying with a loud voice: Fear God and give glory to him, for the hour of his judgment is come;

39 And worship him that made heaven, and earth, and the sea, and the fountains of waters—

40 Calling upon the name of the Lord day and night, saying: O that thou wouldst rend the heavens, that thou wouldst come down, that the mountains might flow down at thy presence.

D&C 133:57-61

57 And for this cause, that men might be made partakers of the glories which were to be revealed, the Lord sent forth the fulness of his gospel, his everlasting covenant, reasoning in plainness and simplicity—

58 To prepare the weak for those things which are coming on the earth, and for the Lord's errand in the day when the weak shall confound the wise, and the little one become a strong nation, and two shall put their tens of thousands to flight.

59 And by the weak things of the earth the Lord shall thrash the nations by the power of his Spirit.

60 And for this cause these commandments were given; they were commanded to be kept from the world in the day that they were given, but now are to go forth unto all flesh—
61 And this according to the mind and will of the Lord, who ruleth over all flesh.

D&C 133:71-74
71 Behold, and lo, there are none to deliver you; for ye obeyed not my voice when I called to you out of the heavens; ye believed not my servants, and when they were sent unto you ye received them not.
72 Wherefore, they sealed up the testimony and bound up the law, and ye were delivered over unto darkness.
73 These shall go away into outer darkness, where there is weeping, and wailing, and gnashing of teeth.
74 Behold the Lord your God hath spoken it. Amen.

CHAPTER FIVE

THE GATHERING OF ISRAEL

"The gathering of Israel—both that which comes before and that which comes after the Second Coming of the Son of Man—consists of two things. It consists, first, of receiving the restored gospel and of joining The Church of Jesus Christ of Latter-day Saints. Next it consists of assembling to whatever places are appointed for the worship of the Lord and the receipt of the fullness of his blessings. Thus, the gathering is both spiritual and temporal."
(Bruce R. McConkie, The Millennial Messiah, p. 198-199.)

Joseph Smith, History of the Church, Vol. 2, Introduction, p. 26.

"The work of God was also greatly enlarged during this Kirtland period, by the appearance of Moses and Elias and Elijah, and bestowing upon the Prophet the keys of their respective dispensations. Let us contemplate the event. 'Moses appeared before us,' says the Prophet, 'and committed unto us the keys of the gathering of Israel, from the four parts of the earth, and the leading of the ten tribes from the land of the north.' Who, at the time comprehended the full import of this incident? Who comprehends it now? From the beginning of the great Latter-day work men had their attention directed to the gathering of Israel and the establishment of Zion and Jerusalem as a part of the purposes of God to be accomplished in the work, the angel Moroni on the occasion of his first visit to the Prophet Joseph, quoted a number of Old Testament scriptures referring to the Lord's promises concerning the redemption of Judah and Jerusalem; also concerning the gathering of Israel from all the lands wither they had been driven. Numerous are the prophecies relating to the return of Israel from the land of the north, and other parts of the earth, into which they were driven in the day of their rebellion and apostasy; but it occurred to no one that before these prophecies could be fulfilled Israel's great prophet, Moses, who held the keys of the dispensation pertaining to the gathering of Israel, must come and give to men the authority to proceed with that work. The moment he appears, however, and gives such authority, the propriety of it, the fitness of it is apparent. The appearance of Moses was also in proper sequence of events in the development of the great Latter-day work. Although, as already stated, the gathering of Israel in the last days had been made a prominent feature in the communication of Moroni to the Prophet Joseph, and the subject also of some other early revelations to the Church not until the foreign ministry had been organized—the Twelve and the Seventy—the quorums of Priesthood on which rests the responsibility to travel in all the world and preach the Gospel and gather Israel—not until this ministry was organized did Moses appear and commit the keys of the gathering of Israel from the four parts of the earth. What order is here? The organization of the foreign ministry to go into all the nations of earth, and then the coming of Moses to commit the keys of the gathering of Israel from the four parts of the earth, and the leading of the ten tribes from the land of the north. In this incident as in a thousand others in the great work of God in the last days, the evidence of a divine wisdom having regard for the eternal fitness of things, for the proper sequence in the order of events in the development of the Lord's purposes, is apparent."

Joseph Smith, History of the Church, Vol. 6, p. 12.

"The Lord does not require every soul to leave his home as soon as He believes. Some may be wanted to go to the isles of the sea, and some to go north, and some south. But He does require them to hearken to counsel, and follow that course which He points out, whether to gather or stay to do some other work."

Joseph Smith, History of the Church, Vol. 6, p. 12.

"Perhaps some of you are ready to ask, 'Cannot the Lord save us as well where we are as to gather together?' Yes, if the Lord says so. But if He commands us to come out and gather together, He will not save us by staying at home."

Joseph Smith, Journal of Discourses, Vol. 6, p. 239, June 2, 1839.

"There will be here and there a Stake for the gathering of the Saints. Some may have cried peace, but the Saints and the world will have little peace from henceforth. Let this not hinder us from going to the Stakes; for God has told us to flee, not dallying, or we shall be scattered, one here, and another there. There your children shall be blessed, and you in the midst of friends, where you may be blessed. The Gospel net gathers of every kind.

I prophesy that the man who tarries after he has an opportunity of going will be afflicted by the Devil. Wars are at hand: we must not delay, but are not required to sacrifice. We ought to have the building up of Zion as our greatest object. When wars come, we shall have to flee to Zion. The cry is to make haste. The last revelation says, 'Ye shall not have time to have' gone over the earth, until these things come. It will come as did the cholera, war, fires, and earthquakes, one pestilence after another, etc., until the Ancient of Days come; then judgment will be given to the Saints.

Whatever you may hear about me or Kirtland, take no notice of it; for if it be a place of refuge, the Devil will use his greatest efforts to trap the Saints. You must make yourselves acquainted with those men who, like Daniel, pray three times a day to the house of the Lord. Look to the Presidency and receive instructions. Every man who is afraid, covetous, etc., will be taken in a snare. The time is soon coming when no man will have any peace but in Zion and her Stakes."

Teachings of the Prophet Joseph Smith, Section Two, 1834–37, p. 71.

"Take away the Book of Mormon and the revelations, and where is our religion? We have none; for without Zion, and a place of deliverance, we must fall; because the time is near when the sun will be darkened, and the moon turn to blood, and the stars fall from the heaven, and the earth reel to and fro. Then, if this is the case, and if we are not sanctified and gathered to the places God has appointed, with all our former professions and our great love for the Bible, we must fall; we cannot stand; we cannot be saved; for God will gather out his Saints from the Gentiles, and then comes desolation and destruction, and none can escape except the pure in heart who are gathered."

Teachings of the Prophet Joseph Smith, Section Two, 1834–37, p. 84.

"Now Enoch was in good company in his views upon this subject: 'And I heard a great voice out of heaven, saying, Behold, the tabernacle of God is with men, and He will dwell with them, and they shall be His people and God Himself shall be with them, and be their God' 21:3).

I discover by this quotation, that John upon the isle of Patmos, saw the same things concerning the last days, which Enoch saw. But before the tabernacle can be with men, the elect must be gathered from the four quarters of the earth."

Teachings of the Prophet Joseph Smith, Section Two, 1834-37, p. 93.

"In speaking of the gathering, we mean to be understood as speaking of it according to scripture, the gathering of the elect of the Lord out of every nation on earth, and bringing them to the place of the Lord of Hosts, when the city of righteousness shall be built, and where the people shall be of one heart and one mind, when the Savior comes: yea, where the people shall walk with God like Enoch, and be free from sin. The word of the Lord is precious; and when we read that the veil spread over all nations will be destroyed, and the pure in heart see God, and reign with Him a thousand years on earth, we want all honest men to have a chance to gather and build up a city of righteousness, where even upon the bells of the horses shall be written 'Holiness to the Lord.'"

Teachings of the Prophet Joseph Smith, Section Two, 1834-37, p. 100.

"As, therefore, the tares are gathered and burned in the fire, so shall it be in the end of the world; that is, as the servants of God go forth warning the nations, both priests and people, and as they harden their hearts and reject the light of truth, these first being delivered over to the buffetings of Satan, and the law and the testimony being closed up, as it was in the case of the Jews, they are left in darkness, and delivered over unto the day of burning; thus being bound up by their creeds, and their bands being made strong by their priests, are prepared for the fulfillment of the saying of the Savior— 'The Son of Man shall send forth His angels, and gather out of His Kingdom all things that offend, and them which do iniquity, and shall cast them into a furnace of fire, there shall be wailing and gnashing of teeth.' We understand that the work of gathering together of the wheat into barns, or garners, is to take place while the tares are being bound over, and preparing for the day of burning; that after the day of burnings, the righteous shall shine forth like the sun, in the Kingdom of their Father. Who hath ears to hear, let him hear."

Teachings of the Prophet Joseph Smith, Section Four, 1839–42, p. 183.

"The greatest temporal and spiritual blessings which always come from faithfulness and concerted effort, never attended individual exertion or enterprise. The history of all past ages abundantly attests this fact. In addition to all temporal blessings, there is no other way for the Saints to be saved in these last days, [than by the gathering] as the concurrent testimony of all the holy prophets clearly proves, for it is written—'They shall come from the east, and be gathered from the west; the north shall give up, and the south shall keep not back.' 'The sons of God shall be gathered from afar, and his daughters from the ends of the earth.'"

Brigham Young, Messages of the First Presidency, Vol. 2, p. 107.

"Let the wicked contend with the wicked, and while they are contending let the Elders preach the Gospel to those who will believe, that the work be not hindered; and where the Saints cannot live in peace, and worship God according to the dictates of their own consciences, being enlightened by the spirit of truth, and the Revelations of Jesus Christ, they may receive it as a sign that it is time for them to arise and flee to Zion, to come home, to come to a land amid the everlasting hills, which is coveted by none, except the Saints; and by them that they may dwell in peace, and enjoy the religion of heaven, and the good of their labours."

Brigham Young, Journal of Discourses, Vol. 12, p. 153, January 12, 1868.

"We are gathered together expressly to build up the kingdom of God. We are not gathered together to build up the kingdom of this world. The voice of God has not called us together from the uttermost parts of the earth to build up and enrich those who are diametrically opposed to His kingdom and its interests. No, but we are gathered together expressly to become of one heart and of one mind in all our operations and endeavors to establish Christ's spiritual and temporal kingdom upon the earth, to prepare for the coming of the Son of Man in power and great glory."

Brigham Young, Journal of Discourses, Vol. 12, p. 281, October 8, 1868.

"We are called upon as individuals, each of us who form this community, to come out from the wicked world, from Babylon. All those who believe the history given by John, the 'beloved disciple,' know that the time would come when the Lord would call upon all people, who believe in Him, delight to do His will, and seek to understand the requirements of heaven, to gather out from the midst of Babylon. John wrote plainly in reference to this gathering, and we have believed it. We are called upon to come out from among the wicked, as it is written, 'Come out of her, O my people,' that is, come out of Babylon. What is Babylon? Why, it is the confused world; come out of her, then, and cease to partake of her sins, for if you do not you will be partakers of her plagues."

Heber C. Kimball, Journal of Discourses, Vol. 4, p. 335, June 7, 1857.

"But we are gathered, and we never will be scattered again—no never, while the earth stands, if you will do as you are told."

Heber C. Kimball, Journal of Discourses, Vol. 8, p. 273, June 3, 1860.

"God has set to his hand again the second time to recover the remnant of his people, which are of the house of Israel, and to gather his elect from the four quarters of the earth. That kingdom is established with its authorities and powers agreeably to the will of God, and they are in the mountains, and all the combines powers of earth and hell can never get them out. They will never leave this land until the Lord God Almighty commands them to go, and then they will go where He directs them. You may set your hearts at rest upon this subject, for I have told you the truth about it, brethren and sisters; and you need not falter by the way, nor find fault about anything that transpires; for this kingdom will stand, whether you do or not. I want you to understand that this is my testimony: it is what I know. I am not telling what I believe, but I am telling you what I know."

Orson Hyde, Journal of Discourses, Vol. 2, p. 68-69, October 8, 1854.

"Says one, 'I really wish I knew how soon it will be when the angels are sent from heaven to gather up the elect at the winding up scene?' I can tell you how soon it will be. 'Have you got the word of the Lord upon this subject?' I do not claim that I have, but when I tell you, you will say it is true; and if it is true, it is just as good as the word of the Lord, and as any other revelation already given. When will it be that the angels are sent to gather in the remnant? It will be just at the time when the Saints have done all that is in their power to do, and can do no more, and have been worn out in the service of their God: then the Lord will send the armies of heaven to aid them. He has had an army under His training from the beginning, and when He gives the word of command they will collect the balance of the Saints from the four winds; and not only so, but they will open the graves, and raise the Saints from the dead."

Orson Pratt, Journal of Discourses, Vol. 2, p. 294, January 7, 1855.

"How did He set His hand the first time, to gather Israel out of Egypt? Did He do it by a company of uninspired men, without miracles, angels, signs, and wonders? No; but He set His hand the first time by signs, wonders, prophets, miracles, sending angels from heaven, by dividing the waters and causing Israel to walk through the midst of the sea without suffering harm, and by coming upon the Mount, and proclaiming the law in the ears of all Israel; when He undertakes to gather them from the nations of the earth, you will find a work of still greater magnitude highly necessary to accomplish that great gathering. To take a nation from the midst of another single nation where they were all collected, and lead them off eleven days journey to another land, is a small work compared with the gathering them from all the nations of the earth, and assembling them in one. When He sets His hand again the second time, He says, 'He shall set up an ensign for the nations;' which is the same thing as spoken of in the 49th chapter. The standard that I have proved should be lifted up to the gentiles, is the same thing as the ensign mentioned in this place. 'He shall set up an ensign to the nations' 'and gather together the dispersed of Judah from the four corners of the earth,' etc.

Do you believe they can be assembled before that standard—that ensign, is raised? Can they be assembled in some other way, and the prophecies be fulfilled? In vain would it be for the nations to undertake to accomplish this thing in any other way than the one the Lord has pointed out by prophecy. Mark what He says in the 15th verse, 'And the Lord shall utterly destroy the tongue of the Egyptian sea; and with his mighty wind shall he shake his hand over the river, and shall smite it in the seven streams, and make men go over dry shod. And there shall be an highway for the remnant of his people, which shall be left, from Assyria; like as it was to Israel in the day that he came up out of the land of Egypt.' Do you believe the words of the Prophet? Do you believe that when the Lord sets His hand the second time to gather Israel from the four quarters of the earth, and lifts up a standard and ensign among the Gentiles to accomplish it, they will go through the sea dry shod, as they did through the Red Sea anciently? If you do not, you do not believe this prophecy. I am now speaking to a people that do believe it; they believe it shall be like as it was in the day that Israel came up out of the land of Egypt; not spiritually, but literally, as then."

Orson Pratt, Journal of Discourses, Vol. 7, p. 186, July 10, 1859.

"A great many have prayed unwisely, and no wonder they cannot get faith to fulfil their prayers. How have they prayed? 'O Lord, gather out all thy Saints from those European countries, and bring them to Zion with songs of everlasting joy upon their heads, that there may be none left abroad upon the earth.'

If the Lord should do this, it would prove the whole system false. When the time comes that the Saints of the Lamb of God are scattered upon all the face of the earth, among all nations and kingdoms of the Gentiles, and the multitudes gather against them to battles, we shall not find such unwise prayers answered. The Saints, instead of being all gathered out, will still be among the nations, for the power of the Lamb of God to descend upon the Saints of the Most High that are among all the nations and kingdoms of the Gentiles, and not only upon these, but also upon his covenant people, the descendants of Jacob; and they are to be armed with righteousness and the power of God in great glory. But gather them all out, and where have you got your Saints? It would completely falsify this saying."

Orson Pratt, Journal of Discourses, Vol. 7, p. 188, July 10, 1859.

"Then many of the Jews will believe, although many of that nation will gather to Jerusalem in unbelief. But the Book of Mormon has told us that the main part of them will believe while yet scattered. They will receive your testimony and gather to Jerusalem; and because of your testimony, the Gentile believers will gather to Zion; and because of your testimony, all the elect of God, of whatever nation, tongue, and people, will be gathered out year after year; and by-and-by, the great and last gathering will be done through instrumentality of angels. There will be two, as it were, grinding at a mill; the faithful one will be taken, and the other will be left: there will be two, as it were, sleeping in one bed; one will be picked up by the angels, and the other will be left; and the remnant of the children of god scattered abroad on all the face of the earth will receive their last gathering by the angels. But between this and that day there will be ship-load after ship-load gathering continually of the elect of God, of the Israel of God, and of the covenant people of the Lord to Zion and Jerusalem."

Orson Pratt, Journal of Discourses, Vol. 13, p. 132, April 10, 1870.

"Another object that the Lord had in view was to gather His people out from all nations before the coming of the great and terrible judgments which are pronounced in this ancient record of the Nephites. God has said, concerning the nation which should inherit this land in the latter days, when this work should be brought forth, if they would not repent of their sins and hearken to the servants of God who should be sent forth among them, if they would reject this divine record which He should bring forth by His power, if they would fight against His Church and His Zion, that when they were fully ripened in iniquity they should be cut off from the face of this land. And for this reason He would gather out from their midst His people and assemble them in one."

Orson Pratt, Journal of Discourses, Vol. 14, p. 332-333, February 11, 1872.

"As it is written by the Apostle Paul, 'Blindness in part hath happened to Israel until the fullness of the Gentiles be come in, and so all Israel shall be saved.' All Israel in that day will hear the voice of the Lord and the voice of his servants; all Israel, in that day, will see the arm of the Lord made bare in signs and mighty wonders in effecting the restoration of his chosen people to their own land. Then will be fulfilled that which is spoken of in the 20th chapter of Ezekiel concerning their restoration: 'For with a mighty hand, saith the Lord, and with fury poured out will I rule over you, and I will gather you out of the nations and from the countries wherein you were driven with a mighty hand, with an outstretched arm and with fury poured out, and I will bring you into the wilderness of the people, and there will I plead with you face to face like as I plead with your fathers in the wilderness of the land of Egypt, so will I plead with you saith the Lord God.' That has never been fulfilled, but it will be fulfilled when scattered Israel return to their own land. A similar scenery is to be enacted to that which was enacted when Israel were brought forth out of the land of Egypt, while they were in the wilderness. Go back to that period and behold the Lord descending upon Mount Sinai, speaking with the voice of a trump in the ears of twenty-five hundred thousand people, the thunders rolling, the lightnings flashing and the voice of Jehovah heard by a whole nation. You marvel at this, it was great and wonderful; but another day is to come when those sceneries enacted in the wilderness of the land of Egypt will be almost entirely forgotten, swallowed up in the greater manifestations of his power, not alone on Mount Sinai, but among all the nations of the earth. Wherever Israel is scattered there will the servants of God be, and his power working wonders, signs and miracles for the gathering of that people and restoring them to their own land. And when they are gathered together in a vast body the Lord intends to take that multitude into the wilderness before he permits them to go into the land of their fathers, and when he gets them into that wilderness, he says, 'I will plead with you face to face, like as I plead with your fathers in the wilderness of the land of Egypt.'"

Orson Pratt, Journal of Discourses, Vol. 15, p. 55-56, December 18, 1870.

"To prepare the people for that great day it is necessary that the Saints should be gathered together, as predicted in the 5th verse, when he should give this great and grand revelation in the last days, when the mighty God, even the Lord, shall speak. He will call to the heavens to assist in the great latter-day work; and all the angels and the heavenly host, who do his bidding, will go forth as swift messengers to execute his decrees and fulfil his purposes in bringing about this grand gathering of his elect from the four quarters of the earth. Who will they be? Those who have made a covenant with him by sacrifice. What kind of a sacrifice? The sacrifice of every earthly thing required, their native countries, their fathers and mothers, for in many instances those who obey the Gospel are compelled to sever the nearest earthly ties—parents from their children, children from their parents and kindred from their kin, in order that they may come forth and be gathered into one grand body preparatory to the coming of the Son of God in flaming fire."

Orson Pratt, Journal of Discourses, Vol. 15, p. 56, December 18, 1870.

"There is to be a grand gathering of all his people from the four quarters of the earth into one body, one family as it were; one people consolidated in one region of country, before he shall come."

Orson Pratt, Journal of Discourses, Vol. 15, p. 180, September 22, 1872.

"But that which the Lord intends to accomplish first by the bringing forth of this book (Book of Mormon), is the redemption of as many as will hearken to its words in all the Gentile nations of the earth, and to gather them together in one; for not only are the house of Israel and the house of

Judah to be gathered back to their own lands, but all Christians throughout the whole earth are to be gathered in one in the latter days, according to a prophecy which you will find in the 43rd chapter of Isaiah: 'I will bring them from the east, and gather them from the west. I will say to the north, Give up; and to the south, Keep not back: bring my sons from far, and my daughters from the ends of the earth; even every one that is called by my name.' This has reference to the sons and daughters of the living God, to the people called Saints; not particularly to the literal seed of the house of Israel, but to all those who believe in him, and who are called by his name. All must be gathered; all must come from the ends of the earth. No Christians will be left, scattered abroad over the nations, as many suppose will be the case so long as time lasts. A complete and full gathering together of the people of God must take place in the latter days, called, by Paul, the dispensation of the fullness of times. You will find this prediction in the first chapter of his epistle to the Ephesians. Paul there declares that a new dispensation must come in, and he denominates it the dispensation of the fullness of times. He tells us that in that dispensation the Lord will gather together in one all things in Christ. Every person that believes in, and has put on Christ by baptism and by repentance of sin, must be gathered in one in that dispensation; not only those on earth, but those in heaven—all the congregations who are in Christ, who have dwelt on the earth in former ages, are to be united with those who are in the flesh on the earth. One great, vast, general assembly of all that are in Christ—the dead as well as the living—from the days of Adam down until the work is completed."

Orson Pratt, Journal of Discourses, Vol. 16, p. 324-325, November 22, 1873.

"And then we have other revelations, showing that when their times (Gentiles) are fulfilled there is a speedy and short work to be accomplished in the gathering of the house of Israel from the four quarters of the earth. They are to be brought out of all nations, kindreds, tongues, and people with a mighty hand and outstretched arm. We are told that God will then perform wonders, miracles and signs, greater than ever have been performed since the creation of the world; that he will bring back his covenant people. After the Jews have rebuilt Jerusalem, and after the Temple is erected, the Lord Jesus will come."

Orson Pratt, Journal of Discourses, Vol. 17, p. 318-319, February 28, 1875.

"'All ye inhabitants of the world, and dwellers on the earth, see ye, when he lifteth up an ensign upon the mountains, and when he bloweth a trumpet hear ye.' It seems then that God is going to lift up an ensign upon the mountains. What do you mean by an ensign? According to the definitions given by our lexicographers an ensign is a kind of standard to which people rally and around which they gather. The Lord is going then, to lift up an ensign on the mountains, and it is to be so wonderful in its nature, something of so much importance that no part of the people are required to understand it; but in the language of Isaiah, 'all ye inhabitants of the world,' all nations, languages and kindreds are required to see, when the Lord lifts up an ensign on the mountains: 'When he bloweth a trumpet hear ye.' What kind of a trumpet? The trumpet of the Gospel, that which takes the Gospel to all these nations, calling upon them to flee out of their own lands. Gather out from the nations, come together in one, go up into the mountains where the kingdom of God is established for the last time. What for? To escape the judgments and tribulations which must come upon the nations of great Babylon."

Orson Pratt, Journal of Discourses, Vol. 17, p. 320, February 28, 1875.

"But there will be a chance to escape from these judgments for all who are willing to gather to the place of refuge which God has appointed in the mountains; all people can rally and gather to that place if they wish to do so. This is spoken of in many places. Let us turn to the fifth Chapter of Isaiah, and see what is said there, concerning the ensign. In the 26th verse we read—'And he will lift up an ensign to the nations from afar, and will hiss unto them from the ends of the earth, and behold they shall come with speed swiftly.' An ensign for the nations lifted up from afar! Isaiah, where were you when you delivered that prophecy? In Palestine. What land would be far off from Palestine where you resided? I think this American continent would be about as far off as almost any portion of the globe.

When the Lord commences this message it will be sent from the nation 'afar off' to the ends of the earth; and there will be a gathering connected with it, of that people who shall come with speed swiftly. The Prophet probably did not know the nature and power of steam in the days to which he referred, and that the gathering would be effected by means of steamboats and railroads; but he did understand that there would be some very swift method of conveyance."

Orson Pratt, Journal of Discourses, Vol. 18, p. 46, July 11, 1875.

"You have heard the proclamation, when the latter-day kingdom was established, to take your lamps and go forth to meet the Bridegroom. Instead of staying in Europe, Asia, Africa, Australia, or among the islands of the sea, you have been commanded to take your lamps and gather out; this is like the fish net that was cast into the sea, and gathered all kinds, both good and bad. 'Do you mean to say,' says one, 'that there are some gathered among you who are bad?' Yes; if there were not the parable of our Savior would not be fulfilled. But by and by there will be a sorting out, and the bad will be cast away unto their own place, while the good will be gathered into vessels and be saved.

This will be fulfilling the words of the Prophet Isaiah, in the 43rd chapter—'I will gather them from the east, and from the west, I will say to the north give up, and to the south keep back. Bring my sons from afar, and my daughters from the ends of the earth, even every one that is called by my name.'—Says one—'Do you really think there will be no Christians left in the north, nor in the south, nor in the east, nor in the west, but that every one that is called by the name of the Lord will be gathered in one?' Yes, that is what we believe and that is one of the peculiarities of what the world call 'Mormonism,' we do not believe there will be a Christian left on the whole face of the earth, but what will be gathered together. 'Well,' says one, 'if that is true, if Isaiah told the truth about that, and the day is at hand for his prophecy to be fulfilled, the nations will truly be in a awful dilemma, when every Christian is gathered out.' I think they will, I think you draw a very correct conclusion.

Why does the Lord gather them out? As the Prophet Isaiah has said in another place, he gathers them out to the mountains, and that say one to another—'Come, let us go up to the mountain of the Lord and to the house of the God of Jacob.' What for? 'That he may teach us of his ways, and that we may walk in his paths.' It seems, than, that the Lord will have one people somewhere on the face of the earth, up in some mountainous region, who are going to teach the nations his ways, and how to walk in his paths."

Orson Pratt, Journal of Discourses, Vol. 18, p. 60, July 25, 1875.

"What other preparation are necessary to be made besides the preaching of this Gospel to all nations? Supposing that among the nations of the earth there were to be raised up a true Christian Church, is there anything particular for that Christian Church to do after having received the ordinances of the Gospel in order to more fully prepare them for the coming of the Son of God? In answer, yes. The Christian Churches built up in the four quarters of the earth after the angel comes, will be required to gather from all these nations unto one place. That is something which no Christian denomination believes in, or if they do believe in it they do not practice it, for the members of the Churches called Christian remain in the respective nations where they receive the truth; it is true that individuals may emigrate, but as Churches they do not. But the Scriptures, speaking of the great day of the coming of the Lord, say there is to be a gathering from all the nations of the earth unto one place of those who have taken upon them the name of the Lord Jesus. That great gathering is referred to in the chapter I have quoted from, also in another chapter in which, referring to the downfall of spiritual Babylon, it is declared that there shall be a gathering of the people, and that too by inspiration, by the command of the Almighty; it will not be left to the wisdom of man, but it will be directed by—'Hear ye the word of the Lord,' as declared to John on the Isle of Patmos. He says—'I heard a great voice from heaven saying—Come out of her, my people!' What people? 'My people.' Who are God's people? Those who obey the everlasting Gospel which the angel brings by authority. 'Come out of her, my people that ye be not partakers of her sins and that ye receive not of her plagues. For her sins have reached unto heaven, and God hath remembered her iniquities;' and now, you who are Saints, you who have obeyed the Gospel restored by the angel, come out of her, for the Lord is going to punish great Babylon. How is he going to punish her? By casting her down, and causing her overthrow. After speaking of the bringing of the Gospel by an angel, the very next verse says—'There followed another angel.' What, two angels come. Yes, and mark the message of the second one. 'There followed another angel, saying, Babylon is fallen, is fallen, that great city, because she made all nations drink of the wine of the wrath of her fornication.'"

Orson Pratt, Journal of Discourses, Vol. 18, p. 61, July 25, 1875.

"Before these terrible judgments are sent forth upon the nation of the earth, God will save all who receive the everlasting Gospel by gathering them to one place, where they can serve him and keep his commandments. He will not merely give them some idea, by reading the Scriptures, that he desires them to gather, but John says there will be a great voice from heaven proclaiming—'Come out of her, my people, that ye be not partakers of her sins, and that ye receive not of her plagues.'

Then there is to be a gathering of the people of God in the latter days? Yes. Do you marvel to see this people coming forth from all the various nations, leaving the homes of their ancestry, the graves of their ancient fathers, leaving their acquaintances and friends, and gathering up here into these mountain vales? Do you see it? Do you marvel at it? Remember, O ye inhabitants of the earth, who are looking upon these things, that you are beholding the fulfillment of prophecy, prophecy spoken by the Apostle Paul, in the first chapter of his epistle to the Ephesians. Paul saw the gathering; he saw that it would be a new dispensation, a dispensation to come after his day. Let me repeat Paul's words—'That in the dispensation of the fullness of times he might gather together in one all things in Christ, both which are in heaven, and which are in earth.' Thus you see that all things in Christ are to be gathered together in one. What does this include? Are the inhabitants of heaven to be made one with the inhabitants of the earth that are in Christ? Yes."

Orson Pratt, Journal of Discourses, Vol. 18, p. 67-68, July 25, 1875.

"We shall after a while, be in Jackson County, in the western borders of Missouri. Why are we going there? Because it is the great central gathering place for the Saints of latter days, for all that will be gathered from South America, Central America, Mexico, and Canada, and from all the nations of the Gentiles—their head quarters will be in Jackson County, in the State of Missouri."

Orson Pratt, Journal of Discourses, Vol. 18, p. 143g, August 30, 1875.

"The great latter-day work has commenced, the kingdom of God has been reorganized on the earth; in other words, the Christian Church in all its purity and with all its ordinances, has been reorganized upon the face of the earth, and the time has at length come when the Spirit of God has been poured out from on high. Until that period arrived, there was no hope for Israel, no hope for the land of Palestine, no hope for the redemption of the tribes scattered in the four quarters of the earth; but when the wilderness should become as a fruitful field, when the spirit should again be poured out from on high, through the everlasting Gospel of the Son of God, then the people should be gathered together by the commandment of the Lord. As is here stated, his Spirit should be the instrument in gathering them together. 'My mouth, it hath commanded this great gathering.' then we may look out for a change upon the face of the land where this gathering takes place; we may look for the deserts to become like the garden of Eden, to blossom as the rose that blossoms in rich and fertile gardens, and to blossom abundantly, and the desert to rejoice with joy and singing. We are to look also, soon after this period of time for the great Redeemer to come. 'Say to them that are of a fearful heart, be strong, fear not, behold your God will come with vengeance; he will come and save you,' having reference to his second coming in the clouds of heaven, with power and with great glory, attended by all the angelic hosts; coming in flaming fire to consume the wicked from the face of the earth as stubble, to burn them up, body root and branch, while the Saints that are left will go forth upon the face of the earth and grow up as calves of the stall, and tread upon the ashes of the wicked."

Orson Pratt, Journal of Discourses, Vol. 18, p. 183, March 26, 1876.

"But one of the great preparatory works in that dispensation of the gathering of Zion to the mountains, will be the construction of a great highway, which is to be cast up in the desert. Let me ask you who have been across these mountains, from Omaha for many hundred miles westward, what kind of a county is it? Is it a country of orchards, vineyards, and alluvial soil, that is calculated to flatter the agriculturist? Says one—'No, I never saw such barren plain for hundreds and hundreds of miles. In the day time, when we had an opportunity of looking at it, it had all one appearance, and was a vast sage plain and desert.' Now Isaiah said that when his people should get up into the mountains a highway should be cast up in the desert. 'Prepare ye the way of the Lord, make straight in the desert a highway for our God.' What! Is it made for the Lord? Yes. What is the Lord going to do with it? He is going to gather his people from all the nations on this highway through the desert. Do you want to know anything more about this highway? Read another chapter in Isaiah; he gives more particulars than what I have mentioned."

Orson Pratt, Journal of Discourses, Vol. 18, p. 184-185, March 26, 1876.

"Would you suppose that the House of Jacob, the ten tribes of Israel, can be gathered from the four quarters of the earth, and brought back to their own land, without the lifting of this ensign? No. Read the 11th chapter of Isaiah. There he says—'I will lift up an ensign for the nations, I will assemble the outcasts of Israel, and I will gather together the dispersed of Judah from the four quarters of the earth.' Until the Lord God sends forth this proclamation to all the inhabitants of the world and dwellers on the earth, in vain may we look for the redemption of the outcasts of Israel and the dispersed of Judah. Israel, the ten tribes called the outcasts, will never return, the scattered Jews will never be restored, until such an ensign is raised. Isaiah, in the fifth chapter, speaks of that ensign—'I will lift up for the nations an ensign from afar.' Why not lift it up in Jerusalem, Isaiah? Why not lift it up in Palestine? Why not commence the work in Asia? Says Isaiah—'I will lift up an ensign to the nations from afar.' How far? Away off to the ends of the earth, from where Isaiah then was."

Orson Pratt, Journal of Discourses, Vol. 18, p. 185-186, March 26, 1876.

"I will quote a passage or two more in relation to the gathering. Paul saw this gathering, and he calls it a new dispensation that should come after his day. He says that in the dispensation of the fullness of times he would gather together in one all things in Christ, whether they be things in heaven or things on the earth. The dispensation of the fullness of times, then, was to be characterized by the gathering of all persons that were in Christ. All the righteous dead that are in heaven, whose bodies are asleep in the grave, together with all the Christians on the earth, will be gathered in one in that dispensation. Fulfilling another prophecy in the 43rd chapter of Isaiah, where the Lord says—'I will say to the north give up, and to the south keep not back; bring my sons from afar and my daughters from the ends of the earth, even every one that is called by my name.' Will it leave a Christian behind? Not one. Go and search New York, Philadelphia, and all the eastern States, and the middle and southern states, and then in Europe, for a Christian after this prophecy is fulfilled, and you can't find one. Why? Because they are all gathered in one. How? By new revelation. The Lord says, 'I will say to the north give up.' The Lord is going to speak, the Lord is going to utter something—'I will say to the south keep not back. I will say, Come ye, my sons and daughters, from the ends of the earth, even every one that is called by my name.' What an awful condition the world will be in when there is not a Christian among them. Amen."

Orson Pratt, Journal of Discourses, Vol. 18, p. 228-229, August 26, 1876.

"But the day will come when the Lord will not spare any who remain in Babylon; that will be, however, when this prophecy of Isaiah is completely fulfilled—'I will gather them from the east, and from the west; I will say to the north, give up, and to the south, keep not back; bring my sons from afar, and my daughters from the ends of the earth, even, every one that is called by name.' All this is to take place in the very dispensation in which the angel should bring the Gospel, which is the dispensation of the fullness of times. The Apostle Paul also refers to the same great event, in the following language: 'That in the dispensation of the fullness of times he might gather together in one all things in Christ, both which are in heaven and which are on earth; even in him.' It is the purpose of God then, not to confine the gathering to earthly Saints alone. 'What,' says one, 'Are immortal beings coming down from heaven to live on this earth?' Certainly, and thus fulfill numerous prophecies in the Scriptures; one of which is, 'They shall reign on the earth.' Who are these person? They are they whom John heard singing in heaven about it. They said, 'Thou hast redeemed us out of every nation, kindred, tongue and people, and hast made us unto our God, kings and priests: and we shall reign on the earth.' What a glorious song! While we are singing about going to heaven, all heavenly beings are singing about coming back to earth to live and to reign. Why? Because this is their inheritance, they have been made worthy through the blood of the lamb, and their redeemer will be their King of Kings and Lord of Lords, and to his dominion there shall be no end. When this takes place, then will be fulfilled the saying, that all things which are in Christ, both in heaven and on earth, shall be gathered together. The wicked, too, shall be gathered, but in bundles ready for the burning. Marvel not, therefore, Latter-day Saints, that you have been exalted out from among the Gentile nations! Marvel not that the Lord has said to the North, give up, and to the south, keep not back, bring my sons from afar, and my daughters from the ends of the earth! Marvel not at the Savior's parable of the gathering of all kinds of fish and bringing them to the shore! By and by, angels will come among the Latter-day Saints who have been gathered from the nations, and they will pluck out one here, and another there, putting them in to their place. The separation of the fish will take place; the bad will be cast away, while the good will be reserved in vessels for the Master's use."

Orson Pratt, Journal of Discourses, Vol. 21, p. 279-280, June 20, 1880.

"In another very plain parable, concerning the gathering in the last days, the kingdom of heaven is compared—that is the kingdom which should exist in the last days—to a net that should be cast into the sea, and gather of all kinds, both good and bad. They are brought up to the shore, not left in their native ocean or native waters, but brought up to the shore. The bad area cast away, and the good were cast into the vessels. Now, this had reference also to the end of the world. This had reference to the great and last dispensation, when the servants of God will go forth, being commissioned of the Lord of Hosts to gather out his Saints, those that have made a covenant with him by sacrifice, and in the gathering out of these Saints from all the lands of the earth, and from the four quarters thereof, they will gather up a great many that are not good, that will not stand the test; but the bad will be cast out, those who have not on the wedding garment they will be cast away, and bound hand and foot, as it were, until the end shall come, that is, the final judgment, which will be more than a thousand years after the time of the coming of the Savior.

This same great gathering is characterized also by Daniel, as a stone cut out of the mountain without hands. This stone is represented as a kingdom, and its location is represented as a mountain, showing that there is to be a kingdom of God set up in the last days by the gathering together of his people in an elevated region of country, called a mountain. By and by that stone will roll forth, until the kingdoms of this world are broken in pieces, and as the Prophet Daniel said, the kingdom shall not be left to other people, but shall stand forever; all those other earthly kingdoms, that Nebuchadnezzar saw in his dream, will vanish away, like a night vision, or, in other words, become 'like the chaff of the summer threshing floors; and the wind carried them away, and no place was found for them.'"

Orson Pratt, Journal of Discourses, Vol. 21, p. 280, June 20, 1880.

"To prove still more clearly the nature of this great latter-day work of gathering, read the writings of John the Revelator. He saw the introduction of the Gospel in the latter-days. He saw 'another angel' should bring it. He saw that it should be published to every nation, kindred, tongue and people. He saw that following that angel there would come great and terrible judgments. He saw that after that angel should come with the Gospel, there would come a voice from heaven, saying, 'Come out of her, my people, that ye be not partakers of her sins, and that ye receive not of her plagues. For her sins have reached unto heaven, and God hath remembered her iniquities.' This voice from heaven, this new revelation, that was promised by the mouth of John the revelator, and the sound to all is: 'Come out from among these nations. Come out from the four quarters of the earth. Come out from Great Babylon, 'Mystery, Babylon the Great,' that you may escape the desolation and plagues that will soon overtake her.' Read concerning the coming of that angel with the Gospel. Read the declaration that that should be the hour of God's judgment. When the Gospel is preached, it is the last message to the human family, the last warning voice that they will hear before the coming of the Lord. If they receive it, they will flee out from the nations; if they receive it not, then know assuredly that the hour of God's judgment is come, and God himself will judge the people, as written in this 50th Psalm."

John Taylor, Journal of Discourses, Vol. 24, p. 123-124, April 8, 1883.

"The Lord has said he would gather together His elect from the four quarters of the earth. And how does He do it? By operating upon the minds of those who obey the Gospel. Jesus said in His day and it is true to-day—'My sheep hear my voice and know it, and follow me and a stranger they will not follow because they know not the voice of a stranger.' It is under the influence of this Spirit that we have been gathered together."

John Taylor, Journal of Discourses, Vol. 26, p.107, October 20, 1881.

"They built a Temple by and by, as we are doing now, in Kirtland, Ohio. And in that Temple the Lord Jesus Christ appeared to them again, the account of which you may read for yourselves in the Doctrine and Covenants. Jesus appeared there, and Moses appeared there, and Moses conferred upon Joseph the keys of the gathering of Israel from the four quarters of the earth, and also the ten tribes. And you are here because that Priesthood was conferred upon the Elders who came to you with the Gospel; and when they laid their hands upon your heads, among other things you received the Holy Ghost and the spirit of the gathering. But you did not know what it was that was working in you like yeast sometimes under certain conditions, producing an influence causing you to come to Zion. Yet you could not help it; if you had wanted to help it, you could not while you were living your religion and were governed thereby, for that spirit brought that influence and power along with it, and it carries it with it wherever it goes. And as men received the Holy Ghost so they received the spirit of the gathering, which was conferred by Moses upon Joseph Smith, and by him upon others, and which created that anxiety you all felt to gather to Zion."

John Taylor, The Government of God, Chapter 11.

"Yes, says Jeremiah, He will taken them one of a city, and two of a family, and bring them to Zion, and give them pastors after his own heart, that shall feed them with knowledge and understanding. iii. 14,15. The proclamation to the world will be the means of establishing this Zion, by gather together multitudes of people from among all nations. For there are multitudes among all nations who are sincerely desirous to do the will of God, when they are made acquainted with it; but having been cajoled with priestcraft and abominations so long, they know not which course to steer, and are jealous of almost everything. As it was formerly, so will it be in the latter times. Jesus said, 'My sheep hear my voice, and know me, and follow me, and a stranger they will not follow, for they know not the voice of strangers.' Those who love truth, and desire to be governed by it, will embrace it, and enter into the covenant which the Lord will make with his people in the last days, and be gathered with them; they will be taught of the Lord in Zion, will form his kingdom on the earth, and will be prepared for the Lord when he comes to take possession of his kingdom."

John Taylor, The Government of God, Chapter11.

"It may be proper here to remark, that there will be two places of gathering, or Zion; the one in Jerusalem, the other in another place; the one is a place where the Jews will gather to, and the other a mixed multitude of all nations. Concerning the house of Israel, Jeremiah says, 'Therefore, behold, the days come, saith the Lord, that it shall no more be said, The Lord liveth, that brought up the children of Israel out of the land of Egypt; but, the Lord liveth, that brought up the children of Israel from the land of the north, and from all the lands whither he had driven them: and I will bring them again into their land that I gave unto their fathers.' According to this passage, and many others, there will evidently be a great display of the power of God manifested towards the house of Israel in their restitution to their former habitations. Another Scripture says, that 'Jerusalem shall be inhabited in her own place, even in Jerusalem.' Here I would remark, that there was a Zion formerly in Jerusalem; but there is also another spoken of in the Scriptures. Hence, in the passage which we quoted from the Psalms, the Kingdoms are to be gathered together in Zion, and the people to fear the name of the Lord, and all the kings of the earth his glory. The law is to issue from Zion, and the word of the Lord from Jerusalem. Again—'The Lord God that gathereth the outcasts of Israel, says, yet will I gather others unto me besides these.' It is very evident from these passages that there are two places of gathering, as well as from many others that might be quoted. For example, Joel, in speaking of the troubles of the last days, says, There shall in the last days be deliverance in Mount Zion, and in Jerusalem. Now, he never could say with propriety in Mount Zion, and in Jerusalem, if these were not two places."

Wilford Woodruff, Conference Report, p. 57, April 1898.

"He said (Joseph Smith) 'It will fill the Rocky Mountains. There will be tens of thousands of Latter-day Saints who will be gathered to the Rocky Mountains, and there they will open the door for the establishing of the gospel among the Lamanites, who will receive the gospel and their endowments and the blessings of God. This people will go into the Rocky Mountains; they will there build temples to the Most High. They will raise up a posterity there, and the Latter-day Saints who dwell in these mountains will stand in the flesh until the coming of the Son of Man. The Son of Man will come to them while in the Rocky Mountains.'"

Wilford Woodruff, Journal of Discourses, Vol. 18, p. 188-189, April 6, 1876.
"Ezekiel says that in the last days the stick of Joseph in the hands of Ephraim should be placed with the stick of Judah, before the eyes of the nations in the hands of the Lord, for a special purpose—to gather the house of Israel in the latter days. These two records were also to be made use of in order to preach the fullness of the everlasting Gospel to both Jew and Gentile; and they will stand in judgment against the generation living on the earth when they come forth."

Teachings of Lorenzo Snow, p. 153.
"There will be a universal gathering to America and Palestine. Mormonism teaches that prior to the Millennial reign of peace, there is to be a universal gathering of scattered Israel, the lineal descendants of Abraham, Isaac, and Jacob; meaning not only the Jews, but also the 'lost tribes' and such of the chosen seed as have for generations been mixed with other peoples. This gathering, which includes the converted Gentiles, is preliminary to the glorious advent of the King of kings, and the resurrection of those who are Christ's at His coming. The places of assembly are America and Palestine, the former taking chronological precedence as the gathering place of 'Ephraim and his fellows,' while the 'dispersed of Judah' will migrate to and rebuild Jerusalem. Here, upon the American continent, will be reared Zion, a new Jerusalem, where the Saints will eventually assemble and prepare for the coming of the Messiah. (January 2, 1902)"

Erastus Snow, Journal of Discourses, Vol. 16, p. 203, September 14, 1873.
"Mark the object of the gathering—the nations shall say, 'Let us go up to the mountain of the Lord, to the house of the God of Jacob, for he will teach us of his ways and we will learn to walk in his paths.' How will this be brought about? Because the law shall go forth out of Zion, and the word of the Lord from Jerusalem. How can this be unless God shall begin to reveal himself to his people and minister in their midst as in ancient days, by his own voice, the voice of Prophets, the spirit of revelation and the ministration of angels?"

Erastus Snow, Journal of Discourses, Vol. 23, p. 182-184, May 6, 1882.
"Another Scripture also says concerning scattered Israel, that Ephraim has mixed himself among the people; and speaking of the gathering of Israel in the latter-day dispensation, the Prophet Jeremiah has said that God would gather Israel and lead them as a shepherd does his flock, and says he, I am Father to Israel, but Ephraim is my first-born. Now, if Ephraim has been scattered and has mixed himself with the people until their identity is lost among the nations, how are they going to be recognized and receive the promised blessings—how is it that Ephraim shall be the first-born of the Lord in the great gathering of the latter-days? If we turn back to the blessing which Moses gave to the twelve tribes of Israel, as found in Deuteronomy, we shall there see that in blessing the tribe of Joseph, he especially charged them with the duty of gathering the people from the ends of the earth. Said he, Joseph's horns are like the horns of unicorns, which shall push the people together from the ends of the earth, and they are the thousands of Manasseh and ten thousands of Ephraim; showing that it shall be the ten thousands of Ephraim and thousands of Manasseh who shall be in the foremost ranks of bearing the Gospel message to the ends of the earth, and gathering Israel from the four quarters of the world in the last days."

The Gathering of Israel

Erastus Snow, Journal of Discourses, Vol. 12, p. 211, April 8, 1868.

"One reason assigned by the Lord for the gathering of His people is set forth in the revelations of St. John, where He says, 'Come out of her O, my people that ye be not partakers of her sins, and that ye receive not of her plagues.' This, in a few words, explains the chief reason for the Lord requiring His people to gather together. But the prophets Isaiah and Micah assign another good reason—they predict that the mountain of the Lord's house in the last days shall be established in the tops of the mountains, and the nations shall flow unto it, saying. 'Let us go up to the mountain of the Lord and to the house of the God of Jacob, for He will teach us of His ways, that we may learn to walk in his paths.'

These two scriptures show unto us that the Lord has required His people to gather in the last days, that they might escape the sins of the wicked, and the plagues which shall be poured out upon them, and that they might be taught in His paths, taught to govern themselves, to correct their foolish habits and customs, and to train themselves and their offspring that they may be able to build up Zion according to the law and order of Heaven."

Franklin D. Richards, A Compendium of the Doctrines of the Gospel, p. 90.

"As general as was the scattering of Israel so must the gathering be. If the dispersion was over all the earth, and among all nations, so the gathering must be out of all nations, and from all parts of the earth."

Franklin D. Richards, A Compendium of the Doctrines of the Gospel, p. 231-232.

"One very significant sign of his coming, he stated would be, that his elect should be gathered from the four quarters of the earth. Through the instrumentality of Joseph Smith and the Holy Priesthood, this great work is now going on: 'And they,' that is those who are being gathered, 'shall hear of wars, and rumors of wars, . . . for nation shall rise against nation, and kingdom against kingdom; there shall be famine, and pestilences, and earthquakes, in divers places; and again, (for the second time) because iniquity shall abound, the love of many shall wax cold.' Again Jesus gave the assurance that he who was not overcome should be saved: 'And again'—that is when the Elect are being gathered and judgments were being poured out upon the nations for the second time—'This Gospel of the kingdom shall be preached in all the world, for a witness unto all nations, and then shall the end come,' or the destruction of the wicked; 'and again'—that is for the second time—'shall the abomination of desolation, spoken of by Daniel the prophet, be fulfilled.'"

George Q. Cannon, Journal of Discourses, Vol. 15, p. 204, October 8, 1872.

"But though we have gathered together, as we have, in this country, there seems to be in the minds of a great many people a disposition to overlook the reasons which God our heavenly Father has had in view in gathering us out, and collecting us together, and making us one people. The prophecies which were recorded in ancient days, as well as those which have been given us in the day in which we live, all point forward to this great dispensation, as a time when God should do a great and mighty work in the midst of the earth, and when a great revolution should be effected and a great reformation accomplished among the children of men; when he should have a peculiar people—a people who should be gathered out from all nations, a people upon whom he should place his name,

275

and whom he should recognize as his. We are told by the Revelator John, that a time would come when the people of God should be commanded to some out of Babylon, out of confusion, when they should be gathered out from every nation, from the remotest parts of the earth, and when he should make of them a great and mighty people."

Joseph F. Smith, Messages of the First Presidency, Vol. 4, p. 222.
    "The establishment of the latter-day Zion on the American continent occasions the gathering of the Saints from all nations. This is not compulsory, and particularly under present conditions, is not urged, because it is desirable that our people shall remain in their native lands and form congregations of a permanent character to aid in the work of proselyting."

Joseph F. Smith, Journal of Discourses, Vol. 19, p. 193-194, September 30, 1877.
    "In various dispensations there are various differences in regard to certain requirements of the Gospel. For instance, in the day of Noah, when he preached the Gospel to the antediluvian world, he was given a special commandment, to build an ark, that in case the people would reject him and the message sent unto them, that himself and all who believed on him might be saved from the destruction that awaited them. In this dispensation there is a principle or commandment peculiar to it. What is that? It is the gathering the people unto one place. The gathering of this people is as necessary to be observed by believers, as faith, repentance, baptism, or any other ordinance. It is an essential part of the Gospel of this dispensation, as much so, as the necessity of building an ark by Noah, for his deliverance, was a part of the Gospel of his dispensation. Then the world was destroyed by a flood, now it is to be destroyed by war, pestilence, famine, earthquakes, storms, and tempests, the sea rolling beyond its bounds, malarious vapors, vermin, disease, and by fire and the lightnings of God's wrath poured out for destruction upon Babylon. The cry of the angel unto the righteous of this dispensation is, 'Come out of her O my people, that ye partake not of her sins, and that ye receive not of her plagues.' We believe also in the principle of direct revelation from God to man . . . The religious world is in this condition today, ripening for the great destruction which awaits them, but there is an ark prepared for such as are worthy of eternal life, in the gathering of the Saints to the chambers of the Almighty, where they shall be preserved until the indignation of God is passed."

Hyrum M. Smith, Doctrine and Covenants Commentary, Sec. 29, p. 160.
    "Zion means the pure in heart, as well as a place of gathering, and it is to be noted that no place can be Zion, unless it is inhabited by those who are pure in heart. Jackson County, Mo., is to be the central place of Zion, and there the New Jerusalem will be built, and this will be just as soon as the Lord has a people prepared to make a Zion and a New Jerusalem there. 'When the Lord shall build up Zion, he shall appear in his glory' (Psalms 102:16)."

Hyrum M. Smith, Doctrine and Covenants Commentary, Sec. 45, p. 264.
    "The remnant shall be gathered. This has reference to the return of the Jews to Jerusalem. This is another important sign of the coming of our Lord. In the day in which we live the children of God have been taught to gather at the various places appointed by revelation, in order to assist in the

building up of the Kingdom of God preparatory to the second advent. The spirit of gathering accompanies the acceptance of the gospel. . . . The very purpose of the gathering is that there may be a people prepared for the coming of the Lord."

Hyrum M. Smith, Doctrine and Covenants Commentary, Sec. 58, p. 345.

"Gathering be not in haste. This is another warning against gathering without deliberate consideration of the duties and responsibilities connected with the settlement in Zion. If the Saints need wisdom and wise counsel at any time, it is when they are moved upon by the spirit of gathering."

Hyrum M. Smith, Doctrine and Covenants Commentary, Sec. 63, p. 379-381.

"Why gather the people together in this place (Jackson County, Mo.)? For the same purpose that Jesus wanted to gather the Jews—to receive the ordinances, the blessings, and glories that God has in store for His Saints.

(63:24-31) In these paragraphs special instructions concerning gathering are given. It was not to be undertaken in haste, but after due preparation, 'lest there should be confusion, which bringeth pestilence' (v. 24). If they went on the long journey without the necessary preparations, proper food and suitable clothing, the consequence would be sickness . . .

The land of gathering belonged to the Lord (v. 25), but the Saints, mindful of the injunction of Christ, to 'render unto Caesar the things which are Caesar's,' were to purchase their inheritance (v. 27). A contrary course would lead to bloodshed (v. 28). But that would mean that the Saints would be slaughtered, for they were forbidden to shed blood (v. 31). They would be 'scourged from city to city, and from synagogue to synagogue.'

The Latter-day Saints are forbidden to make war in order to secure a gathering-place, and especially such a sacred place as that in which the greatest of all God's temples is to be located. They are not forbidden to defend their lives, their homes, their loved ones, their liberty and country, against murderers and thieves, but they are forbidden to be the aggressors.

32-37. In these paragraphs our Lord states one of the most solemn reasons for the gathering of His Saints—a reason which concerns the entire world. He is angry with the wicked (v. 32), and He has decreed wars upon Earth; 'the wicked shall slay the wicked' (v. 33). In order that the Saints might escape this general slaughter, they were commanded to gather upon the land of Zion (v. 36). . . .There are other important reasons for gathering.

34. The Saints also shall hardly escape. Because of their neglect to gather and to build up Zion."

Hyrum M. Smith, Doctrine and Covenants Commentary, Sec. 63, p. 386.

"If they have the spirit of the gospel, their gathering will be for the purpose of building up the Kingdom of God and, as far as depends on them, hasten on the day when the Millennial reign shall begin. Consequently, they will go to Zion duly prepared. They will repent of their weaknesses and imperfections; they will go according to counsel (v. 41), and they will realize that to gather to Zion is a religious undertaking similar to that of joining the Church."

David O. McKay, Messages of the First Presidency, Vol. 2, April 10, 1954, p. 136.

"In these secluded vales we gather the Saints that we may enjoy the rights and privileges of the Constitution, denied to us elsewhere; that we may have he privilege of worshiping God according to the dictates of our own consciences. We gather that we may enjoy not only the rights of citizenship, but live in peace, and have the respect and courtesy extended to ourselves and our families by our associates, which is denied to us in the world. We gather that we may obey the ordinances and keep the commandments of God, and concentrate our ability in rolling forth the great work of God upon the earth, establishing His kingdom, building temples, and preparing the way for the coming of the Son of Man. And when those professing to be Saints, gather with us, we naturally expect them to be influenced by the same motives."

Orson F. Whitney, Saturday Night Thoughts, p. 168.

"Jackson County, Missouri, is the chosen site for the City of Zion. No other place has been or will be appointed for that purpose. All other gathering places for God's people are only Stakes of Zion, holding the outside cords and curtains of the spiritual Tabernacle of the Lord."

Orson F. Whitney, Saturday Night Thoughts, p. 190.

"The present is distinctively a gathering dispensation. But it stands for much more than the assembling of the dispersed House of Israel. It is the spiritual harvest-time of all the ages, the long-heralded Era of Restitution, when the great Garnerer of 'all things in Christ' will reveal himself in power and glory, and place the capstone on the temple of heaven-inspired human achievement. Such is the Dispensation of the Fulness of Times. The gathering of Israel is only the preface to the book, only the prologue to the play. The gathering of the gatherers—such is the meaning of the preliminary work now in progress, a work in which Gods, angels and men have joined."

Orson F. Whitney, Saturday Night Thoughts, p. 196-197.

"The gathering of the House of Israel is to be supplemented by a greater gathering—the bringing together of the Gospel dispensations, with all the sacred powers and mighty personages connected therewith. There is to be a General Assembly, a universal union, in which sainted souls from glorified creations will join. All things that are Christ's, both in heaven and on earth, will eventually be brought together, and the divided and discordant parts attuned and blended in one harmonious Whole."

Joseph Fielding Smith, Answers to Gospel Questions, Vol. 3, p. 152-153.

"Question: 'What is the difference between the keys of the missionary work given the Prophet Joseph Smith by Peter, James, and John and the keys restored by Moses for the gathering of Israel?'

Answer: The answer to this question is a simple one. When Moses was called to gather Israel and lead them back to the land that the Lord had given to Abraham for an everlasting possession, they were members of the Church. Moses was not sent to restore to them the priesthood, nor to convert them, for they were all versed in the knowledge that they were the descendants of Abraham, Isaac, and Jacob, and without doubt had ministers among them. They had been trained in the teachings of Jacob and Joseph. So the work of Moses was to gather Israel who were in a compact body. His mission was to lead them to the land of their fathers and see that they were established there according to the commandment of the Lord. It is verily true that through him the Lord gave many laws and commandments for their government and spiritual development as well as the 'carnal law.'

In these latter days when Israel has been scattered, Moses was sent to restore the keys of the gathering, not the preaching of the gospel. It was after people were converted that the spirit of gathering entered their souls, and it was due to the influence of the Spirit of the Lord, based upon the restoration of the keys given to Moses, that the members of the Church, when they were brought into the Church, obtained the desire to gather to the body of the Church. So these two things went hand in hand."

Joseph Fielding Smith Jr., Doctrines of Salvation, Vol. 3, p. 252.

"It is essential in this dispensation that Ephraim stand in his place at the head, exercising the birthright in Israel . . .Ephraim must be gathered first to prepare the way through the gospel and the priesthood, for the rest of the tribes of Israel when the time comes for them to be gathered to Zion."

John A. Widtsoe, Evidences and Reconciliations, p. 248.

"In the early days of the Church, persecution raged against the Saints in Jackson County, Missouri. For the comfort of the people, the Lord gave several revelations. In one He promised, 'I will raise up unto my people a man, who shall lead them like as Moses led the children of Israel.' (D&C 103:16) There have been many conjectures concerning this statement. There have even been misguided men who have declared themselves to be this man 'like as Moses.'

Yet, the meaning as set forth in the scriptures, is very simple. In modern revelation the President of the Church is frequently compared to Moses. Soon after the organization of the Church, the Lord said, 'no one shall be appointed to receive commandments and revelations in this church excepting my servant Joseph Smith, Jun., for he receiveth them even as Moses.' (D&C 28:2) In oneof the great revelations upon Priesthood, this is more specifically expressed: 'the duty of the President of the office of the High Priesthood is to preside over the whole church, and to be like unto Moses.' (D&C 107:91)

The discussion of this question among the Saints led to the following statement in the Times and Seasons (6:922) by John Taylor, then the editor: 'The President [of the Church] stands in the Church as Moses did to the children of Israel, according to the revelations.' The man like unto Moses in the Church is the President of the Church."

Harold B. Lee, Conference Report, April 1948, p. 55.

"Thus, clearly, the Lord has placed the responsibility for directing the work of gathering in the hands of the leaders of the Church to whom he will reveal his will where and when such gatherings would take place in the future. It would be well before the frightening events concerning the fulfillment of all God's promises and predictions are upon us, that the Saints in every land prepare themselves and look forward to the instruction that shall come to them from the First Presidency of this Church as to where they shall be gathered and not be disturbed in their feelings until such instruction is given to them as it is revealed by the Lord to the proper authority."

The Teachings of Spencer W. Kimball, p. 439-440.

"Now, the gathering of Israel consists of joining the true church and their coming to a knowledge of the true God. Any person, therefore, who has accepted the restored gospel, and who now seeks to worship the Lord in his own tongue and with the Saints in the nations where he lives, has complied with the law of the gathering of Israel and is heir to all of the blessings promised the Saints in these last days. The Saints are no longer to come to a single place. . . .

Now, in the early days of the Church we used to preach for the people to come to Utah as the gathering process, largely because that was the only place in the whole world where there was a temple. . .

The First Presidency and the Twelve see great wisdom in the multiple Zions, many gathering places where the Saints within their own culture and nation can act as a leaven in the building of the kingdom—a kingdom which seeks no earthly rewards or treasures."

Teachings of Ezra Taft Benson, p. 60.

"The Book of Mormon is the instrument that God has designed to 'sweep the earth as with a flood, to gather out His elect unto the New Jerusalem.' This sacred volume of scripture has not been, nor is it yet, central in our preaching, our teaching, and our missionary work. (Salt Lake City, Utah, 5 March 1987.)"

Teachings of Ezra Taft Benson, p. 91.

"In the scriptures there are set forth three phases of the gathering of Israel. One, the gathering of Israel to the land of Zion which is America, this land. That is under way and has been under way since the Church was established and our missions abroad were inaugurated. Then two, the return of the lost tribes, the ten lost tribes, from the land of the north (see D&C 133). And the third phase is the reestablishment of the Jews in Palestine as one of the events to precede the second coming of the Master. Isaiah said they will be gathered together, the dispersed of Judah, from the four corners of the earth and they will be set in their own land, they will build the old wastes and repair the waste cities (see Isaiah 11:11-12). Jeremiah, who predicted the dispersion and the scattering, said that in the last days the Lord would cause them to return to the land that He gave to their fathers and they shall possess it; and they shall build it up as at first (Jeremiah 30:3). ("The Jews Return to Palestine in Fulfillment of Prophecy," Washington D.C. Stake Conference, March 3, 1957.)"

Teachings of Ezra Taft Benson, p. 149.

"To members, the term stake is a symbolic expression. Picture in your mind a great tent held up by cords extended to many stakes that are firmly secured in the ground. The prophet Isaiah likened latter-day Zion to a great tent encompassing the earth. That tent was supported by cords fastened to stakes. (See 3 Nephi 22:2; Isaiah 54:2.) Those stakes, of course, are various geographical organizations spread out over the earth. Presently Israel is being gathered to the various stakes of Zion."

Teachings of Ezra Taft Benson, p. 151.

"As the Church grows, it is very important that we build solidly and well, and that our prospective stakes have the basic ingredients that are necessary for success and that existing stakes work tirelessly for full stakehood in the sense of spiritual achievement. These stakes are to be the gathering spots for the Zion of today, and they need to be spiritual sanctuaries and to be self-sufficient in as many ways as is possible. (Regional Representatives Seminar, Salt Lake City, Utah, April 4, 1974.)"

Teachings of Ezra Taft Benson, p. 151-152.
    "Latter-day Saint chapels are more than just houses of worship. The stakes and districts of Zion are symbolic of the holy places spoken of by the Lord where His Saints are to gather in the last days as a refuge from the storm."

Bruce R. McConkie, Mormon Doctrine, "Ensign to the Nations", p. 228.
    "This ensign is . . . the gospel . . . it is The Church of Jesus Christ of Latter-day Saints."

Bruce R. McConkie, Mormon Doctrine, "Gathering of Israel", p. 306.
    "However, the temporal gathering of Israel will not be completed before the Second Coming (1 Ne. 14:12.) . . . The purpose of the gathering of Israel is twofold: 1. To put the peoples of living Israel in that environment where they may the better work out their salvation . . . 2. To enable the gathered remnants of the chosen lineage to build temples and perform the ordinances of salvation."

Bruce R. McConkie, Mormon Doctrine, "Gathering of Israel", p. 306-307.
    "Israel cannot be gathered . . . without revelation and direction. . . Acordingly the Lord... sent Moses to deliver the keys of the gathering of Israel . . .By virtue of these keys the prophet and his successors . . . have held the directive and presiding authority relative to this great work."

Bruce R. McConkie. The Mortal Messiah, Vol. 3, p. 457.
    "'This he spake, signifying the gathering of his saints; and of angels descending and gathering the remainder unto them: the one from the bed, the other from the grinding, and the other from the field, whithersoever he listeth. For verily there shall be new heavens, and a new earth, wherein dwelleth righteousness.' (JST Luke 17:38). Truly the angels shall complete the gathering of the elect."

Bruce R. McConkie, The Mortal Messiah, Vol. 4, p. 337-338.
    "Why is the Lord gathering Israel in these last days? It is to fulfil the covenant made with Abraham and renewed with Isaac and Jacob and others. What is that covenant? It is not the gathering of Israel per se, but something far more important than the mere assembling of a people in Jerusalem or on Mount Zion or at any designated place. It is not the allocation of Palestine for the seed of Abraham, or the designation of the Americas as the inheritance of Joseph, though each of these arrangements has a bearing on the fulfillment of the covenant. The gathering of Israel, at whatever place Deity specifies, is a necessary condition precedent, something that makes possible the fulfilling of the ancient covenant."

Bruce R. McConkie, The Mortal Messiah, Vol. 4, p. 347-348.

"The restoration of the gospel, the gathering of Israel, and the establishment of Zion are one and the same thing; or, at least, they are so inseparably intertwined as one that they cannot be separated— for it is the Lord who gives the gospel, and it is the gospel that gathers Israel, and it is Israel that builds Zion."

Bruce R. McConkie, The Mortal Messiah, Vol. 4, p. 351-352.

"It is the Book of Mormon that gathers Israel. When the Stick of Judah and the Stick of Joseph, in the hands of Ephraim, become one in the hands of his people, then the Lord God will gather them; then will they come forth from among the heathen and receive the gospel; then shall they come into their own land according to the covenant."

Bruce R. McConkie, The Millennial Messiah, p. 191.

"Ephraim has the birthright and is the presiding tribe; if the other tribes are to receive their blessings from Ephraim . . . Ephraim must be the first tribe to gather in the last days."

Bruce R. McConkie, The Millennial Messiah, p. 247.

"Israel shall be gathered in part before the Millennium . . .Israel shall be gathered in full after the Millennium commences, and that gathering will include the Jews and . . . the Ten Tribes."

Bruce R. McConkie, A New Witness for the Articles of Faith, p. 333-334.

"They (Israel) were scattered for their sins and rebellion. And when they are gathered again in the last days, it is and will be because they . . . accept his everlasting gospel, and join his church."

Bruce R. McConkie, A New Witness for the Articles of Faith, p. 420.

"It is the power of the Book of Mormon that gathers Israel in the last days."

See Bruce R. McConkie, A New Witness for the Articles of Faith, p. 519-520.

"The present assembling of people of Jewish ancestry ... is not the scriptural gathering of Israel ... the scattering of Israel is still going on. . . . when any of the house of Israel forsake the Lord . . . and join apostate churches, have they not joined themselves again with the lost sheep of Israel?"

Bruce R. McConkie, A New Witness for the Articles of Faith, p. 545-546.

"Israel was not scattered at one time . . . Israel will not be gathered all at one time. The gathering commenced with the organization of The Church of Jesus Christ of Latter-day Saints . . . It will thus continue on a worldwide basis until the Second Coming and then go on into the Millennium for as long as is necessary to perfect the work and convert the world."

Bruce R. McConkie, A New Witness for the Articles of Faith, p. 548.

"In that day the whole earth, having become Zion in all its parts, will be a gathering place."

Bruce R. McConkie, A New Witness for the Articles of Faith, p. 552.

"Those who do not repent and gather spiritually into the Church will not be privileged to gather temporally."

Bruce R. McConkie, A New Witness for the Articles of Faith, p. 569.

"Thus, the gathering of Israel is both spiritual and temporal. The lost sheep gather spiritually when they join the Church, and they gather temporally when they come to a prepared place—that is, to Zion or one of her stakes. . . .For the present, the Lord's people, who are Zion, are called to gather in the stakes of Zion as these are established in the lands of their inheritance."

Bruce R. McConkie, A New Witness for the Articles of Faith, p. 574.

"The holy word also affirms that Israel gathers to Zion to escape the abomination of desolation that shall be poured out upon a wicked world in the last days. In Zion there will be safety. (D&C 115:5-6.)"

Bruce R. McConkie, A New Witness for the Articles of Faith, p. 574.

"The crowning reason for gathering to Zion or to her stakes. It is to receive the blessings found in the temples of the Lord."

Bruce R. McConkie, A New Witness for the Articles of Faith, p. 598.

"The Lord's people must . . . gather into congregations where they can strengthen and perfect each other . . .The law of the gospel includes the law of gathering. . . . the gathering is not a hasty, unprepared foray to a new locale. It is a wisely planned and prearranged assembling; provision must be made for food clothing, shelter, travel, and even a future livelihood, if possible."

Boyd K. Packer, Conference Report, Ensign, November 1992, p. 73.

"There are some among us now who have not been regularly ordained by the heads of the Church who tell of impending political and economic chaos, the end of the world. . . .They are misleading members to gather to colonies or cults. . . .Do not be deceived by them—those deceivers. If there is to be any gathering, it will be announced by those who have been regularly ordained and who are known to the Church to have authority. Come away from any others. Follow your leaders who have been duly ordained and have been publicly sustained, and you will not be led astray."

Boyd K. Packer, Conference Report, Ensign, May 1994, p. 21.

"As we continue on our course, these things will follow as night the day: The distance between the Church and a world set on a course which we cannot follow will steadily increase.

Some will fall away into apostasy, break their covenants, and replace the plan of redemption with their own rules.

Across the world, those who now come by the tens of thousands will inevitably come as a flood to where the family is safe. Here they will worship the Father in the name of Christ, by the gift of the Holy Ghost, and know that the gospel is the great plan of happiness, of redemption, of which I bear witness in the name of Jesus Christ, amen."

SCRIPTURAL REFERENCES

Deuteronomy 30:1-4

1 And it shall come to pass, when all these things are come upon thee, the blessing and the curse, which I have set before thee, and thou shalt call them to mind among all the nations, whither the LORD thy God hath driven thee,

2 And shalt return unto the LORD thy God, and shalt obey his voice according to all that I command thee this day, thou and thy children, with all thine heart, and with all thy soul;

3 That then the LORD thy God will turn thy captivity, and have compassion upon thee, and will return and gather thee from all the nations, whither the LORD thy God hath scattered thee.

4 If any of thine be driven out unto the outmost parts of heaven, from thence will the LORD thy God gather thee, and from thence will he fetch thee:

Nehemiah 1:8-9

8 Remember, I beseech thee, the word that thou commandedst thy servant Moses, saying, If ye transgress, I will scatter you abroad among the nations:

9 But if ye turn unto me, and keep my commandments, and do them; though there were of you cast out unto the uttermost part of the heaven, yet will I gather them from thence, and will bring them unto the place that I have chosen to set my name there.

Isaiah 2:2-3

2 And it shall come to pass in the last days, [that] the mountain of the LORD'S house shall be established in the top of the mountains, and shall be exalted above the hills; and all nations shall flow unto it.

3 And many people shall go and say, Come ye, and let us go up to the mountain of the LORD, to the house of the God of Jacob; and he will teach us of his ways, and we will walk in his paths: for out of Zion shall go forth the law, and the word of the LORD from Jerusalem.

Isaiah 11:12

12 And he shall set up an ensign for the nations, and shall assemble the outcasts of Israel, and gather together the dispersed of Judah from the four corners of the earth.

Isaiah 18:Heading

The Lord shall raise the gospel ensign, send messengers to his scattered people, and gather them to mount Zion.

Isaiah 51:Heading

In the last days, the Lord shall comfort Zion and gather Israel—The redeemed shall come to Zion amid great joy.

Isaiah 52:11-12

11 Depart ye, depart ye, go ye out from thence, touch no unclean thing; go ye out of the midst of her;

be ye clean, that bear the vessels of the LORD.

12 For ye shall not go out with haste, nor go by flight: for the LORD will go before you; and the God of Israel will be your rereward.

Isaiah 54:7

7 For a small moment have I forsaken thee; but with great mercies will I gather thee.

Isaiah 57:1

1 The righteous perisheth, and no man layeth it to heart: and merciful men are taken away, none considering that the righteous is taken away from the evil to come.

Jeremiah 3:Heading

Israel and Judah defiled and polluted the land through wickedness—In the last days, the Lord will gather Israel, one of a city and two of a family, and bring them to Zion.

Jeremiah 16:15-16

15 But, The LORD liveth, that brought up the children of Israel from the land of the north, and from all the lands whither he had driven them: and I will bring them again into their land that I gave unto their fathers.

16 Behold, I will send for many fishers, saith the LORD, and they shall fish them; and after will I send for many hunters, and they shall hunt them from every mountain, and from every hill, and out of the holes of the rocks.

Jeremiah 23:3

3 And I will gather the remnant of my flock out of all countries whither I have driven them, and will bring them again to their folds; and they shall be fruitful and increase.

Jeremiah 29:14

14 And I will be found of you, saith the LORD: and I will turn away your captivity, and I will gather you from all the nations, and from all the places whither I have driven you, saith the LORD; and I will bring you again into the place whence I caused you to be carried away captive.

Jeremiah 32:36-39

36 And now therefore thus saith the LORD, the God of Israel, concerning this city, whereof ye say, It shall be delivered into the hand of the king of Babylon by the sword, and by the famine, and by the pestilence;

37 Behold, I will gather them out of all countries, whither I have driven them in mine anger, and in my fury, and in great wrath; and I will bring them again unto this place, and I will cause them to dwell safely:

38 And they shall be my people, and I will be their God:

39 And I will give them one heart, and one way, that they may fear me for ever, for the good of them, and of their children after them:

Ezekiel 20:34

34 And I will bring you out from the people, and will gather you out of the countries wherein ye are scattered, with a mighty hand, and with a stretched out arm, and with fury poured out.

Ezekiel 34:11-13

11 For thus saith the Lord GOD; Behold, I, even I, will both search my sheep, and seek them out.

12 As a shepherd seeketh out his flock in the day that he is among his sheep that are scattered; so will I seek out my sheep, and will deliver them out of all places where they have been scattered in the cloudy and dark day.

13 And I will bring them out from the people, and gather them from the countries, and will bring them to their own land, and feed them upon the mountains of Israel by the rivers, and in all the inhabited places of the country.

Ezekiel 37:21-22

21 And say unto them, Thus saith the Lord GOD; Behold, I will take the children of Israel from among the heathen, whither they be gone, and will gather them on every side, and bring them into their own land:

22 And I will make them one nation in the land upon the mountains of Israel; and one king shall be king to them all: and they shall be no more two nations, neither shall they be divided into two kingdoms any more at all:

Ezekiel 39:Heading

Gog and Magog destroyed—For seven years they burn the weapons of war—For seven months they bury the dead—Then comes the supper of the great God and the continued gathering of Israel.

Zechariah 10:Heading

Judah and Joseph shall be sown among the people in far countries—The Lord will hiss for them and gather them and redeem them.

JST Matthew 1:27

27 And now I show unto you a parable. Behold, wheresoever the carcass is, there will the eagles be gathered together; so likewise shall mine elect be gathered from the four quarters of the earth.

JST Matthew 1:37

37 And whoso treasureth up my word, shall not be deceived, for the Son of Man shall come, and he shall send his angels before him with the great sound of a trumpet, and they shall gather together the remainder of his elect from the four winds, from one end of heaven to the other.

Matthew 13:24-30

24 Another parable put he forth unto them, saying, The kingdom of heaven is likened unto a man which sowed good seed in his field:

25 But while men slept, his enemy came and sowed tares among the wheat, and went his way.

26 But when the blade was sprung up, and brought forth fruit, then appeared the tares also.

27 So the servants of the householder came and said unto him, Sir, didst not thou sow good seed in thy field? from whence then hath it tares?

28 He said unto them, An enemy hath done this. The servants said unto him, Wilt thou then that we go and gather them up?

29 But he said, Nay; lest while ye gather up the tares, ye root up also the wheat with them.

30 Let both grow together until the harvest: and in the time of harvest I will say to the reapers, Gather ye together first the tares, and bind them in bundles to burn them: but gather the wheat into my barn.

Matthew 23:37-38

37 O Jerusalem, Jerusalem, thou that killest the prophets, and stonest them which are sent unto thee, how often would I have gathered thy children together, even as a hen gathereth her chickens under her wings, and ye would not!

38 Behold, your house is left unto you desolate.

JST Matthew 24:40

40 For the Son of man shall come, and he shall send his angels before him with the great sound of a trumpet, and they shall gather together the remainder of his elect from the four winds; from one end of heaven to the other.

Luke 17:34-36

34 I tell you, in that night there shall be two men in one bed; the one shall be taken, and the other shall be left.

35 Two women shall be grinding together; the one shall be taken, and the other left.

36 Two men shall be in the field; the one shall be taken, and the other left.

JST Luke 17:36-38

36 And they answered and said unto him, Where, Lord, shall they be taken.

37 And he said unto them, Wheresoever the body is gathered; or, in other words, whithersoever the saints are gathered, thither will the eagles be gathered together.

38 This he spake, signifying the gathering of his saints; and of angels descending and gathering the remainder unto them; the one from the bed, the other from the grinding, and the other from the field, whithersoever he listeth.

Ephesians 1:10

10 That in the dispensation of the fulness of times he might gather together in one all things in Christ, both which are in heaven, and which are on earth; even in him:

Revelation 18:4-10

4 And I heard another voice from heaven, saying, Come out of her, my people, that ye be not partakers of her sins, and that ye receive not of her plagues.

5 For her sins have reached unto heaven, and God hath remembered her iniquities.

6 Reward her even as she rewarded you, and double unto her double according to her works: in the cup which she hath filled fill to her double.

7 How much she hath glorified herself, and lived deliciously, so much torment and sorrow give her: for she saith in her heart, I sit a queen, and am no widow, and shall see no sorrow.

8 Therefore shall her plagues come in one day, death, and mourning, and famine; and she shall be utterly burned with fire: for strong is the Lord God who judgeth her.

9 And the kings of the earth, who have committed fornication and lived deliciously with her, shall bewail her, and lament for her, when they shall see the smoke of her burning,

10 Standing afar off for the fear of her torment, saying, Alas, alas, that great city Babylon, that mighty city! for in one hour is thy judgment come.

1 Nephi 15:Heading

Lehi's seed are to receive the gospel from the Gentiles in the latter days—The gathering of Israel is likened unto an olive tree whose natural branches shall be grafted in again—Nephi interprets the vision of the tree of life and speaks of the justice of God in dividing the wicked from the righteous.

1 Nephi 22:12

12 Wherefore, he will bring them again out of captivity, and they shall be gathered together to the lands of their inheritance; and they shall be brought out of obscurity and out of darkness; and they shall know that the Lord is their Savior and their Redeemer, the Mighty One of Israel.

1 Nephi 22:24-25

24 And the time cometh speedily that the righteous must be led up as calves of the stall, and the Holy One of Israel must reign in dominion, and might, and power, and great glory.

25 And he gathereth his children from the four quarters of the earth; and he numbereth his sheep, and they know him; and there shall be one fold and one shepherd; and he shall feed his sheep, and in him they shall find pasture.

Jacob 6:2

2 And the day that he shall set his hand again the second time to recover his people, is the day, yea, even the last time, that the servants of the Lord shall go forth in his power, to nourish and prune his vineyard; and after that the end soon cometh.

3 Nephi 5:24-6

24 And as surely as the Lord liveth, will he gather in from the four quarters of the earth all the remnant of the seed of Jacob, who are scattered abroad upon all the face of the earth.

25 And as he hath covenanted with all the house of Jacob, even so shall the covenant wherewith he hath covenanted with the house of Jacob be fulfilled in his own due time, unto the restoring all the house of Jacob unto the knowledge of the covenant that he hath covenanted with them.

26 And then shall they know their Redeemer, who is Jesus Christ, the Son of God; and then shall they be gathered in from the four quarters of the earth unto their own lands, from whence they have

been dispersed; yea, as the Lord liveth so shall it be. Amen.

3 Nephi 20:12-13

12 And verily, verily, I say unto you, that when they shall be fulfilled then is the fulfilling of the covenant which the Father hath made unto his people, O house of Israel.

13 And then shall the remnants, which shall be scattered abroad upon the face of the earth, be gathered in from the east and from the west, and from the south and from the north; and they shall be brought to the knowledge of the Lord their God, who hath redeemed them.

3 Nephi 20:29

29 And I will remember the covenant which I have made with my people; and I have covenanted with them that I would gather them together in mine own due time, that I would give unto them again the land of their fathers for their inheritance, which is the land of Jerusalem, which is the promised land unto them forever, saith the Father.

3 Nephi 20:41-42

41 And then shall a cry go forth: Depart ye, depart ye, go ye out from thence, touch not that which is unclean; go ye out of the midst of her; be ye clean that bear the vessels of the Lord.

42 For ye shall not go out with haste nor go by flight; for the Lord will go before you, and the God of Israel shall be your rearward.

3 Nephi 21:23-29

23 And they shall assist my people, the remnant of Jacob, and also as many of the house of Israel as shall come, that they may build a city, which shall be called the New Jerusalem.

24 And then shall they assist my people that they may be gathered in, who are scattered upon all the face of the land, in unto the New Jerusalem.

25 And then shall the power of heaven come down among them; and I also will be in the midst.

26 And then shall the work of the Father commence at that day, even when this gospel shall be preached among the remnant of this people. Verily I say unto you, at that day shall the work of the Father commence among all the dispersed of my people, yea, even the tribes which have been lost, which the Father hath led away out of Jerusalem.

27 Yea, the work shall commence among all the dispersed of my people, with the Father to prepare the way whereby they may come unto me, that they may call on the Father in my name.

28 Yea, and then shall the work commence, with the Father among all nations in preparing the way whereby his people may be gathered home to the land of their inheritance.

29 And they shall go out from all nations; and they shall not go out in haste, nor go by flight, for I will go before them, saith the Father, and I will be their rearward.

Mormon 3:17-18

17 Therefore I write unto you, Gentiles, and also unto you, house of Israel, when the work shall commence, that ye shall be about to prepare to return to the land of your inheritance;

18 Yea, behold, I write unto all the ends of the earth; yea, unto you, twelve tribes of Israel, who shall

be judged according to your works by the twelve whom Jesus chose to be his disciples in the land of Jerusalem.

D&C 29:7-9
7 And ye are called to bring to pass the gathering of mine elect; for mine elect hear my voice and harden not their hearts;
8 Wherefore the decree hath gone forth from the Father that they shall be gathered in unto one place upon the face of this land, to prepare their hearts and be prepared in all things against the day when tribulation and desolation are sent forth upon the wicked.
9 For the hour is nigh and the day soon at hand when the earth is ripe; and all the proud and they that do wickedly shall be as stubble; and I will burn them up, saith the Lord of Hosts, that wickedness shall not be upon the earth;

D&C 31:8
8 And you shall strengthen them and prepare them against the time when they shall be gathered.
D&C 33:6
6 And even so will I gather mine elect from the four quarters of the earth, even as many as will believe in me, and hearken unto my voice.

D&C 38:42
42 And go ye out from among the wicked. Save yourselves. Be ye clean that bear the vessels of the Lord. Even so. Amen.

D&C 42:35-36
35 And for the purpose of purchasing lands for the public benefit of the church, and building houses of worship, and building up of the New Jerusalem which is hereafter to be revealed—
36 That my covenant people may be gathered in one in that day when I shall come to my temple. And this I do for the salvation of my people.

D&C 42:63-64
63 And behold, it shall come to pass that my servants shall be sent forth to the east and to the west, to the north and to the south.
64 And even now, let him that goeth to the east teach them that shall be converted to flee to the west, and this in consequence of that which is coming on the earth, and of secret combinations.

D&C 45:68-71
68 And it shall come to pass among the wicked, that every man that will not take his sword against his neighbor must needs flee unto Zion for safety.
69 And there shall be gathered unto it out of every nation under heaven; and it shall be the only people that shall not be at war one with another.
70 And it shall be said among the wicked: Let us not go up to battle against Zion, for the inhabitants of Zion are terrible; wherefore we cannot stand.

71 And it shall come to pass that the righteous shall be gathered out from among all nations, and shall come to Zion, singing with songs of everlasting joy.

D&C 57:1-2

1 Hearken, O ye elders of my church, saith the Lord your God, who have assembled yourselves together, according to my commandments, in this land, which is the land of Missouri, which is the land which I have appointed and consecrated for the gathering of the saints.
2 Wherefore, this is the land of promise, and the place for the city of Zion.

D&C 58:56

56 And let the work of the gathering be not in haste, nor by flight; but let it be done as it shall be counseled by the elders of the church at the conferences, according to the knowledge which they receive from time to time.

D&C 63:24

24 And now, behold, this is the will of the Lord your God concerning his saints, that they should assemble themselves together unto the land of Zion, not in haste, lest there should be confusion, which bringeth pestilence.

D&C 63:37

37 And that every man should take righteousness in his hands and faithfulness upon his loins, and lift a warning voice unto the inhabitants of the earth; and declare both by word and by flight that desolation shall come upon the wicked.

D&C 64:24

24 For after today cometh the burning—this is speaking after the manner of the Lord—for verily I say, tomorrow all the proud and they that do wickedly shall be as stubble; and I will burn them up, for I am the Lord of Hosts; and I will not spare any that remain in Babylon.

D&C 77:9-11

9 Q. What are we to understand by the angel ascending from the east, Revelation 7th chapter and 2nd verse?
 A. We are to understand that the angel ascending from the east is he to whom is given the seal of the living God over the twelve tribes of Israel; wherefore, he crieth unto the four angels having the everlasting gospel, saying: Hurt not the earth, neither the sea, nor the trees, till we have sealed the servants of our God in their foreheads. And, if you will receive it, this is Elias which was to come to gather together the tribes of Israel and restore all things.
10 Q. What time are the things spoken of in this chapter to be accomplished?
 A. They are to be accomplished in the sixth thousand years, or the opening of the sixth seal.
11 Q. What are we to understand by sealing the one hundred and forty-four thousand, out of all the tribes of Israel—twelve thousand out of every tribe?

A. We are to understand that those who are sealed are high priests, ordained unto the holy order of God, to administer the everlasting gospel; for they are they who are ordained out of every nation, kindred, tongue, and people, by the angels to whom is given power over the nations of the earth, to bring as many as will come to the church of the Firstborn.

D&C 77:14

14 Q. What are we to understand by the little book which was eaten by John, as mentioned in the 10th chapter of Revelation?

A. We are to understand that it was a mission, and an ordinance, for him to gather the tribes of Israel; behold, this is Elias, who, as it is written, must come and restore all things.

D&C 84:2-4

2 Yea, the word of the Lord concerning his church, established in the last days for the restoration of his people, as he has spoken by the mouth of his prophets, and for the gathering of his saints to stand upon Mount Zion, which shall be the city of New Jerusalem.

3 Which city shall be built, beginning at the temple lot, which is appointed by the finger of the Lord, in the western boundaries of the State of Missouri, and dedicated by the hand of Joseph Smith, Jun., and others with whom the Lord was well pleased.

4 Verily this is the word of the Lord, that the city New Jerusalem shall be built by the gathering of the saints, beginning at this place, even the place of the temple, which temple shall be reared in this generation.

D&C 86:4-7

4 But behold, in the last days, even now while the Lord is beginning to bring forth the word, and the blade is springing up and is yet tender—

5 Behold, verily I say unto you, the angels are crying unto the Lord day and night, who are ready and waiting to be sent forth to reap down the fields;

6 But the Lord saith unto them, pluck not up the tares while the blade is yet tender (for verily your faith is weak), lest you destroy the wheat also.

7 Therefore, let the wheat and the tares grow together until the harvest is fully ripe; then ye shall first gather out the wheat from among the tares, and after the gathering of the wheat, behold and lo, the tares are bound in bundles, and the field remaineth to be burned.

D&C 101:20-22

20 And, behold, there is none other place appointed than that which I have appointed; neither shall there be any other place appointed than that which I have appointed, for the work of the gathering of my saints—

21 Until the day cometh when there is found no more room for them; and then I have other places which I will appoint unto them, and they shall be called stakes, for the curtains or the strength of Zion.

22 Behold, it is my will, that all they who call on my name, and worship me according to mine everlasting gospel, should gather together, and stand in holy places;

D&C 101:67-68

67 Therefore, a commandment I give unto all the churches, that they shall continue to gather together unto the places which I have appointed.

68 Nevertheless, as I have said unto you in a former commandment, let not your gathering be in haste, nor by flight; but let all things be prepared before you.

D&C 103:11-13

11 But verily I say unto you, I have decreed that your brethren which have been scattered shall return to the lands of their inheritances, and shall build up the waste places of Zion.

12 For after much tribulation, as I have said unto you in a former commandment, cometh the blessing.

13 Behold, this is the blessing which I have promised after your tribulations, and the tribulations of your brethren—your redemption, and the redemption of your brethren, even their restoration to the land of Zion, to be established, no more to be thrown down.

D&C 105:14-15

14 For behold, I do not require at their hands to fight the battles of Zion; for, as I said in a former commandment, even so will I fulfil—I will fight your battles.

15 Behold, the destroyer I have sent forth to destroy and lay waste mine enemies; and not many years hence they shall not be left to pollute mine heritage, and to blaspheme my name upon the lands which I have consecrated for the gathering together of my saints.

D&C 105:24

24 Talk not of judgments, neither boast of faith nor of mighty works, but carefully gather together, as much in one region as can be, consistently with the feelings of the people;

D&C 109:38-41

38 Put upon thy servants the testimony of the covenant, that when they go out and proclaim thy word they may seal up the law, and prepare the hearts of thy saints for all those judgments thou art about to send, in thy wrath, upon the inhabitants of the earth, because of their transgressions, that thy people may not faint in the day of trouble.

39 And whatsoever city thy servants shall enter, and the people of that city receive their testimony, let thy peace and thy salvation be upon that city; that they may gather out of that city the righteous, that they may come forth to Zion, or to her stakes, the places of thine appointment, with songs of everlasting joy;

40 And until this be accomplished, let not thy judgments fall upon that city.

41 And whatsoever city thy servants shall enter, and the people of that city receive not the testimony of thy servants, and thy servants warn them to save themselves from this untoward generation, let it be upon that city according to that which thou hast spoken by the mouths of thy prophets.

D&C 109:58-59

58 That from among all these, thy servants, the sons of Jacob, may gather out the righteous to build

a holy city to thy name, as thou hast commanded them.

59 We ask thee to appoint unto Zion other stakes besides this one which thou hast appointed, that the gathering of thy people may roll on in great power and majesty, that thy work may be cut short in righteousness.

D&C 110:11

11 After this vision closed, the heavens were again opened unto us; and Moses appeared before us, and committed unto us the keys of the gathering of Israel from the four parts of the earth, and the leading of the ten tribes from the land of the north.

D&C 113:5-6

5 What is the root of Jesse spoken of in the 10th verse of the 11th chapter?

6 Behold, thus saith the Lord, it is a descendant of Jesse, as well as of Joseph, unto whom rightly belongs the priesthood, and the keys of the kingdom, for an ensign, and for the gathering of my people in the last days.

D&C 115:6

6 And that the gathering together upon the land of Zion, and upon her stakes, may be for a defense, and for a refuge from the storm, and from wrath when it shall be poured out without mixture upon the whole earth.

D&C 124:10

10 For the day of my visitation cometh speedily, in an hour when ye think not of; and where shall be the safety of my people, and refuge for those who shall be left of them?

D&C 125:2

2 Verily, thus saith the Lord, I say unto you, if those who call themselves by my name and are essaying to be my saints, if they will do my will and keep my commandments concerning them, let them gather themselves together unto the places which I shall appoint unto them by my servant Joseph, and build up cities unto my name, that they may be prepared for that which is in store for a time to come.

D&C 133:4-15

4 Wherefore, prepare ye, prepare ye, O my people; sanctify yourselves; gather ye together, O ye people of my church, upon the land of Zion, all you that have not been commanded to tarry.

5 Go ye out from Babylon. Be ye clean that bear the vessels of the Lord.

6 Call your solemn assemblies, and speak often one to another. And let every man call upon the name of the Lord.

7 Yea, verily I say unto you again, the time has come when the voice of the Lord is unto you: Go ye out of Babylon; gather ye out from among the nations, from the four winds, from one end of heaven to the other.

8 Send forth the elders of my church unto the nations which are afar off; unto the islands of the sea;

send forth unto foreign lands; call upon all nations, first upon the Gentiles, and then upon the Jews.

9 And behold, and lo, this shall be their cry, and the voice of the Lord unto all people: Go ye forth unto the land of Zion, that the borders of my people may be enlarged, and that her stakes may be strengthened, and that Zion may go forth unto the regions round about.

10 Yea, let the cry go forth among all people: Awake and arise and go forth to meet the Bridegroom; behold and lo, the Bridegroom cometh; go ye out to meet him. Prepare yourselves for the great day of the Lord.

11 Watch, therefore, for ye know neither the day nor the hour.

12 Let them, therefore, who are among the Gentiles flee unto Zion.

13 And let them who be of Judah flee unto Jerusalem, unto the mountains of the Lord's house.

14 Go ye out from among the nations, even from Babylon, from the midst of wickedness, which is spiritual Babylon.

15 But verily, thus saith the Lord, let not your flight be in haste, but let all things be prepared before you; and he that goeth, let him not look back lest sudden destruction shall come upon him.

Moses 7:62

62 And righteousness will I send down out of heaven; and truth will I send forth out of the earth, to bear testimony of mine Only Begotten; his resurrection from the dead; yea, and also the resurrection of all men; and righteousness and truth will I cause to sweep the earth as with a flood, to gather out mine elect from the four quarters of the earth, unto a place which I shall prepare, an Holy City, that my people may gird up their loins, and be looking forth for the time of my coming; for there shall be my tabernacle, and it shall be called Zion, a New Jerusalem.

Articles Of Faith 1:10

10 We believe in the literal gathering of Israel and in the restoration of the Ten Tribes; that Zion (the New Jerusalem) will be built upon the American continent; that Christ will reign personally upon the earth; and, that the earth will be renewed and receive its paradisiacal glory.

INDEX

Aaron, 1:226, 1:228, 2:230, 3:90, 3:142

Aaronic Priesthood, 1:6, 1:17, 1:112, 3:10, 3:12, 3:90

Abominable church. *See* Great and abominable church.

Abomination, 1:131, 1:142, 1:255, 1:275, 1:283, 2:4, 2:vi, 2:3, 2:27, 2:37, 2:107, 2:115, 2:117, 2:153, 2:241, 3:19, 3:35, 3:38, 3:40, 3:54, 3:294, 3:352

Abomination of desolation. *See* Desolation of abomination.

Abominations, 1:7, 1:50, 1:131, 1:156, 1:213, 1:253, 1:256, 1:273, 2:3, 2:11, 2:13, 2:25, 2:34- 2:35, 2:46, 2:62, 2:70-2:72, 2:76-2:77, 2:98, 2:112, 2:129, 2:138, 2:140-2:141, 2:164, 2:190, 2:230, 2:234-2:236, 2:239, 2:244, 2:246, 2:251-2:252, 2:269, 3:54, 3:81, 3:101, 3:212, 3:231, 3:324, 3:328

Abortion, 1:107, 1:109, 1:201

Abraham, 1:1, 1:1, 1:5, 1:7, 1:8, 1:11, 1:16, 1:63, 1:64, 1:122, 1:136, 1:176, 1:200, 1:274, 2:82, 2:91-2:92, 2:104-2:105, 2:125, 2:127, 2:131, 2:151, 2:246, 2:259, 3:22, 3:72, 3:109, 3:121, 3:149, 3:162, 3:171, 3:185, 3:201, 3:225, 3:270, 3:326, 3:352

Acton, Lord, 1:209

Adam, 1:1, 1:4, 1:8, 1:10, 1:11, 1:13, 1:17, 1:26, 1:32, 1:35, 1:121, 1:161, 1:266, 2:14, 2:160, 2:163, 2:166, 2:170, 2:221, 2:224, 2:226, 2:235, 2:259, 2:4, 3:8, 3:45, 3:66, 3:86, 3:139, 3:151, 3:153, 3:155, 3:158, 3:160, 3:163-3:164, 3:191, 3:196-3:199, 3:201, 3:203, 3:245, 3:248, 3:273, 3:302, 3:307-3:308, 3:311, 3:313, 3:320, 3:331, 3:332, 3:334-3:335, 3:347, 3:348

Adams, John, 1:196, 1:211, 3:241

Adam-ondi-ahman, 2:4, 3:151

Adultery, 1:216, 3:132, 3:260

Adversary, 1:41, 1:78, 1:80-1:81, 1:85, 1:109, 1:115, 1:143, 2:vii, 2:151, 2:171, 2:173, 2:183, 2:192, 2:211, 2:220, 2:234, 3:285

Adversity, 1:114, 1:126, 2:179, 2:183, 2:193

Affection, 1:21, 1:102, 2:15, 2:178, 3:117, 3:260

Affliction, 1:65, 1:89, 1:143, 1:176, 2:10, 2:62, 2:157, 2:159, 2:170, 2:188, 2:190, 3:98, 3:107

Afflictions, 1:17, 1:50, 1:57, 1:72-1:74, 1:81, 1:83, 1:118, 1:121, 1:133, 1:134, 1:237, 1:245, 2:v, 2:33, 2:138, 2:155-2:156, 2:158, 2:175, 2:188, 2:190, 2:193, 3:v, 3:166, 3:260, 3:278

Africa, 1:225, 1:228, 1:232, 1:267, 2:7, 2:9, 2:139, 2:149, 3:4, 3:19, 3:155, 3:179, 3:241

Age, 1:3, 1:7, 1:14, 1:16, 1:30, 1:57, 1:98, 1:101-1:102, 1:109, 1:117, 1:122, 1:160, 1:179, 1:187, 1:211, 1:228, 1:234, 1:236, 1:239, 1:247, 2:3, 2:11, 2:16, 2:40, 2:74, 2:80, 2:158, 2:159, 2:171, 2:174, 2:176, 2:202, 3:vi-3:7, 3:11, 3:21, 3:43, 3:52, 3:108, 3:124, 3:129, 3:152, 3:154, 3:164, 3:189, 3:191, 3:202, 3:203, 3:206, 3:212, 3:213, 3:242, 3:296, 3:311, 3:318-3:319, 3:331

Agency, 1:31, 1:47, 1:56, 1:89, 1:103, 1:151, 1:165, 1:167-1:168, 1:192, 1:199, 1:211, 1:219, 2:17, 2:44, 2:73, 2:150, 2:154, 2:182-2:183, 2:224, 2:234, 3:81, 3:136, 3:201, 3:205, 3:219, 3:234, 3:238, 3:240, 3:247, 3:287, 3:292, 3:342

Ages, 1:vii, 1:3, 1:10, 1:18, 1:42, 1:48, 1:49, 1:91, 1:97, 1:152, 1:166, 1:191, 1:261, 1:266, 1:278, 2:8, 2:50, 2:184, 2:226, 2:235, 2:259, 2:272, 3:vi, 3:5, 3:14, 3:73, 3:138, 3:162, 3:164, 3:220, 3:235, 3:277, 3:315, 3:330, 3:340, 3:347

Albany, 2:136, 2:143, 2:153

Alliance, 1:174

Alliances, 1:175, 1:205, 2:88

America, 1:33, 1:35, 1:101, 1:150, 1:164, 1:172, 1:173, 1:185, 1:189-1:191, 1:193, 1:197, 1:202, 1:206, 1:209, 1:210, 1:238, 1:246, 1:280, 2:7, 2:55, 2:64, 2:79, 2:122, 2:136, 2:139, 2:147, 2:152, 2:267, 2:270, 3:3-3:4, 3:16, 3:18, 3:68, 3:76-3:77, 3:93, 3:115, 3:123, 3:127, 3:135, 3:168, 3:170, 3:289, 3:296, 3:299, 3:305

Anarchy, 1:99, 1:155, 1:156, 1:170, 1:190, 1:210-1:211, 1:220, 2:1, 2:11, 3:133

Ancient of Days, 1:260, 2:1, 2:8, 2:187, 2:264, 2:265, 2:274, 2:277, 3:8, 3:63, 3:153, 3:157, 3:159, 3:235, 3:237, 3:308

Ancients, 1:8, 1:29, 1:46, 2:48, 3:24, 3:31, 3:96, 3:225, 3:340

Angel, 1:17-1:18, 1:53, 1:66, 1:87, 1:133, 1:150, 1:223-1:224, 1:227, 1:236, 1:241, 1:243, 1:252, 1:256-1:257, 1:259, 1:270, 1:272, 1:276, 2:1, 2:12, 2:28, 2:40, 2:46, 2:58, 2:59, 2:87, 2:101, 2:102, 2:116, 2:132, 2:140,

2:209, 2:236-2:239, 2:241, 2:244-2:245, 2:251-2:253, 2:259, 2:261, 2:262, 2:264, 2:270, 2:273, 2:274, 2:278, 2:280, 2:282-2:285, 3:5, 3:7, 3:21, 3:22, 3:46, 3:51, 3:54-3:55, 3:57, 3:75, 3:120, 3:134, 3:149, 3:159, 3:232, 3:235, 3:270, 3:306, 3:320, 3:322-3:323, 3:330, 3:350, 3:351, 3:354

Destroying angel(s), 1:87, 1:223, 1:224, 2:1-2, 2:55, 2:72

Angels, 1:2, 1:29, 1:42, 1:43, 1:102, 1:103, 1:129, 1:132, 1:140, 1:145, 1:224, 1:227, 1:231, 1:254-1:256, 1:261, 1:264, 1:265, 1:268, 1:271, 1:274, 1:278, 1:286-1:287, 1:291-1:292, 2:vi, 2:2, 2:7, 2:14, 2:15, 2:20, 2:21, 2:29, 2:50, 2:53, 2:57, 2:58, 2:61, 2:72, 2:84, 2:157, 2:158, 2:170, 2:174, 2:188, 2:209, 2:215, 2:228, 2:230, 2:231, 2:246, 2:251, 2:260, 2:261, 2:270, 2:281-2:283, 3:10-3:11, 3:16, 3:17, 3:22, 3:24, 3:26, 3:35, 3:37, 3:39-3:42, 3:50, 3:53-3:55, 3:62, 3:66, 3:85, 3:119, 3:125, 3:133, 3:149, 3:152-3:154, 3:185, 3:191, 3:192, 3:199, 3:219, 3:234, 3:282, 3:292, 3:293, 3:305-3:306, 3:315, 3:316, 3:331, 3:333, 3:342, 3:343, 3:348, 3:350-3:351, 3:353, 3:355

Angels of destruction, 1:72, 1:102, 2:14, 2:20, 2:21

Anger, 1:85, 1:133, 1:143, 1:285, 2:4, 2:12, 2:17, 2:18, 2:22, 2:24, 2:25, 2:30-2:31, 2:33, 2:37, 2:41, 2:69, 2:76, 2:97, 2:123, 2:134, 2:154, 2:180, 2:189-2:190, 2:192, 2:240, 2:248, 2:250, 2:254, 3:32, 3:48, 3:58, 3:96, 3:156

Animal, 3:189, 3:190, 3:197, 3:202, 3:204, 3:206

Animals, 1:12, 1:43, 2:56-2:57, 2:65, 2:257, 2:260, 3:5, 3:190, 3:264

Antediluvian, 1:55, 1:276, 2:10, 2:13, 3:286

Anti-Christ(s), 1:165, 2:4, 2:195, 2:201

Anxiety, 1:32, 1:86, 1:272, 3:285, 3:312

Apathy, 1:200,

Apocrypha, 3:178, 3:316

Apostasy, 1:vii, 1:11, 1:13, 1:97, 1:101, 1:259, 1:283, 2:4, 2:vii, 2:121, 2:215, 2:218, 2:221, 2:223, 2:225-2:226, 2:234-2:235, 2:243, 3:7, 3:44, 3:248

Apostate, 1:282, 2:180, 2:182, 2:212, 2:220, 2:221, 2:226, 2:227, 2:234, 2:236, 2:254, 2:257, 3:293, 3:342

Apostates, 1:100, 2:212, 2:215, 3:293, 3:303

Apostles, 1:vii, 1:4, 1:6-1:8, 1:11, 1:13, 1:31, 1:54, 1:67, 1:69, 1:75, 1:116, 1:160, 1:188, 1:224, 1:228, 1:240, 1:242, 1:245, 2:vi, 2:90, 2:143, 2:149, 2:163, 2:167, 2:169, 2:172, 2:181, 2:204, 2:209, 2:224, 2:230, 2:236, 2:237, 2:253, 2:254, 2:269-2:271, 3:11, 3:15, 3:19, 3:22, 3:49, 3:117, 3:128, 3:134, 3:155, 3:158, 3:160, 3:172, 3:193, 3:195, 3:211-3:212, 3:233, 3:248, 3:289, 3:313, 3:323, 3:351, 3:353

Twelve apostles, 2:181, 2:204, 2:236, 2:237, 3:19, 3:117, 3:134, 3:155, 3:158, 3:193, 3:195, 3:250, 3:323, 3:351

April 6, 1:9, 1:28, 1:32, 1:33, 1:42, 1:47, 1:65, 1:87, 1:148, 1:160, 1:161, 1:165, 1:184, 1:274, 2:42, 2:63, 2:73, 2:87, 2:119, 2:134, 2:159, 2:170, 2:171, 2:179, 2:214, 2:243, 3:2, 3:9, 3:21, 3:72, 3:83, 3:116, 3:138, 3:141, 3:190, 3:219, 3:224, 3:234, 3:242, 3:262, 3:274, 3:283, 3:284, 3:313

Ariel, 2:5, 3:70

Aristocracy, 3:276, 3:279

Ark, 1:4, 1:4, 1:55, 1:111, 1:276, 2:12, 2:14, 2:53, 2:67, 2:262, 3:36, 3:37, 3:41, 3:73, 3:124, 3:145, 3:303

Arm of the Lord, 1:51, 1:237, 1:256, 1:264, 2:171, 2:230, 2:254, 3:48

Armageddon, 1:13, 1:121, 2:4, 2:21, 2:59, 2:95, 2:107, 2:116, 2:283, 3:349

Armies, 1:43, 1:50, 1:79, 1:168, 1:214, 1:263, 2:7, 2:23, 2:41, 2:66, 2:83, 2:107, 2:108, 2:123, 2:137, 2:142, 2:203, 2:270, 2:284, 3:vii, 3:6, 3:62, 3:70, 3:72, 3:119, 3:141, 3:149, 3:180, 3:195, 3:238, 3:349, 3:354

Armistice, 2:vii, 2:92

Armour of God, 1:130, 1:130, 1:213

Arms, 1:30, 1:38, 1:42, 1:78, 1:135, 1:136, 2:43, 2:81, 2:93, 2:112, 2:127, 2:161, 2:171, 2:247, 2:264, 2:266, 2:269, 2:276, 3:11, 3:77, 3:86, 3:225, 3:226, 3:229-3:231

Army, 1:viii, 1:39, 1:72, 1:73, 1:115, 1:124, 1:263, 2:15, 2:46, 2:81, 2:83, 2:85, 2:86, 2:93, 2:94, 2:107, 2:110, 2:135, 2:146, 2:147, 2:162, 2:163, 2:280, 2:284, 3:33, 3:46, 3:79, 3:123, 3:149, 3:169, 3:170, 3:217, 3:337, 3:342-3:344

Asia, 1:152, 1:225, 1:228, 1:267, 1:270, 2:15, 2:57, 2:81, 2:107, 2:139, 2:141, 2:149, 2:269, 2:270, 2:272, 3:4, 3:19,

3:119, 3:155, 3:157, 3:171, 3:179, 3:230, 3:241, 3:313

Asleep, 1:22, 1:47, 1:65, 1:75, 1:147, 1:195, 1:270, 2:2, 2:144, 2:236, 2:254, 3:viii, 3:1, 3:43, 3:49, 3:108, 3:138, 3:165, 3:337

Assyria, 1:236, 1:263, 2:12, 2:96, 3:29, 3:101, 3:168, 3:172, 3:176, 3:181, 3:207

Atheism, 1:119, 1:181, 1:205, 1:210, 3:318

Atheists, 3:298

Atlantic ocean. *See* ocean.

Atomic, 1:116

Atonement, 1:122, 2:82, 2:103, 2:204, 2:208, 2:215, 2:223, 3:53, 3:318, 3:323

Authority, 1:1, 1:3, 1:4, 1:13, 1:16, 1:17, 1:29, 1:48, 1:56, 1:62, 1:93, 1:99, 1:112, 1:115, 1:129, 1:167, 1:170, 1:173, 1:174, 1:201-1:203, 1:213, 1:216, 1:236, 1:268, 1:279, 1:281, 1:283, 2:9, 2:73, 2:80, 2:93, 2:119, 2:152, 2:154, 2:181, 2:196, 2:199-2:200, 2:203, 2:212, 2:215, 2:217, 2:218, 2:221, 2:258, 2:260, 2:268, 2:272, 2:281, 3:6, 3:7, 3:11, 3:18, 3:40, 3:84, 3:89, 3:90, 3:111, 3:141, 3:142, 3:154, 3:157-3:158, 3:165, 3:175, 3:196, 3:198, 3:204, 3:223, 3:224, 3:228, 3:230-3:232, 3:239, 3:242, 3:244, 3:256, 3:277, 3:297, 3:311, 3:314, 3:339, 3:350

Autocratic, 3:245

Axis, 3:180

Babel, 2:4, 2:244, 3:154

Babylon, 1:37-1:38, 1:64, 1:66, 1:71, 1:73, 1:82, 1:84, 1:89, 1:128, 1:137, 1:140, 1:146, 1:197, 1:230, 1:266, 1:268, 1:270, 1:285, 1:288, 1:291, 2:4, 2:vi, 2:1, 2:7, 2:12, 2:24, 2:29, 2:41, 2:53, 2:59, 2:71, 2:73, 2:109, 2:116, 2:175, 2:234, 2:236, 2:244, 2:246, 2:249, 2:254-2:255, 2:264-2:267, 2:269, 2:283, 2:284, 3:4, 3:7, 3:29, 3:53, 3:68, 3:85, 3:100, 3:111-3:112, 3:229, 3:231, 3:233, 3:283

Babylonian(s), 2:266, 2:247, 2:267, 2:268, 2:273, 3:229, 3:233, 3:236

Ballot, 1:172, 1:187

Baltimore, 2:134, 2:144

Baptism, 1:2, 1:25, 1:26, 1:35, 1:52, 1:84, 1:199, 1:266, 1:276, 2:68, 2:81, 2:86, 2:88, 2:230, 3:27, 3:199, 3:245, 3:332, 3:337

    baptism of fire, 3:27, 3:199, 3:336, 3:337

Baptize, 1:158, 2:270, 3:27

Baptized, 1:5, 1:35, 1:46, 1:73, 1:158, 1:230, 1:248, 2:86, 2:121, 2:131, 2:142, 3:viii, 3:10, 3:27, 3:68, 3:199, 3:201, 3:279, 3:334

Base of operations, 1:178

Battle, 1:41, 1:48, 1:66, 1:71, 1:109, 1:111, 1:114, 1:115, 1:125, 1:139, 1:148, 1:180, 1:181, 1:199, 1:290, 2:12, 2:15, 2:23, 2:49, 2:81, 2:107-2:110, 2:113-2:114, 2:116, 2:165, 2:176, 2:207, 2:249, 2:274, 2:283, 3:9, 3:83, 3:103, 3:115, 3:148, 3:159, 3:217, 3:252, 3:289, 3:333, 3:342, 3:348-3:349, 3:351

Battles, 1:27, 1:86, 1:94, 1:100, 1:109, 1:120, 1:153, 1:191, 1:264, 2:92, 2:123, 2:164, 2:182, 3:159, 3:241, 3:315, 3:347, 3:354

Bear, 1:vii, 1:19, 1:26, 1:28, 1:32, 1:33, 1:41, 1:70, 1:81-1:82, 1:84, 1:89, 1:97, 1:99, 1:102, 1:114, 1:125, 1:127, 1:140, 1:141, 1:148, 1:150, 1:151, 1:165, 1:170, 1:185, 1:194, 1:207, 1:227, 1:232, 1:283, 1:285, 1:289, 1:290, 1:294, 1:295, 2:2, 2:6, 2:50, 2:144, 2:146, 2:150, 2:155, 2:158, 2:159, 2:161, 2:162, 2:174, 2:183, 2:199, 2:215, 2:233, 2:236, 2:255, 2:257, 2:264, 2:276, 2:281, 3:1, 3:3, 3:53, 3:59, 3:88, 3:97, 3:111, 3:132, 3:146, 3:150, 3:181, 3:187, 3:207, 3:214, 3:218, 3:235-3:236, 3:238, 3:240, 3:250-3:252, 3:255, 3:271, 3:282, 3:287, 3:323, 3:324

Beecher , Henry Ward, 1:70

Beasts, 1:79, 1:252, 2:29, 2:35, 2:52, 2:57, 2:60, 2:65, 2:100, 2:127, 2:129, 2:130, 2:137, 2:253, 2:254, 2:257, 2:259-2:262, 2:264, 2:271, 2:274, 2:277-2:279, 2:282, 3:64, 3:155-3:156, 3:189, 3:192, 3:197, 3:202, 3:211, 3:233, 3:347, 3:353

Beautify, 1:43, 1:45, 3:66-3:67

Belief, 1:27, 1:94, 1:161, 1:167, 1:175, 1:191, 1:193, 1:220, 1:236, 2:74, 2:89, 2:104, 2:179, 2:182, 2:208, 2:258, 3:77,

3:117, 3:161, 3:215, 3:297-3:298

Bethlehem, 3:250

Bible, 1:7, 1:14, 1:18, 1:68, 1:125, 1:150, 1:151, 1:225, 1:238, 1:245, 1:260, 2:10, 2:43, 2:135, 2:147, 2:168, 2:202, 2:213, 2:257, 2:265, 3:7, 3:13, 3:17, 3:63, 3:73, 3:75, 3:85, 3:126, 3:133, 3:141, 3:173, 3:175, 3:178, 3:190, 3:215, 3:224, 3:227, 3:229, 3:232, 3:247, 3:307, 3:309-3:311, 3:313, 3:316, 3:319-3:320, 3:326, 3:333

Bill of Rights, 1:171, 1:175, 1:192, 1:194

Birth, 1:11, 1:16, 1:231, 1:245, 2:122, 3:14, 3:169, 3:191, 3:229, 3:235, 3:282, 3:335

Birthright, 1:279, 1:282, 2:125, 3:135

Bishop, 2:153, 2:272, 3:61, 3:62, 3:111, 3:260, 3:264, 3:266, 3:268, 3:269, 3:276, 3:280, 3:287, 3:289-3:291, 3:293, 3:301-3:303

Bishops, 1:174, 3:128, 3:266, 3:270

Blasphemy, 1:7, 1:102, 2:182, 2:244, 2:252, 2:281, 2:284

Blessing, 1:3, 1:8, 1:53, 1:56, 1:62, 1:69, 1:84, 1:86, 1:87, 1:90, 1:92, 1:102, 1:118, 1:128, 1:161, 1:170, 1:173, 1:188, 1:226, 1:253, 1:284, 2:2, 2:77, 2:79-2:80, 2:96, 2:126, 2:128, 2:129, 2:160, 2:167, 2:174, 2:183, 2:215, 2:260, 3:vi, 3:17, 3:73, 3:90, 3:108-3:109, 3:122, 3:126, 3:140, 3:155, 3:161, 3:164, 3:181, 3:196, 3:262, 3:263, 3:307, 3:308, 3:311, 3:316, 3:344

Blessings, 1:2, 1:3, 1:6, 1:32-1:34, 1:41, 1:46, 1:52, 1:58, 1:72, 1:74, 1:87-1:88, 1:92, 1:98, 1:99, 1:105, 1:175, 1:176, 1:185, 1:187, 1:196, 1:207, 1:237, 1:244, 1:245, 1:259, 1:273, 1:277, 1:280, 1:282, 1:283, 2:17, 2:46, 2:72, 2:78, 2:81, 2:84, 2:89, 2:121, 2:126, 2:131, 2:136, 2:158, 2:161, 2:167, 2:177, 2:215, 2:246, 3:vi, 3:vii, 3:9, 3:11, 3:12, 3:44, 3:68, 3:72, 3:74, 3:88, 3:90, 3:124, 3:126, 3:134-3:135, 3:152, 3:155, 3:159, 3:161, 3:170, 3:172, 3:174-3:175, 3:179, 3:201, 3:203, 3:205, 3:224-3:225, 3:237, 3:238, 3:248, 3:264, 3:272, 3:273, 3:276, 3:293-3:295, 3:311, 3:317, 3:347

Blind, 1:47, 1:76, 1:189, 1:224, 2:38, 2:182, 2:213, 2:237, 3:viii, 3:98, 3:182, 3:286, 3:325

Blood, 1:8, 1:9, 1:12, 1:16, 1:18, 1:24, 1:26, 1:38, 1:52, 1:69, 1:71, 1:116, 1:118, 1:130, 1:136, 1:142, 1:150, 1:159, 1:172, 1:173, 1:181, 1:194, 1:213-1:214, 1:217-1:219, 1:240, 1:260, 1:271, 1:277, 2:2, 2:3, 2:16, 2:23, 2:28, 2:32, 2:33, 2:35-2:38, 2:42-2:43, 2:52, 2:55, 2:57, 2:70-2:73, 2:76, 2:77, 2:80, 2:82, 2:85, 2:89-2:90, 2:92, 2:94, 2:101, 2:102, 2:104, 2:108, 2:111-2:112, 2:122, 2:126, 2:144, 2:157, 2:158, 2:169, 2:172, 2:174, 2:179, 2:183, 2:185, 2:191, 2:250, 2:259, 2:278-2:279, 3:vii, 3:21, 3:31, 3:46, 3:53, 3:58, 3:64, 3:86, 3:89, 3:96, 3:105, 3:143, 3:147, 3:175, 3:223, 3:266, 3:294, 3:328

Bloodshed, 1:40, 1:43, 1:59, 1:60, 1:86, 1:102, 1:103, 1:111, 1:141, 1:147, 1:156, 1:172, 1:181, 1:214, 1:221, 1:244, 1:277, 2:1, 2:19, 2:34, 2:37, 2:43, 2:47, 2:49, 2:133, 2:154, 2:182, 2:191, 2:264, 3:12, 3:133, 3:164, 3:165, 3:257

Body, 1:8, 1:34, 1:62, 1:65, 1:68, 1:175, 1:182, 1:199, 1:200, 1:209, 1:235, 1:265, 1:269, 1:278, 1:279, 1:287, 2:11, 2:22, 2:74, 2:83, 2:84, 2:93, 2:102, 2:157, 2:170, 2:179, 2:211, 2:212, 2:264, 2:273, 3:17, 3:22, 3:24, 3:25, 3:42, 3:66, 3:78, 3:80, 3:156, 3:159, 3:161, 3:167, 3:174, 3:177-3:178, 3:192, 3:199, 3:203, 3:204, 3:215, 3:218, 3:220, 3:226, 3:236, 3:262, 3:296, 3:305, 3:311, 3:315, 3:333, 3:337, 3:338, 3:340, 3:341, 3:343, 3:346-3:348, 3:354

Bomb(s), 1:168, 1:183, 2:44

Bondage, 1:viii, 1:39, 1:97, 1:106, 1:107, 1:134, 1:157, 1:179, 1:214, 1:217, 1:219, 2:74, 2:154, 2:163, 2:226, 3:78, 3:109, 3:122, 3:149, 3:243, 3:276, 3:298, 3:347

Book of Life, 2:195, 2:252, 2:281, 2:284, 3:294, 3:347, 3:352

Book of Mormon, 1:7, 1:14, 1:26, 1:45, 1:46, 1:78, 1:82, 1:100-1:102, 1:104, 1:125, 1:193, 1:196, 1:200, 1:210, 1:235, 1:236, 1:238, 1:245, 1:247, 1:260, 1:264, 1:265, 1:280, 2:5, 2:15, 2:20, 2:43, 2:61, 2:79, 2:84, 2:88, 2:120-2:121, 2:123-2:126, 2:137, 2:142, 2:147, 2:185, 2:213, 2:218, 2:220, 3:5, 3:9, 3:70, 3:82, 3:85, 3:106, 3:117, 3:137, 3:140, 3:157, 3:167, 3:172, 3:173, 3:175, 3:217, 3:229, 3:273, 3:277, 3:283, 3:286, 3:309, 3:310, 3:313, 3:338, 3:343

Book of remembrance, 3:34, 3:89, 3:303, 3:319, 3:320

Born again, 3:335, 3:335

Born of the Spirit, 2:142

Index

Boston, 1:184, 2:136, 2:143, 2:153
Branch, The, 3:251-3:251, 3:253, 3:261
Brass, 2:47, 2:60, 2:129, 2:141, 2:253, 2:266, 2:268, 2:273, 2:277, 2:280, 3:67, 3:155, 3:225, 3:229-3:231, 3:233, 3:236, 3:311, 3:319
Brass plates, 3:311, 3:319
Bridegroom, 1:36, 1:68, 1:95, 1:96, 1:224, 1:256-1:257, 1:267, 2:68, 2:106, 2:253, 3:1, 3:7, 3:22, 3:54, 3:57, 3:112
Brimstone, 1:55, 1:117, 2:46, 2:57, 2:109, 2:111, 2:229, 2:261, 2:280, 2:282, 2:284, 3:14, 3:41, 3:47, 3:102
Britain, 1:166, 1:246, 2:48, 2:66, 2:79, 2:92, 2:153
British Isles, 3:175
Broken heart, 2:223, 3:329
Brother of Jared, 1:136, 1:217, 2:78
Brotherhood, 1:30, 1:74, 3:63, 3:278
Budget, 1:98
Buildings, 1:45, 2:30, 2:189, 3:80, 3:83, 3:262
Bundle, 1:30
Burial, 1:191, 2:139
Burn, 1:4, 1:62, 1:107, 1:137, 1:140, 1:162, 1:269, 1:286, 1:287, 1:290, 1:291, 2:22, 2:39, 2:67, 2:70-2:71, 2:78, 2:111, 2:237, 2:252, 2:254, 2:284, 3:28, 3:48, 3:53, 3:59, 3:68, 3:211, 3:335
Burned, 1:64, 1:77, 1:79, 1:92, 1:114, 1:118, 1:230, 1:256, 1:261, 1:288, 1:292, 2:1, 2:7, 2:11, 2:14, 2:23, 2:29, 2:36, 2:40, 2:41, 2:44, 2:56, 2:61, 2:68, 2:70, 2:189, 2:212, 2:228, 2:231, 2:241, 2:243, 2:251, 2:253, 3:4, 3:13, 3:33, 3:35, 3:44, 3:45, 3:47, 3:53, 3:54, 3:96, 3:109, 3:195, 3:199, 3:210, 3:291, 3:333, 3:335, 3:349
Burning, 1:65, 1:92, 1:141, 1:271, 1:288, 2:2, 2:6, 2:8, 2:29, 2:38, 2:41, 2:56, 2:59, 2:67, 2:68, 2:142, 2:145, 2:183, 2:207, 2:246, 2:271, 2:284, 3:22, 3:25, 3:47, 3:152, 3:163, 3:195, 3:293, 3:303, 3:333, 3:335
Bury, 1:112, 1:286, 2:112, 2:133, 2:140, 2:152
Burying, 2:111
Business, 1:27, 1:36, 1:40, 1:58, 1:85, 1:87, 1:89, 1:90, 1:154, 1:191, 1:202, 1:214, 1:223, 2:41, 2:141, 2:159, 2:226, 2:245, 3:64, 3:81, 3:87, 3:138, 3:220, 3:222, 3:265, 3:266, 3:273, 3:281, 3:282, 3:288, 3:296, 3:314

Cain, 1:215, 2:182, 3:161
Calamities, 1:10, 1:48, 1:51, 1:57, 1:58, 1:66, 1:91, 1:97, 1:106, 1:112, 1:113, 1:116, 1:117, 1:245, 2:1, 2:7, 2:10, 2:12, 2:17-2:19, 2:50, 2:57, 2:123, 2:138, 2:150, 2:211, 3:39, 3:84, 3:157
Calamity, 1:31, 1:97, 1:104, 1:114, 1:126, 1:144, 1:223, 1:224, 1:231, 2:vii, 2:3, 2:6, 2:10, 2:15, 2:19, 2:24, 2:35, 2:43, 2:58, 2:105, 2:108, 2:140, 2:141, 2:191, 3:51
Calling and election, 2:2
Calm, 1:76, 1:85, 2:74, 2:144, 2:184, 2:215, 3:295
Canaan, 2:64, 3:121, 3:167, 3:270, 3:307
Candlesticks, 2:101
Canon, 3:307, 3:307, 3:316
Capitalism, 1:203
Captive, 1:21, 1:64, 1:110, 1:133, 1:230, 1:234, 1:242, 1:251, 1:285, 2:11, 2:86, 2:89, 2:90, 2:100, 2:102, 2:108, 2:182, 3:103, 3:172, 3:178, 3:327
Carnage, 1:59, 1:116, 1:135, 1:229
Carnal, 1:94, 1:132, 1:200, 2:158, 2:229, 2:235, 3:92, 3:102, 3:119, 3:276
Cast out the righteous, 1:133, 2:31, 2:70, 2:76, 2:77
Cataclysm, 1:83
Catastrophe, 1:112, 2:50, 2:66, 2:133, 2:152
Catholic, 2:260, 2:272, 3:67
Celestial, 1:9, 1:11, 1:28, 1:31, 1:60, 1:63, 1:64, 1:72, 1:80, 1:93, 1:107, 2:72, 2:91, 2:159, 2:160, 2:170, 2:233, 2:235, 3:53, 3:68, 3:77, 3:81-3:82, 3:93, 3:94, 3:98, 3:110, 3:118-3:120, 3:125, 3:134, 3:138, 3:140, 3:158,

3:159, 3:197-3:198, 3:201, 3:203, 3:221, 3:225, 3:228, 3:238, 3:248, 3:271, 3:274, 3:290, 3:295, 3:298, 3:333, 3:334, 3:338-3:339, 3:342-3:343, 3:345, 3:347, 3:349, 3:354

Celestial kingdom, 1:11, 1:31, 1:58, 1:63, 1:72, 1:80, 2:72, 2:170, 3:68, 3:74, 3:77, 3:93, 3:94, 3:109, 3:110, 3:159, 3:197, 3:198, 3:225, 3:238, 3:248, 3:276, 3:292, 3:334, 3:348

Celestial law, 1:28, 1:93, 3:118-3:120, 3:131, 3:143, 3:203, 3:276-3:278, 3:290, 3:295, 3:339, 3:343, 3:349

Celestial marriage, 3:134

Central Park, 2:145

Chaff, 1:23, 1:152, 1:271, 2:5, 2:30, 2:107, 2:139, 2:179, 2:200, 2:267-2:269, 2:271-2:272, 2:276, 3:71, 3:226, 3:227, 3:229-3:230, 3:274

Challenge, 1:13, 1:92, 1:103, 1:106, 1:109, 1:110, 1:112, 1:114, 1:184, 1:190, 2:185, 2:223, 2:225

Challenges, 1:112, 1:120-1:123, 1:126, 1:185, 1:207, 2:vii, 2:151

Chaos, 1:114, 1:171-1:174, 1:283, 2:vii, 2:74, 2:203, 2:211, 3:242, 3:336, 3:343

Chapels, 1:102, 1:104, 1:243, 1:281

Chariot(s), 2:8, 2:8, 2:21, 2:24, 2:34, 2:45, 2:107, 2:112, 2:113, 2:248, 2:253, 2:280, 3:156

Charity, 1:73, 1:73, 1:168, 1:183, 1:197, 1:201, 3:101, 3:102, 3:260, 3:298

Chasten, 1:45, 1:52, 1:118, 1:134, 2:33, 3:106, 3:190

Chastening, 1:38-1:38, 1:50, 1:52, 1:102, 1:111, 1:141, 2:16, 2:18-2:20, 2:37, 2:138, 2:154, 2:161-2:162, 2:191, 3:85, 3:164, 3:243, 3:257

Chastise, 1:42, 1:65

Chastity, 1:95, 1:123, 3:260

Cherubim, 2:262

Chicken, 2:203

Chickens, 1:137, 1:254, 1:287, 3:10, 3:50

Child, 1:38, 1:102, 1:130, 1:164, 2:2, 2:11, 2:22, 2:27, 2:115, 2:125, 2:158, 2:162, 2:209, 2:240, 2:281, 3:1, 3:44, 3:97-3:98, 3:146, 3:168, 3:181-3:182, 3:193, 3:196, 3:201, 3:207, 3:208, 3:234, 3:256, 3:282

Children of Israel. *See* Israel, Children of

Children of Light, 1:29, 1:47, 1:75, 1:130, 1:200, 2:27, 3:viii, 3:44, 3:56

China, 1:230, 1:232

Choice, 1:3, 1:13, 1:22, 1:93, 1:111, 1:178, 1:184, 1:188, 1:198, 1:217, 2:77-2:78, 2:138, 3:vi, 3:67, 3:83, 3:124, 3:168, 3:172, 3:179, 3:262, 3:268, 3:292, 3:320

Cholera, 1:51, 1:52, 1:260, 2:1, 3:63, 3:153

Chosen, 1:vi, 1:1, 1:4, 1:13, 1:28, 1:70, 1:77, 1:144, 1:160, 1:169, 1:237, 1:249, 1:251, 1:264, 1:274, 1:278, 1:281, 1:284, 2:14, 2:82, 2:94, 2:121, 2:169, 2:180, 2:188, 2:217, 2:252, 2:284, 3:vi, 3:87, 3:93, 3:98, 3:134, 3:143, 3:153, 3:169, 3:170, 3:219, 3:301

Christendom, 1:225, 1:238, 2:40, 2:107, 2:163, 2:233, 2:271, 3:64, 3:157, 3:190

Christian, 1:1, 1:68, 1:85, 1:105, 1:109, 1:188, 1:196, 1:207, 1:210, 1:245, 1:246, 1:268, 1:270, 2:44, 2:152, 2:157, 2:158, 2:221, 2:235, 2:262, 3:6, 3:7, 3:9, 3:161, 3:190, 3:236, 3:306

Christianity, 1:119, 1:173, 1:185, 2:204, 2:272

Christians, 1:114, 1:267, 1:270, 2:84, 2:134, 2:162, 2:221, 3:6, 3:133, 3:240

Church, great and abominable. *See* Great and abominable church

Church of Jesus Christ of Latter-day Saints, 3:247, 3:248

Church of the devil, 1:211, 2:184, 2:233, 2:238, 2:241, 2:247

Church of the Firstborn, 1:55, 1:141, 1:255, 1:292, 3:53, 3:54, 3:145, 3:170, 3:302

Church of the Lamb, 1:82, 1:104, 1:131, 1:235, 1:252, 2:234, 2:238-2:239

Circuses, 1:207, 1:209

Citizen, 1:164, 1:164, 1:168, 1:170, 1:190, 1:201, 1:203, 1:204, 1:210, 1:220, 3:281

Citizens, 1:99, 1:147, 1:163, 1:166, 1:169, 1:171, 1:179, 1:183, 1:189, 1:192, 1:194, 1:196, 1:201-1:202, 1:204, 1:206, 1:220, 2:133, 2:171, 2:265, 3:122, 3:141, 3:227, 3:228

Citizenship, 1:112, 1:164, 1:190, 1:278, 2:148, 2:152, 2:179, 2:234, 3:122

Civil rights, 1:147, 1:167, 1:182

Class distinctions, 2:220, 3:283, 3:285, 3:289, 3:290

Cleanse, 1:33, 1:35, 1:80, 1:90, 1:103, 1:106, 1:141, 2:9, 2:19, 2:35, 2:40, 2:64, 2:66, 2:68, 2:75, 2:97, 2:111-2:112, 2:162, 2:171, 2:216, 2:272, 3:66, 3:74, 3:93, 3:99, 3:116, 3:144, 3:222, 3:254

Cleansed, 1:vii, 1:33, 1:53, 1:79, 1:97, 1:103, 2:13, 2:20, 2:66, 2:86, 3:42, 3:44, 3:95, 3:99, 3:116, 3:121, 3:135, 3:140, 3:158, 3:199, 3:204, 3:209, 3:213, 3:245, 3:270, 3:336

Cleansing, 1:44, 1:106, 2:64, 2:69, 2:224, 3:175, 3:198, 3:199, 3:246, 3:335-3:337

Climate, 1:34, 1:198, 2:148, 3:170, 3:195, 3:340

Clothing, 1:24, 1:40, 1:41, 1:43, 1:71, 1:86, 1:87, 1:92, 1:96, 1:97, 1:106, 1:107, 1:112, 1:119, 1:177, 1:188, 1:277, 1:283, 2:151, 2:198, 2:205, 2:208, 2:223, 3:69, 3:83, 3:190, 3:274

Cloud, 1:48, 1:78, 1:127, 1:141, 2:2, 2:12, 2:53, 2:67, 2:74, 2:83, 2:85, 2:101, 2:107, 2:116, 2:119, 2:120, 2:153, 2:243, 3:1, 3:5, 3:7, 3:25, 3:26, 3:39, 3:42, 3:43, 3:49, 3:51, 3:53, 3:54, 3:56, 3:63, 3:69, 3:75, 3:78-3:80, 3:115, 3:117, 3:121, 3:126, 3:169-3:170, 3:209

Clouds, 1:46, 1:54, 1:79, 1:114, 1:122, 1:158, 1:226, 1:227, 1:269, 2:21, 2:56, 2:68, 2:112, 2:115, 2:170, 2:277, 3:1, 3:2, 3:5, 3:8, 3:14, 3:17, 3:21, 3:23, 3:25, 3:32, 3:35-3:40, 3:45, 3:50, 3:51, 3:53, 3:71, 3:76, 3:139, 3:160, 3:163, 3:191, 3:199, 3:200, 3:209, 3:228, 3:233, 3:235

Clouds of glory, 3:14, 3:160, 3:199

Colonists, 1:49

Columbus, 1:158, 1:159, 2:136, 3:241

Comet, 2:2, 3:21

Comfort, 1:67, 1:98, 1:101, 1:172, 1:176, 1:183, 1:279, 1:284, 2:vii, 2:58, 2:96, 2:98, 2:151, 2:156, 3:10, 3:44, 3:75, 3:99, 3:100, 3:164, 3:189, 3:274, 3:279, 3:282, 3:308, 3:309

Commission, 1:11, 1:14, 1:110, 1:220, 1:243, 2:213, 2:218, 3:176, 3:204

Communism, 1:164, 1:174, 1:178-1:180, 1:182, 1:207, 1:210, 1:232, 2:200-2:201, 2:235, 3:279, 3:286-3:288, 3:292, 3:295, 3:297, 3:318

Complacency, 1:83, 1:112, 2:183

Compression of events, 1:119

Condemn, 1:137, 1:210, 2:6, 2:33, 2:162, 2:209, 2:211, 2:212

Condemnation, 1:67, 1:69, 1:142, 2:8, 2:19, 2:73, 2:147, 2:166, 2:211, 2:271, 3:72, 3:106, 3:157, 3:243, 3:264, 3:309, 3:310, 3:314, 3:317, 3:328, 3:354

Conduct, 1:44, 1:50, 1:56, 1:65, 1:107, 1:113, 1:119, 1:198, 2:125, 2:135, 2:138, 2:165, 2:223, 3:vii, 3:12, 3:45, 3:122, 3:260, 3:268, 3:270, 3:277, 3:280

Confess, 1:45, 2:207, 3:43, 3:55, 3:64, 3:186, 3:209, 3:217, 3:219, 3:221, 3:234

Confidence, 1:95, 1:112, 2:137, 2:155-2:156, 2:181, 2:222, 2:264, 3:245

Confident, 3:316

Conflict(s), 1:27, 1:100, 1:115, 1:173, 1:174, 1:186, 1:209, 2:43, 2:44, 2:93, 2:109, 2:172, 3:135, 3:200, 3:247

Confusion, 1:58, 1:74, 1:145, 1:151, 1:170, 1:230, 1:276, 1:277, 1:291, 2:4, 2:9, 2:18, 2:41, 2:141, 2:199, 2:214, 2:243, 2:244, 2:264, 3:104, 3:154, 3:216, 3:245, 3:259

Congregation, 1:8, 2:85, 2:119, 2:137, 2:169, 3:127, 3:162, 3:308, 3:331

Congress, 1:155, 1:157, 1:159, 1:174, 1:192, 1:193, 1:203, 2:40, 2:134, 2:144

Conscience, 1:86, 1:164, 1:165, 1:194, 1:220, 2:42, 2:222, 3:298

Consecrate, 1:94, 2:47, 2:129, 2:132, 3:123, 3:261, 3:262, 3:266, 3:268-3:269, 3:290, 3:295, 3:297, 3:300, 3:301, 3:303

Consecration, 1:141, 1:164, 2:4, 3:77, 3:86, 3:93, 3:120, 3:149, 3:263-3:265, 3:267, 3:269, 3:286, 3:289, 3:294, 3:295, 3:299-3:300, 3:303, 3:317

    law of   Consecration, 2:4, 3:77, 3:86, 3:269, 3:280, 3:286, 3:294, 3:295, 3:317

Conspiracy, 1:109-1:110, 1:123, 1:147, 1:166, 1:167, 1:178, 1:181, 1:183-1:184, 1:193, 1:220

Conspire, 1:195

Constitution, 1:3, 1:vii, 1:30, 1:112, 1:147, 1:150, 1:152, 1:156, 1:163, 1:165-1:166, 1:168, 1:170, 1:176-1:181, 1:184, 1:192, 1:196-1:197, 1:200, 1:203, 1:205-1:208, 1:219, 1:278, 2:73, 2:148, 2:152, 2:167, 2:168, 2:180, 3:122, 3:136, 3:219, 3:224, 3:347

Constitutional government, 1:153, 1:161, 1:163-1:165, 1:173, 1:185, 1:193, 1:195, 1:202, 3:242

Constitutional principles, 1:161, 1:185
Consumption, 1:111, 1:141, 1:202, 2:37, 2:127, 2:154, 2:191, 3:164, 3:257
Contention, 1:32, 1:100, 1:153, 1:167, 1:214, 1:217, 2:41-2:43, 2:223, 2:234, 2:258
Contentions, 1:22, 1:41, 1:223, 2:32, 2:33, 2:35, 2:274, 3:237, 3:300, 3:322
Continent, 1:6, 1:49, 1:50, 1:70, 1:81, 1:151, 1:159, 1:164, 1:238, 1:240, 1:267, 1:274, 1:276, 1:295, 2:4, 2:7, 2:11, 2:15,
        2:16, 2:91, 2:147-2:149, 2:235, 2:266, 3:vii, 3:11, 3:16, 3:18, 3:23, 3:73-3:74, 3:80, 3:82, 3:87, 3:88,
        3:114, 3:115, 3:123, 3:125, 3:129, 3:143, 3:150, 3:157, 3:160, 3:161, 3:173-3:174, 3:177-3:179, 3:187,
        3:192-3:193, 3:214, 3:226, 3:229, 3:241, 3:242, 3:271, 3:273, 3:277, 3:306-3:307, 3:310, 3:311, 3:338
    Western continent, 2:50, 2:149, 3:vii, 3:11, 3:74, 3:82, 3:125, 3:143, 3:161, 3:174, 3:177, 3:226, 3:241, 3:306,
        3:336
Continents, 1:26, 2:5, 3:155, 3:166, 3:180, 3:289
Controversy, 1:156, 1:227, 1:228, 2:11, 2:24, 2:146, 3:96
Conversion, 1:247
Convert, 1:241, 1:242, 1:246, 1:278, 1:282, 2:22, 2:82, 2:89, 2:90, 2:152, 2:178, 3:67, 3:190, 3:345
Convulsions, 1:61, 1:63, 1:76, 2:5, 2:18, 2:50, 3:165
Cornerstone, 1:105, 1:189, 3:248, 3:298
Corrupt, 1:95, 1:158, 1:160, 1:200, 1:209, 1:223, 2:3, 2:10, 2:13, 2:19, 2:68, 2:121, 2:167, 2:176, 2:208, 2:215, 2:226,
        2:241, 2:244, 2:254, 2:257, 2:264, 3:vii, 3:66, 3:72, 3:130, 3:143, 3:191, 3:281, 3:336
Corruption, 1:41, 1:55, 1:58, 1:125, 1:145, 1:148, 1:152, 1:153, 1:155, 1:162, 1:181, 2:9, 2:56, 2:72, 2:264, 3:42, 3:67,
        3:81, 3:193, 3:203, 3:209, 3:289, 3:298
Council, 1:28, 1:174, 2:95, 2:144, 2:234, 3:77, 3:117, 3:157, 3:172, 3:216, 3:283, 3:305, 3:331
Council of Fifty, 3:216, 3:216
Council of the Twelve, 2:95
Court, 1:159, 1:181, 1:182, 1:201, 1:210, 2:101, 2:116, 2:200, 2:234, 3:104, 3:148
Courts, 1:172, 1:201, 1:202, 2:74, 3:342
Covenant, 1:11, 1:15, 1:69, 1:78, 1:90, 1:91, 1:96, 1:104, 1:120, 1:131, 1:132, 1:140, 1:144, 1:146, 1:201, 1:232,
        1:252-1:254, 1:257, 1:265, 1:266, 1:271, 1:273, 1:282, 1:290, 1:293, 2:vii, 2:1-2:2, 2:12, 2:23, 2:31,
        2:40, 2:55, 2:61, 2:68, 2:82, 2:84, 2:87, 2:92, 2:94, 2:95, 2:98, 2:102, 2:109, 2:112, 2:115, 2:121,
        2:129, 2:131, 2:157, 2:185, 2:189, 2:205, 2:228, 2:230, 2:239, 2:254, 2:262, 3:23, 3:24, 3:29, 3:30,
        3:34, 3:50, 3:53, 3:90, 3:95, 3:101, 3:110, 3:121, 3:124, 3:145-3:147, 3:185, 3:200, 3:217, 3:255,
        3:257, 3:262, 3:274, 3:278, 3:290, 3:291, 3:293-3:295, 3:303, 3:304, 3:316, 3:328, 3:329, 3:352
    new and everlasting covenant, 2:82, 3:138, 3:200
    new covenant, 2:61, 2:133, 3:53, 3:90, 3:106
Covenant people, 1:104, 1:131, 1:132, 1:232, 1:252, 1:266, 1:290, 2:31, 2:40, 2:84, 2:102, 2:109, 2:189, 2:239, 3:101,
        3:147, 3:217, 3:290, 3:300
Covenants, 1:viii, 1:7, 1:10, 1:26, 1:33, 1:34, 1:42, 1:46, 1:50, 1:61, 1:74, 1:76, 1:85, 1:186, 1:213, 1:238, 1:252, 1:272,
        1:277, 1:283, 2:15, 2:55, 2:74, 2:76, 2:88, 2:92, 2:101, 2:102, 2:108, 2:125, 2:138, 2:147, 2:177, 2:179,
        2:202, 2:218, 2:220, 2:221, 2:234, 2:237, 2:240, 3:vi, 3:70, 3:77, 3:90, 3:91, 3:135, 3:174, 3:197,
        3:201, 3:224, 3:234, 3:250, 3:269, 3:280, 3:290, 3:292, 3:301, 3:309, 3:315, 3:317, 3:322, 3:347
Covet, 3:260
Covetous, 1:21, 1:27, 1:205, 1:207, 1:260, 2:1, 3:80, 3:260
Covetousness, 1:55, 3:92, 3:118, 3:266, 3:267, 3:297, 3:303
Coward, 1:29, 1:188
Cowdery, Oliver, 1:8, 3:10, 3:165, 3:178
Create, 1:53, 1:127, 1:168, 1:177, 1:183, 1:191, 2:179, 2:186, 2:211, 2:217, 3:17, 3:63, 3:95, 3:115, 3:121, 3:126, 3:208,
        3:285
Creation, 1:14, 1:22, 1:25, 1:51, 1:56, 1:58, 1:71, 1:99, 1:104, 1:182, 1:206, 1:209, 1:211, 1:248, 1:266, 2:13, 2:50, 2:56,
        2:221, 2:260, 2:265, 2:285, 3:66, 3:92, 3:129, 3:139, 3:140, 3:153-3:154, 3:189, 3:191-3:192, 3:196,
        3:199, 3:204-3:206, 3:217, 3:227, 3:289, 3:311, 3:313, 3:314, 3:318, 3:338, 3:343, 3:345, 3:348
Creator, 1:173, 1:201, 2:56, 2:136, 3:68, 3:204, 3:213

Creature, 1:59, 1:201, 1:230, 1:253, 1:255, 1:257, 2:145, 2:188, 2:208, 2:259, 2:260, 2:285, 3:27, 3:145, 3:196, 3:335

Creatures, 1:106, 1:140, 1:191, 2:28, 2:56, 2:57, 2:177, 2:246, 2:279, 3:81, 3:199, 3:298, 3:302, 3:304

Creed, 1:161, 3:318

Creeds, 1:145, 1:261, 2:66, 2:196, 2:241, 3:63, 3:206, 3:228

Crime, 1:87, 1:194, 1:211, 2:21, 2:33, 2:208, 2:221

Crises, 1:97, 1:98, 1:102, 1:114, 2:151

Crisis, 1:32, 1:104, 1:126, 1:177, 1:190, 1:198, 1:207, 1:208, 2:viii, 2:150, 3:vii, 3:222

Criticism, 1:190, 1:190, 2:184

Critics, 1:197

Crops, 1:30, 2:2, 2:21, 2:35, 2:41, 2:64, 2:141

Crown, 1:106, 1:188, 2:54, 2:119, 2:170, 2:182, 2:259, 3:7, 3:49, 3:148, 3:164, 3:298, 3:302, 3:304, 3:335

Crowns, 1:31, 1:223, 1:250, 2:21, 2:179, 2:203, 3:46, 3:49

Crumble, 1:46, 1:58, 1:59, 1:62, 1:153, 1:229, 3:71

Crystal, 2:278, 3:351, 3:355

Cult, 2:217

Cults, 1:283, 2:203

Culture, 1:125, 1:280, 3:290

Cumorah, 1:26, 3:306, 3:311

Curse, 1:2, 1:11, 1:21, 1:34, 1:90, 1:128, 1:250, 1:255, 1:284, 2:23, 2:24, 2:32, 2:34, 2:36, 2:48, 2:57-2:58, 2:64, 2:65,
    2:76, 2:96, 2:187, 2:188, 2:193, 2:228, 3:30, 3:56, 3:67, 3:72, 3:86, 3:122, 3:158, 3:177, 3:181, 3:189,
    3:199, 3:204, 3:220, 3:253, 3:263-3:264, 3:278, 3:294, 3:303, 3:332, 3:335, 3:343-3:344

Curses, 1:117, 2:94, 3:111, 3:345

Curtain, 1:41, 1:256, 3:22, 3:55

Curtain of heaven, 1:256, 3:22, 3:55

Cycle(s), 1:96, 1:200

Cyclone(s), 1:71, 2:16, 2:64

Damnation, 1:199, 2:19, 2:72, 2:73, 3:328

Damned, 1:60, 1:139, 1:224, 2:206, 2:228, 2:258, 3:64

Dan, 1:250, 2:202, 2:273, 2:275, 3:8, 3:13, 3:159, 3:162, 3:237

Danger, 1:33, 1:47, 1:57, 1:77, 1:80, 1:92, 1:166, 1:168, 1:172, 1:173, 1:179, 1:189, 1:190, 1:202, 1:204, 1:208, 2:15,
    2:69, 2:166, 2:181, 2:183, 2:213, 2:215, 2:225, 3:vii, 3:115

Daniel, 1:2, 1:40, 1:76, 1:78, 1:128, 1:245, 1:260, 1:275, 2:8, 2:27, 2:45, 2:98, 2:108, 2:112, 2:115, 2:123, 2:155, 2:169,
    2:171, 2:187, 2:246, 2:265, 2:267, 2:270, 2:272, 2:274, 2:277, 3:8, 3:13, 3:35, 3:38, 3:40, 3:63, 3:85,
    3:135, 3:151, 3:154, 3:156, 3:158-3:161, 3:163, 3:164, 3:217, 3:220, 3:228, 3:231, 3:233, 3:236-3:237,
    3:240-3:241, 3:254, 3:258, 3:307, 3:313

Dark Ages, 1:191, 2:235

Darkness, 1:viii, 1:3, 1:8, 1:21, 1:31, 1:66, 1:75, 1:79, 1:85, 1:86, 1:93, 1:95, 1:98, 1:105, 1:108, 1:110, 1:128, 1:130,
    1:138, 1:143, 1:145, 1:146, 1:159, 1:215, 1:226, 1:253, 1:254, 1:261, 1:288, 2:2, 2:7, 2:18, 2:25, 2:27,
    2:30, 2:32, 2:33, 2:35, 2:36, 2:39, 2:59, 2:66, 2:76, 2:123, 2:128, 2:136, 2:149, 2:154, 2:155, 2:158,
    2:173, 2:191, 2:192, 2:201, 2:213, 2:219, 2:239, 2:262, 2:274, 2:283, 3:vi, 3:viii, 3:7, 3:28, 3:33,
    3:43-3:44, 3:49, 3:59, 3:99, 3:101, 3:113, 3:126, 3:130, 3:199, 3:200, 3:204, 3:211, 3:219, 3:222,
    3:225, 3:237, 3:241, 3:244, 3:312, 3:314, 3:317, 3:325, 3:327, 3:328, 3:333, 3:353

Daughter, 1:38, 2:2, 2:24, 2:161, 2:250, 3:103, 3:154, 3:201

Daughters, 1:viii, 1:13, 1:21, 1:39, 1:55, 1:128, 1:161, 1:261, 1:267, 1:270, 1:271, 2:2, 2:113, 2:178, 2:235, 3:33, 3:77,
    3:85, 3:95, 3:99, 3:164, 3:181, 3:194, 3:263, 3:307, 3:339

David, 1:166, 1:169, 1:230, 1:245, 1:278, 2:44, 2:50, 2:55, 2:88, 2:91, 2:122, 2:146, 2:180, 2:185, 2:201, 2:272, 2:274,
    3:viii, 3:23, 3:80, 3:86, 3:91, 3:115, 3:117, 3:121, 3:125, 3:134, 3:171, 3:232, 3:235, 3:237, 3:248,
    3:250, 3:253-3:256, 3:307
    root of David, 3:251

Davidic king, 2:4, 3:249

Day, great and dreadful, 1:10, 1:11, 1:21, 1:25, 1:90, 1:91, 1:103, 2:vi, 3:28, 3:35, 3:162

Day of the Lord, 1:4, 1:10, 1:11, 1:25, 1:45, 1:64, 1:75, 1:91, 1:102, 1:103, 1:128, 1:130, 1:138, 1:141, 1:242, 1:257, 1:295, 2:6, 2:7, 2:12, 2:25, 2:36, 2:80, 2:112-2:114, 2:132, 3:3-3:4, 3:11, 3:12, 3:28, 3:32-3:34, 3:43-3:45, 3:49, 3:54, 3:57, 3:99, 3:103, 3:112, 3:162

Day of transfiguration, 3:52, 3:212, 3:353

Dead, 1:2, 1:5, 1:8, 1:12, 1:25, 1:26, 1:89, 1:127, 1:158, 1:234, 1:248, 1:263, 1:266, 1:270, 1:295, 2:5, 2:29, 2:54, 2:57, 2:58, 2:68, 2:79, 2:81, 2:85, 2:87, 2:88, 2:98, 2:101, 2:119, 2:137, 2:140, 2:143, 2:145, 2:179, 2:191, 2:208, 2:221, 2:226, 2:244, 2:283, 3:1, 3:6, 3:19, 3:21, 3:44, 3:49, 3:52, 3:56, 3:59, 3:69, 3:113, 3:118, 3:140, 3:150, 3:159, 3:166, 3:187, 3:191, 3:197, 3:199, 3:203, 3:205, 3:209, 3:210, 3:212, 3:214, 3:238, 3:247, 3:307, 3:324, 3:328, 3:332, 3:334, 3:341, 3:353, 3:354

    work for the dead, 1:10

Dead Sea, 2:79, 2:81, 2:87, 3:21

Death, 1:7, 1:13, 1:26, 1:30, 1:42, 1:47, 1:49, 1:57, 1:60, 1:64, 1:92, 1:109, 1:118, 1:120, 1:173, 1:209, 1:221, 1:225, 1:245, 1:249, 1:288, 2:1, 2:3, 2:10, 2:15, 2:21, 2:29, 2:33, 2:43, 2:48, 2:49, 2:55, 2:57, 2:61, 2:74, 2:82, 2:83, 2:85, 2:90, 2:123, 2:128, 2:133, 2:144-2:145, 2:156, 2:162-2:164, 2:170, 2:181, 2:188, 2:214, 2:215, 2:234, 2:243, 2:253, 2:260, 2:281, 3:viii, 3:7, 3:21, 3:86, 3:122, 3:135, 3:139-3:140, 3:143, 3:152, 3:160-3:161, 3:164, 3:169, 3:172, 3:177, 3:191, 3:193, 3:196, 3:199-3:203, 3:209-3:210, 3:213, 3:256, 3:303, 3:311, 3:336, 3:338, 3:340-3:341, 3:344-3:345, 3:347, 3:348, 3:350-3:351, 3:355

    second death, 3:209, 3:210, 3:336

Debauchery, 1:48, 1:87

Debt, 1:96-1:98, 1:106, 1:107, 1:178, 1:181, 1:187, 1:205, 1:207, 1:208, 2:160, 3:288

Decadence, 1:209, 3:157

Decay, 1:178, 1:201, 1:209, 2:175, 3:124, 3:129, 3:244

Deceive, 1:viii, 1:39, 1:145, 1:165, 1:179, 1:182, 2:103, 2:196-2:198, 2:200-2:201, 2:203, 2:207, 2:209, 2:228, 2:230, 2:285, 3:89, 3:209, 3:284, 3:286, 3:287, 3:323, 3:337, 3:350, 3:351

Deceiver(s), 1:283, 2:207

Deception, 1:123, 1:193, 1:205, 2:245

Decision, 1:174, 1:188, 2:7, 3:33, 3:274, 3:283

Decisions, 1:vii, 1:98, 1:179, 1:181, 1:187, 1:210, 2:200

Declaration of Independence, 1:156, 1:173

Dedication, 1:96, 1:108, 2:80

Defend, 1:13, 1:47, 1:106, 1:151, 1:160, 1:177, 1:184, 1:185, 1:196, 1:197, 1:205, 1:207, 1:209, 1:277, 2:43, 2:48, 2:73, 2:114, 2:153, 2:169, 3:218

Degree of glory, 3:339

Delegate(s), 1:126, 1:202, 3:137

Delegation, 2:92

Deliver, 1:3, 1:63, 1:65, 1:82, 1:128, 1:134, 1:144, 1:153, 1:214, 1:227, 1:251, 1:258, 1:281, 1:286, 2:24, 2:76, 2:80, 2:86, 2:102, 2:126, 2:127, 2:129-2:131, 2:156, 2:189, 2:205, 3:7, 3:100, 3:122, 3:163, 3:253, 3:304, 3:308, 3:324

Deliverance, 1:viii, 1:27, 1:39, 1:43, 1:63, 1:73, 1:82, 1:85, 1:93, 1:94, 1:126, 1:128, 1:132, 1:260, 1:273, 1:276, 2:12, 2:25, 2:135, 2:143, 2:156, 2:200, 2:229, 3:26, 3:33, 3:62, 3:78, 3:85, 3:86, 3:99, 3:102

Deliverer, 1:15, 1:70, 2:91-2:92, 2:94, 3:vii, 3:viii, 3:7, 3:26, 3:249, 3:256

Delivers, 1:250, 2:155, 2:177, 3:153, 3:158

Delusion, 1:112, 2:182, 2:206, 2:228

Democracy, 1:176, 1:203, 1:211, 1:212, 3:245, 3:248

Democrat, 1:149

Depend, 1:36, 1:41, 1:47, 1:50, 1:65, 1:80-1:81, 1:94, 1:205, 1:239, 2:138, 2:165, 2:172, 2:175, 3:217

Dependence, 1:188

Depression, 1:109, 3:152

Descend, 1:140, 1:228, 1:264, 2:56, 2:68, 2:81, 2:84, 2:87, 2:91, 2:119, 2:122, 3:19, 3:26, 3:27, 3:44, 3:55, 3:84, 3:94, 3:122, 3:140, 3:141, 3:193, 3:196, 3:199, 3:249, 3:298, 3:302, 3:336, 3:344, 3:346-3:347

Descent, 3:154

Desert, 1:56, 1:70, 2:202, 2:205, 2:216, 2:217, 3:10, 3:31, 3:35, 3:38, 3:40, 3:96, 3:97, 3:170, 3:207

Deserts, 1:269, 2:196, 2:215, 3:57, 3:168, 3:180, 3:186

Desire, 1:46, 1:51, 1:73, 1:84, 1:94, 1:116, 1:147, 1:152, 1:160, 1:161, 1:184, 1:195, 1:214, 1:223, 1:231, 1:253, 1:273, 1:279, 2:25, 2:32, 2:57, 2:76, 2:82, 2:93, 2:139, 2:163, 2:164, 2:173, 2:186, 2:269, 2:280, 3:34, 3:140, 3:193, 3:277, 3:278, 3:285-3:286, 3:288, 3:291, 3:309, 3:315

Desolate, 1:152, 1:156, 1:200, 1:287, 2:7, 2:11-2:13, 2:22-2:25, 2:41, 2:66, 2:96, 2:110, 2:130, 2:137, 2:153, 2:228, 2:237, 2:249, 2:252, 2:253, 2:284, 3:1, 3:4, 3:10, 3:32, 3:69, 3:103, 3:168, 3:181, 3:182

Desolation, 1:13, 1:42, 1:50, 1:86, 1:115-1:116, 1:137, 1:139, 1:142, 1:144, 1:156, 1:159, 1:237, 1:255, 1:260, 1:272, 1:275, 1:283, 1:290, 1:291, 2:1, 2:4, 2:1, 2:11, 2:13, 2:27, 2:28, 2:36-2:38, 2:41, 2:68, 2:78, 2:96, 2:105, 2:107, 2:115, 2:117, 2:137-2:138, 2:143, 2:148, 2:249-2:250, 3:19, 3:32, 3:35, 3:38, 3:40, 3:46, 3:48, 3:54, 3:105

Desolation of Abomination, 1:142, 1:255, 2:4, 2:37, 2:107, 2:117, 2:153, 3:54

Desolations, 1:50, 1:105, 1:117, 1:118, 1:137, 1:232, 1:233, 1:255, 2:1, 2:36, 2:39, 2:98, 2:112, 2:138, 2:254

Despair, 1:108, 1:109, 1:113, 1:115, 1:120-1:123, 1:125

Destroyer, 1:51, 1:52, 1:89, 1:156, 1:293, 2:1, 2:11, 2:38, 2:96, 3:108, 3:110, 3:335

Devil, 1:4, 1:7, 1:23, 1:26-1:28, 1:31, 1:61, 1:81, 1:108, 1:130, 1:132-1:134, 1:136, 1:145, 1:156, 1:177, 1:182, 1:188, 1:199-1:200, 1:211, 1:213, 1:217, 1:218, 1:224, 2:2, 2:4, 2:30, 2:47, 2:56-2:57, 2:69, 2:101, 2:107, 2:157, 2:159, 2:161, 2:167, 2:171, 2:195-2:196, 2:207, 2:223-2:224, 2:226, 2:229, 2:230, 2:233, 2:236, 2:238, 2:241, 2:247, 2:261, 2:262, 2:264, 2:281, 2:285, 3:55, 3:102, 3:190, 3:192, 3:200, 3:205, 3:209, 3:213, 3:238-3:241, 3:257, 3:262, 3:263, 3:273, 3:282, 3:330, 3:340, 3:350, 3:351, 3:353-3:354
    Also see Satan.

Devotion, 1:167, 1:198, 1:220, 2:260, 3:117

Devourer, 1:128

Dictatorship, 1:165, 1:168, 1:171, 1:206, 1:211

Disappointment, 3:272, 3:272, 3:275

Disarmament, 1:180, 1:180, 1:181

Disaster, 1:91, 1:97, 1:102, 1:112, 1:116, 1:166, 1:208

Disasters, 1:106, 1:116, 1:118, 1:231, 2:vii, 2:16, 2:18, 3:15

Discern, 1:31, 1:76, 1:143, 1:197, 2:3, 2:134, 2:197, 2:200, 2:222, 3:79, 3:130, 3:306

Discernment, 1:101, 2:200, 2:219

Disciples, 1:vi, 1:11, 1:35, 1:36, 1:75, 1:90, 1:101, 1:120, 1:160, 1:230, 1:234, 1:251, 1:255, 1:290, 2:11, 2:12, 2:27, 2:36, 2:175, 2:176, 2:180, 2:273, 3:12, 3:19, 3:42, 3:50, 3:65, 3:69, 3:132, 3:155, 3:194, 3:196, 3:206, 3:221, 3:227, 3:236, 3:238, 3:295, 3:337

Discouragement, 1:98, 1:102, 1:109, 1:121

Disease, 1:28

Disloyal, 1:168, 1:170

Disobedience, 1:64, 1:82, 1:88, 1:116, 1:224, 2:vi, 3:76, 3:275, 3:276

Dispersion, 1:9, 1:241, 1:275, 1:280, 2:102, 3:103, 3:176, 3:177, 3:346

Dispute, 2:103, 3:229

Disputes, 1:172, 1:201, 1:223, 2:42

Dissension, 1:55, 2:217, 2:220

Division, 1:55, 1:153, 2:70, 2:81, 2:91, 2:214, 2:223, 2:224, 2:258, 2:265, 3:69, 3:81, 3:120, 3:133, 3:177, 3:217, 3:227, 3:263, 3:270, 3:278, 3:342

Divorce, 1:96, 1:109, 1:191

Doctrine and Covenants, 1:viii, 1:7, 1:26, 1:46, 1:85, 1:186, 1:238, 1:272, 1:277, 2:15, 2:55, 2:74, 2:108, 2:125, 2:179, 2:234, 3:77, 3:90, 3:91, 3:135, 3:174, 3:197, 3:201, 3:250, 3:268, 3:269, 3:280, 3:309, 3:317, 3:347

Dollars, 1:45, 3:270, 3:273, 3:277, 3:278

Dominion, 1:31, 1:60, 1:65, 1:109, 1:136, 1:156, 1:157, 1:221, 1:271, 1:288, 2:7, 2:8, 2:47, 2:49, 2:107, 2:160, 2:179, 2:223, 2:234, 2:238, 2:265-2:267, 2:269, 2:273, 3:4, 3:8, 3:26, 3:69, 3:73, 3:85, 3:140, 3:153, 3:156, 3:157, 3:163, 3:199, 3:204, 3:205, 3:215, 3:224, 3:226-3:227, 3:231, 3:235-3:236, 3:244, 3:246, 3:247, 3:254, 3:264, 3:302

Dominions, 1:152, 1:234, 1:250, 1:252, 2:139, 2:239, 2:265, 2:269, 2:278, 3:163, 3:223, 3:254, 3:305, 3:331, 3:341, 3:342, 3:346

Doubt, 1:58, 1:73, 1:80, 1:90, 1:93, 1:101, 1:103, 1:112, 1:137, 1:175, 1:278, 2:18, 2:55, 2:80, 2:85, 2:93, 2:107, 2:170, 2:172-2:173, 2:175, 2:179, 2:206, 2:218, 2:245, 3:23, 3:73, 3:88, 3:123, 3:139, 3:156, 3:175, 3:191, 3:195, 3:198, 3:205, 3:232, 3:233, 3:264, 3:267, 3:285, 3:306-3:308, 3:311, 3:316, 3:340, 3:343

Dragon, 1:108, 1:109, 2:207, 2:250, 2:260, 2:280-2:283, 2:285, 3:209, 3:256, 3:350

Dream, 1:21, 1:23, 1:55, 1:128, 1:271, 2:164, 2:266-2:267, 2:270, 2:272, 3:33, 3:70, 3:71, 3:80, 3:90, 3:99, 3:102, 3:226, 3:229, 3:231, 3:295, 3:307

Dreams, 1:8, 1:21, 1:55, 1:128, 3:32, 3:33, 3:80, 3:99, 3:167, 3:233, 3:307

Drought, 2:150

Drugs, 1:183

Duty, 1:9, 1:28, 1:33, 1:44, 1:66, 1:70, 1:72, 1:83, 1:84, 1:97, 1:103, 1:104, 1:111, 1:145, 1:150, 1:160, 1:190, 1:194, 1:196, 1:199, 1:202, 1:223, 1:248, 1:274, 1:279, 2:43, 2:47, 2:56, 2:136, 2:162, 2:163, 2:176, 2:177, 2:181, 2:197, 2:213, 2:218, 2:219, 2:225, 3:vii, 3:67, 3:87, 3:131, 3:221, 3:247, 3:260-3:262, 3:264, 3:267, 3:288, 3:303

Eagle, 2:278, 2:281

Ear, 1:30, 1:65, 2:13, 2:157, 2:226, 2:229, 2:281, 3:32, 3:55, 3:58, 3:186, 3:249, 3:325, 3:330

Earth, Celestial, 3:336

Earth, end of, 1:90, 1:246, 1:254, 2:4, 3:9, 3:37, 3:50, 3:195, 3:199, 3:211, 3:324, 3:333, 3:350, 3:354
    new earth, 1:281, 2:266, 3:13, 3:15, 3:42, 3:45, 3:48, 3:122, 3:147, 3:185, 3:209, 3:210, 3:228, 3:338, 3:340-3:341, 3:349, 3:351-3:353

Earth, under the, 1:59, 1:142, 2:260, 3:43, 3:196, 3:209

Earthquake, 1:23, 1:47, 1:75, 1:95, 1:111, 1:112, 1:141, 1:226, 2:11, 2:15, 2:21, 2:31, 2:37, 2:50, 2:54, 2:85, 2:91, 2:92, 2:100-2:101, 2:114, 2:133, 2:135, 2:143, 2:154, 2:191, 2:278, 3:6, 3:8, 3:19, 3:27, 3:34, 3:70, 3:71, 3:164, 3:165, 3:175, 3:257

East, 1:53, 1:226, 1:238, 1:261, 1:266-1:267, 1:270, 1:289, 2:2, 2:45, 2:86, 2:98, 2:107, 2:111, 2:113-2:114, 2:129, 2:136, 2:138, 2:143, 2:179, 2:202, 2:205, 2:268, 2:278, 2:283, 3:11, 3:18, 3:21, 3:35, 3:38, 3:40, 3:50, 3:62, 3:73, 3:116, 3:133, 3:161, 3:172, 3:263, 3:326, 3:351

Economic, 1:102, 1:107, 1:109, 1:110, 1:112, 1:125, 1:171-1:172, 1:178, 1:197-1:198, 1:202, 1:283, 2:203, 2:233, 3:288, 3:297

Economy, 1:77, 1:85, 1:177, 1:178, 1:197, 1:198, 1:208, 2:196, 3:190, 3:261, 3:282, 3:285, 3:334

Eden, Garden of, 1:269, 2:113, 2:151, 3:16, 3:32, 3:67, 3:135, 3:153, 3:155, 3:160-3:161, 3:195

Education, 1:107-1:108, 1:112, 1:179, 1:183, 1:204, 1:208, 2:122, 2:200, 2:273, 3:127, 3:263, 3:281-3:282

Educational, 1:100, 1:101, 1:107, 1:110, 1:182, 1:204, 2:151, 2:200, 2:221, 2:222, 2:224, 2:233

Egypt, 1:11, 1:22, 1:42, 1:43, 1:232, 1:236, 1:263, 1:273, 2:5, 2:60, 2:74, 2:82, 2:84, 2:96, 2:101, 2:119, 2:126, 2:200, 3:72, 3:147, 3:162, 3:168, 3:179, 3:181-3:182, 3:193, 3:207-3:209, 3:216, 3:225, 3:253, 3:311

Egyptian, 1:18, 1:73, 1:228, 1:236, 1:263, 3:78, 3:168, 3:276, 3:313

Elders, 1:16, 1:48, 1:69-1:71, 1:142, 1:157, 1:175, 1:177, 1:180, 1:186, 1:195, 1:197, 1:199, 1:229, 1:234, 1:252, 1:256-1:257, 1:262, 1:272, 1:294, 2:vii, 2:3, 2:4, 2:13, 2:18-2:19, 2:37, 2:40, 2:73, 2:75, 2:79, 2:119, 2:121, 2:158, 2:163, 2:164, 2:170, 2:181, 2:254, 2:260, 2:261, 2:264, 2:278, 2:279, 3:62-3:63, 3:69, 3:85, 3:86, 3:103, 3:104, 3:111, 3:115, 3:128, 3:134, 3:148, 3:158, 3:227, 3:239, 3:267, 3:290, 3:300, 3:302

Elect, 1:viii, 1:4, 1:39, 1:43, 1:99, 1:110, 1:123, 1:127, 1:182, 1:223, 1:232, 1:262, 1:265, 1:272, 1:280, 1:281, 1:287, 1:290, 1:295, 2:197, 2:203, 2:228, 3:14, 3:20, 3:24, 3:37, 3:41, 3:49, 3:59, 3:113, 3:145, 3:150, 3:187, 3:208, 3:214

Index

Elements, 1:vii, 1:44, 1:51, 1:62, 1:65, 1:115, 1:157, 1:162, 1:239, 2:50, 2:55, 2:67, 3:23, 3:24, 3:45, 3:47, 3:48, 3:73, 3:129, 3:175, 3:192, 3:262, 3:336, 3:344

Eleventh hour, 1:34, 1:226, 1:243

Elias, 1:14, 1:16, 1:18, 1:140, 1:255, 1:259, 1:291, 1:292, 3:111, 3:158, 3:162, 3:169

Elijah, 1:2, 1:16, 1:21, 1:25, 1:124, 1:259, 2:2, 2:80, 3:162, 3:249

Emergencies, 1:95, 1:106

Emergency, 1:29, 1:97, 1:119, 1:176, 1:230, 2:179, 3:88, 3:116

Emotions, 2:184

Empire, 1:200, 1:201, 1:209, 1:225, 2:8, 2:82, 2:141, 2:265, 2:268, 2:273, 3:11, 3:156, 3:226, 3:236

Empires, 1:58, 1:59, 1:154, 1:156, 1:157, 1:227, 1:234, 2:1, 2:3, 2:9, 2:11, 2:13, 2:81, 2:265-2:267, 2:272, 2:273, 3:130, 3:217, 3:223, 3:227-3:228, 3:236

Endowment(s), 1:31, 1:79, 1:91, 1:273, 3:9, 3:66, 3:200, 3:296

Endure, 1:17, 1:31, 1:39, 1:40, 1:45, 1:46, 1:52, 1:56, 1:83, 1:102, 1:114, 1:172, 1:189, 1:190, 1:197, 1:207-1:208, 1:232, 2:151, 2:155-2:157, 2:164, 2:172-2:175, 2:183, 2:188, 2:192, 2:193, 2:223, 2:225, 2:233, 2:262, 3:3, 3:17, 3:23, 3:24, 3:26, 3:45, 3:88, 3:100, 3:121-3:122, 3:130, 3:133, 3:159, 3:228, 3:244, 3:245, 3:270, 3:350

England, 3:64, 3:223

Enmity, 1:100, 2:143, 2:215, 2:217, 3:55, 3:189, 3:202, 3:204, 3:205, 3:213

Enoch, 1:6, 1:10, 1:26, 1:31, 1:33, 1:48, 1:98, 1:113, 1:121, 1:230, 1:261, 2:5, 2:11, 2:39, 2:165, 2:259, 2:4, 3:22, 3:27, 3:45, 3:53, 3:58-3:59, 3:66, 3:68, 3:72-3:74, 3:77-3:78, 3:84, 3:91, 3:94-3:95, 3:113, 3:124, 3:131, 3:139, 3:143, 3:150, 3:152, 3:154, 3:155, 3:200, 3:201, 3:212-3:214, 3:225, 3:262, 3:264, 3:271, 3:278, 3:284, 3:286, 3:289, 3:316-3:317, 3:320, 3:331, 3:339
  city of Enoch, 1:20, 1:121, 2:4, 3:68, 3:95, 3:124, 3:138, 3:143, 3:200, 3:286, 3:313

Enos, 3:73, 3:152, 3:154, 3:164, 3:319

Ensign, 1:18, 1:20, 1:25, 1:27, 1:93, 1:98, 1:100, 1:102, 1:105, 1:109, 1:110, 1:115, 1:116, 1:184-1:186, 1:211, 1:212, 1:232, 1:263, 1:267, 1:270, 1:281, 1:294, 2:vii, 2:20, 2:21, 2:51, 2:140, 2:152, 2:153, 2:183-2:185, 2:201, 2:203, 2:204, 2:223, 2:225, 2:263, 2:274, 3:15, 3:62, 3:76-3:77, 3:93, 3:96, 3:105, 3:116, 3:168, 3:171, 3:181, 3:248, 3:252, 3:258

Ensign to the nations, 1:267, 1:270, 3:62, 3:171

Environment, 1:195, 1:281

Ephraim, 1:17, 1:18, 1:25, 1:244, 1:247, 1:248, 1:274, 1:282, 2:90, 2:124, 2:126, 3:92, 3:105, 3:112, 3:169, 3:170, 3:172, 3:177, 3:183, 3:194, 3:258, 3:266, 3:289

Error, 1:100, 2:42, 2:43, 2:86, 2:178, 2:215, 2:222, 2:224, 2:225, 2:273, 3:219, 3:277

Escape, 1:27, 1:30, 1:42, 1:44-1:45, 1:73, 1:77, 1:78, 1:84, 1:89, 1:91, 1:100, 1:102, 1:117, 1:129, 1:130, 1:137-1:139, 1:161, 1:176, 1:199, 1:209, 1:216, 1:225, 1:226, 1:255, 1:260, 1:266, 1:267, 1:272, 1:275, 1:283, 2:13, 2:20, 2:27, 2:38, 2:40, 2:50, 2:55, 2:61, 2:62, 2:108, 2:113, 2:138, 2:147, 2:169, 2:173-2:174, 2:181, 2:244, 3:32, 3:43, 3:44, 3:107, 3:278, 3:304, 3:306, 3:340, 3:346

Esdras, 3:172, 3:175, 3:178, 3:179

Esther, 1:73

Eternal life, 1:28, 1:88, 1:103, 1:116, 1:143, 1:176, 1:238, 1:241-1:243, 1:254, 1:276, 2:18, 2:36, 2:119, 2:169, 2:170, 2:192, 2:197, 3:50, 3:53, 3:67, 3:109, 3:172, 3:353

Eternity, 1:15-1:16, 1:18, 1:65, 1:141, 1:211, 1:250, 2:36, 2:94, 2:119, 2:169, 2:173, 2:212, 2:214, 2:258, 3:65, 3:119, 3:201, 3:221, 3:268, 3:278, 3:302, 3:330, 3:339

Ether, 1:136, 1:184, 1:185, 1:193, 1:200, 1:218, 2:77-2:78, 2:104, 2:151-2:152, 2:235, 3:48, 3:121, 3:143, 3:178, 3:185, 3:319, 3:343, 3:352

Ethiopia, 2:110, 2:139, 2:153, 3:77

Euphrates (River), 2:46, 2:57, 2:280, 2:283, 3:5, 3:178

Europe, 1:152, 1:175, 1:203, 1:224-1:225, 1:267, 1:270, 2:9, 2:15, 2:41, 2:74, 2:81, 2:82, 2:107, 2:141, 2:149, 2:265, 2:270-2:272, 3:4, 3:119, 3:155-3:157, 3:166, 3:173, 3:179, 3:229, 3:230, 3:241

Evil spirit(s), 2:209, 3:200, 3:349

Evolution, 1:101

Exaltation, 1:11, 1:28, 1:31, 1:57, 1:58, 1:89, 1:103, 1:104, 1:250, 2:vi, 2:160, 2:166, 2:225, 3:203, 3:276, 3:294, 3:295, 3:348

Example, 1:12, 1:38, 1:78, 1:101, 1:120, 1:147, 1:174, 1:199, 1:273, 2:131, 2:218, 2:246, 2:264, 3:242, 3:260, 3:320

Executive orders, 1:181

Exile, 2:183, 3:177

Expectations, 1:101, 1:122, 1:193, 3:3

Experience, 1:8, 1:14, 1:38, 1:56, 1:74, 1:78, 1:86, 1:94, 1:95, 1:120, 1:124, 1:125, 1:144, 1:179, 1:197, 1:219, 1:246, 2:6, 2:19, 2:21, 2:155, 2:159, 2:162, 2:171-2:172, 2:175, 2:182, 2:203, 2:217, 3:3, 3:27, 3:68, 3:73, 3:88, 3:120, 3:189, 3:193, 3:202, 3:204, 3:270, 3:280, 3:282, 3:286, 3:288

Experiences, 1:113, 3:247, 3:294

Extinct, 1:32

Extravagance, 1:viii, 1:39, 2:163, 3:284

Eye, 1:8, 1:25, 1:47, 1:56, 1:104, 1:109, 1:122, 1:148, 2:146, 2:161, 2:173, 2:201, 2:248, 3:viii, 3:2, 3:32, 3:45, 3:52, 3:58, 3:92, 3:100, 3:132, 3:143, 3:193, 3:196, 3:199, 3:203, 3:205-3:206, 3:209, 3:211-3:213, 3:286, 3:289, 3:303, 3:330, 3:344

Ezekiel, 1:8, 1:228, 1:265, 2:8, 2:25, 2:52, 2:98, 2:107-2:108, 2:111, 2:241, 2:271, 3:19, 3:32, 3:156, 3:253, 3:254

Facts, 1:82, 1:145, 1:186, 1:189, 1:203, 2:141, 2:182, 2:267, 3:316

Failure, 1:108, 1:175, 1:201, 2:55, 2:176, 2:181, 2:218, 3:202, 3:215

Faithfulness, 1:11, 1:32, 1:74, 1:85, 1:91, 1:139, 1:261, 1:291, 2:37, 3:105, 3:138, 3:143, 3:197, 3:219, 3:246, 3:252, 3:279

Falling away, 1:245, 2:206, 2:228

False doctrines, 1:22, 1:89, 1:100, 2:223, 2:226, 2:234, 2:244, 3:322

False educational ideas, 2:221

False idea (s), 1:28, 1:107

False messiah(s), 2:4, 2:103, 2:195, 2:207, 3:323

False prophet, 2:195, 2:197, 2:207, 2:283, 2:284, 3:47, 3:351

False prophets, 1:29, 1:225, 2:195-2:197, 2:200, 2:203, 2:205-2:208

Famine, 1:30, 1:34, 1:36, 1:37, 1:40, 1:44, 1:47, 1:58, 1:60, 1:64, 1:66, 1:71, 1:85, 1:87-1:88, 1:95, 1:105-1:106, 1:112, 1:118, 1:135, 1:141, 1:156, 1:230, 1:275, 1:276, 1:285, 1:288, 2:4, 2:1, 2:4, 2:10, 2:13, 2:14, 2:18, 2:29, 2:33, 2:34, 2:37, 2:39, 2:61, 2:64-2:65, 2:72, 2:82, 2:85, 2:96, 2:102, 2:133, 2:134, 2:137, 2:138, 2:147, 2:154, 2:188, 2:191, 2:243, 2:248, 2:253, 3:2, 3:38, 3:164, 3:165, 3:193, 3:238, 3:257

Famines, 1:40, 1:97, 1:116, 1:126, 1:150, 1:243, 1:254, 2:6, 2:21, 2:26, 2:27, 2:35, 2:36, 2:52, 3:3, 3:40, 3:42, 3:50

Fanaticism, 1:108, 2:227

Farm, 1:92, 3:127, 3:266, 3:268, 3:269, 3:283, 3:287, 3:289

Farmer(s), 2:64, 2:67, 2:142, 3:127

Farms, 1:30, 1:73, 1:85, 2:142, 3:61, 3:66, 3:78, 3:127

Fashion(s), 1:114, 3:128, 3:191, 3:261, 3:279

Fasting, 1:96, 2:55

FBI, 1:183

Feast, 1:75, 1:132, 2:82, 2:100, 3:19, 3:192, 3:209

Federal, 1:167, 1:171, 1:175, 1:178, 1:182, 1:187, 1:191-1:192, 2:134, 2:200

Feeling, 1:18, 1:98, 1:115, 1:118, 1:151, 1:152, 1:165, 1:229, 2:10, 2:141, 2:144, 2:151, 2:169, 2:174, 2:243, 2:246, 3:24, 3:26, 3:77, 3:84, 3:89, 3:118, 3:127, 3:174, 3:266, 3:271-3:274, 3:284

Feelings, 1:8, 1:18, 1:30, 1:31, 1:34, 1:41, 1:43, 1:57, 1:71, 1:160, 1:223, 1:279, 1:293, 2:17, 2:82, 2:89, 2:158, 2:167, 2:174, 2:177, 2:180, 2:181, 2:184, 2:200, 2:213, 3:63, 3:64, 3:68, 3:84, 3:141, 3:263, 3:265, 3:274, 3:277, 3:284

Fidelity, 1:93, 1:123, 2:157

Fig tree, 1:9, 1:20, 1:244, 2:vi, 2:2, 2:4, 2:23, 2:28, 2:278, 3:9, 3:11, 3:14, 3:37, 3:41, 3:42, 3:100, 3:165, 3:255

Parable of the fig tree, 1:120, 3:14, 3:37, 3:41

Figurative, 2:66, 2:285, 3:92, 3:333

Financial, 1:viii, 1:39, 1:97, 2:44, 2:163, 3:274, 3:283

Fire, 1:20, 1:21, 1:23, 1:28, 1:29, 1:40, 1:43, 1:51, 1:53, 1:55, 1:56, 1:64, 1:69, 1:75, 1:77, 1:78, 1:103, 1:117, 1:122, 1:128, 1:137-1:139, 1:143, 1:176, 1:217, 1:223, 1:224, 1:227, 1:254, 1:265, 1:269, 1:276, 1:288, 2:4, 2:vi, 2:vii, 2:1, 2:3, 2:8, 2:9, 2:13, 2:15, 2:16, 2:21, 2:22, 2:24-2:25, 2:27, 2:31, 2:33, 2:36, 2:37, 2:43, 2:46, 2:52-2:54, 2:57, 2:61-2:64, 2:70, 2:71, 2:88, 2:99, 2:101, 2:102, 2:105, 2:107, 2:110-2:111, 2:131, 2:138, 2:143, 2:145, 2:151, 2:152, 2:190, 2:191, 2:197, 2:200, 2:205, 2:229, 2:231, 2:237, 2:240, 2:241, 2:243, 2:244, 2:249, 2:252, 2:253, 2:261, 2:271, 2:272, 2:277, 2:280, 2:283-2:284, 3:1, 3:12, 3:14, 3:24, 3:29, 3:32, 3:33, 3:35, 3:41, 3:43, 3:49, 3:63, 3:68, 3:74, 3:78, 3:95, 3:96, 3:99, 3:102, 3:107, 3:109, 3:115, 3:118-3:121, 3:126, 3:154, 3:163, 3:175, 3:198-3:199, 3:201, 3:209, 3:262, 3:270, 3:334, 3:337, 3:343, 3:344, 3:347, 3:348, 3:350-3:351, 3:353, 3:355

flaming fire, 1:51, 1:127, 1:265, 1:269, 3:26, 3:63, 3:68, 3:78, 3:80, 3:95, 3:115, 3:118-3:119, 3:121, 3:154, 3:170, 3:199

Fires, 1:155, 1:260, 2:1, 2:2, 2:75, 3:63, 3:153, 3:328

First Presidency, 1:25, 1:28, 1:29, 1:84, 1:86, 1:87, 1:105, 1:152, 1:165, 1:174, 1:185, 1:262, 1:276, 1:278-1:280, 2:3, 2:74, 2:81, 2:95, 2:158, 2:159, 2:166-2:167, 2:175, 2:204, 2:213, 3:15, 3:21, 3:63, 3:83, 3:88, 3:89, 3:132, 3:155, 3:158, 3:217, 3:260, 3:261, 3:268

Fitness, 1:259, 1:260

Flag, 1:153, 1:157, 1:183, 2:92, 3:218

Flies, 2:18, 2:21, 2:35, 2:58

Flocks, 1:46, 1:70, 1:73, 1:134, 1:249, 2:45, 2:126, 2:127, 2:129, 2:130, 2:249, 3:71, 3:168, 3:169, 3:264

Flood, 1:vii, 1:4, 1:66, 1:95, 1:97, 1:99, 1:120, 1:126, 1:127, 1:133, 1:176, 1:276, 1:280, 1:283, 1:295, 2:9, 2:16, 2:17, 2:31, 2:51, 2:66, 2:67, 2:69, 2:76, 2:98, 2:112, 2:190, 2:247, 2:281, 3:3, 3:15, 3:59, 3:74, 3:78, 3:80, 3:113, 3:142, 3:150, 3:155, 3:161, 3:178, 3:187, 3:214, 3:306, 3:309, 3:314, 3:336

Floods, 1:64, 2:13, 2:14, 2:21

Follies, 1:42, 1:77, 3:87, 3:280, 3:281

Fooleries, 1:54, 3:194

Foot, 1:63, 1:153, 1:156-1:157, 1:159, 1:160, 1:234, 1:244, 1:271, 2:23, 2:25, 2:54, 2:73, 2:83, 2:88, 2:101, 2:105, 2:116, 2:129, 2:144, 2:153, 2:168, 3:8, 3:51, 3:124, 3:151, 3:209

Forbidden, 1:35, 1:215, 1:218, 2:43, 3:79, 3:86, 3:101, 3:104, 3:155, 3:201

Forehead, 2:234, 2:252, 2:261, 2:282, 2:284

Foreign, 1:33, 1:42, 1:45, 1:48, 1:75, 1:93, 1:148, 1:161, 1:162, 1:168, 1:170, 1:172, 1:175, 1:180, 1:192, 1:194, 1:201, 1:205, 1:257, 1:295, 2:3, 2:21, 2:48, 3:81, 3:111, 3:228, 3:236, 3:328

Foreknowledge, 1:81, 1:83, 1:100, 2:224

Forerunner, 1:15, 3:10, 3:12

Foreshadow, 2:50, 3:284

Forgive, 1:78, 2:78, 2:147, 2:167, 2:177, 2:180-2:181, 3:208

Fornication(s), 1:137, 1:243, 1:256, 1:268, 1:288, 2:7, 2:29, 2:175, 2:241, 2:243, 2:245, 2:253-2:255, 2:261, 2:269, 2:280, 2:284, 3:4, 3:7, 3:54, 3:55, 3:231

Fortifications, 1:93

Foundation, 1:viii, 1:3, 1:10, 1:16, 1:17, 1:25, 1:26, 1:32, 1:67, 1:73, 1:74, 1:81, 1:87, 1:111, 1:134, 1:140, 1:155, 1:158, 1:159, 1:161, 1:179, 1:186, 1:189, 1:204, 1:206, 1:212, 2:16, 2:17, 2:32, 2:121, 2:122, 2:147, 2:150, 2:156, 2:172, 2:176, 2:185, 2:215, 2:217, 2:229, 2:235, 2:252, 2:281, 2:284, 3:vi, 3:39, 3:68, 3:73, 3:108, 3:111, 3:128, 3:136, 3:200, 3:248, 3:275, 3:282, 3:285, 3:310, 3:313, 3:315, 3:316, 3:324, 3:325, 3:330, 3:350, 3:352

Founding Fathers, 1:167, 1:185, 1:189, 1:193, 1:196, 1:200

Fowls, 2:35, 2:52, 2:111, 2:137, 2:140, 2:207, 2:259, 2:260, 2:276, 2:285, 3:46, 3:47, 3:55, 3:211, 3:213, 3:347, 3:353

Franklin, Benjamin, 3:241

Free agency. *See* Agency.

Freedom, 1:49, 1:110-1:111, 1:114, 1:116, 1:134, 1:136, 1:155-1:157, 1:161, 1:163, 1:164, 1:166, 1:168-1:169, 1:172-1:173, 1:181, 1:184, 1:188, 1:190-1:191, 1:196, 1:198, 1:200, 1:202-1:204, 1:208, 1:209, 1:214, 1:217, 1:230, 2:43, 2:64, 2:124, 2:148, 2:151, 2:181, 2:216, 2:264, 3:83, 3:175, 3:234, 3:271, 3:281, 3:287, 3:299

Free-enterprise, 1:197

Friend, 1:70, 1:85, 2:157, 2:163, 2:212, 2:223, 3:26, 3:64, 3:235

Friends, 1:15, 1:30, 1:34, 1:37, 1:42, 1:44, 1:74, 1:86, 1:146, 1:153, 1:158, 1:182, 1:191, 1:214, 1:216-1:217, 1:245, 1:260, 1:268, 2:11, 2:15, 2:88, 2:89, 2:94, 2:99, 2:105, 2:108, 2:178, 2:179, 2:181, 2:184, 2:193, 2:262, 3:51, 3:191, 3:232, 3:274, 3:307, 3:318, 3:334

Friendship, 2:166, 3:275

Frogs, 2:207, 2:259, 2:283

Fruit, 1:22, 1:35, 1:128, 1:237, 1:287, 2:20, 2:61, 2:65, 2:74, 2:205, 2:248, 3:67, 3:101, 3:106, 3:108, 3:155, 3:162, 3:201, 3:208

Fruits, 1:128, 1:174, 1:208, 1:242, 2:18, 2:147, 2:176, 2:202, 2:208, 2:253, 3:10, 3:44, 3:55, 3:172, 3:190, 3:196, 3:255

Fuel, 1:92, 1:97, 1:106

Gabriel, 3:13, 3:162

Gad, 3:316

Gadianton robbers, 1:99, 1:116, 1:135, 1:136, 1:216, 2:21

Garden, 1:92, 1:98, 1:249, 1:269, 2:56, 2:113, 2:151, 3:16, 3:32, 3:67, 3:73, 3:97, 3:99, 3:153, 3:155, 3:160-3:161, 3:166, 3:169, 3:170, 3:195, 3:206, 3:271

Garden of Eden. *See* Eden, Garden of.

Gardens, 1:43, 1:98, 1:269, 3:62, 3:141

Garment, 1:271, 2:24, 2:277, 3:42, 3:78, 3:156, 3:163, 3:197, 3:209, 3:293, 3:301

Gates of hell, 1:83, 1:93

Gates of the New Jerusalem, 2:145, 3:133

Gathering of Israel. See Israel, gathering of.

Genealogy, 3:293, 3:303

General assembly, 1:4, 1:55, 1:266, 1:278, 3:23, 3:53, 3:90, 3:95, 3:117, 3:145

General conference, 1:167

Generosity, 2:181

Gentile, 1:60, 1:77, 1:80, 1:213, 1:228, 1:230, 1:234, 1:238, 1:242, 1:246, 1:247, 1:264, 1:265, 1:271, 1:274, 2:1, 2:40, 2:72, 2:83, 2:84, 2:89, 2:105, 2:126, 2:186, 3:vii, 3:71, 3:86, 3:101, 3:136, 3:167, 3:175, 3:278

Gentiles, 1:3, 1:18, 1:20-1:21, 1:30, 1:95, 1:142, 1:152, 1:156, 1:195, 1:199-1:200, 1:213, 1:218, 1:223, 1:225, 1:227, 1:231, 1:234, 1:236, 1:238, 1:240, 1:242, 1:247, 1:254-1:257, 1:260, 1:264, 1:266, 1:274, 1:288, 1:289, 2:1, 2:4, 2:11, 2:27, 2:31, 2:36, 2:37, 2:47, 2:48, 2:53, 2:72, 2:77, 2:83, 2:85, 2:87, 2:89-2:91, 2:102, 2:107, 2:114, 2:116, 2:120, 2:122, 2:127, 2:129, 2:131, 2:132, 2:153, 2:163, 2:229, 2:233, 2:239, 2:240, 2:246, 3:vii, 3:2-3:3, 3:7, 3:32, 3:43, 3:50, 3:70-3:72, 3:75, 3:85, 3:101, 3:103, 3:112, 3:117, 3:120, 3:130, 3:146, 3:173, 3:175, 3:182, 3:207, 3:221, 3:223, 3:249, 3:252, 3:256, 3:264, 3:301, 3:310, 3:323, 3:328-3:329

   fulness of the gentiles, 1:251, 2:89, 2:101, 2:104, 2:119, 3:184, 3:256

   time of the Gentiles, 1:3, 1:234, 1:235

Germany, 1:198, 2:8, 2:271, 3:64, 3:156, 3:175

Gibbon, Edward, 1:209

Gift, 1:26, 1:29, 1:56, 1:61, 1:80, 1:167, 1:244, 1:283, 2:89, 2:147, 2:208, 2:229, 2:270, 3:viii, 3:100, 3:300, 3:301, 3:305, 3:315, 3:316, 3:331

Gifts, 1:29, 1:52, 1:56, 1:103, 1:136, 1:242, 1:244, 1:245, 2:vi, 2:83, 2:85, 2:89-2:90, 2:101, 2:202, 2:209, 3:68, 3:155, 3:248, 3:296, 3:314

Giving, 1:1, 1:90, 1:94, 1:109, 1:126, 1:142, 2:14, 2:92, 2:94, 2:139, 2:172, 2:175, 2:196, 2:259, 2:260, 3:23, 3:36, 3:37, 3:41, 3:81, 3:157, 3:200, 3:217, 3:232, 3:259, 3:272, 3:283, 3:288, 3:295, 3:307, 3:309, 3:310, 3:313

Glass, 1:28-2:29, 2:135, 2:278, 3:192, 3:338, 3:353, 3:355

Globe, 1:51, 1:55, 1:161, 1:226, 1:227, 1:267, 2:7, 2:57, 2:67-2:68, 2:138, 2:270, 2:272, 3:3-3:4, 3:22, 3:24, 3:73, 3:74, 3:122, 3:123, 3:129, 3:155, 3:158, 3:173-3:174, 3:191, 3:195, 3:202, 3:310, 3:336-3:339, 3:343, 3:355

Goal(s), 1:192, 1:202, 1:204, 3:314

God, faith in, 1:30, 1:65, 1:69, 1:167, 1:189, 1:191, 1:193, 2:44

God, knowledge of, 1:38, 1:69, 1:115, 2:160, 3:126, 3:139, 3:196, 3:308, 3:312-3:313

God, love of, 1:90, 2:171, 2:188

God, manifestations of , 3:316

God, seal of the living, 1:140, 1:255, 1:291, 2:278, 3:185

God, wrath of , 1:62, 1:131, 1:142, 1:217, 1:223, 1:255, 2:37, 2:40, 2:57, 2:70, 2:78, 2:101, 2:189, 2:239, 2:261, 2:282, 3:202

Godhood, 1:97

Gog and Magog, 1:286, 2:107, 2:109-2:111, 2:247, 3:32, 3:333, 3:349, 3:351

Gold, 1:34, 1:37, 1:38, 1:53, 1:61, 1:114, 1:134, 1:208, 1:227, 1:245, 2:12, 2:21, 2:45, 2:53, 2:60, 2:66, 2:82, 2:84, 2:99, 2:100, 2:113, 2:203, 2:213, 2:248, 2:252-2:253, 2:264, 2:267, 2:268, 2:273, 2:274, 2:284, 3:17, 3:29, 3:30, 3:35, 3:47, 3:74, 3:75, 3:79-3:80, 3:123-3:124, 3:126, 3:130, 3:155, 3:221, 3:225, 3:230, 3:231, 3:233, 3:236, 3:264, 3:268, 3:310, 3:311

Gomer, 2:110

Government, 1:3, 1:33, 1:44, 1:49, 1:62-1:64, 1:86, 1:95, 1:99, 1:108, 1:145, 1:147, 1:149, 1:151, 1:153, 1:155, 1:157, 1:159, 1:161, 1:163, 1:165, 1:167, 1:169, 1:175, 1:178, 1:180, 1:183, 1:186-1:187, 1:189, 1:195, 1:197-1:199, 1:203, 1:205, 1:208, 1:216-1:217, 1:220, 1:230, 1:272, 1:273, 1:279, 2:3, 2:16, 2:33, 2:56, 2:64, 2:81, 2:82, 2:133-2:136, 2:139-2:140, 2:149, 2:152, 2:160, 2:161, 2:164, 2:167-2:168, 2:183, 2:193, 2:196, 2:199, 2:213, 2:219, 2:220, 2:234, 2:264, 2:268, 2:269, 3:vii, 3:viii, 3:7, 3:8, 3:11, 3:18, 3:62, 3:70, 3:84, 3:90, 3:117, 3:128, 3:134, 3:157, 3:205, 3:216, 3:218-3:219, 3:222, 3:224, 3:227, 3:230, 3:232, 3:234-3:235, 3:237-3:238, 3:240, 3:243, 3:246, 3:249, 3:250, 3:268, 3:271, 3:298, 3:342, 3:347

world government, 1:180, 1:203, 1:205, 1:209

Grace, 1:ix, 1:67, 1:121, 1:141, 1:168, 1:198, 2:81, 2:99, 2:127, 2:157, 3:106, 3:273, 3:302, 3:314, 3:315

Grain, 1:30, 1:36, 1:37, 1:43, 1:88, 2:63, 2:65, 3:262

Grand Council, 1:28, 3:153, 3:159-3:160

Grass, 2:28, 2:56, 2:127, 3:196

Gratitude, 1:100, 2:215, 3:vii

Grave, 1:29, 1:93, 1:178, 1:202, 1:270, 3:192, 3:338, 3:346

Graven images, 1:94, 2:34, 2:248

Graves, 1:8, 1:228, 1:263, 1:268, 2:5, 2:83, 2:101, 2:111, 3:5, 3:19, 3:25, 3:55, 3:58, 3:112, 3:120, 3:121, 3:150, 3:166, 3:189, 3:197, 3:202-3:203, 3:205, 3:269, 3:270, 3:341, 3:344, 3:353

Great and abominable church, 1:3, 1:131, 2:46, 2:101, 2:109, 2:116, 2:234, 2:237, 2:241, 2:247, 3:100, 3:101

Abominable church, 1:3, 1:131, 2:46, 2:101, 2:109, 2:116, 2:233, 2:236, 2:238, 2:241, 2:247, 3:100, 3:101, 3:322

Great and marvelous work, 1:78

Great Britain, 1:166, 1:246, 2:48, 2:66, 2:79, 2:92, 2:153

Greed, 1:116, 3:92, 3:291, 3:297, 3:299

Greek, 2:56, 2:280, 3:64

Growth, 1:6, 1:80, 1:124, 1:184, 2:176, 2:218, 2:220, 3:88, 3:151, 3:262, 3:285, 3:296

Guilt, 1:220, 2:19, 2:134

Gulf, 1:37, 1:134

Gulliver, 1:110, 1:147, 1:195

Guns, 1:29

Habit(s), 1:110, 1:275, 2:123, 2:215, 3:5, 3:87, 3:290

Hail, 1:55, 1:134, 1:223, 1:224, 2:vii, 2:3, 2:28, 2:53, 2:58, 2:63, 2:81, 2:133, 2:146, 2:163, 2:279, 3:26, 3:165, 3:170

Hailstorm, 2:35, 2:56

Hailstorms, 1:75, 1:254, 2:6, 2:15, 2:36, 2:67, 3:3, 3:50

Hamilton, Alexander, 1:198

Handmaidens, 1:21, 3:307

Harden, 1:90, 1:131, 1:133, 1:137, 1:255, 1:261, 1:290, 2:6, 2:17, 2:36, 2:77, 2:130, 2:189, 2:190, 2:237, 3:3, 3:292, 3:327, 3:333

Hardness of heart, 1:123, 2:57, 3:317, 3:329

Harlot(s), 1:89, 1:243, 2:40, 2:46, 2:101, 2:113, 2:233-2:235, 2:238-2:239, 2:244, 2:246, 2:251, 2:252, 2:284, 3:322

Harvest, 1:4, 1:231, 1:278, 1:292, 2:2, 2:3, 2:63, 2:66, 2:114, 2:138-2:140, 2:231, 2:250, 3:1, 3:2, 3:9, 3:37, 3:108, 3:333

Hate, 1:171, 2:165, 2:169, 2:177, 2:180, 2:181, 2:187-2:188, 2:193, 2:205, 2:237, 2:246, 2:252, 2:284, 3:50, 3:149

Hatred, 1:162, 2:19, 2:42, 2:143, 2:159, 2:169, 2:172, 2:173, 2:181, 2:214

Head, 1:3, 1:150, 1:192, 1:216, 1:269, 1:279, 2:79, 2:123, 2:141, 2:153, 2:173, 2:181, 2:261, 2:266, 2:268-2:270, 2:273, 2:277, 3:7, 3:46, 3:97, 3:127, 3:153-3:154, 3:156, 3:157, 3:163, 3:164, 3:175, 3:199, 3:209, 3:216, 3:218, 3:225-3:227, 3:229-3:231, 3:234, 3:236, 3:247, 3:286, 3:290, 3:346

Heal, 1:115, 1:224, 2:98, 2:225, 3:43, 3:98, 3:327

Health, 1:46-1:46, 3:71, 3:98, 3:199-3:200

Heat, 1:51, 1:53, 1:62, 1:101, 1:120, 1:122, 1:123, 1:127, 1:198, 2:38, 2:283, 3:24, 3:55, 3:63, 3:95, 3:192, 3:213, 3:338, 3:340, 3:343

Heathen, 1:228, 1:256, 1:282, 1:286, 2:7-2:9, 2:34, 2:56, 2:60, 2:87, 2:100, 2:110, 2:111, 2:114, 2:137, 2:140-2:142, 2:262, 3:23, 3:51, 3:178, 3:190, 3:192, 3:200, 3:202, 3:208, 3:212, 3:232, 3:254, 3:307

Heathen nations, 1:228, 1:256, 2:7-2:9, 2:56, 2:262, 3:19, 3:23, 3:51, 3:190, 3:200, 3:212, 3:232, 3:307

Heaven, new, 3:13, 3:15, 3:48, 3:147, 3:185, 3:210, 3:340-3:341, 3:344, 3:349, 3:351-3:353

Heavenly, 1:59, 1:65, 1:70, 1:105, 1:145, 1:152, 1:186, 1:192, 1:195, 1:201, 1:265, 1:271, 1:275, 2:v, 2:1, 2:8, 2:58, 2:86, 2:168, 2:196, 2:197, 2:226, 2:257, 3:v-3:vi, 3:20, 3:24, 3:27, 3:53, 3:67, 3:74, 3:90, 3:129, 3:133, 3:152, 3:161, 3:240, 3:242, 3:248, 3:264-3:266, 3:283, 3:284, 3:300, 3:302, 3:311, 3:318, 3:344, 3:345, 3:349

Heavenly Father, 1:59, 1:145, 1:275, 2:v, 2:58, 2:168, 3:v, 3:67, 3:133, 3:161, 3:240, 3:242, 3:284

Hebrew, 2:108, 2:116, 2:257, 2:280, 2:283, 3:160

Heir, 1:28, 1:280, 2:119, 2:235, 3:2, 3:235, 3:250, 3:259, 3:282

Heirs, 2:132, 3:90, 3:105, 3:282, 3:299, 3:301, 3:315

Hell, 1:29, 1:67, 1:71, 1:83, 1:85, 1:93, 1:96, 1:131-1:133, 1:137, 1:152, 1:197, 1:215, 1:224, 1:231, 1:262, 2:vi, 2:30, 2:72, 2:162, 2:168, 2:169, 2:186, 2:187, 2:195, 2:238, 3:65, 3:199, 3:202, 3:219, 3:251, 3:263, 3:304, 3:318, 3:327, 3:346, 3:354

Hemisphere, 1:152, 1:204, 1:238, 2:9, 2:91, 2:139, 2:220, 2:269, 2:272, 3:3, 3:74, 3:76, 3:87, 3:117, 3:118, 3:136, 3:157, 3:161, 3:171, 3:174, 3:177, 3:338

Heresies, 2:173, 2:203, 2:206

Heresy, 2:226

Heritage, 1:191, 1:293, 2:38, 2:113, 2:170, 2:184, 3:110

Heroes, 1:10

Hide, 1:24, 1:61, 1:249, 1:256, 2:28, 2:38, 2:97, 2:130, 2:133, 2:196, 2:278, 3:23-3:24, 3:26, 3:46, 3:58, 3:324, 3:325

Highway(s), 1:92, 1:99, 1:236, 1:236, 1:263, 1:269, 3:10, 3:31, 3:57, 3:167-3:168, 3:171-3:172, 3:179, 3:182, 3:186

Hitler, 1:199

Holiness, 1:59, 1:93, 1:232, 2:117, 2:199, 2:209, 3:43, 3:105, 3:113, 3:181, 3:209

Holocaust, 1:185, 2:44

Holy Ghost, 1:31, 1:52, 1:53, 1:55-1:56, 1:61, 1:65, 1:66, 1:68, 1:94, 1:132, 1:136, 1:193, 1:227, 1:230, 1:244, 1:245, 1:283, 2:vii, 2:4, 2:89, 2:130, 2:131, 2:142, 2:171, 2:174, 2:212, 2:214, 2:219, 2:220, 2:226, 2:270, 3:viii, 3:27, 3:100, 3:126, 3:164, 3:171, 3:184, 3:201, 3:305, 3:315, 3:316, 3:335, 3:336

Holy places, 1:67, 1:71, 1:93, 1:102, 1:104, 1:141, 1:224, 1:255, 1:281, 1:292, 2:36, 2:95, 2:221, 3:17, 3:54, 3:108, 3:124, 3:297

Index

Home, 1:viii, 1:49, 1:79, 1:86, 1:92, 1:94, 1:96, 1:106, 1:107, 1:109, 1:115, 1:142, 1:159, 1:189, 1:197, 1:199, 1:201, 1:209, 1:223, 1:224, 1:234, 1:240, 1:243, 1:253, 1:262, 1:289, 2:vii, 2:3-2:4, 2:89, 2:102, 2:104, 2:130, 2:134, 2:164, 2:167, 2:175, 2:201, 2:217, 2:222, 3:9, 3:117, 3:171, 3:185, 3:195, 3:261, 3:278, 3:279, 3:292, 3:326, 3:334

Homes, 1:101, 1:102, 1:109-1:110, 1:189, 1:241, 1:268, 1:277, 2:42-2:43, 2:47, 2:136, 2:159, 2:183, 3:116, 3:117, 3:127-3:128, 3:132

Homosexuality, 1:107

Honest, 1:vii-1:7, 1:50, 1:60, 1:73, 1:99, 1:154, 1:156, 1:162, 1:173, 1:185, 1:193, 1:196, 1:219, 1:229, 1:230, 1:261, 2:107, 2:138, 2:143, 2:174, 2:216, 2:218, 3:84, 3:130, 3:242, 3:243, 3:272-3:274, 3:282, 3:288, 3:295

Honesty, 1:88, 1:151, 1:153, 1:189, 2:9, 3:69, 3:84

Honor, 1:27, 1:59, 1:61, 1:72, 1:74, 1:84, 1:89, 1:126, 1:148, 1:195, 1:254, 2:36, 2:91, 2:168, 2:177, 2:260, 3:50, 3:89, 3:107, 3:116, 3:132, 3:140, 3:159, 3:177, 3:196, 3:257, 3:279, 3:280, 3:288, 3:325, 3:330, 3:347

Hope, 1:50, 1:63, 1:70, 1:81, 1:86, 1:92, 1:95, 1:108, 1:110, 1:123, 1:124, 1:165, 1:178, 1:204, 1:207, 1:269, 2:43, 2:52, 2:73, 2:92, 2:93, 2:98, 2:114, 2:122, 2:156-2:157, 2:161, 2:168, 2:176, 2:208, 2:214, 3:33, 3:45, 3:119, 3:265

Horn, 1:240, 2:47, 2:129, 2:187, 2:265, 2:277, 3:159, 3:163

Horne, M. Isabella, 3:189

Horns, 1:274, 2:46, 2:237, 2:258, 2:259, 2:274, 2:277, 2:278, 2:281

Horse, 1:40, 2:60, 2:100, 2:107, 2:207, 2:233, 2:284, 3:47, 3:285, 3:289

Horses, 1:52, 1:261, 2:34, 2:57, 2:87, 2:107, 2:110, 2:112, 2:113, 2:123, 2:137, 2:253, 3:32, 3:209, 3:265, 3:268, 3:273

House of Israel. *See* Israel, house of.

Human, 1:3, 1:59, 1:61, 1:72, 1:84, 1:91, 1:103, 1:104, 1:108, 1:124, 1:155, 1:161, 1:165, 1:168, 1:170, 1:173, 1:179, 1:203, 1:209, 1:232, 1:272, 1:278, 2:13-2:14, 2:17-2:18, 2:20, 2:43, 2:59, 2:66, 2:143, 2:145, 2:147, 2:166, 2:168, 2:171, 2:176, 2:177, 2:182, 2:184, 2:211, 2:244, 2:260, 2:261, 2:265, 2:266, 2:270, 3:vi, 3:22, 3:27, 3:141, 3:157-3:158, 3:161, 3:162, 3:204, 3:220, 3:226, 3:228, 3:230, 3:233, 3:238, 3:242, 3:262, 3:281, 3:309, 3:333, 3:340, 3:345

Humanism, 1:101

Humanity, 1:58, 1:73, 1:89, 1:152, 1:155-1:157, 1:168, 1:175, 1:186, 1:244, 2:10, 2:19, 2:41, 2:120, 2:150, 2:168, 3:273

Humble, 1:24, 1:70, 1:102, 1:118, 1:126, 1:137, 1:156, 1:173, 1:216, 2:20, 2:55, 2:131, 2:160, 2:172, 2:190, 2:223, 2:224, 3:84, 3:123, 3:124, 3:141, 3:288, 3:304

Humility, 1:63, 1:223, 2:119, 2:190, 2:218, 2:219, 3:290, 3:294

Humor, 1:175

Hunger, 1:37, 2:65, 2:158

Hurricane, 1:95

Husband(s), 1:145, 2:84, 2:160, 2:230, 3:138, 3:146, 3:210, 3:341, 3:347

Hutchins, Dr. Robert Maynard, 2:44

Hypocrisy, 1:253, 2:128, 2:140, 2:141, 2:166, 2:216

Hypocrites, 1:73, 1:79, 1:80, 1:143, 2:154, 2:179, 2:192, 2:196, 2:209, 2:230, 3:36, 3:39, 3:96

Idea, 1:28, 1:75, 1:89, 1:193, 1:202, 1:205, 1:268, 2:56, 2:58, 2:136, 2:172, 2:182, 3:5, 3:10, 3:88, 3:131, 3:176, 3:190, 3:191, 3:193-3:195, 3:203, 3:309

Ideal, 1:176

Ideas, 1:6, 1:6, 1:197, 1:212, 2:156, 2:200, 2:221, 2:245, 2:273, 3:124, 3:234, 3:236, 3:262, 3:286, 3:297, 3:318

Idleness, 3:202, 3:297, 3:299

Idol(s), 2:53, 2:60, 2:97, 2:230, 2:254, 2:280, 3:29, 3:232, 3:254, 3:307

Idolaters, 3:336, 3:351

Idolatry, 2:131

Idumea, 1:136, 2:23

Ignorance, 1:135, 1:160, 2:123, 2:166, 2:171, 2:176, 3:159, 3:199, 3:224, 3:262, 3:279, 3:286, 3:327, 3:337

Image, 1:203, 2:29, 2:41, 2:140-2:141, 2:207, 2:259, 2:266, 2:268, 2:270, 2:273-2:274, 2:283-2:285, 3:47, 3:129, 3:155,

3:209, 3:225-3:226, 3:229, 3:232-3:233, 3:236, 3:254, 3:279, 3:346

Immorality, 1:72, 1:99, 1:102, 1:104, 1:205, 2:15, 2:20, 2:21, 2:218

Immortal, 1:5, 1:271, 2:87, 3:82, 3:122, 3:125, 3:139, 3:155, 3:189, 3:192, 3:193, 3:196, 3:202, 3:206, 3:225, 3:250, 3:305, 3:331, 3:336, 3:338, 3:342, 3:344, 3:353, 3:355

Immortal beings, 1:271, 3:82, 3:139, 3:157, 3:195-3:196, 3:198, 3:206, 3:250, 3:338

Immortality, 1:31, 1:226, 2:18, 3:26, 3:196, 3:205-3:206, 3:336, 3:337, 3:347

Import, 1:259, 3:261

Importations, 1:45

Importing, 1:45

Inactive, 2:222

Incense, 2:28

Income, 1:96, 1:194, 1:197, 3:263-3:264, 3:267, 3:295

Independence, Missouri, 1:33, 1:105, 1:156, 1:171, 1:173, 1:175, 1:178, 1:179, 1:188, 1:192-1:193, 1:207-1:209, 2:124, 2:145, 3:104, 3:115, 3:128, 3:136, 3:142, 3:148, 3:153, 3:298

Independent, 1:33, 1:66, 1:104-1:106, 1:140, 1:159, 1:193, 1:194, 1:208, 1:209, 2:63, 2:218, 2:261, 3:74, 3:177, 3:179, 3:218, 3:224, 3:234, 3:240, 3:241, 3:262, 3:288, 3:292, 3:302

Independent American, 1:193

India, 1:230

Indian(s), 1:35, 2:88, 2:120-2:121, 2:125, 3:12, 3:127, 3:142, 3:272

Indoctrination, 2:151

Indulgence, 1:200

Industry, 1:45, 1:177, 3:265, 3:279, 3:281

Inequality, 3:263-3:264, 3:292

Infant, 3:193, 3:201, 3:208, 3:213, 3:283

Infidelity, 2:viii, 2:89

Inflation, 1:177, 1:181, 1:207

Influence, 1:16, 1:66, 1:79, 1:82, 1:83, 1:145, 1:165, 1:186, 1:190, 1:193, 1:206-1:208, 1:211, 1:220, 1:229, 1:272, 1:279, 2:11, 2:12, 2:74, 2:174-2:176, 2:179, 2:201, 2:215, 2:226, 2:262, 3:22, 3:66, 3:84, 3:152, 3:200, 3:218, 3:220, 3:234, 3:235, 3:242, 3:273, 3:284

Information, 1:107, 1:149, 1:178, 1:182, 1:239, 2:v, 2:135, 3:v, 3:11, 3:93, 3:132, 3:177, 3:198, 3:203, 3:267, 3:309, 3:336

Inheritance, 1:49, 1:63, 1:138, 1:141, 1:191, 1:213, 1:253, 1:271, 1:277, 1:281, 1:283, 1:288-1:289, 2:78, 2:80, 2:96, 2:102, 2:104, 2:119, 2:124, 2:131, 2:178, 2:179, 2:231, 2:239, 2:274, 3:52, 3:55, 3:76, 3:79, 3:83, 3:86, 3:89, 3:93, 3:103-3:105, 3:115, 3:134, 3:148, 3:166, 3:168, 3:182-3:183, 3:197, 3:201, 3:212, 3:237, 3:248, 3:250, 3:260, 3:263, 3:265, 3:266, 3:275-3:276, 3:289-3:290, 3:292-3:293, 3:296, 3:301, 3:303, 3:347, 3:352, 3:353

Inheritances, 1:151, 1:232, 1:293, 2:121, 2:199, 3:78, 3:79, 3:92, 3:107, 3:109, 3:117, 3:120, 3:142, 3:263, 3:268, 3:269, 3:280, 3:283, 3:288, 3:291, 3:293, 3:296, 3:303

Iniquity, 1:23-1:24, 1:52, 1:58, 1:65, 1:90, 1:93, 1:99, 1:113, 1:116, 1:128, 1:135-1:136, 1:138, 1:145, 1:151, 1:153, 1:159, 1:196, 1:206, 1:217, 1:224, 1:237, 1:246, 1:254, 1:261, 1:264, 1:275, 1:3, 2:9, 2:10, 2:12, 2:18, 2:19, 2:23, 2:24, 2:31, 2:53, 2:66, 2:74, 2:88, 2:97, 2:105, 2:146, 2:147, 2:151, 2:155, 2:181-2:182, 2:190, 2:191, 2:205, 2:206, 2:211, 2:228, 2:229, 2:234, 2:239, 2:246, 2:247, 2:250, 3:10, 3:30, 3:37, 3:38, 3:40, 3:47, 3:50, 3:51, 3:66, 3:80, 3:86, 3:91, 3:98, 3:99, 3:126, 3:141, 3:175, 3:184, 3:208, 3:255, 3:280, 3:292, 3:293, 3:312, 3:328, 3:329, 3:334

Initiative, 1:188, 3:296

Insects, 1:43, 3:262

Inspiration, 1:7, 1:56, 1:150, 1:158, 1:169, 1:194, 1:211, 1:268, 2:90, 2:176, 2:199, 2:215, 2:0, 3:73, 3:142, 3:171, 3:275

Inspired Version, 3:319

Instruct, 2:122, 3:17, 3:198, 3:203, 3:240, 3:309

Instruction, 1:vii, 1:77, 1:112, 1:126, 1:199, 2:viii, 2:1, 2:25, 2:133, 2:152, 2:225, 2:234, 2:0, 3:63, 3:70, 3:117, 3:173,

316

3:195, 3:232, 3:307, 3:310, 3:314, 3:316, 3:317, 3:340

Insurance, 3:282

Integrity, 1:viii, 1:59, 1:151, 1:156, 1:160, 1:167, 2:4, 2:17, 2:56, 2:135, 2:136, 2:226, 3:69, 3:84, 3:143

Intellectual, 3:83

Intelligence, 1:61, 1:76, 2:v, 2:2, 2:158, 2:161, 2:172, 2:212, 2:214, 3:v, 3:1, 3:65, 3:66, 3:91, 3:190, 3:192, 3:196, 3:271, 3:272, 3:277, 3:305, 3:310, 3:312, 3:314

Intelligences, 3:204, 3:238

Intention(s), 1:77, 1:181, 2:146, 2:179, 3:135, 3:286, 3:293, 3:243

Interpret, 2:124, 2:244, 2:274

Interpretation(s), 1:68, 2:221-2, 2:235, 2:236, 2:257-2:258, 2:260, 2:264, 2:267, 2:273, 2:277, 3:91, 3:225, 3:226, 3:231, 3:236, 3:237, 3:294, 3:329

Intervene, 1:89, 1:99, 2:56, 3:5, 3:225

Intervention, 1:159, 1:183

Invade, 2:91

Invasion, 1:168, 1:194

Invention, 2:244, 3:71

Investment, 1:201

Iron rod, 1:120, 2:222, 3:26

Isaac, 1:31, 1:136, 1:274, 1:278, 1:281, 2:125, 3:22, 3:72, 3:121, 3:162, 3:171, 3:225, 3:270

Isaiah, 1:53, 1:54, 1:56, 1:63, 1:240, 1:267, 1:275, 1:284-1:285, 2:7, 2:8, 2:20, 2:23-2:24, 2:50, 2:55, 2:68, 2:72, 2:86, 2:96, 2:107, 2:108, 2:127, 2:138, 2:146, 2:153, 2:164, 2:228, 2:248, 2:271, 2:275, 3:v, 3:10, 3:16, 3:17, 3:23, 3:26, 3:30, 3:69-3:71, 3:73, 3:75, 3:80, 3:82, 3:85, 3:96, 3:98, 3:103, 3:115, 3:118, 3:120, 3:121, 3:124, 3:126, 3:129, 3:130, 3:132, 3:136, 3:156, 3:168, 3:170-3:171, 3:182, 3:193, 3:195, 3:199, 3:201-3:203, 3:207, 3:208, 3:211, 3:245, 3:258, 3:263, 3:290, 3:307, 3:308, 3:316, 3:320, 3:340, 3:350

Ishmael, 2:124

Islam, 1:119, 1:232

Isle of Patmos, 1:248, 1:261, 1:268, 3:169, 3:313

Israel, Children of, 1:43, 1:64, 1:84, 1:87, 1:130, 1:230, 1:251, 1:285, 1:286, 2:11, 2:52, 2:55, 2:67, 2:84, 2:98, 2:114, 2:246, 2:279, 3:33, 3:48, 3:119, 3:122, 3:124, 3:133, 3:176, 3:182, 3:216, 3:219, 3:232, 3:249, 3:253-3:254, 3:269, 3:276, 3:307, 3:351

Gathering of Israel, 1:3, 1:272, 1:274, 1:281-1:283, 1:286, 1:288, 1:294, 1:295, 2:79, 2:95, 3:93, 3:113, 3:150, 3:165, 3:169, 3:176, 3:178, 3:186, 3:187, 3:214

Israel, House of, 1:8, 1:73, 1:239, 1:242, 1:245, 1:249, 1:252-1:254, 1:262, 1:265-1:266, 1:274, 1:282, 1:289, 2:1, 2:15, 2:25, 2:34, 2:46, 2:79, 2:84, 2:87, 2:96-2:97, 2:101, 2:104, 2:111, 2:116, 2:119, 2:123-2:124, 2:126, 2:130-2:131, 2:189, 2:236, 2:238-2:239, 3:viii, 3:13, 3:49, 3:75, 3:78, 3:99, 3:100, 3:103, 3:146-3:147, 3:166-3:167, 3:169, 3:172, 3:174, 3:178, 3:183, 3:250, 3:301, 3:310, 3:322, 3:323, 3:325-3:326, 3:352

Issue, 1:173, 1:174, 1:177, 1:186, 1:190, 1:197, 1:211, 1:273, 2:16, 2:42, 2:56, 2:57, 2:90, 2:98, 2:233, 3:72, 3:136, 3:215, 3:218, 3:220, 3:238

Issues, 1:27, 1:100, 1:116, 1:188, 1:198, 1:199

Jacob, 1:15, 1:127, 1:136, 1:217, 1:264, 1:267, 1:270, 1:275, 1:281, 1:284, 1:288, 1:289, 1:293, 1:3, 2:22, 2:33, 2:44, 2:83-2:85, 2:94, 2:96-2:97, 2:102-2:104, 2:119-2:120, 2:122, 2:125, 2:127, 2:130, 2:158, 2:189, 3:11, 3:17, 3:22, 3:29, 3:47, 3:64, 3:65, 3:72, 3:95, 3:103, 3:110, 3:121, 3:133, 3:162, 3:174, 3:185, 3:225, 3:235, 3:249-3:250, 3:252, 3:254-3:256, 3:270, 3:320, 3:328

Jacob, Remnant of, 1:289, 1:3, 2:119, 2:120, 2:122, 2:125, 2:129-2:130, 2:132, 3:117, 3:135, 3:136, 3:146, 3:185

Jared, brother of. *See* Brother of Jared.

Jaredites, 1:49, 1:178, 1:196, 2:4, 2:136, 2:152, 3:161

Jefferson, Thomas, 1:178, 1:207, 3:241

Jehoshaphat, 2:85, 2:107, 2:113, 2:114

Jehovah, 1:vii, 1:59, 1:186, 1:248, 1:265, 2:94, 2:136, 2:143, 2:165, 3:6, 3:79, 3:131, 3:153, 3:154, 3:157, 3:251, 3:319

Jeremiah, 1:8, 1:8, 1:66, 1:127, 1:128, 1:241, 1:272-1:274, 1:285, 2:24, 2:45, 2:108, 2:248, 2:250, 3:98, 3:168-3:170, 3:176, 3:182, 3:208, 3:253, 3:311, 3:320

Jerusalem, 1:viii, 1:66, 1:127, 1:128, 1:138, 1:158, 1:213, 1:228, 1:230, 1:234-1:235, 1:238, 1:239, 1:246, 1:254, 1:264, 1:266, 1:270, 1:274, 1:276, 1:280, 1:281, 1:284, 1:295, 1:3, 2:6, 2:7, 2:25, 2:27, 2:39, 2:40, 2:48, 2:50, 2:58, 2:60, 2:79, 2:82, 2:86, 2:88, 2:90, 2:93, 2:96, 2:98, 2:101, 2:103, 2:108, 2:112, 2:115, 2:117, 2:121-2:122, 2:124-2:127, 2:129-2:130, 2:135, 2:145, 2:151, 2:205, 2:250, 2:251, 3:vii, 3:viii, 3:5, 3:6, 3:11-3:12, 3:16, 3:19, 3:21, 3:22, 3:24, 3:30, 3:31, 3:33-3:35, 3:47, 3:49, 3:58, 3:59, 3:66, 3:68, 3:75-3:77, 3:87, 3:90, 3:93, 3:95, 3:102-3:103, 3:106, 3:113, 3:115, 3:122, 3:124, 3:127, 3:131, 3:133, 3:135, 3:142, 3:146, 3:150, 3:160, 3:166, 3:180, 3:186-3:187, 3:193-3:194, 3:196, 3:210, 3:218, 3:228, 3:232, 3:237, 3:248-3:253, 3:267, 3:271, 3:274, 3:275, 3:290, 3:300, 3:305, 3:307, 3:310-3:312, 3:338, 3:341, 3:343, 3:344, 3:347-3:349, 3:351-3:352

Jesse, 1:18, 2:96, 3:207, 3:258
    root of Jesse, 1:18, 1:18, 1:294, 2:96, 3:207, 3:252, 3:258
    stem of Jesse, 1:25, 1:25, 3:252

Jew, 1:213, 1:230, 1:274, 2:88-2:90, 2:93, 2:94, 2:99, 2:105, 2:169, 3:67, 3:86, 3:101, 3:136, 3:322

Jews, 1:viii, 1:80, 1:228, 1:229, 1:231, 1:236-1:238, 1:240, 1:242, 1:244, 1:252, 1:253, 1:256, 1:257, 1:261, 1:264, 1:266, 1:270, 1:273, 1:274, 1:276, 1:282, 1:295, 2:4, 2:6, 2:7, 2:31, 2:40, 2:53, 2:66, 2:84, 2:88, 2:90, 2:102, 2:107-2:108, 2:114, 2:115, 2:120, 2:127, 2:158, 2:168, 2:182, 2:200, 2:205, 2:208, 2:233, 2:236, 2:237, 2:246, 3:vi-3:viii, 3:2, 3:3, 3:5, 3:7-3:9, 3:19, 3:21, 3:34, 3:35, 3:51, 3:111, 3:121, 3:127, 3:135, 3:166-3:167, 3:174, 3:178, 3:183, 3:217, 3:237, 3:240, 3:256, 3:305, 3:307-3:308, 3:319, 3:333

Job, 1:98, 1:115, 1:182, 1:191

John the Baptist, 1:11-3:11, 3:27, 3:162, 3:245, 3:311

John the Revelator, 1:53, 1:61, 1:108, 1:226, 2:85, 2:157, 2:200, 2:223, 2:234, 2:257, 2:262, 2:269, 3:2, 3:80, 3:169, 3:193, 3:196, 3:228, 3:231, 3:342

Jonah, 1:195

Josephus, 1:234

Joshua, 3:254, 3:255

Judah, 1:22, 1:246, 1:249, 1:259, 1:263, 1:266, 1:274, 1:280, 1:282, 1:284-1:286, 1:295, 2:52, 2:79, 2:84, 2:85, 2:92, 2:95-2:96, 2:105, 2:113, 2:114, 2:122, 2:274, 3:vii, 3:8, 3:11, 3:33-3:35, 3:100, 3:112, 3:135, 3:166, 3:168, 3:169, 3:172, 3:176, 3:180-3:182, 3:207, 3:237, 3:250, 3:251, 3:253

Judas, 2:72, 2:181, 2:201, 2:212

Judge, 1:20, 1:101, 1:216, 1:272, 2:87, 2:103, 2:114, 2:134, 2:154, 2:158, 2:192, 2:207, 2:214, 3:46, 3:49, 3:95, 3:105, 3:154, 3:190, 3:192, 3:193, 3:196-3:197, 3:207, 3:216, 3:245, 3:259, 3:264, 3:266, 3:282, 3:323, 3:326, 3:337

Judges, 1:148, 1:214, 2:32-2:33, 3:70, 3:130, 3:197, 3:250

Judging, 1:10, 1:68, 2:87, 2:182, 2:217, 3:19, 3:196, 3:197, 3:246, 3:255, 3:352

Just men made perfect, 3:6, 3:53

Justice, 1:88, 1:112, 1:131, 1:134, 1:150, 1:154, 1:168, 1:210, 1:214-1:216, 1:218, 1:288, 2:17, 2:34, 2:47, 2:64, 2:77, 2:131, 2:133, 2:143, 2:152, 2:156, 3:142, 3:153, 3:201, 3:235, 3:246, 3:251-3:253

Justification, 1:205, 2:49

Justify, 1:24, 1:99, 1:113, 1:192, 1:195, 1:219, 1:220, 1:227, 2:44, 2:49, 2:162, 2:211, 2:222, 3:177

Juvenile, 2:16

Kansas, 2:64, 3:123, 3:126-3:128, 3:142, 3:263

Key, 1:vi, 1:48, 1:80, 1:104, 1:113, 1:180, 2:56, 2:195, 2:215, 2:259, 2:279, 2:285, 3:117, 3:209, 3:315, 3:350

Kindness, 1:96, 2:181, 2:234, 3:115, 3:121, 3:153, 3:260

King, 1:9, 1:48, 1:114, 1:170, 1:213-1:214, 1:216, 1:217, 1:224, 1:228, 1:232, 1:271, 1:274, 1:285-1:286, 2:29, 2:33, 2:34, 2:44-2:45, 2:52, 2:56, 2:76, 2:82, 2:87, 2:89, 2:92, 2:95, 2:105, 2:114, 2:162, 2:228, 2:248, 2:251, 2:252, 2:261, 2:264, 2:269, 2:273-2:274, 2:276, 2:280, 2:284, 2:3, 3:7-3:8, 3:18-3:20, 3:31,

3:39, 3:46, 3:51, 3:52, 3:72, 3:80, 3:120, 3:160, 3:172, 3:176, 3:192, 3:205, 3:212, 3:215-3:217, 3:219, 3:223, 3:227-3:229, 3:231, 3:234, 3:235, 3:238-3:240, 3:245, 3:247, 3:249, 3:251, 3:254, 3:257, 3:259, 3:307, 3:319, 3:333, 3:340

King James Version, 3:319, 3:333

Kingdom of heaven, 1:4, 1:129, 1:133, 1:271, 1:286, 2:187, 2:191, 2:225, 2:257, 2:258, 3:27, 3:62, 3:173, 3:216, 3:218, 3:235, 3:237, 3:239, 3:240, 3:245, 3:247, 3:257, 3:295

Kingdoms of glory, 3:318

Kingdoms of the world, 1:75, 2:15, 2:59, 2:260, 2:265, 2:266, 3:218, 3:224, 3:225, 3:229, 3:240, 3:258

Kings, 1:3, 1:124, 1:213, 1:251, 1:273, 1:274, 1:288, 2:28, 2:29, 2:82, 2:103, 2:116, 2:124, 2:188, 2:203, 2:207, 2:237, 2:251-2:253, 2:264-2:267, 2:269, 2:273, 2:277, 2:278, 2:284, 3:vi, 3:31, 3:45-3:46, 3:64, 3:68, 3:70, 3:77, 3:85, 3:117, 3:118, 3:125, 3:193, 3:197, 3:215-3:216, 3:229, 3:231-3:233, 3:235-3:236, 3:239, 3:244, 3:246, 3:247, 3:254, 3:307, 3:311, 3:339-3:340, 3:342, 3:344, 3:345, 3:352

Kirtland, 1:259, 1:260, 1:272, 2:211, 3:11, 3:63, 3:129, 3:176, 3:178, 3:304

Knee, 3:43, 3:55, 3:64, 3:186, 3:209, 3:217, 3:219, 3:221, 3:234, 3:244

Kolob, 3:201

Labor, 1:1, 1:67, 1:75, 1:90, 1:142, 1:149, 1:172, 1:178, 1:183, 1:205, 1:231, 1:241, 1:243, 1:248, 1:255, 2:37, 2:91, 2:176, 3:5, 3:53, 3:82, 3:87, 3:92, 3:194, 3:202, 3:220-3:221, 3:261, 3:266, 3:278, 3:279, 3:284, 3:285, 3:288, 3:289

Laborer(s), 1:141, 1:248, 3:92, 3:282, 3:289, 3:291, 3:293, 3:301

Ladder, 3:264

Lamanite, 2:124-2:125

Lamanites, 1:29, 1:80, 1:135, 1:178, 1:215, 1:216, 1:218, 1:228, 1:244, 1:273, 1:3, 2:35, 2:47, 2:65, 2:88-2:89, 2:105, 2:119-2:120, 2:126, 2:131-2:132, 2:136, 2:220, 3:9, 3:11, 3:12, 3:52, 3:78, 3:103, 3:117, 3:135-3:136, 3:289, 3:293, 3:300, 3:337

Lamb, 1:60, 1:75, 1:82, 1:235, 1:236, 1:251-1:252, 1:257, 1:271, 2:28, 2:29, 2:40, 2:55, 2:89, 2:104, 2:106, 2:157, 2:180, 2:233-2:234, 2:236, 2:259-2:261, 2:282, 3:23, 3:26, 3:46, 3:48, 3:55, 3:57-3:58, 3:62, 3:91, 3:100, 3:112, 3:134, 3:136, 3:146, 3:147, 3:195-3:197, 3:207, 3:252, 3:294, 3:322-3:323, 3:351-3:352, 3:355

Lament, 1:84, 1:154, 1:288, 2:29, 2:66, 2:97, 2:105, 2:253, 3:51

Lamp, 1:124, 2:28, 2:56, 2:221, 2:279

Lamps, 1:8, 1:63, 1:95-1:96, 1:129, 3:17, 3:22, 3:126

Land of promise, 1:136, 1:196, 1:217, 1:291, 2:77, 2:79, 3:104, 3:121, 3:148, 3:270

Language, 1:14, 1:48, 1:125, 1:150, 1:161, 1:205, 1:243, 1:256, 1:266, 1:270, 2:4, 2:8, 2:21, 2:66, 2:121, 2:143, 2:144, 2:165, 2:215, 2:260, 2:267, 2:271, 3:23, 3:86, 3:154, 3:156, 3:157, 3:206, 3:208, 3:215, 3:216, 3:260, 3:279, 3:320, 3:333

Law of consecration. *See* Consecration, law of

Lawgiver, 1:1, 1:70, 2:134, 2:228, 2:261, 3:31, 3:52, 3:212, 3:216, 3:227

Lawyers, 2:32

Leader, 1:110, 1:111, 1:115, 1:193, 1:216, 1:244, 2:89, 2:221

Leaders, 1:vii, 1:65, 1:66, 1:70, 1:86, 1:92, 1:96, 1:97, 1:106, 1:107, 1:112, 1:187, 1:193, 1:211-1:212, 1:216, 1:231, 1:279, 1:283, 2:147, 2:169, 2:183, 2:184, 2:203, 2:204, 2:222, 2:234, 2:240, 3:161, 3:297, 3:328

Leadership, 1:27, 1:93, 1:98, 1:188, 1:195, 2:93, 2:146, 2:152, 2:221, 2:225

Lebanon, 3:207, 3:325

Legacy, 2:170, 2:174

Legal, 1:149, 1:179, 2:168, 2:181, 2:202, 3:221, 3:245, 3:259, 3:261, 3:315, 3:335

Legislators, 1:148, 3:70

Lehi, 1:120, 1:126, 1:132, 1:213, 2:31, 2:94, 2:124, 2:125, 3:135, 3:147, 3:311

Levi, 1:3, 2:81, 2:85, 2:86, 2:99, 2:231, 3:17, 3:35, 3:47, 3:126

Liar, 1:218, 2:195, 2:207, 2:240, 3:134, 3:243

Liars, 2:178, 2:209, 3:202, 3:351

Liberty, 1:vii, 1:86, 1:89, 1:110, 1:112, 1:121, 1:136, 1:142, 1:152, 1:154, 1:157, 1:159, 1:167, 1:169, 1:174, 1:176, 1:188-1:190, 1:195, 1:198, 1:200, 1:201, 1:204-1:208, 1:216, 1:225, 1:227, 1:256, 1:277, 2:15, 2:37, 2:42, 2:43, 2:128, 2:134, 2:147, 2:149, 2:178, 2:179, 2:182, 2:200, 2:216, 2:234, 3:21, 3:90, 3:127, 3:175, 3:218, 3:219, 3:228, 3:240, 3:242, 3:245, 3:271, 3:286, 3:292, 3:295, 3:313, 3:320

Liberty Jail, 1:121, 3:313, 3:320

Libya, 2:110

Light of Christ, 2:209

Lightning, 1:40, 1:65, 1:66, 1:75, 1:111, 1:141, 2:7, 2:15, 2:37, 2:146, 2:154, 2:191, 3:4, 3:164, 3:257, 3:303

Lightnings, 1:28, 1:71, 1:223, 1:224, 1:254, 1:256, 1:265, 1:276, 2:vii, 2:3, 2:6, 2:18, 2:28, 2:30, 2:36, 2:38, 2:53, 2:116, 2:189, 2:283, 3:3, 3:54

Likeness, 2:230, 2:254, 2:281, 2:285

Limit, 1:viii, 1:106, 1:191-1:193, 2:163, 3:130

Limits, 1:88, 1:100, 2:166

Lineage, 1:245, 1:281, 2:13, 2:19, 2:91, 2:122, 3:111, 3:175, 3:249

Lion, 2:24, 2:89, 2:96, 2:122, 2:124, 2:126-2:127, 2:131, 2:257, 2:264, 2:278, 2:281, 3:172, 3:181, 3:196, 3:209

Liquor, 2:202, 2:214

Listening, 1:126, 1:229

Literature, 1:123, 1:184, 2:225, 3:83

Little season, 1:7, 2:141, 2:158, 2:285, 2:3, 3:92, 3:107, 3:125, 3:209, 3:211, 3:334, 3:340, 3:348-3:350, 3:354

Locusts, 2:21, 2:56, 2:279, 2:280

Lord of Hosts, 1:20, 1:118, 1:137, 1:140, 1:261, 1:271, 1:290, 1:291, 2:12, 2:22, 2:25, 2:26, 2:31, 2:39, 2:54, 2:68, 2:70-2:71, 2:78, 2:82, 2:87, 2:99-2:100, 2:248, 2:250-2:251, 2:254, 3:17, 3:19, 3:28, 3:30, 3:31, 3:34-3:35, 3:47, 3:48, 3:53, 3:58, 3:59, 3:86, 3:126, 3:169, 3:192, 3:211, 3:246, 3:251-3:253, 3:257, 3:293, 3:303

Lord of Lords, 1:271, 2:252, 2:269, 2:284, 3:46, 3:125, 3:194, 3:231, 3:239, 3:244, 3:340

Lost tribes. *See* Ten tribes.

Lot, 1:55, 1:64, 1:102, 1:174, 1:179, 1:230, 1:292, 2:11, 2:12, 2:20, 2:125, 2:151, 2:200, 2:201, 2:264, 3:78-3:79, 3:104, 3:135, 3:176, 3:197, 3:303, 3:304

Love, 1:49, 1:85, 1:101, 1:115, 1:116, 1:120, 1:123, 1:124, 1:160, 1:163, 1:164, 1:178, 1:196, 1:206, 1:246, 1:254, 1:260, 1:273, 1:275, 2:155, 2:165, 2:171, 2:175, 2:177-2:178, 2:180, 2:181, 2:187-2:188, 2:205, 2:206, 2:211, 2:222, 2:228, 2:246, 3:vii, 3:38, 3:40, 3:43, 3:50, 3:64, 3:74, 3:101, 3:153, 3:189, 3:205, 3:217, 3:238, 3:275, 3:287-3:289, 3:294, 3:298

Love of God, 1:90, 2:171, 2:188

Loyal, 1:164, 1:167, 1:170, 1:184

Loyalty, 1:19, 1:168, 1:189, 1:190, 1:198, 1:208, 2:44

Lucifer, 2:vii, 2:226, 3:160, 3:349

Lust, 1:176, 3:8

Luxuries, 1:190, 3:268

Luxury, 1:114, 3:284

Lying, 1:207, 2:83, 2:85, 2:140, 2:141, 2:144, 2:145, 2:178, 2:206, 2:228, 2:259, 3:104, 3:148, 3:328

Maggots, 2:21, 2:35

Magicians, 2:197, 2:197, 2:200, 2:267

Mammon, 3:288

Management, 1:168, 1:216, 2:208, 3:298, 3:299

Manasseh, 1:247, 2:94, 2:124-2:125

Manifestation, 1:54, 1:67, 3:76, 3:133, 3:166

Mansion, 1:15, 3:16, 3:191, 3:336, 3:346

Mansions, 1:224, 2:66, 3:191, 3:193, 3:195, 3:221, 3:302, 3:336, 3:337, 3:344, 3:346

Manufacture, 1:37, 1:37-1:38, 1:41, 1:84, 2:142, 2:245, 3:67

Manufacturing, 1:61, 2:44, 2:142, 3:261, 3:265

Mark, 1:112, 1:119, 1:129, 1:178, 1:251, 1:263, 1:268, 2:26, 2:29, 2:45, 2:55, 2:175, 2:205, 2:207, 2:261, 2:269, 2:283-2:285, 3:40, 3:47, 3:89, 3:93, 3:133, 3:151, 3:179, 3:209, 3:231

Mark of the beast, 2:175, 2:207, 2:283, 2:284, 3:47

Marriage, 1:55, 1:75, 1:90, 1:96, 1:129, 2:14, 3:36, 3:37, 3:41, 3:263

Marriage supper, 3:46

Martyr, 1:15, 1:18

Martyrdom, 2:136, 2:216

Marvelous, 1:13, 1:56, 1:78, 1:237, 1:246, 2:38, 2:44, 2:46, 2:92, 2:103, 2:119, 2:127, 3:vi, 3:5, 3:73, 3:74, 3:93, 3:180, 3:205, 3:308, 3:311, 3:321, 3:323, 3:327

Materialism, 1:101, 2:43, 3:92

Materialistic, 3:298

Mediation, 2:215

Mediator, 3:53, 3:90

Medical, 1:208, 2:59

Meetings, 1:96, 1:108, 2:164, 2:213, 2:218, 3:17, 3:126, 3:155, 3:317

Megiddo, 2:107-2:108

Melchizedek Priesthood, 1:6, 1:16, 2:81, 2:95, 3:90

Member, 1:164, 1:167, 1:170, 1:172, 1:206, 2:196, 2:216, 2:217, 2:219, 2:222-2:223, 3:242

Memory, 3:130

Merchandise, 1:37, 1:38, 1:61, 1:84, 1:89, 2:66, 3:265

Merchants, 1:37, 1:38, 1:61, 2:66, 2:252-2:253

Merciful, 1:123, 1:138, 1:143, 1:285, 2:10, 2:102, 2:154, 2:192, 2:229, 3:71, 3:183, 3:322, 3:330

Mercy, 1:52, 1:63, 1:75, 1:77, 1:92, 1:122, 1:124, 1:188, 1:254, 2:6, 2:15, 2:17, 2:36, 2:64, 2:92, 2:93, 2:97, 2:127, 2:155, 2:156, 2:171, 2:177, 2:181, 2:216, 2:227, 3:3, 3:50, 3:74, 3:89, 3:97, 3:103, 3:153, 3:154, 3:246, 3:321

Meridian of Time, 1:11, 1:246, 2:266, 3:216, 3:227, 3:348

Meshech, 2:110, 2:111

Message, 1:55, 1:86, 1:100, 1:104, 1:126, 1:150, 1:176, 1:185-1:187, 1:190, 1:203, 1:226, 1:228, 1:231-1:232, 1:236, 1:241, 1:247, 1:267, 1:268, 1:272, 1:274, 1:276, 2:6, 2:8-2:9, 2:12, 2:17, 2:20, 2:90, 2:142, 2:152, 2:169, 2:219, 2:262, 2:268, 2:270, 2:271, 2:274, 3:3, 3:7, 3:157, 3:230

Messenger, 1:15, 1:63, 1:64, 1:105, 2:1, 2:196, 2:250, 2:270, 3:10, 3:17, 3:34, 3:50, 3:126

Methodists, 1:148, 1:148, 3:66

Methuselah, 3:141, 3:152, 3:164, 3:319

Micah, 1:20, 1:275, 2:25, 3:86, 3:136, 3:320

Michael, 1:2, 1:26, 1:128, 1:199, 2:280, 3:13, 3:135, 3:152-3:153, 3:160, 3:163-3:164, 3:256, 3:302, 3:349, 3:353-3:354

Midnight, 1:62, 3:40

Military, 1:175, 1:181, 1:184, 1:194, 1:201, 1:206, 1:207, 2:81, 2:152, 2:181, 3:86, 3:217

Millennial, 1:13-1:14, 1:18, 1:29, 1:65, 1:122, 1:124, 1:159, 1:247, 1:259, 1:274, 1:277, 2:4, 2:18, 2:21, 2:66, 2:69, 2:91, 2:93, 2:109, 2:123, 2:126, 2:136, 2:185, 2:196, 2:203, 2:236, 2:245, 2:247, 2:248, 2:3, 3:viii, 3:14-3:15, 3:23, 3:28, 3:95, 3:99, 3:125, 3:136, 3:137, 3:140, 3:165-3:166, 3:174, 3:179-3:180, 3:189, 3:211, 3:215, 3:224, 3:243, 3:285, 3:306, 3:318-3:319, 3:348-3:349

Millennium, 1:12, 1:70, 1:114, 1:122, 1:125, 1:282, 2:21, 2:75, 2:91, 2:0, 2:3, 3:15, 3:56, 3:70, 3:72, 3:94, 3:121, 3:177, 3:189, 3:191-3:193, 3:195, 3:196, 3:199, 3:202, 3:234, 3:249, 3:251, 3:318, 3:333, 3:338, 3:340-3:342

Mind, 1:1, 1:8, 1:17, 1:32, 1:38, 1:40, 1:56, 1:79, 1:87, 1:93-1:95, 1:103, 1:138, 1:160, 1:176, 1:200, 1:201, 1:235, 1:240, 1:248, 1:258, 1:261, 1:262, 1:280, 1:284, 2:68, 2:83, 2:94, 2:96, 2:110, 2:119, 2:143, 2:144, 2:159, 2:171, 2:199, 2:202, 2:208, 2:220, 2:226, 2:237, 2:251-2:252, 2:257, 3:6, 3:73, 3:79, 3:83, 3:88, 3:92, 3:103, 3:105, 3:113, 3:115, 3:120, 3:122, 3:143, 3:147, 3:167, 3:181, 3:197, 3:202, 3:208, 3:217, 3:221, 3:222, 3:243, 3:266, 3:267, 3:270, 3:288, 3:304, 3:307, 3:313, 3:329, 3:342

Minister, 1:17, 1:28, 1:46, 1:116, 1:274, 2:50, 2:93, 2:234, 3:17, 3:90, 3:140, 3:177, 3:184, 3:232, 3:310

Ministers, 1:223, 1:235, 1:278, 2:84, 2:173, 2:203, 3:74, 3:81

Ministry, 1:11, 1:18, 1:121, 1:142, 1:231, 1:239, 1:248, 1:255, 1:259, 2:37, 2:95, 2:103, 2:123, 2:199, 2:220, 3:11, 3:49, 3:140, 3:160, 3:179, 3:184, 3:194, 3:290, 3:295, 3:313, 3:318

Miracle, 1:51, 1:95-1:96, 1:250, 2:92, 2:125, 3:24, 3:79, 3:130

Miracles, 1:viii, 1:23, 1:39, 1:135, 1:136, 1:238, 1:265, 1:266, 2:59, 2:83, 2:92, 2:116, 2:191, 2:233, 2:282-2:284, 3:47, 3:180, 3:325, 3:328, 3:344, 3:345

Miraculous, 1:117, 3:130

Mission, 1:vii, 1:8, 1:11, 1:17, 1:26, 1:48, 1:59, 1:68, 1:71, 1:92, 1:95, 1:98, 1:119, 1:122, 1:142, 1:156, 1:181, 1:195, 1:212, 1:224, 1:228, 1:239, 1:242, 1:243, 1:250, 1:255, 1:279, 1:292, 2:14, 2:15, 2:79-2:80, 2:150, 2:262, 3:10, 3:169, 3:186, 3:197, 3:318

Missionaries, 1:50, 1:101, 1:110, 1:227, 1:249, 2:13, 2:138, 3:7, 3:169, 3:175, 3:190

Missionary work, 1:3, 1:101, 1:223, 1:231, 1:278, 1:280, 2:121, 3:201

Missouri, 1:viii, 1:33, 1:51, 1:151, 1:278, 1:279, 1:291, 1:292, 2:4, 2:121, 2:124, 2:132-2:133, 2:144-2:145, 2:181, 2:233, 2:234, 3:65, 3:89, 3:91, 3:104, 3:115, 3:120, 3:123, 3:126, 3:129, 3:131, 3:133, 3:136, 3:137, 3:143, 3:144, 3:148, 3:153, 3:155, 3:158, 3:160, 3:162, 3:248, 3:267, 3:269, 3:274, 3:277, 3:278, 3:311, 3:313, 3:331

Missouri River, 2:145, 3:313, 3:331

Mistake, 1:vii, 1:10, 1:51, 1:54, 1:91, 1:97, 1:123, 1:173, 1:234, 2:7, 2:217, 3:9, 3:76, 3:274, 3:287

Mistakes, 1:184, 1:184, 3:239

Moab, 2:45

Mob, 1:30, 1:36, 1:71, 1:148, 2:134, 2:136, 2:162, 3:64

Mobocracy, 1:79, 1:151, 2:134, 2:141, 3:263

Mobs, 1:29, 1:79, 1:80, 1:148, 1:155, 2:134, 2:150, 2:157, 2:159, 2:164

Mock, 2:160

Model, 1:198, 3:346

Moderation, 3:281, 3:281

Modesty, 2:199

Monetary System, 1:197, 1:198, 1:202, 1:207, 1:209

Money, 1:85, 1:92, 1:162, 1:183, 1:187, 1:192, 1:194, 1:197, 1:201, 1:202, 1:208, 1:209, 2:230, 3:92, 3:99, 3:102, 3:190, 3:263, 3:268, 3:272, 3:278, 3:283, 3:284, 3:286, 3:297, 3:328

Monroe Doctrine, 1:179

Moon, 1:8, 1:21, 1:50, 1:122, 1:124, 1:128, 1:228, 1:234, 1:247, 1:251, 1:256, 1:260, 2:7, 2:12, 2:18, 2:21, 2:23, 2:25, 2:27-2:28, 2:36, 2:38, 2:52, 2:68, 2:107, 2:108, 2:113-2:115, 2:278, 2:279, 3:19-3:21, 3:24, 3:30, 3:36-3:40, 3:42, 3:43, 3:51, 3:58, 3:64, 3:76, 3:77, 3:79, 3:80, 3:96, 3:99, 3:129, 3:130, 3:140, 3:146, 3:149, 3:200, 3:201, 3:223, 3:305, 3:331, 3:334, 3:352

    turn to blood, 1:260

Moral, 1:60, 1:97, 1:119, 1:121, 1:167, 1:178, 1:179, 1:184, 1:188, 1:191, 1:193-1:194, 1:196, 1:197, 1:202, 1:206, 1:208, 1:219, 2:151, 2:154, 2:223, 3:136, 3:238

Morality, 1:60, 1:112, 1:116, 1:185, 1:208, 1:210, 1:212, 2:133, 2:152, 3:288

Mormon, 1:7, 1:14, 1:26, 1:45, 1:46, 1:78, 1:82, 1:97, 1:99, 1:102, 1:104, 1:125, 1:193, 1:196, 1:200, 1:210-1:211, 1:235, 1:236, 1:238, 1:245-1:247, 1:260, 1:264, 1:265, 1:280, 1:289, 2:5, 2:15, 2:34, 2:43, 2:47, 2:50, 2:59, 2:61, 2:79, 2:84, 2:88, 2:104, 2:108, 2:120-2:121, 2:123-2:126, 2:142, 2:147, 2:185, 2:202, 2:213, 2:218, 2:220, 2:230, 2:233, 2:235, 2:240, 2:257, 3:vi, 3:5, 3:9, 3:48, 3:70, 3:82, 3:85, 3:106, 3:117, 3:136, 3:137, 3:140, 3:157, 3:167, 3:172, 3:173, 3:175, 3:179, 3:217, 3:229, 3:248, 3:251, 3:273, 3:283, 3:286, 3:293, 3:298, 3:299, 3:306, 3:310, 3:318, 3:338, 3:343, 3:349

Moroni, 1:17, 1:18, 1:26, 1:101, 1:105, 1:108, 1:134, 1:196, 1:197, 1:214, 1:246, 2:20, 2:35, 2:128, 2:208, 2:235, 3:162, 3:298

Mortal, 1:11, 1:13, 1:31, 1:72, 1:184, 1:232, 1:246, 1:247, 1:250, 2:151, 2:179, 2:184, 2:185, 2:202, 2:203, 2:226, 2:236, 2:275, 3:4, 3:7, 3:14, 3:18, 3:19, 3:23, 3:72, 3:93, 3:130, 3:144, 3:157, 3:162, 3:179, 3:195, 3:198, 3:203, 3:245, 3:338, 3:340, 3:341, 3:345, 3:349

Mortality, 1:186, 1:188, 1:211, 3:25, 3:82, 3:157, 3:161, 3:189, 3:198, 3:199, 3:202, 3:203, 3:206, 3:337, 3:338, 3:344-3:346

Mortals, 1:14, 1:119, 1:182, 2:226, 3:13, 3:82, 3:156, 3:157, 3:189, 3:202

Mosaic law, 2:91, 3:277

Moses, 1:1, 1:4, 1:5, 1:11, 1:16, 1:17, 1:19, 1:26, 1:40, 1:51, 1:53, 1:64, 1:73, 1:86, 1:97, 1:110, 1:116, 1:122, 1:146, 1:164, 1:205, 1:220, 1:228, 1:244, 1:245, 1:259, 1:272, 1:274, 1:279, 1:281, 1:284, 1:294, 1:295, 2:29, 2:49, 2:79, 2:94, 2:123, 2:129, 2:163, 2:179, 2:195, 2:200, 2:226, 2:235, 2:247, 3:8, 3:17, 3:24, 3:37, 3:43, 3:72, 3:82, 3:90, 3:109, 3:119, 3:122, 3:126, 3:146, 3:149-3:150, 3:158, 3:171, 3:174, 3:176, 3:178, 3:186, 3:187, 3:205, 3:225, 3:276, 3:304, 3:313, 3:315, 3:320, 3:328, 3:350, 3:355

Mother of abominations, 1:131, 1:252, 1:256, 2:46, 2:235, 2:241, 3:54

Mother of harlots, 1:243, 2:40, 2:46, 2:101, 2:233-2:234, 2:238-2:239, 2:244, 2:246, 2:251, 2:252, 2:284, 3:322

Mothers, 1:vii, 1:265, 2:2, 2:103, 2:143-2:145, 2:160, 3:24, 3:77

Mount of Olives, 1:47, 1:228, 2:50, 2:81, 2:86, 2:87, 2:91, 2:92, 2:202, 2:3, 3:vii-3:8, 3:19, 3:80, 3:171, 3:192, 3:197

Mount Sinai, 1:51, 2:54, 3:24, 3:49

Mount Zion, 1:24, 1:64, 1:127, 1:128, 1:237, 1:249-1:250, 1:257, 1:281, 1:284, 1:292, 2:23, 2:25, 2:106, 2:153, 3:17, 3:24, 3:31, 3:33, 3:53, 3:57, 3:58, 3:62, 3:70-3:71, 3:74, 3:80, 3:85, 3:90, 3:91, 3:95-3:96, 3:99-3:102, 3:106, 3:118, 3:120, 3:125, 3:126, 3:148, 3:150, 3:170, 3:171, 3:225

Mourning, 1:67, 1:144, 1:288, 2:1, 2:10, 2:13, 2:29, 2:38, 2:61, 2:114, 2:144, 2:243, 2:253, 3:97, 3:99, 3:122, 3:166, 3:207, 3:338, 3:344

Movie(s), 1:107, 1:183, 2:225

Multitude, 1:23, 1:24, 1:171, 1:251, 1:265, 1:273, 2:12, 2:22, 2:30, 2:55, 2:107, 2:111, 2:164, 2:234, 2:250, 2:271, 3:46, 3:72, 3:98, 3:102, 3:152, 3:156, 3:164, 3:178

Murder, 1:23, 1:145, 1:178, 1:218, 1:220, 2:21, 2:133, 3:128, 3:132

Murderer, 1:179, 3:161, 3:243

Murderers, 1:vii, 1:98, 1:277, 2:32, 2:43, 2:76, 2:148, 2:159, 2:168, 2:264, 3:336, 3:351

Murmuring, 1:84, 1:100

Music, 1:104, 1:123, 1:183

Mysteries, 1:vi, 1:28, 1:249, 2:158, 2:212, 2:258, 2:259, 3:309, 3:327, 3:330

Mysteries of God, 1:133, 3:327

Mystery of God, 3:210

Myth, 1:95

Nationality, 1:44, 2:135, 3:167, 3:242

Natural affection, 1:21, 2:15

Natural man, 1:123

Nauvoo, 1:79, 2:79, 3:129, 3:189

Nebuchadnezzar, 1:51, 1:271, 2:69, 2:260, 2:264, 2:272, 3:24, 3:229

Necessities, 1:37, 1:37, 1:95, 1:96, 1:119, 1:178, 2:64, 3:105, 3:296, 3:301

Neighbor, 1:24, 1:61, 1:66, 1:85-1:86, 1:139, 1:142, 1:154, 1:161, 1:202, 1:255, 1:290, 2:48, 2:74, 2:87, 2:141, 2:147, 2:148, 2:178, 3:11, 3:83, 3:84, 3:86, 3:91, 3:92, 3:103, 3:115, 3:132, 3:148, 3:239, 3:243, 3:260, 3:272, 3:275, 3:278, 3:282, 3:286, 3:303

Neighbors, 1:37, 1:65, 1:158, 1:245, 2:10, 2:166, 2:217, 3:64, 3:243, 3:266

Nephi, 1:12, 1:19, 1:22-1:24, 1:52, 1:82, 1:100, 1:104, 1:110, 1:122, 1:132, 1:135-1:136, 1:184, 1:196, 1:198, 1:200, 1:217, 1:218, 1:252-1:253, 1:280, 2:32, 2:46, 2:47, 2:61, 2:65, 2:71, 2:76, 2:77, 2:91, 2:102, 2:116, 2:127, 2:130, 2:151, 2:152, 2:184, 2:188, 2:190, 2:191, 2:207, 2:208, 2:223, 2:224, 2:228-2:229, 2:233, 2:236, 2:238, 2:240, 3:30, 3:47, 3:48, 3:92, 3:95, 3:102-3:103, 3:159, 3:175, 3:177, 3:180, 3:185, 3:293, 3:308, 3:318, 3:321, 3:325, 3:328

Nephite, 1:56, 2:235, 3:206, 3:285, 3:313, 3:319

Nephites, 1:45, 1:99, 1:113, 1:117, 1:136, 1:178, 1:215-1:216, 1:231, 1:264, 2:4, 2:35, 2:65, 2:88, 2:93, 2:94, 2:129, 2:136, 2:169, 2:220, 3:93, 3:140, 3:161, 3:172, 3:175, 3:179, 3:183, 3:272, 3:273, 3:283, 3:286, 3:293,

3:300, 3:305, 3:326, 3:349
Nephities, three. *See* Three Nephites.
Net, 1:116, 1:260, 1:267, 1:271, 2:224
New Jerusalem, 1:viii, 1:32, 1:39, 1:127, 1:138, 1:274, 1:280, 1:290, 2:48, 2:91, 2:121-2:122, 2:124-2:126, 2:135, 2:145, 2:151, 3:47, 3:58, 3:59, 3:62, 3:66, 3:68, 3:92, 3:93, 3:103, 3:106, 3:112, 3:115, 3:118, 3:120-3:122, 3:124, 3:129, 3:131, 3:133, 3:136, 3:142, 3:146, 3:150, 3:160, 3:177, 3:185, 3:210, 3:267, 3:271, 3:274, 3:275, 3:290, 3:300, 3:312, 3:336, 3:341, 3:344, 3:346-3:348, 3:352
New name, 3:146
New York, 1:180, 1:204, 1:270, 2:136, 2:137, 2:143, 2:145, 2:153, 3:123
Newspaper, 2:51
Newspapers, 2:225
Night vision, 1:9, 1:24, 1:271, 2:164, 2:272, 3:70, 3:71, 3:80, 3:90, 3:102, 3:228
Nile (River), 2:84-2:84, 3:193
Noah, 1:vii, 1:4, 1:11, 1:16, 1:20, 1:31, 1:55, 1:69, 1:74, 1:97, 1:103, 1:111, 1:117, 1:123, 1:125, 1:133, 1:230, 2:3, 2:7, 2:9-2:12, 2:16, 2:31, 2:63, 2:68, 2:69, 2:76, 2:190, 3:2-3:4, 3:14, 3:29, 3:59, 3:66, 3:113, 3:142, 3:162, 3:204, 3:280, 3:308, 3:313, 3:319, 3:336
Noble, 1:16, 1:183, 1:197, 1:209, 2:199, 2:217, 2:260, 3:83, 3:280
North countries, 1:249, 2:39, 2:65, 2:104, 2:106, 3:167-3:169, 3:185-3:186, 3:313, 3:352
North country, 1:235, 1:241, 2:45, 2:83, 2:133, 2:249, 3:21, 3:98, 3:155, 3:165, 3:169, 3:172-3:173, 3:178, 3:253, 3:312
North Pole, 3:167
Nuclear, 1:206, 1:209
Numbers, 1:52, 1:81, 1:252, 2:56, 2:91, 2:92, 2:174, 2:218, 2:220, 2:225, 2:238, 3:62, 3:76, 3:116, 3:175, 3:221, 3:225, 3:311

Oath, 1:20, 1:127, 1:152, 1:164, 1:197, 1:217, 2:235, 3:29, 3:59, 3:113, 3:204
Oaths, 1:210, 1:218, 2:76
Obedience, 1:32, 1:58, 1:78, 1:93, 1:95, 1:96, 1:113, 1:114, 1:188, 2:19, 2:164, 2:218, 3:6, 3:63, 3:89, 3:93, 3:94, 3:110, 3:119, 3:132, 3:202, 3:235, 3:239, 3:264, 3:275, 3:292, 3:293, 3:295, 3:343
Obey, 1:36, 1:56, 1:60, 1:81, 1:82, 1:95, 1:130, 1:157, 1:194, 1:214, 1:265, 1:268, 1:272, 1:278, 1:284, 2:41, 2:73, 2:86, 2:142, 2:155, 2:168, 2:174, 2:195, 2:212, 2:214, 2:218, 2:264, 2:265, 2:274, 2:278, 3:24, 3:26, 3:72, 3:128, 3:163, 3:181, 3:198, 3:237, 3:240, 3:247, 3:254, 3:265, 3:273, 3:277, 3:284, 3:291, 3:294, 3:295, 3:314, 3:317
Obligation, 1:13, 1:103, 1:110, 1:187, 1:194, 2:225, 3:288
Ocean, 1:1, 1:159, 1:271, 2:106, 2:120, 2:244, 2:266, 2:268, 3:57, 3:112, 3:155, 3:167, 3:180, 3:229, 3:241, 3:314, 3:342
    Atlantic Ocean, 2:268, 3:155, 3:180
    Pacific Ocean, 2:120, 3:127
Oceans, 3:117, 3:180
Offering, 1:94, 1:170, 1:193, 1:226, 2:48, 2:231, 2:235, 3:17, 3:22, 3:47, 3:126, 3:158
Offerings, 1:93, 1:128, 2:80, 2:181, 3:291
Official, 1:191, 1:204, 3:160, 3:261
Officials, 1:174, 1:182, 1:190, 1:205, 2:92
Offspring, 1:72, 1:148, 1:156, 1:275, 2:13, 2:160, 3:134, 3:208, 3:256, 3:345
Oil, 1:36, 1:47, 1:63, 1:95-1:96, 1:129, 1:249, 2:99, 2:119, 2:253, 3:viii, 3:17, 3:99, 3:126, 3:166, 3:168, 3:169
Old Testament, 1:125, 1:259, 3:24, 3:311
Olive tree, 1:240, 1:288, 3:172
Omaha, 1:269
One hundred forty-four thousand, 1:3, 1:250
One mighty and strong, 2:202, 3:78, 3:303
Opportunities, 1:119, 1:121, 2:164, 2:166, 2:175, 2:177, 3:124, 3:334
Opportunity, 1:43, 1:65, 1:76, 1:109, 1:229, 1:260, 1:269, 2:85, 2:164, 2:166, 3:63, 3:86, 3:200

Index

Opposition, 1:8, 1:28, 1:40, 1:62, 1:70, 1:78, 1:100, 1:104, 1:111, 1:113, 1:153, 1:181, 1:246, 2:156, 2:160, 2:167, 2:170, 2:171, 2:173, 2:181-2:182, 2:184, 2:185, 2:198, 2:235, 3:266, 3:317
Oppression, 1:62, 1:145, 1:171, 1:175, 1:179, 1:193, 1:232, 2:74, 2:170, 2:180, 2:264, 3:146
Orbit, 3:334, 3:335
Ordain, 1:248
Ordeal, 1:31, 3:26
Ordeals, 1:63, 1:73, 2:173, 2:175, 3:338, 3:339
Order of Enoch, 3:264, 3:269, 3:271, 3:284
Ordinance, 1:10, 1:118, 1:276, 1:292, 2:1, 2:12, 2:23, 2:81, 2:228, 3:30, 3:62, 3:126, 3:186, 3:203, 3:312, 3:335
Ordinances, 1:1-1:3, 1:11, 1:36, 1:48, 1:89, 1:103, 1:113, 1:248, 1:268, 1:269, 1:277, 1:278, 1:281, 2:vi, 2:68, 2:86, 2:90, 2:98, 2:159, 2:168, 2:178, 2:215, 2:220, 2:230, 2:254, 3:65, 3:75, 3:131, 3:198-3:200, 3:203, 3:223, 3:224, 3:243, 3:247, 3:268, 3:318, 3:336, 3:339
Overcome, 1:3, 1:7, 1:35, 1:36, 1:48, 1:80, 1:123, 1:126, 1:138, 1:224, 1:275, 2:vii, 2:101, 2:156, 2:161, 2:182, 2:191, 2:205, 2:223, 2:246, 2:252, 2:261, 2:265, 2:266, 2:271, 2:281, 2:284, 3:38, 3:40, 3:49, 3:52, 3:55, 3:66, 3:88, 3:105, 3:119, 3:212, 3:227-3:228, 3:243, 3:267, 3:296, 3:315, 3:337, 3:342, 3:349, 3:353, 3:354
Overthrow, 1:32, 1:33, 1:63, 1:67, 1:79, 1:82, 1:116, 1:156, 1:157, 1:159, 1:161, 1:184, 1:186, 1:211, 1:217-1:218, 1:243, 1:268, 2:1, 2:11, 2:13, 2:18, 2:34, 2:41, 2:136, 2:141, 2:157, 2:161, 2:163, 2:209, 2:247, 3:vii, 3:86, 3:222, 3:223, 3:238-3:240, 3:342

Pacific Ocean. *See* ocean.
Pagan, 2:220, 2:235
Palestine, 1:47, 1:242, 1:269, 1:270, 1:281, 2:80-2:82, 2:85, 2:93, 2:113, 2:123, 2:138-2:139, 3:viii, 3:25, 3:76-3:77, 3:91, 3:118, 3:129, 3:155, 3:166, 3:173, 3:196, 3:217, 3:250, 3:296
Papyrus, 3:313
Parable, 1:36, 1:36, 1:68, 1:95-1:97, 1:103, 1:120, 1:267, 2:187, 2:192, 2:231, 2:236, 3:36, 3:40-3:42, 3:107, 3:109, 3:123, 3:172, 3:295
Parables, 2:66, 3:173, 3:333
Paradise, 1:175, 1:234, 2:5, 2:119, 2:285, 3:165, 3:189, 3:193, 3:318
Paradisiacal glory, 1:295, 3:13, 3:92, 3:114, 3:150, 3:158, 3:187, 3:214
Parent, 1:28, 1:164, 2:2, 2:166, 3:1, 3:309
Parents, 1:21, 1:38, 1:81, 1:105, 1:190, 1:215, 1:218, 1:265, 2:6, 2:162, 2:166, 3:24, 3:161, 3:196, 3:203
Partridge, Edward, 3:142, 3:142, 3:290
Passion, 1:162
Patience, 1:29, 1:93, 1:95, 1:120-1:122, 1:130, 1:131, 1:143, 2:192, 2:281, 2:282
Patmos, 1:227, 1:248, 1:261, 1:268, 3:169, 3:313
Patriarch, 1:16, 3:151, 3:154, 3:159, 3:296, 3:311
Patriarchal blessings, 2:125, 3:vii, 3:12, 3:161
Patriarchs, 1:3, 1:6, 1:71, 1:110, 3:vi, 3:128, 3:198, 3:274
Patriot, 1:191, 1:207
Patriotism, 1:166, 1:185, 1:198, 1:203, 1:208
Patriots, 1:110, 1:166, 1:188, 1:194, 1:198, 1:207, 2:vii
Pattern, 1:101, 1:155, 1:172, 1:202, 1:208, 2:120, 2:122, 2:269, 3:27, 3:52, 3:70, 3:84, 3:119, 3:120, 3:126, 3:138, 3:212, 3:231, 3:238, 3:248, 3:261, 3:309, 3:353
Paul, 1:8, 1:12, 1:17, 1:55, 1:102, 1:108, 1:166, 1:237, 1:241-1:242, 1:264, 2:1, 2:68, 2:74, 2:90, 2:168, 2:174, 2:178, 3:21, 3:23, 3:25, 3:199, 3:316, 3:337, 3:344
Pearls, 2:252-2:253, 2:284, 3:67, 3:300, 3:352
Peary, Commodore or Commander, 3:174
Peculiar, 1:3, 1:77, 1:111, 1:229, 1:248, 1:275, 1:276, 2:16, 2:122, 2:146, 2:183, 2:269, 3:87, 3:179, 3:216, 3:230, 3:232
Pentecost, 3:245
Perish, 1:37, 1:52, 1:125, 1:127, 1:169, 1:194, 1:213, 1:237, 2:7, 2:31, 2:34, 2:66, 2:70, 2:76, 2:97, 2:102, 2:120, 2:126,

2:128, 2:142, 2:189, 2:190, 2:206, 2:220, 2:228-2:230, 2:240, 2:244, 2:254, 2:266, 3:4, 3:58, 3:75, 3:80, 3:81, 3:92, 3:129, 3:145, 3:224, 3:227, 3:246, 3:251, 3:256, 3:289, 3:325, 3:330, 3:350

Persecute, 1:24, 1:30, 1:144, 1:155, 1:178, 1:219, 1:229, 1:243, 2:86, 2:136, 2:156-2:158, 2:161, 2:163, 2:165, 2:167, 2:168, 2:175, 2:182, 2:184, 2:186-2:188, 2:191, 2:234, 3:64, 3:253

Persecution, 1:viii, 1:36, 1:39, 1:73, 1:79, 1:84, 1:96, 1:101, 1:114, 1:122, 1:125, 1:153, 1:159, 1:279, 1:3, 2:159, 2:164, 2:166-2:167, 2:171, 2:175, 2:180, 2:187-2:188, 2:191, 2:192, 2:221, 2:234, 3:7, 3:296

Persecutions, 1:56, 1:79, 1:80, 1:83, 1:207, 2:94, 2:155-2:157, 2:175, 2:179, 2:183, 2:184, 2:190, 2:212, 2:230, 2:233, 2:234, 3:221, 3:291

Perseverance, 1:130, 2:157, 3:87, 3:275, 3:277, 3:279

Persia, 2:110, 3:161

Pessimism, 2:150, 2:151

Pestilence, 1:12, 1:28, 1:42-1:44, 1:46, 1:50, 1:53, 1:58, 1:60, 1:71, 1:85, 1:87, 1:88, 1:105, 1:116, 1:118, 1:135, 1:143, 1:150, 1:176, 1:226, 1:230, 1:249, 1:260, 1:276, 1:285, 1:291, 2:3, 2:9, 2:12-2:14, 2:20, 2:21, 2:30-2:31, 2:33, 2:39, 2:43, 2:55, 2:57, 2:58, 2:62-2:64, 2:102, 2:110, 2:111, 2:133, 2:138, 2:147, 2:248, 2:272, 3:1, 3:2, 3:32, 3:63, 3:104, 3:107, 3:153, 3:165, 3:169, 3:175, 3:238

Peter, 1:12, 1:16-1:17, 1:21, 1:26, 1:130, 1:176, 1:246, 1:278, 2:10, 2:69, 2:206, 3:43, 3:162, 3:201, 3:316, 3:319, 3:345

Petition, 2:90, 3:244

Pharisees, 2:89, 2:172, 3:256

Philistines, 3:86

Philosophies, 1:101, 1:110, 1:167, 1:211, 2:200, 2:222, 3:287

Philosophy, 1:29, 1:165, 1:167, 2:143, 2:162, 2:222, 2:247, 3:244, 3:287

Physical, 1:97, 2:11, 2:67, 2:246, 3:24, 3:65, 3:86, 3:91

Pilgrims, 3:143

Pillar, 1:51, 1:56, 1:78, 3:24, 3:49, 3:55, 3:79, 3:80, 3:119, 3:126, 3:145, 3:170

Pioneers, 1:114

Pit, 1:24, 1:100, 1:246, 2:46, 2:57, 2:101, 2:116, 2:189, 2:239, 2:252, 2:280, 2:284-2:285, 3:5, 3:31, 3:100, 3:235

Plague, 1:51-1:53, 1:63, 1:66, 1:111, 1:141, 1:143, 1:176, 1:226, 1:249, 2:9, 2:18, 2:37, 2:58, 2:62, 2:81, 2:82, 2:85, 2:100, 2:115-2:116, 2:137, 2:154, 2:191, 2:272, 3:107, 3:164, 3:169, 3:208, 3:238, 3:257

Plagues, 1:34, 1:43, 1:60, 1:67, 1:78, 1:89, 1:131, 1:231, 1:243, 1:262, 1:276, 1:287, 1:288, 1:3, 2:1, 2:11, 2:19, 2:21, 2:29, 2:55, 2:57, 2:61, 2:67, 2:101, 2:107, 2:134, 2:244-2:246, 2:249, 2:280, 2:283, 3:1, 3:12, 3:78, 3:298, 3:351

Plan of salvation, 1:122, 2:165, 2:212, 2:217, 3:161, 3:201, 3:206

Planet, 1:121, 1:203, 2:2, 2:257, 3:21, 3:194, 3:204, 3:222, 3:339, 3:355

Planets, 3:82, 3:213

Planning, 1:66, 1:98, 1:202

Plat, 3:61, 3:125, 3:153

Plates, 2:132, 2:218, 3:310-3:311, 3:319, 3:320, 3:327, 3:329

Pleasure, 1:2, 1:12, 1:15, 1:21, 1:38, 1:43, 1:78, 1:88, 1:90, 1:98, 1:102, 1:209, 2:206, 2:228, 3:152, 3:183, 3:190, 3:198, 3:249, 3:262, 3:273, 3:326, 3:330, 3:345

Polarization, 1:121, 2:vii

Police, 1:168, 1:174, 1:182, 1:201, 1:203, 1:206, 1:209

Political, 1:58, 1:61, 1:86, 1:93, 1:100, 1:102, 1:110, 1:112, 1:116, 1:125, 1:153, 1:160, 1:162, 1:165, 1:169, 1:175, 1:178, 1:182, 1:184-1:185, 1:191, 1:197, 1:203, 1:207-1:208, 1:212, 1:232, 1:234, 1:283, 2:10, 2:81, 2:133, 2:141, 2:152, 2:158, 2:203, 2:217, 2:224, 2:233, 2:247, 3:63, 3:117, 3:215-3:217, 3:223, 3:234, 3:240, 3:243, 3:297-3:298

Politicians, 1:112, 1:152, 1:160, 1:191, 1:212, 2:272

Ponder, 1:69, 1:121, 1:122, 1:185, 3:82

Poor, 1:16, 1:23-1:24, 1:37, 1:64, 1:106, 1:216, 1:227, 1:240, 1:254, 2:66, 2:72, 2:119, 2:120, 2:122, 2:195, 2:213, 2:220, 2:230, 2:282, 3:29, 3:70, 3:93, 3:113, 3:123, 3:132, 3:172, 3:252, 3:260, 3:263, 3:267, 3:273, 3:276, 3:278-3:280, 3:282, 3:285, 3:290, 3:291, 3:294, 3:299, 3:301, 3:302, 3:304, 3:325, 3:354

Popular, 1:196, 1:199, 1:230, 2:186, 2:198, 2:239, 2:244, 2:260, 3:47

Popularity, 1:78, 2:155, 2:171

Population, 1:152, 2:68, 2:139, 2:269, 3:341

Pornographic, 1:184

Posterity, 1:2, 1:11, 1:18, 1:19, 1:112, 1:148, 1:152, 1:273, 2:2, 2:133, 2:152, 2:221, 3:9, 3:13, 3:64, 3:95, 3:135, 3:152, 3:158, 3:160, 3:161, 3:174, 3:175, 3:307-3:308, 3:319, 3:331, 3:337, 3:345

Poverty, 1:33, 1:96, 1:197, 2:186, 3:272, 3:274, 3:280, 3:296, 3:298

Praise(s), 1:60, 1:62, 1:100, 2:174, 2:186, 2:188, 2:230, 2:237, 2:260, 3:84, 3:91, 3:98, 3:101, 3:196, 3:197, 3:207, 3:211, 3:284

Pratt, Orson, 1:viii, 1:4, 1:5, 1:45, 1:47, 1:55, 1:56, 1:62, 1:150, 1:224, 1:226, 1:235, 1:238, 1:240, 1:243, 1:264, 1:269-1:272, 2:7, 2:9, 2:40-2:41, 2:50, 2:56, 2:58, 2:66-2:67, 2:72, 2:83-2:85, 2:121-2:122, 2:136, 2:139, 2:164-2:165, 2:197, 2:234, 2:265-2:267, 2:270-2:272, 3:viii, 3:4, 3:6, 3:7, 3:19, 3:23, 3:25, 3:72, 3:76, 3:80-3:82, 3:115, 3:117, 3:122-3:123, 3:125, 3:129, 3:139, 3:154, 3:155, 3:157, 3:170, 3:171, 3:194, 3:197, 3:198, 3:224, 3:229-3:230, 3:232, 3:233, 3:245, 3:264-3:265, 3:267, 3:270, 3:305, 3:307, 3:312, 3:340, 3:342, 3:345, 3:346

Pray, 1:29, 1:46, 1:65, 1:69, 1:75, 1:78, 1:91, 1:93, 1:137, 1:142, 1:143, 1:149, 1:178, 1:194, 1:207, 1:260, 2:vii, 2:73, 2:90, 2:115, 2:119, 2:147, 2:154, 2:170, 2:177, 2:180, 2:187, 2:188, 2:190, 2:198, 2:212, 2:214, 2:222, 3:27, 3:40, 3:42, 3:63, 3:69, 3:99, 3:121, 3:227, 3:238, 3:240, 3:245, 3:255, 3:260, 3:265, 3:274, 3:324, 3:335

Prayer, 1:32, 1:43, 1:55, 1:66, 1:74, 1:108, 1:109, 1:130, 1:137, 1:165, 1:169, 1:173, 1:182, 1:248, 2:55, 2:80, 2:171, 2:209, 2:216, 2:218, 2:219, 3:11, 3:14, 3:27, 3:69, 3:152, 3:227, 3:249, 3:260, 3:305, 3:317

Prayers, 1:23, 1:78, 1:84, 1:138, 1:190, 1:218, 2:102, 2:131, 2:213, 2:214, 2:267, 3:140, 3:168, 3:172, 3:261
    Prayers of the righteous, 1:133, 1:133, 2:131

Preach, 1:viii, 1:6, 1:11, 1:23, 1:30, 1:38, 1:53, 1:59, 1:64, 1:66, 1:69, 1:88, 1:96, 1:118, 1:136, 1:156, 1:216, 1:225, 1:227, 1:232, 1:233, 1:241, 1:244, 1:245, 1:252-1:254, 1:257, 1:259, 1:262, 1:274, 1:280, 2:vii, 2:10, 2:12, 2:74, 2:85, 2:144, 2:150-2:151, 2:158, 2:163, 2:226, 2:245, 2:261-2:262, 3:7, 3:21, 3:63, 3:67, 3:86, 3:101, 3:219, 3:225, 3:245, 3:272, 3:278

Precedent, 1:281, 3:11, 3:205

Precepts of men, 1:24, 1:254, 2:224, 3:3

Preexistence, 3:318

Prejudice, 2:89, 2:185, 2:212

Premortal existence, 1:111

Preparedness, 1:95, 1:96

Presbyterian, 2:202, 3:64

Presbyterians, 3:64, 3:242

Preserve, 1:31, 1:34-1:36, 1:74, 1:85, 1:87, 1:98, 1:99, 1:113, 1:127, 1:131, 1:134, 1:137, 1:146, 1:150, 1:152, 1:153, 1:160-1:161, 1:175, 1:178, 1:185-1:186, 1:193, 1:197, 1:200, 1:207, 1:215, 1:254, 2:18, 2:39, 2:42, 2:58, 2:70, 2:127, 2:128, 2:175, 2:189, 3:25-3:26, 3:41, 3:59, 3:113, 3:124, 3:129, 3:167, 3:260, 3:280, 3:282, 3:324

President, 1:iv-1:viii, 1:7, 1:12, 1:13, 1:39, 1:84, 1:88, 1:93, 1:107, 1:149, 1:158, 1:159, 1:167, 1:175, 1:178, 1:179, 1:184, 1:204, 1:210, 1:230, 1:231, 2:vi, 2:4, 2:135, 2:146, 2:199, 2:213, 2:221, 3:83, 3:137, 3:141, 3:142, 3:153, 3:216, 3:246, 3:271, 3:277

President of the Church, 1:12, 1:174, 1:193, 2:201, 3:137, 3:142

President of the United States, 1:158, 1:159, 1:178, 1:193

Presidents, 1:162, 1:180, 1:248, 2:143, 2:243, 3:117, 3:239

Prey, 1:28, 1:80, 2:25, 2:85, 2:91, 2:110, 2:189, 3:57, 3:172, 3:186, 3:196

Price, 1:9, 1:103, 1:118, 1:173, 1:200, 1:207, 3:285, 3:308

Price controls, 1:198, 1:207

Pride, 1:23-1:24, 1:100, 1:102, 1:144, 1:219, 1:253, 2:3, 2:20, 2:30, 2:35, 2:77, 2:128, 2:230, 3:83, 3:93, 3:263, 3:280, 3:282, 3:300

Priest, 1:3, 1:68, 1:88, 1:128, 1:227, 2:12, 2:23, 2:170, 3:30, 3:67, 3:89, 3:195, 3:245, 3:254, 3:255, 3:303

Priestcraft, 1:273, 2:31, 2:107, 2:244, 3:234

Priestcrafts, 1:253, 2:34, 2:129, 2:140, 2:141

Priests, 1:3, 1:16, 1:63, 1:88, 1:229, 1:235, 1:255, 1:271, 1:292, 2:82, 2:89, 2:97, 2:243, 3:vi, 3:10, 3:64, 3:68, 3:86, 3:87, 3:99, 3:128, 3:151, 3:154, 3:159, 3:164, 3:193, 3:195, 3:197, 3:209, 3:210, 3:235, 3:246, 3:260, 3:290, 3:300, 3:311, 3:333, 3:339, 3:340, 3:344, 3:345

Prince, 1:128, 1:176, 2:21, 2:82, 2:97-2:98, 2:111-2:112, 2:200, 3:154, 3:158-3:159, 3:161, 3:164, 3:199, 3:252, 3:302, 3:308

Prince of peace, 1:176, 2:21, 3:154, 3:252

Priorities, 1:98

Priority, 1:99

Prison, 1:29, 1:216, 2:56, 2:128, 3:31, 3:55, 3:58, 3:210, 3:334, 3:340, 3:346, 3:350

Private, 1:68, 1:86, 1:177, 1:187, 1:197, 1:204, 1:208, 1:220, 2:186, 3:136, 3:220, 3:261, 3:286, 3:297-3:299

Private enterprise, 1:177, 1:187

Private property, 1:194, 3:136

Problem, 1:123, 1:183

Problems, 1:112, 1:182, 1:188, 1:195, 1:208, 1:209, 2:vii, 2:221, 3:247

Procedure, 1:179, 3:142, 3:277, 3:299

Procedures, 1:96

Proclaim, 1:48, 1:50, 1:115, 1:117, 1:144, 1:153, 1:154, 1:157, 1:229, 1:232, 1:238, 1:241, 1:293, 2:114, 2:138, 2:172, 2:244, 2:268, 3:110, 3:134, 3:230

Procrastinate, 1:95

Profess, 1:29, 1:52, 1:59, 1:68, 1:156, 1:228, 2:6, 2:11, 2:148, 2:195, 2:200, 2:217, 2:221, 3:167, 3:222, 3:226, 3:243, 3:274, 3:282

Profit, 1:118, 2:166, 3:243, 3:281, 3:285, 3:294, 3:298, 3:315

Progress, 1:85, 1:85, 1:124, 1:168, 1:171, 1:183, 1:203, 1:229, 1:230, 1:278, 2:3, 2:108, 2:150, 2:161, 2:167-2:169, 2:180, 2:181, 3:85, 3:122, 3:226, 3:244, 3:283, 3:297

Progression, 1:100, 3:161

Promise, 1:vii, 1:5, 1:8, 1:9, 1:14, 1:19, 1:22, 1:44, 1:56, 1:78, 1:83, 1:91, 1:93, 1:94, 1:102, 1:105, 1:126, 1:136, 1:145, 1:170, 1:196, 1:198, 1:213, 1:217, 1:246, 1:291, 2:58, 2:77, 2:79, 2:91, 2:102, 2:119, 2:121, 2:123, 2:124, 2:169, 2:171, 2:200, 2:202, 3:8, 3:27, 3:45, 3:104, 3:111, 3:124, 3:142, 3:148, 3:162, 3:199, 3:241, 3:242, 3:249, 3:260, 3:272

Promised land, 1:11, 1:131, 1:289, 2:104, 2:120, 3:17, 3:126, 3:185

Promises, 1:viii, 1:1, 1:10, 1:29, 1:45, 1:57, 1:65, 1:68, 1:81, 1:83, 1:85, 1:116, 1:118, 1:138, 1:153, 1:205, 1:259, 1:279, 2:79, 2:80, 2:90, 2:94, 2:103, 2:119, 2:122, 2:130, 2:155, 2:166, 2:179, 2:216, 2:222, 3:vi, 3:7, 3:9, 3:12, 3:50, 3:69, 3:88, 3:123, 3:135, 3:136, 3:177, 3:183, 3:235, 3:242, 3:311, 3:319, 3:325

Promptings, 1:94, 1:97, 1:179, 2:222

Propaganda, 1:108, 1:182, 1:211, 2:222, 2:225

Property, 1:29, 1:79, 1:151, 1:165, 1:175, 1:193-1:194, 1:210, 1:220, 2:16, 2:136, 3:111, 3:120, 3:128, 3:132, 3:136, 3:261, 3:264, 3:267, 3:269-3:270, 3:272, 3:282, 3:285, 3:287, 3:290, 3:293, 3:296, 3:300, 3:303

Prophecies, 1:vi, 1:18, 1:22, 1:29, 1:30, 1:32, 1:47, 1:55, 1:58, 1:126, 1:153, 1:157, 1:223, 1:235, 1:263, 1:271, 1:275, 2:vii-2:9, 2:84, 2:85, 2:90, 2:92, 2:108, 2:121, 2:125, 2:130, 2:133, 2:138, 2:157, 2:266, 2:270, 2:271, 2:274, 3:vi, 3:viii, 3:5, 3:7, 3:11-3:13, 3:24, 3:25, 3:63, 3:73, 3:76, 3:77, 3:88, 3:156, 3:167, 3:175-3:178, 3:226-3:228, 3:306-3:308, 3:311

Prophecy, 1:viii, 1:9, 1:22, 1:28-1:29, 1:48, 1:62, 1:68, 1:99, 1:109, 1:117, 1:125, 1:150, 1:152, 1:225, 1:234, 1:237, 1:242, 1:243, 1:245, 1:266, 1:270, 1:280, 2:3-2:5, 2:10, 2:44, 2:68, 2:85, 2:93, 2:101, 2:123-2:124, 2:139, 2:141, 2:167, 2:204, 2:215, 2:223, 2:259, 2:263, 2:265-2:266, 2:268, 2:273, 2:274, 3:3, 3:7, 3:8, 3:19, 3:24, 3:37, 3:46, 3:70, 3:76-3:77, 3:80, 3:86, 3:117, 3:158, 3:166, 3:167, 3:169, 3:199, 3:216, 3:217, 3:220, 3:227, 3:231, 3:236, 3:249, 3:263, 3:272, 3:313, 3:318, 3:344, 3:350

Prophets,Two, *See* Two prophets.

Index

Prosperity, 1:42, 1:44, 1:49-1:51, 1:57, 1:70, 1:72, 1:78, 1:79, 1:82, 1:112, 1:114, 1:115, 1:134, 1:167, 1:175, 1:184, 1:189, 1:203, 2:98, 2:136, 2:155, 2:162, 2:171, 2:178, 2:220, 3:73, 3:100, 3:273, 3:283
Prosperous, 1:99, 1:189, 2:136, 2:147, 2:179, 3:272, 3:282-3:283
Protection, 1:27, 1:31, 1:51, 1:72, 1:73, 1:88, 1:92-1:94, 1:101, 1:105, 1:112, 1:136, 1:147, 1:154-1:155, 1:166, 1:167, 1:192, 1:196, 1:201, 1:205, 1:206, 1:219-1:220, 2:15, 2:148, 2:152, 2:154, 2:165, 2:168, 2:177, 2:201, 3:24, 3:133, 3:282
Proxy, 3:200
Prune, 1:288, 2:171
Psalm, 1:272, 2:55, 3:62, 3:74, 3:80, 3:130, 3:142
Psalms, 1:273, 1:276, 3:29, 3:249, 3:252, 3:350
Public, 1:30, 1:45, 1:86, 1:99, 1:107, 1:156, 1:166, 1:168, 1:189, 1:192, 1:198, 1:201, 1:203, 1:209, 1:210, 1:212, 1:220, 1:290, 2:225, 2:234, 3:61, 3:147, 3:219, 3:270-3:271, 3:296, 3:300
Punish, 1:64, 1:118, 1:194, 1:220, 2:12, 2:23, 2:133, 2:250, 3:101, 3:281
Punishment, 1:63, 1:77, 2:19-2:20, 3:72
Pure in heart, 1:60, 1:176, 1:226, 1:260, 1:261, 3:16, 3:17, 3:22, 3:27, 3:64, 3:65, 3:72, 3:91-3:92, 3:106-3:107, 3:126, 3:130, 3:143, 3:225, 3:263, 3:278, 3:280
Purified, 1:53, 1:65, 1:138, 1:227, 2:36, 2:55, 2:80, 2:81, 2:179, 2:211, 2:212, 3:84, 3:90, 3:141, 3:158, 3:191, 3:199, 3:333-3:334, 3:338, 3:344, 3:348
Purity, 1:59, 1:61, 1:269, 2:198, 2:236, 3:84, 3:116, 3:224, 3:323

Quality, 1:99, 1:189
Quarrel, 1:58, 1:72, 1:96, 2:15
Queen, 1:73, 1:288, 2:1, 2:29, 2:243, 2:253, 3:83
Queen of Sheba, 3:83
Quickened, 1:226, 1:256, 3:27, 3:55, 3:196
Quorum, 1:110, 1:248, 2:79, 2:180, 2:199, 3:15, 3:155
Quorums, 1:259, 2:183, 2:198, 3:155

Rabbi, 2:93, 2:93, 2:94
Rainbow, 2:21, 3:15, 3:209
Rationalize, 1:112, 2:225
Rebel, 1:44, 1:154, 1:214, 2:135, 2:177, 3:317
Record, 1:7, 1:26, 1:55, 1:69, 1:99, 1:113, 1:114, 1:140, 1:227, 1:238, 1:244, 2:74, 2:88, 2:121, 2:130, 2:142, 2:146, 2:170, 2:220, 2:259, 3:53, 3:88, 3:144, 3:161, 3:167, 3:177, 3:178, 3:239, 3:296, 3:302, 3:303, 3:307, 3:312-3:313, 3:323, 3:329, 3:331
Records, 1:101, 1:215, 1:238, 1:274, 2:224, 2:245, 3:10, 3:21, 3:154, 3:157, 3:172, 3:174, 3:175, 3:177, 3:178, 3:180, 3:203, 3:224, 3:264, 3:293, 3:303, 3:308, 3:311, 3:313, 3:316, 3:319-3:320, 3:330
Red, 1:73, 1:107, 1:173, 1:192, 1:197, 1:198, 1:201, 1:202, 1:263, 2:84, 2:259, 2:280, 3:26, 3:31, 3:58, 3:180, 3:320
Red Sea, 1:73, 1:263, 2:84, 3:180
Redeem, 1:4, 1:158, 1:186, 1:286, 2:121, 3:53, 3:67, 3:91, 3:93, 3:108, 3:125, 3:192, 3:220, 3:234, 3:251
Redemption, 1:1, 1:8, 1:33, 1:45, 1:56, 1:57, 1:73, 1:80, 1:140, 1:248, 1:259, 1:265, 1:269, 1:270, 2:56, 2:89, 2:119, 2:120, 2:154, 2:156, 2:166, 2:176, 2:226, 3:7, 3:8, 3:42, 3:51, 3:55, 3:77, 3:92, 3:94, 3:107, 3:110, 3:111, 3:115, 3:120, 3:122, 3:150, 3:171, 3:192, 3:225, 3:267, 3:269, 3:292, 3:294, 3:304, 3:337, 3:339, 3:354
Refiner, 2:84, 3:17, 3:35, 3:47, 3:126
Refuge, 1:vii, 1:50, 1:53, 1:87, 1:97, 1:102, 1:104, 1:127, 1:138, 1:144, 1:162, 1:260, 1:267, 1:281, 2:3, 2:48, 2:60, 2:137, 2:138, 3:18, 3:56, 3:83, 3:95, 3:103, 3:111, 3:115, 3:147
Religion, 1:15, 1:16, 1:38, 1:41, 1:43, 1:52, 1:56, 1:57, 1:69, 1:77, 1:84-1:86, 1:114, 1:123, 1:125, 1:134, 1:151, 1:160, 1:171, 1:173, 1:175, 1:179, 1:191, 1:199, 1:210, 1:220, 1:225, 1:227, 1:260, 1:262, 1:272, 2:3, 2:47, 2:147, 2:156, 2:159, 2:162-2:163, 2:184, 2:202, 2:215, 2:227, 2:236, 2:246, 3:68, 3:71, 3:84, 3:138,

3:217-3:218, 3:235, 3:280, 3:314, 3:334
    civil religion, 1:119
Religions, 1:viii, 1:39, 1:151, 2:203, 3:217
Remission, 1:35, 1:84, 2:86, 2:142, 2:208, 2:230, 3:viii, 3:27, 3:245, 3:277
Remission of sins, 1:35, 1:84, 2:86, 2:230, 3:27, 3:245, 3:277
Remnant of Jacob. *See* Jacob, remnant of.
Repent, 1:41-1:42, 1:45, 1:49, 1:50, 1:52, 1:89, 1:102, 1:113, 1:117, 1:118, 1:150, 1:156, 1:157, 1:189, 1:216-1:218, 1:223, 1:228, 1:235, 1:253, 1:257, 1:264, 1:277, 1:283, 2:vi-2:7, 2:11, 2:16, 2:31, 2:41, 2:47, 2:58, 2:66, 2:69, 2:70, 2:83, 2:86, 2:89, 2:130-2:131, 2:136, 2:140, 2:170, 2:178, 2:181, 2:211, 2:212, 2:215, 2:218, 2:222, 2:224, 2:229, 2:240, 2:244, 2:258, 2:272, 3:3, 3:4, 3:9, 3:23, 3:58, 3:75, 3:82, 3:101, 3:106, 3:167, 3:172, 3:228, 3:264, 3:266, 3:288, 3:291, 3:329
Repentance, 1:57, 1:102, 1:132, 1:135, 1:208, 1:266, 1:276, 2:17-2:20, 2:33, 2:34, 2:65, 2:74, 2:81, 2:86, 2:132, 2:147, 2:212, 2:220, 2:229, 2:230, 2:240, 2:268, 3:10, 3:19, 3:49, 3:230, 3:245
Republican, 1:149, 1:152, 1:162, 1:163, 1:169, 1:197, 1:204, 1:206, 3:219
Resist, 1:98, 1:102, 1:114, 1:134, 2:64, 2:74, 2:92, 2:175, 2:177
Resistance, 1:29, 1:125, 2:185
Resource(s), 1:33, 1:41, 1:49, 1:92, 1:94, 1:104, 1:106, 1:209
Responsibilities, 1:1, 1:50, 1:159, 1:176, 1:187, 1:190, 1:201, 1:277, 2:125, 2:138, 2:150, 2:152, 2:177, 2:201
Responsibility, 1:11, 1:18, 1:95, 1:108, 1:109, 1:147, 1:151, 1:159, 1:164, 1:166, 1:180, 1:187-1:189, 1:192, 1:197, 1:207-1:208, 1:210, 1:259, 1:279, 2:16, 2:92, 2:198, 2:200, 2:216, 3:224, 3:242, 3:283, 3:297
Restitution, 1:11, 1:13, 1:14, 1:64, 1:90, 1:273, 1:278, 2:5, 2:66, 2:80, 2:81, 3:158, 3:165, 3:315, 3:333
Restoration, 1:8, 1:25, 1:90, 1:116, 1:117, 1:169, 1:232, 1:237, 1:242, 1:264, 1:265, 1:279, 1:282, 1:292, 1:293, 1:295, 2:79-2:80, 2:103, 2:105, 2:125, 2:149, 2:235, 2:243, 2:274, 3:8, 3:13, 3:14, 3:43, 3:69, 3:95, 3:96, 3:106, 3:109, 3:113, 3:135, 3:136, 3:148, 3:150, 3:158, 3:162, 3:171, 3:177, 3:178, 3:187, 3:214, 3:217, 3:241, 3:246, 3:249, 3:319, 3:338, 3:347
Restoration of the gospel, 1:116, 1:282, 2:243, 2:274
Restore, 1:2, 1:3, 1:11, 1:90, 1:140, 1:150, 1:226, 1:237, 1:255, 1:278, 1:279, 1:291, 1:292, 2:5, 2:80, 2:98, 2:103, 2:112, 2:179, 3:3, 3:11, 3:13, 3:98, 3:165, 3:249, 3:322, 3:323
Resurrected, 1:15, 2:87, 2:257, 3:5, 3:17, 3:80, 3:177-3:179, 3:190, 3:193, 3:195, 3:318, 3:337-3:338, 3:341, 3:343, 3:344, 3:346-3:347, 3:349
Resurrected beings, 2:87, 3:318
Resurrection, 1:5, 1:8, 1:76, 1:122, 1:274, 2:56, 3:16, 3:51, 3:197, 3:203, 3:204, 3:210, 3:251, 3:333, 3:335, 3:347, 3:348
    first resurrection, 1:8, 3:5, 3:6, 3:51, 3:53, 3:210, 3:212
    second resurrection, 1:8, 3:200
Retribution, 1:77
Reverence, 1:186, 1:220
Revolution, 1:58, 1:155, 1:162, 1:182-1:184, 1:191, 1:275, 2:6, 2:67, 2:137, 2:266, 3:227
Revolutionists, 1:165
Revolutions, 1:229, 2:15, 2:158, 3:305, 3:331
Rich, 1:76, 1:96, 1:100, 1:205, 1:227, 1:269, 2:28, 2:195, 2:213, 2:220, 2:252-2:253, 2:278, 2:282, 3:45, 3:57, 3:70, 3:120, 3:124, 3:132, 3:151, 3:186, 3:200, 3:221, 3:260, 3:263-3:264, 3:266, 3:267, 3:270, 3:272, 3:273, 3:279, 3:280, 3:282, 3:285, 3:286, 3:289, 3:290, 3:294, 3:300, 3:304
Riches, 1:37, 1:46, 1:78, 1:96, 1:138, 1:141, 1:224, 1:254, 2:36, 2:91, 2:155, 2:171, 2:187, 2:253, 3:50, 3:65, 3:67, 3:76, 3:103, 3:115, 3:124, 3:130, 3:132, 3:147, 3:263-3:264, 3:267, 3:301
Riots, 1:147, 1:181, 1:182
Ripe in Iniquity, 1:3, 2:73, 2:76, 2:190
Ripening, 1:65, 1:113, 1:215, 1:216, 1:276, 2:74, 2:138, 2:140, 2:153
River, 1:26, 1:105, 1:263, 2:46, 2:57, 2:84, 2:86, 2:280, 2:283, 3:5, 3:152, 3:153, 3:166, 3:168, 3:267, 3:313, 3:331
Rivers, 1:48, 1:286, 2:23, 2:28, 2:56-2:58, 2:67, 2:85, 2:137, 2:153, 2:165, 2:244, 2:279, 2:283, 3:27, 3:73, 3:77, 3:98, 3:183, 3:250

Robbers, 1:99, 1:116, 1:135, 1:136, 1:216, 2:21

Rocks, 1:173, 1:285, 2:50, 2:53, 3:1, 3:29, 3:45, 3:46, 3:57, 3:112, 3:158, 3:172, 3:175, 3:178, 3:182, 3:186

Rocky Mountains, 1:273-1:273, 3:10, 3:69, 3:170

Roman, 1:200, 1:201, 1:209, 2:1, 2:8, 2:260, 2:265, 2:270-2:271, 2:273, 3:156, 3:216, 3:229, 3:231, 3:236

Romans, 1:15, 1:21, 1:130, 1:242, 1:251, 2:74, 2:91, 2:176, 2:188, 3:256

Rome, 1:189, 1:197, 1:207, 1:209, 3:216

Root of David. *See* David, root of.

Root of Jesse. *See* Jesse, root of.

Rothschilds, 2:107

Ruin, 1:46, 1:50, 1:64, 1:87, 1:147, 1:155, 1:185, 1:230, 2:11, 2:72, 2:107, 2:138, 2:143, 2:150, 2:151, 3:71, 3:281-3:283, 3:348

Rumors, 1:40, 1:135, 1:246, 1:254, 1:275, 2:2, 2:45-2:47, 2:205, 3:21, 3:50, 3:328

Russia, 1:173, 1:225, 1:230, 1:232, 2:7, 2:8, 2:64, 2:107, 2:271, 3:156, 3:166, 3:223

Sabbath, 1:70, 1:156, 2:115, 2:160, 2:226, 3:129, 3:198, 3:250, 3:260

Sacrament, 1:96, 1:185, 2:129, 2:213, 2:218, 3:23, 3:317

Sacred, 1:103, 1:147, 1:152, 1:153, 1:156, 1:186, 1:193, 1:195, 1:220, 1:277, 1:278, 1:280, 2:vi, 2:43, 2:88, 2:150, 2:178, 2:268, 3:62, 3:87, 3:124, 3:129, 3:134, 3:177, 3:195, 3:198, 3:230, 3:260, 3:275, 3:294, 3:306-3:307, 3:309, 3:310, 3:315, 3:316

Sacrifice, 1:5, 1:45, 1:50, 1:57, 1:71, 1:73, 1:92, 1:114, 1:118, 1:164, 1:181, 1:186, 1:188, 1:203, 1:260, 1:265, 1:271, 2:1, 2:98, 2:112, 2:172, 2:179, 3:23-3:24, 3:26, 3:29, 3:33, 3:53, 3:63, 3:254, 3:279, 3:287

Safety, 1:28, 1:35, 1:40, 1:46, 1:50, 1:55, 1:60, 1:61, 1:66, 1:73, 1:77, 1:85, 1:86, 1:91, 1:93, 1:108, 1:115, 1:126, 1:130, 1:136, 1:138, 1:139, 1:148, 1:154, 1:155, 1:161, 1:164, 1:167, 1:189, 1:210, 1:220, 1:283, 1:290, 1:294, 2:viii, 2:10, 2:14, 2:15, 2:27, 2:41, 2:91, 2:92, 2:137, 2:138, 2:140-2:142, 2:147, 2:158, 2:174, 2:197, 2:246, 3:9, 3:11, 3:19, 3:44, 3:56, 3:71, 3:84, 3:113, 3:147, 3:148, 3:218, 3:228, 3:275

Saint, 1:31, 1:37, 1:39, 1:40, 1:104, 1:238, 1:281, 2:150, 2:166, 2:169, 2:223, 2:245, 3:62, 3:86, 3:220, 3:275, 3:279

Salt, 1:viii, 1:13, 1:39, 1:65, 1:80, 1:102-1:104, 1:106, 1:110, 1:112, 1:172, 1:187, 1:280, 1:281, 2:72, 2:73, 2:129, 2:163, 2:217, 2:224, 2:225, 2:246, 3:63, 3:125, 3:264

Salt Lake City, 1:viii, 1:13, 1:39, 1:102-1:104, 1:106, 1:110, 1:112, 1:172, 1:187, 1:280, 1:281, 2:73, 2:163, 2:224, 2:225, 2:246, 3:125, 3:264

Samuel, 1:211, 3:320

Sanctification, 1:32, 1:143, 3:76, 3:118, 3:335, 3:337

Sanctified, 1:7, 1:8, 1:37, 1:38, 1:50, 1:124, 1:260, 2:55, 2:97, 2:110, 2:117, 2:174, 3:9, 3:23, 3:42, 3:53, 3:74, 3:76, 3:77, 3:80, 3:85, 3:90, 3:92, 3:110, 3:119, 3:135, 3:139, 3:140, 3:143, 3:149, 3:195, 3:209, 3:280, 3:286, 3:298, 3:329, 3:334, 3:336, 3:339, 3:341, 3:344, 3:348, 3:353

Sanctify, 1:35, 1:48, 1:56, 1:71, 1:141, 1:146, 1:294, 2:111, 2:162, 3:23, 3:53, 3:57, 3:65, 3:76, 3:87, 3:89, 3:92, 3:118, 3:119, 3:191, 3:204, 3:213, 3:336

Sanctuary, 2:81, 2:98, 3:63, 3:147, 3:189, 3:254

Satan, 1:15, 1:54, 1:64, 1:77, 1:81, 1:82, 1:87, 1:91, 1:98-1:100, 1:110, 1:111, 1:116, 1:117, 1:140, 1:147, 1:165, 1:166, 1:170, 1:179, 1:188, 1:193, 1:198, 1:215, 1:217, 1:218, 1:220, 1:261, 2:2, 2:4, 2:17, 2:49, 2:66, 2:70, 2:131, 2:157, 2:161, 2:175, 2:185, 2:189, 2:191, 2:202, 2:206, 2:209, 2:212, 2:213, 2:215, 2:216, 2:219, 2:221, 2:223, 2:226, 2:228, 2:230, 2:235, 2:236, 2:238, 2:246, 2:254, 2:263, 2:281, 2:285, 3:47, 3:51, 3:55, 3:56, 3:104, 3:106, 3:189, 3:190, 3:192, 3:194, 3:199, 3:202, 3:209, 3:212-3:213, 3:240, 3:244, 3:257, 3:278, 3:287, 3:289, 3:308, 3:327, 3:330, 3:334, 3:337, 3:344, 3:352-3:354

Saturday, 1:89, 1:278, 2:18, 3:91, 3:92, 3:158, 3:165, 3:201, 3:289

Saturn, 3:82, 3:194

Scatter, 1:155, 1:284, 3:108, 3:282

Schemers, 3:281

School, 1:43, 1:56, 1:171, 1:187, 3:5, 3:124, 3:276, 3:282

Schools, 1:107, 1:121, 1:178, 1:183, 3:61, 3:125, 3:127

Science, 2:44, 2:108, 3:83, 3:86, 3:117, 3:141

Scoffers, 1:21, 2:69, 3:8, 3:45

Scorn, 1:120

Scourge, 1:36, 1:42, 1:43, 1:49, 1:52, 1:100, 1:102, 1:176, 1:255, 1:3, 2:6, 2:19, 2:21, 2:22, 2:36, 2:56, 2:61, 2:64, 2:133, 2:136, 2:137, 2:220, 3:96, 3:106

Scripture, 1:vi, 1:6, 1:54, 1:68, 1:200, 1:241, 1:261, 1:273, 1:274, 1:280, 2:44, 2:108, 2:136, 2:179, 2:215, 3:2, 3:6, 3:117, 3:132, 3:192, 3:199, 3:215, 3:312, 3:316, 3:320

Scroll, 1:256, 2:5, 2:23, 2:28, 2:52, 2:131, 2:266, 2:278, 3:5, 3:6, 3:22, 3:45, 3:55, 3:166, 3:227

Scrolls, 3:320

Sea, 1:26, 1:51, 1:64, 1:73, 1:85, 1:115, 1:130, 1:140, 1:217, 1:234, 1:236, 1:237, 1:243, 1:255, 1:260, 1:271, 1:276, 1:291, 1:294, 2:3, 2:5, 2:11, 2:15, 2:21-2:22, 2:25, 2:27, 2:38, 2:39, 2:52, 2:66, 2:79, 2:81, 2:84, 2:87, 2:96, 2:102, 2:106, 2:127, 2:138, 2:153, 2:222, 2:245, 2:253, 2:260-2:262, 2:268, 2:275, 2:279, 3:4, 3:21, 3:34, 3:42, 3:46, 3:54-3:55, 3:57, 3:59, 3:64, 3:82, 3:96, 3:111, 3:112, 3:122, 3:150, 3:166, 3:170, 3:173, 3:180-3:181, 3:185, 3:192, 3:197, 3:202-3:204, 3:208, 3:210-3:211, 3:245, 3:252, 3:308, 3:310, 3:322, 3:327, 3:330, 3:338, 3:340, 3:341, 3:347, 3:351, 3:355

    sea of glass, 2:29, 2:29, 2:278, 3:192, 3:338, 3:353, 3:355

Seal, 1:15, 1:38, 1:90, 1:140, 1:142, 1:224, 1:230, 1:241, 1:255, 1:293, 2:2, 2:28, 2:37, 2:38, 2:52, 2:59, 2:147, 2:169, 2:202, 2:285, 3:1, 3:12, 3:15, 3:46, 3:53, 3:54, 3:108, 3:110, 3:185, 3:186, 3:190, 3:192, 3:209, 3:210, 3:324, 3:339, 3:350

Sealed, 1:8, 1:14, 1:18, 1:23-1:24, 1:26, 1:53, 1:69, 1:71, 1:84, 1:116, 1:130, 1:140, 1:226, 1:244-1:245, 1:248-1:249, 1:251, 1:258, 1:291, 1:292, 2:2, 2:136, 2:179, 2:195, 2:278-2:279, 3:53, 3:137, 3:185, 3:191, 3:192, 3:194, 3:211, 3:295, 3:306, 3:311, 3:313, 3:324, 3:327, 3:329-3:330, 3:339

Sealed in their foreheads, 1:53, 1:226, 1:248-1:249, 2:2, 3:194

Sealed records, 3:311

Sealing power, 1:14

Seals, 2:259, 3:195

Season, 1:7, 1:56, 1:117, 1:121, 2:18, 2:65, 2:74, 2:141, 2:158, 2:185, 2:240, 2:277, 2:285, 2:3, 3:1, 3:36, 3:38, 3:44, 3:82, 3:90, 3:92, 3:107, 3:118, 3:125, 3:139, 3:143, 3:191, 3:204, 3:209, 3:211, 3:213, 3:334, 3:336, 3:340, 3:348-3:350, 3:354

    Season, little. *See* Little season.

Seasons, 1:29, 1:75, 1:96, 1:279, 2:38, 2:43, 2:58, 2:186, 3:11, 3:14, 3:44, 3:69, 3:180, 3:212, 3:213, 3:226, 3:314

Second Coming, 1:vii, 1:14, 1:18, 1:51, 1:54-1:55, 1:62, 1:68, 1:75, 1:76, 1:87, 1:90, 1:97, 1:99, 1:101, 1:110, 1:112, 1:116, 1:117, 1:119-1:120, 1:122, 1:124-1:126, 1:199, 1:227, 1:259, 1:269, 1:280-1:282, 2:vi, 2:3, 2:21, 2:28, 2:44, 2:50, 2:59, 2:69, 2:74, 2:92, 2:94, 2:95, 2:108, 2:126, 2:0, 3:vii, 3:2, 3:1, 3:3, 3:8, 3:9, 3:12, 3:15, 3:17-3:19, 3:21-3:24, 3:28, 3:30, 3:34, 3:35, 3:46, 3:49, 3:52, 3:94, 3:96, 3:136-3:137, 3:143, 3:162, 3:206, 3:297, 3:318, 3:333

Secret, 1:23, 1:28, 1:67, 1:99, 1:102, 1:110, 1:154, 1:163, 1:166, 1:168, 1:178, 1:185-1:186, 1:213, 1:216, 1:218, 1:221, 1:253, 1:290, 2:2, 2:20, 2:32-2:33, 2:36, 2:49, 2:76, 2:108, 2:129, 2:140, 2:141, 2:149, 2:175, 2:191, 2:202, 2:220, 2:230, 2:260, 3:1, 3:6, 3:35, 3:38, 3:40, 3:48, 3:101, 3:162, 3:211, 3:213, 3:260, 3:262, 3:312, 3:327, 3:328

Secret combination, 1:178, 1:185, 1:186, 1:217-1:218

Secret combinations, 1:23, 1:99, 1:154, 1:166, 1:184, 1:186, 1:290, 2:191, 3:328

Secret societies, 1:110, 1:178, 2:175

Sect(s), 1:145, 1:149, 1:230, 2:viii, 2:160, 2:173, 2:186, 3:63, 3:64, 3:221, 3:334

Secular, 1:119, 1:211, 3:247, 3:295, 3:317

Security, 1:92, 1:105, 1:115, 1:116, 1:132, 1:149, 1:151, 1:167, 1:172, 1:176, 1:177, 1:179-1:181, 1:183, 1:190, 1:198, 1:200, 2:149, 2:151, 2:183, 2:213, 2:229, 3:92, 3:102

Seed, 1:4, 1:18-1:19, 1:22-1:23, 1:34, 1:108, 1:118, 1:131, 1:152, 1:232, 1:236, 1:244, 1:252, 1:266, 1:274, 1:281, 1:286, 2:2, 2:3, 2:22, 2:44, 2:63, 2:84, 2:90, 2:101, 2:103, 2:104, 2:119, 2:124, 2:128, 2:130-2:131, 2:172, 2:187, 2:223, 2:236, 2:238, 2:262, 2:276, 2:281, 3:1, 3:2, 3:8, 3:103, 3:109, 3:145, 3:149, 3:158, 3:175,

3:184, 3:185, 3:216, 3:253, 3:263, 3:304, 3:311, 3:320, 3:322, 3:323, 3:325, 3:326, 3:352

Seeds, 1:98, 1:159, 1:177, 2:147, 2:148, 2:221

Seer, 1:19, 1:22, 1:26, 1:45, 1:176, 3:263, 3:310, 3:322

Seers, 1:24, 3:31, 3:297, 3:316

Self, 1:33, 1:45, 1:66, 1:67, 1:104, 1:113, 1:125, 1:147, 1:184, 1:189, 1:194, 1:198, 1:200, 1:204-1:205, 1:208, 1:231, 1:281, 2:74, 2:197, 2:213, 2:218, 2:260, 3:87, 3:142, 3:269, 3:281, 3:284, 3:288, 3:298, 3:299

Selfish, 1:173, 3:204, 3:273

Selfishness, 1:94, 1:95, 1:121, 1:160, 3:132, 3:267, 3:281, 3:285-3:286, 3:288-3:289, 3:292, 3:297, 3:299

Senators, 1:162, 1:208

Serpent, 2:135, 2:261, 2:281, 2:285, 3:55, 3:209, 3:213, 3:257, 3:330, 3:350

Service, 1:118, 1:166, 1:169, 1:192, 1:263, 2:3, 2:172-2:173, 3:288, 3:290, 3:291

Seven, 1:8, 1:30, 1:51, 1:263, 2:7, 2:53, 2:57, 2:61, 2:98, 2:101, 2:116, 2:146, 2:211, 2:278, 2:282, 3:4, 3:13, 3:24, 3:26, 3:54, 3:154, 3:155, 3:161, 3:168, 3:170, 3:191, 3:192, 3:209-3:210, 3:215, 3:229, 3:255, 3:306, 3:312, 3:313, 3:341, 3:351

Seventh, 1:161, 1:248, 1:249, 2:53, 2:57, 2:59, 2:101, 2:116, 2:273, 2:279, 2:283, 3:5, 3:13, 3:45, 3:46, 3:120, 3:153, 3:155, 3:189, 3:210, 3:213, 3:236, 3:256, 3:270, 3:296, 3:330, 3:336, 3:352, 3:354

seventh seal, 2:28, 2:28, 2:59, 2:279, 3:1, 3:12, 3:15, 3:46, 3:54

seventh thousand years, 1:248, 1:249, 2:59, 3:1, 3:12, 3:13, 3:53, 3:191, 3:192

Seventies, 1:225, 1:229, 2:40, 2:83, 2:243, 3:128, 3:158

Seventy, 1:248, 3:151, 3:155

Sex, 1:112, 1:123, 1:201

Sex education, 1:112, 1:183

Sexual, 1:102, 1:107, 1:201, 2:20

Shalmaneser, 3:176

Shame, 1:128, 2:97, 2:116, 2:133, 2:212, 2:251, 2:283, 3:26, 3:58, 3:163

Sheep, 1:51, 1:115, 1:242, 1:272, 1:273, 1:282, 1:283, 1:286, 2:89, 2:99, 2:127, 2:129, 2:130, 2:168, 2:188, 2:240, 2:248, 2:253, 3:26, 3:69, 3:173, 3:180, 3:184, 3:268

Shepherd, 1:115, 1:274, 1:286, 1:288, 2:41, 2:97, 2:122, 2:131, 3:16, 3:39, 3:98, 3:118, 3:179, 3:254, 3:310, 3:323

Shepherds, 2:197, 2:248, 3:182

Shoot, 3:42, 3:51

Showdown, 1:vii, 1:98, 1:109

Sickle, 1:227, 2:114, 3:7, 3:9

Sickness, 1:42, 1:43, 1:47, 1:51, 1:255, 1:277, 2:21, 2:36, 2:72, 2:215, 3:189, 3:200, 3:348

Siege, 1:23, 2:50, 2:81, 2:85, 2:92, 3:34

Siegel, Alberta, 1:125

Sign, 1:8, 1:152, 1:232, 1:256, 1:262, 1:275, 1:276, 2:2-2:3, 2:21, 2:26, 2:29, 2:43, 2:88, 2:112, 2:115, 2:144, 2:195, 2:230, 2:281, 3:1-3:2, 3:22, 3:27, 3:35-3:38, 3:40, 3:42, 3:54, 3:103, 3:143

Sign of the Son of Man, 2:2, 2:21, 2:26, 2:115, 2:195, 3:20, 3:21, 3:36-3:38, 3:40, 3:143

Signs, 1:5, 1:21, 1:29, 1:47, 1:48, 1:65, 1:76, 1:84, 1:90, 1:102, 1:126, 1:135, 1:138, 1:149, 1:154, 1:155, 1:211, 1:225, 1:234, 1:236, 1:237, 1:247, 1:251, 1:255, 1:264-1:266, 2:vii, 2:2, 2:5, 2:8, 2:17, 2:19, 2:21, 2:27, 2:32, 2:35, 2:36, 2:40, 2:52, 2:107, 2:108, 2:195, 2:196, 2:201, 2:203, 2:205, 2:206, 2:228, 2:230, 3:vii-3:viii, 3:1, 3:9, 3:12, 3:14, 3:21, 3:22, 3:39, 3:43, 3:49, 3:131, 3:176, 3:178, 3:223, 3:317

Signs of the times, 1:9, 1:10, 1:47, 1:65, 1:84, 1:117, 1:140, 1:149, 1:239, 2:vii, 2:19, 2:108, 2:203, 3:viii, 3:11, 3:12, 3:14, 3:53, 3:143, 3:176, 3:317

Silence, 1:62, 1:68, 1:124, 1:203, 1:256, 2:28, 2:36, 2:225, 2:279, 3:23, 3:29, 3:54

Sinai, 1:51, 2:54, 3:24, 3:49

Sister, 2:160, 2:170, 2:178, 2:196, 3:120, 3:189, 3:270

Sisters, 1:27, 1:34, 1:71, 1:76, 1:86, 1:111, 1:114, 1:120, 1:163, 1:170, 1:181, 1:262, 2:11, 2:42, 2:63, 2:160, 2:166, 2:170, 2:171, 2:173-2:174, 2:183, 2:214, 2:243, 3:93, 3:155, 3:284, 3:285, 3:288, 3:289, 3:315, 3:334

Six, 1:vii, 1:13, 1:34, 1:97, 1:110, 1:243, 2:3, 2:56, 2:63, 2:81, 2:123, 2:133, 2:195, 2:196, 2:212, 2:258, 2:264, 2:278,

3:2, 3:13, 3:53, 3:124, 3:127, 3:155, 3:167, 3:189, 3:191-3:194, 3:201, 3:228, 3:249, 3:306, 3:311, 3:313

Sixth, 1:11, 1:25, 1:227, 2:28, 2:52, 2:111, 2:245, 2:255, 2:278, 2:283, 3:5, 3:55, 3:300, 3:352

    sixth seal, 1:255, 1:291, 2:28, 2:52, 2:278, 3:186

    sixth thousand years, 1:255, 1:291, 2:56, 3:186

Slave, 1:172, 3:259

Slavery, 1:171, 1:173, 1:187, 2:200

Slaves, 1:173, 2:48, 2:123, 2:153, 2:253

Slay, 1:34, 1:85, 1:118, 1:135, 1:139, 1:154, 1:157, 1:217, 1:277, 2:13, 2:17, 2:20, 2:37, 2:46, 2:74, 2:184, 2:185, 2:249, 2:280, 3:5, 3:29, 3:133, 3:252

Smite, 1:21, 1:25, 1:216, 1:226, 1:236, 1:263, 2:17, 2:22, 2:25, 2:48, 2:58, 2:99-2:101, 2:107, 2:111, 2:115, 3:29, 3:36, 3:38, 3:46, 3:57, 3:96, 3:112, 3:130, 3:168, 3:178, 3:186, 3:208, 3:252

Smith, Joseph, 1:4, 1:7-1:9, 1:14, 1:17-1:18, 1:26, 1:28, 1:40, 1:87, 1:105, 1:113, 1:121, 1:125, 1:147-1:148, 1:150, 1:153-1:155, 1:157, 1:160, 1:175, 1:180, 1:185, 1:186, 1:197, 1:199, 1:223-1:224, 1:246, 1:248, 1:259, 1:272, 1:273, 1:275, 1:278, 1:279, 1:292, 2:2-2:4, 2:35, 2:40, 2:55, 2:63, 2:66, 2:79, 2:90, 2:95, 2:134, 2:141, 2:148, 2:157, 2:163, 2:170, 2:172, 2:181, 2:185-2:186, 2:195-2:197, 2:201, 2:216, 2:218, 2:235, 2:241, 2:243, 2:257, 2:259, 2:260, 2:264, 2:266, 3:vi, 3:3, 3:9-3:11, 3:13, 3:21, 3:59, 3:61, 3:63, 3:85, 3:91, 3:93, 3:115, 3:128, 3:131, 3:135, 3:136, 3:139, 3:140, 3:148, 3:151, 3:153, 3:158, 3:171, 3:178, 3:189, 3:190, 3:202, 3:216, 3:217, 3:228, 3:229, 3:242, 3:249, 3:258-3:260, 3:306, 3:308, 3:310, 3:319, 3:333

Smoke, 1:21, 1:53, 1:127, 1:128, 1:288, 2:21, 2:24, 2:25, 2:27, 2:36, 2:43, 2:70, 2:107, 2:189, 2:243, 2:254, 3:5, 3:17, 3:33, 3:43, 3:51, 3:63, 3:80, 3:95, 3:99, 3:118, 3:126, 3:152, 3:328, 3:350

Smoking, 1:37

Socialism, 1:101, 1:173, 1:178, 1:208, 2:200, 2:225, 3:297

Socialist, 2:151

Socialistic, 1:116, 1:211, 3:297

Society, 1:31, 1:38, 1:107, 1:121, 1:123, 1:157, 1:166, 1:168, 1:172, 1:173, 1:183, 1:186, 1:209, 1:224, 2:4, 2:74, 2:159, 2:179, 2:181, 2:196, 3:26, 3:90, 3:283, 3:334

Sodom, 1:55, 1:64, 1:72, 1:117, 1:176, 1:230, 2:12-2:14, 2:20, 2:101, 2:248, 3:14, 3:41

Solomon, 3:83, 3:177, 3:316, 3:320

Son(s) of perdition, 2:206, 2:212, 2:228

Song, 1:203, 1:248, 1:249, 1:271, 2:259, 3:58, 3:70, 3:112, 3:150, 3:212, 3:215

Songs, 1:139, 1:264, 1:291, 1:293, 2:55, 3:83, 3:97, 3:103, 3:107, 3:110, 3:148, 3:181, 3:186

Sorcerer, 3:243

Sorcerers, 3:35, 3:134, 3:202, 3:336, 3:351

Sorceries, 2:57, 2:254, 2:280

Sores, 2:57, 2:59, 2:283

Sorrow, 1:30, 1:44, 1:51, 1:83, 1:102, 1:115, 1:145, 1:157, 2:1, 2:4, 2:10, 2:11, 2:17, 2:57, 2:119, 2:135, 2:160, 2:174, 2:211, 2:213, 2:243, 2:250, 3:48, 3:98-3:99, 3:122, 3:139, 3:166, 3:168, 3:170, 3:181, 3:210, 3:213, 3:294, 3:336, 3:338, 3:340-3:341, 3:343

Soul, 1:vii, 1:61, 1:87, 1:94, 1:109, 1:113, 1:122, 1:128, 1:131, 1:176, 1:185, 1:189, 1:204, 1:220, 1:231, 1:260, 1:284, 2:7, 2:22, 2:24, 2:97, 2:123, 2:145, 2:184, 2:193, 2:217, 2:218, 2:227, 2:238, 2:247, 2:253, 2:283, 3:4, 3:68, 3:78, 3:80, 3:82, 3:99, 3:146, 3:166, 3:181, 3:203, 3:250, 3:251, 3:354

South America, 1:35, 1:49, 1:246, 1:269, 2:123, 2:124, 2:139, 2:147, 2:267, 3:3, 3:63-3:64, 3:68, 3:76-3:77, 3:127, 3:170, 3:289

South Carolina, 2:48

Sovereignty, 1:174, 1:181, 1:192, 1:205, 1:209, 3:234, 3:243

Soviet Union. *See* Russia.

Spare, 1:113, 1:115, 1:140, 1:242, 1:270, 1:291, 2:71, 2:77, 2:190, 2:213, 2:248, 2:254, 3:50, 3:53, 3:109, 3:146, 3:181, 3:304, 3:353

Spend, 1:85, 1:197

Spirit, contrite, 1:94, 2:223, 3:317, 3:329

Spirit of God, 1:vi, 1:1, 1:7, 1:48, 1:74, 1:82, 1:83, 1:236, 1:269, 2:vii, 2:viii, 2:3, 2:15, 2:18, 2:40-2:42, 2:55, 2:57, 2:73, 2:149, 2:179, 2:197-2:198, 2:207, 2:215, 2:216, 3:9, 3:83, 3:84, 3:152, 3:190, 3:196, 3:219, 3:244, 3:312

Spirits, 1:5, 1:8, 1:12-1:13, 1:29, 1:38, 1:81, 1:123, 1:158, 1:180, 1:249, 2:13, 2:116, 2:158, 2:168, 2:195, 2:197, 2:199-2:200, 2:207, 2:209, 2:217-2:219, 2:278, 3:6, 3:85, 3:153, 3:162, 3:193, 3:334, 3:346, 3:348, 3:349, 3:354

Spiritual, 1:2, 1:34, 1:37, 1:73, 1:95, 1:97-1:99, 1:103, 1:106, 1:108, 1:110, 1:119, 1:123, 1:125, 1:130, 1:167, 1:178, 1:183, 1:188, 1:202, 1:208, 1:211-1:213, 1:236, 1:243, 1:259, 1:261, 1:262, 1:268, 1:279, 1:283, 1:295, 2:vi, 2:15, 2:95, 2:158, 2:200, 2:211, 2:219, 2:222, 2:223, 2:244, 2:247, 2:255, 2:262, 2:272-2:274, 3:18, 3:65, 3:68, 3:84, 3:112, 3:132, 3:134, 3:136, 3:143, 3:152, 3:183, 3:192, 3:198, 3:216, 3:220, 3:221, 3:247, 3:248, 3:262, 3:268, 3:272, 3:275, 3:276, 3:278, 3:309, 3:318, 3:354

Spirituality, 1:111, 1:185, 1:189, 3:91

Spoil, 2:90, 2:107, 2:108, 2:110, 2:111, 3:34, 3:100, 3:108

Spring Hill, Missouri, 3:161, 3:164

Stake, 1:32-1:33, 1:103, 1:104, 1:106, 1:108, 1:110, 1:126, 1:174, 1:182, 1:190, 1:211, 1:260, 2:64, 2:68, 2:93, 2:173, 2:217, 3:65, 3:67-3:68, 3:94, 3:124, 3:127, 3:128, 3:132, 3:199, 3:262, 3:278, 3:280, 3:338, 3:340

Stakes, 1:27, 1:102, 1:104, 1:144, 1:190, 1:232, 1:257, 1:278, 1:283, 1:292, 1:295, 2:1, 2:161, 2:217, 2:228, 3:31, 3:62, 3:63, 3:87, 3:94, 3:103, 3:105, 3:107, 3:112, 3:124, 3:127, 3:129, 3:132, 3:143, 3:146, 3:176, 3:181, 3:289

Standard, 1:4, 1:33, 1:60, 1:101, 1:153-1:154, 1:156, 1:157, 1:189, 1:208, 1:230, 1:266, 2:12, 2:48, 2:96, 3:15, 3:50, 3:62, 3:63, 3:72, 3:88, 3:175, 3:182, 3:220, 3:237, 3:243, 3:277, 3:325

Star, 1:65, 1:159, 2:4, 2:18, 2:66, 2:91, 2:123, 2:136, 2:151, 2:196, 2:245, 2:279, 3:viii, 3:78, 3:125, 3:134, 3:140, 3:165-3:166, 3:174, 3:224, 3:243, 3:256, 3:306, 3:308

Stars, 1:8, 1:164, 1:194, 1:247, 1:251, 1:256, 1:260, 2:7-2:8, 2:12, 2:18, 2:23, 2:36, 2:38, 2:107, 2:108, 2:113-2:115, 2:264, 2:278, 2:279, 3:20, 3:30, 3:36-3:40, 3:42, 3:51, 3:58, 3:131, 3:201, 3:223, 3:290, 3:305, 3:346

Stars fall, 1:8, 1:260, 2:36, 2:108, 3:20, 3:51

Starve, 1:37, 2:74, 2:220

State, 1:viii, 1:14, 1:39, 1:46, 1:51, 1:100, 1:117, 1:145, 1:151, 1:165, 1:169, 1:175, 1:177, 1:180-1:182, 1:186-1:188, 1:191-1:192, 1:194, 1:195, 1:197, 1:198, 1:203, 1:208, 1:211-1:212, 1:269, 1:292, 2:4, 2:44, 2:91, 2:93, 2:103, 2:135-2:137, 2:141-2:142, 2:151, 2:160, 2:200, 2:202, 2:215, 2:226, 2:234, 2:238, 2:267, 2:273, 2:274, 3:26, 3:72, 3:84, 3:91, 3:115, 3:120, 3:131, 3:133, 3:148, 3:153, 3:189, 3:196, 3:202-3:204, 3:216, 3:219, 3:226, 3:236-3:238, 3:243, 3:246, 3:262-3:263, 3:269, 3:277, 3:283, 3:287, 3:298, 3:299, 3:323, 3:329, 3:334, 3:337, 3:339, 3:340, 3:344, 3:346-3:348, 3:353, 3:355

State control, 1:204

States, 1:vii, 1:40, 1:42, 1:69, 1:147, 1:150, 1:154, 1:158-1:160, 1:162, 1:165, 1:166, 1:168, 1:172, 1:175, 1:177-1:178, 1:180, 1:183-1:184, 1:187, 1:189, 1:191, 1:193-1:194, 1:201, 1:210-1:211, 1:220, 1:237, 1:277, 1:3, 2:11, 2:13, 2:16, 2:48, 2:56, 2:92, 2:122, 2:134-2:136, 2:144, 2:150, 2:152-2:153, 2:162, 2:164, 2:168, 2:180, 2:183, 2:224, 2:264, 2:268, 3:3, 3:11, 3:63, 3:64, 3:74, 3:117, 3:123, 3:133, 3:156, 3:160, 3:165, 3:173, 3:190, 3:223-3:224, 3:230, 3:240, 3:241, 3:246, 3:248

Statue, 3:232, 3:307

Status, 1:191

Statutes, 2:97, 3:87, 3:111, 3:178, 3:254, 3:316

Stem of Jesse. *See* Jesse, stem of.

Steward, 1:141, 3:108, 3:120, 3:259, 3:266, 3:268, 3:270, 3:279, 3:286, 3:300, 3:302, 3:304

Stewards, 1:143, 2:154, 2:192, 3:120, 3:121, 3:266, 3:268, 3:270, 3:290

Stewardship, 2:224, 3:121, 3:123, 3:153, 3:263, 3:265, 3:269-3:270, 3:283, 3:284, 3:286, 3:289, 3:293, 3:295

Stewardships, 3:120, 3:121, 3:124, 3:151, 3:158-3:160, 3:269-3:271, 3:299, 3:302

Stick, 1:17, 1:110, 1:238, 3:272

Stocks, 1:92

Stone, 1:32, 1:93, 1:94, 1:116, 1:152, 1:234, 1:244, 1:271, 2:85, 2:116, 2:145, 2:158, 2:169, 2:253, 2:261, 2:265, 2:268, 2:272-2:274, 2:276, 2:280, 3:8, 3:34, 3:62, 3:75, 3:86, 3:89, 3:96, 3:124, 3:126, 3:151, 3:155, 3:156, 3:170, 3:215-3:216, 3:226-3:227, 3:229, 3:231, 3:233, 3:236, 3:249, 3:257, 3:274

Stones, 2:252-2:253, 2:284, 3:75, 3:80, 3:130, 3:136, 3:151, 3:158, 3:182, 3:352

Storehouse, 1:106, 1:128, 3:105, 3:149, 3:267, 3:271, 3:288, 3:292, 3:294, 3:298, 3:302, 3:303

Storm, 1:23, 1:53, 1:64, 1:102, 1:108, 1:126, 1:127, 1:134, 1:144, 1:145, 1:194, 1:281, 1:294, 2:5, 2:11, 2:31, 2:54, 2:56, 2:63, 2:74, 2:81, 2:110, 3:63, 3:70, 3:95, 3:111

Storms, 1:50, 1:71, 1:79, 1:95, 1:142, 1:276, 2:11, 2:13, 2:14, 2:16, 2:18, 2:63, 2:138, 3:124, 3:129

Strange act, 1:143

Stranger, 1:272, 1:273, 2:197, 3:35

Strangers, 1:79, 1:243, 1:273, 2:114, 2:197, 2:251, 3:33, 3:64, 3:65, 3:140, 3:143, 3:283, 3:312

Structure, 1:182, 1:206, 2:211, 2:221, 3:136

Stubble, 1:117, 1:137, 1:140, 1:269, 1:290, 1:291, 2:25, 2:30, 2:39, 2:66, 2:67, 2:75, 2:78, 2:113, 2:185, 2:240, 2:254, 3:24, 3:32, 3:35, 3:48, 3:53, 3:58, 3:59, 3:199, 3:210, 3:211, 3:335

Student(s), 1:109, 1:230, 2:151, 2:181

Studying, 1:vi, 1:85, 1:96, 1:185, 2:217, 3:25, 3:86

Styles, 1:110

Subversive, 2:181, 2:225

Success, 1:110, 1:181, 1:184, 1:281, 3:277, 3:283, 3:288, 3:292, 3:295

Suffer, 1:28, 1:30, 1:34, 1:43, 1:45, 1:49, 1:52, 1:54, 1:62, 1:63, 1:68, 1:85, 1:91, 1:94, 1:97, 1:131, 1:135, 1:152, 1:154, 1:155, 1:195, 1:207, 1:215, 1:217-1:218, 1:225, 1:234, 1:237, 1:238, 2:31, 2:47, 2:59, 2:65, 2:70, 2:83, 2:92, 2:101, 2:120, 2:129, 2:142, 2:156, 2:157, 2:160, 2:166, 2:171, 2:174, 2:184, 2:188-2:192, 2:236, 2:238, 3:26, 3:83, 3:102, 3:106, 3:110, 3:118, 3:202, 3:259, 3:296, 3:341

Suffering, 1:28, 1:36, 1:62, 1:97, 1:102, 1:116, 1:121, 1:126, 1:170, 1:171, 1:228, 1:243, 1:263, 2:10, 2:20, 2:41, 2:42, 2:89, 2:91, 2:159, 2:166, 2:179, 3:315

Suicide, 1:109, 1:166

Summer, 1:122, 1:152, 1:156, 1:238, 1:244, 1:271, 2:vii, 2:137, 2:153, 2:267-2:269, 2:271-2:272, 2:276, 3:1, 3:9, 3:11, 3:36, 3:37, 3:39, 3:41, 3:42, 3:51, 3:142, 3:226, 3:227, 3:229-3:230, 3:274

Sun, 1:8, 1:12, 1:21, 1:49, 1:50, 1:59, 1:76, 1:120, 1:123, 1:124, 1:128, 1:152, 1:153, 1:162, 1:228, 1:247, 1:251, 1:256, 1:260, 1:261, 2:7-2:8, 2:12, 2:18, 2:21, 2:23, 2:25, 2:27-2:28, 2:36, 2:38, 2:52, 2:59, 2:66, 2:107, 2:108, 2:113-2:115, 2:168, 2:187, 2:212, 2:278-2:279, 2:283, 3:1, 3:19, 3:22-3:24, 3:26, 3:29, 3:35-3:40, 3:42, 3:43, 3:46, 3:51, 3:58, 3:64, 3:75-3:77, 3:79, 3:80, 3:99, 3:118, 3:127, 3:131, 3:140, 3:143, 3:146, 3:149, 3:200, 3:209, 3:223, 3:305, 3:331, 3:352

Supreme Court, 1:159, 1:181, 1:192, 2:200

Surplus, 3:111, 3:279, 3:284, 3:290, 3:294, 3:298-3:299

Survival, 1:97-1:97, 1:104, 1:205

Survive, 1:97, 1:101, 1:111, 1:189, 1:190, 1:208-1:209, 2:16

Sustenance, 1:33, 1:87, 1:165, 1:167, 1:188, 3:274, 3:287

Sword, 1:20, 1:29, 1:46, 1:52, 1:53, 1:61, 1:66, 1:69, 1:86, 1:88, 1:105, 1:111, 1:130, 1:137, 1:139, 1:141, 1:143, 1:154, 1:161, 1:176, 1:214, 1:218, 1:223, 1:224, 1:234, 1:236, 1:242, 1:251, 1:254, 1:255, 1:285, 1:290, 2:vi, 2:vii, 2:1, 2:3, 2:8, 2:10, 2:18, 2:23, 2:31, 2:34, 2:36, 2:37, 2:39-2:41, 2:46-2:48, 2:62, 2:74, 2:90, 2:96-2:97, 2:99, 2:100, 2:110-2:111, 2:113, 2:134, 2:136-2:138, 2:146-2:148, 2:154, 2:161, 2:188, 2:230, 2:234, 2:239, 2:251, 2:254, 2:259, 2:268, 2:269, 2:271, 2:282, 3:31-3:32, 3:46, 3:65, 3:83, 3:84, 3:95, 3:99, 3:103, 3:107, 3:115, 3:148, 3:156, 3:164, 3:207, 3:230, 3:231, 3:239, 3:250, 3:257

Symbols, 1:92, 1:105, 2:149, 2:275

Sympathy, 1:151, 1:160, 1:165, 1:167, 3:275, 3:287

Tabernacle, 1:53, 1:278, 1:295, 2:29, 2:57, 2:144-2:145, 2:156, 2:226, 2:281, 2:282, 3:17, 3:55, 3:59, 3:63, 3:67, 3:85, 3:95, 3:113, 3:125, 3:126, 3:128, 3:130, 3:143, 3:145, 3:146, 3:150, 3:187, 3:189, 3:210, 3:214, 3:254,

Index

3:336, 3:341, 3:347
Talent, 2:60, 2:116, 2:273, 2:283, 3:302
Talents, 1:1, 1:94, 1:120, 3:14, 3:234, 3:262, 3:295-3:297, 3:302
        parable of the talents, 3:14
Tame, 1:242
Tares, 1:4, 1:72, 1:103, 1:181, 1:200, 1:231, 1:256, 1:286-1:287, 2:7, 2:14, 2:36, 2:198, 2:223, 2:236, 2:241, 3:4, 3:14,
        3:37, 3:54, 3:333
Tax, 1:46, 1:207, 3:71
Taxation, 1:174, 1:175, 1:183, 1:201, 1:202, 1:205, 1:208
Taxes, 1:177, 1:192, 1:202, 1:209
Teach, 1:20, 1:24, 1:48, 1:54, 1:57, 1:90, 1:99, 1:135, 1:169, 1:201, 1:228, 1:240, 1:274, 1:275, 1:284, 1:290, 2:11, 2:96,
        2:125, 2:158, 2:169, 2:180, 2:216, 2:226, 2:234, 2:241, 3:17, 3:67, 3:71, 3:76, 3:87, 3:95, 3:98-3:99,
        3:195, 3:208, 3:240, 3:252, 3:286, 3:290, 3:294, 3:314
Teacher, 2:195
Teachers, 1:vii, 1:24, 1:174, 2:93, 2:195, 2:196, 2:200, 2:206, 2:221-2:222, 2:230, 2:240, 3:2, 3:3, 3:62, 3:128, 3:243,
        3:328
Technology, 1:208
Telestial, 2:44, 3:140, 3:143, 3:202, 3:334, 3:339, 3:348
Tempest, 1:23, 2:5, 2:30, 2:31, 2:54, 2:81, 2:102, 2:163, 3:70
Tempests, 1:43, 1:85, 1:223, 1:224, 1:254, 1:256, 1:276, 2:vii, 2:3, 2:11, 2:36, 2:38, 2:63, 3:50, 3:54, 3:328
Temple, 1:8, 1:9, 1:11, 1:12, 1:72, 1:78-1:79, 1:84, 1:95, 1:101, 1:110, 1:158, 1:227, 1:234, 1:242, 1:245, 1:266, 1:278,
        1:280, 1:290, 1:292, 2:vi, 2:7, 2:15, 2:53, 2:57, 2:75, 2:79, 2:83, 2:86, 2:88-2:91, 2:101, 2:119, 2:120,
        2:122, 2:124, 2:145, 2:151, 2:206, 2:221, 2:228, 2:249, 2:282, 2:283, 3:vii-3:9, 3:11-3:12, 3:16-3:19,
        3:21, 3:34, 3:35, 3:47, 3:55, 3:56, 3:61, 3:62, 3:67, 3:68, 3:74, 3:75, 3:83, 3:90, 3:99, 3:104, 3:115,
        3:117, 3:120, 3:123, 3:125, 3:131, 3:134, 3:136, 3:137, 3:141, 3:145, 3:147, 3:161, 3:175, 3:178,
        3:194, 3:203, 3:243, 3:250-3:251, 3:255, 3:257, 3:267, 3:300, 3:306-3:307, 3:312, 3:318
        temple ordinances, 3:203, 3:318
Temples, 1:10, 1:32, 1:65, 1:79, 1:88, 1:89, 1:96, 1:99, 1:102, 1:273, 1:277, 1:278, 1:281, 1:283, 2:vii, 2:43, 2:87, 2:88,
        2:113, 3:18, 3:61, 3:62, 3:67, 3:69, 3:83, 3:106, 3:122, 3:124-3:125, 3:128-3:129, 3:179, 3:191, 3:271,
        3:334
Temporal, 1:33, 1:35, 1:37, 1:71, 1:77, 1:97, 1:104, 1:106, 1:111, 1:112, 1:116, 1:119, 1:259, 1:262, 1:281, 1:283, 2:15,
        2:245, 3:7, 3:13, 3:23, 3:24, 3:81, 3:84, 3:91, 3:183, 3:191-3:192, 3:220-3:221, 3:237, 3:244, 3:259,
        3:262, 3:271-3:273, 3:279-3:280, 3:283, 3:285, 3:287, 3:292, 3:297, 3:313, 3:339, 3:341, 3:346
Temptation, 1:65, 1:98, 1:125, 2:177, 2:186, 2:213, 3:285, 3:340, 3:346
Temptations, 2:156, 2:175, 3:189, 3:199, 3:202
Ten commandments, 1:165, 1:193, 3:78
Ten Tribes, 1:47, 1:80, 1:224, 1:229, 1:241, 1:244, 1:249, 1:259, 1:260, 1:272, 1:282, 1:294, 1:295, 2:95, 2:274, 2:3,
        3:viii, 3:21, 3:113, 3:150, 3:155, 3:165, 3:167, 3:169, 3:173, 3:176, 3:186, 3:187, 3:214, 3:237, 3:250,
        3:305, 3:311, 3:313
        Lost tribes, 1:232, 2:133, 3:11, 3:138, 3:165, 3:176-3:180, 3:184, 3:308, 3:310, 3:319
Ten virgins, parable of, 1:62, 1:68, 1:75, 1:95, 1:129, 2:231, 3:51, 3:295
Tent, 1:280-1:280, 2:248, 3:146, 3:181
Tenth Amendment, 1:187, 1:206
Terrestrial, 2:44, 3:13, 3:140, 3:143, 3:202-3:204, 3:206, 3:334, 3:348, 3:349
Test, 1:39, 1:95, 1:97, 1:111, 1:115, 1:124, 1:202, 1:207, 1:271, 2:150, 2:157, 2:173, 2:211, 2:216, 3:284
Testament, 1:116, 1:117, 1:125, 1:246, 1:259, 2:44, 2:53, 2:107, 2:184, 2:247, 3:1, 3:6, 3:7, 3:9, 3:12, 3:13, 3:24, 3:132,
        3:140, 3:162, 3:205, 3:217, 3:258, 3:311, 3:319
Tests, 1:viii, 1:39, 1:120, 2:4, 2:135, 2:173, 2:175
Theocracy, 1:151, 3:18, 3:205, 3:216, 3:219, 3:243, 3:248
Theocratic government, 3:218-3:219

Thermonuclear, 2:108

Thief, 1:40, 1:47, 1:75, 1:87, 1:117, 2:36, 2:113, 2:116, 2:283, 3:viii, 3:2, 3:9, 3:11, 3:14, 3:21, 3:32, 3:36, 3:38, 3:41, 3:45, 3:160

Thieves, 1:205, 1:277, 2:43

Thoughts, 1:54, 1:56, 1:89, 1:96, 1:133, 1:278, 2:18, 2:78, 2:202, 2:217, 3:9, 3:55, 3:91, 3:92, 3:158, 3:165, 3:213, 3:220, 3:289, 3:330

Thread, 1:147, 1:148, 1:166, 1:169-1:170, 1:175, 1:195, 1:210

Threaten, 1:169, 2:63

Three and a half, 2:85, 3:5, 3:6

Three Nephites, 1:45, 1:231, 2:93, 2:94, 3:140

Thrift, 3:299

Throne, 1:48, 1:58, 1:60, 1:81, 1:158, 1:188, 1:224, 1:251-1:252, 2:53, 2:82, 2:87, 2:116, 2:119, 2:156, 2:229, 2:254, 2:260, 2:261, 2:270, 2:277, 2:283, 3:16, 3:23, 3:39, 3:46, 3:102, 3:127, 3:154-3:156, 3:163, 3:182, 3:186, 3:194, 3:197, 3:210, 3:213, 3:216, 3:224, 3:226, 3:228, 3:232, 3:235, 3:251, 3:307, 3:330, 3:334, 3:336-3:337, 3:340-3:341, 3:346, 3:351, 3:354, 3:355

Thrones, 1:58-1:60, 1:62, 1:153, 1:157, 1:227, 1:234, 1:235, 2:1, 2:6, 2:13, 2:264, 2:277, 2:285, 3:19, 3:22, 3:130, 3:160, 3:163, 3:190, 3:195-3:196, 3:209, 3:223, 3:228, 3:233, 3:239, 3:246, 3:250, 3:255, 3:305, 3:312, 3:331, 3:346

Thunder, 1:23, 1:40, 1:75, 1:108, 1:111, 1:141, 1:252, 2:7, 2:13, 2:15, 2:18, 2:31, 2:37, 2:38, 2:54, 2:106, 2:146, 2:154, 2:191, 2:259, 3:4, 3:57, 3:70, 3:71, 3:112, 3:164, 3:257

Thunders, 1:28, 1:71, 1:223, 1:224, 1:265, 2:vii, 2:3, 2:7, 2:18, 2:53, 2:116, 2:283, 3:4, 3:50, 3:209-3:210, 3:306

Tidings, 1:26, 1:50, 1:53, 1:64, 1:227, 1:229, 2:45, 2:138, 3:3, 3:25, 3:73, 3:76, 3:100, 3:132, 3:198, 3:225

Time of the Gentiles. *See* Gentiles, time of Time:

Tithe, 1:141, 3:303

Tithing, 1:65, 1:92, 1:93, 1:95, 1:96, 1:108, 2:218, 2:226, 3:53, 3:86, 3:87, 3:92, 3:93, 3:111, 3:118, 3:120, 3:131, 3:263-3:264, 3:267, 3:269, 3:271, 3:273, 3:276-3:277, 3:280, 3:289, 3:295

Tobacco, 2:226

Token, 1:108, 3:138

Tolerance, 2:225

Tongue, 1:3, 1:124, 1:164, 1:186, 1:227, 1:241, 1:252, 1:255-1:257, 1:263, 1:264, 1:271, 1:272, 1:280, 1:292, 2:12, 2:48, 2:49, 2:56, 2:60, 2:77, 2:84, 2:100, 2:115, 2:116, 2:196, 2:245, 2:259, 2:261, 2:283, 3:vi-3:7, 3:21, 3:43, 3:55, 3:69, 3:79, 3:85, 3:86, 3:91, 3:102, 3:160, 3:168, 3:186, 3:205, 3:209, 3:215, 3:217, 3:219, 3:221, 3:234, 3:237, 3:327

Tongues, 1:51, 1:75, 1:224, 1:226, 1:231, 1:236, 1:238-1:239, 1:248, 1:249, 1:251, 1:266, 2:7, 2:15, 2:35, 2:79, 2:83, 2:93, 2:101, 2:103, 2:137, 2:157, 2:162, 2:238, 2:252, 2:261, 2:264, 2:268, 2:269, 2:271, 2:274, 2:281, 2:283, 2:284, 3:24, 3:25, 3:63, 3:75, 3:87, 3:157, 3:170, 3:194, 3:205, 3:226, 3:230, 3:231, 3:237, 3:323

Tool(s), 1:98, 1:165, 1:167, 3:268, 3:287, 3:289

Torment, 1:288, 1:288, 2:229, 2:243, 2:253, 2:282, 3:5, 3:58, 3:102, 3:202, 3:304

Tornadoes, 2:14

Tower of Babel, 2:4

Tradition, 1:135, 1:196, 1:250, 2:202, 3:73, 3:264

Traditions, 1:28, 1:54, 1:77, 1:109, 1:119, 1:207, 1:232, 2:226, 3:13, 3:71, 3:243, 3:267, 3:315

Train, 1:60, 1:74, 1:106, 1:118, 1:161, 1:275, 3:189, 3:290

Transfiguration, 3:52, 3:212, 3:353
    day of transfiguration, 3:52, 3:212, 3:353

Transfigured, 3:23, 3:52, 3:121, 3:212, 3:270, 3:328, 3:353

Transgression, 1:134, 2:56, 2:76, 2:136, 2:181, 2:197, 2:219, 3:30, 3:191, 3:193, 3:304, 3:335, 3:338

Translated, 1:11, 1:26, 1:235, 1:249, 2:218, 3:73, 3:84, 3:88, 3:139, 3:141, 3:198, 3:206, 3:296, 3:308, 3:310, 3:333

Translated beings, 3:318

Translation, 1:6, 1:9, 1:18, 1:25, 1:56, 1:125, 1:225, 2:124, 2:257, 3:84, 3:138-3:140, 3:143, 3:206, 3:332

Trap(s), 1:179, 2:200, 1:260, 3:63

Travail, 1:130, 2:27, 3:44, 3:146, 3:181

Treason, 1:193, 1:220

Treasure, 1:54, 1:138, 1:218, 2:143, 3:132

Treasures, 1:44, 1:198, 1:280, 2:45, 2:66, 3:57, 3:80, 3:105, 3:172, 3:186, 3:221, 3:264, 3:305, 3:312

Treasury, 1:178, 3:69, 3:264, 3:284, 3:287, 3:296

Treaty, 1:174-1:175, 1:194

Tree of life, 1:98, 1:288, 2:5, 3:165

Trespass, 1:73

Trial, 1:28, 1:31, 1:82, 1:93, 1:113, 1:121, 1:122, 1:153, 1:207, 2:157, 2:164, 2:168, 2:173, 2:185, 3:44, 3:88, 3:284

Trials, 1:8, 1:34, 1:41, 1:44, 1:57, 1:59, 1:63, 1:73, 1:74, 1:81, 1:84, 1:109, 1:115, 1:116, 1:119, 1:133, 1:188, 2:viii, 2:143, 2:150, 2:151, 2:156, 2:164, 2:175, 2:215, 2:217, 2:218, 3:7, 3:88

Tribe, 1:216, 1:240, 1:250, 1:255, 1:274, 1:291, 2:79, 2:82, 2:89-2:90, 2:117, 2:124, 3:135, 3:196, 3:249

Tribes, 1:47, 1:80, 1:130, 1:216, 1:217, 1:224, 1:228, 1:229, 1:231, 1:232, 1:235, 1:240, 1:241, 1:244, 1:247, 1:249-1:251, 1:253, 1:255, 1:259, 1:260, 1:269-1:270, 1:272, 1:274, 1:279-1:280, 1:291, 1:292, 1:294, 1:295, 2:26, 2:79, 2:83, 2:93-2:95, 2:104, 2:115, 2:120, 2:122, 2:126, 2:130, 2:133, 2:274, 2:279, 2:3, 3:viii, 3:11, 3:21, 3:36-3:38, 3:40, 3:63, 3:113, 3:133, 3:138, 3:150, 3:155, 3:166, 3:168, 3:171, 3:173, 3:176, 3:180, 3:186, 3:187, 3:193-3:194, 3:197, 3:214, 3:232, 3:237, 3:246, 3:255, 3:305, 3:307, 3:308, 3:310, 3:311, 3:313, 3:319, 3:326, 3:351

twelve tribes, 1:140, 1:255, 1:274, 1:289, 1:291, 3:19, 3:117, 3:133, 3:134, 3:169, 3:185, 3:193, 3:232, 3:246, 3:250, 3:255, 3:307, 3:351

Tribulation, 1:14, 1:28, 1:35, 1:36, 1:44, 1:50, 1:52, 1:56, 1:93, 1:95, 1:98, 1:105, 1:112, 1:121, 1:125, 1:137, 1:140, 1:226, 1:290, 1:293, 2:2, 2:26, 2:27, 2:78, 2:115, 2:116, 2:120, 2:157, 2:167, 2:186-2:188, 2:205, 2:233, 3:37, 3:48, 3:52, 3:109, 3:134, 3:291, 3:298, 3:302, 3:335

Tribulations, 1:8, 1:26, 1:50, 1:59, 1:106, 1:109, 1:114, 1:123, 1:127, 1:146, 1:225, 1:227, 1:266, 2:21, 2:138, 2:156, 2:215, 3:79, 3:113, 3:150, 3:205, 3:298, 3:305

Trump(s), 1:5, 1:38, 1:47, 1:254, 1:256, 1:265, 2:7, 2:36, 2:54, 2:56, 2:57, 2:68, 2:255, 3:viii, 3:4-3:6, 3:13, 3:22, 3:25, 3:44, 3:51, 3:54-3:56, 3:78, 3:330, 3:340, 3:353-3:354

Trumpet, 1:4, 1:47, 1:286, 1:287, 2:28, 2:46, 2:57, 2:96, 2:112, 2:132, 2:139, 2:140, 2:153, 2:209, 2:228, 2:259, 2:279, 2:280, 3:viii, 3:6, 3:32, 3:36, 3:37, 3:40, 3:77, 3:121, 3:159, 3:270, 3:306

Trumpets, 1:248, 2:53, 2:57, 2:58, 3:5-3:6, 3:22, 3:180, 3:192, 3:194

Trust, 1:21, 1:60, 1:63, 1:64, 1:70, 1:82-1:84, 1:94, 1:127, 1:133, 1:134, 1:149, 1:153, 1:159, 1:164, 1:167, 1:214, 2:153, 2:171, 2:184, 2:201, 2:218, 2:223, 2:229, 3:242, 3:261, 3:295

Twinkling, 3:52, 3:143, 3:196, 3:199, 3:203, 3:205-3:206, 3:211-3:213, 3:344

Two prophets, 2:59, 2:93, 2:95, 2:101, 2:105

Type, 1:100, 2:248, 3:33, 3:127, 3:147, 3:162, 3:251, 3:338

Tyranny, 1:62, 1:86, 1:99, 1:111, 1:145, 1:147, 1:160, 1:162, 1:171, 1:175, 1:178, 1:190, 1:191, 1:195, 2:124, 2:151, 2:264

Tyrants, 1:107

Unbelief, 1:15, 1:69, 1:117, 1:136, 1:138, 1:237, 1:242, 1:264, 2:vi, 2:30, 2:46, 2:84, 2:89, 2:93, 2:101, 2:104, 2:108, 2:131, 2:163, 2:246, 3:viii, 3:7, 3:9, 3:179, 3:184, 3:312, 3:317, 3:327, 3:329, 3:337

Understanding, 1:14, 1:29, 1:44, 1:47, 1:69, 1:80, 1:88, 1:90, 1:102, 1:113, 1:114, 1:127, 1:152, 1:169, 1:179, 1:201, 1:243, 1:273, 2:139, 2:171, 2:172, 2:199, 2:213, 2:233, 2:238, 2:244, 2:262, 2:268, 2:282, 3:viii, 3:3, 3:16, 3:64, 3:68, 3:89, 3:130, 3:140, 3:199, 3:203, 3:263, 3:276, 3:288, 3:296

Ungodliness, 1:15, 2:94, 3:249, 3:256

Unicorn, 3:172

United Nations, 1:174, 1:175, 1:206

United order, 1:74, 1:105, 1:164-1:165, 2:201, 2:3, 3:92, 3:131, 3:261, 3:262, 3:271, 3:274, 3:279-3:280, 3:285, 3:287,

3:291, 3:294, 3:296, 3:298-3:299

United States, 1:vii, 1:40, 1:69, 1:147, 1:150, 1:154-1:155, 1:158-1:160, 1:163, 1:165, 1:166, 1:168, 1:178, 1:180, 1:184, 1:187, 1:189, 1:193, 1:201, 1:206, 1:210-1:211, 1:237, 1:3, 2:11, 2:13, 2:16, 2:56, 2:92, 2:122, 2:135, 2:136, 2:150, 2:152, 2:164, 2:168, 2:180, 2:264, 3:64, 3:74, 3:117, 3:133, 3:156, 3:160, 3:165, 3:173, 3:190, 3:223-3:224, 3:240, 3:248

Universe, 1:249, 2:67, 2:134, 3:64, 3:153, 3:204, 3:245, 3:296, 3:346

Upheavals, 1:92, 2:59

Urim and Thummim, 1:8, 3:201, 3:310, 3:311, 3:315-3:316, 3:334

Usurpations, 1:171, 1:173, 1:181

Utah, 1:13, 1:50, 1:86, 1:102, 1:106, 1:108, 1:110, 1:112, 1:187, 1:190, 1:191, 1:202, 1:281, 2:138, 2:144, 2:224, 2:225, 2:233, 3:63, 3:131, 3:135, 3:287

Valiant, 1:65, 1:103, 1:110, 1:188, 1:199, 2:225

Valley Forge, 1:200

Valleys, 1:32, 1:35, 1:37, 1:39, 1:40, 1:47, 1:82, 1:87, 2:5, 2:25, 2:38, 2:50, 2:86, 2:106-2:107, 2:132, 2:150, 2:159, 2:169, 2:209, 3:viii, 3:3, 3:22, 3:25, 3:56, 3:57, 3:63, 3:65, 3:76, 3:92, 3:112, 3:123, 3:131, 3:195

Values, 1:107, 1:115, 1:125, 1:202, 1:208, 1:212, 2:246, 3:296

Vanity, 1:87, 2:61, 3:106, 3:282

Vapors, 1:276, 2:21, 2:36, 2:43, 3:51, 3:328

Veil, 1:33, 1:138, 1:146, 1:261, 2:35, 2:39, 2:75, 2:157, 3:49, 3:55, 3:59, 3:113, 3:204, 3:329

Vengeance, 1:20, 1:32, 1:50, 1:65, 1:87, 1:118, 1:128, 1:141, 1:143, 1:144, 1:176, 1:226, 1:269, 2:25, 2:32, 2:34, 2:35, 2:61, 2:62, 2:66, 2:76, 2:123, 2:124, 2:137, 2:140-2:142, 2:178, 2:181, 2:191, 3:27, 3:29, 3:44, 3:58, 3:59, 3:96, 3:107, 3:113, 3:202, 3:204, 3:293, 3:303

Venus, 3:82, 3:194

Victim(s), 1:62, 1:114, 2:vii, 3:205, 3:348

Victory, 1:15, 1:31, 1:39, 1:173, 1:200, 1:209, 2:29, 2:81, 2:92, 2:156, 2:161, 2:164, 2:173, 2:182, 3:222

Vine, 1:20, 1:128, 2:23, 3:100, 3:162, 3:255

Vineyard, 1:142, 1:248, 1:256, 1:288, 2:37, 2:44, 2:109, 2:171, 2:185, 3:8, 3:107-3:108, 3:283, 3:304, 3:349

Virgins, parable of the ten. *See* Ten Virgins.

Virtue, 1:32, 1:58-1:59, 1:151, 1:153, 1:156, 1:160, 1:167, 1:181, 1:281, 2:2, 2:9, 2:161, 2:168, 3:159, 3:203, 3:235, 3:280

Vision, 1:7-1:9, 1:13, 1:24, 1:55-1:56, 1:78, 1:81, 1:204, 1:227, 1:231, 1:242, 1:245, 1:246, 1:248, 1:271, 1:288, 1:294, 2:46, 2:68, 2:108, 2:139, 2:164, 2:166, 2:196, 2:200, 2:257-2:259, 2:261, 2:264, 2:272, 2:274, 2:275, 2:280, 3:62, 3:70, 3:71, 3:77, 3:80, 3:90, 3:102, 3:151, 3:159, 3:186, 3:215, 3:228, 3:233, 3:257

Visions, 1:21, 1:29, 1:65, 1:76, 1:128, 1:148, 1:249, 1:3, 2:15, 2:199, 2:202, 2:213, 2:257-2:259, 2:262, 2:270, 2:276-2:277, 3:8, 3:32, 3:33, 3:62, 3:99, 3:139, 3:167, 3:233, 3:235, 3:306-3:307, 3:316

Volunteer, 1:122, 1:122

Vote, 1:107, 1:149, 1:154, 1:178, 1:186, 1:192, 1:196, 2:214, 3:261, 3:265

Voting, 1:192, 1:203

Vulture, 2:3

Wages, 1:198, 1:202, 3:35

Wander, 1:169, 3:121, 3:270

War, 1:vii, 1:7, 1:10, 1:13, 1:28, 1:30, 1:33-1:34, 1:40, 1:41, 1:44, 1:45, 1:47, 1:58-1:60, 1:75, 1:76, 1:101, 1:102, 1:105, 1:108-1:109, 1:111-1:113, 1:115, 1:116, 1:127, 1:139, 1:153, 1:156, 1:165, 1:186, 1:194, 1:203, 1:208, 1:209, 1:214, 1:228, 1:231, 1:232, 1:236, 1:243, 1:244, 1:260, 1:276, 1:277, 1:290, 1:3, 2:viii, 2:4, 2:6, 2:8, 2:14-2:15, 2:19, 2:40, 2:42, 2:44, 2:59, 2:72, 2:74, 2:91, 2:98, 2:101, 2:108-2:110, 2:113-2:114, 2:116, 2:123, 2:124, 2:126, 2:135, 2:141, 2:143, 2:146, 2:151, 2:157, 2:159, 2:166, 2:167, 2:170, 2:182, 2:187, 2:201, 2:223, 2:226, 2:234, 2:245, 2:246, 2:249, 2:250, 2:252, 2:261-2:263, 2:265-2:266, 2:268-2:269, 2:273, 2:274, 2:277, 2:280-2:281, 3:vii, 3:11, 3:12, 3:26, 3:27, 3:32, 3:63, 3:83, 3:95,

Index

3:99, 3:100, 3:103, 3:115, 3:148, 3:153, 3:156, 3:163, 3:172, 3:207, 3:226-3:228, 3:230, 3:238-3:239
Civil War, 1:208, 2:123, 2:124, 2:148, 2:152
nuclear war, 1:209
war in heaven, 1:111, 1:180-1:181, 2:280, 3:349
Warfare, 1:8, 1:68, 1:159, 1:160, 1:244, 2:18, 2:21, 2:43, 2:123, 2:135, 2:141, 2:147, 2:172, 2:173, 2:235, 2:245, 3:10, 3:240, 3:242
Warn, 1:1, 1:viii, 1:39, 1:42, 1:54, 1:55, 1:64, 1:126, 1:147, 1:165, 1:171, 1:181, 1:185, 1:209, 1:224, 1:226, 1:227, 1:230, 1:293, 2:vii, 2:11, 2:14-2:15, 2:142, 2:153, 2:197, 3:9, 3:86, 3:110
Warning, 1:vi, 1:vii, 1:11, 1:64, 1:67, 1:74, 1:75, 1:90, 1:95, 1:97, 1:101-1:103, 1:117, 1:139, 1:140, 1:150, 1:164, 1:167, 1:175, 1:189, 1:190, 1:198, 1:203, 1:226, 1:227, 1:230, 1:237, 1:240, 1:243, 1:245, 1:261, 1:272, 1:277, 1:291, 2:vi, 2:1, 2:6, 2:11, 2:12, 2:17, 2:20, 2:37, 2:55, 2:69, 2:83, 2:133, 2:140, 2:265, 2:268, 3:2, 3:3, 3:14, 3:105, 3:166, 3:223, 3:230, 3:333
Warnings, 1:10, 1:75, 1:90, 1:242, 1:0, 2:15, 2:20, 3:21
Warriors, 3:108
Washington, George, 1:184
Waste, 1:35, 1:44, 1:51, 1:75, 1:87, 1:135, 1:145, 1:150, 1:151, 1:156, 1:201, 1:223, 1:240, 1:280, 2:3, 2:11, 2:12, 2:23, 2:25, 2:38, 2:41, 2:72, 2:94, 2:96, 2:110, 2:121, 2:147, 3:17, 3:30, 3:74, 3:85, 3:97, 3:98, 3:102, 3:107, 3:109, 3:110, 3:118-3:119, 3:121-3:122, 3:124, 3:129, 3:133, 3:239, 3:263
Watchmen, 2:197, 3:63, 3:97-3:98, 3:107-3:108, 3:149, 3:227
Water, 1:43, 1:48, 1:57, 1:73, 1:85, 1:148, 1:157, 2:14, 2:57, 2:59, 2:79, 2:81, 2:85-2:87, 2:92, 2:131, 2:165, 2:178, 2:245, 2:262, 2:281, 2:283, 3:21, 3:49, 3:57, 3:68, 3:144, 3:186, 3:193, 3:201, 3:335, 3:345
Waters, 1:64, 1:83, 1:153, 1:236, 1:251-1:252, 1:256, 1:263, 1:271, 2:7, 2:9, 2:25, 2:27-2:28, 2:38, 2:50, 2:56-2:58, 2:79, 2:81, 2:84, 2:85, 2:87, 2:98, 2:101, 2:106, 2:135, 2:137, 2:144, 2:153, 2:170, 2:234, 2:239, 2:241, 2:244, 2:252, 2:275, 2:279, 3:4, 3:21, 3:32, 3:54, 3:73, 3:78, 3:98, 3:112, 3:125, 3:139, 3:170, 3:172, 3:173, 3:178, 3:181, 3:183, 3:196, 3:202, 3:203, 3:207, 3:208, 3:211, 3:245, 3:252, 3:277, 3:307, 3:308, 3:310, 3:312-3:313, 3:322, 3:327, 3:331, 3:335, 3:336, 3:338
Weakness, 1:22, 1:28, 1:91, 1:123-1:124, 1:138, 1:154, 1:155, 2:212, 2:274, 3:91, 3:131, 3:237, 3:322, 3:330
Weaknesses, 1:81, 1:124, 1:126, 1:187, 1:277, 2:175, 2:176, 2:201, 2:211
Wealth, 1:46, 1:55, 1:79, 1:94, 1:96, 1:156, 1:179, 1:183, 1:201, 1:202, 1:204, 1:205, 1:208, 2:64, 2:74, 2:91, 2:100, 2:148, 3:71, 3:120, 3:123, 3:268, 3:270, 3:272, 3:282, 3:285, 3:294
Weapon, 1:53, 1:91, 1:207, 2:268, 3:86, 3:230
Weapons, 1:29, 1:48, 1:286, 2:23, 2:92, 2:136, 2:158, 2:165, 2:245, 2:249
Weeping, 1:44, 1:55, 1:143, 1:144, 1:258, 2:13, 2:35, 2:38, 2:92, 2:135, 2:154, 2:192, 3:37, 3:39, 3:98, 3:182, 3:208, 3:295, 3:345
Welfare, 1:8, 1:48, 1:65, 1:67, 1:71, 1:92-1:93, 1:96, 1:105-1:106, 1:111, 1:134, 1:165, 1:172, 1:180, 1:183, 1:190, 1:197-1:199, 1:202, 1:204, 1:208, 1:229, 2:18, 2:40, 2:82, 3:101, 3:273, 3:275, 3:285, 3:293, 3:299, 3:309
welfare program, 1:105, 1:106, 3:297
welfare state, 1:180, 1:197, 1:198, 1:204, 3:299
West, 1:261, 1:266-1:267, 1:270, 1:289-1:290, 2:52, 2:85, 2:86, 2:100, 2:114, 2:129, 2:136, 2:138, 2:139, 2:144-2:145, 2:202, 2:205, 2:266, 2:270, 3:8, 3:34, 3:35, 3:38, 3:40, 3:50, 3:62, 3:68, 3:77, 3:116, 3:133, 3:151, 3:161, 3:166, 3:229, 3:263, 3:273, 3:326, 3:351
Wheat, 1:4, 1:38, 1:43, 1:72, 1:79, 1:96, 1:103, 1:181, 1:200, 1:249, 1:261, 1:286-1:287, 2:14, 2:66, 2:179, 2:198, 2:200, 2:223, 2:253, 2:254, 3:14, 3:66, 3:99, 3:166, 3:169, 3:218
Wheat and tares, parable of, 1:200
Whirlwind, 1:44, 1:53, 1:75, 1:86, 1:91, 1:103, 1:134, 1:144, 1:159, 1:170, 1:227, 2:37-2:38, 2:45, 2:61, 2:107, 2:135, 2:147, 3:32, 3:156
Whore, 1:82, 1:213, 2:116, 2:235, 2:240, 2:241, 2:251-2:252, 2:283-2:284, 3:100, 3:101
Widow, 1:143, 1:288, 2:1, 2:29, 2:243, 2:253, 3:35, 3:260
Widows, 1:145, 2:230

Wight, Lyman, 3:151

Wild, 1:79, 1:122, 1:177, 1:242, 2:65, 2:126, 2:217, 3:142, 3:196

Wilderness, 1:26, 1:30, 1:48, 1:79, 1:80, 1:84, 1:217, 1:265, 1:269, 2:90, 2:113, 2:132, 2:135-2:136, 2:145, 2:165, 2:236, 2:250, 2:252, 2:254, 2:281, 2:284, 3:10, 3:11, 3:17, 3:31, 3:32, 3:78, 3:97, 3:103, 3:126, 3:128, 3:133, 3:170, 3:207, 3:290

Wind, 1:44, 1:86, 1:122, 1:145, 1:152, 1:263, 1:271, 2:4, 2:28, 2:139-2:141, 2:144, 2:145, 2:198, 2:219, 2:249, 2:267-2:269, 2:276, 3:165, 3:226, 3:230

Windows, 1:92, 1:128, 2:113, 3:30, 3:32

Winds, 1:4, 1:53, 1:134, 1:142, 1:155, 1:226, 1:263, 1:286, 1:287, 1:294, 2:4, 2:5, 2:179, 2:228, 2:255, 2:275, 2:278, 3:36, 3:37, 3:39, 3:40, 3:71, 3:73, 3:100, 3:183, 3:338

Wine, 1:24, 1:137, 1:243, 1:249, 1:256, 1:268, 2:7, 2:53, 2:102, 2:113, 2:116, 2:129, 2:143, 2:189, 2:241, 2:243, 2:245, 2:250, 2:253-2:255, 2:269, 2:282-2:284, 3:4, 3:7, 3:54-3:55, 3:99, 3:162, 3:166, 3:169, 3:231